Praise for Peter Dale Scott's *The Road to 9/11*

"Peter Dale Scott exposes a shadow world of oil, terrorism, drug trade, and arms deals, of covert financing and parallel security structures—from the Cold War to today. He shows how such parallel forces of the United States have been able to dominate the agenda of the George W. Bush administration, and that statements and actions made by Vice President Cheney and Defense Secretary Rumsfeld before, during, and after September 11, 2001, present evidence for an American 'deep state' and for the so-called Continuity of Government in parallel to the regular 'public state' ruled by law. Scott's brilliant work not only reveals the overwhelming importance of these parallel forces but also presents elements of a strategy for restraining their influence to win back the 'public state,' the American democracy."

Ola Tunander, International Peace Research Institute, Oslo

"*The Road to 9/11* is vintage Peter Dale Scott. Scott does not undertake conventional political analysis; instead, he engages in a kind of poetics, crafting the dark poetry of the deep state, of parapolitics, and of shadow government. As with his earlier work *Deep Politics and the Death of JFK,* Scott has no theory of responsibility and does not name the guilty. Rather, he maps out an alien terrain, surveying the topography of a political shadow land, in which covert political deviancy emerges as the norm. After reading Scott, we can no longer continue with our consensus-driven belief that our so-called liberal order renders impossible the triumph of the politically irrational."

Eric Wilson, Senior Lecturer of Public International Law, Monash University, and co-editor of *Government of the Shadows*

"A powerful study of the historic origins of the terrorist strikes of September 11, this book offers an indispensable guide to the gluttonous cast of characters who, since Watergate and the fall of Nixon, fashioned an ever-more-reckless American empire. By exposing the corrupt U.S. 'deep state'—transfer of public authority to America's wealthy and to the nation's unaccountable secret intelligence agencies—Peter Dale Scott's *The Road to 9/11* illuminates the path toward a more democratic and inclusive republic."

David MacGregor, King's University College at the University of Western Ontario

"*The Road to 9/11* provides an illuminating and disturbing history of the American government since World War II. Scott's account suggests that the 9/11 attacks were a culmination of long-term trends that threaten the very existence of American democracy, and also that there has been a massive cover-up of 9/11 itself. This book, which combines extensive research, perceptive analysis, and a fascinating narrative, will surely be considered Scott's *magnum opus.*"

David Ray Griffin, author of *Debunking 9/11 Debunking*

The publisher gratefully acknowledges the generous support of Stephen M. Silberstein as a member of the Publisher's Circle of University of California Press.

THE ROAD TO 9/11

BOOKS BY PETER DALE SCOTT

9/11 and American Empire: Intellectuals Speak Out, edited with
David Ray Griffin (2007)

*Drugs, Oil, and War: The United States in Afghanistan, Colombia,
and Indochina* (2003)

Minding the Darkness: A Poem for the Year 2000 (2000)

Crossing Borders: Selected Shorter Poems (1994)

Deep Politics and the Death of JFK (1993, reissued 1996)

Listening to the Candle: A Poem on Impulse (1992)

Cocaine Politics: Drugs, Armies, and the CIA in Central America,
with Jonathan Marshall (1991, reissued 1998)

Coming to Jakarta: A Poem about Terror (1989)

*The Iran-Contra Connection: Secret Teams and Covert Operations in the
Reagan Era*, with Jonathan Marshall and Jane Hunter (1987)

*Crime and Cover-Up: The CIA, the Mafia, and the Dallas-Watergate
Connection* (1977, reissued 1993)

*The Assassinations: Dallas and Beyond—A Guide to Cover-Ups and
Investigations*, edited with Paul L. Hoch and Russell Stetler (1976)

The War Conspiracy: The Secret Road to the Second Indochina War (1972)

Zbigniew Herbert: Selected Poems, translated with Czeslaw Milosz (1968,
reissued 1986)

The Politics of Escalation in Vietnam, with Franz Schurmann and
Reginald Zelnik (1966)

THE ROAD TO 9/11

WEALTH, EMPIRE,
AND THE FUTURE OF AMERICA

Peter Dale Scott

UNIVERSITY OF CALIFORNIA PRESS

BERKELEY   LOS ANGELES   LONDON

University of California Press, one of the most
distinguished university presses in the United States,
enriches lives around the world by advancing scholar-
ship in the humanities, social sciences, and natural
sciences. Its activities are supported by the UC Press
Foundation and by philanthropic contributions from
individuals and institutions. For more information,
visit www.ucpress.edu.

University of California Press
Berkeley and Los Angeles, California

University of California Press, Ltd.
London, England

First paperback printing 2008

Library of Congress Cataloging-in-Publication Data

Scott, Peter Dale.
    The road to 9/11 : wealth, empire, and the future of
America / Peter Dale Scott.
        p.   cm.
    Includes bibliographical references and index.
    ISBN 978-0-520-25871-6 (pbk : alk. paper)
        1. Transparency in government—United States.
2. Privacy, Right of—United States. 3. War on
Terrorism, 2001—Political aspects. 4. September 11
Terrorist Attacks, 2001—Political aspects. 5. United
States—Politics and government—1945–1989.
6. United States—Politics and government—1989–
7. Democracy—United States. 8. Elite (Social
sciences)—United States. 9. National security—
United States. 10. Political corruption—United
States—History—20th century. I. Title.
    JK468.S4S36   2007
    973.931—dc22   2007018905

Manufactured in the United States of America

16   15   14   13   12   11   10   09   08

10   9   8   7   6   5   4   3   2   1

This book is printed on Natures Book, which contains
50% postconsumer waste and meets the minimum
requirements of ANSI/NISO Z39.48-1992 (R 1997)
(*Permanence of Paper*).

To *the many trailblazers for a sane society, whose message must be rediscovered by each generation. And among them in particular to*

William Lloyd Garrison (1805–1879)

Leo Tolstoy (1828–1910)

Carl Schurz (1829–1906)

David Graham Phillips (1867–1911)

W. E. B. DuBois (1868–1923)

Mahatma Gandhi (1869–1948)

Scott Nearing (1883–1983)

A. J. Muste (1885–1967)

Khan Abdul Ghaffar Khan (Badshah Khan) (1890–1988)

Franz Jägerstätter (1907–1943)

I. F. Stone (1907–1989)

Simone Weil (1909–1943)

Czeslaw Milosz (1911–2004)

Nelson Mandela (b. 1918)

Paolo Freire (1867–1911)

Fred Shuttlesworth (b. 1922)

Martin Luther King Jr. (1929–1968)

Mario Savio (1942–1996)

Adam Michnik (b. 1946)

Contents

Acknowledgments

It has taken more than five years to write this book, longer than any other nonfiction book project I have ever undertaken. It draws on many years of research and discussion that have led me to the positions I articulate here for the first time. My first debt of gratitude is to the University of California Press for supporting me in this project, despite warnings about the risk the press was undertaking and attacks on the press for publishing two earlier books of mine. In particular, I want to thank my longtime editor Naomi Schneider for her inspiration, editorial skills, and patience. Thanks also to her helpful assistant, Valerie Witte. Two other editors have also provided invaluable help: Russell Schoch and Karen Croft. I am grateful to my agent, Victoria Shoemaker, to David Peattie of BookMatters, for overseeing the book's production, to my copyeditor, Amy Smith Bell, and my indexer, Leonard Rosenbaum, as well as to Lisa Macabasco and my other fact-checkers. I am grateful also to Global Research.com, *The Spokesman*, *Nexus*, and Lobster.com, where portions of this book first appeared.

As I was writing this manuscript, a number of other books were published that helped me with their perspectives and documentation. I must mention in particular two books by Kevin Phillips: *Wealth and Democracy* and *American Dynasty*, his portrait of the Bush family. Particular chapters in my book are indebted to the following works: Seymour Hersh's classic *The Price of Power* (on Kissinger), Robert Parry's *Secrecy & Privilege* (on the Republican countersurprise and Iran-Contra), Robert

Dreyfuss's *Devil's Game* (on the United States and Islamism), Peter Truell and Larry Gurwin's *False Profits* (on the Bank of Credit and Commerce International), Steve Coll's *Ghost Wars* (on Afghanistan), James Bamford's *A Pretext for War* and James Mann's *Rise of the Vulcans* (on continuity of government planning), David Ray Griffin's *The New Pearl Harbor* and *The 9/11 Commission Report* along with Paul Thompson's *The Terror Timeline* (on 9/11), and Jonathan Schell's *The Unconquerable World* (on nonviolence and America's future). Many other important books that strengthened my argument were published after mine was essentially completed. Very late in the game I was able to draw on research by peace researcher Ola Tunander about the "dual state" to reinforce my own distinction between the open politics of the public state and the deep, or covert, politics of the deep state.

Most of the book was written in the San Francisco Bay Area, where as with my previous books I profited from discussions with such friends as Daniel Ellsberg and Jonathan Marshall. But as I write in the preface, I profited also from extended periods of seclusion in Thailand and from the generosity of such new friends as Terry Kong and Thanis Kanjanaratakorn. A profound shift in my perspective ensued, which profited further from discussions with the talented and experienced monks of Wat Abhayagiri in Northern California—Ajahn Pasanno, Ajahn Amaro, and Ajahn Sudanto. Also very relevant to the development of my perspectives were the two months that, thanks to the generosity of the Lannan Foundation, I spent among the citizens of Marfa and Fort Davis in West Texas.

My final and most profound debt of gratitude is to the person who has patiently supported and encouraged me throughout the writing of this book: my wonderful wife of fourteen years, Ronna Kabatznick.

THE AMERICA WE KNEW AND LOVED

Can It Be Saved?

On March 17, 2003, President George W. Bush presented Saddam Hussein with an ultimatum; it became clear that he would soon declare a pre-emptive war against Iraq. It was a shock—a shock that forced me to recognize, against my will, how much America had changed since I immigrated here from Canada in 1961. Acute social problems beset the 1960s, but dreams of justice and equality were still alive. Today many of these same dreams are being abandoned, at least by the state.

When dreams are abandoned, a nation's fate is altered. The America of 1961 has not vanished, but it has changed direction. The country has swerved from its traditional path, toward a different post-America where traditional rights, freedoms, and openness have been seriously eroded. When I say this, I am not just referring to the corporate crimes of Enron and others that have helped finance the gap between our political parties and the quest for social justice. I am not just referring to the Bush administration's scrapping of international treaties on topics ranging from arms limitation to torture, nor to its boorish diplomatic behavior and defiance of the UN charter itself. I am not just recalling the abuse of electoral procedures in Florida, nor the judicial abuse that ratified it. Nor am I just talking about the redefinition of our government and civil rights in the name of "homeland security."[1] I am talking about deeper changes beneath all this corruption, ineptitude, malevolence, and hysteria.

Empires always become "bad news" for their home countries, as the economist J. A. Hobson pointed out a century ago.[2] Spain, one of

Europe's most progressive nations in the early 1500s, lost its progressive economy and middle class as a result of a deluge of gold from Mexico and the Andes. In a more complex fashion, an influx of foreign wealth converted Britain from an industrial country to a financial one, even before its social structure was further weakened by two disastrous world wars.

This transformation is happening to America as well. In 1961, when I came to teach at the University of California for one year, there were no tuition fees, and almost anyone who qualified could afford a university education. I remember teaching a student who after seven years in the coal mines was using his savings to put himself through law school. As late as 1970, 31 percent of the California state budget went to higher education and 4 percent to prisons. In 2005, however, these expenditure shares were on the order of 12 percent and 20 percent, respectively. In other words, the state's priorities have shifted from higher education to prisons. Or take housing. In 1961, with two years' salary as a beginning lecturer, I could have bought a house in Berkeley. Today, however, an entering lecturer might have to pay twenty years' salary to afford the same house. As I wrote in my long poem *Minding the Darkness*, you can expect no less when foreign capital, much of it hot money or flight capital, enters the United States at a rate of $100 billion a year.

Similar changes are occurring in many other countries, including my native Canada. Until recently I would have accepted these changes as inescapable everywhere. However, between 2002 and 2005, I spent three six-month periods in Thailand, where my wife, Ronna, had a temporary teaching post. I have been more influenced by this experience than I could have expected. Thailand has its own severe and quite different problems, including, most recently, a benign military coup (which most urban Thais welcomed). Before this, the Thai army and police oversaw a ruthless campaign against drug traffickers in which well over a thousand people were murdered. But from Thailand one can look back on America and, out of love for America, recognize a cultural sickness we would prefer not to acknowledge. What I am talking about goes far beyond the policies of the current administration in Washington. These policies grow out of what I now see as a deformed lifestyle, a condition of involuntary affluence that oppresses even the supposed beneficiaries by its imposed obligations. (For most Americans this affluence is either beyond their reach or slipping away, as the U.S. economy is twisted further and further out of equilibrium. The affluence affects them nonetheless.)

What I discovered in Thailand with Ronna was a happiness that comes from a greater simplicity, much as we experienced in the United

States when we were younger. In the small provincial city of Phayao, in northern Thailand, we lived out of two suitcases in a single dormitory room with no kitchen. We had no car. We walked each night to dine in a modest restaurant by the highway that had a roof but no walls. There the prices were cheap, fantastically so for us, but inexpensive also for Thais. The newly opened restaurant was crowded with all kinds of people— from students to the rich and their families. Night after night we dined at the same table with Thai professionals, some of whom became our best friends.

America presents a sad contrast to this more simple existence. Here my closet is crowded with clothing I seldom wear, and the kitchen with gadgets we seldom use. Our commitments in Berkeley are so widespread that we own two cars. And the high prices in restaurants dissuade us from seeing friends, except very occasionally and in small numbers. This personal account is anecdotal, of course, and some of our happiness in Thailand should perhaps be attributed to luck. Nevertheless, we saw vividly in Thailand what the eco-philosopher E. F. Schumacher learned in Burma (now Myanmar) a half century earlier: Small is beautiful. Less is more. Happiness is found close to the necessities of life, not in needless complexity and meaningless multiplicity of choice.

I believe these lessons have important political consequences. When speaking and writing about what I find wrong in America's exploitation of the third world, I have observed that a healthier policy may require cutbacks in the current lavish style of many Americans—particularly in our consumption of oil and gas. After my experience in Thailand, I see much more clearly how the current political overreaching of U.S. policy into the oil-rich regions of Azerbaijan, Iraq, and even Kyrgyzstan is grounded in the social malaise of habitual, unchosen, and even unwanted affluence. Like Schumacher, I need to relate this perspective to questions of spirituality. America is and always has been a deeply spiritual country. But that spirituality is not communally shared among all Americans; on the contrary, the country is now divided rather than united by strongly held fundamentalist religious beliefs.

Almost everyone Ronna and I met in northern Thailand was Buddhist. But even the few Christians and Muslims we encountered during our stay exhibited a common spirituality with the majority. This spirituality expressed itself in how the Thais lived. People were extraordinarily generous; we received gifts even from virtual strangers. People seemed relatively uninterested in possessions or money. For example, when two dormitory cleaning women came in at my request to clean our room, they were reluctant to accept any money: "Mai ao; mai ao!" (We don't want it!) The Thais we got to know well were like Americans in that they sought, competitively, the best possible education for their children. For themselves, however, they seemed much more interested in enjoying the life they already had than in advancement or promotion. No doubt this was a consequence of our living in a small provincial city.

After our stay in Phayao, I wondered what experience I might gain from living in a small American town. Then by chance, thanks to a grant from the Lannan Foundation, I was able for two months in 2004 to become familiar with two small towns in West Texas: Marfa and Fort Davis.[3] Until this experience Texas had always seemed somewhat alien to me, as the source of presidents and policies that we in Berkeley were always voting against. But what a pleasure to find essentially the same virtues in West Texas that Ronna and I had enjoyed in Phayao: simplicity, generosity, friendship, considerateness, and also spirituality—even among people who were not so-called believers or churchgoers.

My two months in Texas made clearer to me than ever before the gap between the American people and their leaders. During this same period, the U.S. government was revealed to have engaged in torture, arbitrary detentions, illegal eavesdropping, and the punitive destruction of Iraqi cities like Fallujah. My despair about the country developed into a confidence that the war in Iraq, along with the horrors that have accompanied it elsewhere, would become increasingly unpopular. My experience in Texas reinforced my vision of America as a country that is healthiest at the level of local community but culturally underdeveloped and divided and thus vulnerable to special interests at the higher levels.

The United States has not yet fully healed the divisions that surfaced during the Civil War. The healing efforts to overcome those divisions—in the civil rights movement of the 1960s, for example—have been followed by lapses into hostile and uncommunicative opposition, like that characterized by the gap between the Red and Blue states in the 2000 and 2004 elections. The country's history of Reconstruction and segregation should remind us that such advances and regressions have occurred before.

These divisions did not begin with the Civil War, however. Historian Michael Lind, in a brilliant study, has analyzed the Old World roots of the different political cultures in the northern and southern states. He sees George W. Bush in particular as the product of a southern culture of violent dominance, as opposed to a majority culture (also found in Texas) of egalitarianism and meritocracy.[4] Lind points out how the trading North has been traditionally internationalist, while the militaristic

South has traditionally favored unilateral expansionism.[5] "From the earliest days of the American Republic," he adds, "white southerners have been represented above their proportion of the U.S. population in the armed forces—and greatly under-represented among members of the Foreign Service, which until recently was a bastion of patrician Northeasterners. The Mason-Dixon line might as well run through the Potomac River between the Pentagon and the State Department."[6]

Lind observes that although over the years there have been both southern presidents and conservative presidents, "George W. Bush is the first Southern conservative to be elected president of the United States since James Knox Polk in 1844."[7] One could argue that it is no accident that both these presidents initiated expansionist wars. The Mexican-American War of 1846 indeed had features similar to the U.S. invasions of Afghanistan and Iraq in 2001 and 2003. Polk's war too was essentially unprovoked, dubiously justified, attacked as an abuse of presidential power, and so divisive along North-South lines as to have produced an American political crisis.[8]

These differences in American culture are enduring but not insuperable. On the contrary, as prizewinning historian Garry Wills has reminded us, the history of America is precisely a history of *making* a nation out of radically disparate communities. There is nothing in that history of our nation making to cause us despair of further progress: "Ours is not only the world's oldest democracy (it can even be argued that we are the first real democracy), but one of the few governments not to have been overthrown by revolution or conquest. We are the standing refutation of the classical political theory that democracies are by nature unstable."[9]

The history of the United States has been precisely a history of creative responses to oppressive top-down power. The civil rights movement, like the Polish Solidarity movement, has shown that oppression and deprivation can still rouse people to the call of liberation, even in modern conditions of government surveillance and crowd control. The great American dreamer Walt Whitman wrote: "The word democracy is a great word whose history . . . remains unwritten because that history has yet to be enacted."[10] Today we can wonder if the next chapter of democracy's unwritten history will even be written in the United States. Our times are clearly abnormal and in flux. The question is whether a mood of despair, when shared widely enough, can become a source of hope.

The answer is up to us, and it goes beyond politics. We must address the crisis of America's deep cultural divisions and fractured civil society. Our current political process, which once worked by building coalitions, now tends to have the opposite effect of dividing us: Red states against Blue states, country against city, believers against nonbelievers, so-called ethnic whites (a term I do not believe in) against the rest.

Why is there such a gap today between the values of ordinary Americans throughout the country and those who control us?[11] One obvious answer, which I touch on in the introduction, is the rapidly increasing gap between America's richest and its poorest, with the middle class, the heart of any public democracy, also losing ground. The wealthiest top fifth of U.S. citizens now make 11.0 times more than those in the poorest bottom fifth, as opposed to 4.3 times more in Japan and 7.1 times more in Canada or France.[12] Thus America, which historically flourished by being less class-bound than Europe, has now surpassed the Old World with respect to income disparity.

But there is another problem affecting the United States: our supposed open society is in fact partly driven by deeper forces many of us do not clearly see, especially in matters of foreign policy. This weakness of civil society at the federal level allows policy to be dictated by special interests. This is particularly true of foreign policy, more and more of which is driven by covert bureaucracies in the Central Intelligence Agency (CIA) and the Pentagon, uncontrolled by the checks and balances of the public state. In this book I designate as the "deep state" (a term borrowed from Turkish analysts) that part of the state driven by top-down policy making, often by small cabals.

In the book's final chapter I sketch ways in which we can begin to address these problems of the deep state. But first we must analyze them. Chapters 2 through 6 explore this more or less continuous train of unauthorized intrusions, often illegal, into the public political process. It is a story about individuals and cabals whose power derives not from the Constitution but from their proximity to wealth and private power. In chapters 7 through 9, I talk about al Qaeda. Chapter 7 examines the origins of al Qaeda in CIA's Operation Cyclone of the 1980s, the recruitment, training, and arming of "Arab Afghans" to fight in Afghanistan and points north. Chapter 8 looks at the U.S. government sponsorship of recruitment in America for what became al Qaeda. Chapter 9 examines the case of Ali Mohamed, an Egyptian double agent who trained recruits for al Qaeda in terror while still on the payroll of the U.S. Army. Chapter 10 discusses the relationship of al Qaeda operatives to Americans in oil and pipeline regions like Azerbaijan and Kosovo.

In chapters 11 through 14, I discuss the history of American strategic thinking about global oil reserves and also about so-called continuity of government or COG (the pre-planned response to crisis, which Dick Cheney and Donald Rumsfeld worked on with Oliver North in the 1980s), which was partially implemented on 9/11. In chapters 12 and 13, I examine a relevant aspect of 9/11 itself: Cheney's actions on the morning of 9/11 and his implementation of COG. I conclude, largely from the misrepresentations of them in the *9/11 Commission Report*, that a venue should be established in which the vice president would testify for the first time about 9/11 under oath.

In my conclusion I suggest ways to help restore and advance the America we once knew. I still have the faith that brought me to this country in 1961: that the history of the human species is one of slowly increasing self-knowledge, so that there is a slow—painfully slow—evolution toward greater openness and mutual understanding of diversity in society and politics. The United States, for all its obvious faults, was once a leader in this evolution. Whether it will continue to be one is less certain. But I believe America's values are still a possibility worth striving for, with all the energy we can muster. And as this book goes to press in 2007, I find more reasons to believe in America's future than in those dark weeks preceding the Iraq War.

Peter Dale Scott
March 2003–March 2007

ONE

INTRODUCTION

Wealth, Empire, Cabals, and the Public State

I hope we shall crush in its birth the aristocracy of our monied corporations which dare already to challenge our government to a trial of strength, and bid defiance to the laws of our country.

Thomas Jefferson, 1816

We hold it a prime duty of the people to free our government from the control of money.

Theodore Roosevelt, 1912

The real truth . . . is, as you and I know, that a financial element in the larger centers has owned the Government ever since the days of Andrew Jackson.

**Letter from Franklin D. Roosevelt
to Colonel E. M. House, 1933**

THE GROWTH OF GREAT WEALTH
AT THE EXPENSE OF THE PUBLIC STATE

In this book I try to explain the paradoxes that distress most of the Americans I've met over the past few years. Whether they live in Berkeley, New England, or West Texas, these people wonder why the United States steered deliberately—and seemingly inevitably—into a war with Iraq that had little domestic support. They wonder why so many open processes of our government have been replaced by secret decisions at the uppermost levels. They wonder why our country, which is not currently facing any major enemies, is increasing its defense budget more rapidly than ever before.

A stock answer often used to explain these changes is to invoke the terrorist attacks of September 11, 2001. But pressures for them had been building long before 9/11. Even more disturbing, some of those lobbying for a "revolution in military affairs," including huge new defense budgets and military action against Iraq, stated before 2001 that such changes would not occur quickly without "some catastrophic and catalyzing event—like a new Pearl Harbor."[1] Since the 9/11 attacks, leading members of the Bush administration have spoken of the attacks as a "great opportunity" (President Bush) or (in Donald Rumsfeld's words) "the kind of opportunities that World War II offered, to refashion the world."[2]

I wrote this book in an effort to contextualize 9/11. In one sense, 9/11 is an event without precedent, and one that threatens to move America beyond the age of public politics to a new era in which power, more than ever before, is administered downward from above. But at the same time, 9/11 must be seen as a culmination of trends developing through a half century: toward secret top-down decision making by small cabals, toward the militarization of law enforcement, toward plans for the sequestering of those who dissent, toward government off-the-books operations, transactions, and assets, and toward governance by those who pay for political parties rather than those who participate in them.

Essentially, I agree with political commentator Kevin Phillips that a major answer to these questions, although not a complete one and insufficiently discussed, is found in an area beyond politics: the "connecting lines . . . between tainted government, corrupted politics, corporate venality, and the unprecedented two-decade build-up of wealth itself."[3] Domination of the public state by private wealth is not a novelty in America, as the epigraphs at the beginning of this chapter make clear. The novelty since World War II, however, lies in the secret growth and articulation of this top-down power *within* government. In particular, the Office of Policy Coordination (OPC), a group hidden from the public eye, was secretly created in June 1948 and dominated at first by a small ex–Office of Special Services (OSS) elite from Wall Street. Wall Street's secret intrusion of its views and personnel into American covert policy justifies our speaking of an American "overworld"—that realm of wealthy or privileged society that, although not formally authorized or institutionalized, is the scene of successful influence of government by private power.

Of all the political systems in the world, America's has traditionally been characterized by its openness to self-analysis, self-criticism, and ultimately self-correction. Past periods of wealth disparity, notably in the Gilded Age, have been followed by reform movements that compressed the income gap. But, as Phillips has warned, the type of reforms that have followed past excesses of wealth in politics must happen again soon, or they may not happen at all: "As the twenty-first century gets underway, the imbalance of wealth and democracy in the United States is unsustainable. . . . Either democracy must be renewed, with politics brought back to life, or wealth is likely to cement a new and less democratic regime—plutocracy by some other name."[4]

Economist Paul Krugman has transmitted statistics for the staggering increases in income for America's most wealthy: "A new research paper by Ian Dew-Becker and Robert Gordon of Northwestern University, 'Where Did the Productivity Growth Go?,' gives the details. Between 1972 and 2001, the wage and salary income of Americans at the 90th percentile of the income distribution rose only 34 percent, or about 1 percent per year. . . . But income at the 99th percentile rose 87 percent; income at the 99.9th percentile rose 181 percent; and income at the 99.99th percentile rose 497 percent."[5] Many of these increases are marked by the transfer rather than the creation of wealth and derive from what Phillips has called the "financialization" of America: the "process whereby financial services, broadly construed, take over the dominant economic, cultural, and political role in a national economy."[6]

THE OVERWORLD, THE DEEP STATE, AND BUREAUCRATIC PARANOIA

Obviously, as the wealth of the top 1 percent has increased radically, so has its power, particularly over communications. Conversely, the public state—the realm of open and deliberated policy decisions—has diminished at the hands of private manipulators. Under both presidents Bill Clinton and George H. W. Bush, for example, the United States was committed to controversial commitments and interventions, from Uzbekistan to Kosovo, which were the product of secret lobbying by cabals, not public debate. The political power of money has been analyzed in the media and Congress chiefly as the external problem of what is often called corruption, the role of money in choosing and influencing Congress and the White House.[7] To this, since the 1970s, has been added a coordinated campaign by a few wealthy individuals (such as billionaire publisher

Richard Mellon Scaife), foundations (such as Coors, Allen-Bradley, Olin, Smith Richardson), and their media (such as Rupert Murdoch's News Corporation) to shift the political culture of the country radically to the right.[8]

But this book also focuses on something else: the top 1 percent's direct or indirect control of certain specific domains of government, beginning in the 1940s with the creation of CIA. It is a story that looks beyond the well-defined public entities of open politics to include the more amorphous and fluid realm of private control behind them. This realm of wealthy private influence, the overworld, is a milieu of those who either by wealth or background have power great enough to have an observable influence on their society and its politics.[9] Those parts of the government responding to their influence I call the "deep state" (if covert) or "security state" (if military). Both represent top-down or closed power, as opposed to the open power of the public state or res publica that represents the people as a whole.[10]

I argue in this book that the power of the American public state needs to be revived, and its out-of-control deep state radically curtailed. I am not an opponent of deep states per se: publics are not infallible and sometimes need to be opposed. But in our current crisis the proper balance between the public state and the deep state has been lost, and the deep state's secret top-down powers have become a major threat to democracy. A well-functioning deep state serves to impose needed wisdom and discipline, but in recent years America's unchecked deep state has been imposing both folly and indiscipline. The tension between an open public state and a closed deep state or security state existing within it is an old and widespread phenomenon.[11] In the United States it has become more acute since the beginning of the Cold War in the 1940s, when the investment firms of the Wall Street overworld provided President Harry Truman with his secretary of defense, James V. Forrestal. This same overworld provided them both with the ideas and personnel for a new Central Intelligence Agency.

The policy making of the closed deep state, shielded by secrecy, has tended increasingly toward global dominance at any price, without regard to consequences. The collective wisdom of foreign policy experts, usually most represented in the State Department, has been powerless to restrain it. Over and over throughout this book I reveal occasions where the relatively sane proposals of the State Department have been trumped by the bureaucratic paranoia of people whose career success was based on their commitment to worst-case scenarios. This "paranoid style in

American politics" has traditionally referred to marginal elements that exist remote from true power. But there has been a paranoid tradition of the deep state as well, dating back to the Alien and Sedition Acts of 1799 (recently cited by the Department of Homeland Security as a model for its Endgame program).[12]

Closed policy making that puts security first above all, especially when protected by secrecy, is a formula for bureaucratic paranoia. The United States experienced such paranoia with the Alien Act and the Palmer Raids of 1918 and again with the State Department and Treasury personnel purges after World War II. In this book I argue that the bureaucratic paranoia of the deep state was a major cause (as well as a result of) 9/11. I believe our present course of ever more heightened paranoia is a sure formula for more 9/11s.

This book will not address the often asked questions of to what extent the Bush-Cheney administration knew in advance of the impending attacks on 9/11, and then either let them happen or even possibly made them happen. Instead, this book makes a more general argument that the bureaucratic paranoia inside the American deep state, undisciplined by the available wisdom of the public state, helped years ago to create al Qaeda and then to create the circumstances in which, almost inevitably, elements in al Qaeda would turn against the United States.[13]

Having worked briefly in the Canadian bureaucracy, I have observed that bureaucratic debate where power is involved tends to favor paranoid or worst-case analyses, especially those that justify budget and bureaucratic growth. Today's bureaucratic paranoia has indeed been institutionalized by what has been popularized as Vice President Cheney's "one percent doctrine": "Even if there's just a one percent chance of the unimaginable coming due, act as if it is a certainty. It's not about 'our analysis,' as Cheney said. It's about 'our response' . . . Justified or not, fact-based or not, 'our response' is what matters. As to 'evidence,' the bar was set so low that the word itself almost didn't apply. If there was even a one percent chance of terrorists getting a weapon of mass destruction . . . the United States must now act as if it were a certainty."[14]

This doctrine is a license for untrammeled expansion of the secret deep state. As the deep state metastasizes, its origins in the overworld become less clear and possibly less relevant. In using the term "overworld," we must be careful not to reify it or attribute to it a unity and coherence it does not possess. It is a term of convenience to indicate, at least initially, a somewhat amorphous realm of sociopolitical change on which we should focus attention. The overworld is emphatically less cohesive than a class, despite what popular historian Frederick Lundberg and others have suggested.[15] Ultimately its much discussed institutions, like the Council on Foreign Relations (CFR) and the Trilateral Commission, are more significant as symptoms and evidence rather than as sources of overworld power.

The overworld was clearly centered in Wall Street in the 1940s, and CIA was primarily designed there. With the postwar shifts of U.S. demographics and economic structure southward and westward, the overworld itself has shifted, becoming less defined by geography than by the interrelated functions of the petroleum-industrial-financial complex. Cheney's global oilfield services firm Halliburton, today a "bridge between the oil industry and the military-industrial complex,"[16] was nowhere near the Wall Street power center in the 1940s. This shift in the overworld led by 1968 to a polarizing debate over the Vietnam War. The expanding military-industrial complex, dedicated to winning that war at any cost, found itself increasingly opposed by elements on Wall Street (which at the time I labeled the "CIA-financial establishment") who feared the impact of the war's costs on the stability of the dollar.[17] I argue that Nixon's inability to satisfy either of the two polarized factions—symbolized by the American Security Council and the Council on Foreign Relations—was a major factor in the unprecedented and ultimately unresolved drama of Watergate.

Today, with the relative decline of the domestic civilian economy and the proliferation of military business, we can see an emerging military-financial complex. This is symbolized by the easy movement up from the Pentagon to Wall Street of such key players as the director Bruce P. Jackson of the Project for the New American Century.[18] One can measure the emergent power of the military in the establishment by comparing the relatively critical stance of the mainstream media toward the Vietnam War and the recent misleading White House propaganda about Iraq that was published uncritically in the *New York Times*.[19] Increasingly a gap has widened between the mainstream press and television—the so-called old media—and the emerging new media of open communications via the Internet.

In a sense, the current American political crisis can be seen as a tension between the goals of this military-financial complex, on the one hand, and the requisite conditions for a healthy civilian economy and civil society on the other. This is another way of understanding the tension, described throughout this book, between the deep/security state and the public state. Through all these shifts certain essential continuities can be traced in the overworld's influence—first on CIA and increasingly on national security policy in general. Most recently, private power consolidated its influence by managing to establish a small but extremely important "shadow government," or "parallel government." The overworld did this through planning for what is officially known as continuity of government (COG), with its own secret, parallel institutions.[20] Toward the end of this book I show how the plans for COG in a time of crisis were first implemented on 9/11. More important, they may also have contributed to changes in U.S. emergency defense responses that perhaps escalated a much smaller terrorist attack into "a new Pearl Harbor."

THE DIALECTICS OF WEALTH, EXPANSION, AND RESTRAINT

History has demonstrated, four or five times over, the dialectics of democratic openness. This process determined the fates of the ancient city-states of Athens and Rome, and since the Renaissance we have seen it again with the empires of Spain, the Netherlands, and Great Britain. An urban civil society that was relatively free and open surpassed its neighbors in generating wealth. As wealth increased, it expanded the reach of the state beyond that society's borders.[21] And then, as Yale historian Paul Kennedy wrote in *The Rise and Fall of the Great Powers*, a military overstretch ensued that weakened the homeland economically and precipitated its decline.

To the extent that wealth expanded, these extra-societal institutions came to lie outside the transparency of domestic civil society. In effect, they become both powerful and secret, and new elements of the state developed to interact with these institutions on a secret level. Paradoxically, as the power, scope, and exposure of the state increased, so did that society's paranoia—the fear of being surpassed by competing states.[22] Within the state secrecy trumped openness. There is a political sociology of secrecy: those with higher clearances participated in policy making at a level where those without clearances were denied access.[23] The result was the increasing dominance over the officially organized public state by an undemocratic top-down deep state, one that answered to other interests than those of the homeland public. Institutions and relationships outside the geographic bounds of civil society consolidated more and more into an overworld, usually strengthened by offshore resources, that had the wealth and de facto power to influence and eventually determine the policies of the public state.

America since World War II has differed from these empires before it in two respects. On the one hand, the modern nation-state system is now global; on the other, America's overwhelming military preeminence has contributed to the impression of a unipolar world.[24] Because of these two factors, the flag imperialism of a century ago (such as the Spanish-American War) has evolved into trade imperialism: the flag now follows trade and investment, rather than vice versa. (Admiral George Dewey sent the U.S. Navy to the Philippines in 1898 before any major American firms had invested there. But when President George W. Bush dispatched U.S. troops to Georgia in 2002, it was only after U.S. oil firms had begun to develop a major oil pipeline across the country.)

This subordination of the flag to trade has satisfied most U.S. economic interests, or so-called traders, symbolized by Wall Street and the Council on Foreign Relations. But it also created a so-called Prussian backlash, especially in the military, from those who believed that as long as America had the military capacity to overwhelm its enemies, it should not hesitate to do so. As a result, postwar presidents from Harry Truman through Richard Nixon repeatedly had to restrain rebellious hawkish elements in the armed forces of which they were the commanders in chief. President Dwight Eisenhower was able to restrain Admiral Arthur Radford's demand in 1954 for direct U.S. intervention in the French Indochina War, when the French were being defeated at Dien Bien Phu.[25] But the top CIA and Pentagon leadership plotted for further engagement in Indochina in the late 1950s, planning not so much *with* Eisenhower as *against* him. As I have described in detail in my book *Drugs, Oil, and War*, key decisions in escalating U.S. support in Laos were only belatedly approved by Eisenhower, at times when he was away from his office, either to play golf or for a planned check-up in a hospital.[26]

Economist James Galbraith has revealed how, in the midst of the 1961 Berlin crisis, President John Kennedy angered the U.S. generals, and possibly CIA director Allen Dulles, by rejecting "the military's drive for a vast U.S. nuclear build-up" and possible first strike as well.[27] A few days later Kennedy was told about a study by White House aide Carl Kaysen "that showed that a 'disarming first strike' against Soviet strategic forces could be carried out with a high degree of confidence that it would catch them all on the ground."[28] Galbraith also notes the report of Nikita Khrushchev that at the peak of the Cuban Missile Crisis in 1962, Robert Kennedy told the Russian ambassador Anatoly Dobrynin: "Even though the President himself is very much against starting a war over Cuba, an irreversible chain of events could occur against his will. . . . If the situation continues for much longer, the President is not sure that the military will not overthrow him and seize power. The American military could get out of control."[29]

A recent study of the second Tonkin Gulf incident on August 4, 1964, which led eventually to the Vietnam War, indicates that the crucial decision to bomb North Vietnam did not come from President Lyndon Johnson, who "was deliberately prevented" by those below him "from making an informed decision" on that day.[30] Later, we shall see that Nixon also faced opposition from the bureaucratic faction that wished for a more unrestrained exercise of U.S. military power. America's ignominious departure from Vietnam silenced, for a generation, the "Prussians'" demand for the reckless use of American military force. But it also gave rise to a compensatory belief, articulated by Marine Colonel Oliver North, that the war effort in Vietnam was not lost on the battlefield; rather, it was lost in the streets of America. Quietly and secretly, North and his allies began to make arrangements, through continuity of government planning, to ensure that in any future military engagement, American dissent at home would not be allowed to endanger the outcome.

THE SPREAD OF SECRECY AND THE ROAD TO 9/11

In the 1987 Iran-Contra hearings the congressman Jack Brooks tried vainly to question Colonel North about his "work on plans for continuity of government in the event of a major disaster."[31] Denied an answer, Brooks then accused North of being part of a secret "government within a government." Author Theodore Draper later echoed the charge when he wrote of a "junta-like cabal."[32] North's work on so-called COG was important, and the planning was continued after his departure by a small cabal-like committee, including Dick Cheney (then a congressman) and Donald Rumsfeld (who at the time was a private citizen). Eventually North's most secret and controversial recommendations, including plans for the warrantless roundup and detention of minorities, saw fruition after 9/11.[33] Chapter 14 of this book explores in detail how 9/11, or more accurately the U.S. response to that attack, is the fruit of COG planning in the 1980s.

These two apparently unrelated episodes—Iran-Contra and the U.S. response to 9/11—are in fact part of a continuous expansion of secret policy making by cabals going back to the 1940s. More and more, major redirections of U.S. foreign policy have been initiated and conducted not by those who are publicly charged with the responsibility for them, but by others, often in secret. This practice can be traced back chiefly to the creation, in 1947, of two related institutions: the National Security Council and the Central Intelligence Agency. Indeed, one political motive for these institutions was to create a larger space for secrecy at the heart of what had been traditionally a more open form of government. Since then, secrecy, invoked at first as necessary to the defense of the public state, has become increasingly an enemy to the public state.

Perhaps no one in 1947 could have predicted the extent to which the public power of the open democratic state would be overridden by secret edicts and processes, imposed within government from outside sources, rather than publicly arrived at. But anyone interested in saving the American Republic will want to identify these secret forces that have been eroding it. This erosion was not an inevitable historical process. Rather, it was the result of recurrent intrusions into the public political process by a few individuals, above all from the overworld, who have influenced the course of American politics.

This influence is exercised both publicly and covertly. The most obvious influence is through money, changing hands both above and below the table. The right of the wealthy to donate to political parties and causes is a legally circumscribed one. Beyond the reach of the law, however, is the ability of wealth to subvert true public discourse by creating an artificial realm of media discourse, in which the honest reporters of unpleasant truths are marginalized and sometimes lose their jobs. One such example is that of Gary Webb, whose Pulitzer Prize–winning journalistic career ended after he wrote about the CIA and drugs.[34]

The sustained maintenance of bias in media discourse is thus reflected and enhanced by bureaucratic discourse. It is unusual for the overworld to intervene directly in the higher processes of government. More common is the maintenance of artificial consensus by influencing the selection and promotion of power experts *within* the government. Throughout this book I document how, time after time, solid expert advice on policy was overridden by power experts who knew next to nothing about the foreign region affected but everything about self-advancement in a corrupt Washington.[35]

There are also less visible institutions that mediate and serve as a more secret interface between the American people and overworld power.[36] Besides CIA itself, an institution initially guided more from Wall Street than from Washington, there are less-known institutions, such as the President's Foreign Intelligence Advisory Board and, more recently, the group set up under Ronald Reagan to plan for so-called COG. As we shall see, the history of COG planning, which originated in the 1950s, assumed its current shape in response to the mobilization of U.S. Army intelligence and CIA against left-wing Americans during the civil disorder of the 1960s and 1970s. The reactive planning under Presidents Johnson and Nixon became increasingly proactive in the 1980s administration of President Reagan. Under him the COG project was developed by the Federal Emergency Management Agency (FEMA) operating under the White House National Program Office (NPO), a group so supersecret it was not publicly named until a 1991 CNN news story.[37]

This increasing articulation and institutionalization of secret power corresponds to an increasing subordination of public power to the private realm. Many Americans have become inured to the fact that major policy decisions, ranging from defense strategies to the initiation of preemptive war, are no longer formulated by the public state. Rather, many of these decisions are now imposed on it from outside.

The beginnings of this public implementation can be traced to the creation of CIA in 1947. This was the most important of a series of secret decisions made in the 1940s and 1950s, decades before many of the events I detail throughout this book. Right after World War II the chances seemed greater than ever before for a more peaceful, orderly, legal, and open world. The United States was then wealthy enough to finance postwar reconstruction in devastated Europe. Later the U.S. government would fund health and agriculture programs in the newly liberated former colonies of the third world. The world's two great superpowers—the United States and the Soviet Union—had apparently agreed on rules and procedures for mediating their serious differences through a neutral body, the United Nations.

But the United Nations was to prove inadequate for the resolution of international conflict. One major reason for this was that the Soviet Union, the United States, and (after 1949) China all pursued covert expansive policies that brought them into conflict and occasionally into war. The Marxist-Leninist nations of the USSR and China lent support to other Marxist-Leninist parties and movements, some of them insurrectionary, in other parts of the world. The immediate concern of the United States was Europe, where it appeared that the French and Italian Communist parties might be elected to power in 1948.

From the beginning of the postwar era, Washington looked for assets and "proxy armies" of its own, to combat the threat it perceived from the Soviet Union and China. Some of these proxies, like the Nationalist Chinese Kuomintang (KMT) troops in Burma, or the mafias in Italy and

Marseilles, soon outgrew their U.S. support to become de facto regional players, or parastates (exhibiting some but not all of the features of states) in their own right.

From 1945 to 1947 elements in the U.S. Army conspired to maintain contacts with former German anti-Communists in Europe and their German Army commander, General Reinhard Gehlen. Five men were involved, of whom three (William J. Donovan, Allen Dulles, and Frank Wisner) were representatives of the Wall Street overworld and also of the New York Social Register, which listed the members of New York high society.[38] They were awaiting a new agency to succeed Donovan's Office of Strategic Services (OSS) and take over the Nazis' ethnic armies in Eastern Europe. But the idea of a centralized intelligence agency encountered fierce competitive opposition from the FBI's J. Edgar Hoover, who was backed at first by elements of army intelligence.[39]

Although it took two years to overcome their opponents, the Wall Street lawyers and bankers in Truman's administration succeeded in 1947 in establishing CIA, which would report to the president through the new National Security Council (NSC). This new agency, based on the precedent and personnel of the OSS, had been urged on Washington by the War-Peace Studies Project of the Council on Foreign Relations in the early 1940s.[40] It was reinforced by a report commissioned in 1945 by navy secretary James V. Forrestal. The report was written by Ferdinand Eberstadt, who like Forrestal was a private Wall Street banker from the investment bank Dillon Read.[41]

As CIA director Richard Helms narrates in his memoirs, Allen Dulles (then a Republican lawyer at Sullivan and Cromwell in New York) was recruited in 1946 "to draft proposals for the shape and organization of what was to become the Central Intelligence Agency in 1947."[42] Dulles promptly formed an advisory group of six men, all but one of whom were Wall Street investment bankers or lawyers.[43] In 1948, Forrestal appointed Dulles chairman of a committee, along with two other New York lawyers, to review CIA's performance.[44] "The three lawyers conferred for close to a year in one of the board rooms at J. H. Whitney," another Wall Street investment firm.[45]

In its first two decades, CIA, like its intellectual parent the Council on Foreign Relations, was dominated internally and externally by the aristocratic elements of the New York overworld. All seven of the known deputy directors of CIA during this period came from the same New York legal and financial circles; and six of them were listed in the New York Social Register as well.[46] When joined by the young James Angleton, son of an international corporate executive, this early core became the basis for an inner "agency-within-an-agency" that survived into the 1960s.[47]

Within a year the NSC was authorizing covert operations overseas through CIA. In fact, these operations were being implemented by an even more secret group within CIA, the Office of Policy Coordination (OPC). The CIA at least had been publicly empowered by the 1947 National Security Act, even though it contained a "loophole" through which CIA launched covert operations in a way Congress had "not intended."[48] In June 1948 the National Security Council secretly launched OPC, without any congressional authorization at all.[49]

The decision to create OPC was "based on what was seen as a CIA success in Italy," the election of a Christian Democratic government in April despite widespread fears of a Communist electoral victory.[50] Key to this success was the rapid supply of millions of dollars to the non-Communist parties, another decision that had its origins in New York. As journalists David Wise and Thomas B. Ross wrote: "[Defense Secretary] Forrestal felt that secret counteraction was vital, but his initial assessment was that the Italian operation would have to be private. The wealthy industrialists in Milan were hesitant to provide the money, fearing reprisals if the Communists won, and so the hat was passed at the Brook Club in New York. But Allen Dulles felt the problem could not be handled effectively in private hands. He urged strongly that the government establish a covert organization."[51]

This episode is instructive. The defense secretary felt the operation should be a private undertaking, but a private Wall Street lawyer (from the political party that was not currently in power) determined that it should be carried out by the government. For years, we as common taxpayers have similarly unwittingly been taxed to pay for projects like those of the Brook Club and the wealthy industrialists in Milan. More important, a practice had been consolidated of subordinating public policy to overworld policy (as we shall see again in 1979, with respect to the shah of Iran).

Even more than CIA, OPC was a creation of the New York overworld. It was the work principally of four men associated with the Council on Foreign Relations: the career diplomat George Kennan and the three-man committee in 1948 chaired by CFR president Dulles.[52] Dulles and his allies also arranged for the OPC chief to be Frank Wisner, another Wall Street lawyer who in 1947 had joined the State Department with the deliberately understated title "deputy assistant secretary for occupied countries."[53] OPC set in motion at least three projects that acquired a life, culture, and momentum of their own. These projects—collectively and much later, long after the demise of OPC itself—contributed to the catastrophe of 9/11.

The first project was an arrangement for the creation and support of right-wing "stay-behind" groups in Europe to combat the risk of Communist takeover.[54] This arrangement in Italy, known later as Operation Gladio, led in turn to a shadow system of parallel intelligence agencies, shielded from the overview of Italy's public and more centrist government. These CIA-linked agencies developed a strategy of tension in which a series of lethal terrorist bombings, falsely presented as left-wing, were used to drive Italy further to the right.[55] (The Piazza Fontana bombing of December 1969 killed sixteen people; the Bologna Station massacre of May 1983 killed eighty-five.)

Guido Giannettini, one of the Italian authors of this strategy of tension (and of the Piazza Fontana bombing eight years later), came to America in 1961 to lecture at the Naval War College on "Techniques and Possibilities of a Coup d'Etat in Europe."[56] In March 1962 the Joint Chiefs of Staff prepared their own documents developing Giannettini's strategy. This was Operation Northwoods, which many books have cited as a "precedent" for "U.S. complicity in the attacks of 9/11."[57] As journalist James Bamford wrote of Northwoods: "The plan, which had been written with the approval of the Chairman and every member of the Joint Chiefs of Staff, called for innocent people to be shot on American streets."[58]

In addition to this stay-behind project, OPC began a psychological warfare campaign to go beyond the State Department's official policy of containing Communism, by mobilizing public opinion and covert resources for the destabilization of eastern Europe.[59] OPC's third project, which eventually had global consequences affecting both Afghanistan and al Qaeda, was to combat Communism by using assets supported by illegal drug trafficking.

OPC, THE DRUG TRAFFIC, AND GOVERNMENT OFF-THE-BOOKS ASSETS

One of Wisner's projects in 1950 was so-called Operation Paper, the U.S. government's support for the remnants of the Nationalist Chinese KMT forces in Burma and Thailand. These forces worked off and on with OPC and CIA for more than a decade. Operation Paper's assets were off the books and self-financing—mostly by profits from drug dealing.[60] By restoring the global drug traffic out of Southeast Asia, the KMT proxy institutionalized what would become a CIA habit of turning to drug-supported, off-the-books assets for fighting wars—in Indochina and the South China Sea in the 1950s, 1960s, and 1970s; in Afghanistan and Central America in the 1980s; in Colombia in the 1990s; and again in Afghanistan in 2001. As I have written elsewhere, nearly all these wars were in defense of the overseas interests or aspirations of major U.S. oil companies.[61]

Because the use of drug-supported proxy armies was at odds with Washington's official antidrug policies, the practice had to remain secret. This meant that major programs with long-term consequences were being initiated and administered by small cliques that were almost unknown in Washington. Operation Paper brought OPC into contact not only with drug traffickers abroad but also with organized crime at home. OPC officer Paul Helliwell was the key figure involved in creating an infrastructure in Thailand (SEA Supply Inc.) and a supporting airline (Civil Air Transport, later Air America). Helliwell's infrastructure linked top CIA officials from the Wall Street overworld with leaders from the organized crime underworld. For example, he was the legal counsel for the small Miami National Bank used by gangster financier Meyer Lansky to launder his foreign profits.[62]

Operation Paper became a precedent for other, even larger operations where OPC (and later CIA) worked with criminals in off-the-books, self-financing operations. The OPC's use of the KMT as a proxy for U.S. power was followed without interruption by similar programs, first in Thailand and Laos and later against Cuba.[63] In 1996 veteran Senate staffer Jack Blum told the Senate Intelligence Committee that "a careful review of covert operations in the Caribbean and South and Central America shows a forty-year connection between crime and covert operations that has repeatedly blown back upon the United States."[64] Some of these drug-supported programs continued to receive direct overworld and/or CIA guidance. For example, the sponsor of CIA's drug-financed Thai Paramilitary Police Unit (PARU) operation in Thailand and Laos was former Office of Strategic Services (OSS) director William Donovan, who in 1953 returned from private life as a Wall Street lawyer to serve as America's ambassador to Thailand.[65] Helliwell also worked after 1959 for CIA on anti-Castro projects; some of these Cuban recruits later became drug traffickers.[66]

Today's vastly expanded global heroin traffic is largely the product of

CIA's work with two different sets of proxy forces: the drug-supported KMT and PARU troops in Southeast Asia in the 1950s and 1960s, and the drug-supported Afghan networks in the 1980s. When OPC/CIA began to support the KMT troops in Burma in the 1950s, local opium production in the region was on the order of eighty tons a year. At the height of the Vietnam War, production reached a thousand tons in 1970, before declining at the war's end.[67] Later, as first Pakistan and then CIA started supporting guerrillas in Afghanistan after 1973, opium production in this region began to rise spectacularly. From a hundred tons in 1971, it reached eight hundred tons in 1979, the year of CIA intervention, and then two thousand tons by 1991.[68] With the U.S. occupation in Afghanistan, opium production, which the Taliban had nearly eliminated for the single year of 2001, reached a new high of five thousand six hundred tons in 2006.[69]

The result of all of this is not just a worldwide drug scourge; the flow of drugs also supplies the socioeconomic infrastructure for the scattered terrorist groups collectively known as al Qaeda.[70] Those who blame CIA for the rise of al Qaeda usually point to CIA's supply of training and arms during the 1980s Afghan war. But U.S. operations in conjunction with jihadi drug armies after the end of that war have been perhaps even more responsible. In chapters 8 and 9, I show that U.S. toleration of and even alliance with al Qaeda–backed jihadi groups—notably in Afghanistan, Azerbaijan, Bosnia, and Kosovo—have been in areas of major interest to U.S. oil companies.

In sum, OPC established the practice of using off-the-books forces, some of which broke domestic drug laws. This practice endured and has had lasting consequences, affecting even the catastrophic events of 9/11.[71] Eventually, the more bureaucratic and hierarchical CIA raised objections to the practices of the freewheeling "Fifth Avenue Cowboys" in OPC, with particular respect to the KMT in Burma and Thailand. By 1952 scandals over the KMT drug trafficking, some possibly involving OPC officers, had become so offensive that CIA director Walter Bedell Smith abolished OPC altogether, merging its personnel with CIA's own covert operations staff.[72] But this merger, far from suppressing or even controlling the former "cowboys" of OPC, gave them a more permanent home inside CIA.

Since the events of 9/11, it is clear that America has begun to turn away radically from its own professed ideals of a democratically governed state in an open civil society. But from as early as the 1940s the public power of the public state has been increasingly overridden by the covert power of elite and nonaccountable intelligence and security bureaucracies. Covert operations today represent a serious challenge to the Enlightenment hopes of the great liberal historian Lord Acton, that now "all information is within reach, and every problem . . . capable of solution."[73]

The chronological record of events as reconstructed by archival historians from public records has become increasingly subverted by suppressed or deep history. We now have a chronology for which the public records are either nonexistent or have been falsified. The result is a serious challenge to the democratic hopes of the philosopher Jürgen Habermas for an expanding public sphere of rational discourse, protected against the intrusive policies of nongovernment groups.[74]

THE REPUBLICANS AND ROLLBACK IN THE 1950S: A NEW RUTHLESSNESS

In 1953 America's strategic objectives expanded from a containment of the Soviet Union to a rollback of it. An era of covert interventions in countries with large non-Communist populations (notably in France and Italy) was succeeded by an era of trying to eradicate Communist and other movements that had demonstrably high support (specifically in Indochina and Indonesia). A sign that the United States had assumed more expansive ambitions was its participation in the overthrow of the democratically elected premier Mohammed Mossadeq and his government in Iran in 1953.[75] In doing so, the United States intervened to rescue the Anglo-Iranian Oil Company, a British company that had the backing of the British and U.S. overworld but no significant popular support in Iran.

A year later the United States intervened in Guatemala against another elected leader, on behalf of United Fruit, which faced expropriation of its lands not under cultivation. Both of these interventions, in Iran and Guatemala, were initially advocated within the Council on Foreign Relations.[76]

I call rollback's expansion of U.S. intervention an overreach, not just on ethical grounds but because in these cases there was no lasting support for the operation from the local people.[77] Both in Iran and Guatemala the pro-U.S. dictatorships established could only maintain themselves by brutal repressive tactics that eventually led to their overthrow.[78] In the case of Iran it seems inevitable in retrospect that finally, in 1979, this overreach would be annulled by the victory of anti-American ayatollahs who are among America's chief problems today. The first postwar political victory of Islamist extremism, can be attributed in part to CIA expansive overreach in 1953.

In a more general way the expansions of rollback contributed to the militarization of U.S. foreign policy and specifically to the type of U.S. military interventions, common in Central America a century ago, that Franklin Roosevelt appeared to have renounced with his "Good Neighbor" policy. After World War II rollback was supported inside the United States by a number of sources—from ethnic groups appalled by Roosevelt's acceptance at the 1945 Yalta Conference of Soviet troops in Eastern Europe, to the lavish funds of T. V. Soong and the China lobby, seeking to prevent U.S. recognition of the People's Republic of China. There were elite pressures as well, from people like William Donovan, Henry Luce of the Time-Life empire, and the former Trotskyite James Burnham, who was taken up both by Luce and OPC.[79]

Official National Security Council doctrine for the Cold War was set down in the 1950 document *NSC-68*, drafted by Forrestal's longtime protégé Paul Nitze. *NSC-68* assumed that conflict with the "inescapably militant" Kremlin was inevitable, U.S. policy must be "to check and to roll back the Kremlin's drive for world domination."[80] The document's paranoid exaggeration of Soviet strength and American weakness would be repeated: in the Gaither Report of 1957 (also drafted by Nitze), which became the basis of false fears about a "missile gap," and (as I discuss later) in the 1970s anti-Soviet campaign mounted by the Committee on the Present Danger (CPD), in which Nitze was again prominent.[81]

Thanks largely to the Korean War, the U.S. annual military budget, which was at $14.5 billion in 1950, more than tripled by 1953 to $49.6 billion. It would remain over $40 billion throughout the 1950s.[82] Soon what Eisenhower would label the "military-industrial complex" was asserting itself through new lobbying groups, notably the American Security Council (ASC), founded in 1955. The ASC united old-wealth oil and military corporations with new-wealth businesses in the South and the West, some of which incorporated investments from organized crime.[83]

As the goal of rollback became more ambitious and overreaching, U.S. foreign policy became more ruthless. OPC/CIA proclivity for so-called dirty tricks was sanctioned by the report of a special committee chaired by Lieutenant General James Doolittle, a friend of the CIA's covert operations chief Frank Wisner.[84] The whole of American foreign policy now reached for more costly and difficult goals. The most egregious example was the U.S. engagement in Indochina after 1959, urged by oil interests through the Council on Foreign Relations and by the military-industrial complex through the American Security Council.[85]

The deep state's expansion abroad was matched domestically. CIA developed covert relationships "with about 50 American journalists or employees of U.S. media organizations."[86] According to one CIA operative: "You could get a journalist cheaper than a good call girl, for a couple hundred dollars a month."[87] The agency arranged for the publication of books to be read in America, and for at least one of these works to be reviewed favorably in the *New York Times*.[88] CIA also developed covert relationships with "several hundred American academics" on U.S. campuses.[89]

Violent U.S.-supported overthrows of democratically elected leaders in the 1960s—such as those in Brazil, Ghana, and Indonesia—were followed by a radical increase of overseas U.S. direct and indirect investment in these same countries, particularly in fossil fuels. This was reflected in changes in the American overworld (now less dominated by the Europe-oriented Council on Foreign Relations) and in the deep state. The CFR became more and more allied with the traditionally powerful petroleum lobby, once primarily domestic but now increasingly global in its concerns.[90] Especially before the withdrawal after 1967 of the British Navy from the Indian Ocean, U.S. strategy in the Middle East was dominated by CIA and international oil players, rather than by the Pentagon. Their policies were in the main pro-Arab and above all pro-Saudi, with the oil companies acquiescing in and even subsidizing the Saudi policy of expanding the influence of its extremist and anti-Western Wahhabi sect throughout the Muslim world.

The oil industry is the largest, richest, and most powerful in the world. But the power in Washington of the pro-Arab oil lobby (which journalist Ovid Demaris once characterized as "in itself a subgovernment, with roots planted deep in the soil of the real government") was increasingly matched by the legislative lobbying of the American Israel Public Affairs Committee (AIPAC).[91] Today, U.S. policies on the Middle East, particularly with respect to Iraq and Iran, reflect a consensus of the expansionist agendas of both lobbies.

FROM ROLLBACK TO GLOBALIZATION AND FULL-SPECTRUM DOMINANCE

Since the collapse of the Soviet Union, the term "rollback" has also become a historical memory. But the forces that worked for it are very much alive in contemporary American foreign policy and characterize both sides of the two main global strategies—civilian and military—dominating it. This overarching policy has been characterized by scholar Richard Falk and others as a "global domination project." U.S. foreign policy specialist Andrew Bacevich has described it as a "strategy of openness," with a dual emphasis on "free trade and investment" complemented by "a belief in the necessity of American hegemony."[92] The civilian strategy is for what I call top-down globalization—government-enforced market fundamentalism, or global economic integration on American terms, which include the opening of foreign markets to U.S. investment.

The military strategy is for full-spectrum dominance of the globe. "Full-spectrum dominance" was the key term in *Joint Vision 2020*, the U.S. Department of Defense blueprint for the future, endorsed on May 30, 2000, by General John M. Shalikashvili, chairman of the Joint Chiefs of Staff.[93] The term was taken from U.S. Space Command's *Vision for 2020* in 1998, which spoke of USSPACECOM as "dominating the space dimension of military operations to protect U.S. interests and investment."[94] The same sense of mission as protecting investment can be seen in an article from the Foreign Military Studies Office of Fort Leavenworth, Kansas, which was published three months before the 2001 World Trade Center attacks: "The Caspian Sea appears to be sitting on yet another sea—a sea of hydrocarbons. . . . The presence of these oil reserves and the possibility of their export raises [*sic*] new strategic concerns for the United States and other Western industrial powers. As oil companies build oil pipelines from the Caucasus and Central Asia to supply Japan and the West, these strategic concerns gain military implications."[95]

U.S. oil companies had worked actively to ensure this military interest. Since 1995, they had been united in a private foreign oil companies group to lobby in Washington for an active U.S. policy to promote their interests in the Caspian basin. Their meeting with NSC energy expert Sheila Heslin in the summer of 1995 was followed shortly by the creation of an interagency governmental committee to formulate U.S. policy toward the Caspian. Heslin told Congress in 1997 that U.S. policy in Central Asia was "to in essence break Russia's monopoly control over the transportation of oil [and gas] from that region, and frankly, to promote Western energy security through diversification of supply."[96] A former CIA officer later complained about Heslin's subservience to the oil lobby in the Clinton administration.[97] That oil company influence did not diminish with the election, financed in large part by oil companies, of

President George W. Bush (formerly a Saudi-financed oilman) and Vice President Dick Cheney (formerly CEO of Halliburton and board member of the U.S.-Azerbaijan Chamber of Commerce).

The disastrous policy failure of the Vietnam War saw the first serious dissatisfaction expressed, by both the left and the right, with the role of America's foreign policy establishment in creating that war. The publication of such books as Noam Chomsky's *American Power and the New Mandarins*, Richard J. Barnet's *The Roots of War*, and David Halberstam's *The Best and the Brightest* supplied serious critiques of the roles played by men like national security adviser McGeorge Bundy, whom the mainstream media had previously treated as icons.[98] The war produced unprecedented unrest and violence in the United States. In 1967 and 1968 this violence led to the creation of a special army directorate with plans to coordinate with local police in surveillance and control of left-wing protesters. This led to de facto use of right-wing gangs in surveillance and control, one of many factors that signaled a shift of the country to the right.

Nixon inherited these programs, but he also augmented them. Later I discuss how one vastly expanded army plan, known as Garden Plot, continued to proliferate after Nixon's fall from office. Garden Plot is the direct ancestor of the planning for continuity of government, which I see as contributing to the catastrophic events of 9/11. In the Nixon era the multilateralist policies of the once-dominant Council on Foreign Relations came to yield place to the unilateralist and neocon policies of the once-marginal American Enterprise Institute. A key moment was the split in the CFR establishment after 1968, dividing the "traders" (those who were concerned for international economic order) from the "Prussians" or "warriors" (those who were concerned for preserving U.S. predominance over the Soviet Union.)[99] This last group included the first neocons.

Let's look in particular at what neocon founder Irving Kristol called the right wing's "intellectual counterrevolution" in the late 1960s and early 1970s.[100] This counterrevolution arose from the fear, approaching panic, at the spread of chaos, violence, and revolutionary rhetoric in the United States during this period. Author and editor Lewis Lapham recalled the grave anxiety with which the overworld watched America coming apart: "I remembered my own encounter with the fear and trembling of what was still known as 'The Establishment,' . . . at the July encampment of San Francisco's Bohemian Club. . . . In the summer of

1968, the misgivings were indistinguishable from panic. . . . [The] country's institutional infrastructure, also its laws, customs . . . seemed to be collapsing into anarchy and chaos—black people rioting in the streets of Los Angeles and Detroit, American soldiers killing their officers in Vietnam."[101]

Future Supreme Court Justice Lewis Powell, in a 1971 confidential memorandum for the U.S. Chamber of Commerce, warned that survival of the free enterprise system lay "in organization, in careful long-range planning and implementation, in consistency of action over an indefinite period of years, in the scale of financing available only through joint effort, and in the political power available only through united action and national organizations."[102] Soon, funding for this right-wing ideological offensive was being provided "by a small sewing circle of rich philanthropists—Richard Mellon Scaife in Pittsburgh, Lynde and Harry Bradley in Milwaukee, John Olin in New York City, the Smith Richardson family in North Carolina, Joseph Coors in Denver, [and] David and Charles Koch in Wichita."[103] With support from these foundations America saw a spate of new and well-funded right-wing organizations, such as the Scaife-backed Moral Majority and the interlocking Coors-backed Council for National Policy (once called by ABC News "the most powerful conservative group you've never heard of").[104]

The stage was set for what political commentator Kevin Phillips and others have called the "greed decade" of the 1980s, when "the portion of the nation's wealth held by the top 1 percent nearly doubled, skyrocketing from 22 percent to 39 percent, probably the most rapid escalation in U.S. history."[105] With the spreading gap between rich and poor, the ideal of a public state in which all classes participated was further weakened by the reality of a deep state or security state in which, more than ever before, a few manipulated the many. This was facilitated by a parallel development in the media, with the emergence of new press barons like Rupert Murdoch and Conrad Black. As journalist David Brock wrote: "In the late 1970s and early 1980s, Keith Rupert Murdoch [the prime example] went on a buying spree in the United States, purchasing papers in San Antonio, New York City, Boston, and Chicago. American journalism was never the same."[106]

In addition, the Reagan administration instituted its own Office of Public Diplomacy in the State Department, staffed by "perception management" experts from CIA and Special Forces, to plant anti-Communist propaganda in the American press.[107] As a result of these trends, the old media—the mainstream press and television—became less and less likely to present critical perspectives on controversial government policies.

"A NEW PEARL HARBOR"

Once in power, Ronald Reagan, his CIA director William Casey, and vice president George H. W. Bush initiated emergency planning, building from the Garden Plot plan, for what Alfonso Chardy of the *Miami Herald* called "suspension of the Constitution, turning control of the government over to FEMA [the Federal Emergency Management Agency], emergency appointment of military commanders to run state and local governments and declaration of martial law."[108] The plan also gave FEMA, which had been involved in drafting it, sweeping new powers, including the power "to surveil political dissenters and to arrange for the detention of hundreds of thousands of undocumented aliens in case of an unspecified national emergency."[109]

What is most astonishing about this 1980s planning is that Congress was "completely bypassed."[110] Once again, as in the early days of OPC, private power allied with the extreme wealth of the overworld was imposing policies and structures by secret procedures that radically redirected the course of the public state. It was doing so at a constitutional level. COG—more properly characterized as *change* of government rather than *continuity* of government—was not seeking to influence or assist constitutional authority, but to control it, and if necessary, to override it. Questions about this program emerged briefly in the 1980s, particularly in the Iran-Contra hearings of July 1987 when Oliver North was asked (but did not get to answer) whether he had worked on "a contingency plan . . . that would suspend the American constitution."[111]

Public alarm was alleviated by the false assurance that this referred to a proposed executive order from FEMA and that this had already been "effectively killed" by the attorney general William French Smith.[112] In fact, FEMA planning continued up to the day of September 11, 2001, when COG was first implemented.[113] Worse, however, there are indications that COG planning may have helped set the stage for 9/11 to happen. Two members of the ultra-secret private group drafting COG in the 1980s were Dick Cheney (then a congressman) and Donald Rumsfeld (then the CEO of G. D. Searle, a pharmaceutical company).[114] In the fall of 2000, a year before 9/11, Cheney and Rumsfeld signed on to a major study, *Rebuilding America's Defenses*, by the lobbying group Project for the New American Century (PNAC). The study called for a major increase in the defense budget, the removal of Saddam Hussein from Iraq, and the maintenance of U.S. troops in the Gulf area even after Saddam's disappearance.

The PNAC study was a blueprint for the George W. Bush foreign policy that has been and still is being implemented. It also reflected support from the private sector for the blueprint of full-spectrum dominance that had been articulated in the Pentagon's *Joint Vision 2020*. The similarity between the two blueprints was not coincidental. *Joint Vision 2020* built on a draft known as *Defense Planning Guidance* written in 1992 for then Defense Secretary Cheney by future PNAC members Paul Wolfowitz, I. Lewis Libby, and Zalmay Khalilzad.[115] Every critical study of 9/11 has noted the PNAC report's frank assertion that the policy changes it advocated would be difficult to implement quickly, "absent some catastrophic and catalyzing event—like a new Pearl Harbor."[116]

Rumsfeld, in addition to being a PNAC member and a member of the COG secret team, endorsed the same idea as the chair of the so-called Rumsfeld Commission, which made proposals with regard to the projected multibillion-dollar project for the U.S. Space Command. This commission's report, issued January 7, 2001, said with respect to attacks in space: "The question is whether the U.S. will be wise enough to act responsibly and soon enough to reduce U.S. space vulnerabilities. Or whether, as in the past, a disabling attack against the country and its people—a 'Space Pearl Harbor'—will be the only event able to galvanize the nation and cause the U.S. government to act."[117]

From these various quotations we can see that the high-profile PNAC report was merely the public face of a consensus that had already emerged at a high level. Throughout the 1990s both the U.S. oil industry and the Pentagon had contributed to the consensus that America would need full-spectrum dominance to guarantee access to oil and other resources in the rest of the world.[118] This program would require massive expenditures, perhaps as much as a trillion dollars, and this could not be expected from Congress—except in response to an attack as massive and frightening as Pearl Harbor.[119] This leads us to recall that America's entry into wars has frequently been triggered by disputed attacks, including the Tonkin Gulf incidents in Vietnam.[120] With respect to the events of 9/11 it is clear that the administration's settled goal of invading Iraq *depended* on the attack. What we have been witnessing, to quote the Oslo researcher Ola Tunander, is "the use of terrorism to construct world order."[121]

Almost two centuries ago the French statesman Alexis de Tocqueville wrote of America's "great democratic revolution" as being irresistible "because it is the most uniform, the most ancient, and the most permanent tendency that is to be found in history."[122] The political developments of the past few years have led many Americans to fear that proponents of top-down power have at last found the means to frustrate that tendency. In this book's concluding chapter, I suggest ways to give renewed strength to what I call the prevailable will of the people—that potential for solidarity that, instead of being checked by top-down repression, can actually be awakened and reinforced by it. Whether the United States can again be counted among the forces working for democratic revolution may well depend on the future of the Internet, and whether the new media, profiting from the increasing limitations of the old media, can help create the public arena for a more democratic society.

TWO

NIXON, KISSINGER, AND THE DECLINE
OF THE PUBLIC STATE

That there was a Rule of Law and a Rule of Government, and
that many things which might not be done by the Rule of Law
might be done by the Rule of Government.

Rex [Charles I] v. Richard Chambers, 1642

Use of this technique is clearly illegal; it amounts to burglary.
It is also highly risky and could result in great embarrassment
if exposed. However, it is also the most fruitful tool and can
produce the type of intelligence which cannot be obtained in
any other fashion.

White House Huston Memorandum, 1970

CHAOS, PARANOIA, AND SUPPRESSION
IN THE WHITE HOUSE

In 1968, roiled in domestic conflict and paranoia, the United States
elected its most paranoid president ever—Richard Nixon.[1] Six years
later, as the Vietnam War was winding down, Nixon resigned from
office and the public paranoia subsided. Especially with the election of
Jimmy Carter in 1976, there was a prevailing sense that an era of domestic conflict was over and that with peace would come a healing of divisions. On the surface this may have been true. Only a few secret players

knew that plans for martial law and so-called psychological warfare or mind control in America, far from disappearing with the Nixon presidency, were still in place and would be increased over the next three decades. At the time of Nixon's election the country was coming apart. Both the left and the right were suffering from internal divisions. Meanwhile, centrist politicians of both parties were going down to defeat, as "liberal" became a term of opprobrium to the left and right alike. The term "compromise," long the touchstone for American democratic resolution of differences, acquired more and more negative, almost sinister connotations.[2]

Two chief pressures on the body politic were responsible for distorting it: the backlash to the civil rights movement and Vietnam. The whole world has been inspired and changed by the U.S. struggle to end segregation and heal ancient divisions, particularly in the South.[3] There movement activists redressed injustice with demands for changes that the majority of Americans would ultimately come to accept; their successes were due chiefly to nonviolent Gandhian techniques and processes of *satyagraha* (open participatory power), or what author and *Nation* correspondent Jonathan Schell has defined as "cooperative power."[4] By persuading public opinion to accept overdue changes to unite the American nation, they made U.S. democracy stronger and greatly increased what Harvard international relations professor Joseph Nye has called its soft power in the world (an "ability . . . associated with intangible power resources such as an attractive culture, ideology, and institutions").[5] These steps toward racial equality also incurred an inevitable backlash.

Then the shadow of the Vietnam War fell across the land, and some of these same social activists began working for violent revolution. In so doing, they clearly passed the bounds of what was acceptable to the nation. They became foes of public opinion, what I call the prevailable will of the people.[6] Soon most Americans saw democracy as imperiled, and for good reason. In 1967 the National Guard was called out twenty-five times to deal with rioting, gunfire, arson, and looting. In Detroit that summer forty-three people died, while the National Guard was reinforced by U.S. Army paratroopers of the 81st and 103rd divisions. In 1968, acting on the recommendations of the hastily convened Kerner Commission, the Pentagon took unusual steps to combat civil disturbance. A plan and command, named Operation Garden Plot, was devised for "DOD components [that is, U.S. armed forces] to respond to reasonable requests from the FBI for military resources for use in combating acts of terrorism."[7] Under this plan

> Military Intelligence—working with the FBI, local county and state
> police forces—undertook and directed a massive domestic intelligence-
> gathering operation. . . .
>
> Security forces ranging from Army troops to local police were trained to
> implement their contingency plans.
>
> The Army task force that had designed this program took on a new name,
> the Directorate of Civil Disturbance Planning and Operations, and
> became a national coordinating center for these different efforts.

The army task force's transformation into the Directorate of Civil Disturbance Planning and Operations occurred during the massive rioting
that broke out in black ghettos of nineteen cities after the assassination of Martin Luther King Jr. in April 1968. The directorate's headquarters was in the Pentagon's basement, known as "the domestic war
room."[8]

In effect, plans and programs were being established to institutional-
ize martial law on a long-term or even permanent basis. A number of
steps were taken toward eroding the prohibition, established in the
Posse Comitatus Act of 1876, against the ongoing use of the army in
civilian law enforcement.

In 1970 this army program, code-named Garden Plot, was partially
exposed by Senator Sam Ervin's Senate Subcommittee on Constitutional
Rights. In 1975 journalist Ron Ridenour gave further revelations of one
of Garden Plot's "subplans—code name Cable Splicer, covering California, Oregon, Washington and Arizona, under the command of the Sixth
Army. It is a plan that outlines extraordinary military procedures to stamp
out unrest in this country. Developed in a series of California meetings
from 1968 to 1972, Cable Splicer is a war plan that has adapted for
domestic use procedures used by the U.S. Army in Vietnam."[9] The massive army intelligence program was supplemented at various stages by
CIA, the Secret Service, the Internal Revenue Service, and the National
Security Administration.[10]

The FBI's Cointelpro program also created bogus revolutionary
movements that were accused of provoking violence, notably during the
Wounded Knee uprising at the Pine Ridge Reservation.[11] The *Pike Committee Report*, prepared for the House of Representatives in 1975 but
then suppressed by it, corroborated that the FBI provoked violence in
order to discredit the left. The committee's hearings documented the
problem of FBI informants turned agents provocateurs. One such example was William Lemmer, who infiltrated the Vietnam Veterans Against

the War (VVAW). In May 1972, while on the FBI payroll, Lemmer instigated an illegal VVAW action at Fort Tinker Air Force Base.[12] Later, together with Miami city police informant Pablo Fernandez, Lemmer attempted to involve VVAW leaders (the so-called Gainesville Eight) in violence at the Democratic National Convention.[13]

Army-police collaboration led to a number of dirty tricks, including the supply of arms to unauthorized right-wing gangs, like the so-called Legion of Justice in Chicago, in exchange for intelligence.[14] In the army's surveillance of Martin Luther King Jr., the 20th Special Forces Group is reported to have used reservists from the Alabama National Guard, who in turn traded arms for intelligence from the Ku Klux Klan.[15] In other words the U.S. Army with these programs, consciously or not, was countering a militant left by building up and arming a militant right.

In the chapters that follow, I show that some of these programs outlived Nixon and in fact were substantially expanded by President Reagan. The consequences of these programs are still with us. They interface with the problem of jihadi terrorism in the United States today, and above all with the events of 9/11.

Nixon inherited these anti-disturbance and surveillance programs, but he also took great interest in expanding them and in bringing CIA more actively into the surveillance business.[16] In 1971, in response to the leak of the Pentagon Papers by former Pentagon analyst Daniel Ellsberg, Nixon authorized the creation of the White House Plumbers unit to spy on Ellsberg. The unit was soon engaged in an illegal break-in at the office of Ellsberg's psychiatrist. They were also involved with orders to a small unit of Cuban exiles to attack Ellsberg physically, either to "punch him" or possibly to "break both his legs."[17] Ultimately the break-in and other surveillance excesses of the Plumbers, which we remember collectively as part of the Watergate scandal, would force Nixon from office. At the time, however, his concern for more forceful restraint of dissent was widely shared, within both the nation and its establishment.

As previously noted, author and editor Lewis Lapham described the "fear and trembling" in 1968 "of what was still known as 'The Establishment,' . . . at the July encampment of San Francisco's Bohemian Club."[18] In response to the feared left-wing offensive against the nation's institutions, many on the right began to organize a counteroffensive of their own. Future Supreme Court justice Lewis Powell expressed it in a 1971 confidential memorandum to the U.S. Chamber of Commerce: "Survival of what we call the free enterprise system lies in organization, in careful long-range planning and implementation, in consistency of action over an indefinite period of years, in the scale of financing available only through joint effort, and in the political power available only through united action and national organizations."[19]

Nixon himself may have played a role in the implementation of this program. The *Haldeman Diaries* for September 12, 1970, record: "P[resident] . . . pushing again on project of building *our* establishment in press, business, education, etc."[20] A visible public step was when rightwing billionaire Joseph Coors launched the Heritage Foundation in 1973 to defend Nixon's already embattled presidency.[21] Coors and the Heritage Foundation failed to save Nixon, but they would play a significant role in electing Reagan six years later.

After the first oil embargo of 1973 was followed by congressional moves to regulate the American oil companies, they too mobilized to prevent further such interference. Michael Wright, the chairman of Exxon U.S.A., warned in a pamphlet called "The Assault on Free Enterprise": "Let there be no mistake, an attack is being mounted on the private enterprise system in the U.S. The life of that system is at stake."[22]

All these projects contributed to a controlled rightward shift of public discourse: above all, by redirecting private funding from the great central and institutionalized foundations (Ford, Rockefeller, Carnegie) to ideologically driven conservative competitors (Coors, Allen-Bradley, Olin, Smith Richardson).[23] (Eventually both the Rockefeller and the Ford families became estranged from the mainstream foundations that still bore their names.)[24] The shift in funding meant that the once dominant and Atlanticist Council on Foreign Relations would be increasingly challenged, and in the end superseded, by the unilateralist, neocon American Enterprise Institute.

Interestingly, as the establishment overworld shifted toward Nixonian and eventually Reaganite Republicanism, the mafia underworld reportedly did so too. This has been offered as an additional explanation why the entertainer Frank Sinatra, who in the 1960s was the close friend of both Chicago mob leader Sam Giancana and President John F. Kennedy, became in 1970 an intimate friend of Republican Vice President Spiro Agnew.[25]

THE NIXON-KISSINGER BALANCING ACT:
THE TWIN PILLARS STRATEGY AND ITS CONSEQUENCES

In March 1969 senior members of the Council on Foreign Relations establishment journeyed from Wall Street to Washington, D.C., to warn

Nixon "of the disastrous possibilities for the international economic order if the war were continued."[26] But the old CFR consensus on the world had been shattered by the challenge of the Vietnamese Tet offensive in 1968, and they no longer spoke for Wall Street as a whole. The "traders" whose priority was economic order were now challenged by a minority of "warriors" or "Prussians" within the CFR, notably Paul Nitze, whose overriding concern was, as in earlier years, not to yield world dominance to the Soviet Union.

Many of those who once passionately disliked the policies of Nixon and Kissinger in Chile, Vietnam, and other countries have come to give them credit for helping to stabilize a particularly dangerous period of potential nuclear war and for hammering out the basis of a crude global equilibrium that included China. But in 1974 Nitze publicly attacked Nixon and Kissinger before the Senate Armed Services Committee for promoting their "myth of détente."[27] In so doing, he represented what was still a small but significant overworld minority (who in 1976 would organize as the Committee on the Present Danger). Within the U.S. government a similar gulf had emerged between the State Department and the Joint Chiefs of Staff. Nitze, still in the minority under Nixon, would soon see his position prevail under presidents Ford and Reagan.

With the nation, the establishment, and the government itself so deeply divided, there was no solution for Vietnam that could gain general acceptance. Nixon chose to pursue a middle course, which was certain to please almost no one and to arouse resistance approaching revolt, even within his own cabinet. His solution to this problem, as Kissinger later recalled, was to cut out whole sections of the Washington bureaucracy that he distrusted and "to run foreign policy from the White House."[28] To do this, Nixon, the former darling of the American Security Council, appointed as his national security adviser perhaps the only figure whom both he and the CFR could trust—Henry Kissinger.[29]

In his seminal work, *Wealth and Politics*, political commentator Kevin Phillips regards the election of Nixon in 1968 as the last of the "seven U.S. political watersheds—the American Revolution and the elections of 1800, 1828, 1860, 1896, 1932, and 1968—[involving] a major party campaign against a national elite. . . . [During Nixon's campaign] the anti-establishment 'outsider' conservatism gaining influence in the Republican Party targeted both the party's 'eastern establishment'—the axis of Rockefellers, Scrantons, and Lodges—and a larger 'eastern liberal establishment' clustered around the prestige media, foundations, think tanks, and Ivy League universities."[30] All of this is true. But the victory of the

Sunbelt outsiders in campaign rhetoric was not matched in Nixon's subsequent appointments and policies. In particular, Nixon's new defense
secretary, Melvin Laird—a former congressman from Wisconsin who had
been highly critical of former defense secretary Robert McNamara's style
of management—was completely subordinated to, and frequently
bypassed by, Nixon and Kissinger.[31]

Like McGeorge Bundy under Presidents Kennedy and Johnson,
Bundy's Harvard protégé Kissinger was named to be national security
adviser after having chaired an important policy "study group" at the
Council on Foreign Relations. As a former assistant to Nelson Rockefeller, Kissinger had been paid by Rockefeller to write a book on limited
warfare for the CFR. He had also campaigned hard in Rockefeller's losing campaign for the presidential nomination in 1968.[32] Thus Rockefeller and the CFR might have been excluded from control of the Republican Party, but not from the Republican White House.

Nixon and Kissinger were also radical innovators, at times virtually a
two-man cabal that conducted U.S. policy in novel and more secretive
ways. They felt that they had to be. America was losing not just a war in
Vietnam, but also its ability to dominate world finance and its traditional
share of world trade and manufacturing. According to Phillips: "Whereas
in the late 1940s the United States had produced 60 percent of the industrial world's manufactures and 40 percent of its goods and services, both
portions were halved by the late 1970s. . . . The convergence of inflation
and weaker U.S. trade balances in turn undercut the dollar, encouraging
foreign governments to trade in their greenbacks for gold."[33]

Under Nixon in 1973 the United States experienced its first major oil
shock, as America gradually shifted from being an oil exporter to becoming an oil importer, today the world's largest.[34] At the same time the
country changed from being the world's largest creditor to becoming one
of the world's largest debtors. The two conditions were interrelated, as
the United States sought to maintain financial stability by secret political
agreements to recycle petrodollars into the American bond and stock
markets.

Also at this time there was widespread concern, which Kissinger shared
with Nitze, that with the setbacks in Vietnam the United States was losing
ground to the Soviet Union, not just in Asia but also in Africa, South
America, and even Europe.[35] Kissinger later believed "that the United
States had essentially won the Vietnam War in 1972, only to lose it
because of weakened resolve by the public and Congress."[36] After 2003
both George W. Bush and Cheney consulted with Kissinger more than

with any other outside adviser. His message to both men was what he had learned from Vietnam, and in 2005 he proclaimed in the *Washington Post*: "Victory over the insurgency is the only meaningful exit strategy."[37]

Nixon and Kissinger were in power through difficult and almost unmanageable times. Their policies led to many positive outcomes. But I shall focus on the darker aspects of their strategies, many of which had a particular bearing on 9/11.

Nixon and Kissinger developed the habit of imposing geostrategic policies of the greatest long-term importance, which they had discussed with almost no one else in the government. There are many examples of such secret diplomacy, including Kissinger's famous July 1971 mission to Beijing to meet with Premier Zhou Enlai, which was handled so secretively that it excluded the State Department.[38] In May 1972, according to foreign affairs specialist James A. Bill, "President Richard Nixon and National Security Advisor Henry Kissinger visited the Shah on their way back from a summit meeting in Moscow. Here, against the best advice from the Department of Defense, they gave the Shah a blank military check enabling him to purchase the sophisticated F-14 aircraft. Between 1972–1977, the value of U.S. military sales to the Shah amounted to $16.2 billion."[39]

These arms sales were in general implementation of the Nixon Doctrine enunciated by Nixon in 1969, by which the United States scrapped the Dulles system of anti-Communist alliances in favor of containing Communism by arms sales to designated regional powers. But the arms sales were implemented by two men, Nixon and Kissinger, talking alone with the shah. "Joseph Sisco, the under-secretary for the Middle East, was left in his hotel room, uninformed about the outcome. . . . There had been no major review beforehand and Nixon's decision was passed to the Pentagon with no chance to revise it."[40]

Nixon's policy for the Middle East has been called a "twin pillars" policy, "in which Iran and Saudi Arabia would serve as anti-Soviet regional proxies."[41] The fall of the shah in 1979 would leave only one pillar remaining, but the core of Nixon's Middle East policy has lasted to the present day. This was the formula of higher oil prices balanced by increased arms sales to the countries earning windfall petrodollars. On the one hand, the new policy helped stabilize the dollar; on the other, it filled the vacuum left by the departure of the British in 1971 from the Persian Gulf area.

The Nixon arms deal with Iran in 1972 has since been analyzed as a double gift to Nixon's most affluent political backers: the U.S. oil majors seeking protection and the U.S. arms industry, which was facing cutbacks at the end of the Vietnam War.[42] To pay for these huge arms purchases, the shah, with encouragement from Nixon and Kissinger, "took the initiative for OPEC's enormous increase of oil prices in 1973; the oil revenues thus obtained helped him order more weapons and launch more big projects."[43]

In the new quasi equilibrium, massive U.S. arms sales helped pay for massive U.S. oil imports, and vice versa. This exchange helped consolidate what economist James Galbraith first called the "military-petroleum complex"[44] and foreign policy analyst Walter Russell Mead has recently labeled the "finance-security-hydrocarbon complex."[45] According to the *Washington Post*, "Kissinger's policy which was quietly adopted by the Carter administration" was explicitly defended by Kissinger: "In exchange for paying higher oil prices, Kissinger argued that the United States and its allies would receive an ensured and politically stable source of supply. Also, America's major oil companies and other corporations would be in a position to garner billions of dollars and a competitive advantage in trade with the OPEC countries."[46]

There were other momentous and ill-considered consequences. Both Saudi Arabia and later Iran used their enormous new wealth to strengthen the worldwide forces of Islamic fundamentalism, using such CIA-approved vehicles as the Muslim Brotherhood and the Muslim World League. The League had been founded by Saudi king Faisal in 1972, as part of his strategy "to set up an 'Islamic bloc,' complete with American support," against his enemy, Egypt's secular ruler Gamal Abdel Nasser.[47] European sources claim that the League was funded in part by the Arabian-American Oil Company (Aramco), even before it was nationalized by Saudi Arabia after 1974.[48]

From America to Indonesia mosques and madrassas multiplied and sidelined traditional Islam in favor of the reactionary views of Saudi Wahhabis and Pakistani Deobandis (a faction similar to Wahhabis but originating historically in reaction to the assimilationist practices of British colonialism in India). (A Wahhabi eminence in Saudi Arabia, Sheikh Abd al-Aziz bin Baz, later head of the Muslim World League, argued in 1966 that the sun revolved around the earth, and the earth was flat. Anyone who disagreed was guilty of "falsehood toward God, the Koran, and the Prophet."[49])

This wave of proselytizing helped in particular to polarize and destabilize Afghanistan, where, as oil profits skyrocketed in the 1970s, representatives of the Muslim Brotherhood and the Muslim World League, with Iranian and CIA support, "arrived on the Afghan scene with bulging bankrolls."[50]

The oil-for-arms policy also profoundly affected U.S. domestic politics. In addition to increasing oil company revenues, the policy perpetuated and expanded the military-industrial complex that had grown fat on Vietnam, thus increasing the flow of funds for both parties from the petroleum-industrial complex. It also increased the flow of illegal contributions into American domestic politics from foreign arms salesmen and recipients, notably the Saudi Lockheed salesman Adnan Khashoggi and the shah of Iran. Khashoggi had contributed $50,000 to Nixon's campaign in 1968. In 1972, according to what Khashoggi told Pierre Salinger, he contributed $1 million to Nixon; he is rumored to have called on Nixon in San Clemente and to have "forgotten" his briefcase with the money when he left.[51] Khashoggi attended the 1973 Nixon inaugural, along with even more dubious figures like Michele Sindona, a member of the conspiratorial Italian Masonic Lodge Propaganda Due (P-2). Sindona was later convicted after having looted and bankrupted the Franklin National Bank. Eight years later P-2 chief Licio Gelli was a guest at Reagan's inauguration.[52]

In like manner the shah, after receiving his "military blank check" in May 1972, is said to have contributed hundreds of thousands, maybe more than $1 million, to Nixon's 1972 campaign.[53] Sampson's comment is worth repeating: "It was a poignant coincidence that after 1973, just when the United States was painfully seeking to clean up its business methods and to limit the influence of money on politics, the new Arab wealth was encouraging a much more easy-going attitude to commissions and bribes. While the Arabs were being westernised, the West was being Arabised."[54]

Khashoggi's corrupting influence in America did not only work through bribes; he was also a supplier of sex. Just as his uncle Yussuf Yassin had been a procurer of women for King Abdul-Aziz, so Khashoggi himself was said to have "used sex to win over U.S. executives." The bill for the madam who supplied girls en masse to his yacht in the Mediterranean ran to hundreds of thousands of dollars.[55] The corrupting power represented by Khashoggi's wealth and female companions attracted favorable CIA interest, and he was listed in the 1992 *Kerry-Brown BCCI Report* as one of the "principal foreign agents of the U.S."[56] Such "former" CIA officers as Miles Copeland and James Critchfield became part of his milieu. They advised Khashoggi on diplomatic initiatives, such as a proposed Mideast Peace Fund that would reward both Israel and Palestine for recognizing each other.[57]

Khashoggi represented the postwar emigration offshore of immense wealth and the power it conveyed. He served as a "cut-out," or representative, in a number of operations forbidden to those he represented. Lockheed, for one, was conspicuously absent from the list of military contractors who contributed illicitly to Nixon's 1972 election campaign. But there was no law prohibiting their official representative Khashoggi from cycling $200 million through the bank of Nixon's friend Bebe Rebozo.[58] In the 1980s, following much adverse publicity, Khashoggi's role as cut-out would be inherited and expanded by his friend Kamal Adham, former chief of Saudi intelligence and by this time a major influence behind the activities of the Bank of Credit and Commerce International.

Nixon admirers defend the two Nixon-Kissinger policies—of closing the gold window and of seeking a balance-of-payments equilibrium of arms and oil in its place—as a successful strategy for containing the USSR, and ultimately overcoming it. However, these policies enriched the United States in unexpected ways that have clearly harmed the overall social equilibrium of the world and (in the eyes of some critics) of the United States itself.

In the case of demonetizing gold, according to economist Michael Hudson: "By going off the gold standard at the precise moment that it did, the United States obliged the world's central banks to finance the U.S. balance-of-payments deficit by using their surplus dollars to buy U.S. Treasury bonds, whose volume quickly exceeded America's ability or intention to pay. All the dollars that end up in European, Asian, and Eastern central banks as result of American's excessive import-imbalance, have no place to go but the U.S. Treasury. Because of the restrictions placed on the central banks—there is no place else for this money to go—these countries were forced to buy U.S. treasuries or else accept the worthlessness of the dollars received through trade."[59] Meanwhile the increases in the U.S. balance-of-payments deficits were now being partially offset by arms sales, first to the twin pillars and increasingly to the rest of the world.

This is an example of how a policy, not closely monitored, can metastasize.[60] What began as a program to make the world "secure" by selling U.S. arms abroad is today a major source of U.S. and global insecurity.[61] Many of the weapons America has pumped into the world—notably the Stingers sent to Afghanistan in the 1980s—are now a threat to be dealt with. In the 1976 presidential campaign Jimmy Carter declared: "We can't have it both ways. We can't be both the world's leading champion of peace and the world's leading supplier of arms." But the arms sales program has generated a political constituency, and has continued to expand under every president since Nixon, including Carter. The United States today is the world's largest arms exporter, selling $14 billion of arms a year, the great bulk of it in Asia and North Africa.[62]

The distinguished social scientist Chalmers Johnson has shown how today the foreign policies of both parties in many areas—such as the expansion of NATO—are encouraged in the Pentagon as opportunities for more arms sales.[63] As he wrote in his *Sorrows of Empire*: "The military-industrial complex warmly welcomed the wars against Yugoslavia, Afghanistan, and Iraq as good for business. Actions just short of war, such as bombings and missile strikes, are also . . . 'giant bazaars for selling the wares of the armaments manufacturers.'"[64]

U.S. balance-of-payments deficits have also been eased by the high price of oil, since America made secret deals to ensure that petrodollars would be recycled and later that all OPEC oil sales would be dollar denominated.[65] (The first step was when Nixon's treasury secretary, William Simon, "negotiated a secret deal so the Saudi central bank could buy U.S. Treasury securities outside the normal auction."[66]) Thus the biggest demand for dollars overseas is the need of oil-importing countries to maintain dollar reserves to pay for their oil. What this has meant in practice is that the U.S. dollar is strengthened at the expense of third-world countries, which now have to pay much more in dollars for their oil. After 1972 the continents of Africa and South America became burdened with unmanageable debt. (One exception was Colombia, which maintained a stable balance of payments through its export of drugs to the United States.[67])

The final irony is that the unlimited commitment made by Nixon and Kissinger to the shah in 1972 contributed within a few years to the collapse of his overmilitarized and underdeveloped regime.[68] It was later termed by Zbigniew Brzezinski's White House assistant Gary Sick to be the crucial error leading to the fall of the shah. Iran, "the regional tail wagging the superpower dog," swiftly destabilized itself by imports its economic infrastructure could not absorb.[69]

The Nixon Doctrine can be seen as a substitute for a worse one proposed at the time: that the United States should directly assume the role, which Britain was forced for financial reasons to abdicate in 1971, of being the major military power in the region. America would assume that role directly with the Carter Doctrine of 1980. But it is obvious in retrospect that the Nixon Doctrine became a major factor in the destabilization of Iran that forced the departure of the shah only seven years later. Its primary motivation was neither America's security nor Iran's. Instead, it had everything to do with the oil companies' concern for their investments in the Persian Gulf, and their fear, not so much that they would be overrun by Soviet attack, as that they would lose the ability to negotiate from strength with their host countries.

NIXON, KISSINGER, THE ROCKEFELLERS, AND DÉTENTE

Nixon's and Kissinger's arrival in the White House in 1969 coincided with David Rockefeller's becoming CEO of the Chase Manhattan Bank. The Nixon-Kissinger foreign policy of détente was highly congruous with Rockefeller's push to internationalize Chase Manhattan banking operations. Thus in 1973 Chase became the first American bank to open an office in Moscow. A few months later, thanks to an invitation arranged by Kissinger, Rockefeller became the first U.S. banker to talk with Chinese Communist leaders in Beijing.[70] Rockefeller also served as intermediary between the White House and other foreign leaders, such as Gamel Abdel Nasser and Anwar Sadat in Egypt, King Faisal of Saudi Arabia, and the leaders of Oman.[71]

The Kissinger-Rockefeller relationship was complex and certainly intense. As investigative author Jim Hougan wrote: "Kissinger, married to a former Rockefeller aide, owner of a Georgetown mansion whose purchase was enabled only by Rockefeller gifts and loans, was always the protégé of his patron, Nelson R., even when he wasn't directly employed by him."[72] I have found no documentation for any direct interventions by the Rockefellers in the Nixon-Kissinger conduct of the war in Southeast Asia. But David Rockefeller, in his *Memoirs*, speaks candidly of his total support of the Vietnam War and of General William Westmoreland's strategy of troop escalations, until the Tet Offensive in 1968 persuaded him "that we had no choice but to negotiate our withdrawal on the most acceptable terms possible."[73]

The Nixon-Kissinger phase of the Vietnam War was one of a series of short-term violent escalations, in order to achieve their notions of "acceptable terms" at the conference table. This led to the notorious bombings of North Vietnam in 1972, which Nixon authorized after contemplating a nuclear attack. (He was recorded as saying, "I want that place bombed to smithereens. If we draw the sword, we're going to bomb those bastards all over the place. Let it fly, let it fly."[74]) Both Nixon and Kissinger expressed later the thought that (in Kissinger's words) "we could have ended the war much sooner if we had been willing to do in 1969 what we ended up doing in 1972."[75]

A violent example of Nixon-Kissinger secrecy serving oil interests was the secret expansion of the U.S.-Vietnam bombing campaign to Cambodia, with the result that, as Christopher Hitchens has written, as many as 1,350,000 people may have been killed. To do this, Kissinger restructured the chain of command to exclude a reluctant Defense Secretary Laird, so that he himself could take personal charge of bombing raids.[76] As international affairs analyst Asad Ismi reported, "Although the U.S. military informed Kissinger that there would be substantial Cambodian civilian casualties, he told the Senate that Cambodian areas selected for bombing were 'unpopulated,' a blatant lie."[77]

In my book *Drugs, Oil, and War*, I show how the overthrow of Cambodian prime minister prince Norodom Sihanouk, and the Cambodian incursion of 1970, were preceded by years of unauthorized geomagnetic exploration of Cambodian offshore waters by the U.S. Navy, with the UN's Economic Commission for Asia and the Far East acting as a flimsy cover. The change of government was followed two years later with the signing of oil exploration agreements by Sihanouk's U.S.-installed successor, Lon Nol, and the U.S. oil companies Unocal and Chevron.[78]

The importance of Cambodia to oilmen probably explains why Nixon, on the day of his decision to invade Cambodia (April 28, 1970), shared his decision with "several private citizens [from] veterans and patriotic organizations," two days before he notified Congress. Almost certainly one of these "patriotic organizations" was the American Security Council, a group representing both arms and oil interests (including Unocal) that had helped push Nixon into national prominence.[79]

NIXON, KISSINGER, DAVID ROCKEFELLER, AND CHILE

Perhaps the most blatant example of Nixon's intervention on behalf of corporate interests was in engineering the overthrow of the elected president Salvador Allende in Chile. As investigative reporter Seymour Hersh wrote years ago: "There is compelling evidence that [in Chile] Nixon's tough stance against Allende in 1970 was principally shaped by his concern for the future of the American corporations whose assets, he believed, would be seized by an Allende government."[80] Here, on occasion, Nixon and Kissinger gave major directions for covert operations to CIA without consulting the 40 Committee, the administrative group formally responsible for approving all sensitive covert operations.[81]

However, the covert operational planning with CIA director Richard Helms brought in Nixon's "corporate benefactors"—Jay Parkinson of Anaconda Copper, Donald Kendall of Pepsi, and Harold Geneen of ITT.[82]

David Rockefeller's hidden instigation of the Allende overthrow is amply acknowledged in his own *Memoirs*. His two pages on Chile reveal the limitations of this overworld mind, in some ways gentle and benevolent but concerned first and foremost for U.S. corporate property in Latin America's "miasma of confrontation and suspicion." He wrote: "The Andean Pact, for example, formed in 1970 by Chile, Bolivia, Peru, Ecuador, and Colombia . . . severely restricted the operations of foreign corporations, and there were a number of outright expropriations. I was so concerned about the situation that I met with Secretary of State William P. Rogers and National Security Advisor Henry Kissinger."[83]

David Rockefeller's solution was to have them send his brother Nelson on a fact-finding mission to Latin America. This naïve idea produced such violent anti-American demonstrations in Venezuela and elsewhere that Christian Democratic president Eduardo Frei canceled the projected visit to Chile (which the U.S. ambassador had opposed from the outset). "Clearly," David Rockefeller concluded without irony, "it would take more than a presidential emissary . . . to repair hemispheric relations."[84]

Other accounts of Allende's overthrow have pointed to Nixon's and Kissinger's initial disinterest in the subject, as evidenced by Kissinger's reference to Chile as the "dagger pointed to the heart of Antarctica."[85] But Kissinger did a volte-face in 1970, leading to his famous remark that "I don't see why we have to let a country go Marxist just because its people are irresponsible."[86] In his own words the establishment by election of "a Cuba-style Communist dictatorship . . . was judged [note the passive construction] to be extremely inimical to American national interests."[87]

Allende's election was so "judged" by David Rockefeller

> In March 1970, well before the election, my friend Augustin [that is, Agustin] (Doonie) Edwards, publisher of *El Mercurio*, Chile's leading newspaper, told me that Allende was a Soviet dupe who would destroy Chile's fragile economy and extend Communist influence in the region. If Allende won, Doonie warned, Chile would become another Cuba, a satellite of the Soviet Union. He insisted the United States must prevent Allende's election.
>
> Doonie's concerns were so intense that I put him in touch with Henry Kissinger. I later learned that Doonie's reports confirmed the intelligence already received from official intelligence sources, which led the Nixon administration to increase its clandestine financial subsidies to groups opposing Allende.[88]

That Edwards's reports corroborated the CIA's is hardly surprising. CIA was drawing its intelligence from Edwards and his allies in the first place.

Helms in his autobiography confirms that CIA initially failed, despite repeated urgings, to get Nixon and Kissinger interested in stopping the election of Allende. It was in the same month of March 1970 that finally "the 40 Committee [of the National Security Council] authorized CIA to spend $135,000 on what it referred to as 'spoiling operations.' "[89] To understand what then developed, it is necessary to know that Rockefeller knew Edwards from the Business Group for Latin America (the BGLA, later the Council of the Americas, or the CLA). With the encouragement of Robert Kennedy, Rockefeller had founded the BGLA in 1963, "as cover for [CIA's] Latin American operations."[90] From the outset the BGLA worked closely with CIA in Chile, where the "principal contact" for both the BGLA and CIA was "the organization of Agustin Edwards."

CIA and BGLA/CLA "relied heavily on Edwards to use his organization and his contacts to channel their covert monies into the 1964 political campaign," and again into the 1970 campaign.[91] In addition, the joint CIA/CLA funding for the 1970 election campaign was approved, over Ambassador Edward Korry's strong objections, by the assistant secretary of state for Latin America, Charles Meyer. Meyer was a former active member of the CLA who "told a private Council luncheon that he had been 'chosen' for the post [at State] 'by David Rockefeller.' "[92]

Hersh has revealed how Edwards took part with other corporate executives in key CIA meetings.[93] Right after the election of Allende on September 4, Edwards and his family left Chile for the United States, where (to quote Rockefeller again) "Donald Kendall, CEO of Pepsico, hired Doonie as a vice president, and Peggy and I helped get them established."[94] Hersh supplies the denouement: "On September 14, according to Kissinger's memoirs, Kendall met privately with Richard Nixon. . . . The next morning, Mitchell and Kissinger, at Nixon's direction, had breakfast with Kendall and Edwards: hours later, Kissinger asked Helms to meet Edwards. . . . Helms later told an interviewer that Kendall was with Edwards when they met in a Washington hotel. The two men appealed passionately for CIA help in blocking Allende—an argument, Helms realized, they must have made to Nixon. In the early afternoon, Nixon summoned Helms, Mitchell, and Kissinger to his office and gave Helms a blank check to move against Allende without informing anyone—even [Ambassador] Korry—what he was doing."[95]

Author and journalist Walter Isaacson adds that after the morning meeting between Edwards and Kissinger, and before Kissinger called Helms, "Kissinger met privately with Mitchell and then David Rockefeller, chairman of the Chase Manhattan Bank, which had interests in Chile that were more extensive than even Pepsi-Cola's."[96] A subsequent FBI interview of David Rockefeller recorded that for some time he "had allowed the Chase Manhattan Bank to be used in the CIA's anti-Allende Chilean operations."[97] Complacent that Allende's overthrow was for the best, even though "what followed can only be described as a reign of terror," Rockefeller was proud of having helped persuade Kissinger and Nixon to plot against Allende, and thus pave the way for the kind of Chicago-school free market economy he admired. (As Rockefeller wrote, "The economic side of the story is a more constructive one [and a] model for other hemispheric nations."[98])

The overthrow of Allende in 1973 deeply affected developments in Iran six years later. An explicit reason for the 1979 occupation of the U.S. embassy in Tehran was the legitimate fear that the embassy would play a role similar to the role the U.S. embassy in Santiago had played in overthrowing Allende. In chapter 11, I discuss the European charges that Nixon, Kissinger, and CIA used tactics, similar to those used against Allende, to frustrate Italian democracy as well.

THE NIXON-KISSINGER USE OF
THE RIGHT-WING MUSLIM CARD IN PAKISTAN

Another secret Nixon-Kissinger policy helped define the future of U.S.-Pakistan relations for three decades, including the U.S. presence in Afghanistan and America's relation (along with that of Pakistan's intelligence service) to al Qaeda. I am referring to Nixon's and Kissinger's acquiescence (and ultimate assistance) in the killing by the Pakistani Army of from one to three million civilians in Bangladesh (then called East Pakistan) in 1970 and 1971. At the time Nixon and Kissinger were determined to support General Yahya Khan of Pakistan, who was the go-between in arranging privately for Kissinger's secret mission to open up U.S.-Chinese relations in Beijing.[99] In October 1970, Nixon and Kissinger had lifted a longtime embargo on arms sales to Pakistan, thus beginning what became known as America's "tilt" toward Pakistan over India.[100]

When Yahya's party was roundly defeated by the Bangladeshi vote in the Pakistani elections of December 1970, Yahya, confident of U.S. backing as evidenced by U.S. arms and aid, felt empowered to prevent a peaceful transfer of power to a new government headed by Sheikh Mujibur Rahman of the Awami League. U.S. diplomats in Dhaka implored Kissinger to stop the resulting tide of killings, but Kissinger instead sent a message to Yahya, thanking him for his "delicacy and tact."[101] Kissinger's support for Yahya provoked a cable of protest signed by twenty U.S. diplomats in Dhaka, headed by Consul General Archer Blood. They were later joined by nine senior members of the State Department's South Asia division. Hitchens later called the inevitably named Blood Telegram "the most public and the most strongly worded demarche from State Department servants . . . that has ever been recorded."[102] The only result of the protest, however, was that Archer Blood was recalled immediately from his post.[103]

On the Pakistani side Nixon and Kissinger, using CIA, had just encouraged the first massive intervention into domestic Pakistani politics of Pakistan's military intelligence service, the Inter-Services Intelligence (ISI), together with the fundamentalist Jamaat-e-Islami political party.[104] The ISI spent millions of rupees in vain to block the electoral victory of the Awami League, whose goals were socialism, secularism, and democracy. Subsequently, the Jamaat-e-Islami supported the army's massacre in Bengal and even formed armed groups like Al Shams and Al Badr to participate in the killings.[105]

Drawing on the careful research of foreign correspondent Lawrence Lifschultz, Hitchens reports that after Kissinger's brief visit to Bangladesh in 1974, "a faction at the U.S. embassy in Dacca began covertly meeting with a group of Bangladeshi officers who were planning a coup against Mujib[ur]. On 14 August 1975, Mujib and forty members of his family were murdered in a military takeover. His closest former political associates were bayoneted to death in their prison cells a few months after that."[106] The leader of the coup and murder, Khondakar Mustaque (a right-wing Islamic fundamentalist), had had conspiratorial contact with Kissinger personally since 1971.[107] This is an example, extreme but not isolated, of the way U.S. interventions have destroyed progressive tendencies in South Asian Islam and left ascendancy by default to the fundamentalist right.

Furthermore, according to the renowned Indian observer B. Raman: "When Dr. Henry Kissinger was the National Security Adviser, the intelligence community of the U.S. and the ISI worked in tandem in guiding and assisting the so-called Khalistan movement in the Punjab. The visits of prominent Sikh Home Rule personalities to the U.S. before the Bangladesh Liberation War in December, 1971, to counter Indian allegations of violations of the human rights of the Bengalis of East Pakistan through counter-allegations of violations of the human rights of the Sikhs in Punjab were jointly orchestrated by the ISI, the U.S. intelligence and some officials of the U.S. National Security Council (NSC) Secretariat, then headed by Dr. Kissinger."[108]

America's interest in Islamist reactionaries to oppose progressives dates back to the 1950s. In 1953, Eisenhower received in the Oval Office a delegation including Said Ramadan of the Muslim Brotherhood, an organizer associated in Pakistan with the World Muslim Congress and the Jamaat-e-Islami.[109] Freelance investigative journalist Robert Dreyfuss has reported that when Ramadan was in Karachi, he helped organize an Islamist cadre among university students; he also cites Swiss reports that Ramadan was "an intelligence agent of the English and the Americans."[110]

In 1971, CIA joined Saudi intelligence in backing the Muslim Brotherhood and its allies in a worldwide campaign against communism, particularly in Egypt.[111] Kissinger became personally involved in the cut-out, or intermediary, role played by Kamal Adham between King Faisal in Saudi Arabia and Anwar Sadat (himself once secretary of the World Muslim Congress) in Egypt. In Dreyfuss's words, "Not only was Adham acting as an intermediary for Faisal, but he was also secretly working as a conduit for communications between Sadat and Kissinger. In his memoirs, Kissinger describes the connection, noting that the Saudi role allowed Sadat and Nixon to stay in touch while *bypassing both foreign ministries.*"[112]

Thanks in part to Kissinger, the subsequent decade saw a significant "Islamification" of Pakistan and increased CIA support for both the ISI and the Jamaat-e-Islami (the local representatives of the Muslim Brotherhood).[113] A 2003 article in the Pakistani *Defence Journal* declared that in the 1970s "the initial groundwork for the anti-Communist Jihad in Afghanistan was laid as a result of cooperation between Pakistan and American (and British) intelligence agencies. Indeed, the three sets of intelligence services were one in purpose in those days."[114]

CIA was on familiar ground. Together with its longtime ally the British intelligence service MI6, it had recruited right-wing mullahs for the coup against Mossadeq in Iran in 1953.[115] CIA in the 1950s also turned to the Muslim Brotherhood, which had a long and complex history with British intelligence. Citing the former CIA agent Miles Copeland, Said Aburish has written that "around 1955 . . . the CIA began to cooperate with the Muslim Brotherhood, the Muslim mass organization founded in Egypt but with followers throughout the Arab Middle East. . . . This signalled the beginning of an alliance between the traditional regimes and mass Islamic movements against Nasser and other secular forces."[116]

The increase of Muslim Brotherhood–Jamaat-e-Islami influence in Pakistan, subsidized by Saudi Arabia, was accompanied by an increase in the number of fundamentalist madrassas, today the core of opposition to Pakistani prime minister Pervez Musharraf's efforts to modernize Pakistan. Kissinger's actions in Pakistan further reinforced the emerging CIA-ISI-Islamist coalition that would "Islamize" Pakistan and its army, distort CIA efforts in Afghanistan under Casey, and finally contribute to the rise of al Qaeda.[117] Today, with the wisdom of hindsight, I doubt whether Kissinger's end justified the means, even from a ruthlessly American point of view.

Kissinger had proceeded on the assumption that his political skills and Nixon's could manage a U.S. response to Pakistan's problems better than the bureaucracy could as a whole. In the case of Pakistan, this assumption was demonstrably foolish. Kissinger's memoirs report his impression at the time that "India was bent on a showdown with Pakistan. . . . China might then act," and the Soviet Union might then intervene to teach Beijing a lesson. As Hersh later responded, events "over the next five months would prove every aspect of Kissinger's analysis wrong. Pakistan initiated the war with India; China did not move; and the Soviet Union urged restraint upon the Indians."[118] But we are living today with the disastrous fallout from the Pakistan-Islamist tilt.

My overall assessment of the Nixon-Kissinger legacy is mixed. On the one hand, Nixon, like Johnson before him, must be given credit for avoiding nuclear confrontation with the Soviet Union. On the other hand, Nixon's insistence on conducting foreign policy in secret, without broad participation, led ultimately to major errors, a crisis and breakdown in his relations with Congress, and lasting negative consequences for the third world. With Nixon's resignation in 1974, there was an illusory sense that the Watergate crisis had ended. But some of the damage to the body politic was permanent. The open procedures for policy resolution in the common ground of the public state had fallen still further into desuetude. Public politics had become, as they remain today, contests in which dissident minorities exert their own wills, ignoring that of the rest.

The divisions existing throughout the United States antedated Nixon's election and should not be attributed principally to him. However, there is no doubt that his personal paranoia aggravated rather than healed the breakdown in comity or civility in American politics.[119] By bypassing regular bureaucratic policy development, Nixon also contributed greatly to what has replaced it: the imposition of radical policy innovations from the outside by small, unrepresentative cabals. In my opinion the specific crimes for which Nixon was impeached and lost public favor were less serious than his deeper, less visible alterations of the body politic. One of the chief of these was Garden Plot, the secret plans and arrangements for the military suppression of dissent. Greatly expanded under Nixon's paranoid direction, Garden Plot continued after his downfall to gather its own momentum. In chapters 11 to 13, I shall show how this augmentation of secret power would contribute to the events of 9/11.

WATERGATE AND ITS COMPETING CABALS: THEIR IMPLICATIONS FOR 9/11

With the breakdown of Nixon's relationship to a Democratic Congress, it was probably inevitable that Congress would fight back. As the world knows, that retaliation took place chiefly in the form of the Watergate investigations and the ultimate resolutions of impeachment. In a general way this process represented the attempt of Congress, representing the public state, to respond to encroachments upon it. When we look more closely, however, we see competing cabals at work, striving by strategic leaks to restrain (or in the end, to remove) the president and his White House clique. By the end of the 1970s these cabals would be more, not less, powerful than before.

The complete picture of what we call the Watergate scandal is dialectical, starting with leaks about Nixon to the press, which provoked White House investigations and cover-ups, which were followed by a third stage of leaks about the investigations and cover-ups. The event that became the center of the scandal—the Watergate break-in—was a domestic matter, but most of the initial leaks and passionate controversy concerned foreign policy. The first resolution for Nixon's impeachment, introduced by the congressman Robert Drinan on July 31, 1973, called for inquiry into four other matters besides Watergate, including Nixon's secret bombing of Cambodia.[120] Although the Cambodian bombing did not ultimately figure in the articles of impeachment, the sensational leak of it (by the *New York Times* on May 9, 1969) led immediately to the first dramatic wiretaps of NSC staffers and reporters that would ultimately help bring Nixon down.[121]

Other leaks of Nixon-Kissinger excesses in foreign policy, notably the leak in December 1971 of the "tilt towards Pakistan," provoked frenzied investigation by the White House Plumbers.[122] Eventually this investigation revealed that the source of the leak, navy yeoman Charles Radford, had been systematically stealing White House documents and passing them, via his navy superior, Admiral Robert Welander, to the chairman of the Joint Chiefs of Staff (JCS), Admiral Thomas Moorer.[123] In retrospect, it seems clear that the primary JCS motive for conspiratorial spying on the White House was dislike of Nixon's and above all Kissinger's policies of détente and coexistence with the Soviet bloc and China. As historian Stanley Kutler wrote in his *Wars of Watergate*: "Moorer bitterly remembered what he regarded as foolish and soft policies toward North Vietnam. His successor as chief of naval operations, Admiral Elmo R. Zumwalt, Jr., came close to accusing Nixon and Kissinger of treason and Kissinger of being a Soviet sympathizer."[124]

With the Cambodia and Pakistan leaks it is possible to see Nixon as caught in the middle between two competing (and conspiratorial) cabals. One group, reflecting the hopes of the "traders" in New York for a scaling down of the Vietnam War, sought by leaks—for example, Cambodia—to curb the secret escalations of the war. A competing cabal of "Prussians," centered in but not restricted to the Joint Chiefs of Staff, sought in contrast to win in Vietnam and put an end to Nixonian plans for coexistence with the Soviet Union.

James McCord, the principal architect of the Watergate break-in, which was surely set up to be disclosed,[125] expressed a paranoia about Kissinger that exceeded even that of Moorer and Zumwalt. In a newsletter he put out in the aftermath of Watergate, "McCord put forward a right-wing conspiracy theory that the Rockefeller family was lunging for complete control over the government's critical national security functions, using the Council on Foreign Relations and Henry Kissinger as its surrogates."[126] McCord's mind-set is of interest not only because he was a principal conspirator in the Watergate break-in, but also because of his role as an Air Force Reserve colonel in an obscure program of the Office of Emergency Preparedness (the predecessor to FEMA). His group was responsible for contingency plans, "in the event of a national emergency . . . for imposing censorship [and] preventive detention of civilian 'security risks,' who would be placed in military 'camps.'"[127] (These plans continued to be developed throughout the 1980s, with the secret participation of Dick Cheney and Donald Rumsfeld, as part of the supersecret continuity of government planning that was partially implemented for the first time on September 11, 2001.)

Much more threatening to the presidency was probably the opposition of James Angleton, head of CIA counterintelligence. Angleton eventually came to "pronounce Kissinger 'objectively, a Soviet agent.'"[128] But Angleton had a more immediate reason to oppose Nixon after November 20, 1972, the day Nixon at Camp David notified Richard Helms he would be replaced as head of CIA.[129] Helms and Angleton had been two of the last survivors of the Dulles "inner circle" within CIA.[130]

I cannot adequately emphasize the exceedingly complex relationship to Watergate of what Hougan has called "the counterintelligence establishment," including Angleton at CIA and John Mohr at the FBI. I will say only that when chief Watergate burglar Howard Hunt "retired" from CIA in 1970, the paperwork (now at the U.S. National Archives and Records Administration) specified that he was to go to another assignment.[131] At the Mullen Company, a CIA proprietary firm, and later at the White House, Hunt proceeded to commit crimes and other questionable activities "on behalf of" the president, some of which were clearly not authorized by the Nixon White House and for nearly all of which he deposited irrefutable evidence in the files of CIA.[132] This evidence remained at CIA until the firing of Helms in November 1972, after which it soon began to reach the Justice Department.

Many highly placed people in Washington—including Nixon himself, his troubleshooter Charles Colson in the White House, and Senator Howard Baker on the Senate Watergate Committee—suspected the hand of CIA behind Watergate.[133] Others have claimed that CIA was eavesdropping on Nixon in the Oval Office, as Colson and others in the White House believed, and that Nixon's knowledge of this explains why he complied, disastrously, with orders to hand over his tapes.[134]

The firing of Helms was only one part of Nixon's dramatic plans for a wholesale reorganization of the Washington bureaucracy in his second term. These plans seem to have united a coalition that no longer wished merely to curb his actions, but to unseat him. That coalition, I am convinced, included the composite of insiders, notably Mark Felt of the FBI, who leaked information to reporter Bob Woodward as "Deep Throat." That coalition also appears to have united members of both the trader and the Prussian cabals against the president, who now threatened both factions. Woodward, for example, was no ordinary journalist, but a veteran of the navy and naval intelligence who at one point, according to Hougan, "seems to have become a protégé of his [and Radford's] commanding officer, Admiral Robert O. Welander."[135] Woodward was part of an elite group selected to brief top intelligence officials, and it was in this capacity that he probably first made contact with the FBI part of the "Deep Throat" composite, Mark Felt.[136]

In 1993, in my extended study of the CIA inner circle's relationship to the Kennedy assassination, I noted analogies between that event, Watergate, and Contragate:

> The in-house coalition of conservatives who opposed the Nixon-Kissinger moves toward detente in 1972 was similar to the one which opposed the Kennedy-Harriman detente initiatives in 1963. It still included James Angleton in the CIA, who in the 1960s had suspected Harriman of being a Soviet spy, and who in the 1970s "reportedly 'objectively' believed Kissinger to be a Soviet spy." Nixon, like Kennedy was having trouble with his Joint Chiefs of Staff, one of whom, Admiral Zumwalt, resigned over his differences with Kissinger. Those who believe that Nixon's betrayer "Deep Throat" was a real official, and not a composite, advanced well-argued reasons that he must have been a senior FBI official, probably Mark Felt, John Mohr, or L. Patrick Gray. In all [these] crises, one sees the recurrence of CIA and other intelligence officials and assets, repeatedly those with more militant anti-Communist stances than the Presidents they have worked under.[137]

The CIA's official historian, Thomas Troy, attributes a less manipulative role than I do to CIA in Watergate, but he offers an assessment I agree with of the scandal's major consequences for CIA:

> Thomas Powers was absolutely correct in his analysis of the significance of the CIA's unfortunate and reluctant involvement in the Watergate scandal. Writing in 1979, he said that Watergate "marks a violent break in Agency history, the first step in a process of exposure which has pretty much destroyed the unwritten charter established by Allen Dulles." Watergate "undermined the consensus of trust in Washington which was a truer source of the Agency's strength than its legal charter . . ." And Watergate "ended the long congressional acquiescence to the special intimacy between the CIA and the Presidency, an intimacy which allowed Presidents to use CIA as they might, beholden to no one so long as congressional oversight remained a kind of charade. Watergate, in short, made the CIA fair game."[138]

CIA's new vulnerability became highly visible with the disclosures in 1974 and especially 1975, the so-called year of intelligence, about CIA's role in domestic surveillance and political assassinations.[139] As I explore in the next chapter, this public scrutiny of CIA served the purposes of those who wished to diminish it, in pursuit of a more powerful Pentagon and increased defense budget.

THREE

THE PIVOTAL PRESIDENCY

Ford, Rumsfeld, and Cheney

> We had to struggle with the old enemies of peace: business and financial monopoly, speculation, reckless banking, class antagonism, sectionalism, war profiteering. They had begun to consider the Government of the United States as a mere appendage to their own affairs. We know now that Government by organized money is just as dangerous as Government by organized mob.
>
> **Franklin Delano Roosevelt, 1936**

A PIVOTAL SHIFT: THE HALLOWEEN MASSACRE OF NOVEMBER 1975

Historians of the 1970s once tended to overlook Gerald Ford's presidency as an unimportant interlude, a time of relatively tranquil confusion and indecision between the more dynamic eras of Nixon-Kissinger and Carter-Brzezinski. The events of 9/11 suggest the opposite, however: that the Ford presidency, in which the management team of Rumsfeld-Cheney first emerged, was a pivotal moment, one during which the prerogatives of the deep state and the military-industrial complex were reasserted, following the massive (and at first glance apparently successful) congressional revolt against them in the Watergate crisis.

Books about Watergate inevitably structure that crisis as an Aeschylean drama about the hubris and retributive downfall of a man. It is time to reassess Watergate as a single chapter in an ongoing American (and not only American) crisis of authority, whose origins are as old as the

Republic itself but which became acute in the two decades between the election of John F. Kennedy in 1960 and of Ronald Reagan in 1980. The most dramatic moment of that crisis may well have been the palace revolution of August 1974, still imperfectly understood, when Kissinger told his president bluntly that "he had to resign" because "an impeachment trial would paralyze foreign policy and be too dangerous for the country."[1] But Nixon's forced resignation did little to resolve the ongoing crisis. It left in place a barely prepared successor, who had hardly had time to arrange for the transition. As a result, Ford's White House was peopled with a surfeit of conflicting constituencies: Nixonian holdovers, Ford's congressional staff (the so-called Grand Rapids group), Kissinger's team of advisers, and (after Nelson Rockefeller became vice president in December 1974), old Rockefeller liberals.

This conflicted scene mirrored the confusion inside the Republican Party. Ford slowly realized that by keeping on Kissinger as secretary of state, he faced an ever more powerful challenge from the Reagan forces in the party who might deny Ford renomination in 1976. Governance was made still more difficult by the Democratic landslide in the November 1974 elections. In Kissinger's words the new Congress "was violently opposed to intervention abroad . . . [,] ever suspicious of the CIA, deeply hostile to covert operations, and distrustful of the veracity of the executive branch."[2] Congressional mistrust had been increased by Ford's pardon of Nixon on September 8, 1974.

Meanwhile, the country was in the midst of a catastrophic post-Vietnam economic recession, one that "convinced most American elites that they were facing a true long-term crisis."[3] On December 6, 1974, the Dow Jones Industrial Average fell to 577.60. Through most of the next year the City of New York, despite a number of emergency bailouts, hovered on the brink of declaring bankruptcy.[4] Small wonder, then, that members of the threatened overworld called for a resumption of Vietnam-level defense spending as a means to jump-start the ailing economy. As I wrote in chapter 1 and will discuss further, a well-financed "intellectual counterrevolution" was mustered, one of whose goals was to ensure that disarmament talks did not endanger the Pentagon's budget.[5]

A key figure in this avalanche of right-wing money was Ford's treasury secretary, William Simon at the Olin Foundation, where he "was joined by the legendary John J. McCloy . . . the recognized chairman of all things Eastern and established" (and longtime Rockefeller representative).[6] As a result of backing from Olin and others, the American Enterprise Institute in Washington, formerly a marginal group, emerged as an energetic opponent of Kissinger's foreign policy of détente.[7] By 1976 their lavish activities and expenditures were bearing fruit: a number of different polls showed that in just seven years a majority of Americans had shifted from wanting cuts in defense spending to wanting an increase.[8]

The near anarchy in government, in the Republican Party, and in the White House made short work of Ford's initial plans to administer without a Haldeman-like chief of staff. In September he appointed Donald Rumsfeld to be his new coordinator, and Rumsfeld in turn brought in his unknown protégé, Dick Cheney, then only thirty-three years old. Ford and Rumsfeld's initial priority was, as Rumsfeld later put it, "to restore a sense of legitimacy to the executive branch."[9] In addition, Rumsfeld insisted, successfully, on the need to exercise a more aggressive leadership within the White House.[10]

The post-Watergate crisis of authority was partially resolved on November 2, 1975, with Ford's so-called Sunday Morning Massacre, also known as the Halloween Massacre. No less than nine leading administration figures either were fired or changed positions. In one concerted move, Rumsfeld became secretary of defense and Cheney his successor as chief of staff. Kissinger was stripped of his second role as national security adviser, William Colby was fired as CIA director, and Ford told Kissinger's mentor Nelson Rockefeller that he would not be Ford's running mate in 1976.[11] When the dust had cleared, what emerged was an ideologically pruned White House dominated by two new personalities: Rumsfeld, now in the Pentagon, and his protégé Cheney in the White House.

Especially in the wake of 9/11, some scholars have interpreted the Halloween Massacre as an ideological "palace coup" engineered by Rumsfeld and Cheney themselves.[12] Both Nelson Rockefeller and Kissinger believed at the time that Rumsfeld was responsible, acting out of ambition for his own political future.[13] But the authorship and motives of the shift have been disputed. An in-depth analysis by Ford's domestic policy assistant James Reichley argues that Ford himself, "apparently consulting no one except [his Kitchen Cabinet adviser] Bryce Harlow . . . put together the series of job changes."[14]

Because I seriously question Rumsfeld's and Cheney's behavior on 9/11, I want to make it clear that I regard the case for their authorship of the important Halloween Massacre as unproven. Although further research is needed, I regard Rumsfeld and Cheney as molded *by* the intrigues of 1975 as much as molders *of* those intrigues.[15] There is no doubt that by the end of 1976 both men had emerged as foes of détente and of congressional oversight of foreign policy. In time their positions would harden even more into rigid ideological ones. But in 1975 and 1976 the two may have reflected a more expedient search to strengthen the Ford presidency against its enemies right and left.

This leaves open the question whether the initiative for the massacre came from inside the White House, as most treatments have assumed, or from forces in the overworld. Ford is not generally remembered as a president of forceful initiatives. Both Nixon and Carter were (as this book documents) remarkably responsive to policy initiatives thrust on them by the powerful Rockefeller family. Did Ford really not seek or receive overworld backing for a surprise decision that "devastated" Nelson Rockefeller—"his hopes of becoming president were now permanently dashed"—and left him "an angry and bitter man"?[16] (If there was such backing, it might well have involved William Casey, a bitter enemy of both Rockefeller and Kissinger, whom Ford appointed to the President's Foreign Intelligence Advisory Board in March 1976.)[17]

A slightly different question is how much, and when, Rumsfeld and Cheney helped change Ford's initial emphasis—on restoring the White House's status in the eyes of public opinion and the Democratic Congress—to a strategy of ensuring his nomination at the 1976 party convention.[18] The first course was one of restoring the public state, as suggested by Ford's autobiography's title, *A Time to Heal*. The eventual strategy, in which Cheney emerged as a mastermind, paved the way for presidencies more imperial than Nixon ever conceived of. This makes the question an important one, and once again, the answer is uncertain. The eighteenth-century moral philosopher Adam Smith, discussing economic activity, wrote famously in *The Wealth of Nations* that an individual is "led by an invisible hand to promote an end which was no part of his intention."[19] It is almost as if there is a comparable invisible hand operating in political affairs as well—an impersonal calculus that dictates where a presidency, when guided only by the pursuit of power, will end up, despite the president's stated intentions. We shall see this process even more dramatically in the case of President Jimmy Carter.

In truth, Ford himself was already reverting, even before the massacre, toward his traditional conservative preference for military spending over domestic spending. His decision to diminish Rockefeller and Kissinger (which Rumsfeld endorsed) reflected his increasingly urgent desire to win the support of his party, rather than the Democratic Congress. Ford's concern with Kissinger, in particular, may have derived from his awareness, formally expressed in a pollster's November 12 memorandum to Cheney, that "detente is a particularly unpopular idea with most Republican primary voters and the word is worse."[20]

This pivotal conservative shift went unnoticed at the time. Publicly it appeared that Secretary of State Kissinger had survived, losing only his position as national security adviser (where his successor was his former deputy, Brent Scowcroft). Along with right-wing congressmen the press focused on the firing of the secretary of defense James Schlesinger, the leading opponent in the administration of Kissinger's proposals for parity with the Soviet Union. But whereas in November 1974 Ford had agreed with Soviet first secretary Leonid Brezhnev at Vladivostok on a Strategic Arms Limitation Talks (SALT II) negotiation aiming at parity, Rumsfeld was able, after becoming defense secretary, to frustrate Kissinger's pursuit of this goal.

This means that after November 1975 the team of Rumsfeld and Cheney occupied roughly the same positions of dominance in the Pentagon and White House that they would come to occupy in the George W. Bush administrations after 2001. Increasingly, they would use their positions in pursuit of the same goals. One extreme instance of this was when "at the Republican Party Convention, acting as Ford's representative, Cheney engineered the adoption of Reagan's foreign policy plank in the platform."[21] Echoing Reagan, this plank argued that "agreements . . . such as the one signed in Helsinki, must not take from those who do not have freedom the hope of one day gaining it."[22] It thus repudiated what Kissinger had achieved with the Helsinki Accords of 1975, perhaps the most constructive and important achievement of Kissinger's career.

THE CONSEQUENCES OF HELSINKI, EAST AND WEST

The Helsinki Accords were negotiated in July 1975 at the Conference on Security and Cooperation in Europe (CSCE) meetings, the chief business of which, as part of détente, was to regularize and ratify the borders of Eastern Europe. As a quid pro quo, and partly to quiet critics who saw in this a betrayal of such states as Poland, Kissinger insisted on including the so-called Basket III, which established human rights as a formal component of European security. The Helsinki human rights provisions of Basket III "became a key weapon of Soviet-bloc dissidents in the '80s."[23] Kissinger later made it clear that these provisions were his primary reason for agreeing to the accords: "As one of the negotiators of the Final Act of the Helsinki conference, I can affirm that the administration I represented considered it primarily a diplomatic weapon to use to thwart the communists' attempts to pressure the Soviet and captive peoples."[24]

As Soviet ambassador Anatoly Dobrynin later wrote, the Helsinki Accords "gradually became a manifesto of the [Soviet bloc] dissident and liberal movement, a development totally beyond the imagination of the Soviet leadership."[25] Robert Gates, then on the National Security Council staff, later claimed that, by unleashing forces of criticism and debate inside the Soviet bloc, the Helsinki Accords led directly to the collapse of the Soviet Union: "The Soviets desperately wanted CSCE, they got it, and it laid the foundations for the end of their empire. We resisted it for years, went grudgingly. Ford paid a terrible political price for going—perhaps reelection itself—only to discover years later that CSCE had yielded benefits beyond our wildest imagination. Go figure."[26]

But, as Kissinger himself wrote: "this was not how the [Helsinki] conference was perceived in the United States [at the time]. . . . *Newsweek* magazine sneered at Helsinki as 'considerable ceremony, little substance.' Ronald Reagan, gearing up for his political campaign, argued: 'Mr. Ford flew halfway around the world to sign an agreement at Helsinki which placed the American seal of approval on the Soviet empire in Eastern Europe.' . . . [However] as I predicted in a speech . . . on August 14, 1975: . . . 'At Helsinki, for the first time in the postwar period, human rights and fundamental freedoms became recognized subjects of East-West discourse and negotiation. The conference put forward *our* standards of humane conduct, which have been—and still are—a beacon of hope to millions.' "[27]

Both Kissinger the German and Brzezinski the Pole were self-defined realists and as such were attacked in the 1980s by Straussian neocons around Reagan, who argued that to have ignored the immorality of the Soviet Union was itself immoral. But Kissinger at least recognized that a realism that ignores the driving strength of idealism is not realistic. Consciously or unconsciously, he had helped set the stage for Solidarnosc and the Velvet Revolution in Eastern Europe—movements that some day may be emulated in America.

From the viewpoint of those who believe in social change through nonviolent action, the "paradox" presented by Gates's judgment is no paradox. Recognizing the postwar frontiers of Poland in the eastern bloc did not mean abandoning them to perpetual Soviet rule, as the Reagan camp charged at the time. Rather, it meant liberating the Poles from the fear of an invasion from the west by NATO, which in their eyes would have meant a German occupation once again. Thus for the first time Polish dissent could mobilize the deep-seated national resistance to the Soviet presence without fearing it would precipitate an East-West war. Far from imprisoning Poland behind a legitimated iron curtain, Helsinki liberated Poles for the resistance of Solidarnosc, which began just four years later.[28]

In Poland the opportunities created at Helsinki were exploited swiftly. In 1976 Adam Michnik and leftist dissidents founded KOR (the Workers Defense Committee), a group that enjoyed the support of Archbishop Karol Wojtyla of Kraków (soon to become Pope John Paul II). Incoming president Carter wasted no time in exploiting Helsinki to support the new movement. As British historian Timothy Garton Ash later commented: "In early 1977 the most active younger members of KOR were arrested, and materials collected for a trial. Then, in July 1977, they were all quite unexpectedly amnestied. . . . By 1977 [Polish Party Secretary Edward] Gierek was already in desperate financial straits, while the 'Helsinki process' was in full swing and the Carter administration made the most explicit 'linkage' between the economic and human rights components of detente. That year both Chancellor Schmidt and President Carter visited Warsaw. At a press conference Carter loudly praised the Polish record on human rights and religious tolerance, in the next breath announcing a further $200 million of U.S. credits. 'Linkage' could hardly be more explicit than that."[29]

I regard Helsinki as a defining moment for two reasons. First, it showed a successful way to spread democracy through nonviolent rollback—not by attempting to impose democracy militarily (the neocon agenda in Afghanistan and Iraq), but by persuading authoritarian regimes to lighten their oppression of an alienated public. Helsinki was not a unique example of such a U.S. initiative. In the mid-1980s CIA director William Casey and Republican senator Paul Laxalt were similarly able to persuade President Ferdinand Marcos to hold the elections that ended his hold over the Philippines. Second, and even more important, if the seeds for Soviet dissolution were planted nonviolently by Helsinki in 1975, and fostered by follow-up nonviolent support in the 1980s for Solidarnosc and Russian dissidents, then there was no state need or purpose for a number of other much more aggressive later programs, from whose costly blowback we are still suffering. I am thinking specifically of America's use of Islamist terrorists and drug traffickers in programs directed externally against the Soviet Union. These programs began in the late 1970s under Brzezinski, as I explore in detail in the next chapter.

But even while the Helsinki Accords were liberalizing Eastern Europe, backlash to them was driving America farther to the right. This became apparent at the August 1976 Republican convention. The foreign policy plank amendment criticized Helsinki and praised Soviet dissident Alexandr Solzhenitsyn, the notorious and controversial foe of détente whom Ford had declined, on July 4, 1975, to invite to the White House. (Later in July, Solzhenitsyn turned down an open invitation from Ford. He denounced détente in general, and the upcoming Helsinki conference, as a "betrayal of Eastern Europe."[30]) The adoption of this policy plank amendment signaled a definitive Republican rejection of Kissinger and his policies; Kissinger himself, still Ford's secretary of state, was booed when he appeared at the convention in the presidential box. The man who had engineered the passage of the amendment, and its acceptance by Ford, was Cheney, Ford's chief of staff.

THE GRADUAL EMERGENCE OF THE NEOCON ANTI-KISSINGER COALITION

The Cheney-Rumsfeld opposition to Kissinger and his policies had been crystallized by the snub of Solzhenitsyn, which Cheney had opposed in a memo to Rumsfeld on July 8, 1975, and by the Helsinki agreements three weeks later.[31] But the root issue may have been Kissinger's efforts to limit U.S. defense spending under a second SALT agreement with the Russians. According to reporter Robert G. Kaiser in a lengthy *Washington Post* news story in June 1977, Kissinger's negotiation of SALT II was derailed by a leak from a "cabal" (neocon Richard Perle, his friend John F. Lehman Jr., and Lieutenant General Edward Rowny) in a Rowland Evans and Robert Novak column published in December 1975. "That column," Kaiser wrote, "may have changed the course of history."

> The [Evans and Novak] column concluded that Kissinger was about to fly off to Moscow to offer these dangerous concessions and that only the then-new Secretary of Defense, Donald Rumsfeld, could stop him. Rumsfeld's actions could "decide the fate of SALT II and influence the future of the country," Evans and Novak wrote.
>
> Soon afterward, according to informed officials, Rumsfeld did intervene with Ford and blocked a Kissinger mission to Moscow that December. The delay allowed hard-liners to muster support for their opposition to the compromises Kissinger favored. By the time Kissinger got to Moscow in January, 1976—with Ronald Reagan's shadow already large on the

Republican Party horizon—Gerald Ford was not interested in Kissinger's compromise proposals.[32]

This Evans-Novak alliance with Rumsfeld and the neocons presaged the leak to Robert Novak in 2003, when from neocon sources he leaked the identity of CIA covert operative Valerie Plame. But just a year earlier, in 1974, the Evans-Novak column had voiced frequent criticisms of Rumsfeld and Cheney, who in turn had referred bitterly to the two as "Errors and No-facts."[33]

Kissinger's and Rockefeller's decline in power reflected the decline in power of the old Wall Street–Council on Foreign Relations consensus, which in the wake of Vietnam was bitterly split. In 1973, David Rockefeller had created a new Trilateral Commission, with Zbigniew Brzezinski as its director. The commission brought together—from Canada, Europe, Japan, and the United States—investment bankers and multinational corporate directors.[34] It sought, in a Trilateralist paper's words, to build a new consensus about "the management of interdependence . . . the central problem of world order for the coming years"—as opposed to the containment of communism, which had dominated elite thinking for the previous quarter century. A key Trilateral document, *Towards a Renovated International System*, established three major tasks for the new global system: "managing the world economy, satisfying basic human needs, and keeping the peace. . . . [T]he last [addressed] the policy of detente with the Soviet Union. . . . Acknowledging the realities of transnational investment that had already integrated the economies of the three regions . . . the Trilateral position maintained that unilateral positions were inherently destabilizing and no longer tolerable."[35]

This influential challenge of traders to U.S. militarism and unilateralism was opposed, not for the first or last time, by an overworld faction of Prussians, far more militant and better funded, who maintained that America's top priority was not international trade and investment, but military superiority over the Soviet Union. The impetus for the Prussians' campaign came initially from a relatively small group of anti–New Left and pro-Israel Democrats around Senator Henry Jackson—the original self-described neoconservatives—in the Coalition for a Democratic Majority Foreign Policy Task Force. Allying themselves with veteran cold warrior Paul Nitze (the author of *NSC-68* in 1950 and of the 1957 *Gaither Report*), they formed what went public in 1976 as the Committee on the Present Danger (CPD).[36]

The pivotal importance of this CPD has often been missed, inasmuch as it reiterated the scare tactics of the first CPD in 1950, reiterated by a third CPD in 2004.[37] But the differences are significant. The first CPD in 1950 was created by a consensus *within* the state in support of government mobilization against a threat (the USSR) whose size was uncertain and open to misunderstanding.[38] The second CPD in 1975 and 1976 was mounted in *opposition* to a government policy that threatened to establish a more peaceful and less militarized world. In short, the interests now being defended were not those of the nation but of the military-industrial complex itself. In economic terms, capitalism in general was not being defended but (in economist Seymour Melman's phrase) "Pentagon capitalism," which has bloated our arms industries while draining resources from the peacetime economy.

Insufficient attention has been paid to the fact that "David Packard, a former undersecretary of defense, provided the founding grant to establish CPD II [the second incarnation of the committee]."[39] Packard was a major owner of Hewlett-Packard, the maker of computer systems for antiballistic missiles (ABMs); ABMs in turn were the program most significantly limited by the Kissinger-Nixon SALT I treaty of 1972. Nitze had first made contact in 1969 with Richard Perle and Paul Wolfowitz, in a short-lived committee lobbying for continued development of ABMs.[40] SALT I had been amended in 1974 to permit only one ABM site, and this site had been abandoned unilaterally by the United States in 1975. This was partly because the ABM system did not work and (according to expert congressional testimony) would not work.[41] It was also because, as Secretary of Defense McNamara had argued since 1968, the system was strategically destabilizing, making sense only as preparation for a first-strike capacity.[42]

KISSINGER'S DEFEAT ON SALT II

Reinforcing the case against antiballistic missiles development and against increased defense spending in general was the assessment of Soviet capabilities and intentions by CIA analysts. These had already been challenged in 1974 by Major General Daniel Graham, the new head of the Defense Intelligence Agency.[43] In 1975, Graham's challenge to CIA estimates was taken up by the Committee on the Present Danger (CPD). In the committee's view the agency chronically minimized the Soviet military threat, thus creating a false basis for what the CPD saw as insufficient U.S. defense expenditures.

This attack on CIA came at a time when CIA faced unusual criticism from the left, the right, and, most extraordinarily, from the establishment media. As federal arms control expert Anne Hessing Cahn wrote: "In the mid-1970s, the CIA was vulnerable on three counts. First, it was still reeling from the 1975 congressional hearings about covert assassination attempts on foreign leaders and other activities. Second, it was considered 'payback time' by hard-liners, who were still smarting from the CIA's realistic assessments during the Vietnam war years—assessments that failed to see light at the end of the tunnel. And finally, between 1973 and 1976, there were four different directors of central intelligence, in contrast to the more stately progression of four directors in the preceding 20 years."[44] What had once been the agency of overworld control would now be overridden by a maneuver in which the CPD faction of the overworld was complicit.

Through 1975 the CPD group pressured Ford to allow for outside analysis of the CIA's assessments. CIA director William Colby stubbornly resisted these demands, even after they were endorsed by the President's Foreign Intelligence Advisory Board, a part-time board composed of private citizens.[45] The board's diverse membership included William Casey, John Connally, John Foster, Clare Booth Luce, Edward Teller, and Robert Galvin, CEO of Motorola and head of the American Security Council. Its chairman in 1975, and the man applying pressure to Ford, was Admiral George W. Anderson Jr. Anderson was a right-winger appointed by Nixon and president of the Metropolitan Club in Washington, where the CPD group was meeting.[46]

This impasse ended with the Halloween Massacre and the firing of Colby as CIA director. His replacement was America's representative in Beijing, George H. W. Bush.[47] At the direction of the President's Foreign Intelligence Advisory Board, Bush appointed a team of twelve men from outside the CIA, which came to be known as Team B, to critique the current CIA's annual assessment of Soviet Union strength. Whereas Colby had resisted the plan, new CIA director Bush signed off on the Team B proposal "with gusto, 'Let her fly!!—OK, G.B.' "[48]

The team's hawkish outcome was predictable, as all twelve men were hardliners who regarded CIA analysts as "soft" on the Russians.[49] The chair of Team B, Richard Pipes, had been "discovered" by neocon Richard Perle. Pipes in turn picked Perle's colleague Wolfowitz.[50] Four Team B members (including Pipes and Nitze) would soon join the CPD. Their outlook reflected that of the President's Foreign Intelligence Advisory Board itself, six of whose sixteen members soon became members of the CPD.[51] Their report forced a more hawkish reevaluation of Soviet strength by CIA, which helped doom Kissingerian arms control and détente as pillars of U.S. foreign policy.

A few people, including Team B member Major General George Keegan, immediately leaked the Team B dissent, to fan their misleading campaign that America faced a "window of vulnerability" requiring huge increases in the U.S. defense budget. Two other leakers, after President Carter's election, were outgoing CIA Director Bush and outgoing Defense Secretary Rumsfeld.[52] The leaks failed to earn Ford reelection in 1976, but they were a major factor in the Reagan victory four years later. As Cahn told the BBC in 2005, with Team B finally in power: "The United States embarked on a trillion dollar defense buildup. As a result, the country neglected its schools, cities, roads and bridges, and health care system. . . . From the world's greatest creditor nation, the United States became the world's greatest debtor—in order to pay for arms to counter the threat of a nation that was collapsing."[53]

The Team B report was in part the product of rollback hawks from the 1950s, such as Galvin and Nitze (the principal author of *NSC-68*). But it was also the first victory for the triumvirate of Rumsfeld, Cheney, and Wolfowitz, who would later dominate the war policies of George W. Bush.[54] The three men had key allies in 1976, notably Bush the elder, who created Team B, and Wolfowitz's close friend Perle, who as a staff aide to Senator Henry Jackson "emerged as the driving force behind congressional opposition to arms control with the Soviet Union."[55]

In 1976 the triumvirate's victory was not yet apparent. Carter and his running mate Walter Mondale were both members of the Trilateral Commission, and they campaigned that year on trilateral issues—even promising to cut the defense budget. After his election Carter picked twenty-five members of the Trilateral Commission for top policy positions. His new secretary of state, Cyrus Vance, had previously authored a report downplaying the Soviet threat. The Coalition for a Democratic Majority and the newly formed Committee of the Present Danger nominated fifty-three hawks for government service, but not one was selected.[56]

Nevertheless, the Team B advocates prevailed. Carter presided over huge defense budget increases. With the election of Ronald Reagan, no fewer than thirty-three members of the CPD would be brought into the new administration, including Reagan himself, Richard V. Allen, the new national security adviser Perle, CPD founder and chairman Eugene Rostow, and eventually Rumsfeld.[57]

OFFSHORED CIA ASSETS:
THE SAFARI CLUB AND A ROGUE CIA

The Halloween Massacre reversed another apparent victory for the public state over the deep state. Outgoing CIA director Colby had been cooperating with investigation of CIA launched by the so-called McGovernite 94th Congress that had been elected in 1974.[58] However, the new CIA director, George H. W. Bush, found a way to avoid the newly imposed rules of congressional oversight. He accelerated the delegation of covert operations to foreign intelligence services and also to assets not only off-the-books but sometimes offshore. These offshore assets—notably the Bank of Credit and Commerce International (BCCI)—were of great use to CIA director Casey and Bush himself as vice president in escaping congressional review.[59] Above all, "Bush cemented strong relations with the intelligence services of both Saudi Arabia and the shah of Iran. He worked closely with Kamal Adham, the head of Saudi intelligence, brother-in-law of King Faisal and an early BCCI insider."[60]

In 1972, as I mentioned in chapter 2, Adham had acted as a channel between Kissinger and Anwar Sadat in negotiations for the sudden expulsion of Soviet advisers from Egypt.[61] Now, in 1976, faced with the congressional crackdown on unsupervised CIA operations, Adham, Sadat, and the shah of Iran formed their own anti-Communist coalition—the so-called Safari Club—to conduct through their own intelligence agencies operations that were now difficult for CIA.[62] A key figure in securing a formal agreement to this effect was Alexandre de Marenches, head of the French intelligence service SDECE (the Service de Documentation Extérieure et de Contre-Espionnage).[63] De Marenches surfaces again in connection with the 1980 Republican-CIA plots against President Carter.

In February 2002, Saudi intelligence chief Prince Turki bin Faisal, nephew of and successor to Adham, gave Georgetown University alumni a frank account of the Safari Club's formation in response to post-Watergate restrictions: "In 1976, after the Watergate matters took place here, your intelligence community was literally tied up by Congress. It could not do anything. It could not send spies, it could not write reports, and it could not pay money. In order to compensate for that, a group of countries got together in the hope of fighting Communism and established what was called the Safari Club. The Safari Club included France, Egypt, Saudi Arabia, Morocco, and Iran."[64]

The Safari Club met at an exclusive resort of the same name in Kenya, which in the same year, 1976, was visited and eventually bought by Adham's friend Adnan Khashoggi.[65] According to investigative journalist Joseph Trento, "The Safari Club needed a network of banks to finance its intelligence operations. With the official blessing of George H. W. Bush as the head of the CIA, Adham transformed a small Pakistani merchant bank, the Bank of Credit and Commercial International (BCCI), into a world-wide money-laundering machine, buying banks around the world to create the biggest clandestine money network in history."[66]

Trento further charges that Adham, his successor Prince Turki, and their Saudi agency the GID, or Mukhabarat, funded off-the-books worldwide covert operations for CIA. These included support for an alleged "private CIA" close to Bush and dominated by former CIA men like Ed Wilson, Theodore Shackley (who had served as Bush's associate deputy director for operations), and Tom Clines.[67] Unquestionably, the brief period in which Bush served as the director of central intelligence was one of off-the-books operations by allegedly "rogue" agents like Wilson, working with Shackley.[68] "Contracting-out," or "offshoring," became a device to escape the new oversight procedures established after Watergate by the Senate Church Committee, which had been established by the McGovernite Congress to investigate government intelligence activities.

These offshore events in 1976 were mirrored by a similar arrangement for off-loading former CIA agents and operations in Latin America. This was the Confederación Anticomunista Latinoamericana (CAL) and its death-squad collaboration Operation Condor. Operation Condor was a coalition of intelligence agencies of CAL countries, chiefly Argentina, Brazil, Chile, and Paraguay. The CAL was funded through the World Anti-Communist League by the governments of South Korea and Taiwan and—once again—the petrodollars of Saudi Arabia.[69]

After Carter's election, Bush was replaced as CIA director by Admiral Stansfield Turner, who began to marginalize or fire the "Bush team" associated with Shackley. These men, notably Clines, were accused of forming a "private CIA" or "rogue CIA" from 1977 to 1980 that was loyal to Bush (and possibly involved him) and was supported by connections to BCCI and the Safari Club.[70] After the Camp David Accords were signed in 1979, Clines became partner in a lucrative shipping company, Tersam, backed by Ali Mohammed Shorafa of the United Arab Emirates, a nominee of the elite BCCI group permitted to buy out the First American Bank in Washington.[71]

These offshore relationships gave Shackley, de Marenches, and others an offshore base for assisting active and retired CIA officers, most notably Shackley's friend Bush, to defeat Carter in his bid for reelection.[72] The overall result of this off-loading and offshoring was not just loss of accountability, but also loss of control over major policies. A key example would soon be the 1980s CIA support of the resistance in Afghanistan, where CIA's disastrous favoring of drug traffickers had grown directly out of the Safari Club arrangement and was partly handled through BCCI. This loss of control will emerge as a major factor in our nation's slouching toward the tragedy of 9/11.

FOUR

BRZEZINSKI, OIL, AND AFGHANISTAN

> In a democracy, important questions of policy with respect to
> a vital commodity like oil, the lifeblood of an industrial soci-
> ety, cannot be left to private companies acting in accord with
> private interests and a closed circle of government officials.
>
> **Senate Committee on Foreign Relations, Subcommittee on
> Multinational Corporations, 1975**

THE DEMISE OF DÉTENTE

In 1976 Jimmy Carter campaigned vigorously against both Donald
Rumsfeld's plans for increased defense spending and Henry Kissinger's
style of secret diplomacy, attacking "a one man policy of international
adventure" that "is not understood by the people or the Congress."[1]
Carter's speeches proclaimed a vision of replacing "balance of power
with world order politics" and of reducing war-peace issues to be "more
a function of economic and social problems than of . . . military security
problems."[2]

But after four years "Carter had come full circle—from an enthusiast
of global interdependence who hoped to develop concrete structures of
cooperation that would put detente on a firm and lasting basis, to the
leadership of a doctrine of global confrontation that brought with it
prospects of Cold War tension for many years to come."[3] In this chapter
I analyze how the populist from Georgia, who promised to shift America
away from military toward economic global strategies, came in the end
himself to create a U.S. military presence in the Persian Gulf. This reversal is one of the reasons that Carter is remembered as an uncertain and
indecisive president. In fact, however, he was presiding over, or perhaps

better trying to keep up with, a reversal of opinion within the overworld, one that would eventually maintain Cold War tension, or a substitute for it, into the twenty-first century.

In 1976 it appeared that trilateralism had defeated the Committee on the Present Danger. Carter and his running mate, Walter Mondale, were both members of the Trilateral Commission, and they campaigned on trilateral issues, even promising to cut the defense budget. On his election Carter picked twenty-five members of the Trilateral Commission for top policy positions. His new secretary of state, Cyrus Vance, had previously authored a report downplaying the Soviet threat. The Coalition for a Democratic Majority and the newly formed Committee of the Present Danger nominated fifty-three hawks for government service; not one was selected.[4] It appeared on the surface that with the blessing of David Rockefeller's Trilateral Commission, the traditional U.S. search for unilateral domination would be abandoned. But, as detailed in chapter 3, the 1970s were a period in which a major "intellectual counterrevolution" was mustered, to mobilize conservative opinion with the aid of vast amounts of money.

A key figure in this avalanche of right-wing money was Nixon's former treasury secretary, William Simon at the Olin Foundation, where he "was joined by the legendary John J. McCloy . . . the recognized chairman of all things Eastern and established" (and longtime Rockefeller representative).[5] Thanks in large part to these lavish expenditures, public opinion had shifted in favor of wanting an increase in defense spending.[6] Meanwhile, the case against détente was helped by Soviet military adventurism in Africa, where the USSR introduced shiploads of weapons and fifteen thousand Cuban troops in support of a new Marxist dictatorship in Ethiopia.

An early blow to trilateralist détente, however, was delivered by two establishment trilateralists *within* the Carter administration. Zbigniew Brzezinski, former director of the Trilateral Commission and now Carter's national security adviser, brought in his friend and former coauthor Samuel Huntington to oversee a reconciliation between the conflicting CIA and Team B views on the U.S.-USSR balance of power.[7] Huntington, like George H. W. Bush before him, brought in a number of hawkish outsiders.[8] Thus the resulting product, *Presidential Review Memorandum #10*, or *PRM-10*, was not a reconciliation but a two-part document of opposing views. The *PRM-10* conclusion proclaimed a new era in U.S.-Soviet relations: "ERA TWO . . . a period that embodies 'both the competition of the Cold War era and the cooperation of the detente period.' "[9] "Cooperation and competition" became Brzezinski's set formula for describing American-Soviet relations when talking to the press; in private, however, he pressed for competition.[10]

As a result, the Carter administration was bedeviled by two competing foreign policies, with Brzezinski pursuing supremacy over the Soviet Union and Vance pursuing a SALT II disarmament agreement and détente. The Vance-Brzezinski opposition "spread into one of the most bitter rivalries in executive branch history."[11] As Strobe Talbott later commented, it was so profound that "almost every issue provoked a fight."[12] Brzezinski, like Kissinger, used a small network staff inside the National Security Council (or the deep state) to trump the policy recommendations from the experts in the State Department (or the public state).

On the basis of *PRM-10* Brzezinski secured a presidential directive, PD-18 of August 24, 1977, that affirmed the need to maintain "a 'deployment force of light divisions with strategic mobility' for global contingencies, particularly in the Persian Gulf region and Korea."[13] By the time SALT II was signed in 1979, Carter had consented to significant new weapons programs and arms budget increases (reversing his campaign pledge).[14] By the end of his presidency both Vance and his ally Paul Warnke, the chief negotiator of SALT II, were gone. Most significantly, *PRM-10* reinforced Brzezinski's ideological overreactions in the Middle East. In a speech before the Foreign Policy Association, Brzezinski identified a so-called arc of crisis around the Indian Ocean, where the Soviet Union was poised to capitalize on regional instability.[15] As State Department official Henry Precht later recalled: "There was this idea that the Islamic forces could be used against the Soviet Union. The theory was, there was an arc of crisis, and so an arc of Islam could be mobilized to contain the Soviets. It was a Brzezinski concept."[16] Soon both the fall of the shah and the Soviet invasion of Afghanistan were interpreted by Brzezinski—paranoically rather than accurately—as proof of Soviet expansiveness and designs on the region.[17]

The success of Team B and Huntington in redirecting the Carter administration toward militarism "created an important precedent." As James Mann wrote in *Rise of the Vulcans*: "From that point onward, whenever members of Congress believed that the CIA was minimizing the seriousness of a foreign policy problem, there were calls for a Team B to review the intelligence and make its own independent evaluation. During the mid-1990s the Republican majority in Congress set up a special commission, modeled upon Team B, to study the threat to the United States from ballistic missiles. After reviewing the intelligence, an independent commission concluded that the danger of a missile attack was considerably greater than the U.S. intelligence community had reported. That missile defense commission was headed by Donald Rumsfeld, and one of its leading members was Paul Wolfowitz."[18]

Brzezinski mobilized support for his positions by creating a special coordination committee (SCC) in the White House, chaired by himself, to deal among other things with sensitive operations, covert activity, and crisis management. In his memoir Brzezinski wrote that he "used the SCC to try to shape our policy toward" a number of issues, of which the first listed by him is the Persian Gulf.[19] In this way, in the words of South Asia specialists Diego Cordovez and Selig Harrison: "As he boasts in his memoirs, Brzezinski had steadily eroded Vance's power. . . . This control over covert operations enabled Brzezinski to take the first steps toward a more aggressively anti-Soviet Afghan policy *without the State Department's knowing much about it.*"[20]

More specifically, Brzezinski stymied Vance's efforts to negotiate a Soviet withdrawal from Afghanistan, coupled with "a broader 'mutual restraint' agreement covering both Iran and Pakistan."[21] Again, from Cordovez and Harrison: "The United States government was itself divided from the start between 'bleeders,' who wanted to keep Soviet forces pinned down in Afghanistan and thus to avenge Vietnam, and 'dealers,' who wanted to compel their withdrawal through a combination of diplomacy and military pressure."[22] This led to the killing of Vance's proposal by Brzezinski, "in one of the least-noticed but most important of his many clashes with Vance." Even in the late 1980s "the 'bleeders' fought against the Geneva Accords until the very end."[23]

Since then, and to this day, America has had to cope with the consequences of Brzezinski's reckless adventurism.

Although right-wingers like Barry Goldwater and the John Birch Society continued to complain about Carter's trilateral administration, the trilateralist ideology had shown in practice to be less relevant than the trilateralists' sociology. In the latter the dominant figure was ultimately Brzezinski because of his proximity to his former mentor, David Rockefeller, and those around him.[24] Two events, both of which I explore more deeply in this chapter, contributed to the demise of détente during the Carter presidency. These were the fall of the shah in 1979 and the Soviet invasion of Afghanistan a year later.

Carter had been elected as the so-called energy president, and his first steps, with energy secretary James Schlesinger, were to introduce a number of largely successful conservation programs.[25] But fears of a Soviet threat to the Persian Gulf led the president, in his January 1980 State of the Union address, to proclaim the Carter Doctrine: "An attempt by any outside force to gain control of the Persian Gulf region will be regarded as an assault on the vital interests of the United States of America, and such an assault will be repelled by any means necessary, including military force."[26] As historian Daniel Yergin has commented: "The Carter Doctrine made more explicit what American presidents had been saying as far back as Harry Truman's pledge" in 1945 to the king of Saudi Arabia.[27]

Carter's military approach to his Persian Gulf problems went beyond words. He authorized the creation of what Brzezinski had envisaged—a Rapid Deployment Joint Task Force.[28] In April 1980, Carter mounted a disastrous attack, in an attempt to free the hostages being held in the Tehran U.S. embassy. There were rumors that he planned for a second, bigger operation. The uneasy team of Carter, Vance, and Brzezinski could point to one major foreign policy breakthrough: the Camp David agreement in 1978 that brought peace between Israel and Egypt. Intertwined with the negotiations for Camp David, in which Saudi Arabia played a big role, were other issues of moment. This book is concerned with two of these: (1) the joint policies to combat inflation and protect the weakening U.S. dollar and (2) the various Saudi-U.S. projects for collaboration to diminish the threat of the Soviet Union in Asia.[29]

BRZEZINSKI, HUNTINGTON, AND FEMA

Before looking at Brzezinski's moves in Afghanistan, however, we have to look at one other way in which Brzezinski helped set the stage for 9/11. This was his bringing of Samuel Huntington back to the White House in 1979 to draft Presidential Memorandum 32, which created the Federal Emergency Management Agency (FEMA). What Huntington envisaged as FEMA's future role is uncertain.[30] But hostile critics have pointed to what he had written for the Trilateral Commission in the mid-1970s, in his coauthored book *Crisis in Democracy*: "A government which lacks authority will have little ability, short of a cataclysmic crisis, to impose on its people the sacrifices which may be necessary to deal with foreign policy problems and defense. . . . We have come to recognize that there are potential desirable limits to economic growth. There are also potentially desirable limits to the indefinite extension of political democracy."[31]

Huntington's words were attacked at the time for their unfashionable questioning of democracy. What may have been more significant was the warning that in a full democracy, "necessary" sacrifices can only be imposed by a cataclysmic crisis. Brzezinski echoed this thought in his case for American empire, in *The Grand Chessboard*, when he wrote that "democracy is inimical to imperial mobilization."[32] What would make the American public willing to sacrifice for "imperial mobilization," he suggested, would be "a truly massive and widely perceived direct external threat."[33]

Although Huntington's intentions for FEMA remain unknown, it is clear that FEMA soon became, under President Ronald Reagan, the agency responsible for preserving and refining the Garden Plot strategies for surveillance and detention of domestic protest. It may be relevant that FEMA was authorized on July 20, 1979.[34] This was in the midst of mounting disagreement within the Carter administration about what to do concerning Iran and the deposed shah.[35] Carter's key decision on Iran in November 1979, to freeze all Iranian assets (discussed further in chapter 5), was carried out under legislative powers that had just been given to FEMA in July. At the time Carter's director of FEMA, John W. Macy, made it clear that the agency's chief task was crisis management and civil defense against external enemies, including terrorists; natural disasters were to be a secondary preoccupation.[36] (With this mandate FEMA presumably answered to Brzezinski's special coordination committee in the White House.) Later I show how FEMA did help prepare precisely for mobilization against an external threat, and also for dealing with protesters.

BRZEZINSKI, AFGHANISTAN, AND CENTRAL ASIA

As the son of a displaced aristocratic Pole, Brzezinski had never concealed his interest in breaking up the Soviet bloc. As early as 1966 he had cosigned, with political science professor William Griffith, a confidential report criticizing the programming of Radio Free Europe and Radio Liberty, for being "too passive." The men "argued for adopting a more militant line in the non-Russian broadcasts, which would stimulate anti-Russian antagonism."[37]

As national security adviser, Brzezinski pursued the same goal of stirring up antagonism by convening a Nationalities Working Group to exploit Muslim dissatisfaction inside the Soviet Union. The core of this group were disciples of another displaced aristocrat, Russian count Alexandre Bennigsen, who in his prolific writings saw fundamentalist

Islam in Central Asia as a major threat to the Soviet State.[38] (Robert Dreyfuss has commented astutely that "radical political Islam was not a factor in the dissolution of the USSR after perestroika . . . and the establishment of Central Asia's republics."[39] The importance of Islamism came in the next decade, by which time it presented a threat to the interests of both the United States and Russia.)

The efforts of the Nationalities Working Group were at first minor, with "the distribution of Korans in Central Asian languages and stepped-up efforts, in conjunction with Saudi Arabia's intelligence service, to contact Soviet Muslims visiting Mecca for the hajj."[40] A defining shift in Carter's Islamic policy—one whose consequences for 9/11 would be significant—was when Brzezinski and his aide Robert Gates from CIA, on July 3, 1979, persuaded Carter to send secret aid to Islamist militants in Afghanistan, six months before the Soviet invasion in December 1979.[41] Brzezinski has since, in an interview with *Le Nouvel Observateur*, said that he explained to Carter that in his opinion "this aid was going to induce a Soviet military intervention." Brzezinski explained: "We didn't push the Russians to intervene, but we knowingly increased the probability that they would."[42] In another interview Brzezinski said he had hoped "to make the Soviets bleed for as much and as long as is possible."[43]

Immediately after the catastrophic events on 9/11, the influential British intelligence review, *Jane's,* traced the al Qaeda attack back to its "origins" in this 1979 decision by Carter and Brzezinski:

> The origins of last Tuesday's attack on the United States arguably have their roots in the 1970s. At this time, during the height of the Cold War, a Washington shamed by defeat in Vietnam embarked on a deep, collaborative enterprise to contain the Soviet Union.
>
> The genesis of the policy came to a head following the Soviet occupation of Afghanistan, when President Jimmy Carter set up a team headed by National Security Advisor Zbigniew Brzezinski to employ its "death by a thousand cuts" policy on the tottering Soviet empire, especially the oil- and mineral-rich Central Asian Republics then ruled by Moscow.[44]

As a Pole, Brzezinski had geostrategic motives for tempting the Soviet Union into an imperial overstretch that would weaken it and contribute to its eventual dissolution. As someone unhappy with both Vance and SALT II, he also had domestic reasons. One consequence of the Soviet invasion was the failure of the U.S. Senate, by one vote, to ratify the SALT II arms reduction treaty that Vance had negotiated and with which Brzezinski and the Pentagon were extremely uncomfortable.[45] This could have been predicted: one hardliner in the Carter administration told the *Christian Science Monitor* that "Afghanistan is finally shaking people into shape. . . . I think the Soviets have done us a big favor."[46]

Brzezinski was unambiguously in favor of destabilizing the Soviet Union, not in normalizing relations with it. He later described how "as early as 1978, President Carter approved proposals prepared by my staff to undertake, for example, a comprehensive, covert action program designed to help the non-Russian nations in the Soviet Union pursue more actively their desire for independence—a program in effect to destabilize the Soviet Union."[47] Under this program, CIA began to infiltrate written materials to diverse ethnic regions of the USSR, above all to the Ukraine.[48] This also apparently began the operation whereby CIA helped the Pakistani Inter-Services Intelligence Agency (ISI), Saudi Arabia, and the Saudi International Islamic Relief Organization (IIRO)[49] to distribute in the Soviet Union thousands of Wahhabi-glossed Korans, an important contribution to the spread of Islamism in Central Asia today.[50] A January 1979 article in *Time* magazine endorsed the idea: "From Islamic democracies on Russia's southern tier, a zealous Koranic evangelism might sweep across the border into these politically repressed Soviet states, creating problems for the Kremlin."[51]

Note that Brzezinski's first stirring up of the jihadi hornet's nest occurred before either the fall of the shah in Iran (February 1979) or the Soviet invasion of Afghanistan (December 1979). In the history of oil exploration, this occurred at a time when U.S. oil companies, shaken by the power of OPEC in the 1973 oil crisis, were casting eyes on the potential for oil and gas exploration in the trans-Caspian basin.[52] Whether oil was on Brzezinski's mind in his decision is an open question to which I shall shortly return.

A year later, as already mentioned, Brzezinski initiated his better-known destabilization program, south of the Amu Darya River in Afghanistan. By using Islamic fundamentalism against the Soviets, Brzezinski clearly regarded himself as a master chess player (to adapt the metaphor of his book *The Grand Chessboard*). In a subsequent interview with *Le Nouvel Observateur*, he famously showed no regrets:

> Asked whether he in any way regretted these actions, Brzezinski replied: "Regret what? The secret operation was an excellent idea. It drew the Russians into the Afghan trap and you want me to regret it? On the day that the Soviets officially crossed the border, I wrote to President Carter, saying, in essence: 'We now have the opportunity of giving to the USSR its Vietnam War.'"

Nouvel Observateur: And neither do you regret having supported Islamic fundamentalism, which has given arms and advice to future terrorists?

Brzezinski: What is more important in world history? The Taliban or the collapse of the Soviet empire? Some agitated Muslims or the liberation of Central Europe and the end of the Cold War?[53]

BRZEZINSKI OPENS THE FAZLE HAQ – HEKMATYAR DRUG CONNECTION

The ultimate costs of Brzezinski's adventure included not only the "agitated Muslims" of al Qaeda and Iraq, but also what former CIA al Qaeda expert Mike Scheuer has called "the Afghan heroin factories that have killed more Americans than the 11 September attacks."[54] Others have with good reason described Brzezinski as "the Sorcerer's Apprentice."[55] For generations in both Afghanistan and the Soviet Muslim Republics the dominant form of Islam had been local and largely Sufi. The decision to work with the Saudi and Pakistani secret services meant that billions of CIA and Saudi dollars would ultimately be spent in programs that would help enhance the globalistic and Wahhabistic jihadism that are associated today with al Qaeda.[56]

These dollars also went directly into expanding the drug traffic. It is now quite clear that this would be the consequence of Pakistan president Muhammad Zia-ul-Haq's choice of Lieutenant General Fazle Haq (or Huq) to consult with Brzezinski on developing an Afghan resistance program.[57] Haq, whom Zia had appointed to be military governor of Pakistan's North-West Frontier Province, soon became known as a CIA asset. He was considered the man for visiting dignitaries like William Casey or Vice President George Bush to see when reviewing the CIA Afghan operation.[58] By 1982, Haq was also listed with Interpol as an international narcotics trafficker.[59] An informant from the Bank of Credit and Commerce International (BCCI) told U.S. authorities that BCCI president Agha Hasan Abedi's influence with Zia benefited from the backing of Haq, who was "heavily engaged in narcotics trafficking and moving the heroin money through the bank."[60]

Brzezinski did not initiate this contact. Haq's claim of a Pakistani rather than a U.S. initiative is corroborated by Robert Gates, who writes of "an approach by a senior Pakistani official to an Agency officer" in March 1979, one month before Brzezinski authorized CIA to work with the ISI, and four months before Carter signed the presidential finding to help the mujahideen.[61] But only Brzezinski's witting authority can explain why by 1980 psychiatrist David Musto of the White House Strategy Council on Drug Abuse was being excluded, illegally, from access to White House documents about the opium-growing Afghan mujahideen.[62]

In May 1979 the ISI put CIA in touch with Gulbuddin Hekmatyar, the mujahideen warlord with perhaps the smallest following inside Afghanistan. Hekmatyar was also the leading mujahideen drug trafficker, and the only one to develop his own complex of six heroin labs in an ISI-controlled area of Baluchistan (Pakistan).[63] This decision by the ISI and CIA belies the usual American rhetoric that the United States was assisting an Afghan liberation movement.[64] Instead, it was assisting Pakistani (and also Saudi) assets in a country about which Pakistan felt insecure. As an Afghan leader in 1994 told Tim Weiner of the *New York Times*: "We didn't choose these leaders. The United States made Hekmatyar by giving him his weapons. Now we want the United States to shake these leaders and make them stop the killing, to save us from them."[65] Foreign correspondent Robert D. Kaplan reported his personal experience that Hekmatyar was "loathed by all the other party leaders, fundamentalist and moderate alike."[66]

It is easy to understand why Pakistan insisted that Hekmatyar receive the bulk of U.S. (and Saudi) aid. He was the mujahideen leader most dependent on the ISI for survival, and allegedly the only one willing to accept the British-drawn Durand Line as the Afghan-Pakistan boundary. (The Durand Line, dividing clans and even families, left a large number of Pashtuns inside Pakistan.) The question is rather why Brzezinski agreed to an alliance with this drug connection, and proceeded almost immediately to protect it from critical snoops like David Musto. My answer to this important question will be more obvious by the end of this chapter. It is important to establish why the United States accepted an arrangement whereby of the $2 billion it supplied to the mujahideen in the 1980s, Hekmatyar, a leading drug trafficker, is estimated to have received more than half.[67]

Let me clarify the blowback from Brzezinski's two decisions: Hekmatyar and Saudi-backed Islamist Abdul Rasul Sayyaf—the two principal instruments of his policies—became, far more conspicuously than Osama bin Laden, the protectors of the first al Qaeda plots against America. Al Qaeda itself can be traced principally to the thousands of Ikhwan (Muslim Brotherhood) followers that Egypt released in the 1980s to fight in Afghanistan. Khalid Shaikh Mohammed, said by the *9/11 Commission Report* to have been the "principal architect" of the 9/11 plot, first conceived of it when he was with Sayyaf, a leader with whom bin Laden was still at odds.[68] Meanwhile, several of the men convicted of blowing up the World Trade Center in 1993, and the subsequent New York "day of terror" plot in 1995, had trained or fought with, or raised money for, Brzezinski's "agitated Muslims."[69]

This irony has been noted before. Less noted, but equally important, is that eventually through Pakistani channels the United States and its allies (chiefly Saudi Arabia) gave Hekmatyar more than $1 billion in armaments.[70] This was more than any other CIA client has ever received, before or since. Those weapons, including the lethal ground-to-air Stingers, have since armed terrorists around the world. This unparalleled support to one of the world's leading drug traffickers, who later became one of America's primary enemies, occurred at a time when the United States was talking of a "war on drugs."

The consequences of Brzezinski's decision were felt immediately, in the form of a sudden flood of heroin from the Afghan border into the United States. In May 1980, only five months after arms began to flow to the Afghan guerrillas, Carter's White House adviser on drugs, Musto, complained publicly of the risks "in befriending these tribes as we did in Laos." Musto noted that the number of drug-related deaths in New York had risen by 77 percent.[71] The key to this relationship may have been BCCI. Well into the 1980s the bank continued the cut-out activities for CIA that had been performed earlier by billionaire Saudi arms dealer Adnan Khashoggi and Kamal Adham, who became one of BCCI's principal shareholders.

As already noted, Fazle Haq was allegedly "heavily engaged in narcotics trafficking and moving the heroin money through the [BCCI] bank."[72] The use of this drug trafficking to finance CIA's off-the-books assets in Afghanistan would explain what a highly placed U.S. official told Jonathan Beaty, coauthor of the book *The Outlaw Bank*: that Haq "was our man . . . everybody knew that Haq was also running the drug trade" and that "BCCI was completely involved."[73]

On the Pakistan side this criminal relationship may even have been institutionalized. According to B. Raman, a well-informed Indian analyst writing in the *Financial Times*: "In the 1980s, at the insistence of the Central Intelligence Agency (CIA) of the U.S., the Internal Political Division of the Inter-Services Intelligence (ISI), headed by Brig (retd). Imtiaz, . . . started a special cell for the use of heroin for covert actions. This cell promoted the cultivation of opium and the extraction of heroin in Pakistani territory as well as in the Afghan territory under Mujahideen control for being smuggled into the Soviet controlled areas in order to make the Soviet troops heroin addicts. After the withdrawal of the Soviet troops, the ISI's heroin cell started using its network of refineries and smugglers for smuggling heroin to the Western countries and using the money as a supplement to its legitimate economy. But for these heroin dollars, Pakistan's legitimate economy must have collapsed many years ago."[74]

The Congressional Research Service confirms that "according to some experts, Pakistan's drug economy amounts to as much as $20 billion. Drug money reportedly is used to buy influence throughout Pakistan's economic and political systems."[75]

BRZEZINSKI'S BUREAUCRATIC PARANOIA

Brzezinski's decisions to intervene in Soviet Asia (1978) and in Afghanistan (1979) merit close consideration. The first may be said to define the moment when the United States moved away from goals of coexistence and containment to the goal of dismantling the Soviet Union. The second decision rapidly generated a commitment of U.S. power to the Gulf (the Carter Doctrine) that broadly explains why the United States is in Iraq today. Brzezinski, in short, was the first unilateralist national security adviser, even while working for a Democratic president with the trilateralist agenda of peaceful coexistence with the Soviet bloc. What motivated this naturalized American to embark on such groundbreaking and consequential initiatives? Was it triumphalism? Or paranoia? Was he fulfilling his own Polish agenda? Or was he fulfilling someone else's?

The usual explanation indeed is the conventional bureaucratic paranoia by which Brzezinski repeatedly outflanked the more moderate Secretary of State Cyrus Vance. Political commentator Eric Alterman has expanded on former CIA director Gates's account of the Afghanistan decision in Gates's 1996 memoir *From the Shadows* (from 1978 to 1979, Gates was detached from CIA to become a member of Brzezinski's staff): "The $500 million in nonlethal aid was designed to counter the billions the Soviets were pouring into the puppet regime *they had installed in Kabul*. Some on the American side were willing—perhaps even eager—to lure the Soviets into a Vietnam-like entanglement. Others viewed the program as a way of destabilizing the *puppet government* and countering the Soviets, whose undeniable aggression in the area was helping to reheat the cold war to a dangerous boil. . . . A key meeting took place on March 30, 1979. Under Secretary of Defense Walter Sloc[o]mbe wondered aloud whether there was value in keeping the Afghan insurgency going, 'sucking the Soviets into a Vietnamese quagmire.' Arnold Horelick, CIA Soviet expert, warned that this was just what we could expect."[76]

The italicized phrases accurately summarize what was being spoken in Washington at the time about the Soviet presence in Afghanistan. In 2001, Brzezinski told Alterman on the phone that he had sold the plan to Carter on the grounds that "the Soviets had *engineered a Communist coup* [in 1978] and they were providing direct assistance in Kabul. We were facing a serious crisis in Iran, and the entire Persian Gulf was at stake."[77] Vance, who saw no such threat, "recalls that the April [1978] coup was depicted by Brzezinski as the opening gambit in a Soviet master plan for achieving hegemony in Southwest Asia."[78] It is certainly true that the United States was facing a crisis in the Persian Gulf. The Nixon-Kissinger strategy of détente with Moscow had been based on the assumption that this détente would stabilize the world. But instead of stability, the Middle East was shocked by a number of destabilizing developments, almost none of which were in fact attributable to the Soviet Union.

One key shock was the April 1978 coup in Afghanistan by a group of Soviet-trained army officers under Khalq leader Nur Mohammed Taraki.[79] Although some scholars still suspect Soviet backing for this coup, it is usually acknowledged to have been in fact initiated by the extremist Khalq faction of the Afghan communist People's Democratic Party of Afghanistan (PDPA), whose style acutely embarrassed Moscow.[80] Vance wrote later that "we had no evidence of Soviet complicity in the coup."[81]

One precipitating cause in fact was the shah of Iran's advice to Afghan president Mohammed Daoud Khan, who was on good terms with both the West and the Soviet Union, to purge his army of left-wing officers and clamp down on their party the PDPA. In the resulting confrontation, it was Daoud himself who was purged and killed.[82] Another factor was the work of SAVAK- and CIA-supported Islamist agents who arrived from Iran "with bulging bankrolls."[83] (SAVAK was the shah's domestic security and intelligence service from 1957 to 1979.)

The USSR was acutely embarrassed by this Khalq faction and the reform program it immediately instituted.[84] As British foreign aid expert Peter Marsden wrote in *The Taliban: War, Religion, and the New Order in Afghanistan*, the "PDPA's use of force in bringing the changes to fruition, combined with a brutal disregard for societal and religious sensitivities, resulted in a massive backlash from the rural population."[85] The result was the first broad-based Islamist coalition for jihad in Afghanistan, a cause that the USSR (because of its own Muslim populations) had at this time much more to fear than did the United States.

A second challenge was the fall in February 1979 of the shah of Iran, the ruler who under the so-called Nixon Doctrine had been deputized to serve as the defender of U.S. interests in the Gulf. Brzezinski analyzed the shah's problems in terms of the Soviets "asserting themselves in Iran" and saw his fall as in part "a Soviet threat to Persian Gulf oil fields."[86] The Soviets feared that events in Iran might further feed the cause of U.S.-backed Islamism in Afghanistan. Again, from Marsden: "Indications that the USA might strengthen the Islamic resistance . . . combined with a growing rapprochement between Washington and Peking to create an acute sense of paranoia in the Kremlin."[87] This paranoia was aggravated in mid-March 1979, when a violent rebellion in Herat, an Afghan city close to the Iran border, "resulted in the deaths of some 5,000 people including fifty Soviet advisers and their families."[88]

Fearing the consequences of the Khalq's follies, the Soviets exerted increasing pressure on Kabul.[89] They probably encouraged the overthrow of the Khalq leader, Taraki, in September 1979. I agree with historian Douglas Little that three months later "Moscow's military intervention in Kabul was probably a defensive measure and not the first step in a Kremlin master plan to drive the United States out of the Persian Gulf."[90] There is no doubt that a chief purpose of the Soviet invasion was to replace an unpredictable extremist leader, Hafizullah Amin, with the more moderate Babrak Karmal from the other PDPA faction.[91]

What was being played out in short between the world's two superpowers was apparently not a masterful chess game, but its opposite: a frightened descent into mutually assured paranoia that would eventually prove costly to both players. Both Brzezinski and the Soviets described as threatening moves by their opponents what were in fact indigenous or local developments that owed little or nothing to either camp. The American paranoia was still further heightened by America's recent and ignominious exit from Vietnam—"the specter of Vietnam" that in 1979 still seemed so much more dangerous than it really was.

The Soviet occupation of Afghanistan in December 1979 was presented first by Brzezinski, and later by Casey, as "a potential threat to the Persian Gulf" and its oil fields.[92] (In the eyes of Casey, about to become Reagan's director of central intelligence, it was part of Soviet "creeping imperialism," aimed at the two specific targets of the Central American isthmus and "the oil fields of the Middle East.")[93] Carter responded with the Carter Doctrine, threatening military force if necessary to repel "an attempt by any outside force to gain control of the Persian Gulf region."[94]

This was followed by a massive buildup in the U.S. armed forces, around the novel concept of a Rapid Deployment Joint Task Force (RDF), operating from the new U.S. base of Diego Garcia in the Indian Ocean.[95] (In 1983 the RDF was renamed the United States Central Command, or USCENTCOM, the command responsible for the war in Iraq today.) As Brzezinski could subsequently tell an interviewer: "It was our response in those years which provided the basis for what subsequently was done by Reagan."[96] During the 1980s the RDF would grow into a $45 billion per year enterprise.[97]

The question remains whether Brzezinski's paranoia was genuine, or the rhetoric of a *power expert* skilled at winning bureaucratic contests. It is noteworthy how completely Brzezinski's defense of U.S. oil investments in the Middle East was in line with Kissinger's and Casey's, even though his style of implementation was different. It is also striking that he injected CIA into the Caspian basin, at a time when American oil companies were already looking there for alternative oil sources that would diminish their dependence on OPEC. The RDF, for which Brzezinski and Paul Wolfowitz (until 1980 the U.S. deputy assistant secretary of defense for regional programs) can take credit together, can also be seen as a multibillion-dollar gift to the oil majors.[98]

It is likely that Kissinger, Brzezinski, and Casey were not just reflecting the mind-set of one faction of Wall Street, but receiving advice and encouragement from that very quarter. This was certainly the case when Brzezinski and Kissinger, in alliance with David Rockefeller, were able to force Carter to reverse himself with respect to the shah.

FIVE

CARTER'S SURRENDER TO
THE ROCKEFELLERS ON IRAN

Iran is not in a revolutionary or even pre-revolutionary situation.

**Draft of a top-secret CIA intelligence assessment
for the White House, 1978**

The President glared at Jordan. "The hell with Henry Kissinger," he said. "I am President of this country!"

President Jimmy Carter

THE ROCKEFELLER OVERWORLD DEFEATS
THE U.S. GOVERNMENT

Not since World War II has there been such a naked exercise of overworld power as in the disastrous decision of October 1979 to permit the shah, in flight from Iran, to enter the United States. President Carter's reluctant action—"the crowning indignity" in the sad history of postwar U.S.-Iran relations[1]—has been called "one of the most controversial and detrimental decisions any president has made since the end of World War Two."[2] In this matter Carter and Secretary of State Cyrus Vance were ultimately overruled, in support of a policy decision dictated and enforced by David Rockefeller.[3]

As had been predicted, the shah's arrival in October 1979 soon resulted in the November seizure of hostages at the U.S. embassy in Tehran.[4] (Carter, in caving in to Rockefeller's demands, asked on October 19, "What are you guys going to recommend that we do when they take our embassy and hold our people hostage?"[5]) This was followed in short order by the collapse of the admittedly precarious pro-American governments in Tehran succeeding the shah, their permanent replacement by Islamist ayatollah rule, the unnecessarily protracted detention of the U.S. hostages, and a freeze in U.S.-Iran relations that persists to this day.[6]

The decision was due first to the sustained pressure, private and public, of four Rockefeller men who successfully overruled the informed opposition of Secretary of State Vance, Undersecretary of State Warren Christopher, the State Department, the U.S. embassy in Tehran, and finally the president himself. (Rockefeller men, including Nelson before he died in January 1979, had been intervening on behalf of the shah since at least May 1978.[7]) Three of these men—Henry Kissinger, David Rockefeller, and John McCloy—were outside the government.[8] The fourth was Brzezinski, "a leading pro-Pahlavi partisan within the Carter administration."[9] Of the four, Brzezinski was the best situated to influence policy, or at least to frustrate it.[10]

Many scholars believe that Brzezinski, in his zeal to support the shah, contributed to the shah's downfall. For example, the shah banned demonstrations on September 6, 1978, and the next day, known as Black Friday, "somewhere between 700 and 2000 people were gunned down." The shah's orders followed advice from Brzezinski to be firm, which Ardeshir Zahedi, the shah's son-in-law and ambassador in Washington, had transmitted to Tehran directly.[11] Carter's official expressions of regret for the bloodshed then made both the shah and Washington look vacillating and ineffectual.[12]

After Black Friday most American policy makers, apart from Brzezinski, gradually came to recognize that the shah's dictatorship had fostered a prevailable will against it in Iran that could no longer be resisted by force.[13] The shah's inevitable departure in January 1979 was followed by increased pressures to admit him to the United States, from "a handful of powerful people inside and outside of the government. Particularly intense were National Security Adviser Zbigniew Brzezinski, banking magnate David Rockefeller, former Secretary of State Henry Kissinger, and the esteemed elder statesman John J. McCloy, a coterie which Brzezinski labeled 'influential friends of the shah.'"[14]

David Rockefeller's *Memoirs* are on some subjects disarmingly candid but not with respect to the shah's return. He claims that despite the insistence of journalists and revisionists, there was never a "Rockefeller-Kissinger behind-the-scenes campaign" to have the shah admitted to the

United States.[15] This is belied by accounts such as that of Pulitzer Prize–winning author Kai Bird, relying on the Rockefeller and McCloy papers:

> With the shah . . . in the Bahamas, Rockefeller and Kissinger turned their attention back to Washington, where they were determined to persuade the Carter administration to allow their friend permanent U.S. asylum. To this end, they organized a "special project," code-named Project Alpha. David Rockefeller dipped into his private funds to pay Chase Bank and [McCloy's law firm] Milbank, Tweed employees for the time they spent working on Project Alpha. . . . Thousands of dollars were spent on phone, travel, and legal expenses over the next year. At one point, they paid an academic specialist on the Middle East $40,000 to write a short book intended to answer the shah's critics. It was a remarkable effort, something only a Rockefeller could have mounted. . . . The shah was given his own code name—the "Eagle"—and [Rockefeller's assistant Joseph V.] Reed referred to Rockefeller, Kissinger, and McCloy as the "Triumpherate" [*sic*]. Over the next seven months, Project Alpha pestered the Carter administration into providing sanctuary for the "Eagle."[16]

Kissinger's trump card was played when in July 1979 he told Brzezinski that his continued support for SALT II depended on a "more forthcoming attitude on our part regarding the Shah."[17] McCloy, after conferring with Brzezinski by telephone, pestered Vance, his deputy Warren Christopher, the undersecretary of state David Newsom, and Carter's UN ambassador Donald McHenry.[18]

In addition, McCloy set the lawyers of his firm, Milbank, Tweed, Hadley & McCloy, to work gathering evidence for what has been called the Mullah Theory. This theory would use the pervasive influence of the clergy to support the dubious "claim that Iranian loans and deposits were to and from the same entity." The theory was necessary to support what became the Rockefeller-Reed-McCloy strategy, to engineer a technical default of interest payments on one Chase loan and then use this default to seize all loans and deposits to Iran.[19] As financial analyst Mark Hulbert has written: "McCloy's firm had quite a task before it. . . . [I]nternational law recognizes that different government agencies are separate legal entities, and that a bank cannot seize the assets of one to satisfy a claim against another. Nevertheless, Chase's law firm gamely set out to make the Mullah Theory plausible. . . . Whether or not the courts would have recognized the Mullah Theory as valid, the crucial point is that by the summer of 1979, Chase's preparations for offsetting Iranian loans and deposits were already quite advanced."[20]

Carter came more and more to resent all this pressure to admit the shah. As the *New York Times* reported: "The President himself had been adamantly opposed and had lost his temper more than once on the subject."[21] Informed by his adviser Hamilton Jordan that his opposition to the pressure from Kissinger and his team was politically dangerous, "the President glared at Jordan. 'The hell with Henry Kissinger,' he said. 'I am President of this country!'"[22] It was true that Carter was the president, and Kissinger was only part of the Rockefeller team. But that team prevailed. There can be no denying whatsoever, at least in this particular moment of truth, that the power of the Rockefeller overworld exceeded that of the man they had previously selected to be president of the United States. Furthermore, although one should not force the analogy between Carter's fate and that of the shah's, there is this point of comparison: both men lost their power, not by defying the Rockefeller team, but by capitulating to it.

Another unintended irony is that in contributing as they did to Carter's downfall and electoral defeat, Brzezinski and the rest of the Rockefeller team contributed also to a permanent shift away from Rockefeller and Council on Foreign Relations influence over the U.S. government.[23] With the election of Reagan, the unilateralists of the Committee on the Present Danger (whose members included both Reagan and his campaign manager, William Casey) would take their place.

THE ROCKEFELLER TEAM DIRECTING THE SHAH

The Rockefellers also might not have overcome Carter if Nelson and David Rockefeller had not also designated three Rockefeller men to advise the shah. These men may have played an even more important role. The first was David Rockefeller's personal assistant, Joseph V. Reed, "assigned to handle the shah's finances and his personal needs."[24] A second was Robert Armao, sent by his employer Nelson Rockefeller to act as the shah's public relations agent and lobbyist.[25] A third, perhaps most important of all, was Benjamin H. Kean, described as "a longtime associate of Chase Manhattan Bank chairman David Rockefeller"[26] and as David Rockefeller's "personal physician."[27] (There is some confusion as to whether Kean was dispatched by David Rockefeller,[28] by his assistant Reed,[29] or by Armao.[30])

Kean flew twice to Mexico to establish the shah's medical condition and reportedly advised "that it was 'preferable' for the shah to be treated at an American hospital."[31] His full report on the shah's condition, as mediated through Armao and the State Department's chief medical officer, Dr. Eban H. Dustin, was responsible first for Vance's surrendering his opposition and then for Carter, as the last holdout, surrendering as well. Kean's report, in other words, led indirectly to a permanent break in U.S.-Iranian relations. Kean's responsibility for this is still unknown, partly because he responded to an early description of his role, in *Science* magazine, with a $4 million libel suit.[32] But whether the fault lay with Kean, or with Armao, the responsibility of the shah's Rockefeller team of advisers is unambiguous.

Carter's recollection of the transmitted Kean report was "that the medical equipment and treatment the Shah required was available only in New York and that the Shah was 'at the point of death.' However, Dr. Kean . . . contended that that was not what he had told Dr. Dustin. His opinion at the time, Dr. Kean said, was that it would be preferable to have the Shah treated at New York Hospital, or elsewhere in the United States, but that if necessary, it could be done in Mexico or virtually anywhere. Despite this fact, Armao contended shortly after the Shah arrived in New York that his employer had left Mexico because such equipment was not available there and that the Shah's doctors claimed that the particular radiation treatment he was undergoing was not available anywhere else in the world."[33]

To understand Carter's catastrophic decision, it is important to understand that Iran and U.S.-Iran relations, because of Iran's oil, were both unique. With respect to Iran, the Rockefeller overworld had directed U.S. policy in Iran since the CIA coup of 1953 (a coup negotiated by Theodore Roosevelt's grandson Kermit Roosevelt). Thus the flagrant Rockefeller intervention in 1979 had, by its intended or unintended lack of disguise, a distinct impact on the outcome. Panama, Mexico, and above all Iran resented the actions of Kean and others, precisely because, rightly or wrongly, they sensed a sinister and manipulative Rockefeller influence behind them.

On November 1, 1979, for example, the new Iranian prime minister, Mehdi Bazargan, discussed the shah's presence in New York with Brzezinski at a ceremonial celebration in Algiers. The meeting aroused great alarm in Tehran.[34] As Brzezinski himself has noted: "On November 4, the Iranian militants stormed the Embassy, and two days later Bazargan was forced out of office."[35] Iran's new foreign minister, Abolhassan Bani-Sadr, promptly announced his government's plan to withdraw its assets from the United States, citing the intervention on the shah's behalf by Kissinger and David Rockefeller.[36] His decision precipitated a U.S. freeze on Iranian assets on November 14.

Again in March 1980, after the removal of the shah from New York to Panama, the *Washington Post* reported: "On Saturday, Iranian Foreign Minister Sadegh Ghotbzadeh charged that the shah's U.S. friends, including former secretary of state Henry A. Kissinger and David Rockefeller, chairman of the Chase Manhattan Bank, were plotting to get him out of Panama before today's formal deadline for Iran to present an extradition request to Panamanian officials."[37]

One might almost say that U.S.-Iran relations from 1953 to 1979 had been less between two states than between two overworlds.[38] One overworld was that of the shah, out of touch with his own country, who served Western wishes with respect to oil, the Soviet Union, and Israel. Meanwhile, "U.S. ambassadors to Iran during the 1960s and 70s were . . . mediocre. In fairness to them, however, they had to pursue the party line, promoted back in Washington, where the Shah was considered a close friend and one whose leadership was not to be questioned. The imposing figures, such as Kermit Roosevelt, Richard Helms, Henry Kissinger, John Jay McCloy, and David Rockefeller served as the Shah's public relations men in the United States. . . . There were always a few embassy folks and political consuls and economic consuls who were very good, but the policy was not made at that level."[39] In other words Brzezinski, while failing to serve either U.S. or Iranian *national* interests at the moment of the shah's crisis, was not deviating from twenty years of U.S. deferral to overworld interests in Iran.

WHY DID DAVID ROCKEFELLER PLAY SUCH AN ACTIVE ROLE?

The question remains why David Rockefeller broke with his usual low-profile behavior in lobbying directly with the president and later publicly on the shah's behalf.[40] In his book *Interlock*, Hulbert noted that "one of the companies most indebted to the Shah—was Chase Manhattan Bank. The Shah ordered that all his government's major operating accounts be held at Chase and that letters of credit for the purchase of oil be handled exclusively through Chase. The bank also became the agent and lead manager for many of the loans to Iran. In short, Iran became the crown jewel of Chase's international banking portfolio."[41]

Hulbert argued that Rockefeller and his allies precipitated the November 1979 crisis (that is, the hostage taking) in order to give Chase Manhattan Bank legal cover to seize enough Iranian assets to erase billions in questionable loans that now presented a threat to the bank's liquidity.[42] (Unquestionably, the Chase Manhattan Bank "had by far the biggest exposure of any of the U.S. banks [in Iran], since it was owed both in its own right and as agent bank around four times the amount of Iranian deposits which it held."[43]) This crisis came after a series of press reports on Chase Manhattan's banking problems, some of which hinted that David Rockefeller might be fired as chairman.[44]

Though since ignored, Hulbert's theory received close attention and partial support in Iran political expert James Bill's landmark study, *The Eagle and the Lion: The Tragedy of American-Iranian Relations*:

> The . . . admission of the shah into the United States . . . triggered the subsequent taking of American diplomats hostage. On the morning of November 14, 1979, just ten days after the hostages were taken, President Carter, acting on the advice of Secretary of Treasury G. William Miller, froze all Iranian governmental assets in American banks. Like so many other of the key actors, Miller had ties with the Chase Manhattan Bank and with Iran. . . . The timing of the freeze announcement was crucial to Chase Manhattan. On November 5 the Iranian Central Bank had telexed Chase instructing them to make the forthcoming interest payment of $4.05 million due on November 15 from the surplus funds available in their London office. This interest was owed on a $500 million loan [of questionable legality] negotiated in January 1977 with the shah's government. . . . Once it had declared the $500 million loan in default, Chase then used "cross-default" clauses in the contract to declare all other loans to Iran in default. "Chase then seized Iran's deposits to offset these loans. When the dust had cleared, Chase had no loans to Iran left on its books."[45]

The seizures of Iranian assets were enforced by the Treasury Department under the International Emergency Economic Powers Act, which enables the president to seize the property of a foreign country or national. These powers had only just been transferred to the Federal Emergency Management Agency (FEMA) under the reorganization engineered by Brzezinski and his friend Samuel Huntington on July 20, 1979.[46] A Lyndon Larouche publication quoted a FEMA official seconded to Treasury, Randy Kau, as saying: "We at FEMA had this plan to freeze the Iranian assets two weeks before we did it, and I spent the entire two weeks on the phone [at Treasury] trying to kill the rumors that we would do it."[47] If FEMA did in fact arrange the freeze plan, then FEMA in its first year, 1979, was already playing the "emergency" role of secret super-government that would surface again—potentially with Oliver North's alleged plans in the 1980s to suspend the U.S. Constitution and in fact with the partial establishment of continuity of government (COG) plans on 9/11.

Chase's bargaining position was immensely strengthened, and the suffering of the American hostages considerably prolonged, by what Bill called the Treasury's "puzzling decision to permit American banks to 'offset' the funds that Iran had deposited in their vaults against the monies that the banks had loaned Iran. This effectively turned control [Hulbert says, "title"] of the frozen assets over to the banks and deprived the U.S. government of much of the leverage it needed to solve the hostage crisis. The Carter administration 'relinquished control over Iran's assets. If the banks had not been allowed to take the offsets, the government would have been able to negotiate with the Iranians directly.'"[48]

The offset decision affected banks in foreign countries. It was of questionable legality in international law and was immediately challenged in European courts.[49] Nevertheless, the administration, apparently at the instigation of FEMA, had bought the Mullah Theory of Rockefeller, Reed, and McCloy and effectively lumped all of the claims together. Henceforth, as deputy treasury secretary Robert Carswell later wrote: "The President had no legal power to force loan settlements."[50] He, like Iran, "could only negotiate with the banks, not tell them what to do."[51]

The phrase "weakened" or "failing" state has been used to describe Iran at this time because the nominal governments in Tehran had lost negotiating power, permanently as it turned out, to Ayatollah Khomeini and the Revolutionary Guards who had seized the embassy. It seems to have escaped notice that by ceding the same negotiating power to its banks, America then, as later, exhibited the same feature of becoming a "weakened state." Carter himself became a major victim, as the prolonged negotiations by the banks' law firms, dominated by McCloy, doomed his chance for reelection. As Hulbert wrote: "Before one begins to feel too sorry for Carter, however, it is important to recall that it was his administration that relinquished control over Iran's assets."[52]

ROCKEFELLER AND IRAN'S EFFORTS TO MARKET ITS OIL

Bill's extended examination of Hulbert's argument looks only at the benefits for banking from the crisis over the shah's return (and at Chase's particular vulnerability because several of its loans were possibly illegal under the Iranian constitution).[53] As his book title suggests, Hulbert looks also at the benefits that the freeze bestowed on the oil companies and arms industries with which Chase Manhattan and the Rockefellers interlocked. In February 1979, as earlier in 1953, the Iranian government took steps to market its oil independently of the Western oil majors. In 1979, as in 1953, a freeze of Iranian assets made this action more difficult. As was foreseen by McCloy, who was attorney for both Chase Manhattan and the oil majors: "It could halt the lion's share of trade denominated in dollars. Because most oil [and all OPEC] commerce is conducted in dollars, this would make it difficult for Iran to sell much oil."[54]

Hulbert saw no evidence that the oil companies themselves urged the United States to freeze Iranian assets. But Chase had a powerful motive to return to the old status quo in Iranian oil sales, which before 1979 had supplied about half of a regular deposit flow on the order of $15 billion a year.[55] By effectively restricting the access of Iran to the global oil market, the Iranian assets freeze became a factor in the huge oil price increases of 1979 and 1981 (and thus an indirect cause of Carter's electoral defeat in 1980).[56] Americans should be mindful of the West's actions taken against Iran in 1953 and 1979, the two previous times that Iran attempted to market its own oil independently of the West. There have been reports that Iran will try for a third time to establish its own marketing system for oil, independent of not only American oil companies and banks but also the U.S. dollar.

Hulbert's argument about Chase's motivations, while lucidly argued, is perhaps too monochromatic. International political economist Benjamin J. Cohen has written that the freeze was motivated by two concerns. The first was "that an abrupt liquidation of Iranian assets could trigger an even more widespread run on U.S. currency. . . . In the words of Anthony Solomon, then under secretary of the Treasury, 'Our central concern that morning was the dollar.'"[57] (In August 1978 David Rockefeller himself had expressed concern that lack of confidence in the dollar would persuade many foreign holders of dollars, such as Saudi Arabia, to seek diversification by selling dollars and buying stronger currencies.[58]) Cohen concedes, however, that there was a second "danger": "Officials were determined to avert any threat to the safety or competitive position of U.S. financial institutions."[59]

Whatever its limitations, Hulbert's argument deserves to be considered seriously.[60] Unquestionably, as investigative journalist Robert Parry has noted: "The new Iranian government . . . wanted Chase Manhattan to return Iranian assets, which Rockefeller put at more than $1 billion in 1978, although some estimates ran much higher. The withdrawal might have created a liquidity crisis for the bank which already was coping with financial troubles."[61] David Rockefeller conceded in his *Memoirs* that the

Iranian "government did reduce the balances they maintained with us during the second half of 1979. . . . Carter's 'freeze' of official Iranian assets protected our position, but no one at Chase played a role in convincing the administration to institute it."[62]

However, it would in my opinion be wrong to assign a single motive to the momentous and disastrous decision to admit the shah. It is clear from utterances at the time that both Kissinger and Brzezinski, by backing the shah, wished to squelch doubts about U.S. support for other threatened clients at the time, particularly Nicaraguan strongman Anastasio Somoza and Egyptian president Anwar Sadat. They were concerned with what Kissinger called "momentum," not wishing America to look like a weak, unreliable ally. Brzezinski also explicitly welcomed the opportunity for a crisis to which the United States could retaliate with a show of force. As we have seen, he favored the military coup that the Carter administration, according to the *New York Times*, had started planning in January 1979.[63] Brzezinski continued to chair a series of super-secret "military committee" meetings in his office that led to the ill-fated attempt in April 1980 to rescue the hostages.[64] There are rumors that Brzezinski had still more projects up his sleeve, possibly another military coup attempt.[65]

By most accounts, Carter in 1980 "made it clear to Iran and the rest of the world that the lives of the hostages were his first order of priority."[66] Yet the negotiations for their release, almost concluded in September, were pushed aside by Iraq's invasion of Iran in the same month.[67] Once again, Brzezinski's behavior suggests that he was less interested in resolving the hostage crisis through negotiations than in provoking a larger confrontation to restore the shah. In the words of radical journalist Larry Everest,

> On April 14, 1980, five months before Iraq's invasion, Zbigniew Brzezinski, President Carter's National Security Advisor, signaled the U.S.'s willingness to work with Iraq: "We see no fundamental incompatibility of interests between the United States and Iraq . . . we do not feel that American-Iraqi relations need to be frozen in antagonisms." In June, Iranian students revealed a secret memo from Brzezinski to then-Secretary of State Cyrus Vance recommending the "destabilization" of Iran's Islamic Republic via its neighbors.
>
> According to Iran's president at the time, Abol Hassan Bani-Sadr, Brzezinski met directly with Saddam Hussein in Jordan two months before the Iraqi assault. Bani-Sadr wrote, "Brzezinski had assured Saddam Hussein that the United States would not oppose the separation of Khuzestan (in southwest Iran) from Iran."[68]

CARTER LOSES THE ROCKEFELLER
"MANDATE FROM HEAVEN"

Torn as he was between the conflicting priorities of Vance on the one hand and Brzezinski and Rockefeller on the other, Carter's presidential term finished in fiasco. Salt II did not receive Senate approval. The hostages were neither rescued nor returned until Reagan's inauguration. Vance resigned in the wake of the hostage rescue attempt. More than was known at the time, the Camp David agreement earned Carter the mistrust and even enmity of Saudis and Israelis alike.[69] This generated enemies for Carter inside the United States, for the Saudis were close to the Arabists in CIA and the Israelis to the American Israel Public Affairs Committee lobby's friends in Congress. Elements from both CIA and Israel were allied in the Republicans' plans to defeat Carter by delaying the return of the hostages.[70]

What Brzezinski thought of Carter is not clear from his memoir. It is clear, however, that he saw greater value in Carter's human rights program than did Rockefeller, because of his correct perception that human rights could be a useful means of loosening Russia's grip over Poland and the rest of Eastern Europe.[71] In June 1980, however, David Rockefeller did not hesitate to voice publicly his growing displeasure with both Carter and his emphasis on human rights:

> Under Carter, he told the World Affairs Council, America's "vital interests" had been "subordinated to worthy but fuzzily defined moral issues—such as human rights and the proliferation of nuclear technologies." David insisted that while it was "only proper" for the U.S. to press the cause of human rights, "it should be prudent since our interference may be capable of toppling regimes whose substitutes are unknown."[72]
>
> Another concern of David's was America's declining economic fortunes. The failure of Carter "to put our economic house in order" was proving damaging: "the international monetary system has been shaken and America's global leadership has been weakened." David also complained of a "regulatory rampage" emanating from Washington, that was reducing corporate profits and productivity.[73]

Three months later, Rockefeller and members of his shah team visited Reagan's campaign manager, William Casey, during a "pivotal period of Carter's hostage negotiations." As Parry wrote in *Secrecy & Privilege*: "According to a campaign log dated September 11, David Rockefeller and several of his aides who were dealing with the Iranian issue signed in to see Casey at his campaign headquarters in Arlington, Virginia. With

Rockefeller were Joseph Reed, whom Rockefeller had assigned to coordinate U.S. policy toward the Shah, and Archibald Roosevelt, the former CIA officer who was monitoring events in the Persian Gulf for Chase Manhattan and who had collaborated with Miles Copeland on the Iran hostage-rescue plan."[74]

This was at a time when Ayatollah Khomeini, concerned no doubt by the increasing signs of a possible Iraq-Iran war, authorized his son-in-law Sadegh Tabatabai to approach the Carter representatives with an acceptable offer for release of the hostages. Tabatabai received a favorable response, and so, he told Parry, a meeting with an American delegation was arranged for Bonn, West Germany.[75] Carter later wrote that these "exploratory conversations were quite encouraging, [but as] . . . fate would have it, the Iraqis chose the day of [Tabatabai's] scheduled arrival in Iran, September 22, to invade Iran and to bomb the Tehran airport."[76]

The negotiations, had they succeeded, would have constituted the October Surprise about which the Reagan campaign was so worried.[77] It would seem possible that Rockefeller and his shah team were making contact with the Reagan campaign to forestall this issue. This possibility is increased by Parry's discovery that after Princess Ashraf, the shah's twin sister, had met with David Rockefeller, $20 million from her account with Chase Manhattan was passed in October 1980 to a bank account benefiting Casey's close friend John Shaheen. The money was transmitted by Jean A. Patry, David Rockefeller's lawyer in Geneva, Switzerland.[78]

That the Rockefeller-Reed visit to Casey concerned an October Surprise was corroborated by sworn testimony from a CIA officer, Charles Cogan. Cogan was present when Joseph Reed, by then Reagan's new ambassador to Morocco, visited Casey in early 1981 and reportedly said something to the effect that "we did something about Carter's October Surprise." In a less formal setting Cogan told an investigator that Reed's words to Casey were "We fucked Carter's October Surprise."[79]

Chapter 6 further explores these mysterious dealings and the Republicans' own October Surprise: the deals made in 1980 by Casey and his overworld with the Shi'a fundamentalists around Khomeini. Today it seems certain that Republicans plotted with Islamists, in a possibly treasonable arrangement to keep American hostages imprisoned until Reagan's inauguration. No Americans died from this deal, but it was a precedent for 9/11 nonetheless. Furthermore, the Republican deal was with the extremists around Khomeini and spelled political death for the pro-American Iranian moderate politicians, chiefly Prime Minister Abolhassan Bani-Sadr and Foreign Minister Sadeq Qotbzadeh. They had made the unfortunate mistake of dealing straight up with the Carter administration.[80]

Some observers have suggested that the Republican dealings, which involved Casey and also possibly Bush the elder, may have constituted treason.[81] What is certain is that they played a major part in delivering Iran into the hands of Shi'a Muslim extremists, a revolution that inspired Sunni Muslim extremists in their own jihad.

SIX

CASEY, THE REPUBLICAN COUNTERSURPRISE, AND THE BANK OF CREDIT AND COMMERCE INTERNATIONAL, 1980

William Casey, in 1980, met three times with representatives
of the Iranian leadership. The meetings took place in Madrid
and Paris. . . . R[obert] Gates, at that time a staffer of the
National Security Council in the administration of Jimmy
Carter and former CIA director George Bush also took
part. . . . In Madrid and Paris, the representatives of Ronald
Reagan and the Iranian leadership discussed the question
of possibly delaying the release of 52 hostages from the staff
of the U.S. Embassy in Teheran.

Sergey Vadimovich Stepashin, 1993

CASEY, THE NEW YORK OVERWORLD, AND THE BCCI BANKING MILIEU

In the previous chapters I have detailed how first Kissinger and then
Brzezinski used private assets and foreign cut-outs to implement policies,
some of which were grievously shortsighted and detrimental to the cause
of freedom and democracy. In so doing, they often excluded the agencies
of the public American state from their stratagems. This set the stage for
the off-the-books machinations of William Casey, the last survivor of the
freewheeling style of William J. Donovan and the Office of Strategic
Services (OSS). Casey carried secretive and unilateral behavior even fur-

ther than his two predecessors, often cutting himself off even from the very CIA "he was meant to lead."[1] It was his style to commit the United States, after a cursory authorization from President Ronald Reagan, to off-the-books actions in collusion with a small cabal of outside business-men (Casey's so-called Hardy Boys), politicians, and intelligence officers, among whom he was on a few occasions *the only American* present.

Superficially Casey's career resembled that of his friend Donovan before him, but the similarities masked far more important differences. Both men were self-made Republican Irish Catholic millionaires who rose high into society as Wall Street lawyers. But Donovan was able to join exclusive Protestant clubs at an early age and married into a Prot-estant family whose wealth dated back to before the American Revolu-tion.[2] Casey, however, was socially ill at ease until his death. In 1967, when his friend and OSS roommate Milton Katz sponsored him for membership in the Council on Foreign Relations (CFR) (Allen Dulles was another cosponsor), the CFR rejected Casey's application.[3] The CFR also failed to act on the application of Casey's close friend Leo Cherne, who in 1976 became chairman of the President's Foreign Intelligence Advisory Board.[4] CFR snobbery and exclusiveness helped weaken their links to the new class, backed by the military-industrial complex, which would become dominant during the Reagan administration. Paradoxi-cally, Casey's exclusion from New York's highest social circles facilitated his alliance with the emerging new overworld, "the cabal of Texan, Californian, and Floridian nouveaux riches" who were backing the so-called Reagan Revolution.[5] He fit this role even better than had George H. W. Bush, the Skull-and-Bones Yaleman who had made the prescient decision to seek wealth and power in the up-and-coming state of Texas, rather than in his declining home state of Connecticut.

Casey's business contacts, even when they reinforced his connections to intelligence, were like himself—from the world of nouveaux riches, which was becoming the new corrupt overworld. In 1967, while lawyer John McCloy was representing the oil majors, Casey was representing the corrupt Indonesian general Ibnu Sutowo, head of the Indonesian oil firm Pertamina. The Securities and Exchange Commission (SEC) had filed a stock fraud action against Sutowo for the "investments" (or pay-offs) he was soliciting for his New York restaurant, from oil companies doing business with Pertamina.[6] But Sutowo had pleased the big U.S. oil companies by accepting funds from them for the CIA-supported plot to overthrow Indonesian president Sukarno in 1965 through 1967. After the pro-American Suharto had replaced Sukarno, *Fortune* wrote that

"Sutowo's still small company played a key part in bankrolling those crucial operations, and the army has never forgotten it."[7]

Casey was a close business associate and friend of Sutowo's mentor in payoffs, Bruce Rappaport. In their definitive book on BCCI, *False Profits*, authors Peter Truell and Larry Gurwin wrote that Rappaport was "an oilman thought to have ties to U.S. and Israeli intelligence."[8] But when he drove out to play golf with Casey at Deepdale Golf Club on Long Island, Rappaport's chauffeur was often Louis Filardo, "an alleged associate of New York area mobsters."[9] Rappaport is a gray eminence one encounters again frequently in connection with the Iran-Contra scandal, with BCCI, and with the investment circles of the bin Laden family. His Inter Maritime Bank (IMB) of Geneva and New York together with the Bank of New York (of which he became a major stockholder) became major players in the criminal looting of Russia in the 1990s.[10] IMB's vice president, Alfred Hartmann, a BCCI director, was also chairman of a BCCI-owned bank, the Banque de Commerce et de Placements (BCP), which in 1986 brokered a $25 million investment, triggered by George W. Bush, in Bush's oil company, Harken Energy.[11]

Rappaport was only one of the businessmen, described contemptuously by a CIA veteran as "the Hardy Boys," to whom Casey would grant informal intelligence assignments after sneaking them upstairs to his Langley CIA office in his own private elevator. This special status failed to protect all of them from the law, however. Robert B. Anderson, once treasury secretary in the 1950s, went to prison in 1987 for tax evasion. Max Hugel, whom Casey first picked to be CIA deputy director for operations in 1981, resigned after being implicated in an illicit insider stock transaction.[12] John Shaheen, whom we meet again later in this chapter, involved the Canadian Province of Newfoundland in a costly oil refinery development that went bankrupt without having ever produced a drop of gasoline.[13]

Casey was at ease with businessmen of this color. When nominated by President Nixon to be SEC chairman in the 1960s, Casey himself was involved in two civil suits alleging breach of the securities laws. (Both suits were settled out of court.) Before leaving the SEC, he was again accused in a civil lawsuit concerning mismanagement of funds in the company Multiponics, of which he was a director.[14] Casey's shadowy connections are of major relevance to this book, as we next encounter Casey, Shaheen, and Rappaport in a sequence of wrongdoings far more serious than anything mentioned thus far.

Both Casey and Bush, in other words, were at some remove from the

Rockefeller CFR milieu that had placed first Kissinger and then Brzezinski in the White House. By the time of Reagan's election, however, power was shifting away from the Northeast, and CFR's influence was being severely challenged by the upstart and more unilateralist American Enterprise Institute (AEI). Conservative Jude Wanniski "long characterized [the AEI] as the HQ of what President Eisenhower called 'the military-industrial complex.' "[15] Reagan himself was the second non-CFR presidential candidate (after Barry Goldwater) since Dwight Eisenhower, and the first to be elected.

One factor in the increasing importance of the Sunbelt and its resentments was the relative decline in economic importance of New York itself. This was dramatically illustrated by a shift of the oil majors out of New York. During the Reagan presidency there was a massive and protracted struggle for dominance in which Texaco, ironically a New York company, ultimately lost a $10 billion lawsuit to Pennzoil, ironically a Texas oil company, and one close to then vice president Bush. Illustrating the climax of this shift, Exxon (formerly Standard Oil of New York and the largest oil major of all) decamped in 1990 from New York City to Irving, Texas. Separated from the more traditionalist law firms and investment banks of Wall Street and the CFR, the culture of wealth, particularly that of the oil industry, shifted away from the pieties of trilateralism and Carter and toward the shortsightedly ruthless acquisitive style symbolized by the energy trading company Enron. The stage was set for what political commentator Kevin Phillips and others have called the "greed decade," when "the portion of the nation's wealth held by the top 1 percent nearly doubled, skyrocketing from 22 percent to 39 percent, probably the most rapid escalation in U.S. history."[16]

CASEY, THE CORPORATE COUNTEROFFENSIVE, AND THE REAGAN REVOLUTION

With the spreading gap between rich and poor, the ideal of a public state in which all classes participated was slowly supplanted by the dominance of a deep state in which a few manipulated the many. This was facilitated by a parallel development in the media, thanks in large part to huge influxes of foreign money invested by new press barons like Rupert Murdoch and Conrad Black. The prime example of this was the Reverend Sun Myung Moon's Unification Church, with links to the Korean CIA. From 1965 on Moon invested millions in media and other ways of influencing American media culture. Before spending a year in a U.S. prison for income tax evasion in the mid-1980s, Moon had seen his American empire grow, thanks to both Japanese money and direct-mail campaigns by Richard Viguerie (a cofounder of the Moral Majority), to the point where in 1982 he launched the *Washington Times* to compete with the *Washington Post*.[17] Since that time the *Washington Times* has regularly lost $20 million or more a year, for total losses estimated up to $1 billion.[18]

Behind this visible shift in the media was partly the increasing power of a new "cowboy" overworld, as radical social theorist Carl Oglesby once suggested.[19] But there was also a new emerging consensus within the overworld, uniting both old and new wealth, that America's rich needed to go on a counteroffensive to take the country away from the radical left. William Simon, after stepping down as treasury secretary under Nixon, became a business partner of Casey's. In addition, he "became president of [the] Olin [Foundation] in 1976 with the explicit intention of redirecting its grant-making to achieving partisan political results for the right. He also founded the Institute for Educational Affairs, which bankrolled the right-wing campus reviews. 'The only thing that can save the Republican Party . . . is a counter-intelligentsia,' Simon said."[20]

Casey was a partner with Simon not only in business but also in the cause of counterrevolution. In 1962, Casey had helped establish the National Strategy Information Center (NSIC), along with his protégé Frank Barnett, as well as brewery magnate Joseph Coors and Prescott Bush Jr., brother of George H. W. Bush. In 1976, the NSIC received $1 million for a pro-defense spending campaign, which Barnett coordinated with his newly formed Committee on the Present Danger.[21] Casey himself became a member of the Committee on the Present Danger. In addition, he was a member of the President's Foreign Intelligence Advisory Board when its chairman, Casey's close friend and fellow businessman Leo Cherne, launched the Team B project that scuttled détente in the 1970s.

Together with Sir Antony Fisher, a British disciple of the free-market economist Frederick von Hayek, Casey in 1978 founded what would become the Manhattan Institute. It is said to have supplied the intellectual foundation for the Reagan Revolution in the 1980s, just as Fisher's sister-creation, the Institute of Economic Affairs in Great Britain, supplied the intellectual foundation for the Thatcher Revolution.[22] From the mid-1970s funding for this right-wing ideological offensive "was provided by a small sewing circle of rich philanthropists—Richard Mellon Scaife in Pittsburgh, Lynde and Harry Bradley in Milwaukee, John Olin in New York City, the Smith Richardson family in North Carolina, Joseph Coors in Denver, David and Charles Koch in Wichita."[23] By the

end of the 1970s total estimated corporate spending on advocacy adver-
tising and grassroots lobbying ran to $1 billion annually.[24]

Scaife meanwhile, with CIA encouragement, was funding $100,000 a
year to a joint CIA-British intelligence psychological operation, the
Institute for the Study of Conflict (ISC), and its controversial chief Brian
Crozier.[25] The ISC, created in 1970, was driven by a paranoia about left-
wing subversion, similar to that in future Supreme Court justice Lewis
Powell's confidential memorandum a year later.[26] Crozier in turn was a
member of the Pinay Circle, a European cabal of intelligence personnel
and veterans and their overworld backers. Of these the most important
was former French intelligence chief Alexandre de Marenches, organizer
of the Safari Club. De Marenches was a key figure in the evolution of
Casey's covert anti-Soviet operations in Afghanistan, discussed in chapter
7.[27] The Pinay Circle in the 1970s was actively engaged in trying to elect
right-wing governments (most notoriously Margaret Thatcher in the
United Kingdom). Crozier himself appeared to claim the credit for
Thatcher's election at a meeting of the Pinay Circle.[28]

Through his client Paul Weyrich, Scaife, along with the Coors family
and Viguerie, also helped in 1979 to launch the top-down Moral Majority.[29] The organizers' motives were political as well as religious—to use
abortion as an electoral issue to split the Democratic Catholic voting
block and elect Reagan.[30] Rich Catholics, like Casey's friend Bill Simon,
launched a similar right-wing campaign opposing the Catholic bishops'
pastoral letter on poverty.[31]

Casey played an important role in securing for Reagan the Republican
presidential nomination. After it was clear that Simon could not be nominated, Casey arranged for Reagan "a Sunday brunch with two dozen of
the richest, most powerful Republicans in New York." Later, on November 9, 1979, Casey organized a highly successful dinner, at which sixteen
hundred guests raised more than $800,000 for Reagan.[32] Four days later,
Reagan formally announced his candidacy. In February 1980, after Reagan's defeat in the Iowa primary, Casey replaced Nixon Republican John
Sears as Reagan's campaign director. At this late stage it was Reagan who
picked Casey. But a year earlier Casey had in a sense selected Reagan. He
also helped design the consensus that would elect Reagan.

By 1980, Casey could write of himself, as he did in the press release
announcing his appointment as Reagan's campaign chairman, "*Fortune*
magazine recently proclaimed him a member of the Eastern establishment, while saying he hates to admit it."[33] He was now in a position to
collaborate with other establishment figures, notably David Rockefeller,

in an intrigue to block Carter's reelection that would involve far more dubious and marginal figures. This was the Republican countersurprise of 1980.

CASEY, BUSH, AND THE REPUBLICAN COUNTERSURPRISE

To understand the road to 9/11, it is necessary to revisit an almost forgotten episode in U.S. political history—the Republican negotiations with Muslim fundamentalists before the 1980 election to stop Carter from successfully negotiating the return of the American hostages in Tehran. These illicit contacts generated partnerships in secrecy that united at least two key Republican politicians, William Casey and the elder George Bush, with unlikely co-conspirators from Iran, Israel, and the scandal-ridden Bank of Credit and Commerce International (BCCI).

The illicit liaison produced a flow of U.S. arms, brokered by BCCI, from Israel to Iran. The arrangements, that could not be acknowledged, continued unchecked until they were exposed in the Iran-Contra scandal of 1986. By then they had also generated U.S. dependence on the drug-laundering BCCI for U.S. arms deliveries to Afghanistan. They also figure in the personal financial involvement of both George Bushes, father and son, in a cluster of BCCI-connected Saudi investors who have been accused of funding Osama bin Laden. At least some of the strange events surrounding and leading up to 9/11 can only be understood in the light of this Texas-Saudi connection. A celebrated example is the permission granted bin Laden family members to fly out of the United States in the days after the attacks.[34]

What has been less noticed, however, is that the powerful influence of neocons from the American Enterprise Institute in the two Bush administrations can also be dated back to the intrigues of the 1980 Republican countersurprise. A section of the unpublished *House October Surprise Task Force Report* of 1993 revealed that the Reagan-Bush campaign created "a strategy group, known as the 'October Surprise Group.'" Its ten members included Laurence Silberman from the AEI; and Fred Iklé, Michael Ledeen, and Richard Perle (all from the AEI) "also participated in meetings although they were not considered members."[35] Ledeen, a major figure in the Iran-Contra scandal, has since the 1990s been a leading advocate for the U.S. invasion of both Iraq and Iran.

In 2005, Silberman cochaired the commission that exonerated President George W. Bush from responsibility for the false stories linking Iraq to weapons of mass destruction. The commission report, called by many a whitewash, was praised in the *National Review* by Ledeen.[36] In short, the intimate and overlapping Bush family links to both pro-Muslim bankers and pro-Israeli politicians can be dated back to the 1980 Republican countersurprise, negotiated in part with Muslim fundamentalists. People who have once collaborated secretly in an impeachable if not treasonable offense cannot dispense lightly with their co-conspirators.

Through 1980 there were two competing sets of secret American negotiations with Iranians for the return of the captured U.S. hostages. The first set, official and perforce Democratic, was labeled Carter's October Surprise by vice presidential candidate Bush on October 2, 1980.[37] In competition with it was a second set of negotiations, Republican and possibly illegal, to delay the hostages' return until Reagan's inauguration in 1981. The Republican countersurprise (often also called "October Surprise") had a precedent: Nixon's secret deals with Vietnamese president Nguyen van Thieu in 1968, to delay President Johnson's own "October surprise"—his hopes of Vietnam peace talks—until after the presidential election.[38]

It is now certain that Nixon, acting through his intermediary Anna Chennault, persuaded the head of the Saigon regime not to participate until after Nixon had been elected.[39] (His action of interfering in a major diplomatic negotiation has been called illegal—in this case by Democrats.[40]) In this way Nixon helped to secure not only his election, but also the further loss of Vietnamese and American lives in a fruitless extension of the Vietnam War. Thus the actions of Bush the elder and Casey in October 1980 had antecedents. But in one respect they were unprecedented: Nixon in 1968 was negotiating privately with America's client and ally Nguyen van Thieu. Casey in 1980 was negotiating with representatives of a country that President Carter had designated as an enemy. This is why Gary Sick wrote of a "political coup," Robert Parry of possible treason, and Kevin Phillips of the possibility whether the deal "would have violated federal law."[41]

Even in 2005, accounts of the 1980 Republican surprise remain outside the confines of mainstream U.S. political history. This is in part because, as I detail in this book, the events brought in elements from powerful and enduring forces in Washington—oilmen and CIA on the one hand (CIA is traditionally close to the U.S. oil majors and the oil-rich countries of the Persian Gulf) and the pro-Israel lobby on the other. Just as oil is powerful in the federal bureaucracy, so the pro-Israel lobby, represented by the American-Israel Political Action Committee (AIPAC), is powerful in Congress. The two groups have grown powerful through the years in opposition to each other, but on this occasion they were allied against Jimmy Carter.

The Republican countersurprise of 1980 was originally described in two books by Washington insiders Barbara Honegger (a former Reagan campaign aide) and Gary Sick (the Iran desk officer under Brzezinski for Carter's National Security Council). A desultory House Task Force investigation in 1992, chaired by the congressman Lee Hamilton, was closed down in 1993, after reporting that its ten-month investigation found "no credible evidence" to support allegations that the Reagan-Bush campaign in October 1980 sought to delay the release of Americans held hostage in Iran until after that year's presidential election.[42]

There matters might have rested had it not been for the indefatigable researches of journalist Robert Parry. Parry had twice had fallings-out with his employers from his pursuit of the truth about Iran-Contra: first at the Associated Press after breaking the contra-drugs story, and then at *Newsweek*. After resigning his position to write a book, Parry gained access to the stored records of the House Task Force. There he found clear evidence of a major cover-up, particularly with respect to Casey: "The [House Task Force] investigators learned that William Casey's calendars, passports and travel records had been catalogued by CIA and were turned over to his family after his death in 1987. When the investigators searched Casey's two homes, they found all the catalogued records, except Casey's passport for 1980, a "hostages" file, two personal calendars and loose pages from a third calendar which covered the period of July 24, 1980 to December 18, 1980. Checked against CIA's index, the only folders missing were the ones relevant to the October Surprise issue."[43]

At the same time, during the investigation of BCCI by Senators John Kerry and Hank Brown of the Senate Subcommittee on Terrorism, Narcotics, and International Operations, the subcommittee was denied the records of principal hostage negotiator (and Iranian arms dealer) Cyrus Hashemi's bank records at BCCI. They were "withheld from disclosure to the Subcommittee by a British judge."[44] Over at the FBI two wiretap tape recordings of Hashemi's American office telephone disappeared, ruining a potential arms-trafficking case against Hashemi and his Republican lawyer, Stanley Pottinger.[45] As he pored through the evidence collected by the House investigators, but ignored or discarded by them, Parry found corroboration for all of the key elements of the Republican countersurprise story.

THE ROLE OF CYRUS HASHEMI, THE GOKALS, AND BCCI

In the hostage negotiations key player Hashemi was playing a double game. At the same time that he was negotiating on behalf of Carter, he was also anxiously raising funds in a vain effort to save a failing investment (the Come-by-Chance oil refinery in Newfoundland) with his business partner and close Casey associate John Shaheen.[46] Hashemi quickly gained influence with the new Khomeini regime in Iran. By arranging in 1979 for clandestine transfers of Iranian navy funds into his own bank in the Netherlands Antilles, First Gulf and Trust, he helped the regime evade the U.S. offset orders (discussed in chapter 4) freezing Iranian funds in European banks. According to his brother, Jamshid Hashemi, this was done with Shaheen's assistance, and the attorney advising both of them about the transactions was Casey.[47] The contact led swiftly to a CIA connection, as CIA then used the Hashemis to forward funds in support of the Iranian Navy Chief, Admiral Ahmad Madani.[48]

Hashemi met in March 1980 with Donald Gregg, a CIA officer who knew Bush the elder and would later work in his vice president's office, and who in 1980 was a member of Carter's White House team. Hashemi continued to meet secretly during this period with Casey.[49] The House Task Force heard testimony from Jamshid Hashemi that he and his deceased brother, Cyrus, had attended a July meeting in Spain with Casey and an Iranian leader, the mullah Mehdi Karrubi.[50] This claim was swiftly challenged. As investigative journalist Steven Emerson later wrote, the task force concluded that Casey could not have attended this meeting, since they found that he "was in California from July 25 through July 27, that he flew to London on July 27 and arrived there the following day. He remained in London until late in the day on July 29 and then flew back to the United States."[51]

However, Robert Parry has shown that Casey's "Bohemian Grove alibi" is almost certainly false.[52] The reference is to Casey's attendance at the annual Bohemian Club camp on the Russian River, and all the credible evidence puts him there one week later, on August 1 and 2.[53] According to Parry, dated chits from the club do indicate that Casey's host Darrell Trent bought drinks and shot skeet there on July 24 and 25. However, Casey's personal calendars indicate that he had meetings in Virginia on July 24, in New York on July 25, and that he purchased a Washington–New York plane ticket on July 25.

Jamshid Hashemi testified that in July 1980 he brought a Khomeini representative, Hassan Karrubi, to Madrid. There they met with Hassan's brother, Mehdi Karrubi, with Casey, and with Donald Gregg, the CIA officer working at the Carter-Brzezinski National Security Council. In exchange for delaying the return of the hostages, Casey promised to release $150 million in military hardware that had been already purchased by the shah but held back after the seizure of the hostages. After the deal was agreed to at a second Madrid meeting in mid-August, "Jamshid said his brother, Cyrus, began organizing military shipments— mostly artillery shells and aircraft tires—from Eilat, in Israel, to Bandar Abbas, an Iranian port."[54] The Hashemi deal was threatened, however, by a separate deal being negotiated by the White House. As discussed in chapter 5, Carter's negotiations for release of the hostages were almost successful in September, until they were pushed aside by Iraq's invasion of Iran in the same month.[55] A note written for the Reagan-Bush campaign recorded that "the fighting, now in its third day, forced Iran's Parliament to 'FREEZE INDEFINITELY' the debate on the fate of the 52 [hostages]."[56]

Hashemi's dealings in 1980 were henceforth documented by FBI wiretaps installed at his New York office in September.[57] Studying these records over a decade later, Parry found evidence linking Hashemi's activities to his bank, BCCI:

> Another box contained a "secret" summary of FBI wiretaps placed on phones belonging to Cyrus Hashemi, an Iranian financier who had worked for the CIA in 1980. Hashemi also was a key Carter intermediary in the hostage talks. But in fall 1980, the wiretaps showed Hashemi receiving a $3 million deposit arranged by a Houston lawyer who claimed to be associated with then-vice presidential candidate George Bush.
>
> After the 1980 election, the Houston lawyer was back on the phone promising Hashemi help from "the Bush people" for one of Hashemi's failing investments. And shortly after President Reagan's Inauguration, a second mysterious payment to Hashemi arrived from London by Concorde, via a courier for the Bank of Credit and Commerce International (BCCI).[58]

Hashemi's own companies interlocked with BCCI.[59] Although it has not been proven that BCCI was a vehicle for countersurprise payments, it is extremely likely. According to Truell and Gurwin: "BCCI was an important part of Iran's efforts to obtain weaponry and materiel. . . . Through most of the [1980–88] Iran-Iraq war, BCCI's head office in London ran large accounts for Iran's Bank Melli which were used to pay for weapons, military supplies, pharmaceuticals, and other needs. Bank Melli periodically replenished the accounts with payments that were sometimes as large as $100 million, according to Arif Durrani, a Palestinian arms dealer who used BCCI to finance the export of arms to Iran."[60]

In addition, arms were almost certainly being shipped from Israel to Iran by the BCCI-linked Gulf Group shipping lines of the Gokal brothers. The Gokals were close to BCCI owner Agha Hasan Abedi; they invested heavily in BCCI, and in return they received from the bank perhaps as much as $1.3 billion in loans that were never repaid.[61] One brother, Abbas Gokal, was a board member of Rappaport's Inter Maritime Bank from 1978 to 1982 and owned 19.9 percent of the bank's stock. According to coauthors Alan Block and Constance Weaver: "The Gokals were prime shippers to Iran in its decade long war with Iraq. One brother, Mustapha Gokal, was a financial adviser to Iran's Ayatollah Khomeini, as well as to General Zia, Pakistan's president. Concerning Iran, a former manager of the Gokals' Karachi office told reporters from *The Guardian* that they 'did *everything* for Iran. *Everything.*'"[62]

Although Parry was unable to track down the BCCI money shipment, he did trace a $20 million payment by the shah's sister Princess Ashraf through David Rockefeller's Swiss lawyer Jean Patry. It was used by Shaheen on January 22, 1981, two days after the Reagan inauguration, to fund a business deal that Cyrus Hashemi and Shaheen had been discussing for months. This was the founding of the Hong Kong Deposit and Guaranty Bank, whose other directors included Ghanim al-Mazrouie (an Abu Dhabi official who controlled 10 percent of BCCI), and Hassan Yassin ("a cousin of Saudi financier Adnan Khashoggi and an adviser to BCCI principal Kamal Adham, the former chief of Saudi intelligence").[63] The bank had a short history much like that of BCCI. Although it quickly attracted hundreds of millions of petrodollars, it collapsed in 1984 and an estimated $100 million disappeared.[64] Princess Ashraf lost her own $20 million but showed no regrets. She later told the House Task Force that the $20 million, which looks very much like a payoff to Shaheen and Hashemi, was just a routine investment.[65]

THE CASEY MEETING IN PARIS, OCTOBER 1980

Republican panic about Carter's progress in negotiations produced a spate of meetings in September 1980. As detailed in chapter 5, one of these meetings was on September 11, when David Rockefeller and several of his aides dealing with the Iranian issue signed in to see Casey at his campaign headquarters in Arlington, Virginia. With Rockefeller was Joseph V. Reed, whom Rockefeller had assigned to coordinate U.S. policy toward the shah, and Archibald Roosevelt, the former CIA officer who was monitoring events in the Persian Gulf for Chase Manhattan.[66]

Charles Cogan, a CIA officer who had earlier met Jamshid Hashemi with Shaheen, attended a 1981 meeting at CIA headquarters in Langley in which Reed commented to Casey about their success in disrupting Carter's "October Surprise."[67] Parry has reported Cogan's testimony about Reed but has offered no explanation of it. I think the answer lies in the disclosure of the last chapter: that because of the Treasury ruling on banking offsets, "the President had no legal power to force loan settlements."[68] He, like Iran, "could only negotiate with the banks, not tell them what to do."[69] In effect, the banks (above all Rockefeller's Chase Manhattan with its chief lawyer John J. McCloy) had acquired the whip hand on determining when the hostages would be released.

Five days after his meeting with Rockefeller, Casey met to discuss the "Persian Gulf Project" with Reagan-Bush aides, including Richard Allen and Michael Ledeen.[70] Allen, accompanied by Laurence Silberman and Robert McFarlane, later met with what Allen told Parry was a "swarthy" Iranian or Egyptian who proposed a hostage deal. Parry presents evidence to suggest that this was Houshang Lavi, an experienced Iranian arms dealer, whose hostage proposal eventually went nowhere. Lavi's meeting with the Republicans probably took place on October 2, the same day that he presented a hostage proposal at CIA headquarters.[71]

Later in October, according to many witnesses, Casey met with Iranian and Israeli representatives in Paris and promised delivery to Iran via Israeli third parties of needed U.S. armaments and spare parts.[72] The meetings were arranged by Alexandre de Marenches, former head of French intelligence (and a Knight of Malta like Casey and William Simon). Casey is supposed to have cleared his promise with vice presidential candidate George Bush.[73]

The role of de Marenches is significant, and explains a lot about his subsequent impact on U.S. policy in Afghanistan. De Marenches was a right-winger, a member of the Pinay Circle that claimed credit for the election of Margaret Thatcher's government in Britain.[74] De Marenches had also helped with Kamal Adham of Saudi intelligence (and later BCCI) to organize the so-called Safari Club that worked in the 1970s to reconcile Egypt, Iran, Saudi Arabia, and Morocco in the face of the Soviet threat. In conjunction with BCCI (which Adham joined in 1977), "the Club was able to help bring about President Sadat's historic peacemaking visit of November 1977 to Jerusalem, leading eventually to the U.S.-Egyptian-Israeli peace treaty of 1979."[75]

Parry reported that in December 1992, "deMarenches's biographer, David Andelman, an ex-*New York Times* and CBS News correspondent, had testified before the task force that deMarenches had discussed the Paris meetings while the two were writing deMarenches's autobiography, *The Fourth World War*. After Andelman's testimony, the task force called deMarenches. But when the imperious French spymaster failed to return the call, the task force concluded, paradoxically, that Andelman's testimony was 'credible' but lacked 'probative value.'"[76]

Later Parry found corroboration for Andelman's sworn testimony in the original French edition of *P.S.*, the memoirs of Pierre Salinger, press secretary to John F. Kennedy and ABC News's longtime Paris bureau chief. In the English edition of the memoir the eight paragraphs on the October Surprise (some of which is excerpted below) were deleted by the U.S. publisher, St. Martin's Press:

> Salinger knew Andelman and urged him to "push (deMarenches) toughly to get the truth about the Paris meeting. Andelman came back to me and said that Marenches had finally agreed (that) he organized the meeting, under the request of an old friend, William Casey. . . . Marenches and Casey had known each other well during the days of World War II. Marenches added that while he prepared the meeting, he did not attend it."
>
> [. . .] In the deleted passage, Salinger said he had other information to corroborate deMarenches's statement to Andelman. "In the mid-80s, I had a long and important meeting with a top official in French intelligence," Salinger wrote. "He confirmed to me that the U.S.-Iranian meeting did take place on October 18 and 19 and he knew that Marenches had written a report on it which was in intelligence files. Unfortunately, he told me that file had disappeared."[77]

Parry collected further corroboration from top Iranians and Arabs of the period, including Iran's president Abolhassan Bani-Sadr and defense minister Ahmed Madani, as well as Palestine Liberation Organization chairman Yasir Arafat.[78] Still other testimony supporting the October Surprise charges had come from intelligence agents with confirmed ties to Israel, France, and the United States. Parry continues: "Then, last year, senior representatives of Iran's current government held informal talks in Europe with Americans close to President Clinton. Like de Marenches, these Iranians were amused at how wrong the House task force had been. Casey indeed had made secret overtures to Iran during the hostage crisis of 1980, these Iranians said."[79]

Among the documents of the task force, Parry found a six-page report from Russia's legislature the Supreme Soviet, summarizing Moscow's intelligence information that also placed Casey in Europe, in order to arrange a politically favorable outcome to the 1980 hostage crisis. The Russian report had arrived in Washington on January 11, 1993, two days before the task force report was released that challenged this conclusion.[80]

THE ISRAELI-IRAN ARMS CONNECTION AND IRAN-CONTRA

Shipments of arms and equipment from Israel to Iran began months before Reagan was elected and were augmented after the hostages were released. These included American weapons, which required approval from the U.S. government. Bits of this story have been leaked over the years. The *Wall Street Journal* reported on November 28, 1986, that the Reagan administration had known about and had given tacit approval to Israel for arms sales to Iran since 1981.[81] Journalist Daniel Schorr later confirmed that, following Inaugural Day in 1981, "Israel was shortly thereafter authorized by the Reagan administration to resume delivery of American-made arms to Iran, which President Carter had embargoed."[82] In 1982, Israel's ambassador to the United States, Moshe Arens, told the *Boston Globe* that Israeli arms shipments to Iran were sanctioned and coordinated by the United States government "at almost the highest level."[83]

These shipments of U.S. arms from Israel to Iran began in 1980. They led to a complaint in April 1980 by Carter to Israeli prime minister Begin about a shipment of three hundred tires.[84] A second shipment of tires and tank parts, arranged through de Marenches, produced further protests by Carter to Begin.[85] Soon after the release of the hostages, "in March 1981, Israel signed an agreement to ship arms to Iran. One planeload left immediately. *The Washington Post* says the shipment was authorized by then-Secretary of State Alexander Haig and was worth $10 to $15 million. Haig denies this, but adds, 'I have a sneaking suspicion that someone in the White House winked.' Another report says the weapons sent to Iran were worth $53 million. Still another estimates their value at $246 million. One aircraft chartered in Argentina and carrying American arms to Iran from Israel crashed in Turkey on July 18, 1981."[86] Shipments continued throughout the 1980s, even though there was no official authorization for the sales until the presidential finding of January 1986, in connection with the Iran-Contra deliveries. But there is no record of any official American protests after Reagan replaced Carter in the White House.

Cyrus Hashemi, the Iranian financier close to John Shaheen, continued to be involved in these deals.[87] Hashemi had been indicted with his brother Jamshid by U.S. federal prosecutors in 1984 for supplying arms to America's enemy Iran. But as the result of a tip-off from someone inside the government in Washington, the Hashemis avoided arrest and shifted their base to London.[88] In 1985, Hashemi figured at the margins of an Israeli arms sale to Iran brokered by Michael Ledeen and involving a number of other Republican countersurprise figures: Casey, Robert McFarlane, Shaheen, Shaheen's friend Roy Furmark, and Hashemi's former partner Hassan Karrubi.[89] The next year Hashemi was indicted again in a U.S. Customs sting. And $10 million obtained from the sultan of Brunei, ostensibly for Oliver North's support of the Contra cause, allegedly ended up instead in the Swiss bank account of Bruce Rappaport.[90]

Underlying all the confusion and intrigue of Iran-Contra was the gap between official U.S. policy, which quietly backed Iraq in its war against America's enemy Iran, and neocon-Israeli policy, which regarded Iraq as Israel's greater enemy. In addition, the Israelis were anxious to unload the huge stocks of weapons they had acquired from their enemies in the 1967 war and again from American resupply after the 1973 war.[91]

Israeli arms were also reaching Pakistan for CIA's Afghan mujahideen, even though the regular CIA establishment wanted their links to jihadi warriors to be free from Zionist taint. The Israeli arms flowed to the Afghans via Pakistan from 1982 if not earlier, thanks to a deal brokered between Israel and Pakistan's President Zia by Casey and Representative Charlie Wilson, a key Afghan backer, supporter of Israel, and Casey ally.[92] According to BCCI operative Sami Masri, "We did joint [Mossad-CIA] operations. BCCI was financing Israeli arms going into Afghanistan. There were Israeli arms, Israeli planes, and CIA pilots."[93]

The Kerry-Brown Senate report on BCCI speculated Casey might have facilitated the flow via BCCI, possibly involving his off-the-record contacts with his close friend and golfing partner Rappaport. The report sketched links between Rappaport and a BCCI subsidiary in Oman, through which "BCCI may have been moving money . . . to fund the war in Afghanistan."[94] As can be shown by comparing early and later versions of the Senate BCCI report, "Rappaport's key man in the Omani interlude was Jerry Townsend, an allegedly *former* CIA operative."[95]

In addition, arms were being shipped from Israel by the BCCI-linked Gulf Group shipping lines of the Gokal brothers. In the wake of the Republican countersurprise, "BCCI became an important tool of U.S. intelligence," and the Gokals' Gulf Group enjoyed major contracts shipping goods to third-world countries supplied by U.S. aid programs.[96] But BCCI already enjoyed good relations, both above and below the counter, with Carter and his administration as well.

Kamal Adham, the chief of Saudi intelligence, was a close Abedi associate and investor in BCCI. He was also a leading CIA agent of influence in Saudi Arabia and had been the intermediary or cut-out between Anwar Sadat of Egypt and Henry Kissinger when Sadat was persuaded to evict Soviet advisers from Egypt. Later, "when Carter was urging Egypt to make peace with Israel, Adham's close ties to the Sadat family were of vital importance."[97] On a more venal level Abedi in 1979 had solved the financial crisis of Carter's former budget director Bert Lance by arranging for a friend, Ghaith Pharaon, to purchase Lance's stock interest in the ailing Bank of Georgia.[98] In return, Lance became prominent in BCCI's devious efforts to take over a major bank, First American, in Washington, D.C.

The following is a surmise, but I think a well-founded one. Cyrus Hashemi, attempting to negotiate a hostage-for-arms deal, would have involved his bank BCCI in the outcome, no matter whether it had been Carter's deal or Casey's that ultimately prevailed. It is likely that the veiled and illegal BCCI purchase of First American in early 1981 fooled no one but was permitted as a quid pro quo. Citing the beginning of the takeover battle, Truell and Gurwin have speculated that it was a quid pro quo for Adham's help on Camp David.[99] This does not explain why under Carter, despite BCCI's Democratic connections, the acquisition was never approved. I consider that it was more likely a reward for BCCI's and the Gokals' influence in Tehran that contributed to the success of the Republican countersurprise. (William Middendorf, who controlled First American at the time its shares were sold to BCCI clients, was one of the six nonmembers who in 1980 participated in meetings of the Reagan-Bush "October Surprise Group."[100])

The bank's immunity from regulation and prosecution in the ensuing Reagan years became notorious. As treasury secretary, James Baker flagrantly declined to prosecute BCCI after it had been exposed for illegally acquiring First American. A former National Security Council economist told author Jonathan Beaty that "Baker didn't pursue BCCI because he thought a prosecution of the bank would damage the United States reputation as a safe haven for flight capital and overseas investments."[101] A simpler explanation might be that Baker knew what secrets could be told by the highest-level surviving BCCI officials.[102]

The full story of BCCI was never officially told, nor was the story of the Republican countersurprise. The Iran-Contra hearings successfully covered up the arms shipments to Iran before 1984, and the House Task Force investigation of the Republican Surprise went nowhere. As *Newsweek* correspondent Eleanor Clift correctly predicted in 1991, "Congress will not formally investigate charges that the Reagan campaign stole the election in 1980, in large part because Israel's supporters on Capitol Hill do not want to put the spotlight on Israel's role, which during that period sold weapons to Iran in blatant disregard of President Carter."[103]

The key figure in both cover-ups was the congressman Lee Hamilton, a friend of the pro-Israel AIPAC lobby who chaired the House Iran-Contra Committee in 1987 and the House Task Force from 1992 to 1993.[104] The bland results of the House Task Force report were hardly surprising. Hamilton had earlier participated in a dishonest defense of the Contras against charges of drug trafficking.[105] The chief counsel of the House Task Force was E. Lawrence Barcella, who had received $2 million in legal fees as the lead attorney for BCCI in the late 1980s. At that time Barcella also was a law partner of Paul Laxalt, who had been chairman of the Reagan-Bush campaign in 1980. Finally, Barcella had close personal connections to Michael Ledeen, from whom he had bought a house and shared a housekeeper.[106]

In 2003, Hamilton would be resurrected to cochair the 9/11 Commission, investigating a third crisis that involved both right-wing Republican politicians and Muslim fundamentalists. Many people, including U.S. government officials, had alleged a number of links between BCCI investors, the bin Laden family, and the financing of al Qaeda. For example, a French book has charged that "after dominating the financial news through the 1990s, the BCCI is now at the center of the financial network put in place by Osama bin Laden's main supporters."[107] But in the 2004 *9/11 Commission Report* these allegations were completely ignored.

DID CIA OFFICERS COMBINE TO OUST AN ELECTED PRESIDENT?

It is time to repeat an observation made in chapter 5 that I continue to develop throughout this book. In time, it became known that Pakistan, America's chief ally in South Asia, had become radically corrupted by the combined influence of its Inter-Services Intelligence Agency (ISI) and BCCI. Partly because these two organizations had clearly more influence over the Pakistani state than the Pakistani state over them, it has been fashionable to describe Pakistan, like Afghanistan, as exhibiting the features of a failed or failing state. As we reflect on this chapter and those that follow, we must ask the analogous question: Does not America also exhibit these same features, so that to some extent it too should be classified as a failing state?

Up to this point I have narrated the story of the Republican countersurprise as a party intrigue involving some dubious marginal characters, Muslim fundamentalists, and foreign banks. But when looked at a little closer, the hand of active and retired CIA operatives and assets can be seen at almost every point. As Carter's CIA director Stansfield Turner has remarked, in 1980 "there was no doubt that the CIA was more Republican and didn't like Democrats."[108] At least two dozen former CIA officers joined Vice President Bush's nomination campaign in 1980, while "the seventh floor of Langley was plastered with 'Bush for President' signs."[109]

A key figure was Theodore Shackley, promoted by Bush in 1976, fired by Turner in 1979, and allegedly (according to investigative journalist Joseph Trento) at the center of a "private, shadow spy organization within" CIA and responsible for contracting out operations that were funded in part by offshore funds from Kamal Adham of the GID (the Saudi intelligence agency Mukhabarat), the Safari Club, and BCCI.[110] Former CIA operative Miles Copeland also told Parry of "the CIA within the CIA," men with an allegiance to the former director of Central Intelligence, Bush, who "had an understanding with the Iranians" that the hostages would not be returned before Reagan's election.[111] In 1980, Shackley was coordinating the Republican monitoring of hostage negotiations for Richard Allen of the Reagan-Bush campaign. At the same time he was working with neocon journalist Michael Ledeen, who in late October 1980 wrote a damaging story about Carter's brother, Billy Carter, in the *New Republic*.[112]

Meanwhile, Cyrus Hashemi, who reportedly attended the July meeting in Madrid with Casey, was used by CIA with his bank, First Gulf, as "a conduit for funneling CIA funds to a variety of covert operations."[113] This began with funds for the Iranian admiral Madani in the January 1980 Iranian presidential election. It would appear that CIA was helping to consolidate the connection that would be used for hostage negotiations by Carter and Casey alike. But interestingly CIA assets being exploited in 1980—First Gulf, BCCI, and the Gokals' Gulf Group—were all already associated with Casey, who would not become CIA director until 1981.

The clearest signs of CIA involvement in the Republican countersurprise are in these institutions that were involved. We have already observed that at this time "BCCI became an important tool of U.S. intelligence." In chapter 7, I cite evidence that BCCI's role as a CIA asset dates back to at least 1976, if not 1972. It is often suggested that the same BCCI connection involved Casey's old friend, the alleged CIA and Mossad agent Bruce Rappaport.[114]

Rappaport's longtime connection to the world of the old Office of Policy Coordination drug master Paul Helliwell, with its interface between CIA and organized crime, forces us to focus on a more sinister consequence of what we should now perhaps call the Republican-CIA countersurprise. This is that the arms shipments henceforward financed through BCCI and authorized (if that is the word) by Bush and Casey in 1980, first from Israel to Iran and almost immediately from Israel to Afghanistan, helped open up the United States, for the first time in its history, to a sudden inrush of heroin from the Golden Crescent of the Afghan-Pakistan border. As I note in chapter 7, this is the same heroin connection that (according to most sources but not the *9/11 Commission Report*) has been financing the jihadi operations of al Qaeda.

THE CONSOLIDATION OF OFF-THE-BOOKS GOVERNMENT

If I have taken such lengths to document the October Surprise of 1980, it is because the consequences are with us to this day. One consequence of course was the launching of the Bushes in the White House and of their cabals in the executive office building next door—coordinated with the aid of FEMA by Oliver North in the 1980s and by Dick Cheney today. Another consequence was the restoration of major CIA covert operations and of FBI spying on dissidents. Carter, acting on recommendations drawn up under Gerald Ford after Watergate, had largely returned CIA to its original function of intelligence gathering and analysis, while the FBI had already abolished its Internal Security Branch in 1976.[115]

A third consequence was the melding of covert operations, even against a sitting president, with offshore funding from the superwealth of Saudi Arabia. This was in the context of recycled U.S. largesse to South Korea returning in the form of pro–Vietnam War and other right-wing propaganda inside the United States.[116] By 1987, as I can attest from my brief personal experience in Washington, independent journalists were being placed under direct surveillance for the crime of having reported honestly about the drug trafficking of Contras and their supporters.[117]

In the 1980s CIA's budget soared, with half of it going to sustain a major "covert" war in Afghanistan. As a result, CIA also spent millions training the cadres of non-Afghan mujahideen who later swelled the ranks of al Qaeda.[118] The Reagan-Bush team in 1980 was not the first example of a cabal manipulating American covert politics, nor was it the last. We can almost blame television for the recurring situation in which a smiling president without any particular depth in international affairs (Eisenhower, Ford, Reagan, or the younger Bush) is backed by a shadowy cabal with its own agenda (Dulles, Bush, Casey, or Cheney and the Project for the New American Century).[119]

But there is a significant difference between Dulles in the 1950s and Casey in the 1980s. The instrument of Dulles's covert policies was CIA, which Congress, rightly or wrongly, had authorized by the National Security Act of 1947. Casey and Bush supplemented their vigorous CIA programs with other activities, often illegal, that were supported by unauthorized networks. To quote from the *Final Report of the Independent Counsel for Iran/Contra Matters*: "Reagan Administration officials decided to conduct foreign policy *off the books*, outside of congressional funding and oversight channels."[120]

The inner cabals and outside networks that colluded with Casey and Bush in the 1980s, first in the Republican countersurprise and then later in Iran-Contra, are still with us today. In 2003, to be sure, the war conducted against Iraq was overt and handled through the regular channels of the Pentagon. But in the planning and lobbying for that war, and in the manipulation of evidence to justify it, we see the manipulative hands of some of the same groups. We see the same pattern of informal networks permeating through and outside the bureaucracy. In some cases we see even the same names.

A second part of the legacy of the Casey-Bush cabal is the resort to outside countries such as Israel to help determine and execute U.S. policy. The disastrous consequences of this are considered in chapter 7, when I examine the 1980 U.S. intervention in Afghanistan.

SEVEN

AFGHANISTAN AND THE ORIGINS
OF AL QAEDA

It was the original concept that covert activities undertaken
under the [National Security] Act were to be carefully limited
and controlled. You will note that the language of the Act
provides that this catch-all clause is applicable only in the
event that national security is affected. . . . However, as the
Cold War continued . . . I have read somewhere that as time
progressed we had literally hundreds of such operations going
on simultaneously. It seems clear that these operations have
gotten out of hand.
Clark Clifford, 1975

For God's sake, you're financing your own assassins.
Afghan exile to U.S. State Department official, 1980s

THE BANK OF CREDIT AND COMMERCE INTERNATIONAL
AND THE DEEP HISTORY OF AFGHANISTAN

The CIA-backed resistance to the 1980s Soviet occupation of Afghanistan has been called "the largest covert operation in history."[1] It was
also in some respects the worst conceived. I am not talking about earlier
decisions—the CIA's backing of the SAVAK's efforts in the 1970s to destabilize Afghanistan and incite disruption by Islamic fundamentalists, or
national security adviser Zbigniew Brzezinski's blocking of secretary of
state Cyrus Vance's efforts to neutralize the region, or the almost inevitable decision to support the Afghan resistance.

I'm talking about the disastrous details of the U.S. covert support policy under CIA Director William Casey and Vice President George H. W. Bush: (1) to favor Islamist fundamentalists over native Sufi nationalists, (2) to sponsor an "Arab Afghan" foreign legion that from the outset hated the United States almost as much as the USSR, (3) to help them to exploit narcotics as a means to weaken the Soviet army, (4) to help expand the resistance campaign into an international jihadi movement, to attack the Soviet Union itself, and (5) to continue supplying the Islamists after the Soviet withdrawal, allowing them to make war on Afghan moderates.

By such shortsighted miscalculations, CIA's powers, by means of proxies and offshore-subsidized assets, were used to help propagate, almost to help invent, the Islamist extremism that produced both the Taliban and al Qaeda. From its related dealings with the discredited drug bank the Bank of Credit and Commerce International (BCCI), CIA also became further enmeshed in ongoing criminal activities with the drug-trafficking Pakistani Inter-Services Intelligence Agency (ISI) and with many of the Islamist financial agencies that President George W. Bush has now attacked. These miscalculations helped turn Afghanistan, a country that before 1979 was not an important factor in the global drug traffic, into what it is today: by far the world's leading source of heroin.

America's out-of-control entanglements with jihadi Islamists, and particularly with the ISI, underlie the still misunderstood events of 9/11, and the ongoing inability of the U.S. bureaucracy and media to report honestly either on what happened that day, or on what those events reveal about the deep structure of U.S. global politics. Admittedly the mistakes can be attributed in part to America's limited resources in the area and above all to America's need to act through proxy networks like Saudi Arabian and Pakistani intelligence. But many conscious American decisions were made to compound the support for Wahhabist and Deobandi jihadis.

Consider, for example, the testimony of Michael Springman, the former head of the American visa bureau in Jeddah, Saudi Arabia. Springman told the BBC that since 1987 CIA had been illicitly issuing visas to unqualified applicants from the Middle East and bringing them to the United States for training in terrorism for the Afghan war. In his words: "In Saudi Arabia I was repeatedly ordered by high level State Dept. officials to issue visas to unqualified applicants. These were, essentially, people who had no ties either to Saudi Arabia or to their own country. I complained bitterly at the time there. I returned to the U.S., I complained to the State Dept. here, to the General Accounting Office, to the Bureau of Diplomatic Security and to the Inspector General's office. I was met with silence. What I was protesting was, in reality, an effort to bring recruits, rounded up by Osama bin Laden, to the U.S. for terrorist training by the CIA. They would then be returned to Afghanistan to fight against the then-Soviets."[2]

This and other disastrous policy errors should not be blamed primarily on the officers of CIA, who often opposed some of the worst decisions made in the Casey era. They should be blamed on the existence of history-changing secret powers, enabling a small clique controlling the deep state to embark on a reckless course that knowledgeable experts, some of them with bureaucratic appointments, warned against at the time.[3]

In the 1980s Casey and Vice President Bush, using covert networks, embarked on a number of their own initiatives. Some of these were actively opposed by other cabinet members and also—in the case of the Contras—by the Democratic-controlled Congress. The result was the conduct of operations by a cabal of inner cadres, working with proxies and off-the-books assets like the Saudi GID and BCCI. Americans do not yet have access to the true history of that era. Indeed, we have a schizophrenic history: exhaustive parallel accounts that do not refer to each other and that contribute to the profound divisions and mistrust in the country.

For decades we have had on the one hand the archival history of professional historians, and on the other hand tentative and fallible outsider accounts of deep historical events. Today, however, we have mainstream accounts in different fields that take no note of each other. This schizophrenia is particularly prominent with respect to BCCI as a component of covert U.S. foreign policy, dating back to its involvement in the 1980 Republican countersurprise. The three most thorough histories of U.S. involvement in Afghanistan—those by Diego Cordovez and Selig Harrison, George Crile, and Steve Coll—do not once mention BCCI.[4] Neither is there any mention of the drug money-laundering bank BCCI in two intimate biographies of Casey and the Bush family.[5]

However, the role of BCCI in America's Afghan operations is acknowledged by mainstream journalists. A book coauthored by *Wall Street Journal* reporter Peter Truell tells us that in the "campaign to aid the Afghan rebels . . . BCCI clearly emerged as a U.S. intelligence asset."[6] A book by two senior writers for *Time* confirms that in the words of a U.S. intelligence agent, "Casey began to use the outside—the Saudis, the Pakistanis, BCCI—to run what they couldn't get through Congress. [BCCI president] Abedi had the money to help."[7] (Both books corroborate that Casey met repeatedly with BCCI president Abedi.)[8] Thus BCCI enabled Casey to conduct foreign policy without the constraints imposed by the public democratic state. Our archival and mainstream histories have not yet acknowledged this.

As the U.S. commitment to the anti-Soviet campaign in Afghanistan increased, the relative importance of BCCI's contribution probably diminished. But one of the causes for the disastrously skewed U.S. campaign in Afghanistan was the importance of BCCI and the drug traffic at the outset. Relevant also is BCCI's role as a cut-out, using its wealth throughout the 1980s to corrupt members of the U.S. Congress and other politicians, much as the billionaire arms dealer and CIA asset Adnan Khashoggi had done in preceding decades.

This corruption explains the inability of Congress to deal honestly with the problem of BCCI's intelligence-related drug activities; some prominent members of Congress have even cooperated in suppressing the truth.[9] It is true that Senators John Kerry and Hank Brown (a Democrat and a Republican) submitted an exhaustive report, *The BCCI Affair*, to the Senate Foreign Relations Committee, of which they were members. But the report remained just that—a report *to* the committee from two very isolated senators, while no report *from* the committee was ever issued.[10]

If we are ever to see a more reasonable U.S. foreign policy in the Persian Gulf, we must begin by recovering more of the truth of what has driven the dark side of foreign policy. This includes the full story of why the United States, in invading Afghanistan in 2001, overthrew the Taliban (who had eliminated 94 percent of opium production in the country) with the aid of the Northern Alliance (who had just more than doubled opium production in their limited area.)[11] In this chapter I focus on what appear to have been disastrous miscalculations in Afghanistan, all made with little or no public debate and all implemented through the covert powers of CIA. These ill-considered U.S. ventures were launched by a few. The public state was barely involved: there was neither public discussion of these policies nor even clear awareness of their consequences, not in the entire administration and certainly not in Congress.

THE U.S. MISCALCULATIONS IN AFGHANISTAN

The First Miscalculation:
Backing Islamists over Traditionalists

The downing of U.S. Black Hawk and Chinook helicopters in Iraq in October and November 2003 was a typical example of how the aid supplied by CIA to Islamist terrorists in the 1980s contributed to the escalation and spread of terrorism in the world. At least two of the U.S. Black

Hawk helicopters that crashed in Iraq were brought down by the same sophisticated technique: taking out the ship's vulnerable tail rotor with a rocket-propelled grenade (RPG).[12] As right-wing columnists and Web sites were quick to point out, this was exactly the technique that brought down three Black Hawks in Mogadishu, Somalia, in October 1993. Three weeks after this devastating attack, the United States pulled out of Somalia—an event Osama bin Laden has cited as proof that America can be defeated.

But at first no one pointed out what Mark Bowden, author of the best account of that battle, reported: that the Somalis on the ground had been trained by Arabs who had fought against the Soviets in Afghanistan.[13] As Bowden wrote, it was these Arabs who taught that the best way to bring down a helicopter with an RPG was to shoot for the tail rotor (which keeps the helicopter from spinning by countering torque from its main rotor).[14] In his book on al Qaeda print and television journalist Peter Bergen said of the Mogadishu battle: "A U.S. official told me that the skills involved in shooting down those helicopters were not skills that the Somalis could have learned on their own."[15] In other words the training that the United States supplied to Islamists in the Afghan war in the 1980s, when the emphasis was on bringing down Soviet helicopters, was still coming back to haunt the United States in 2003. That training, according to author George Crile, included "urban terror, with instruction in car bombings, bicycle bombings, camel bombings, and assassination."[16]

We now know that some of the Arab trainers of the Somalis were members of al Qaeda. Ali Mohamed, the chief al Qaeda terrorist trainer (and also an FBI informant) later confessed that he trained the al Qaeda teams in Somalia and fought there himself.[17] The Egyptian-born Mohamed was also a veteran of the U.S. Army and CIA.[18] As I discuss in chapter 9, while allegedly still on the U.S. payroll, Mohamed had been recruiting and training Arabs at the al-Kifah Center in Brooklyn, New York.[19] This served as the main American recruiting center for the network that after the Afghan war became known as al Qaeda.[20]

It is easy in retrospect to challenge the wisdom of having imparted such skills to jihad-waging Islamists. These were extremists who even at the time made it clear they despised the West almost as much as they did the Soviet Union. But what remains is the dangerous system whereby small cliques of policy makers, acting at the highest levels of secrecy, are able to make ill-considered decisions, focused on the techniques and materiel of violence, that will have long-term and tragic effects worldwide.

This system also preserves itself by cover-up. The establishment version of U.S. involvement in Afghanistan and al Qaeda has been set out in two excellent books—*Charlie Wilson's War* by George Crile of *60 Minutes*, and *Ghost Wars* by Steve Coll of the *Washington Post*. Both works give finely woven narratives based on extensive interviews with former and current CIA officers and other high-level officials. This wealth of detail, however, makes it the more striking that they make no mention whatsoever of Ali Mohamed, the al-Kifah training camp, or Springman's statements about CIA visas for Islamists and jihadis. Nor does either of these privileged and apparently exhaustive accounts say anything about ISI and CIA use of the drug traffic against the Soviet Union or the CIA-favored bank BCCI, which was caught up in supplying both the mujahideen and this lucrative drug trade.

The United States is not the first country to have been derailed in Afghanistan. Great Britain's original disastrous involvement there, in 1839, had the modest intention, like Washington's in 2001, of lending support to a supposedly friendly Afghan ally. Of the sixteen-thousand-man expedition dispatched to Kabul in 1842, when Britain believed itself invincible, only one person survived.

The disastrous Soviet adventure with Afghanistan in the 1980s also began with a march to Kabul, to support a challenged pro-Soviet government there. A Pakistani military observer commented later that it took the Red Army tanks only two days to reach Kabul and eight years to begin to leave it. In like fashion the United States and its Northern Alliance allies reached Kabul swiftly in 2001 but came under increasingly heavy fire a year later. Despite the second President Bush's original resolve to keep the United States out of pacification operations in Afghanistan, the dialectic of events there is exerting more and more pressure to increase the U.S. pacification effort with American forces on the ground and a complement of long-term military and civilian advisers in place.

What forces are behind these pressures? The Soviets in 1980 were clearly opposed from the outset by mujahideen (called "freedom fighters" in Washington but "terrorists" in Moscow), who had been armed, financed, and trained since 1978 or earlier by the combined secret services of Pakistan, Saudi Arabia, and CIA. The forces opposing the United States in the wake of the latest Afghanistan war, in contrast, are almost entirely of its own making. This is true of the Pashtun remnants of the Taliban, who can be traced back to the organizational arrangements (involving the Pakistani ISI, the Saudi GID, and CIA) for their antecedents in the mujahideen.[21] It is if anything even more true of the so-called Arab Afghans of al Qaeda—the jihadi Muslims who were drawn (by the same three agencies) to fight against the USSR in the 1980s and have never been completely disbanded since.[22]

We can debate whether the United States should have opposed Soviet aggression by aggressively backing an indigenous opposition. The disaster for the United States is that the *indigenous* opposition, the traditional tribal-based parties ("decentralized, unideological and non-hierarchical"), lost out "as the CIA-ISI arms pipeline supported the more radical Islamic parties," particularly the drug-trafficking network of Gulbuddin Hekmatyar.[23]

It is important to understand that "inspired by the pan-Islamic Muslim Brotherhood . . . and by orthodox [and well-financed] Wahhabi groups in Saudi Arabia, the Afghan fundamentalists had a dedicated but *negligible* organization prior to the Communist takeover and the Soviet occupation."[24] An extreme instance was the Islamist party of Abdul Rasul Sayyaf. It was "virtually nonexistent in the field," but because of Sayyaf's close connections to Saudi Arabia and "impeccable Wahhabite credentials," he and Hekmatyar were ideologically "in a position of clear advantage" to obtain funds.[25]

The Saudis, Pakistanis, and above all the ISI had no interest in seeing Afghan nationalism prevail. Instead, the ISI set up an artificial council of seven parties, of which four were fundamentalist. Local commanders had to join one of these parties to get weapons, of which "67 to 73 percent" went to the four fundamentalist parties.[26] Of the two major fundamentalist parties, Hekmatyar's was based on detribalized Pashtuns from the north, while the Cairo-trained Burhanuddin Rabbani's "consisted almost entirely of Tajiks."[27] Thus the tribal Pashtun nationalists, whose dreams of a united "Pushtunistan" threatened Pakistan's borders, were deliberately underrepresented.

The United States missed an important opportunity in 1980 to rectify this fundamentalist bias. A *loya jirga*, or national assembly, convened to represent all of Afghanistan's divergent groups, called for a loose federal structure, nonaligned foreign policy, and nonsectarian Islam. Although the *loya jirga* was praised by the *Christian Science Monitor* for its representative character, the United States did not intervene when the ISI scuttled the venture by threatening to cut off the supply of U.S. weapons. The religious consequence of this unbalanced ISI support was that the traditional moderate Sufism that had been widespread in Afghanistan, and was represented by one of the two traditionalist parties, lost ground to the radical Salafi Islamism that was favored by Saudi Arabia as well as the ISI and its factions.[28] This mirrored a longtime evolution inside

Pakistan, where traditional Sufism had also been eroded by state-assisted radical elements, the Jamaat-e-Islami and the Jamiat-e-Ulema-Islam, backed by Pakistan president Muhammad Zia-ul Haq.[29]

The American journalist Selig Harrison has observed that this had a deleterious impact on the Pashtun resistance effort: "Ideologically, most commanders, with their tribal ties and their attachment to traditional forms of Islam, were repelled by fundamentalist demands for the abolition of the tribal structure as incompatible with their conception of a centralized Islamic state."[30] Nevertheless, as discussed in chapter 4, the ISI preferred the fundamentalist Hekmatyar precisely because he lacked a popular base in Afghanistan and thus was more dependent on Pakistani support. Zia also allegedly "thought he could count on Hekmatyar to work for a pan-Islamic entity," one embracing not just Pakistan and Afghanistan but eventually Central Asia and Kashmir.[31] In 2001 the drug network developed by Hekmatyar and his supporters in ISI was said by foreign observers to be a key element in the financial backing of al Qaeda.[32] In 2002 there was increasing speculation that with bin Laden on the run, the remnants of the Taliban and al Qaeda were being led in their violent opposition to the American-backed Hamid Karzai regime by Hekmatyar, possibly with rump ISI backing.[33]

Elsewhere it is acknowledged that CIA accepted the ISI's use of the drug trade to supplement the anti-Soviet campaign in the 1980s and consequently prevented U.S. Drug Enforcement Administration officers in Pakistan from pursuing well-known traffickers.[34] CIA failed to foresee that the heroin traffic, having been allowed to flourish, could not be turned off, and in time would come to subsidize the independent, anti-U.S. operations of al Qaeda. In other words the United States in this new millennium is confronting forces that it helped launch two decades ago, without any clear idea of the consequences of doing so, or of how to close these forces down. It is as if CIA had learned nothing from the "disposal problem" it consciously faced with the Cuban exiles after the disastrous Bay of Pigs fiasco, one eighth of whom at least (according to U.S. government estimates) ended up as organized drug traffickers.

As I have argued in *Drugs, Oil, and War*, most of the U.S. operations abroad have been to consolidate U.S. influence in oil-producing areas, and the great majority of the major covert actions have been conducted with the assistance of local drug-trafficking proxies.[35] This recurring convergence between oil and drugs is not a coincidence, but a feature of what I have called the deep politics of U.S. foreign policy—those factors in policy formation that are usually repressed rather than acknowledged.

The role of oil in U.S. geostrategic thinking is generally acknowledged. Less recognized has been the role of drug proxies in waging and financing conflicts that would not have been financed by Congress and U.S. taxpayers.

This phenomenon is sometimes characterized as blowback: the CIA's own term for unintended consequences at home of covert (and usually illegal) programs implemented abroad. But the term, by suggesting an accidental and lesser spin-off, misrepresents the dimensions and magnitude of the drug traffic the United States helped relaunch after World War II. That drug traffic has multiplied and spread throughout the world like a malignant cancer. It has also branched out into other areas— notably money laundering and people smuggling—which, like the drug traffic itself, have contributed to the problem of terrorism we now face.

The Second Miscalculation:
Strengthening the Antecedents of al Qaeda

The U.S. error in the 1980s of strengthening Islamic radicals inside Afghanistan was compounded by a second disastrous miscalculation: creating conditions for the recruitment and training of a worldwide foreign legion of jihadi Muslim terrorists. At first the United States helped to facilitate the recruitment of jihadi Muslims (often called "Arab Afghans") to serve against the USSR in Afghanistan. Under the encouragement of CIA chief William Casey in 1986, the United States then participated in the decision to deploy these Muslims outside Afghanistan and inside the Soviet Union. Since the Soviet withdrawal from Afghanistan in 1989, Osama bin Laden has provided leadership to these same forces, which today continue to threaten both Russia and the United States. These forces will continue to threaten the secular world even if bin Laden and his immediate associates are captured or killed.

In the 1980s, Casey of CIA, Prince Turki bin Faisal of Saudi intelligence, and the ISI worked together to create a foreign legion of jihadi Muslims or so-called Arab Afghans (who in fact were never Afghans and not always Arabs) in Afghanistan.[36] The foreigners were supported by the Services Center (Makhtab al-Khidmat, or MAK) of the Jordanian Palestinian Abdullah Azzam, in the offices of the Muslim World League and Muslim Brotherhood in Peshawar, Pakistan.[37] This project did not emanate from the Afghan resistance but was imposed on it. According to the Spanish author Robert Montoya, the idea originated in the elite Safari Club that had been created by French intelligence chief Alexandre de Marenches in

1976, bringing together other intelligence chiefs such as General Akhtar Abdur Rahman of ISI in Pakistan and Kamal Adham of Saudi Arabia.[38]

The relationship of CIA to the Arab Afghans, the MAK, and bin Laden has been much debated. Journalist Jason Burke denies the frequently made claim that "bin Laden was funded by the CIA."[39] The *9/11 Commission Report* goes further, asserting that "bin Ladin and his comrades had their own sources of support and training, and they received little or no assistance from the United States."[40]

Australian journalist John Pilger argues for a much stronger direction of Arab Afghans and al Qaeda by U.S. and British intelligence: "[In 1986] CIA director William Casey had given his backing to a plan put forward by Pakistan's intelligence agency, the ISI, to recruit people from around the world to join the Afghan jihad. More than 100,000 Islamic militants were trained in Pakistan between 1986 and 1992, in camps overseen by CIA and MI6, with the SAS training future al-Qaida and Taliban fighters in bomb-making and other black arts. Their leaders were trained at a CIA camp in Virginia. This was called Operation Cyclone and continued long after the Soviets had withdrawn in 1989."[41]

Unquestionably, as I explore in chapter 8, MAK centers in America, such as the al-Kifah Center in Brooklyn, were in the 1980s a major source of both recruitment and finance for the MAK, if only because the United States was one of the few countries in which such recruitment and financing were tolerated and even protected. "Millions of dollars each year" are said to have been raised for the MAK in Brooklyn alone.[42]

In addition, Jalaluddin Haqqani, the chief host in Afghanistan to the so-called Arab Afghans, "received bags of money each month from the [CIA] station in Islamabad."[43] (This was an exception to the general rule that CIA aid was funneled through General Zia and the ISI in Pakistan, cited by Burke as the reason why CIA funding "would have been impossible."[44]) Bergen, in arguing that CIA "had very limited dealings" with the Arab Afghans, concedes that "the CIA did help an important recruiter for the Arab Afghans, the Egyptian cleric Sheikh Omar Abdel Rahman." Sheikh Rahman, despite his known involvement with Egyptian terrorists, "was issued a visa for the United States in 1987 and a multiple-entry visa in 1990 [and] at least one of the visas was issued by a CIA officer working undercover in the consular section of the American embassy in Sudan."[45] (This was in addition to the visas reluctantly issued in Jeddah by Michael Springman, as noted earlier.)

Journalist John Cooley has described the sheikh as "helpmate to the CIA in recruiting young zealots, especially among Arab-Americans in the

United States, for the jihad in Afghanistan."[46] Those recruited through the al-Kifah Center were trained by a former CIA contract agent, Ali Mohamed, another Egyptian with connections to the same terrorist group as Rahman. Eventually both Rahman and Mohamed would be convicted for their involvement in 1990's al Qaeda plots. But before that both men enjoyed a surprising degree of FBI protection, in Mohamed's case because he was a top FBI informant on al Qaeda.

The Third Miscalculation: Using Drugs against the USSR

The United States probably had complex motives for assisting and protecting the al-Kifah Center. Like other countries it had security reasons for encouraging Islamist extremists to leave the United States and fight elsewhere. But another motive was their suitability for a Casey-endorsed plan, which Casey discussed with the ISI in 1984: to carry the Afghan jihad north into the Soviet Union.[47] This plan was facilitated by the corrupting power of the drug trade, and it was thus convenient that Hekmatyar, the mujahideen leader closest to Pakistan and the United States, was already a major heroin trafficker.

Before 1979, Pakistan and Afghanistan exported very little heroin to the West. By 1981, however, the drug lords (many of them high-ranking members of Pakistan's political and military establishment) supplied 60 percent of America's heroin. As journalist Robert Friedman wrote in the *Village Voice*: "Trucks from the Pakistan army's National Logistics Cell arriving with CIA arms from Karachi often returned loaded with heroin—protected by ISI [Pakistan's internal security service] papers from police search."[48] It is ironic that CIA helped set up and protect these networks of heroin terrorists in the first place. The ability of secret power to deform and corrupt public policy is perhaps best illustrated by a policy that was opposed by CIA professionals: CIA Director Casey's ill-fated decisions in the 1980s to use first heroin and later heroin-financed guerrillas to destabilize the USSR in the regions north of Afghanistan. The little that is known about these decisions suggests that Casey overrode his own officers and accepted advice from his wide circle of contacts abroad.

As a first step, Casey appears to have promoted a plan suggested to him in 1981 by the former French intelligence chief Alexandre de Marenches that CIA supply drugs on the sly to Soviet troops.[49] Although de Marenches subsequently denied that the plan, known as Operation Mosquito, went forward, there are reports that heroin, hashish, and even cocaine from Latin America soon reached Soviet troops. Along with the

CIA-ISI-linked bank BCCI, "a few American intelligence operatives were deeply enmeshed in the drug trade" before the war was over.[50] Maureen Orth, a correspondent for *Vanity Fair*, heard from Mathea Falco, head of International Narcotics Control for the State Department under Jimmy Carter, that CIA and the ISI together encouraged the mujahideen to addict the Soviet troops.[51]

CIA apparently returned to these narco-trafficking allies in 2001, when it developed a strategy for ousting the Taliban in Afghanistan. The informed Indian observer B. Raman charged in 2002 that "the Central Intelligence Agency (CIA) of the USA, which encouraged these heroin barons during the Afghan war of the 1980s in order to spread heroin-addiction amongst the Soviet troops, is now using them in its search for bin Laden and other surviving leaders of the Al Qaeda, by taking advantage of their local knowledge and contacts."[52] The drug lords selected by CIA, according to Raman, were "Haji Ayub Afridi, the Pakistani narcotics baron, who was a prized operative of the CIA in the 1980s," Haji Abdul Qadeer, Haji Mohammed Zaman, and Hazrat Ali.[53]

Philip Smucker, a journalist for the *Christian Science Monitor*,[54] has confirmed that in 2001 the drug trafficker Haji Mohammed Zaman was recruited again in France for the anti-Taliban cause, by "British and American officials." In his words, "When the Taliban claimed Jalalabad[,] . . . Zaman had fled Afghanistan for a leisurely life in Dijon, France. Just a few years at the top of the heroin trade in Jalalabad had given 'Mr. Ten Percent' a ticket to just about any destination he could have chosen. In late September 2001, British and American officials, keen to build up an opposition core to take back the country from the Taliban, met with and persuaded Zaman to return to Afghanistan."[55] The *Asian Times* corroborated Raman's claim that Zaman's longtime Pakistani drug-trafficking partner, Haji Ayub Afridi, was also released from a Pakistani jail at this time.[56]

The Fourth Miscalculation:
Recruiting Radical Muslims to Attack the USSR

But Casey's offensive plans against the Soviet Union went beyond heroin. In 1984, during a secret visit by Casey to Pakistan, "Casey startled his Pakistani hosts by proposing that they take the Afghan war into enemy territory—into the Soviet Union itself. . . . Pakistani intelligence officers—partly inspired by Casey—began independently to train Afghans and funnel CIA supplies for scattered strikes against military installations, factories and storage depots within Soviet territory. . . . The attacks later alarmed U.S. officials in Washington, who saw military raids on Soviet territory as 'an incredible escalation,' according to Graham Fuller, then a senior U.S. intelligence [CIA] official who counseled against any such raids."[57]

According to Steve Coll, "Robert Gates, Casey's executive assistant and later CIA director, has confirmed that Afghan rebels 'began cross-border operations into the Soviet Union itself' during the spring of 1985. These operations included 'raising Cain on the Soviet side of the border.' The attacks took place, according to Gates, 'with Casey's encouragement.' "[58] Cordovez and Harrison agree that Casey "urged Pakistani intelligence officials to carry the war into the Soviet Central Asian republics by smuggling written propaganda across the Oxus and conducting sabotage operations. . . . Casey's quiet encouragement emboldened the ISI to keep up the Central Asian operations throughout most of the war."[59] Earlier, Casey had already discussed the proposal with King Fahd of Saudi Arabia, which had its own Islamist operations in the trans-Caspian area.[60] But Casey, Zia, and King Fahd may all have been encouraged in this program by Alexandre de Marenches, who from the 1970s had been seeking ways, beginning with Islamic broadcasts, to detach the Muslim areas of Central Asia from the Soviet Union.

This state decision did far more than bin Laden's ideological speeches to enhance the autonomous development of an Islamist foreign legion, whose scope of operations, as well as its membership, became international. As Pakistani observer Ahmed Rashid has noted: "In 1986 the secret services of the United States, Great Britain, and Pakistan agreed on a plan to launch guerrilla attacks into Tajikistan and Uzbekistan. Afghan Mujahedeen units crossed the Amu Darya River in March 1987 and launched rocket attacks against villages in Tajikistan. Meanwhile, hundreds of Uzbek and Tajik Muslims clandestinely traveled to Pakistan and Saudi Arabia to study in madrassahs or to train as guerrilla fighters so that they could join the Mujahedeen. This was part of a wider U.S., Pakistani, and Saudi plan to recruit radical Muslims from around the world to fight with the Afghans. Between 1982 and 1992 thirty-five thousand Muslim radicals from forty-three Islamic countries fought for the Mujahedeen."[61]

"Thus it was," according to Pakistani brigadier Mohammed Yousaf, "the U.S. that put in train a major escalation of the war which, over the next three years, culminated in numerous cross-border raids and sabotage missions" north of the Amu Darya.[62] Rashid has written that the task "was given to the ISI's favorite Mujaheddin leader Gulbuddin Hikmetyar,"[63] who by this time was already supplementing his CIA and

Saudi income with the proceeds of his heroin labs "in the Koh-i-Sultan area [of Pakistan], where the ISI was in total control."[64] But former CIA officer Robert Baer gives credence to the Russian belief that jihadis north of the Amu Darya "were under the command of Rasool Sayyaf . . . , bin Laden's Afghani protector," and Sayyaf's backer, the Saudi IIRO (International Islamic Relief Organization)."[65]

My impression is that both Hekmatyar and Sayyaf were central to the Trans-Oxus campaign, and that this (along with their Saudi and ISI backing) helps explain why the two leaders were the largest recipients of funds. At the same time, CIA was also helping the ISI, the IIRO, and Saudi Arabia distribute throughout the Soviet Union thousands of CIA-printed Korans that had been translated into Uzbek in the United States, an important contribution to the spread of Islamism in Central Asia today.[66]

Casey's Central Asian initiative of 1984 was made at a time when right-wing oil interests in Texas already had their eyes on Caspian basin oil. Casey's cross-border guerrillas were recruited at first from ethnic Uzbeks and Tajiks, but Hekmatyar "gathered around him the most radical, anti-Western, transnational Islamists fighting in the jihad—including bin Laden and other Arabs who arrived as volunteers."[67] Some of Hekmatyar's cadres evolved in time into the heroin-financed Islamist groups like the Islamic Movement of Uzbekistan, who became the scourge of Central Asia in the 1990s.[68] Others were recruited by bin Laden directly into al Qaeda.[69]

In retrospect, no one should have been surprised at this outcome. Of all the mujahideen leaders, Hekmatyar and Sayyaf were the ultra-Islamists with the least following inside Afghanistan itself. A detribalized Kharufi from the northern Pashtun pocket of Kunduz, Hekmatyar lacked tribal backing and was thus the most amenable to ISI influence.[70] By nearly all accounts he was also the principal drug trafficker and perhaps the only leader who was dealing not only in opium but heroin.[71] I suspect that Casey, like Brzezinski before him, went along with the anti-Western Hekmatyar because he was attracted by the capacity of Hekmatyar's networks to disrupt the Soviet Union. The fact that these were heroin networks did not dissuade Casey, but would have been in keeping with CIA practice.

The Fifth Miscalculation:
Prolonging the Conflict to Destroy Gorbachev

Selig Harrison has written how, as a result of the November 1985 summit between U.S. president Ronald Reagan and Soviet president Mikhail

Gorbachev, both Reagan and secretary of state George Shultz showed a new interest in negotiating an Afghan settlement with Gorbachev. The following month, a State Department spokesman expressed a new U.S. willingness to accept and guarantee a UN-negotiated agreement, which would require the United States and Pakistan to cut off aid when the Soviets withdrew.

Almost immediately this new position was attacked by "bleeders" in the Pentagon and the National Security Council, who saw the Afghan war as a means to weaken and embarrass Gorbachev.[72] In addition, members of a Pentagon faction, led by undersecretary Fred Iklé, were anxious to win in Afghanistan by deploying antiaircraft Stingers to the mujahideen.[73] Even in the late 1980s "the 'bleeders' fought against the Geneva Accords until the very end."[74] For the details of this prolonged fight between Washington's so-called dealers and bleeders, I refer readers to the important book *Out of Afghanistan* by Cordovez and Harrison. As late as 1998, Brzezinski defended this strategy. Today we have to ask which opponent it would be better for America to deal with: Mikhail Gorbachev or Osama bin Laden and his allies? What was it that the bleeders feared most? A militant and threatening Soviet Union? Or a reformed and peaceful Soviet Union committed to coexistence—and thus constituting a threat to Pentagon and CIA budgets. Whatever the motive, the Iklé faction had succeeded by February 1986 in trumping the negotiations approach with a new and controversial policy decision: to supply the Stingers.[75]

The signing of the Geneva Accords and withdrawal of Soviet troops in 1988 would, in retrospect, have been a good moment to terminate CIA support for the rebels. We can now recognize, in the words of journalist James Bamford, "how much better off the United States would have been had the CIA stopped with the ouster of the Soviet military and simply left [their premier] Muhammad Najibullah in office."[76]

As Ahmed Rashid predicted accurately in 1990: "If Afghanistan fragments into warlordism, the West can expect a flood of cheap heroin that will be impossible to stop. . . . Afghanistan's President Najibullah has skillfully played on Western fears of a drugs epidemic by repeatedly offering co-operation with the DEA and other anti-narcotic agencies, but the West, which still insists on his downfall, has refused. If President [George Herbert] Bush and Margaret Thatcher continue to reject a peace process, they must prepare for an invasion of Afghan-grown heroin in Washington and London."[77] Within a decade Afghanistan had become by far the world's leading heroin producer.

Instead the United States continued its program of support to the mujahideen. The CIA's campaign in 1991 included the shipping of T-55 and T-70 tanks captured in Iraq to Gardez, the stronghold of Haqqani, Hekmatyar, and the Arab Afghans.[78] But by early 1991, U.S. efforts had declined into interagency sector intrigue. Both "the State department and the CIA . . . sought a change of government in Kabul, but they had different clients. [State] channeled guns and money to the new rebel commanders' shura [from which Hekmatyar had been excluded] . . . and they emphasized the importance of [Ahmed Shah] Massoud. . . . The CIA . . . continued to collaborate with Pakistani intelligence on a separate military track that mainly promoted Hekmatyar."[79]

This was after State Department officer Edmund McWilliams had reported that "Hekmatyar—backed by officers in ISI's Afghan bureau, operatives from the Muslim Brotherhood's Jamaat-e-Islami, officers from Saudi intelligence, and Arab volunteers from a dozen countries—was moving systematically to wipe out his rivals in the Afghan resistance."[80] The CIA persisted, even having received reports that ISI's new plan for Hekmatyar, which involved the Arab Afghans of al Qaeda, was receiving millions of dollars in support from Osama bin Laden.[81] Once again, covert power was overriding public policy.

Secrecy, Folly, and Vested Interests in Afghanistan: The Stingers

Another tragic mistake was the decision in 1986 to equip the mujahideen in Afghanistan with Stinger missiles to bring down Soviet aircraft. The folly of this decision, increasingly recognized in retrospect, serves as a case study of how covert power corrupts when the pressures of special interests thrive and there is no alerted public opinion to correct them. First I must contest the widespread impression that it was the introduction of Stingers into the Afghan war in September 1986 that led to the Soviet defeat and withdrawal. Declassified Kremlin documents give no indication that this was a factor in Gorbachev's and the Politburo's decision two months later to adopt a withdrawal deadline. "At the key November 1986 Politburo meeting," wrote foreign affairs specialist Alan J. Kuperman, "no mention was made of the Stinger nor any other U.S. escalation."[82]

The continuance of the Stinger policy was also a symptom of the reckless and unhealthy relationship that had built up between CIA and the ISI. From the outset it was an open secret to those in the know that the ISI was not forwarding the bulk of the U.S.-supplied arms, including the Stingers, to the mujahideen in Afghanistan. Rather, the ISI was keeping the lion's share for itself.[83] As early as January 1987, Andrew Eiva, director of the Federation for American-Afghanistan Action, complained publicly that in fact only eleven of the promised forty Oerlikon weapons had reached the mujahideen, prompting speculation at the time that the funds were being diverted for other purposes.[84]

The concern of congressmen that Stingers might be diverted "proved to be justified when a resistance commander sold sixteen Stingers to Iran in 1987. One of the missiles narrowly missed a U.S. helicopter in the Persian Gulf on October 8, 1987, prompting U.S. insistence on tightened procedures for distribution of Stingers to resistance units."[85] In 1990 foreign correspondent Christina Lamb wrote a series of articles in which she accused the ISI of selling off Stingers that had been allocated to the mujahideen.[86] In the following years, Stingers turned up in connection with a number of covert Islamist projects, including Osama bin Laden's.[87]

Why did CIA tolerate ISI's abuse of the program? Partly because it is a general characteristic of CIA, like other intelligence agencies, to put the preservation of structural relationships ahead of promoting particular national policies. (This is probably less a conscious doctrine than the result of a promotional system that rewards individuals for the number of assets they recruit.) Furthermore, intelligence agencies tend to share covert assets, like the BCCI bank; and the milieu of these connections becomes independent of the policy decisions to establish contact in the first place. Thus CIA would have been unlikely to break completely with the ISI, or any other unsavory agency, even if ordered to do so.

THE CIA, THE ISI, AND AL QAEDA

There is evidence that elements of the U.S. government continued, even after 1990, to collaborate with elements of the ISI in support of mutual goals, including conflicting goals. Many observers, for example, are convinced that the rise of the Taliban in Afghanistan had not only the active support of ISI elements, but the benign approval of the United States (which saw the Taliban as the best hope for a united Afghanistan through which oil and gas pipelines could be built).[88] In 1997 the *Wall Street Journal* declared: "The Taliban are the players most capable of achieving peace. Moreover, they are crucial to secure the country as a prime transshipment route for the export of Central Asia's vast oil, gas and other natural resources."[89]

It also seems quite clear that Western intelligence (at least British) found al Qaeda itself to be a useful ally against a common enemy—the secular dictator Muammar Gadhafi of Libya. As the French authors Jean-Charles Brisard and Guillaume Dasquié have pointed out, Gadhafi's Libya in 1998 asked Interpol to issue an arrest warrant for Osama bin Laden. They argue that bin Laden and al Qaeda elements were collaborating with the British MI5 in an anti-Gadhafi assassination plot.[90]

As I detail in the next chapters, jihadi Muslims connected to al Qaeda continued to be used for Western causes throughout the 1990s. In the months before the 1993 coup by strongman Heydar Aliyev in Azerbaijan, allegedly paid for in part by Western oil companies, hundreds of jihadis were recruited in Afghanistan by Hekmatyar and shipped to Azerbaijan on an airline set up by CIA veteran Ed Dearborn.[91] Jihadis also took part in two Balkan campaigns in the 1990s, on the same side as the United States and NATO. In Bosnia in the mid-1990s NATO and al Qaeda were on the same side, although it is not clear how closely they collaborated directly with each other.

The Kosovo Liberation Army (KLA or UCK), directly supported and politically empowered by NATO in 1998, had in the same year been listed by the U.S. State Department as a terrorist organization supported in part by the heroin traffic as well as loans from Islamic individuals, among them allegedly Osama bin Laden.[92] The closeness of the KLA to al Qaeda was acknowledged in the western press after Afghan-connected KLA guerrillas proceeded in 2001 to conduct guerrilla warfare in Macedonia. Press accounts included an Interpol report alleging that one of bin Laden's senior lieutenants, Muhammed al-Zawahiri, was the commander of an elite KLA unit operating in Kosovo in 1999.[93] Al-Zawahiri later supplied the guerrillas in Macedonia, along with Ramush Haradinaj, a former KLA commander. Haradinaj, today an indicted war criminal, was the key U.S. military and intelligence asset in Kosovo during the civil war and the NATO bombing campaign that followed.[94] The London *Sunday Times* reported that "American intelligence agents have admitted they helped to train the Kosovo Liberation Army before NATO's bombing of Yugoslavia."[95]

Thus there have been at least two decades of collaboration by the United States and CIA with Islamist elements who made no secret of their hostility toward America. It is striking that this collaboration continued even after bin Laden in 1996 issued the first of his fatwas declaring the United States to be an enemy. It came long after the identification of the 1993 World Trade Center bombers Ramzi Yousef and Mahmud Abouhalima, who had trained in Afghanistan.[96]

To repeat: The story of CIA's involvement shows how its covert powers are governed by secret decision-making processes that are far too restricted to cope wisely with today's complex world. It is these powers, rather than the individuals who compose CIA, that are the source of the problem. CIA officers opposed the decision, backed by Casey against his advisers, to send Islamist terrorists across the Amu Darya to conduct raids in the Soviet Union.[97] And CIA officers voiced concern about the decision to equip the mujahideen in Afghanistan with Stinger missiles.[98]

Journalist George Crile has written that the Democratic congressman Charlie Wilson was almost single-handedly responsible for converting the CIA Afghan operation from assisted harassment into a full-fledged anti-Soviet offensive war. His book, *Charlie Wilson's War*, is an object lesson in how inadequate analysis and understanding of the CIA secrecy problem can lead to bad politics. Inspired by Arthur Schlesinger's anti-Nixon book, *The Imperial Presidency*, the reforms of the Church Committee subjected CIA to increased congressional review and control through such devices as beefed-up intelligence committees in both houses. The intention was to restrain CIA through an enlarged network of checks and balances.

As the corrupting environment of secrecy was not challenged, however, the result of these reforms was just the opposite: a door opened still wider for unrestrained boondoggle. Backed by lobbyists for the defense industries, Israel, and Egypt, Wilson was able to force on CIA hundreds of millions of dollars in weapons programs it had not asked for. From his position in the House Intelligence Committee, Wilson even put an extra $200 million into the CIA's Afghan pipeline in 1991, after the Russians had withdrawn from Afghanistan. This was against the unanimous agreement of the U.S. Embassy in Pakistan, Secretary of State Baker, and the Bush White House that it was time to cut off aid altogether.[99]

PAKISTAN, AL QAEDA, AND 9/11

Was Pakistan's ISI Involved in 9/11?

In October 2001, shortly after the catastrophic events of 9/11, U.S. and British newspapers briefly alleged that the paymaster for the 9/11 attacks was a possible agent of the Pakistani intelligence service ISI, Ahmed Omar Saeed Sheikh (or Sheik Syed). There was even a brief period in which it was alleged that the money had been paid at the direction of the then ISI chief, Lieutenant-General Mahmoud Ahmad.[100]

The London *Guardian* reported on October 1, 2001, that "U.S. investigators believe they have found the 'smoking gun' linking Osama bin Laden to the September 11 terrorist attacks. . . . The man at the centre of the financial web is believed to be Sheikh Saeed, also known as Mustafa Mohamed Ahmad, who worked as a financial manager for Bin Laden when the Saudi exile was based in Sudan, and is still a trusted paymaster in Bin Laden's al-Qaida organization."[101] This story was corroborated by CNN on October 6, citing a "a senior-level U.S. government source" who noted that "Sheik Syed" had been liberated from an Indian prison as a result of an airplane hijacking in December 1999.

The man liberated in this way was Ahmed Omar Saeed Sheikh, a notorious kidnapper raised in England and widely reported as a probable agent of the ISI.[102] One newspaper, the *Pittsburgh Tribune-Review*, suggested he may have been a double agent, recruited inside al Qaeda and the ISI by CIA.[103] Others have since argued that Saeed Sheikh worked for both the United States and Britain, since "both American and British governments have studiously avoided taking any action against Sheikh despite the fact that he is a known terrorist who has targeted U.S. and UK citizens."[104]

Subsequent newspaper stories reported on the undoubted relationship of Saeed Sheikh to the ISI, to FBI claims that he wired $100,000 to 9/11 hijacker Mohamed Atta's bank account,[105] to a CNN report that these funds came from Pakistan,[106] and to the uncontested statement that (as later stated in the indictment of the so-called twentieth hijacker Zacarias Moussaoui) "on September 11, 2001, Mustafa Ahmed al-Hawsawi left the U.A.E. for Pakistan."[107]

The most sensational charge, alluded to earlier, came from Indian intelligence sources: that Saeed Sheikh had wired the money to Atta at the direction of Lieutenant-General Mahmoud Ahmad, then director of the ISI.[108]

All these important and alarming charges are ignored in the *9/11 Commission Report*, in which the Saeed Sheikh born in London is not mentioned.[109] Instead, the report assured its readers in a carefully drafted comment that "we have seen no evidence that any foreign government— or foreign government official—supplied any funding."[110] It was later reported, however, that "the Pakistan foreign office had paid tens of thousands of dollars to lobbyists in the U.S. to get anti-Pakistan references dropped from the 9/11 inquiry commission report."[111]

The U.S. government and the mainstream media's decisions to drop the Saeed Sheikh story in October 2001 were clearly political. On September 20, 2001, President Bush delivered his memorable ultimatum to "every nation, in every region. . . . Either you are with us, or you are with the terrorists." There was probably no leader for which the choice was more difficult, or the outcome more unpredictable, than General Pervez Musharraf in Pakistan. But on October 7, Musharraf fired his pro-Taliban ISI chief, General Mahmoud Ahmad, along with two other ISI leaders.[112] As the historian John Newman, a former U.S. Army Intelligence analyst, has commented: "The stakes in Pakistan were very high. As Anthony Zinni explained to CBS on 60 Minutes, 'Musharaf may be America's last hope in Pakistan, and if he fails the fundamentalists will get hold of the Islamic bomb.' Musharaf was also vital to the war effort, and was the key to neutralizing Islamists and rounding up Al Qaeda operatives in Pakistan."[113]

A number of books, in reporting the Saeed Sheikh story, have focused on the fact that General Ahmad was in Washington on 9/11, meeting with such senior U.S. officials as CIA director George Tenet.[114] In my opinion the mystery of 9/11 must be unraveled at a deeper level, the ongoing groups inside and outside governments, in both Pakistan and America, which have continued to use groups like al Qaeda and individuals like Ahmad, for their own policy purposes. I examine these ongoing relationships further in the chapters that follow. They are far too complex to be reduced to two or three individuals. The ongoing collaboration of the ISI and CIA in promoting terrorist violence has created a complex conspiratorial milieu, in which governments now have a huge stake in preventing the emergence of the truth. That U.S. and British intelligence may have had an agent—Saeed Sheikh—at a high level in al Qaeda was only one indication of that milieu; Ali Mohamed was another.

PAKISTAN, THE TALIBAN, AL QAEDA, AND AMERICA

The events of 9/11 set the United States at war with its former protégés, both in the Taliban and in al Qaeda. In the months after the September attacks, the United States launched bombs and missiles in futile efforts to assassinate two top al Qaeda allies: Gulbuddin Hekmatyar, once the main recipient of CIA weaponry, and his disciple Jalaluddin Haqqani, now no longer "the CIA's favorite commander" but the Taliban military chief and the third U.S. target after Osama bin Laden and Mullah Omar of the Taliban.[115]

Investigative journalist Seymour Hersh has claimed that in November 2001, as the Taliban defenses at Kunduz were crumbling, Pakistan evacuated its fighters "in a series of night time airlifts that were approved by the Bush Administration" and that "an unknown number of Taliban and Al Qaeda fighters managed to join in the exodus." According to

Indian intelligence, these al Qaeda fighters included Uzbek, Arab, and Chechen jihadi militants, some of whom probably became active in Kashmir.[116] According to Hersh, "Some C.I.A. analysts believe that bin Laden eluded American capture inside Afghanistan with help from elements of the Pakistani intelligence service."[117]

Immediately thereafter the world's largest concentration of active international jihadi militants was probably in or near Kashmir. In June 2002, Pakistani national police sources estimated "that some 10,000 Afghan Taliban cadres and followers and about 5,000 al Qaida fighters" were hiding in Pakistan, "with the full support of intelligence authorities, as well as religious and tribal groups," according to one source.[118] This claim would corroborate that of Yossef Bodansky, director of the U.S. Congressional Task Force on Terrorism and Unconventional Warfare: "The ISI actively assists bin Laden in the expansion of an Islamist infrastructure in India."[119] Others have alleged ISI collaboration with al Qaeda in financing and arming the Islamic Movement of Uzbekistan (IMU) in Central Asia, supported also by the drug traffic.[120]

Also pertinent are the reports that journalist Daniel Pearl's researches in Pakistan "may have strayed into areas involving Pakistan's secret intelligence organizations."[121] One of his lead contacts was Ahmed Omar Saeed Sheikh, the suspected paymaster of the 9/11 bombings.[122] Another was "Khalid Khawaja, a Muslim militant and a onetime agent with Pakistan's Inter-Services Intelligence agency (ISI) who counts among his very best friends Osama bin Laden."[123] Former CIA officer Robert Baer has claimed that he had been collaborating with Pearl in the ill-fated Pakistan investigation and that the true target had not been the eccentric shoe-bomber Richard Reid but Khalid Shaikh Mohammed, "one of the masterminds" of 9/11 and (until his seizure in 2003) "the operational chief of al Qaida."[124]

I am surprised that so few journalists have noted how well 9/11 and its consequences have served the purposes of Islamist extremists in the ISI. The ISI owes its strength in Pakistan chiefly to past inputs of U.S. support. The current crisis has cast Musharraf anew in the role of Zia before him. Pakistani debts and nuclear weapons development are alike forgiven. The U.S. arms pipeline is reopened. ISI's extracurricular activities are again given a boost by a new wave of needed heroin from Afghanistan. That Musharraf has been forced, albeit reluctantly, to play a role as a U.S. ally is just what Islamists like ex-ISI chief General Hamid Gul desire: to polarize the country and mobilize Islamists more militantly against the infidel status quo. According to some reports, they were initially successful. As the *Guardian* reported in 2002: "All the evidence suggests Pakistan's many-headed terrorism and security problems are if anything worsening as the religious parties agitate, assassination plots brew, and public opinion, according to one poll, swings against extradition of terror suspects to the U.S."[125]

It is not paradoxical that the ISI could have contributed to the demise of its own creation, the Taliban. The Taliban government in Afghanistan had become, from a Pakistani perspective, a disaster. What had been intended to end conflict and the refugee problem, stabilize government, and provide strategic depth to Pakistan in its struggle against India had by 2001 failed in every way. The secularists in the ISI found their country being drawn into conflict with the governments they had hoped to trade with, while India and its allies were increasingly influential with the Northern Alliance. From the Islamist perspective the cadres of militants who had been trained for guerrilla war in the Central Asian Republics were instead being expended in bloody pitched support battles for which they were ill-suited and that had no prospect of ending soon. As the *Washington Times* observed on June 17, 2002: "For Pakistani extremists, the loss of Afghanistan was no more than the destruction of an outpost in a global battlefield. Pakistan has now taken Afghanistan's place. Al Qaida's underground in Pakistan emerged unscathed from Operation Enduring Freedom across the 1,300-mile border."[126]

From afar it is easy to see the lasting damage that CIA and ISI schemes have done to the causes of political and religious moderation, not only in Afghanistan but also in Pakistan. No external enemy has done as much to weaken and threaten the values that should join this region to the rest of the democratic world. We in America need now to turn our gaze toward our own country. We should not be surprised that CIA's special powers, having done so much to impose brutes, criminals, and terrorists on other parts of the world, have weakened the cause of decency and democracy at home as well.

The erosions of American civil liberties since 9/11 cannot be just blamed on the Bush administration. They are the outcome of a tension, between the public state and covert notions of security, that has been deforming U.S. politics since the special powers assumed at the outset of the Cold War. Many civilians thought that the disaster of U.S. intervention in Vietnam had resolved this crisis and resulted in reforms that would restore constitutional priorities. But the other camp, the proponents of the deep state who agreed with Oliver North that the Vietnam

War was lost in Washington, were waiting all along to neutralize those reforms.

9/11 was a victorious moment for the proponents of the deep state. And prominent in this camp, for at least two decades, have been Dick Cheney and Donald Rumsfeld.

EIGHT

THE AL-KIFAH CENTER, AL QAEDA, AND THE U.S. GOVERNMENT, 1988–98

In the late '80s, Pakistan's then head of state, Benazir Bhutto, told the first President George Bush, "You are creating a Frankenstein."

Newsweek, 2001

THE MAKHTAB AL-KHIDMAT AND THE AL-KIFAH CENTER

The *9/11 Commission Report*, although widely decried by its critics, is useful for having provided a footnoted account of the government's claims concerning the events of 9/11. If the report is read in context, it can be used to define and highlight the key matters that these claims either ignore altogether or brazenly distort. One ignored background area in the report is the lengthy U.S. relationship with those in al Qaeda and its allies, whom today the press and the administration call terrorists but whom President Reagan and the U.S. Congress once referred to as "freedom fighters."[1] As discussed in chapter 7, a key example of this is Jalaluddin Haqqani, said to have been "the CIA's favorite commander" in the 1980s, who after 9/11 "would emerge as the number three target of the U.S. forces in Afghanistan."[2]

The changes in this relationship evolved at different rates with different U.S. agencies; they left a trail of intrigues in which lead U.S. agencies were at times battling with each other. By 1991 CIA was supporting the mujahideen warlord Gulbuddin Hekmatyar and other ISI-backed Islamist commanders in Afghanistan, in opposition to the State Department, which was emphasizing support to a coalition behind Hekmatyar's and

Pakistan's enemy Ahmed Shah Massoud.[3] This trumping of public policy with covert policy (in the tradition of Zbigniew Brzezinski and William Casey) strengthened the covert connection between the United States, the ISI, and al Qaeda. The connection was protected by the secrecy which necessarily surrounded an off-the books program that, as so often before in U.S. history, was funded in part by the heroin traffic.

If anyone personified the United States–al Qaeda connection, it was the FBI and CIA informant Ali Mohamed, a close ally of Osama bin Laden. As I explore in chapter 9, Mohamed was on the U.S. Army payroll at the same time he was training Arab Afghans from the Brooklyn al-Kifah Center.[4] Some of these trainees were later convicted for the 1993 World Trade Center bombing. The CIA, reviewing the case five years later, concluded in an internal document that CIA itself was "partly culpable" in this first World Trade Center attack.[5] The ongoing governmental de facto protection and cover-up of Ali Mohamed's terrorist activities ("at [a] minimum, he was an irreplaceable link in the 1993 bombing plot"[6]) is considered in chapter 9.

The U.S. connection to al Qaeda was also epitomized by the protection afforded to al Qaeda's al-Kifah recruitment and support center in the al-Farook mosque in Brooklyn, New York. From 1985 until the end of the Afghan war in 1988, the senior recruiters of non-Afghan Muslims for the war (the so-called Arab Afghans) were Palestinian Sheikh Abdullah Azzam and his disciple Osama bin Laden. It was difficult for Azzam to recruit in Muslim countries, where there were usually severe restrictions on free speech, and radical Islamists were often suspect if not indeed in prison. Instead, recruitment activity was centered in Great Britain and above all America. As journalist Steven Emerson reported:

> The First Conference of *Jihad* was held by Azzam not in Peshawar or Riyadh or Damascus, but in Brooklyn, at the Al-Farook Mosque on Atlantic Avenue. There, in 1988, Azzam exhorted the nearly two hundred Islamic militants who attended the conference with the following words: "Every Muslim on earth should unsheathe his sword and fight to liberate Palestine. The *jihad* is not limited to Afghanistan. . . . You must fight in any place you can get. . . . Whenever *jihad* is mentioned in the Holy Book, it means the obligation to fight. It does not mean to fight with the pen or to write books or articles in the press or to fight by holding lectures."
>
> The terrorist centers created by Azzam were embedded in mosques and Islamic community centers across the United States. He opened branches of Al-khifa in Atlanta, Boston, Chicago, Brooklyn, Jersey City, Pittsburgh, Tucson and thirty other American cities as well as in Europe and the Middle East.[7]

Azzam's travels took him not just throughout the United States but all over the globe. He "crossed the world from 1985 to 1989. He visited dozens of U.S. cities and began setting up a network of offices designed as recruiting posts and fund-raising centers for the mujahadeen in their battle with the Soviets. . . . The first center, established in the early 1980s in Peshawar [Pakistan], was called Alkifah. Over the next decade, Azzam set up branches at mosques in the United States, the United Kingdom, France, Germany, Norway, and throughout the Mideast. The network was known formally as the Services Office for the Mujahadeen, or Makhtab al-Khidimat (MAK). The flagship Alkifah center in the United States was established on the ground floor of the Al Farooq Mosque in Brooklyn."[8] Both the mosque and later the center financed and trained jihadis, including Americans, for al Qaeda operations overseas. From as early as 1979, the mosque had been a center of international Islamist activity, as part of the U.S.-approved struggle against the Soviets in Afghanistan.[9]

Like the U.S. involvement in Afghanistan itself, the U.S. involvement in the al-Kifah Center was for the most part oblique and secondary. But the MAK network was clearly an integral part of the U.S.-Saudi-Pakistani coalition effort in Afghanistan, and it has been said more than once that CIA found it a more reliable asset than the strife-ridden Afghan jihadis.[10] In the words of *Jane's Intelligence Review*, "MaK channeled several billion dollars' worth of Western governmental, financial and material resources for the Afghan jihad. MaK worked closely with Pakistan, especially the Inter-Services Intelligence (ISI), the Saudi government and Egyptian governments, and the vast Muslim Brotherhood network."[11]

As we saw in the last chapter, the Casey-Saudi-ISI project of a "foreign legion" in Afghanistan, and of a services center to support it, was urged on the Afghan resistance by Casey, Saudi intelligence, Pakistani intelligence, and the elite Safari Club created by French intelligence chief Alexandre de Marenches in 1976. From a legal and technical point of view the al-Kifah Center in Brooklyn may have been established too late to be part of support for the Afghan war. Victory in Afghanistan was achieved in April 1988, when the Soviets agreed to pull out their troops over the next nine months.[12] According to its founding documents, the al-Kifah Center was founded in 1988 as the local chapter of the Makhtab al-Khidimat (service center), the Pakistan-based organization for the recruitment and care of "Arab Afghan" jihadis in Afghanistan.[13]

The U.S. government showed its support by a secret program of providing U.S. visas for known members of organizations it officially considered terrorist. Prominent al Qaeda associates admitted to the United States, despite being on a State Department "watch list," included the blind Egyptian Sheikh Omar Abdel Rahman, Ali Mohamed, Mohamed Jamal Khalifa, and possibly the lead 9/11 hijacker, Mohamed Atta.[14]

Al Qaeda foot soldiers were also admitted to the United States for training under a special visa program.[15] In addition, CIA-trained ISI instructors transmitted CIA techniques for urban terrorism, allegedly including CIA training manuals that al Qaeda later used for terrorist activities around the world.[16] Clearly the al-Kifah Center was prospering, even after 1989, in part from U.S. government protection. Although the FBI had been surveilling the training of terrorists from the al-Farooq mosque, it terminated this surveillance in the fall of 1989.[17]

In 1990 CIA influenced the evolution of the al-Kifah Center into a site for future terrorism by enabling the Egyptian jihadist leader Sheikh Omar Abdel Rahman to come to Brooklyn and take it over: "Even though he'd been on a U.S. terrorism Watch List for three years, the Sheikh was granted a visa [actually a second visa, a multiple-entry visa in 1990] to enter America. This was another blunder on the part of U.S. intelligence. . . . Later, the CIA would try to blame his admission on a corrupt case officer. . . . But the State Department later determined that, although he was on the list of 'undesirables,' the Sheikh obtained three sanctioned visas from CIA agents [*sic*, that is, officers] posing as State Department officials at the U.S. embassy in Khartoum."[18]

A U.S. official argued forcefully that Rahman was an "untouchable" being protected by no fewer than three agencies: " 'It was no accident that the sheikh got a visa and that he's still in the country,' replied the agent, visibly upset. 'He's here under the banner of national security, the State Department, the NSA [National Security Agency], and the CIA.' The agent pointed out that the sheikh had been granted a tourist visa, and later a green card, despite the fact that he was on a State Department terrorist watch-list that should have barred him from the country. He's an untouchable, concluded the agent. 'I haven't seen the lone-gunman theory advocated [so forcefully] since John F. Kennedy.' "[19] As he had done earlier in Egypt, the sheikh "issued a fatwa in America that permitted his followers to rob banks and kill Jews."[20]

Richard Clarke, America's national counterterrorism coordinator under Presidents Clinton and George W. Bush, concedes that in the 1980s "America sought (or acquiesced in) the importation into Afghanistan and Pakistan of an army of 'Arabs'. . . . The Saudis took the lead in assembling the group of volunteers. The Saudi intelligence chief, Prince

Turki, relied upon . . . Usama bin Laden, to recruit, move, train, and indoctrinate the Arab volunteers in Afghanistan."[21]

THE MAK, AL-KIFAH, SAUDI ARABIA, AND PAKISTAN

The al-Kifah Center in Brooklyn was eventually dominated by two Egyptians with a common Islamist background: Ali Mohamed and Sheikh Omar Abdel Rahman. However, the early history of the MAK in America was dominated by Saudis and Pakistanis. The first MAK center in America was started before 1986 at the Al Bunyan Information Center in Tucson.[22] Its first chief was the Saudi mainstream figure Wael Hamza Jalaidan, who together with Abdullah Azzam and Osama bin Laden created al Qaeda in 1988.[23] (The *9/11 Commission Report*, like most American sources, mentions only Azzam and bin Laden as creators of the MAK and al Qaeda.[24] Jalaidan's role, however, is corroborated by terrorist consultants Matthew Epstein and Evan Kohlmann in their testimony to Congress.[25]) Jalaidan's senior status with the Saudi and Pakistani governments is demonstrated by his other formal posts. In the late 1980s he was head of the Saudi Red Crescent Society and the Muslim World League in Afghanistan. He also headed one of the league's charitable affiliates, the Rabita Trust in Pakistan (of which Pakistani president Zia ul-Haq was the founding chairman).[26]

It has often been claimed that Azzam and bin Laden, who were close throughout the 1980s, had a serious falling out in 1988 and 1989 at the end of the Afghan war. Two issues came to divide them. It is alleged that Azzam was focused on limited goals: first completing the liberation of Afghanistan and then possibly turning to the problem of his native Palestine. Bin Laden, however, was focused on the threat of America and the West to Islam globally.[27] Related to this was a dispute "over Azzam's support for Ahmadshah [Ahmed Shah] Massoud, the current [nationalist] leader of the Northern Alliance fighting the Taliban. Bin Laden preferred [the Islamist] Gulbuddin Hekmatyar, former prime minister and leader of the Hizb-i-Islami (Islamic Party), who was both anti-communist and anti-Western."[28] In 1989, Azzam was murdered (it is unclear by whom), and the focus of the former MAK, now al Qaeda, expanded from Afghanistan to the world. Official Saudi support for the group is said to have ended in 1990.[29] But a deeper look shows that little had changed.

Jalaidan's movements illustrate the continuity underlying the shifting focus of the MAK into al Qaeda. Like bin Laden himself, Jalaidan returned briefly to Saudi Arabia to operate as a businessman. Sometime after 1992 he "then joined the 'aid operations' to Bosnia, where he supervised temporarily the Saudi Aid Committee, the largest aid organization then in Bosnia.[30] He also assumed the office of the supervisor of the Muslim World League endowments [in that country]."[31]

The Saudi presence in first the MAK and then al Qaeda parallels the activities of a longtime agent of Pakistan's ISI, Sheikh Mubarik Ali Hasmi Shah Gilani. According to neocon Mira Boland, Gilani trained jihadis to operate in first Afghanistan and then (after the Afghan war had ended in 1989) Kashmir, Chechnya, and Bosnia.[32] Coming to America in 1980, the first year of the Afghan war, he established the Jamaat-al-Fuqra, recruiting both Arabs and African-Americans. Two of his alleged recruits, Wadih el-Hage and Clement Rodney Hampton-El, became involved in the Brooklyn al-Kifah Center and were later indicted and convicted for their involvement in bin Laden's terror plots.[33] Hampton-El was also prominent in the Brooklyn al-Kifah campaign to aid Bosnia.[34]

The Indian analyst B. Raman, reflecting the perspective of security managers, sees the Jamaat-al-Fuqra as a local front for the South Asian Tablighi Jamaat (TJ), a group that also recruited jihadis for Afghanistan and has spread from India through Pakistan to become a worldwide Muslim movement: "The TJ operates in the U.S. and the Caribbean directly through its own preachers deputed from Pakistan and also recruited from the Pakistani immigrant community in the U.S. as well as through front organisations such as the Jamaat-ul-Fuqra founded in the 1980s under the leadership of Sheikh Mubarik Ali Gilani, who generally lives in Pakistan, but travels frequently to the U.S. and the Caribbean."[35]

It is customary in America to speak of al Qaeda as an example of non-state-supported terrorism, as opposed to the state-supported terrorism attributed to such countries as North Korea, prewar Russia, or Syria. What we have seen of the roles of Jalaidan (the Saudi) and Gilani (the Pakistani) shows that the truth is far more complex.[36] The controls exerted by governments over al Qaeda were relatively weak. This was due in part to the increasing autonomy of the group's covert operations, but it was also partly due to the increasing weakening, or if you will "failure," of the states sponsoring the organization. This book has attempted to illustrate this in the case of Saudi Arabia and especially Pakistan, where the state was recurrently redefined, and leaders deposed, at the whim of the ISI. But in the case of 9/11, and the Iraq war that followed, the same domination of public state authority by a private cabal has also been visible in the United States.

A Warning about Indiscriminate Group Characterizations

Both Jamaat-al-Fuqra and especially Tablighi Jamaat defy easy characterization. The bulk of academics and other observers see Tablighi Jamaat as peaceful, apolitical, and law-abiding: As political scientist Mumtaz Ahmad has written: "In fact the Tablighi Jamaat detests politics, and does not involve itself in any issues of sociopolitical importance."[37] But French intelligence officials have called Tablighi Jamaat the "antechamber of fundamentalism."[38] A senior FBI official, Michael J. Heimbach, told the *New York Times* that "we have a significant presence of Tablighi Jamaat in the United States, and we have found that Al-Qaeda used them for recruiting now and in the past."[39]

There is anecdotal confirmation of this. Zacarias Moussaoui, the so-called twentieth hijacker, was recruited for the war in Chechnya through Tablighi Jamaat. The shoe-bomber Richard Reid and the American Taliban partisan John Walker Lindh were also first recruited to Islam through Tablighi Jamaat. The four Saudis convicted for the 1995 bomb attack against Americans in Riyadh "had started their activism" with the pacifist Tablighi Jamaat.[40] From interviews with North Africans journalist John Cooley has confirmed that Tablighi Jamaat there too "was able to play a behind-the-scenes but important role in winning recruits for the Afghan jihad."[41]

The amenability of Tablighi Jamaat to political exploitation became a factor in the internal politics of Pakistan and above all the ISI. In the 1990s the deeply religious retired lieutenant general Javed Nasir, who was the director general of the ISI until 1993, also played an institutional role with the Tablighi Jamaat.[42] His firing under U.S. pressure in April 1993 mobilized Tablighi Jamaat elements in the army to act politically, climaxing with a coup attempt by some Tablighi Jamaat officers in the fall of 1995 against Pakistan prime minister Benazir Bhutto.[43]

From this and other anecdotal evidence right-wing sources are now claiming that the "Tablighi missionaries reportedly active in the United States present a serious national security problem."[44] It is true, as they argue, that Tablighi Jamaat missionary work in prisons, in America as in France, occasionally results in recruitment of converts for the Islamist jihad. Similar fears have been raised about other Muslim groups, from the Muslim Brotherhood to the Hizb-ut-Tahrir.[45] But the logic would be analogous to suggesting that fundamentalist Christian groups constitute a threat to law and order because some of their members have been recruited for violence against abortion clinics.

It can be argued that a far greater threat to U.S. national security is the high percentage of young Hispanic and African American males currently incarcerated, often as a result of racially discriminatory punishments for possession of crack cocaine. The anger of these young men is dangerous and likely in some cases to induce not only conversion to Islam but also organized violent response.[46] The situation is serious in itself and also an analogue to the dangerous multinational anger the United States has created abroad by its invasion of Iraq.

THE MAK, AL-KIFAH, EGYPT, AND SUDAN AFTER 1989

Other governments, notably those of Sudan and of Egypt, were also obliquely involved in the activities of the MAK and al Qaeda, albeit at a lower level and very ambivalently. Egypt was eager to have its Islamic extremists occupied in Afghanistan and other places, rather than continue to plot against the government of Egypt itself. To this end, Egypt liberated a number of convicted terrorists from its cells to travel to Afghanistan. The most prominent of these was the blind Sheikh Omar Abdel Rahman, who first joined Gulbuddin Hekmatyar's faction in Afghanistan in 1987 and then in 1990 came to New York permanently and headed up the al-Kifah Center.

Happy to see these people go, the Egyptian government also wished to keep an eye on them. Thus it is not surprising that Emad Salem, a member of Ali Mohamed's Egyptian unit, was rumored to work for Egyptian intelligence.[47] Unambiguously, Jamed Ahmed al-Fadl, a Sudanese man who worked as MAK recruiter and assistant to the emir of the Brooklyn al-Kifah Center, was also a member of Sudan's intelligence service. He so testified as a witness for the U.S. government in its trial of Osama bin Laden.[48]

All three of these men ended up supplying information to the U.S. government as well. (Salem was the key witness in the conviction of Sheikh Rahman, and al-Fadl in the conviction in absentia of bin Laden.) It was in 1993, after Egyptian president Hosni Mubarak learned that Rahman was still plotting against him, that Salem became an FBI informant.[49] His testimony, like Mohamed's, served the interests of both the U.S. government and Egypt. In like manner, al-Fadl's volunteered information was a factor in improving U.S.-Sudan relations.

THE ARAB AFGHANS AFTER 1990

Journalist Peter Lance has written that by 1994 New York—that is, al-Kifah—had become "the flashpoint for a new global jihad."[50] By this time some of Ali Mohamed's trainees there had murdered the Jewish racist Meir Kahane and participated in the 1993 bombing of the World Trade Center. Yet al-Kifah in Brooklyn continued to train and assist jihadis for other projects, some of which had U.S. approval and support. In 1990 CIA was still involved in a covert war in Afghanistan. America had agreed to end its direct assistance to the Afghan mujahideen. But it assumed that the Soviets would continue with covert assistance to its client government, and al-Kifah was a means of countering with covert support for the opposition.[51]

In September 1991 the United States and the Soviet Union agreed formally to terminate all aid to Afghanistan by the year's end. Gorbachev had already decided to stop propping up the Najibullah government in Kabul, after barely surviving a coup attempt by KGB hard-liners in August.[52] With the cut-off of aid, Washington became instantly, if belatedly, focused on the flood of heroin exiting Afghanistan and set up a new Counter-Narcotics Center to deal with it.[53] Najibullah was ousted in April 1992, and the mujahideen promptly started fighting among themselves, with Hekmatyar and some other warlords clearly fighting to gain control over the heroin traffic.

For the first time, Pakistan and Saudi Arabia began to take action against the threat to themselves from disorganized mujahideen and Arab Afghan forces. In the light of increasing Islamist pressures at home, Pakistan in January 1992 cut off all arms supplies to the mujahideen in Afghanistan.[54] After the fall of Najibullah, Pakistan and Saudi Arabia pushed for reconciliation between the competing factions of Hekmatyar and Massoud. This push was led by General Asad Durrani of the ISI and Prince Turki of the GID. Osama bin Laden, still in 1992 an occasional ally of Prince Turki, "flew to Peshawar and joined the effort."[55]

As part of the effort to restore peace, the Pakistan government, in January 1993, ordered the closure of all Afghan mujahideen offices, along with their aid organizations, in its country.[56] In April 1993, under U.S. pressure, Pakistan prime minister Nawaz Sharif fired the ISI's profoundly Islamist director, Lieutenant General Javed Nasir, and replaced him with a more secular general, Javed Ashraf Qazi. These decisions particularly impacted the Arab Afghans, whose deportation from Pakistan was ordered, although most had nowhere other than Afghanistan to go. "The Algerians cannot go to Algeria, the Syrians cannot go to Syria or the Iraqis to Iraq. Some will opt to go to Bosnia, the others will have to go into Afghanistan permanently," commented one Jeddah source.[57] The order was enforced, and the FBI soon heard a jihad leader complaining that all the camps were closed: "Even the Base [al Qaeda] is closed completely."[58]

THE NIMBY-BOSNIA PHASE
OF AL QAEDA TERRORISM, 1993–95

Because Hekmatyar's power derived from his backing in Pakistan's ISI, one might think that his dispatch of Arab Afghans into Azerbaijan, Uzbekistan, and other parts of Central Asia was part of some Pakistani grand design. That indeed was the conclusion argued energetically in the 1990s by Yossef Bodansky, the director of the U.S. Congressional Task Force on Terrorism and Unconventional Warfare. He saw Pakistan, Iran, and Sudan allied in a "quest for hegemony over the Hub of Islam." This, he claimed "has already become apparent in the rejuvenated Islamist activities in Chechnya and the Islamists' surge into Central Asia and the Caucasus. The ultimate objective, furthered by Pakistan and Iran and actively supported by the Taliban, is to evict the United States from this strategically important region, the untapped energy resources of which are considered a substitute for Persian Gulf resources."[59]

I have quoted Bodansky's remarks on Iran because of Bodansky's status as a Washington insider who influenced U.S. policy in the 1990s. Not only was he able to testify to congressional intelligence committees, the United States at the time, with little evidence, continued to look at al Qaeda, and even the 1993 World Trade Center bombing, as manifestations of a state-supported Hizbollah International backed by Iran.[60] After 9/11, right-wing sources, such as *Insight* magazine, have continued to talk of a "clear pattern of operational contacts between the Iranian government and Osama bin Laden's al Qaeda organization."[61] The *9/11 Commission Report* itself, noting contacts with al Qaeda made back in 1995 and 1996, concluded cautiously that the question of Iranian and Hizbollah involvement in 9/11 "requires further investigation by the U.S. government."[62]

The evidence presented in this chapter about al-Kifah (and by implication al Qaeda) suggests that the strongest state connections by far were with Pakistan and Saudi Arabia. But this relationship after 1993, when Pakistan ordered the deportation of Arab Afghans from its territory, became very complex. This was the climax of what I call the NIMBY (not in my backyard) phase of their sponsorship. Pakistan was issuing a number of visas in 1993 to al Qaeda leaders. But one motive for what might appear as assistance was in fact to get them out of the country. Many went only as far as back to Afghanistan. There many of them eventually fought for the Taliban, and others trained for guerrilla activities in Kashmir and Chechnya.[63] Those Arab Afghans bound for Kashmir were used by "retired military intelligence personnel and Afghan mujahideen working through the Jamaat-i-Islami and other extremist groups with close ties to the ISI."[64] Journalist Loretta Napoleoni, relying in part on Indian sources, has alleged further that in keeping with Pakistan's search for "strategic depth . . . the ISI continued to export Islamist warriors from Pakistan to Central Asia and the Caucasus. . . . When the republics of Kazakhstan, Kyrgyzstan, Tajikistan, Turkmenistan and Uzbekistan reluctantly gained their independence from Moscow in 1991, the ISI played a pivotal role in supporting Islamist armed insurgencies which destabilized them."[65]

Meanwhile Bosnia had declared its independence from Yugoslavia in April 1992, the month of Kabul's downfall, and the subsequent revolt of Bosnian Serbs had been accompanied by headline-grabbing atrocities. As most of the Arab Afghans could not safely return home, it is no surprise that a great many of them swiftly emerged as the vanguard of foreign Muslim volunteers in Bosnia, furnishing professional aid to the inexperienced Bosnian army.[66] At this time Sudan, the only home country with an Islamist government, opened its doors to bin Laden and the homeless jihadis. For five years it supplied a new base for al Qaeda and "also served as a major transit point and source for illegal arms shipments to Bosnia."[67]

The outrage of the Pakistani and Saudi governments at Serbian atrocities was sincere. But the help they provided to get jihadis to Bosnia and support them there had more complex motives. Bosnia solved their "disposal problem"—what to do with warriors whose return home was feared. As former State Department official Martin Indyk has observed, "The Saudis had protected themselves by co-opting and accommodating the Islamist extremists in their midst, a move they felt was necessary in the uncertain aftermath of the Gulf War."[68] In the fall of 1992, ensconced now in Sudan, bin Laden personally arranged for top-level consultations in Zagreb, Croatia, "with key Arab-Afghan leaders operating as Al-Qaida emissaries in Bosnia."[69]

THE UNITED STATES, AL-KIFAH, AND THE BOSNIAN JIHAD

The United States after 1992 also found itself with a "disposal problem." As with the Bay of Pigs veterans three decades earlier, the country feared the wrath of the well-trained militants if their long-established channels of support were suddenly broken off. For America too, an easy solution was to divert its Arab Afghans to Bosnia. According to *Independent* correspondent Andrew Marshall, "In December 1992, a U.S. army official met one of the Afghan veterans from Al-Kifah [in Brooklyn] and offered help with a covert operation to support the Muslims in Bosnia, funded with Saudi money, according to one of those jailed for assisting with the New York bombings. But that effort quickly disintegrated, leaving a great deal of bad feeling."[70]

Bosnia became a chief target of al-Kifah at this time. By 1993 the center in New York had established a "Bosnian branch office in Zagreb, Croatia, housed in a modern, two-story building," which "was evidently in close communication with the organizational headquarters in [Brooklyn,] New York. The deputy director of the Zagreb office, Hassan Hakim, admitted to receiving all orders and funding directly from the main United States office of Al-Kifah on Atlantic Avenue controlled by Shaykh Omar Abdel Rahman."[71] Fliers for a Bosnian Jihad were also distributed by the al-Kifah office in Boston.[72]

Clement Rodney Hampton-El, before being convicted for his role in the New York "Day of Terror" plot, testified that in December 1992 he had been summoned to the Saudi embassy in Washington and given a budget of $150,000 by Saudi Prince Faisal to train mujahideen for Bosnia and to support their families.[73] The next day he went to Fort Belvoir, Virginia, and was given a list of U.S. soldiers who were completing their tours of duty to recruit as potential mujahideen fighters in a Bosnian insurgency.[74] Hampton-El testified that the list was given him by a noted Jamaican-Canadian Muslim convert and cleric, Bilal Philips, who was teaching at the American University in Dubai, after having gained a degree in 1979 at the Islamic University of Medina. (Philips has since spoken out repeatedly to denounce terrorism against civilians.)[75]

> Immediately after the Saudi embassy meeting, Philips and a "Marine Sergeant" named Carson gave Hampton-El contact information for servicemen about to complete their tours of duty.
> "I was given several names of individuals who would be leaving the military in the very near future, those who would be getting out in a week or

two; different states that would provide training also or themselves was [*sic*] interested in going to Bosnia," Hampton-El testified.

Hampton-El said he had previously been given the contact information for potential recruits in Philadelphia, Baltimore and Ohio. Hampton-El said Bilal Philips had received the list from Sgt. Carson.

In response to a question, Hampton-El testified that "Carson" was a pseudonym. It's unclear from the testimony whether he was an active duty serviceman at the time. Carson was not formally identified during the trial.[76]

Hampton-El's actions in December 1992 suggest that his recruitment for Bosnia was a covert action project sponsored not only by Saudi Arabia but also in part by the U.S. government. We know that "by the early fall of 1992 a new base for jihad was quickly growing in the Balkans. With the help of influential clerics and Al-Qaida military commanders, the foreign Bosniak brigade was coalescing together various disparate elements in the international Arab-Afghan network."[77]

The official position of Clinton advisers like Richard Clarke is that as late as 1993 "the Clinton administration did not think about bin Laden or al Qaeda, because they did not know that terrorist or his organization existed."[78] But there is abundant evidence that the relationships between the U.S. government and the Arab Afghans, well established in the 1980s, did not simply vanish after the Russian withdrawal. One example is the apparent Department of Defense assistance to Hampton-El's recruitment efforts for Bosnia, whether the reasons for this were imperialist (to dismantle Serbia) or simply defensive (to get Islamists out of the U.S. Army). And as I detail in chapter 10, by 1991, Richard Secord, a seasoned veteran of Defense and CIA operations, was already preparing to bring Arab Afghan mujahideen from Afghanistan to a country of major interest to both al Qaeda and American oil companies: Azerbaijan.

But the strongest example of a 1990s United States–al Qaeda connection, and until recently one of the most carefully covered up, was the U.S. intelligence relationship to al Qaeda's senior trainer in terrorism: Ali Mohamed.

NINE

THE PRE–9/11 COVER-UP
OF ALI MOHAMED AND AL QAEDA

I cannot consider Islam a religion without political domina-
tion. So what we have, we have what we call a *darul Harb*,
which is the world of war, and *darul Islam*, the world of
Islam. . . . So as a Muslim, I have obligation to change *darul
Harb* to *darul Islam*, to establish Islamic law. It's obligation.
It's not choice.

Ali Mohamed, ca. 1988

Americans see what they want to see, and hear what they
want to hear.

Ali Mohamed, ca. 1988

ALI MOHAMED, AL QAEDA, AND U.S. INTELLIGENCE

The extraordinary cover-up concerning the United States' relationship to
the 9/11 plot is the denouement of this book. But it is inseparable from
the extraordinary cover-up preceding 9/11, with respect to one of the
plot's central figures: Ali Abdelsaoud Mohamed. In the last chapter we
looked at Mohamed as a man who was important in al Qaeda and personally close to Osama bin Laden.[1] He was also intimate and important
to U.S. intelligence, although one would never guess this from the *9/11
Commission Report*.[2] Finally, he was the principal trainer for the al
Qaeda terrorists who bombed the World Trade Center in 1993 and destroyed it eight years later.

Mohamed, who worked at times for the FBI, CIA, and U.S. Army, was in the 1980s a sergeant on active duty with the Fifth U.S. Special Forces at Fort Bragg.[3] In 1989, while still on the U.S. Army payroll, he was training candidates at the al-Kifah Center for al Qaeda's jihad.[4] Special Forces had since the 1950s been training foreign nationals in terrorism, both at Fort Bragg and also in Germany.[5] Only in 2006 did the American public learn that in Afghanistan he trained al Qaeda terrorists in how to hijack airliners—including "how to smuggle box cutters onto airplanes."[6]

Ali Mohamed was known in the al Qaeda camps as Abu Mohamed al Amriki—"Father Mohamed the American."[7] A member of the Egyptian Islamic Jihad, he swore allegiance in 1984 to that group's cofounder, the terrorist Ayman al-Zawahiri, who later became a top aide to bin Laden. (It was on al-Zawahiri's instructions that Mohamed first infiltrated U.S. intelligence services; and in addition, Mohamed helped al-Zawahiri to enter America in 1993 and 1994 to raise money).[8] The *9/11 Commission Report* mentioned Ali Mohamed and said that the plotters against the U.S. Embassy in Kenya were "led" (their word) by Ali Mohamed.[9] That is the report's only reference to him, although it is not all the commission heard.

U.S. attorney Patrick Fitzgerald, who had negotiated a plea bargain with Mohamed, testified at some length about him to the 9/11 Commission:

> Ali Mohamed . . . trained most of al Qaeda's top leadership—including Bin Laden and Zawahiri—and most of al Qaeda's top trainers. Mohamed taught surveillance, countersurveillance, assassinations, kidnaping, codes, ciphers and other intelligence techniques. Mohamed surveilled the American embassy in Nairobi in 1993. And he was well trained to do it: Mohamed spent 17 years in the Egyptian military (with commando training and experience in embassy security). He left the Egyptian army to join the United States Army and was stationed at the Special Warfare School at Fort Bragg from 1986 to 1989, when he became an United States citizen. He gave some training to persons who would later carry out the 1993 World Trade Center bombing, he arranged Bin Laden's security in the Sudan in 1994 after an attempt on Bin Laden's life, and he visited the al Qaeda cell in Kenya. From 1994 until his arrest in 1998, he lived as an American citizen in California, applying for jobs as an FBI translator and working as a security guard for a defense contractor.[10]

Interesting as Fitzgerald's information was, what he omitted was far more interesting. To begin with, Mohamed was not just an FBI job *applicant*. He was an FBI *informant*, from at least 1992 if not earlier.[11] Furthermore, from 1994 "until his arrest in 1998 [by which time the 9/11 plot was well under way], Mohamed shuttled between California, Afghanistan, Kenya, Somalia and at least a dozen other countries."[12] Shortly after 9/11, Larry C. Johnson, a former State Department and CIA official, faulted the FBI publicly for using Mohamed as an informant, when it should have recognized that the man was a high-ranking terrorist plotting against the United States. In Johnson's words, "It's possible that the FBI thought they had control of him and were trying to use him, but what's clear is that they did not have control."[13]

Mohamed's contacts with U.S. intelligence antedated his relationship to the FBI. In the early 1980s Mohamed was employed by CIA in Germany as a "contract agent," then dismissed as a security risk.[14] Despite being on a State Department "watch list," he was able to return to America in 1985 (on what an FBI consultant has called "a visa program controlled by the CIA") and obtain a job as a defense industry security officer with American Protective Services in Sunnyvale, California.[15] As mentioned already, in 1986 he became a sergeant with U.S. Army Special Forces.[16]

For someone on a watch list to be admitted in the United States on a special visa program suggests that he may have been already recruited as a U.S. intelligence agent. What happened next is even more suggestive: "In 1988, he apparently used his leave [from the U.S. Army] to take an unauthorized trip to Afghanistan to fight against the Soviets. Upon achieving the rank of sergeant, he received an honorable discharge from the army three years after joining."[17] It is not unheard of for members of the U.S. armed forces to violate regulations and join other armies, but this is nearly always in order to operate for the United States in a covert capacity.[18] The public has since been told that Mohamed, while on a leave from the U.S. Army, went to Afghanistan and trained "the first al-Qaeda volunteers in techniques of unconventional warfare, including kidnappings, assassinations, and hijacking planes."[19] This was in 1988, one year before he left active U.S. Army service and joined the Reserve.

In 1993, Mohamed had been detained by the Royal Canadian Mounted Police (RCMP) in Vancouver airport, when he inquired after an incoming al Qaeda terrorist who turned out to be carrying two forged Saudi passports. Mohamed immediately told the RCMP to make a phone call to the United States. The call, to Mohamed's FBI handler, John Zent, secured his release.[20] The FBI-directed release of Mohamed by the RCMP affected history. The encounter took place before Mohamed flew to Nairobi, photographed the U.S. Embassy in December 1993, and delivered the photos to bin Laden. According to Mohamed's negotiated confession in 2000, after the 1998 bombing of that embassy, "Bin Laden looked at the picture of the American Embassy and pointed to where a truck could go as a suicide bomber."[21]

However, the 9/11 report is utterly silent about Mohamed's links to CIA and the FBI. It is clear the report's authors did not want to admit that as late as 1998 the U.S. government had continued to work with and protect a trainer of al Qaeda terrorists, even after al Qaeda had already launched a lethal attack against U.S. citizens in the first World Trade Center bombing.

In August 2006 there was a *National Geographic* TV special on Ali Mohamed.[22] This presentation should be taken as the next official fallback position on Ali Mohamed, because John Cloonan, the FBI agent who worked with Fitzgerald on Mohamed, helped narrate it. Here's what TV critics wrote about its contents: "Ali Mohamed manipulated the FBI, CIA and U.S. Army on behalf of Osama bin Laden. Mohamed trained terrorists *how to hijack airliners*, bomb buildings and assassinate rivals. [D]uring much of this time Mohamed was . . . an operative for the CIA and FBI, and a member of the U.S. Army.[23] . . . Mohamed turned up in FBI surveillance photos as early as 1989, training radical Muslims who would go on to assassinate Jewish militant Meir Kahane and detonate a truck bomb at the World Trade Center. He not only avoided arrest, but managed to become an FBI informant while writing most of the al Qaeda terrorist manual and helping plan attacks on American troops in Somalia and U.S. embassies in Africa."[24] That Mohamed trained al Qaeda in hijacking planes and helped write the al Qaeda terrorist manual is confirmed by Lawrence Wright, who has seen U.S. government records.[25]

According to Cloonan, Mohamed was also familiar with the 9/11 plot. "I don't believe he was privy to all the details, but what he laid out was the attack as if he knew every detail," Cloonan said in the *National Geographic* documentary. "'This is how you position yourself. I taught people to sit in first class.'" Mohamed described teaching al Qaeda terrorists how to smuggle box cutters onto airplanes.[26] If these latest revelations about Ali Mohamed are true, then:

1. A key planner of the 9/11 plot, and trainer in hijacking, was also an informant for the FBI.

2. This operative trained the members for *all* of the chief Islamist attacks inside the United States—the first World Trade Center bombing, the New York landmarks plot, and finally 9/11—as well as the attacks against Americans in Somalia and Kenya.

3. And yet for four years Mohamed, already named as an unindicted conspirator, was allowed to move in and out of the country. Then, unlike his trainees, he was allowed to plea-bargain.[27] As of March 2007, Ali Mohamed had not yet been sentenced for any crime.[28]

U.S. PROTECTION OF MOHAMED AND
AL-KIFAH TERRORISTS IN BROOKLYN SINCE 1990

Peter Lance has charged that U.S. attorney Patrick Fitzgerald had evidence before 1998 to implicate Mohamed in the Kenya embassy bombing, yet did nothing and let the bombing happen.[29] In fact, the FBI was aware in 1990 that Mohamed had engaged in terrorist training on Long Island, yet it acted to protect Mohamed and his trainees from arrest, even after one of his trainees had moved beyond training to an actual assassination.[30]

Mohamed's trainees were all members of the al-Kifah Center in Brooklyn, which served as the main American recruiting center for the Makhtab-al-Khidimat, the services center network that after the Afghan war became known as al Qaeda.[31] The al-Kifah Center was headed in 1990 by the blind Egyptian Sheikh Omar Abdel Rahman, who like Ali Mohamed had been admitted to the United States, despite being on a State Department watch list.[32] As he had done earlier in Egypt, the sheikh "issued a fatwa in America that permitted his followers to rob banks and kill Jews."[33]

In November 1990 three of Mohamed's trainees conspired together to kill Meir Kahane, the racist founder of the Jewish Defense League. The actual killer, El Sayyid Nosair, was caught by accident almost immediately, and by luck the police soon found his two coconspirators, Mahmoud Abouhalima and Mohammed Salameh, waiting at Nosair's house. The police found much more: "There were formulas for bomb making, 1,440 rounds of ammunition, and manuals [supplied by Ali Mohamed] from the John F. Kennedy Special Warfare Center at Fort Bragg marked 'Top Secret for Training,' along with classified documents belonging to the U.S. Joint Chiefs of Staff. The police found maps and drawings of New York City landmarks like the Statue of Liberty, Times Square—and the World Trade Center. The forty-seven boxes of evidence they collected also included the collected sermons of blind Sheikh Omar, in which he exhorted his followers to 'destroy the edifices of capitalism.'"[34]

All three had been trained by Mohamed back in the late 1980s at a rifle range, where the FBI had photographed them, before terminating this surveillance in fall 1989.[35] The U.S. government was thus in an excellent position to arrest, indict, and convict all of the terrorists involved, including Mohamed. Yet only hours after the killing, Joseph Borelli, chief of NYPD detectives, struck a familiar American note and pronounced

Nosair a "lone deranged gunman."[36] Some time later he actually told the press that "there was nothing [at Nosair's house] that would stir your imagination. . . . Nothing has transpired that changes our opinion that he acted alone."[37] Borelli was not acting alone in this matter. His position was also that of the FBI, who said it too believed "that Mr. Nosair had acted alone in shooting Rabbi Kahane." "The bottom line is that we can't connect anyone else to the Kahane shooting," an FBI agent said.[38]

In thus limiting the case, the police and the FBI were in effect protecting Nosair's two Arab coconspirators in the murder of a U.S. citizen. Both of them were ultimately convicted in connection with the first World Trade Center bombing, along with another Mohamed trainee, Nidal Ayyad. More important, the police and the FBI were in effect protecting Ali Mohamed himself: the top-secret Fort Bragg training manuals in Nosair's home could have been used to embarrass the prosecution by Nosair's attorney, William Kunstler, in any trial involving conspiracy. The congressional joint inquiry examining intelligence failures before 9/11 later concluded that "the NYPD and the District Attorney's office . . . reportedly wanted the appearance of speedy justice and a quick resolution to a volatile situation. By arresting Nosair, they felt they had accomplished both."[39] Peter Lance has revealed that in fact the district attorney's office wanted to prosecute a much bigger conspiracy, but it was frustrated by federal agencies.[40] It is likely that the Feds wanted to cover up an ongoing covert relationship to al-Kifah: two years later, as detailed in the last chapter, U.S. agencies and al-Kifah members were in contact with respect to Bosnia.

The protection of Ali Mohamed was repeated in 1995, when Nosair was tried again along with Sheikh Rahman and others for conspiracy to blow up New York landmarks including the Statue of Liberty and the World Trade Center. In this trial Nosair's new attorney, Roger Stavis, was shown the Fort Bragg training manuals; he immediately chose to build a defense that Nosair's training in terrorism had been part of the CIA-sanctioned support for the mujahideen in Afghanistan.[41] As he told the court, Mohamed's "date of release from active duty was November 9 of 1989, many months after he came to Jersey City to train Mr. Nosair and other brothers to go to Afghanistan."[42] Over prosecutor Andrew McCarthy's objections, Stavis argued that Nosair was clearly receiving manuals "for jihad in Afghanistan . . . not here in America."[43]

The prosecutors (of whom Patrick Fitzgerald was one) consistently objected to the efforts of Stavis to have the jury learn about the role of Ali Mohamed.[44] As Stavis later told Lance: "The Feds didn't want

Afghanistan in the case at all. It undermined the entire theory of their prosecution" (which was that the al-Kifah terrorists were training only for a jihad against America).[45]

Stavis issued a subpoena for Mohamed to appear, but Mohamed, even though he returned to the United States at this time to speak to an FBI agent (Harlan Bell), failed to appear at the trial. Instead, the government introduced a document stipulating that, after the subpoena was issued, Bell along with prosecutor McCarthy interviewed Mohamed in California. It stipulated further that two weeks later McCarthy "sent by facsimile from New York a letter to Ali Mohamed" concerning the subpoena. Terrorism researcher J. M. Berger concluded from this stipulation that "U.S. Attorney Andrew McCarthy made some sort of signed (but still sealed) agreement with Ali Mohamed that resulted in Mohamed being unable to testify."[46]

Lance pointed out that to have intervened with a witness to keep him from honoring a subpoena "might constitute a violation of the Brady rules" concerning suppression of evidence.[47] From Lance's perspective the prosecutors' motives for keeping Mohamed out of the case were (1) as in 1991, to make it simpler to convict the accused and (2) to cover up the previous failure to stop the World Trade Center bombing. But the possibility exists of a quite different motivation: that a federal agency, perhaps one that earlier had sanctioned Mohamed's trip to Afghanistan (while he was on active service in the U.S. Army), would be interested in maintaining its relationship to Mohamed as an asset. It would thus be important to not blow his cover, because he was a covert informant or possibly even an operative. There is no question that CIA will intervene in criminal proceedings to ensure that assets deemed important to the agency are not prosecuted, or have to appear in court.[48]

On September 10, 1998, Mohamed was finally arrested, after the August 1998 embassy bombings for which he had been directly responsible.[49] Yet when indictments were handed down two months later, the name of Ali Mohamed, the ringleader, was not among the thirteen people indicted. Instead, he was allowed to avoid a court appearance through a plea bargain, the terms of which are still unknown. As of March 2007, more than eight years after his arrest, he had not yet been sentenced.

Once again, according to Lance: "Ali Mohamed was a precious commodity for the Justice Department—not just because of the intelligence he could give up, but for the embarrassment he could save the Feds if he cooperated under the right conditions. So Patrick Fitzgerald and his boss, U.S. Attorney Mary Jo White, did everything they could to keep him a secret while they tried to cut a deal with him. . . . Whenever Ali was brought into the courtroom for any proceeding, the room was sealed. All pleadings referred to him as 'John Doe.'"[50]

ALI MOHAMED AND THE 9/11 PLOT

Did the U.S. government (including the CIA) continue to use Mohamed as an informant, even after 1998 when he was under arrest? According to Berger, "Mohamed was one of the primary sources for the infamous Aug. 6, 2001, presidential daily brief (PDB) entitled 'Bin Laden Determined to Strike in U.S.'"[51] But Mohamed may have supplied this information before his arrest, as much of the relevant information in the PDB would appear to date from 1998 or earlier. At the heart of the August 6 brief was a disguised double reference to Mohamed himself: "Al-Qa'ida members—including some who are U.S. citizens—have resided in or traveled to the U.S. for years, and the group apparently maintains a support structure that could aid attacks. Two al-Qa'ida members found guilty in the conspiracy to bomb our embassies in East Africa were U.S. citizens, and a senior EIJ [Egyptian Islamic Jihad] member lived in California in the mid-1990s."[52]

Ali Mohamed is simultaneously one of the two found guilty in the embassies plot (the other was his friend Wadih el-Hage) and also the EIJ member who lived in California.[53] CIA, in its warning to President Bush about Mohamed's "support structure," did not reveal that he had been in federal custody for almost three years. But Berger, who was a researcher for the *National Geographic* show, adds flesh to the possibility that Mohamed's "support structure" was capable of helping to create 9/11: "Ali A. Mohamed . . . knew al Qaeda was sponsoring flight training for terrorists. He knew of at least one specific terrorist operation centered on a suicide airplane attack. And he knew at least three terrorist pilots personally. He was linked to at least one of the specific schools visited by the 9/11 hijackers. He knew the internal procedures of the security company that maintained two checkpoints used by hijackers at Boston's Logan Airport.[54] . . . Whether or not Mohamed knew the particulars of the 9/11 plot, he knew a lot. Businesses and institutions exploited by Mohamed and his close associates were re-used by virtually all of the 9/11 hijackers as they prepared for the attack."[55]

What is clear is that shortly after 9/11, Mohamed readily confessed to FBI Agent Cloonan that he had taught al Qaeda terrorists how to hijack airplanes. Such powerful admissions against self-interest are hard to explain without some unusual immunity having been conferred upon him. Even harder to explain is the fact that Mohamed has not to date been sentenced for the crimes to which he had confessed earlier.

THE *9/11 COMMISSION REPORT*'S PRAISE
FOR THE HANDLERS OF ALI MOHAMED

The 9/11 report, summarizing the convictions of Mohamed's trainees for the World Trade Center bombing and New York landmarks plots, talks of "this superb investigative and prosecutorial effort."[56] It says nothing about the suppressed evidence found in Nosair's house, including "maps and drawings of New York City landmarks," which if pursued could have prevented both plots from developing in the first place.

What explains the 9/11 report's gratuitous and undeserved praise for the "superb" effort of Patrick Fitzgerald and the FBI in the New York landmarks case? Did the report's authors recognize that this was an especially sensitive area, which if properly investigated would lead to past U.S. protection of terrorists? This question returns us to Peter Lance's charge that Fitzgerald had evidence before 1998 to implicate Mohamed in the Kenya embassy bombing, yet did nothing and let the bombing happen. Did U.S. authorities have advance evidence before the 9/11 attack, and again do nothing?

As a first step all U.S. agencies should release the full documentary record of their dealings with Ali Mohamed, the FBI and CIA informant who allegedly planned the details of the airline seizures. Of particular relevance would be everything to do with Mohamed's December 1994 interview with authorities after the subpoena that he ignored, one month before he applied successfully to work with the Burns International Security Company. Only a full investigation of these facts will satisfy those who accuse members of the U.S. government of assisting the 9/11 plot or of failing to prevent 9/11 from happening.[57]

The 9/11 Commission probably knew more about this situation than they let on. It cannot be just a coincidence that the person they selected to write the staff reports about al Qaeda and the 9/11 plot, and to conduct the relevant interviews, was a man who had a personal stake in preventing the full truth about Mohamed from coming out. This man was Dietrich Snell, who had been Fitzgerald's colleague in the Southern District of New York U.S. Attorney's office, and had helped Fitzgerald prosecute Ramzi Yousef. It was Snell who presumably drafted the praise for the superb effort by his former colleague Fitzgerald and the FBI. Of the nine people on Snell's team, all but one had worked for the U.S. government, and all but two for either the Justice Department or the FBI.[58]

What we have examined so far is a government-Mohamed cover-up that goes back to at least 1990, long before the Bush-Cheney administrations. But the 9/11 Commission staff reports went out of their way to cover up this cover-up. The 9/11 report, based on the Snell staff reports, mentioned Mahmoud Abouhalima and Mohammed Salameh, two co-conspirators of Ramzi Yousef in the first World Trade Center bombing of 1993.[59] It did not mention that these two men had been trained by Ali Mohamed, even though Fitzgerald referred obliquely to this fact in his testimony. Nor did the report mention that, had it not been for a police and FBI cover-up protecting Mohamed back in 1990, Abouhalima and Salameh would probably have been in jail at the time of the World Trade Center bombing—for their involvement in the murder of Meir Kahane by Mohamed's trainees three years earlier.[60]

I consider the scandal of Ali Mohamed's tolerated terrorism to be symptomatic of an ongoing fundamental problem, for which we need a more serious remedy than a change in the White House. As has happened after past intelligence fiascoes, the U.S. intelligence agencies were strengthened as a result of the 9/11 Commission and their budgets increased. It is time to confront the reality that these agencies themselves, by their own sponsorship and protection of terrorist activities, have aggravated the greatest threats to our national security.

TEN

AL QAEDA AND THE U.S. ESTABLISHMENT

Democratic government is not possible without trust between
the branches of government and between the government and
the people. Sometimes the trust is misplaced and the system
falters. But for officials to work outside the system because
it does not produce the results they seek is a prescription for
failure.

Congressional *Iran-Contra Report*, 1987

U.S. OPERATIVES, OIL COMPANIES, AND AL QAEDA

What is slowly emerging from the revelations of al Qaeda's activities in
Central Asia throughout the 1990s is the extent to which the group acted
in the interests of both American oil companies and the U.S. government.[1] In one way or another a few Americans in the 1990s cooperated
with al Qaeda terrorists in Afghanistan, Azerbaijan, Kosovo, and possibly Bosnia. In other countries—notably Georgia, Kyrgyzstan, and
Uzbekistan—al Qaeda terrorists have provided pretexts or opportunities
for a U.S. military commitment and even troops to follow. This has been
most obvious in the years since the end of the Afghan war in 1989.
Deprived of Soviet troops to support it, the Soviet-backed Najibullah
regime in Kabul finally fell in April 1992. What should have been a glo-
rious victory for the mujahideen proved instead to be a time of troubles
for them, as Tajiks behind Ahmed Shah Massoud and Pashtuns behind
Gulbuddin Hekmatyar began instead to fight each other.

The situation was particularly difficult for the Arab Afghans, who
found themselves no longer welcome. Under pressure from America,
Egypt, and Saudi Arabia, the new interim president of Afghanistan,

Sibghatullah Mojaddedi, announced that the Arab Afghans should leave. In January 1993, Pakistan followed suit, closed the offices of all mujahideen in its country, and ordered the deportation of all Arab Afghans.[2] Shortly afterward Pakistan extradited a number of Egyptian jihadis to Egypt, some of whom had already been tried and convicted in absentia.[3] Other radical Islamists went to Afghanistan but without the foreign support they had enjoyed before.

Fleeing the hostilities in Afghanistan, some Uzbek and Tajik mujahideen and refugees started venturing or returning north across the Amu Darya.[4] In this confusion cross-border raids of the kind originally encouraged by CIA director William Casey back in the mid-1980s continued, with or without U.S. backing.[5] Both Hekmatyar and Massoud actively supported the Tajik rebels in the years leading up to 1992, when both men continued to receive aid and assistance from the United States.[6] The Pakistani observer Ahmed Rashid has documented further support for the Tajik rebels from both Saudi Arabia and the Pakistani intelligence directorate ISI.[7]

These raids into Tajikistan and later Uzbekistan contributed materially to the destabilization of the Muslim republics in the Soviet Union (and after 1992 in its successor, the Commonwealth of Independent States). This destabilization was an explicit goal of U.S. policy in the Reagan era and did not change with the end of the Afghan war. On the contrary the United States was concerned to hasten the breakup of the Soviet Union and increasingly to gain access to the petroleum reserves of the Caspian basin, which at that time were still estimated to be "the largest known reserves of unexploited fuel in the planet."[8]

The collapse of the Soviet Union had a disastrous impact on the economies of its Islamic republics. Already in 1991 the leaders of Central Asia "began to hold talks with Western oil companies, on the back of ongoing negotiations between Kazakhstan and the US company Chevron."[9] The first Bush administration actively supported the plans of U.S. oil companies to contract for exploiting the resources of the Caspian region and also for a pipeline not controlled by Moscow that could bring the oil and gas production out to the West. The same goals were enunciated even more clearly as matters of national security by Clinton and his administration.[10] Eventually the threat presented by Islamist rebels persuaded the governments of Kyrgyzstan, Tajikistan, and Uzbekistan to allow U.S. as well as Russian bases on their soil. The result has been to preserve artificially a situation throughout the region where small elites have grown increasingly wealthy and corrupt, while most citizens have suffered from a sharp drop in living standards.[11]

The gap between the second Bush administration's professed ideals and its real objectives is well illustrated by its position toward the regime of Islam Karimov in Uzbekistan. America quickly sent Donald Rumsfeld to deal with the new regime in Kyrgyzstan installed in March 2005 after the popular Tulip Revolution and the overthrow there of Askar Akayev.[12] But Karimov's violent repression of a similar uprising in Uzbekistan at this time did not diminish U.S. support for the dictator, as long as he allowed U.S. troops to be based in his oil- and gas-rich country.[13]

U.S. OPERATIVES AND AL QAEDA IN AZERBAIJAN

In one former Soviet Republic, Azerbaijan, Arab Afghan jihadis clearly assisted the effort of U.S. oil companies to penetrate the region. In 1991, Richard Secord, Harry "Heinie" Aderholt, and Ed Dearborn—three veterans of U.S. operations in Laos and later of Oliver North's operations with the Contras—turned up in Baku under the cover of an American company MEGA Oil.[14] This was at a time when the first Bush administration had expressed its support for an oil pipeline stretching from Azerbaijan across the Caucasus to Turkey.[15] MEGA never found oil, but the company did contribute materially to the removal of Azerbaijan from the sphere of post-Soviet Russian influence.

Secord, Aderholt, and Dearborn were all career U.S. Air Force officers, not part of CIA. However, Secord has explained in his memoir how Aderholt and he were occasionally seconded to CIA as CIA detailees. Secord describes his own service as a CIA detailee with Air America in first Vietnam and then Laos, in cooperation with the CIA station chief Theodore Shackley.[16] Secord later worked with Oliver North to supply arms and materiel to the Contras in Honduras; he also developed a small air force for them, using many former Air America pilots.[17] Because of this experience in air operations, Casey and North had selected Secord to troubleshoot the deliveries of weapons to Iran in the Iran-Contra operation.[18] (Aderholt and Dearborn also served in the Laotian CIA operation and later in supporting the Contras.)

As MEGA operatives in Azerbaijan, Secord, Aderholt, Dearborn, and their men engaged in military training, passed "brown bags filled with cash" to members of the government, and set up an airline on the model of Air America, which soon was picking up hundreds of mujahideen mercenaries in Afghanistan.[19] (Secord and Aderholt claim to have left Azerbaijan before the mujahideen arrived.) Meanwhile, Hekmatyar, who at the time was still allied with bin Laden, was "observed recruiting Afghan mercenaries [that is, Arab Afghans] to fight in Azerbaijan against Armenia and its Russian allies."[20] At this time, with the blessings of the ISI, heroin flooded from Afghanistan through Baku into Chechnya, Russia, Europe, and even North America.[21] It is difficult to believe that MEGA's airline (so much like Air America) did not become involved.[22]

The operation was not a small one. According to one source, "Over the course of the next two years, the company they founded [MEGA Oil] procured thousands of dollars worth of weapons and recruited at least two thousand Afghan mercenaries for Azerbaijan—the first mujahedin to fight on the territory of the former Communist Bloc."[23] In 1993 the mujahideen also contributed to the ouster of Azerbaijan's elected president, Abulfaz Elchibey, and his replacement by an ex-Communist Brezhnev-era leader, Heidar Aliyev. At stake was an $8 billion oil contract with a consortium of Western oil companies headed by the multinational BP. Part of the contract would be a pipeline that would, for the first time, not pass through Russian-controlled territory when exporting oil from the Caspian basin to Turkey. Thus the contract was bitterly opposed by Russia and required an Azeri leader willing to stand up to the former Soviet Union.

The Arab Afghans helped supply that muscle. Their own eyes were set on fighting Russia in the disputed Armenian-Azeri region of Nagorno-Karabakh and in liberating the neighboring Muslim areas of Russia, Chechnya and Dagestan. To this end, as the 9/11 Commission Report notes, the bin Laden organization established an NGO in Baku, which became a base for terrorism elsewhere.[24] It also became a transshipment point for Afghan heroin to the Chechen mafia, whose branches "extended not only to the London arms market, but also throughout continental Europe and North America."[25] The Arab Afghans' Azeri operations are said to have been financed in part with Afghan heroin.[26]

This foreign Islamist presence in Baku was also supported by bin Laden's financial network.[27] With bin Laden's guidance and Saudi support, Baku soon became a base for jihadi operations against Dagestan and Chechnya in Russia.[28] An informed article argued in 1999 that Pakistan's ISI, facing its own disposal problem with the militant Arab-Afghan veterans, trained and armed them in Afghanistan to fight in Chechnya. The ISI also allegedly encouraged the flow of Afghan drugs westward to support Chechen and Kashmiri militants, thus diminishing the flow into Pakistan itself.[29]

As author and consultant Michael Griffin has observed, the regional conflicts in Nagorno-Karabakh and other disputed areas, including Abkhazia, Turkish Kurdistan, and Chechnya "each represented a distinct, tactical move, crucial at the time, in discerning which power would ultimately become master of the pipelines which, some time in this century, will transport the oil and gas from the Caspian basin to an energy-avid world."[30] Two Arab oil companies, Delta Oil and Nimir Oil, participated in the Western oil consortium, along with the American firm Unocal.

It is unclear whether MEGA Oil was a front for the U.S. government or for U.S. oil companies and their Saudi allies. U.S. oil companies have been accused of spending millions of dollars in Azerbaijan, not just to bribe the government but also to install it. According to a Turkish intelligence source who was an alleged eyewitness, major oil companies, including Exxon and Mobil, were "behind the coup d'état" that in 1993 replaced the elected president, Abulfaz Elchibey, with his successor, Heydar Aliyev. The source claimed to have been at meetings in Baku with "senior members of BP, Exxon, Amoco, Mobil and the Turkish Petroleum Company. The topic was always oil rights and, on the insistence of the Azeris, supply and arms to Azerbaijan." Turkish secret service documents allege middlemen paid off key officials of the democratically elected government of the oil-rich nation just before its president was overthrown.[31]

The true facts and backers of the Aliyev coup may never be fully disclosed. But before the coup the efforts of Secord, Aderholt, Dearborn, and Hekmatyar's mujahideen helped contest Russian influence and prepare for Baku's shift away to the West.[32] Three years later, in August 1996, Amoco's president met with Clinton and arranged for Aliyev to be invited to Washington.[33] In 1997, Clinton said that "in a world of growing energy demand . . . our nation cannot afford to rely on a single region for our energy supplies. By working closely with Azerbaijan to tap the Caspian's resources, we not only help Azerbaijan to prosper, we also help diversify our energy supply and strengthen our energy's security."[34]

But the interest in Azerbaijan was bipartisan. James Baker, George H. W. Bush's secretary of state, was then and still was a decade later a member of the United States–Azerbaijan Chamber of Commerce. So was Dick Cheney. During the 1990s the council's cochairman was Richard Armitage, later one of the so-called Vulcans or neocons in George W. Bush's State Department, who in this period visited Aliyev in Azerbaijan on behalf of Texaco.[35]

UNOCAL, THE TALIBAN, AND BIN LADEN IN AFGHANISTAN

The accusations against Amoco, Exxon, and Mobil in Azerbaijan parallel those from European sources against Unocal in Afghanistan, which has been accused of helping, along with Delta Oil, to finance the Taliban's seizure of Kabul in 1996. (At this time the Taliban was also receiving funds from Saudi Arabia and Osama bin Laden.) The respected French observer Olivier Roy has charged that "when the Taleban took power in Afghanistan (1996), it was largely orchestrated by the Pakistani secret service [the ISI] and the oil company Unocal, with its Saudi ally Delta."[36] Unocal executive John Maresca then testified in 1998 to the House Committee on International Relations on the benefits of a proposed oil pipeline through Afghanistan to the coast of Pakistan.[37] A second natural gas pipeline (Centgas) was also contemplated by Unocal.

For Unocal to advance its own funds for the Taliban conquest would have been in violation of U.S. law, which is why such companies customarily resort to middlemen. No such legal restraints would have inhibited Unocal's Saudi partner in its Centgas consortium, Delta Oil. But Delta Oil has asserted emphatically that it took no part in orchestrating or financing the Taliban's assumption of power in Afghanistan. (Delta was already an investor with Unocal in the oilfields of Azerbaijan and may have been a factor in the October 1995 decision of Turkmenistan's president Saparmurat Niyazov to sign, in New York, a new pipeline contract with Unocal/Delta.[38])

As I wrote in 1996, in my book *Deep Politics and the Death of JFK*, citing the case of a U.S. oil company in Tunisia, "it is normal, not unusual, for the entry of major U.S. firms into Third World countries to be facilitated and sustained, indeed made possible, by corruption."[39] This has long been the case, but in the Reagan 1980s this practice was escalated by a new generation of aggressively risk-taking, law-bending "cowboy" entrepreneurs. The pace was set by new corporations like Enron, a high-debt merger that was in part guided by the junk-bond impresario Michael Milken. Some have speculated that Enron also had a potential interest in the Unocal gas pipeline project through Afghanistan.

By 1997 Enron was negotiating a $2 billion joint venture with Neftegas of Uzbekistan to develop Uzbekistan's natural gas. This was a huge project backed by a $400 million commitment from the U.S. government through the Overseas Private Investment Corporation (OPIC). Uzbekistan also signed a memo of agreement to participate in the

Centgas gas pipeline. The Enron Uzbek negotiations collapsed in 1998.[40] Enron's short-term plans had been to export Uzbek gas west to Kazakhstan, Turkey, and Europe. However, some have claimed that Enron hoped eventually to supply, via the Centgas pipeline, its failing energy plant in Dabhol, India. (Without a cheap gas supply, the cost of electricity from Dabhol was so great that Indians refused to buy it.[41])

In the first half of 2001 the Bush administration attempted to revive negotiations with the Taliban for the pipeline, as a quid pro quo for agreeing to a national unity government with Ahmed Shah Massoud's Northern Alliance and extraditing Osama bin Laden.[42] As the distinguished social scientist Chalmers Johnson has commented, "Support for this enterprise [the dual oil and gas pipelines] appears to have been a major consideration in the Bush administration's decision to attack Afghanistan on October 7, 2001."[43] Political commentator Kevin Phillips has agreed that "plans were discussed in the spring and summer of 2001—well before the events of September—for hamstringing Iraq and convincing the Taliban in Afghanistan to accept construction of an American (Unocal) pipeline from Turkmenistan through Kabul to Karachi, Pakistan."[44]

In my book *Drugs, Oil, and War*, I quote again from Olivier Roy: "It is the Americans who have made inroads in Central Asia, primarily because of the oil and gas interests. Chevron and Unocal are political actors who talk as equals with the States (that is, with the presidents)."[45] It is clear they talk as equals in the current Bush administration. Both the president and vice president are former oilmen, as were some of their oldest friends and political backers, such as Kenneth Lay of Enron.[46]

AL QAEDA, THE KOSOVO LIBERATION ARMY, AND THE TRANS-BALKAN PIPELINE

The United States, al Qaeda, and oil company interests converged again in Kosovo. Although the origins of the Kosovo tragedy were rooted in local enmities, oil became a prominent aspect of the outcome. There the al Qaeda-backed UCK (or Kosovo Liberation Army, KLA) was directly supported and politically empowered by NATO, beginning in 1998. But according to a source of freelance journalist Tim Judah, KLA representatives had already met with American, British, and Swiss intelligence agencies in 1996 and possibly "several years earlier."[47] Some of these connections may have been through American private military companies like

MPRI. Sources have spoken of "the longstanding relationship between KLA Commander Agim Çeku and MPRI General Richard Griffiths," dating back to their joint involvement in the planning of Operation Storm in 1995 by the Croatian Armed Forces against the Serbians.[48] This was back when Arab Afghan members of the KLA, like Abdul-Wahid al-Qahtani, were fighting in Bosnia.[49]

Mainstream accounts of the Kosovo war are silent about the role of al Qaeda in training and financing the KLA, yet this fact has been recognized by experts and to my knowledge never contested by them.[50] For example, James Bissett, former Canadian ambassador to Yugoslavia, has said: "Many members of the Kosovo Liberation Army were sent for training in terrorist camps in Afghanistan. . . . Milosevic is right. There is no question of their [al Qaeda's] participation in conflicts in the Balkans. It is very well documented."[51] In March 2002, Michael Steiner, the United Nations administrator in Kosovo, warned of "importing the Afghan danger to Europe," because several cells trained and financed by al Qaeda remained in the region.[52]

As late as 1997 the KLA had been recognized by the United States as a terrorist group supported in part by the heroin traffic.[53] The *Washington Times* reported in 1999 that "the Kosovo Liberation Army, which the Clinton administration has embraced and some members of Congress want to arm as part of the NATO bombing campaign, is a terrorist organization that has financed much of its war effort with profits from the sale of heroin."[54] Drug historian Alfred McCoy supplies a detailed and footnoted corroboration: "Albanian exiles used drug profits to ship Czech and Swiss arms back to Kosovo for the separatist guerrillas of the Kosovo Liberation Army (KLA). In 1997–98, these Kosovar drug syndicates armed the KLA for a revolt against Belgrade's army. . . . Even after the 1999 Kumanovo agreement settled the Kosovo conflict, the U.N. administration of the province . . . allowed a thriving heroin traffic along this northern route from Turkey. The former commanders of the KLA, both local clans and aspiring national leaders, continued to dominate the transit traffic through the Balkans."[55]

Yet once again, as in Azerbaijan, these drug-financed Islamist jihadis received American assistance, this time from the U.S. government.[56] While the American deep state was developing links with the KLA, the State Department (on behalf of the public state) was trying to promote the legitimacy of Ibrahim Rugova, the elected Kosovo Albanian president with a dedicated commitment to Gandhi-like nonviolence and reconciliation. But Rugova's standing in Kosovo had been fatally weakened in

1995, when he sent a delegation to the Dayton Conference dealing with Bosnia and it was totally ignored.[57]

At the time critics charged that U.S. oil interests were interested in building a Trans-Balkan pipeline with U.S. Army protection. Although initially ridiculed, these critics were eventually proven correct.[58] BBC News announced in December 2004 that a $1.2 billion pipeline, south of a huge new U.S. Army base in Kosovo, had been given a go-ahead by the governments of Albania, Bulgaria, and Macedonia.[59] Much of the financing came from the U.S. government's Overseas Private Investment Corporation and private American firms, as originally proposed in 1996, when the corridor involved had been laid out as part of the Clinton administration's South Balkan Development Initiative.[60]

The closeness of the KLA to al Qaeda was acknowledged again in the Western press, after Afghan-connected KLA guerrillas proceeded in 2001 to conduct guerrilla warfare in Macedonia. Press accounts included an Interpol report containing the allegation that one of bin Laden's senior lieutenants was the commander of an elite KLA unit operating in Kosovo in 1999.[61] This was probably Mohammed al-Zawahiri. The American right wing, which opposed Clinton's actions in Kosovo, has transmitted reports "that the KLA's head of elite forces, Muhammed al-Zawahiri, was the brother of Ayman al-Zawahiri, the military commander for bin Laden's Al Qaeda."[62] Meanwhile, analyst Marcia Kurop has written in the *Wall Street Journal* that "the Egyptian surgeon turned terrorist leader Ayman Al-Zawahiri has operated terrorist training camps, weapons of mass destruction factories and money-laundering and drug-trading networks throughout Albania, Kosovo, Macedonia, Bulgaria, Turkey and Bosnia."[63]

According to Yossef Bodansky, director of the U.S. Congressional Task Force on Terrorism and Unconventional Warfare: "Bin Laden's Arab 'Afghans' also have assumed a dominant role in training the Kosovo Liberation Army. . . . [By mid-March 1999 the KLA included] many elements controlled and/or sponsored by the U.S., German, British, and Croatian intelligence services."[64] Ramush Haradinaj, described by the London *Observer* as a drug trafficker and "the key U.S. military and intelligence asset in Kosovo during the civil war," was later tried as a war criminal before the Hague War Crimes Tribunal.[65] Meanwhile, by 2000, according to DEA statistics, Afghan heroin accounted for almost 20 percent of the heroin seized in the United States—nearly double the percentage taken four years earlier. Much of it is now distributed by Kosovar Albanians.[66]

AL QAEDA AND THE
PETROLEUM-MILITARY-FINANCIAL COMPLEX

It is important to understand that the conspicuous influence of petroleum money in the administration of two Bush presidents was also prominent under President Clinton. A former CIA officer, Robert Baer, complained about the oil lobby's influence with Sheila Heslin of Clinton's National Security Council staff: "Heslin's sole job, it seemed, was to carry water for an exclusive club known as the Foreign Oil Companies Group, a cover for a cartel of major petroleum companies doing business in the Caspian. . . . Another thing I learned was that Heslin wasn't soloing. Her boss, Deputy National Security Adviser Sandy Berger, headed the inter-agency committee on Caspian oil policy, which made him in effect the government's ambassador to the cartel, and Berger wasn't a disinterested player. He held $90,000 worth of stock in Amoco, probably the most influential member of the cartel. . . . The deeper I got, the more Caspian oil money I found sloshing around Washington."[67]

The oil companies' meeting with Heslin in summer 1995 was followed shortly by the creation of an interagency governmental committee to formulate U.S. policy toward the Caspian. The Clinton administration listened to the oil companies, and in 1998 began committing U.S. troops to joint training exercises in Uzbekistan.[68] This made neighboring countries like Kazakhstan and Turkmenistan, wary of Russia, more eager to grant exploration and pipeline rights to American companies.[69] But Clinton did not yield to Unocal's strenuous lobbying in 1996 for U.S. recognition of the Taliban as a condition for building the pipeline from Turkmenistan. Clinton declined in the end to do so, responding instead to the strongly voiced political opposition, especially from women's groups, over the Taliban's treatment of women.[70]

The three-way symbiosis of al Qaeda, oil companies, and the Pentagon is still visible in the case of Azerbaijan, for example. Now the Pentagon is protecting the Aliyev regime (where a younger Aliyev, in a dubious election, succeeded his father). As Chalmers Johnson wrote in his *Sorrows of Empire*: "The Department of Defense at first proposed that Azerbaijan also receive an IMET [International Military Education and Training] grant of $750,000 and an FMF [Foreign Military Financing] grant of $3 million in 2003 as part of the war on terrorism but later admitted that the funds were actually intended to protect U.S. access to oil in and around the Caspian Sea."[71]

Thanks to al Qaeda, U.S. bases have sprung up close to oilfields and pipelines in Georgia, Kosovo, Tajikistan, and Uzbekistan. As petroleum scholar Michael Klare has noted, "Already [U.S.] troops from the Southern Command (Southcom) are helping to defend Colombia's Caño Limón pipeline. . . . Likewise, soldiers from the European Command (Eurcom) are training local forces to protect the newly constructed Baku-Tbilisi-Ceyhan pipeline in Georgia. . . . Finally, the ships and planes of the U.S. Pacific Command (Pacom) are patrolling vital tanker routes in the Indian Ocean, South China Sea, and the western Pacific. . . . Slowly but surely, the U.S. military is being converted into a global oil-protection service."[72]

A survey of U.S. history since World War II suggests that the American deep state has consistently used the resources of drug-trafficking terrorists, and more recently those of al Qaeda, to further its own ends, particularly with respect to oil, at the expense of the public order and well-being of the American public state.[73] But underlying this symbiosis is another factor—the interpenetration of the U.S. political and financial establishment with the establishments of nations supporting terrorists, most notably Saudi Arabia and Pakistan.

MUSLIM GROUPS, AL QAEDA, AND THE WEST

The Muslim World League (MWL, or Rabita al-Alam al-Islami) was founded by Crown Prince Faisal of Saudi Arabia back in 1962 with funds contributed partly by the oil company Aramco, in those days still controlled by U.S. oil majors.[74] The scholar Saïd Aburish has noted CIA's approval of this ideological use of Islam against both Communism and above all pan-Arabist Nasserism: "Faisal . . . decided to play his country's Muslim card by convening an International Islamic Conference in Mecca. The main outcome of the conference was the emergence of the Saudi-financed Muslim World League. . . . Internally, Faisal, with considerable help from the CIA in the form of operatives attached to Aramco, encouraged the formation of anti-socialist Muslim groups, particularly around the oil centre of Dhahran. (There is reason to believe that some of the anti-Saudi and anti-American Islamic groups today are the radicalized successors of these groups.) . . . The then leader of the Egyptian Muslim Brotherhood, Sayed Kuttub, a man Faisal sponsored to undermine Nasser, openly admitted that during this period [the 1960s] 'America made Islam.'"[75]

Many sources agree that in supporting the Afghan jihad, "Prince Turki al-Faisal Saud, the head of the Saudi General Intelligence agency, managed the Saudi contribution, aided by Prince Salman, the governor of Riyadh. Bin Laden worked closely with Prince Turki during this period, effectively working as an arm of Saudi intelligence. In addition the Muslim World League, headed by the leading Saudi cleric Shaikh Abd al-Aziz bin Baz, provided funding."[76] As late as 1995 and 1996, the MWL was still close to al Qaeda elements like the Harkat-ul-Ansar (HuA), an ISI-supported terrorist group active in Kashmir, Tajikistan, Chechnya, and Bosnia.[77] At that time the HuA deputy chief Maulana Fazlur Rehman Khalil was invited to the 34th MWL Congress in Mecca and also spoke there to the World Assembly of Muslim Youth (WAMY).[78] Two years later, in February 1998, he cosigned bin Laden's 1998 edict that declared it a Muslim duty to kill Americans and Jews. By 2004, through his journal *Al Hilal*, Khalil was urging volunteers to fight U.S. forces in Afghanistan and Iraq.[79]

Organizations like the MWL and WAMY are hard to characterize because of their range of connections from their nations' establishments to radicals with al Qaeda. The U.S. branch of WAMY in particular has aroused conflicting responses from U.S. authorities, with investigations repeatedly overruled. It seems clear that, as a legacy of Saudi Arabia's special status, such organizations have been protected from investigation. According to former federal prosecutor John Loftus and others, there was a block in force in the 1980s against antiterrorism actions that might embarrass the Saudis.[80] This block was still in place in the 1990s with respect to the chair of WAMY in Virginia, Osama bin Laden's nephew (or cousin) Abdullah bin Laden. The FBI opened an investigation of Abdullah bin Laden in February 1996, calling WAMY "a suspected terrorist organization," but the investigation was closed down six months later.[81]

Journalist Steven Emerson later testified to the 9/11 Commission that WAMY "has openly supported Islamic terrorism . . . [and] has consistently portrayed the United States, Jews, Christians, and other infidels as enemies who have to be defeated or killed."[82] But as of mid-2004, WAMY had not yet been listed as a terrorist organization. Even a month after 9/11, WAMY's leader, Abdullah bin Laden, said that his only contact with the FBI had been a brief phone call.[83]

WAMY, THE SAFA GROUP, PTECH, AND 9/11

In March 2002 the home of Jamal Barzinji, WAMY's former U.S. representative, was raided as part of Operation Green Quest, a terrorist financing probe. But before that Barzinji had been used by the U.S. Army as a resource for vetting Muslim chaplains in the U.S. Army.[84] Barzinji was a member of "what U.S. investigators have dubbed the 'Safa Group,' a complicated array of individuals and interlocking for-profit and non-profit entities allegedly involved in financing Islamic terrorism." According to a Customs official's affidavit, "Barzinji is an officer of at least 14 Safa Group entities, and his neighbor, M. Yaqub Mirza, is an officer of 29 Safa Group entities. Mirza was also a board member of Ptech, a Quincy[, Massachusetts–]based computer software company raided by federal agents last year as part of Operation Green Quest."[85]

The *Boston Herald* reported later that another "subject of the probe is Ptech, which was bankrolled by Yasin al-Qadi, a wealthy Saudi investor who has been officially designated by the U.S. government as a terrorism financier. Ptech was raided by federal agents in December 2002 and remains under investigation, sources said. No officers or employees of the company have been charged with a crime and al-Qadi has denied any involvement in financing terrorists. The company's close relationship with al-Qadi is of concern to investigators because Ptech provided software and consulting to numerous federal agencies, including the FBI, the Federal Aviation Administration and the Department of Defense."[86] Yassin al-Qadi (or al-Kadi), who managed and directed the Muwafaq Foundation, was added to the U.S. list of specially designated global terrorists in October 2001, one month after 9/11. As a result his assets were frozen.

It is extremely difficult to accept uncritically, or even objectively criticize, U.S. judgments about Muslim foundations in America and their donors, because of the passions and commitments of most sources. On the one hand we have journalists like Greg Palast who allege that "investigators were ordered to 'back off' from any inquiries into Saudi Arabian financing of terror networks," because "Clinton and the Bushes were reluctant to discomfort the Saudis by unearthing their connections to terrorists."[87] A specific instance was the complaint of FBI agent Robert Wright that FBI headquarters systematically obstructed his efforts in Chicago to investigate Yassin al-Qadi and his investment company BMI. In a subsequent suit against the FBI, Wright charged that this block "allowed foreign-born terrorist operatives, such as the perpetrators of the Sept. 11 attacks, to engage in illegal activities in the United States."[88]

On the other hand, al-Qadi denied vigorously that he had ever sent money to Osama bin Laden or his al Qaeda organization. Al-Qadi's foundation had been sending money to such charitable causes as Bosnian

Muslims, before it was shut down in 1996.[89] The Treasury Department's designation did not disclose the reason for designating al-Qadi as a terrorist. However, pro-Israel sources pointed to his foundation's support for the Quranic Literacy Institute (QLI), one of whose employees, Mohammed Abdul Hamid Khalil Salah, was convicted in Israel in 1993 of distributing money and weapons to operatives of Hamas.[90] QLI leaders were subsequently found liable in a multimillion dollar damage suit brought by the family of an American Jew slain in Palestine. But the moderate Council on American Islamic Relations complained that the trial was a travesty, inasmuch as the QLI, whose funds were also frozen by Treasury decree, could not begin to mount an adequate legal defense.[91]

The case against al-Qadi remains conflicted and (in my opinion) unproven. However, there were different, security-related questions with respect to the al-Qadi/BMI-related firm Ptech. Ptech was a company that specialized in enterprise architecture—essentially "the blueprints of the information contained on computer networks." Ptech's software was used for sensitive operations by many U.S. government agencies, including both houses of Congress, the White House, Treasury Department (Secret Service), CIA, the FBI, Army, Air Force, Navy, Department of Energy, the FAA, the IRS, IBM, Enron, and NATO.[92]

Indira Singh, a onetime senior employee of J. P. Morgan, shared her concerns about Ptech with her bank, the FBI, and eventually Senator Chuck Grassley. Customs then raided Ptech headquarters on the night of December 5–6, 2002, but the next day White House spokesman Ari Fleischer gave Ptech an extraordinary clean bill of health.[93] The Customs investigation was subsequently taken over by the FBI and went nowhere. Singh later told a public meeting that "when Ari Fleischer said there was nothing wrong with Ptech I became *persona non grata*, blacklisted everywhere."[94] Specifically, Singh's employers told her to forget the subject, and the FBI investigation came to a stop. Her employment at J. P. Morgan was soon terminated.

So, in short order, was Operation Green Quest. On the same day as the Ptech raid, December 6, 2002, treasury secretary Paul O'Neill was unexpectedly fired. Customs, the lead agency in Green Quest, was then taken from Treasury and moved into the new Department of Homeland Security. In April 2003, Green Quest investigators told *Newsweek* that their work was being stymied by the FBI.[95] On May 13, 2003, homeland security secretary Tom Ridge signed a memo of understanding giving the FBI sole control over terrorist-related financial investigations. Less than two months later, on June 30, Green Quest was formally dissolved.[96]

Singh, however, had confided her concerns about Ptech to a CBS newsman, Joe Bergantino. He later told NPR's *All Things Considered* that "the worst-case scenario is that this is a situation where this was planned for a very long time to establish a company in this country and in the computer software business that would target federal agencies and gain access to key government data to essentially help terrorists launch another attack."[97] Singh explained how well positioned Ptech was to create a crisis like 9/11: "Ptech was with Mitre [Corporation] in the basement of the FAA for two years prior to 9/11. Their specific job is to look at interoperability issues the FAA had with NORAD [North American Aerospace Defense Command] and the Air Force in the case of an emergency. If anyone was in a position to know that the FAA—that there was a window of opportunity or to insert software or to change anything it would have been Ptech along with Mitre."[98]

Just as alarming was what Singh had to say about drugs: "I did a number of things in my research and when I ran into the drugs I was told that if I mentioned the money to the drugs around 9/11 that would be the end of me. That is a current threat that I'm under and therefore I will speak out about the drugs at another forum."[99] (Singh's remarks about 9/11 and drugs have been obliquely echoed on many occasions, principally in *Vanity Fair*, by another fired whistleblower, former FBI translator Sibel Edmonds.[100])

THE SAUDI-TEXAS-GENEVA CONNECTION

Singh also told another journalist that disgruntled Boston FBI agents had told her privately that their hands were tied on Ptech, because "Saudis have been given a free pass for 9/11."[101] This echoes the complaints of two other FBI agents: Robert Wright and John O'Neill.[102] As already noted, Wright formally complained in 2000 about the obstruction of his investigation of Yassin al-Qadi and his firm BMI, an investment banking firm of which Ptech was allegedly "the crown jewel."[103] (Two of Ptech's founding directors were former employees of BMI; and one of them, former BMI director Hussein Ibrahim, became Ptech's vice president and chief scientist.[104])

Eventually in June 2003 the FBI arrested BMI's administrator, Soliman S. Biheiri, on charges that through BMI Biheiri had handled investments for several designated terrorists, including Yassin al-Qadi, Hamas leader Mousa Abu Marzouk, and Sheikh Youssef al-Qaradawi, a radical cleric banned from the United States since 1999.[105] Undoubtedly Ptech, despite being at the nerve center of a U.S. response to aerial attack, also had its own independent al-Kifah/al Qaeda connection. A Ptech employee, Muhamed Mubayyid, was treasurer of a little-known Arab charity, Care International, which "was the Boston branch of the Al-Kifah Refugee Center, based in Brooklyn, N.Y." In May 2005, Mubayyid was indicted on federal charges of lying to authorities investigating the charity's alleged ties to terrorist organizations.[106]

In 2001 the *Toronto Star* reviewed the intricate interplay of oil politics, Saudi Arabia, and al Qaeda, and commented:

> Earlier this month, the *Guardian*, a U.K. newspaper, reported that FBI agents had been told by the Bush administration to back off investigating members of the bin Laden clan living in the U.S. In September, the *Wall Street Journal* documented the lucrative business connections between the bin Laden family and senior U.S. Republicans, including the president's father, George Bush Sr.
>
> What are we to make of all this? One possible conclusion is that the bin Laden terror problem was allowed to get out of hand because bin Laden, himself, had powerful protectors in both Washington and Saudi Arabia.[107]

Indeed. Many observers have noted, from as early as 1992, that George W. Bush's first oil venture, Arbusto, received a $50,000 investment from Texan James Bath, who first made his fortune by investing money for Saudi millionaires.[108] Such little investments purchased political influence. According to Kevin Phillips, "James Bath, who invested fifty thousand dollars in the 1979 and 1980 Arbusto partnerships, probably did so as U.S. business representative for rich Saudi investors Salem bin Laden and Khalid bin Mahfouz. . . . Both men were involved with the Bank of Credit and Commerce International. . . . A decade later, Harken Energy, the company willing to handsomely buy out George W.'s crumbling oil and gas business, had its own CIA connections. . . . 17.6 percent of Harken's stock was owned by Abdullah Baksh."[109] (Khalid bin Mahfouz has categorically denied being an investor in either Arbusto or Harken Energy. This would imply that George W.'s original Saudi benefactor was Osama bin Laden's half-brother, Salem bin Laden.)

The first deals with Arbusto were negotiated as George W.'s father was preparing to run for the presidency in 1979 and 1980. The second deal with Harken began in 1987, as he "was positioning himself to succeed Reagan."[110] There are other Saudi-Bush investments. Much has been written about "the Carlyle Group . . . an integral part of the Military-Industrial-Government Complex," some of whose more prominent members are James A. Baker III, former secretary of defense Frank C. Carlucci, and former president George H. W. Bush. "Until shortly after September 11," journalist Ben. C. Toledano has written, "the Bin Laden family of Saudi Arabia had substantial investments in the Carlyle Group."[111]

More relevant to 9/11 was the Kuwait-American Corporation (Kuw-Am), in which major investors were the elder President Bush's younger brother Marvin Bush and Mishal Yousef Saud al-Sabah of the Kuwaiti royal family.[112] KuwAm backed the security firm for the World Trade Center on 9/11: Securacom, later renamed Stratesec. [(Securacom also provided security for United Airlines and Dulles International Airport.) A director of Securacom until June 2000 was Marvin Bush.[113]] But these investments are only particular symptoms of the Saudi stake in the ravenous U.S. financial establishment, not clues to some central role in it. Since the "twin pillars" doctrine of 1974, a great deal of Saudi wealth has been lavished on the *eminenti* of American political parties in general and the Bush family circle in particular.

For example, Khalid bin Mahfouz helped finance the construction of Houston's tallest building, the Texas Commerce Tower, in conjunction with the family bank of James Baker, the close friend of Bush the elder and Reagan's chief of staff after 1981. The building was completed in 1982, and the thirty-two-year-old bin Mahfouz then "shared business interests with the chief of staff to the president of the United States."[114] In 1985, bin Mahfouz was one of the Saudi financiers who bought out the Baker bank interest in the tower for $200 million. This was $60 million more than it had cost to build the bank tower four years earlier. The sale was made "in the depth of Texas' real estate crash . . . at a time when it was difficult to give away office space in Houston."[115]

One glaring example of Saudi influence was the federal government's reluctance to prosecute BCCI (in which bin Mahfouz was for a few belated years a leading shareholder), after the bank had been exposed for illegally acquiring a U.S. affiliate, First American. A former National Security Council economist told coauthors Jonathan Beaty and S. C. Gwynne that "Baker didn't pursue BCCI because he thought a prosecution of the bank would damage the United States reputation as a safe haven for flight capital and overseas investments."[116]

Toledano has summarized the opinions of those who see a more Texan motivation: "Kevin Phillips writes that 'no other political family in the United States has had anything remotely resembling the Bushes' four decade relationship with the Saudi royal family and the oil sheiks of the Persian Gulf.' All of the arrangements—'arms deals and oil deals and consultancies,' according to William Hartung of the World Policy Institute—

have made our government reluctant to investigate the Saudis."[117] BCCI patronage extended also to Democrats, even to the Democratic Senate Campaign Committee, which in 1990 was cochaired by Senator John F. Kerry and by David L. Paul of the notorious S & L CenTrust Savings Bank of Miami. CenTrust's major stockholder and close associate of Paul was Ghaith Pharaon of BCCI.[118]

Phillips, looking over three decades of Saudi penetration and immunity, has observed:

> [George H. W.] Bush, while running the CIA in 1976, enlisted as a CIA asset James Bath, the U.S. representative of major BCCI investor Khalid bin Mahfouz, as well as the BCCI-linked bin Laden family. . . . One of Bush's major 1976 priorities was expanding its cooperation with Saudi intelligence, at the time run by Sheikh Kamal Adham, who also had close financial ties to BCCI. The possibility that George H. W. Bush was an architect, not a victim or dupe, of BCCI's emerging and corrupting international role would help to explain why Bush could have been so centrally involved in the three major political scandals of the 1980s—October Surprise (1980–81), Iran-Contra (1984–86), and Iraqgate (1981–90)—that partly involved covert financing of clandestine arms deals and relationships with Iraq and Iran. . . . His son's restoration in 2000 renewed [these scandals'] political and legal relevance.[119]

The failure to be more aggressive about Saudi involvement in the BCCI scandal was indeed replicated with respect to 9/11. Toledano observed: "[In 2003] the House and Senate Intelligence Committees prepared a joint report concerning September 11 and how it might have been prevented. Before the report was released, the Bush White House demanded certain deletions, including a 28-page section relating to the Saudis."[120] A diplomatic reason for this was given on the BBC by journalist Greg Palast: "State wanted to keep the pro-American Saudi royal family in control of the world's biggest oil spigot, even at the price of turning a blind eye to any terrorist connection so long as America was safe."[121]

Thus a number of authors, such as Kevin Phillips, have portrayed a Bush-Saudi or Texas-Saudi connection, targeting Khalid bin Mahfouz and the Carlyle Group in particular.[122] It would be more accurate to talk of a Texas-Saudi-Geneva connection. Bruce Rappaport's Inter Maritime Bank in Geneva, mentioned earlier, also had business connections with BCCI, the bin Laden family, and the Bush family. Alfred Hartmann, vice president of Rappaport's Inter Maritime Bank and a BCCI director, was also chairman of a BCCI-owned bank, the Banque de Commerce et de

Placements (BCP), which in 1986 brokered a $25 million investment, triggered by George W. Bush, in the oil company Harken Energy.[123] Only a racial bias can lead one to focus on the Saudis in this Bush-Harken connection, while excluding Rappaport.

It would be more accurate to say that there is a global overworld, in which American, Arab, and Jewish superwealth have become thoroughly intermingled. We live in an era when Arabs have become major shareholders in such major U.S. corporations as Citigroup, Chase Manhattan Bank, Hyatt Hotels, Mobil, Chevron, and News Corp.[124] Arab bankers and CEOs also are represented on the policy task forces of the Council on Foreign Relations. Rappaport, meanwhile, has been located at "the intersection of illicit Russian money and the Bank of New York," through which perhaps as much as $10 billion in Russian flight money passed in less than a year.[125]

In the wake of Harken Energy, Arab investors, along with Russian oligarchs like Boris Berezovsky, still contribute start-up capital for the dubious ventures of those now close to the White House, notably Neil Bush's educational firm Ignite! Inc.[126] One of these ventures is the private military company Diligence Middle East in Iraq. This is headed by former FEMA chief Joe Allbaugh, whom I discuss further in consideration of 9/11 itself.

I have argued elsewhere that in this global overworld there exist metagroups transcending ideological and religious differences, which collaborate with, and are capable of modifying, governmental policy (particularly but not exclusively with respect to the international drug traffic). BCCI was one such meta-group. Berezovsky representatives participated in another, which allegedly met in Saudi billionaire arms dealer Adnan Khashoggi's villa in France and has been accused of plotting the "Russian 9/11" of Moscow bombings in 1999.[127] Somewhere within the shadowy Texas-Saudi-Geneva milieu there is surely room for a meta-group as well.

Much of the debate over 9/11 has been focused on what I have called a false dilemma: whether it was Islamists or the U.S. government who were responsible for the disaster. We should at least contemplate the possibility that it was a global meta-group, working as "an unrecognized Force X operating in the world," that had the various resources and far-reaching connections necessary for the successful plot.[128]

ELEVEN

PARALLEL STRUCTURES AND PLANS FOR CONTINUITY OF GOVERNMENT

We're there because the fact of the matter is that part of the world controls the world supply of oil, and whoever controls the supply of oil, especially if it were a man like Saddam Hussein, with a large army and sophisticated weapons, would have a stranglehold on the American economy and on— indeed on the world economy.

Secretary of Defense Dick Cheney, 1990

To initiate a war of aggression, therefore, is not only an international crime; it is the supreme international crime, differing only from other war crimes in that it contains within itself the accumulated evil of the whole.

Judge Robert H. Jackson,
Nuremberg War Crimes Tribunal, 1946

I don't care what the international lawyers say, we are going to kick some ass.

George W. Bush, September 11, 2001

THE STRATEGY OF TENSION IN EUROPE AND AMERICA

The idea that sectors of government might sponsor extremists in acts of terrorism against their own people is, initially, almost unthinkable. Yet this unthinkable possibility has clearly happened in Italy, with the celebrated bombings of Milan's Piazza Fontana in 1969 and the Bologna railway station in 1980. (Sixteen people were killed in Milan, and eighty-five in Bologna.) Although anarchists took part in these bombings, and were initially blamed for them, it developed that the bombings were part of a "strategy of tension" orchestrated by Italian military intelligence.[1]

The responsibility of Italian intelligence services has been definitively established by Italian courts and parliamentary investigations. As Stanford historian Thomas Sheehan wrote in the *New York Review of Books*, "Later the [Piazza Fontana] massacre was traced to two neofascists, Franco Freda and Giovanni Ventura, and to an agent of the Secret Services (SID) named Guido Giannettini. Giannettini fled the country, but continued to receive checks from SID for a full year. He and three high SID officials were eventually jailed for conspiracy in the massacre."[2] But the Italians found responsible have implicated U.S. covert actions in Italy, beginning with the efforts by the Office of Policy Coordination to defeat the Communists in the 1948 Italian elections. General Vito Miceli, the Italian head of military intelligence, after his arrest in 1974 on a charge of conspiring to overthrow the government, testified "that the incriminated organization, which became known as the 'Parallel SID,' was formed under a secret agreement with the United States and within the framework of NATO."[3]

Former Italian defense minister Paulo Taviani told Magistrate Casson during a 1990 investigation "that during his time in office (1955–58), the Italian secret services were bossed and financed by 'the boys in Via Veneto'—i.e. the CIA agents in the U.S. Embassy in the heart of Rome."[4] In 2000 "an Italian secret service general said . . . that the CIA gave its tacit approval to a series of bombings in Italy in the 1970s to sow instability and keep communists from taking power. . . . 'The CIA wanted, through the birth of an extreme nationalism and the contribution of the far right, particularly Ordine Nuovo, to stop (Italy) sliding to the left,' he said."[5]

The evidence for some degree of U.S. involvement is massive but also problematic.[6] There is no doubt that the United States, operating partly through NATO, sponsored and funded so-called stay-behind paramilitary groups in Italy and other NATO countries (in Operation Gladio); and there is no doubt also that the cadres and munitions of these groups were used in the strategy of tension. For some time critics of U.S foreign policy have stressed the role of CIA assets and Gladio terrorism in the Greek Colonels' coup of 1967: "The Gladio 'Sheepskin' group was involved in a campaign of terrorist bombings, which were blamed on the left, and two days before the election campaign was to begin, a military coup brought to power a junta led by George Papadopoulos, a member of the Greek intelligence service KYP [who had been on CIA payroll since 1952]."[7] This was the climax of a period in which Greece was afflicted with "an intelligence service gone wild" and "a shadow government with powers beyond the control of the nation's nominal leaders."[8]

Even clearer is the continuous U.S. intervention in Italian politics after 1948, to block the formation of any government supported by the Communist Party. In 1972, for example, CIA disbursed $10 million to political parties, affiliated organizations, and twenty-one candidates, mostly Christian Democrats. Ambassador Graham Martin, against CIA advice, gave a further $800,000 to General Miceli, the Italian head of military intelligence.[9] Miceli would be tried two years later for his involvement in the 1970 Borghese coup attempt, which the Piazza Fontana bombing of 1969 was designed to assist. Eventually he and all other defendants would be acquitted.[10]

What is not yet clear, at least to me, is the degree and level of conscious U.S. direction for Italian state violence against civilians. The official Italian Senate investigation into Gladio concluded "without the shadow of a doubt that elements of the CIA started in the second half of the 1960s to counter by the use of all means the spreading ... of the left."[11] But at what level were these elements, and with what central authorization? Undoubtedly Gladio units contributed to the Eurofascism of the 1980s, but by then many if not most Eurofascists were anti-American as well as anti-Soviet. Whatever the details, the perversion of Operation Gladio into sanctioned attacks on innocent civilians illustrates the dangers of top-down power, especially when it is off-shored and removed from the checks and balances of an open public state.[12]

At least some Americans believed themselves in the strategy of tension. William Harvey, when CIA station chief in Rome, reportedly recruited his own "action squads" and suggested that the head of the Italian intelligence service SIFAR (later SID) "use his 'action squads' to 'carry out bombings against Christian Democrat Party offices and certain newspapers in the north, which were to be attributed to the left.'"[13]

More important, European sources allege that one of the masterminds of the 1969 plot, Guido Giannettini, was invited in late 1961 to give a three-day lecture course to U.S. military officers in Annapolis, on "Techniques and Possibilities of a Coup d'Etat in Europe."[14] A few weeks later Pentagon officials began drafting the plans known as Operation Northwoods, the first known American application of a strategy of tension. As summarized by ABC News, "the plans reportedly included the possible assassination of Cuban émigrés, sinking boats of Cuban refugees on the high seas, hijacking planes, blowing up a U.S. ship, and even orchestrating violent terrorism in U.S. cities."[15] This was at a time of developing U.S. Army interest in so-called counterterror as a technique in counterinsurgency, as developed by Nazis, French theorists of *guerre révolutionnaire*, and East European émigrés now attached to the U.S. Army.

Thus one cannot clearly distinguish between the managed violence advocated by Italian strategists of tension and those aping them in the United States. International security analyst John Prados has put the issue very forcibly: "In this age of global concern with terrorism it is especially upsetting to discover that Western Europe and the United States collaborated in creating networks that took up terrorism. In the United States such nations are called 'state sponsors' and are the object of hostility and sanction. Can it be the United States itself, Britain, France, Italy, and others who should be on the list of state sponsors?"[16] It is alarming moreover to note that the Piazza Fontana bombing was planned by a "parallel" structure, outside government control, as a prelude for a military coup.[17]

CHENEY, RUMSFELD, AND COG PLANNING IN THE 1980S

Dick Cheney and Donald Rumsfeld have been associated since the 1980s with a parallel planning structure in the United States. The formal goal of this planned parallel structure was called "continuity of government" (COG), but the name is misleading. The *Progressive Review* referred more descriptively to plans for "a possible military/civilian coup."[18]

The plans for what journalist James Bamford has called the "secret government" of COG had been slowly developing, chiefly but not only under Republican administrations, since the 1950s.[19] As mentioned in chapter 4, a major step was the creation in 1979 of the Federal Emergency Management Agency (FEMA). But FEMA's emergency planning was radically politicized under President Reagan. By 1984, in the words of journalist Ross Gelbspan, "Lt. Col. Oliver North was working with officials of the Federal Emergency Management Agency . . . to draw up a secret contingency plan to surveil political dissenters and to arrange for the detention of hundreds of thousands of undocumented aliens in case of an unspecified national emergency. The plan, part of which was codenamed Rex 84, called for the suspension of the Constitution under a number of scenarios, including a U.S. invasion of Nicaragua. . . . But in addition to groups opposing United States policies in Central America, the FEMA plan reportedly included environmental activists, opponents of nuclear energy and refugee assistance activists."[20]

Earlier, Governor Reagan in California had authorized the development of a counterinsurgency plan (known as Cable Splicer) and exercises to deal with such crises, in conjunction with the U.S. Sixth Army and the Pentagon (Operation Garden Plot). The cadres developing Cable Splicer (headed by Louis Giuffrida), were with Reagan's elevation to the presidency transferred into FEMA. As head of FEMA, Giuffrida pursued plans for massive detention of dissidents; these became so extreme that even Reagan's attorney general, William French Smith, raised objections.[21]

As developed in the mid-1980s by Oliver North in the White House, the plans called for not just the surveillance but also the potential detention of large numbers of American citizens. During the Iran-Contra hearings North was asked by the congressman Jack Brooks about his work on "a contingency plan in the event of emergency, that would suspend the American constitution." The chairman, Democratic senator Daniel Inouye, ruled that this was a "highly sensitive and classified" matter, not to be dealt with in an open hearing. This dramatic exchange was virtually ignored by the establishment media.[22]

In the wake of Brooks's question in Congress, the public was told how attorney general William French Smith, in an August 1984 letter to NSC chair Robert McFarlane, had written that FEMA's proposed executive order "exceeds its proper function as a coordinating agency for emergency preparedness."[23] To this day it is usually reported that "Smith's objections apparently killed the draft executive order."[24] But the authorizing National Security Decision Directive (NSDD 55 of September 14, 1982, on "Enduring National Leadership") continued in effect for a decade. It was augmented by President Reagan on September 16, 1985, with National Security Decision Directive 188 (NSDD 188, "Government Coordination for National Security Emergency Preparedness"). The directives were part of a series, augmented by additional executive orders, that authorized ongoing "continuity planning."[25]

Some of the highest-level planning for COG was conducted by a parallel extragovernmental group. This parallel structure, operating outside normal government channels, included the head of G. D. Searle & Co., Donald Rumsfeld, and then congressman from Wyoming Dick Cheney.[26] Overall responsibility for the program, hidden under the innocuously named National Program Office, was assigned to Vice President George H. W. Bush, "with Lt. Col. Oliver North . . . as the National Security Council action officer."[27]

It is not fanciful to link this private parallel government to 9/11. As detailed in chapter 12, Cheney and FEMA were reunited in May 2001: President George W. Bush appointed Cheney to head a terrorism task force and created a new office within FEMA, the innocuously named Office of National Preparedness, to assist him. In effect, Bush was authorizing a resumption of the kind of planning that Cheney and FEMA had conducted under the heading of COG. And on September 11 the planning bore fruit: a classified "continuity of operations plan" was implemented, at least partially, for the first time.[28]

This chapter and especially the next explore the consequences of this arresting coincidence: that the COG planning team of the 1980s was essentially reconstituted by Bush the younger in May 2001 as a terrorism task force, and then (after planning activities of which we know next to nothing) a major attack on the United States (of which we also still know next to nothing) resulted in implementation of COG. The public also knows next to nothing about COG, except that its powers to disrupt constitutional government are considerable.

"Continuity of government" is a reassuring title. It would be more honest, however, to call it a "change of government" plan, since according to Alfonso Chardy of the *Miami Herald*, the plan called for "suspension of the Constitution, turning control of the government over to FEMA, emergency appointment of military commanders to run state and local governments and declaration of martial law during a national crisis."[29] The plan also gave the Federal Emergency Management Agency, which had been involved in drafting it, sweeping new powers, including internment.[30]

The team was planning, in effect, for the supplanting in a major crisis of the public state by an alternative one. According to author and journalist James Mann: "Rumsfeld and Cheney were principal actors in one of the most highly classified programs of the Reagan Administration. Under it U.S. officials furtively carried out detailed planning exercises for keeping the federal government running during and after a nuclear war with the Soviet Union. The program called for setting aside the legal rules for presidential succession in some circumstances, in favor of a secret procedure for putting in place a new 'President' and his staff. The idea was to concentrate on speed, to preserve 'continuity of government,' and to avoid cumbersome procedures; the speaker of the House, the president pro tempore of the Senate, and the rest of Congress would play a greatly diminished role."[31]

But the planning eventually called for suspension of the Constitution, not just "after a nuclear war" but for any "national security emergency." This was defined in Executive Order 12656 of 1988 as "any occurrence, including natural disaster, military attack, technological emergency, or other emergency, that seriously degrades or seriously threatens the national security of the United States."[32] Clearly 9/11 met this definition.

COG planning was eventually integrated into planning by a number of groups corresponding to different departments, dealing with different functions. One group, the Continuity of Government Interagency Group, dealt with devolution and relocation of government leaders, to prevent decapitation of the government in a crisis. Another group dealt with "command and control" problems, to ensure security for communications and computers so that decisions could be made and implemented. Another group, focused on the Department of Defense, planned for retaliation against the nation's attackers.[33]

In April 1994, Tim Weiner announced in the *New York Times* that in the post-Soviet Clinton era, "the Doomsday Project, as it was known" was to be closed. "The nuclear tensions of that era having subsided, the project has less than six months to live. 'On Oct. 1, it's history,' a Pentagon official said." Weiner added that "while some 'continuity of government' programs continue under the aegis of Pentagon planners, they are pale versions of the vision laid out by President Reagan in 1983. 'They are realizing these requirements are throwbacks to the cold war,' [nuclear analyst Bruce] Blair said. 'They are not relevant to today's world.'"[34]

This article persuaded authors James Mann and James Bamford that Reagan's COG plans had now been abandoned, because "there was, it seemed, no longer any enemy in the world capable of . . . decapitating America's leadership."[35] In fact, however, only one phase of COG planning had been terminated, a Pentagon program for response to a nuclear attack. Instead, according to author Andrew Cockburn, a new target was found:

> Although the exercises continued, still budgeted at over $200 million a year in the Clinton era, the vanished Soviets were now replaced by terrorists. . . . There were other changes, too. In earlier times the specialists selected to run the "shadow government" had been drawn from across the political spectrum, Democrats and Republicans alike. But now, down in the bunkers, Rumsfeld found himself in politically congenial company, the players' roster being filled almost exclusively with Republican hawks. "It was one way for these people to stay in touch. They'd meet, do the exercise, but also sit around and castigate the Clinton administration in the most extreme way," a former Pentagon official with direct knowledge of the phenomenon told

me. "You could say this was a secret government-in-waiting. The Clinton administration was extraordinarily inattentive, [they had] no idea what was going on."[36]

Cockburn's account requires some qualification. Richard Clarke, a Clinton Democrat, makes it clear that he participated in the COG games in the 1990s and indeed drafted Clinton's Presidential Decision Directive (PDD) 67 on "Enduring Constitutional Government and Continuity of Government."[37] But COG planning involved different teams for different purposes. It is quite possible that the Pentagon official was describing the Department of Defense team dealing with retaliation.

The Pentagon official's description of a "secret government-in-waiting" (which still included both Cheney and Rumsfeld) is very close to the standard definition of a cabal, as a group of persons secretly united to bring about a change or overthrow of government. In the same era Cheney and Rumsfeld projected change also by their public lobbying, through the Project for the New American Century, for a more militant Middle East policy. In light of how COG was actually implemented in 2001, one can legitimately suspect that, however interested this group had been in continuity of government under Reagan, under Clinton the focus of Cheney's and Rumsfeld's COG planning was now a change of government.

So we should not be surprised that with the implementation of COG came the warrantless detentions that Oliver North had planned two decades earlier, and the warrantless eavesdropping that is their logical counterpart. The only question is this: Were these practices decided on after 9/11, as the Bush administration maintains? Or were they already being prepared for as part of the COG planning revived by Cheney and FEMA in May 2001? I return to this question in chapters 12 through 14.

OIL AND CHENEY'S ENERGY TASK FORCE

There is the same impression of preparation for 9/11 and its consequent war from Cheney's other task force, the Energy Task Force. By May 2001 it had already set out, urgently and in some detail, plans for taking control over Iraqi oil. As many observers have pointed out, the second Bush administration was the first in which the vice president and his own national security staff wielded powers comparable to, perhaps even surpassing, those of the president. Some have gone even a step further, as journalist Steve Perry wrote in 2005: "Cheney's office is the Pandora's Box of the Bush administration campaign to invade Iraq. Most of the planning as to both the waging and selling of the war occurred under his direction, along with that of Donald Rumsfeld and Paul Wolfowitz at the Pentagon. It was Cheney who played the point in beating up CIA for its unhelpful analysis of the nonthreat posed by Saddam, and Cheney along with his Defense Department pals who effectively circumvented CIA by setting up the Office of Special Plans at the Pentagon to funnel the administration the kind of intelligence it wanted, largely courtesy of their longtime double-dealing stooge, Ahmed Chalabi."[38]

Perry also quotes an op-ed by former Powell chief of staff Colonel Lawrence B. Wilkerson (U.S. Army, retired): "In President Bush's first term, some of the most important decisions about U.S. national security—including vital decisions about postwar Iraq—were made by a secretive, little-known cabal. It was made up of a very small group of people led by Vice President Dick Cheney and Defense Secretary Donald Rumsfeld. . . . I believe that the decisions of this cabal were sometimes made with the full and witting support of the president and sometimes with something less. . . . It's a disaster. Given the choice, I'd choose a frustrating bureaucracy over an efficient cabal every time."[39]

The vice president's first major assignment was to discuss energy policy in his Energy Task Force, which brought in leaders from the petroleum industry. In fact, Cheney could be called an oil industry leader himself. As reported in *The New Yorker*, he served "immediately before becoming Vice-President, as chief executive of Halliburton, the world's largest oil-and-gas-services company. The conglomerate, which is based in Houston, is now [2004] the biggest private contractor for American forces in Iraq; it has received contracts worth some eleven billion dollars for its work there. Cheney earned forty-four million dollars during his tenure at Halliburton. Although he has said that he 'severed all my ties with the company,' he continues to collect deferred compensation worth approximately a hundred and fifty thousand dollars a year."[40]

It is clear that from at least February 2001 Cheney's task force discussions extended to the "capture" of oil resources in Iraq: "One intriguing piece of evidence pointing in this direction was a National Security Council document, dated February 2001, directing NSC staff to cooperate fully with Cheney's task force. The NSC document, reported in *The New Yorker* magazine, noted that the task force would be considering the 'melding' of two policy areas: 'the review of operational policies towards rogue states' and 'actions regarding the capture of new and existing oil and gas fields.' This certainly implies that the Cheney task force was considering geopolitical questions about actions related to the capture of oil and gas reserves in 'rogue' states, including presumably Iraq."[41]

The task force's concerns are well illustrated by two documents, released to the public-interest law firm Judicial Watch only after a fierce court struggle. The first document is a map of Iraq, whose "detail is all about Iraq's oil. The southwest is neatly divided, for instance, into nine 'Exploration Blocks.' Stripped of political trappings, this map shows a naked Iraq, with only its ample natural assets in view. It's like a supermarket meat chart, which identifies the various parts of a slab of beef so customers can see the most desirable cuts. . . . Block 1 might be the striploin, Blocks 2 and 3 are perhaps some juicy tenderloin, but Block 8— ahh, that could be the filet mignon."

The second "task force document, also released under court order, was a two-page chart titled 'Foreign Suitors for Iraqi Oilfields.' It identifies 63 oil companies from 30 countries and specifies which Iraqi oil fields each company is interested in and the status of the company's negotiations with Saddam Hussein's regime. Among the companies are Royal Dutch/Shell of the Netherlands, Russia's Lukoil and France's Total Elf Aquitaine, which was identified as being interested in the fabulous, 25-billion-barrel Majnoon oil field. Baghdad had 'agreed in principle' to the French company's plans to develop this succulent slab of Iraq. There goes the filet mignon into the mouths of the French!"[42]

Cheney's task force was the final stage in a lobbying process by the oil majors that had begun under Clinton. As early as April 1997, a report from the James A. Baker Institute of Public Policy at Rice University addressed the problem of "energy security" for the United States, noting that the country was increasingly threatened by oil shortages. It concluded that Saddam Hussein was still a threat to Middle Eastern security and still had the military capability to exercise force beyond Iraq's borders. The second Bush administration returned to this theme as soon as it took office in 2001, by following the lead of a second report from the same institute. This task force report was cosponsored by the Council on Foreign Relations in New York, another group historically concerned about U.S. access to overseas oil resources.[43] The report, *Strategic Energy Policy: Challenges for the 21st Century*, concluded that "the U.S. should conduct an immediate policy review toward Iraq including military, energy, economic and political/diplomatic assessments."[44]

Meanwhile, the BBC heard from State Department insiders that plan-

ning for regime change in Iraq "began 'within weeks' of Bush's first taking office in 2001, long before the September 11th attack on the U.S."[45]
The administration's concern for controlling oil in the Middle East intermingled with strategic concerns in the area, especially with increasing
uncertainty about the future of U.S. bases in Saudi Arabia. The White
House was also impressed by the report of an AEI-based discussion
group, commissioned by Paul Wolfowitz, that a strategy to deal with
Middle East terrorism would require two generations of conflict, in
which 'Iran is more important. . . . But Saddam Hussein was . . . weaker,
more vulnerable.' "[46]

RUMSFELD, CHENEY, L. PAUL BREMER, AND THE NSC

But in late 2002, Donald Rumsfeld, taking the line of many other senior
Bush officials, told CBS News that the projected war "has nothing to do
with oil, literally nothing to do with oil."[47] One of the few commentators
to speak more candidly was Anthony H. Cordesman, senior analyst at
Washington's Center for Strategic and International Studies: "Regardless
of whether we say so publicly, we will go to war, because Saddam sits at
the center of a region with more than 60 percent of all the world's oil
reserves." Another was former CIA director James Woolsey, who hinted
publicly that if France and Russia contributed to "regime change," their
oil companies would be able to "work together" with the new regime
and with American companies. Otherwise, commented the *Asia Times*,
"they would be left contemplating passing cargoes in the Gulf."[48]

As I have argued elsewhere, the need to dominate oil from Iraq is also
deeply intertwined with the defense of the dollar.[49] The dollar's current
strength is supported by the requirement of the Organization of the
Petroleum Exporting Countries (OPEC), secured originally by a secret
agreement between the United States and Saudi Arabia, that all OPEC oil
sales be denominated in dollars.[50] This requirement was threatened by
the desire of some OPEC countries, following the lead of Saddam Hussein's Iraq in 2000, to allow some OPEC oil sales to be paid in euros.[51]

The United States acted swiftly to ensure that oil would remain dom-
inantly a dollar commodity, by an executive order empowering Iraqi oil
sales to be returned from euros to dollars.[52] Bush's order of May 22,
2003, declaring a "national emergency," did not directly mention the
dollar as such; but it directed all oil earnings into a central fund, controlled by the United States, for reconstruction projects in Iraq. The

Financial Times, on June 6, 2003, confirmed that Iraqi oil sales were now switched back from euros to dollars.[53]

This was only one example of the energetic program being implemented by L. Paul Bremer, who since May had been running Iraq as head of the Coalition Provisional Authority. His stated priorities were to privatize Iraq and open up opportunities for U.S. banks and corporations.[54] Bremer's reckless dismantling of the Iraqi state won him the support of free-market neocons like Charles Krauthammer at the time.[55] In retrospect, however, Bremer has been blamed by most observers, such as Bob Woodward in *State of Denial* and Thomas Ricks in *Fiasco*, for having lost the battle for the hearts and minds of the Iraqi people. His program's open disregard of Iraqi public opinion was noted pointedly at the time by the conservative *Financial Times*.[56]

What was particularly striking about Bremer's program was that some aspects of it clearly contradicted U.S. policy decisions that had been reached in National Security Council meetings held just before the war, on March 10 and March 12, 2003.[57] A "very senior official within the administration" later told writer David Rothkopf that Bremer's disregard for the White House decisions was due to Rumsfeld, whom he accused of "high-level insubordination."[58] But Bremer's coconspirator in destatification and privatization was Peter McPherson, a former Bank of America executive and close Cheney friend who had served in the Ford White House with Rumsfeld and Cheney.[59]

CHENEY, OIL, AND THE PROJECT FOR
THE NEW AMERICAN CENTURY

In the 1990s the most militant and outspoken advocates of invading Iraq were the neocons of the Project for the New American Century (PNAC). Many of these were active supporters of Israel's Likud, and at least one of them helped write policy advice for the Israeli prime minister Benjamin Netanyahu and Likud in 1996.[60] PNAC itself was founded the following year, in 1997. By 2004, PNAC neocons, who desired to smash OPEC by lowering oil prices, had lost in a struggle with the U.S. oil majors, who preferred to maintain OPEC and by so doing see oil prices rise.[61] (According to journalist Greg Palast in *Harper's*, the "the switch to an OPEC-friendly policy for Iraq was driven by Dick Cheney himself."[62]) But before 2003, PNAC and the oil majors were united in their desire to see a U.S. move to take over control of Iraqi oil.

Among PNAC's important supporters in the 1990s were five men who had previously held office in Republican administrations: Donald Rumsfeld, Dick Cheney, Paul Wolfowitz, Lewis Libby, and Zalmay Khalilzad. Aligned with these was James Woolsey, CIA chief for the first two years of the Clinton administration. It is striking that three of these power veterans—Cheney, Rumsfeld, and Woolsey—had also been the most prominent members of the secret group in the 1980s planning for continuity of government (COG).[63] In open letters to Clinton and GOP congressional leaders in 1997, PNAC called for "the removal of Saddam Hussein's regime from power" and a shift toward a more assertive U.S. policy in the Middle East, including the use of force if necessary to unseat Saddam.[64] Their ideology was summarized in a major position paper, *Rebuilding America's Defenses*, in September 2000. This document advocated a global Pax Americana unrestrained by international law and spoke frankly of the need to retain forward-based U.S. troops in the Middle East, even if Saddam Hussein were to disappear.[65]

The paper was planned as an agenda in the event of a Republican victory. Even before victory had been secured by the Supreme Court in December 2000, Cheney was at work securing key posts for PNAC in the White House as well as in the State and Defense departments. Of the project's personnel, Lewis Libby became deputy to Vice President Cheney, Wolfowitz became deputy defense secretary under Rumsfeld, and Perle became chairman of the Defense Policy Board.[66] In addition, former PNAC director John Bolton became the leading hawk under Colin Powell in the State Department. In 2002 the PNAC goals of unchallenged military dominance, plus the right to launch preemptive strikes anywhere, were embodied in the new National Security Strategy of September 2002 (known as "NSS 2002").[67] (A key figure in drafting this document was Philip Zelikow, who later became the principal author of the *9/11 Commission Report*.)[68]

In the days after 9/11 a small PNAC-led group in the Pentagon's Office of Special Plans produced a series of intelligence reviews to justify the desired goal of action against Iraq. According to investigative journalist Seymour Hersh, the eight or nine PNAC-sympathizers in the Pentagon, centered in this office, actually "call[ed] themselves, self-mockingly, the Cabal."[69] The director of the Office of Special Plans was PNAC study participant Abram Shulsky; Shulsky reported to undersecretary of defense William Luti, who in the summer of 2001 had served with Libby on Vice President Cheney's staff and was a passionate advocate of overthrowing Saddam Hussein.[70] Using a flow of very controversial intelligence from Ahmad Chalabi of the Iraqi National Congress, the "cabal" inside the Pentagon enabled Shulsky, reporting through Wolfowitz, to override pessimistic but valid intelligence predictions about an Iraq war with useless assurances that the Americans would be welcomed in Iraq "with open arms."[71]

In other words Cheney and Rumsfeld had by the summer of 2001 set up both the goals and the implementation agencies for a war on Iraq. The course was set, and it became abundantly clear in time that the administration was prepared to lie and distort in order to maintain it. But it was clear from polls taken both before and after the Iraq invasion that for the American people to support this course of action, they had to believe they had been attacked. The Bush agenda, in other words, depended on 9/11, or something like it.

The PNAC study, *Rebuilding America's Defenses*, had itself foreseen the need for such a belief. "The process of transformation," it reported, "even if it brings revolutionary change, is likely to be a long one, absent some catastrophic and catalyzing event—like a new Pearl Harbor."[72] This was only one instance of a widely accepted truism: that it would take something like a Pearl Harbor to get America to accept an aggressive war.[73] So the question to be asked is whether Cheney, Rumsfeld, or any others whose projects depended on "a new Pearl Harbor" were participants in helping to create one. In chapter 12, I provide some reasons why Cheney should be considered a suspect in the 9/11 disaster, and his actions investigated further.

TWELVE

THE *9/11 COMMISSION REPORT* AND VICE PRESIDENT CHENEY

Therefore many judge that a wise prince must, whenever he has the occasion, foster with cunning some hostility so that in stamping it out his greatness will increase as a result.

Niccolò Machiavelli, *The Prince*, 1513

WHY 9/11 STILL NEEDS TO BE INVESTIGATED:
THE COMMISSION AND THE REPORT

9/11 was the largest homicide by far in American history, yet it has never been adequately investigated. The public has been told of a conspiracy that included terrorist conspirators organized and financed abroad. But if U.S. defenses had functioned on that day as they had previously, the four planes at a minimum should have been intercepted by fighter aircraft. Yet we are told that even this did not happen. There is a domestic side to 9/11 as well, about which we still know next to nothing. Key evidence requested by the commission was initially withheld until subpoenas were issued, and some evidence was deliberately destroyed. Worse, there are systematic suppressions of evidence in the *9/11 Commission Report* itself, along with unresolved contradictions in testimony and occasional misrepresentations of some crucial facts.

This chapter and the next will explore these issues and make the case that Vice President Cheney is himself a suspect in the events of 9/11 who needs to be investigated further. To do this I do not, like so many, simply attack the *9/11 Commission Report*. Instead, I use its distortions as clues to what in the report is being suppressed. For the 9/11 report is an example of concerted cover-up, partly by omissions and just as important by its cherry-picking of evidence and contrived misrepresentations. More important, there is a consistent pattern in all this: to minimize Cheney's responsibility for what happened that day and conceal unexplained and disturbing actions by him.

I will argue the following:

1.   There has never been an adequate investigation of what happened on 9/11.

2.   The White House is principally responsible for the failure to investigate this massive homicide.

3.   The 9/11 Commission endorsed Vice President Cheney's account of his behavior that day and ignored other contradictory first-hand accounts from eyewitnesses inside the White House, including Cheney himself.

4.   Unexplained gaps in the documentary record remain that indicate cover-up; these gaps must be resolved.

5.   When a better record has been assembled, the man principally responsible for the U.S. responses (and lack of responses) on 9/11, Cheney himself, should be required to testify for the first time under oath.

THE OFFICIAL RESISTANCE TO INVESTIGATING 9/11

One of the conspicuous facts about 9/11 was the ongoing White House obstruction to an objective investigation of what happened. Initially President Bush "asked that only the House and Senate intelligence committees look into the potential breakdowns among federal agencies that could have allowed the terrorist attacks to occur, rather than a broader inquiry that some lawmakers have proposed."[1]

Thanks chiefly to sustained campaigning by a twelve-member Family Steering Committee of 9/11 victims' families (including the so-called Jersey Girls), Congress eventually created the 9/11 Commission, composed of five Republicans and five Democrats not currently in government.[2] In 2004 commission chair Thomas Kean paid lavish tribute to the Jersey Girls: "They call me all the time. . . . They monitor us, they follow our progress, they've supplied us with some of the best questions we've asked. I doubt very much if we would be in existence without them."[3] In the end, as this chapter shows, the 9/11 Commission and report simply ignored some of the best questions the Jersey Girls raised. In keeping with its statutory charge, the commission did a better job in dealing with the breakdowns of command and control communications on that day, an urgent and politically sensitive issue, than in addressing the Jersey Girls' questions about the circumstances of the attacks.

An account of the commission's activity by its cochairs, Republican Thomas Kean and Democrat Lee Hamilton, chronicles how difficult it was for the commission to produce a unanimous report in insufficient time and "a dramatically insufficient [initial] budget of $3 million."[4] One of its conclusions was that initially there had been what it called "incorrect" accounts by officials of the FAA and NORAD concerning their responses on 9/11.[5] This included contested testimony to the commission itself. Journalist Michael Bronner wrote later in *Vanity Fair*: "As the tapes reveal in stark detail, parts of [William] Scott's and [Larry] Arnold's testimony were misleading, and others simply false."[6]

Furthermore, as commission senior counsel John Farmer wrote later, "many of the Federal Aviation Administration and Defense Department records that establish the truth of that day were withheld from the commission until they were subpoenaed."[7] These withheld records included FAA and NEADS (Northeast Air Defense Sector of NORAD) audio tapes of the events on 9/11, as well as other internal documents that could someday be invaluable in any final reconstruction of what really happened. In short, the commission tacitly acknowledged that there had been a 9/11 cover-up, the crucial point made originally by the Jersey Girls and other so-called conspiracy theorists. The cover-up continues.

Critics of the official view of 9/11 tend to be completely dismissive of the *9/11 Commission Report*. It is more constructive to recognize that in many areas the report gives a useful and accurate summary of events. This recognition allows us to use the other parts of the report, the parts that are consistently misleading, as evidence—evidence of what is being suppressed. In their preface to the 9/11 report, Kean and Hamilton wrote that "we have endeavored to provide the most complete account we can of the events of September 11, what happened and why."[8] In their subsequent book, *Without Precedent*, they made the even bolder claim that the commission "cleared up inconsistencies . . . inconsistencies that had fed so many bizarre theories. Those who chose to continue believing conspiracy theories now had to rely solely on imagination, their theories having been disproved by facts."[9]

But there are still many serious problems, first raised by members of the Family Steering Committee, that the *9/11 Commission Report*, like the Kean-Hamilton book, simply failed to address.[10] To give one obvious example raised by the Jersey Girls: the FBI's executive assistant director for counterterrorism, Dale Watson, told Richard Clarke, the national counterterrorism coordinator, he had a list of alleged hijackers by 9:59 A.M. on 9/11, even before the crash of United Flight 93.[11] Within two weeks the identities of at least six of the hijackers identified by the FBI were unclear; men in Arab countries with the same names and histories (and in at least one case the same photograph) were protesting that they were alive and innocent.[12] In response to these protests, FBI director Robert Mueller acknowledged on September 20, 2001, that the identity of several of the suicide hijackers was in doubt.[13] But there is no trace of this doubt, or any discussion whatsoever of the problem, in the detailed treatment of the alleged hijackers in the *9/11 Commission Report*.[14]

Nor did the *9/11 Commission Report* address the Jersey Girls' question number 12, about the collapse of the forty-seven-story steel-framed building, World Trade Center 7 (WTC-7).[15] WTC-7 was 355 feet from the nearest of the two towers hit by planes, yet it collapsed neatly into its footprint some seven hours after the towers fell. The first alleged reason was fire, but, as the *New York Times* observed, "No other modern, steel-reinforced skyscraper except for the trade towers themselves has ever collapsed in a fire."[16] More recently, official investigators have pointed to debris damage from the collapsing North Tower, but this does not easily explain the vertical precision with which WTC-7 collapsed into its own footprint.[17] Although I myself am an agnostic concerning how WTC-7 collapsed, I find it symptomatic that the 9/11 report failed to discuss it.

A CENTRAL QUESTION:
WAS CHENEY IN CHARGE ON 9/11?

More serious are the places where the report presents a claim as true that is contested and simply ignores the powerful evidence against the claim. Central to the report's analysis of the U.S. failure to stop the 9/11 attacks was the claim that crisis management on that day was decentralized among three independent teleconferences—in the FAA, the White House, and the National Military Command Center (NMCC). For this reason, says the report, the government failed to generate a timely and coordinated response to the hijackings.[18] As famously summarized by the 9/11 Committee cochairs on the *Jim Lehrer News* hour: "When everyone is to blame . . . no one is to blame."[19]

However, it is pretty clear that the two most important orders of that day—an order grounding planes and a later shoot-down order—were both issued to all three teleconferences from a single source. The source was Dick Cheney in (or near) the Presidential Emergency Operations Center, in the bunker underneath the White House. Cheney himself told NBC's Tim Russert on September 16, 2001, only five days later:

Vice Pres. Cheney: I went down into what's call[ed] a PEOC, the Presidential Emergency Operations Center, and there, I had Norm Mineta . . .

Mr. Russert: Secretary of Transportation.

Vice Pres. Cheney: . . . secretary of Transportation, access to the FAA. I had Condi Rice with me and several of my key staff people. We had access, secured communications with Air Force One, with the secretary of Defense over in the Pentagon. We had also the secure videoconference that ties together the White House, CIA, State, Justice, Defense—a very useful and valuable facility. We have the counterterrorism task force up on that net. And so I was in a position to be able to see all the stuff coming in, receive reports and then make decisions in terms of acting with it. But when I arrived there within a short order, we had word the Pentagon's been hit.[20]

I shall argue that this early account by Cheney of his central role is far more accurate than his later account, repeated in the *9/11 Commission Report*, in which he claimed to have arrived in the PEOC shortly before 10:00 A.M. (twenty minutes after the Pentagon was hit at 9:37 A.M.), by which time (I shall argue) both of these two important orders had already been made. There is no doubt that the first order was issued around 9:42 A.M. I shall argue that before 9:54 A.M. a later order was issued through the PEOC, which for the first time, according to Clarke, included a shoot-down order for "the use of force against aircraft deemed to be hostile." Clarke claims he himself received this order by telephone from the PEOC and promulgated it to his teleconference, including Defense Secretary Rumsfeld and General Myers, vice chairman of the Joint Chiefs of Staff.[21]

WHO ISSUED THE ORDER FOR PLANES TO LAND?

There are a number of other occasions when the report, suppressing contrary accounts, presents only those versions of events that will exonerate or minimize the role of Cheney. This happens regularly enough to establish what I have elsewhere called a "negative template" or significant pattern of recurring suppression.[22] The details thus suppressed can be seen as indications or clues as to what is being suppressed. An example that at first may seem insignificant, but is not, is the question of who ordered all planes to land, shortly after 9:42 A.M., at the nearest airport. In the 9/11 report the order is attributed to the man who promulgated it, FAA national operations manager Benedict Sliney (who was on his first day at the job).[23] This is in accord with Sliney's own testimony to commission member Slade Gorton:

Mr. Gorton: And would you describe how you came to that decision and why you felt it imperative enough to make that decision without going through the usual command structure?

Mr. Sliney: I believed I had the authority to do those things on that day. I was charged with the safe and efficient operation of the national airspace system. . . .

As to the order to land, that was the product of the men and women in the Command Center who gave me advice on that day, the supervisors and the specialists. We were searching for something more to do, and that was made and decided on, and the impetus for that of course was the crash into the Pentagon when we gave that order.[24]

According to Sliney, the order was subsequently approved by his superiors, including FAA deputy administrator Monte Belger and eventually "minutes later" by transportation secretary Norman Mineta in the PEOC.[25]

But a year earlier Mineta had testified to Congress (as he would later to the 9/11 Commission) that he himself, from the PEOC, issued the order: "On the morning of September 11th, on first word of the attack, I moved directly to the Presidential Emergency Operations Center in the White House. As soon as I was aware of the nature and scale of the attack, I called from the White House to order the air traffic system to land all aircraft, immediately and without exception."[26]

According to a Bob Woodward story, the order was given to Belger by Mineta in the PEOC, with Cheney nearby and nodding approvingly:

Mineta shouted into the phone to Monte Belger at the FAA: "Monte, bring all the planes down." It was an unprecedented order—there were 4,546 airplanes in the air at the time. Belger, the FAA's acting deputy administrator, amended Mineta's directive to take into account the authority vested in airline pilots. "We're bringing them down per pilot discretion," Belger told the secretary.

"[Expletive] pilot discretion," Mineta yelled back. "Get those goddamn planes down."

Sitting at the other end of the table, Cheney snapped his head up, looked squarely at Mineta and nodded in agreement.[27]

Interviewed by *Aviation Security International Magazine* a few months later, Mineta confirmed that he had issued the order to Belger: "I said to

Monte, 'bring all the planes down.' . . . Monte said, 'we'll bring all the planes down per pilot discretion.' . . . I said to Monte, 'to hell with pilot discretion, get all the planes down.'"[28] Nine months later Mineta confirmed this account again to the 9/11 Commission, in testimony the 9/11 report ignores: "And so at approximately 9:45 A.M., less than one hour after I had first been notified of an airplane crash in New York, I gave the FAA the final order for all civil aircraft to land at the nearest airport as soon as possible. It was the first shutdown of civil aviation in the history of the United States."[29]

The commission thus heard two conflicting accounts of who ordered the order to land and simply suppressed one of them. As on other occasions, it also passed over an obvious opportunity to reconcile the two stories. On June 17, 2004, Belger testified publicly to the commission, on the same panel as Sliney.[30] Like Mineta earlier, Belger was not asked about the order from the PEOC, which Cheney reportedly agreed to by nodding his head.

In the end the 9/11 Commission reported only the story from Sliney that distanced Cheney from the 9:45 A.M. decision, ignoring Mineta's and Woodward's. It had to. The report's chronology was not compatible with the Mineta-Woodward story, because of its claim, ignoring other Mineta testimony, that Cheney did not arrive in the PEOC *until thirteen minutes later, at 9:58*. We see here a phenomenon in the report that we will encounter over and over. As elsewhere, the report promoted a story minimizing Cheney's importance and suppressed a conflicting firsthand story from an important eyewitness. I agree with author David Ray Griffin that this repeated suppression suggests intentionality, "not to provide the fullest possible account of 9/11 but to defend the account provided by the Bush administration and the Pentagon."[31]

WHEN *DID* CHENEY ARRIVE AT THE PEOC?

Every serious critique of the *9/11 Commission Report* has focused on the conflict between Mineta's testimony to the commission, that when he entered the PEOC at about 9:20, Cheney was already there, and the claim in the 9/11 report, ignoring Mineta's testimony, "that the Vice President arrived in the room shortly before 10:00, perhaps at 9:58."[32]

David Ray Griffin calls the report's claim, that the vice president arrived in the room shortly before 10:00, an "obvious lie."[33] But it is arguably not a lie in the sense of a deliberate baseless falsehood; I shall argue in the following pages that Cheney did enter the room at this time, as logs are said to indicate. But I suspect there is misrepresentation in the word "arrived." I believe that in fact Cheney had first arrived a half hour or more earlier and then returned from the PEOC to the tunnel to have an important phone call in seclusion with the president, before returning at 9:58.

The important claim that Cheney had first arrived well before 9:58 does not rely on Mineta's testimony alone. Clarke wrote that he saw Cheney preparing to leave the White House with an extra contingent of Secret Service, some time long before 9:28.[34] As just noted, Cheney himself told Tim Russert of *Meet the Press* on September 16, 2001, in an interview still available five years later on the White House Web site, that he arrived in the PEOC before the Pentagon was hit—that is, before 9:37 A.M.[35] In a brief note, *Newsweek* on December 31, 2001, repeated this story.[36] But the 9/11 report follows a second and much longer account in the same issue of *Newsweek*, based on an interview with Cheney six weeks earlier, which now had him leave his office at 9:35 and arrive in the PEOC "shortly before 10 A.M."[37] New evidence, which only surfaced in 2006, makes Cheney's revised timetable extremely unlikely.

The issue of when Cheney arrived in the PEOC is not trivial. What is at stake here is whether he was present to give or approve two and possibly three important orders before 10 A.M.: one alleged order (whose content is unknown) at about 9:25, a second unquestioned order to land at about 9:45, and a third (an important tripartite order we shall return to) at about 9:50. By Mineta's account, corroborated by Clarke, Cheney would have arrived in the PEOC in time to give all three of these orders; by Cheney's revised account, he arrived after they were all given. The report flagrantly, and symptomatically, failed to deal with Mineta's and Clarke's testimony.

NEW EVIDENCE FOR MINETA'S STORY:
A "THIRD AIRCRAFT" INCOMING AT 9:21 A.M.

There was another, even more disturbing aspect of Mineta's testimony to the 9/11 Commission, also ignored, for which there was also corroboration. Mineta testified that he arrived at the PEOC "at about 9:20 A.M.," at which point Cheney was already present and in charge. Shortly ("probably five or six minutes") after, Mineta observed the following: "During the time that the airplane [was] coming in to the Pentagon [t]here was a young man who had come in and said to the vice president, 'The plane is 50 miles out. The plane is 30 miles out.' And when it got down to 'The plane is 10 miles out,' the young man also said to the vice president, 'Do the orders still stand?' And the vice president turned and whipped his neck around and said, 'Of course the orders still stand. Have you heard anything to the contrary?' "[38]

Commissioner Timothy J. Roemer, questioning Mineta, established that this would have been "about 9:25 or 9:26." As 9/11 chronicler Paul Thompson has observed in his book *Terror Timeline*, ABC News on September 11, 2002, quoting a comment on the episode from deputy FAA administrator Monte Belger, supplied the same PEOC dialogue and time frame, about a plane fifty miles out, at approximately 9:27 A.M.[39] However, the 9/11 Commission claimed that "a primary radar target tracking eastbound at a high rate of speed" toward Dulles airport (Flight 77) was only discovered at 9:32 A.M.[40]

In 2006, in connection with the release of the movie *Flight 93*, the public learned for the first time that tapes from the Northeast Air Defense Sector of NORAD (NEADS), contained the following relevant event, corroborating Mineta's story:

9:21:37

[Master Sergeant Maureen] Dooley: Another hijack! It's headed towards Washington!

[Major Kevin] Naspany: Shit! Give me a location.

Unidentified Male: Okay. Third aircraft—hijacked—heading toward Washington.[41]

This urgent message is not repeated in the 9/11 report. It should have been. It explains the order to launch fighter aircraft from Langley at 9:24 A.M.[42] It corroborates Cheney's original account of his movements (that he arrived in the PEOC before the Pentagon was hit at 9:37). And it discredits the 9/11 report's estimate that an approaching plane *at 9:34 or 9:35* "prompted the Secret Service to order the immediate evacuation of the Vice President [from his White House Office] just before 9:36."[43]

Richard Clarke revealed in his book that "Secret Service had a system that allowed them to see what FAA's radar was seeing."[44] Thus Secret Service probably knew instantly of the 9:21 alarm. It is inconceivable that they first did nothing for fourteen minutes and then at 9:35 acted so precipitously that (according to Cheney himself) they grabbed the vice president by his belt, "hoisted" him up so that his feet barely touched the ground, and propelled him to the PEOC.[45]

The footnotes to this claim in the *9/11 Commission Report* appear to have been constructed with great care. But there has been cherry-picking of the evidence. The footnotes cite a Secret Service timeline memo for the vice president's entry into the PEOC (9:58) and also into the tunnel (9:36). (These times would be accurate, if Cheney entered the tunnel around 9:36—but from the PEOC end, thus not for the first time that day—and then returned to the PEOC at 9:58.) But what about the report's estimated departure from the vice president's office "just before 9:36"? This should be easily verifiable or falsifiable from the Secret Service timeline, but here the timeline is significantly not cited.[46]

At first glance the NEADS report of an incoming third aircraft at 9:21 A.M. would appear to be the plane Mineta referred to. The event also fits neatly with NORAD general Larry Arnold's initial testimony to the commission that NORAD learned of Flight 77's hijacking at 9:24 A.M.[47] The 9/11 report rejected Arnold's testimony as "incorrect." It meant by this that the plane reported was not *identified* as Flight 77; instead, these were "reports about a plane that no longer existed: American 11" (that had already struck the World Trade Center).[48] Thus, the report claimed, NEADS air defenders had "no advance notice on the third" plane (Flight 77).[49]

However, the real issue is not the identification of the plane, but the fact of urgent concern that a plane was indeed "headed toward Washington." This corroborates Mineta's detailed account of this moment to *Aviation Security International Magazine*: "I was sitting across the table from the Vice President with a set of telephones providing us with a direct line to FAA. Someone came in and said, 'Mr. Vice President there's a plane 50 miles out.' I was on the phone with the Deputy Administrator of FAA, Monte Belger, and he said, 'we have a target but the transponder's turned off, so we have no identification, no ident, on the aircraft.' I said, 'Can you tell in relationship to the ground where it is?' He said, 'no that's difficult to do but I would imagine it's somewhere between Great Falls and National Airport coming in.' It seemed it was on what they call the DRA—the down river approach."[50]

The route allegedly described by Belger approximates the eastward route that was being followed in this timeframe by American 77. Once again, there is no sign that Belger was interrogated about this. His testimony could have been pertinent to the report's claim that there was no awareness of Flight 77 at this time.[51] More important, it could have confirmed or refuted Mineta's detailed account of what happened at this time in the PEOC.

The Scrambling of Planes from Langley

Unquestionably the 9:21 report of a third hijack was a crucial event on September 11. It led immediately to the launching by NEADS of planes from Langley, Virginia:

9:21:50

Naspany: O.K. American Airlines is still airborne—11, the first guy. He's heading towards Washington. O.K., I think we need to scramble Langley right now. And I'm—I'm gonna take the fighters from Otis and try to chase this guy down if I can find him.[52]

The *9/11 Commission Report* confirmed this: "After consulting with NEADS command, the crew commander issued the order at 9:23: 'Okay . . . scramble Langley. Head them towards the Washington area. . . . [I]f they're there then we'll run on them. . . . These guys are smart.' That order was processed and transmitted to Langley Air Force Base at 9:24. Radar data show the Langley fighters airborne at 9:30."[53] Because of the misidentification, the report referred to this as "a response to a phantom aircraft . . . an aircraft that did not exist."[54]

Coauthors Thomas Kean and Lee Hamilton, relying on the same quibble about the plane's identification, are even more misleading: "NORAD claimed that the Langley jets were scrambled in pursuit of . . . American 77. Yet that was impossible. At 9:24, NORAD had not yet been notified that American 77 had been hijacked."[55] It was not impossible. On the contrary it was almost certainly the case, even if controllers were not yet aware of the identity of the plane to which they were responding.

This handling of the plane alarm illustrates the distinction between an outright lie and a deliberately constructed deception. The report's claim, that aircraft were scrambled in "response to a phantom aircraft," is carefully crafted language, which a lawyer could conceivably persuade a courtroom judge to accept as not untrue. Yet the impression created, that NORAD was not warned early enough to deal with the approaching plane, was materially misleading, indeed false.[56]

THE REPORT'S UNLIKELY ALTERNATIVE TO MINETA'S STORY

Mineta, in telling his story to the 9/11 Commission, stated unambiguously that the story referred to "the plane coming in to the Pentagon"— that is, Flight 77. In 2002, after Mineta had already testified about the incoming plane to Congress, the White House floated an alternative story, implying that Mineta got both the time and the plane wrong.

In September 2002, relying on interviews with Cheney and his chief of staff Joshua Bolten, CNN suggested that a dialogue similar to that reported by Mineta did occur but with respect to Flight 93, some time after the Pentagon was hit at 9:37:

> After the planes struck the twin towers, a third took a chunk out of the Pentagon. Cheney then heard a report that a plane over Pennsylvania was heading for Washington. A military assistant asked Cheney twice for authority to shoot it down.
>
> "The vice president said yes again," remembered Josh Bolten, deputy White House chief of staff. "And the aide then asked a third time. He said, 'Just confirming, sir, authority to engage?' And the vice president—his voice got a little annoyed then—said, 'I said yes.'"[57]

The *9/11 Commission Report* did not refer to this important Cheney-Bolten allegation. Indeed, it tacitly implied that the story was false, by suggesting that there was no military response to Flight 93 and that the only shoot-down order occurred after Cheney entered the PEOC at 10:00.[58]

Instead, by relying on the notes of Cheney's wife, Lynne Cheney, and of Bolten, the *9/11 Commission Report* recorded a slightly different refinement of the Cheney-Bolten story, unambiguously postponing the dialogue until *after* Flight 93 was downed at 10:03:

> At some time between 10:10 and 10:15, a military aide told the Vice President and others that the aircraft was 80 miles out. . . . The Vice President authorized fighter aircraft to engage the inbound plane. . . . The military aide returned a few minutes later, probably between 10:12 and 10:18, and said the aircraft was 60 miles out. He again asked for authorization to engage. The Vice President again said yes. . . . Bolten watched the exchanges and . . . suggested that the Vice President get in touch with the President and confirm the engage order. . . . The Vice President was logged calling the President at 10:18 for a two-minute conversation that obtained the confirmation. . . . At approximately 10:30, the shelter started receiving reports of another hijacked plane, this time only 5 to 10 miles out. . . . [T]he Vice President again communicated the authorization to "engage" or "take out" the aircraft.[59]

No one has suggested that nearly identical versions of the incoming plane story occurred two or three times in the space of less than an hour.[60] Thus investigators should be granted access to the notes of Lynne Cheney and Lewis Libby, which suggested that the story of the incoming plane occurred an hour later than Mineta claimed.[61] As we shall see in a moment, this is not the only situation where someone's account of what happened not only must be wrong, but may possibly have been falsified.

With respect to the earlier Mineta version of the story, we must ask what would have been the orders that Mineta claims to have heard Cheney allude to. We do not know of a shoot-down order at this time. And above all, as Griffin notes, it would make little sense for the young man to ask, when the plane was ten miles out, if *shoot-down* orders still stood.

Griffin raised the alternative, that it was a *stand-down* order: "Some critics of the official account have suggested therefore that "the orders" in question were orders *not* to have the aircraft shot down. But of course this interpretation, while arguably being the more natural one, would also be very threatening to the Bush administration and the Pentagon."[62]

THE DISPUTED TRIPARTITE ORDER OF ABOUT 9:50 A.M.: WAS THIS A SHOOT-DOWN ORDER?

With respect to the shoot-down order, all accounts agree that it emerged from an important call between the president and vice president, about which I say more in the next chapter. The 9/11 Commission, having received no record of the call, wrote that "we believe this call would have taken place some time before 10:10 to 10:15."[63] Their time estimate is consistent with their claim that the shoot-down order was given too late to affect the fate of Flight 93 (down between 10:03 and 10:07 A.M.).[64]

But the 9/11 report ignored the account of the national counterterrorism coordinator, Richard Clarke. In his book *Against All Enemies*, he wrote that he was first instructed from the PEOC, "Air Force One is getting ready to take off. . . . Tell the Pentagon they have authority from the President to shoot down hostile aircraft, repeat, they have authority to shoot down hostile aircraft." He transmitted the shoot-down order by telephone to his teleconference, which included both Rumsfeld and General Myers at the Pentagon: "Gen. Myers asked, 'Okay, shoot down aircraft, but what are the ROE [Rules of Engagement]?'"[65] As Air Force One took off at 9:54 A.M., this account would mean that the shoot-down order came some time before the downing of Flight 93.

The 9/11 report ignored Clarke's account, which like Mineta's was incompatible with their chronology. Instead, the report wrote, using lawyerly language: "We do not know who from Defense participated [in Clarke's teleconference], but we know that in the first hour none of the personnel involved in managing the crisis did."[66] Against the very explicit claim of Clarke that he engaged in dialogue with both Rumsfeld and Myers at this time, the report cites a minor Pentagon official—"On the absence of Defense officials, see John Brunderman interview (May 17, 2004)"[67]—an official who almost certainly was *not* part of the White House teleconference.[68]

The White House teleconference was videotaped. I would expect such videotape typically to have been retained, and the commission, even before facing this discrepancy, to have reviewed it. There is no sign that they ever obtained it, however, or even tried to. In tacit rejection of Clarke's version, furthermore, they accepted the conflicting claim (which I examine in chapter 13) that "after the Pentagon was struck, Secretary Rumsfeld went to the parking lot to assist with rescue efforts."[69]

To sum up: If Mineta and Clarke are correct, two important orders were issued on the morning of 9/11 before 10 A.M., both from the PEOC, where Cheney was in command. With respect to both orders, the commission presented a different and incompatible account and made no effort to reconcile the conflicting accounts. On the contrary, it ignored the contradictory and authoritative claims made by Mineta and Clarke, even though Mineta's claims were made in testimony to the commission itself, and Clarke was also a witness. These two orders must be considered in conjunction with a third important order that preceded 9/11 and reportedly changed the rules of command for dealing with suspected hijackings of aircraft.

WAS THERE A CHANGE IN THE RULES OF COMMAND BEFORE 9/11?

The failure to intercept the hijackings demands a more thorough explanation than the report offers. The FAA reported sixty-seven interceptions between September 2000 and June 2001.[70] The *Calgary Herald* reported that in 2000 there were 425 instances of pilots who aroused concern and that fighters were scrambled in response to 129 cases whose problems were not immediately resolved.[71] A celebrated example of interception was with the crippled airplane of golfer Payne Stewart in 1999, which had fighter aircraft close to seventy-nine minutes after it first failed to respond to air controllers.[72]

If interceptions of off-course aircraft were, as late as June 2001, a standard procedure, why, according to the *9/11 Commission Report*, were there none on 9/11?[73] A number of professionals have raised this question. Perhaps the strongest indictment of Bush and Cheney for their role in the 9/11 disaster came from Robert M. Bowman, a former director of Advanced Space Programs Development for the U.S. Air Force during the Ford and Carter administrations, and a former U.S. Air Force lieutenant colonel with 101 combat missions. He said in 2005: "If our government had merely done nothing—and I say that as an old interceptor pilot and I know the drill, I know what it takes, I know how long it takes, I know what the procedures are, I know what they were and I know what they changed them to—if our government had merely done nothing and allowed normal procedures to happen on that morning of 9/11, the twin towers would still be standing and thousands of dead Americans would still be alive."[74]

When I asked Bowman what procedural changes he was referring to, he replied: "A few months before 9/11 (June 2001, I think), the Pentagon issued a new document stating that any request for intercept must be approved by the SecDef [Secretary of Defense Rumsfeld]."[75] Like other critics, he was referring to the issuance, on June 1, 2001, of a Joint Chiefs of Staff (JCS) memo, specifying that (in the words of the report) "military assistance from NORAD required multiple levels of notification and approval at the highest levels of government."[76]

The report itself blamed the failure of the U.S. government to respond appropriately to the hijackings in large part to an existing procedural protocol that "was unsuited in every respect for what was about to happen."[77] It too cited the JCS memo of June 1, 2001, specifying that (in the words of the report) "military assistance from NORAD . . . required approval at the highest levels of government."[78] The effect of the JCS memo, as so interpreted, was to erase the earlier distinction between an intercept decision in an emergency (a plane off course) and a shoot-down order (in the case of a confirmed hijacking). It had always been the case that, as Richard Clarke noted in his memoir, "the military would expect clear instructions before they used force." But the normal request from the FAA to NORAD for "military assistance" is for an interception, not a shoot down. After 9/11, according to the *Boston Globe*, "Marine Corps Major Mike Snyder, a spokesman for NORAD headquarters . . . said its fighters *routinely* intercept aircraft. When planes are intercepted, they typically are handled with graduated response. The approaching fighter may rock its wingtips . . . or make a pass in front of the aircraft. Eventually it can fire tracer rounds in the airplane's path, or, under certain circumstances, down it with a missile."[79]

As noted earlier, the FAA reported sixty-seven interceptions between September 2000 and June 2001.[80] It is inconceivable that in this period requests for *interceptions* were cleared by "the highest levels of government." Yet Department of Defense records obtained by the 9/11 Commission show that only at 10:31 on September 11 did Major General Larry Arnold tell NORAD: "[the] Vice president has cleared us to intercept tracks of interest and shoot them down if they do not respond."[81] The NEADS audio file has essentially the same message.[82] Cheney himself referred to the intercept order as the "toughest decision" Bush and he made that day, equating interception of a plane with shooting it down.[83]

But the report showed no curiosity whatsoever as to why this problematic memo was promulgated ten weeks before 9/11, or who was responsible for it. It would have been easy to have asked this question of General Richard B. Myers, vice chairman of the Joint Chiefs of Staff, who was interviewed three times by the commission.[84] As far as is known, the commission did not ask the question. Because most emergency response regulations are secret, it is impossible to evaluate the degree to which changes in regulations complicated NORAD's ability to respond to the hijacked planes. What can be said is that the 9/11 report failed to investigate the origins of the June 1 JCS memo that apparently made interceptions a matter for the White House. (I have been told that the old more permissive procedure was restored in December 2001.)[85]

WHO WAS RESPONSIBLE FOR THE CHANGE?

To explain the lack of interceptions on 9/11, researcher Michael Ruppert also pointed to the issuance of the June 1, 2001, memo. Ruppert, who interviewed many people inside the military and especially NORAD, concluded that the change can be traced to the White House announcement of May 8, 2001, in which President Bush "asked Vice President Cheney to oversee the development of a coordinated national effort" against terrorist weapons of mass destruction.[86] Cheney's group, known as the National Preparedness Review, was tasked to evaluate and make recommendations to strengthen preparedness against acts of domestic terrorism.[87]

As the *Houston Chronicle* reported the next day, "President Bush on Tuesday directed [FEMA] . . . to tackle the additional task of dealing with terrorist attacks. . . . To accomplish that goal, Bush appointed Vice President Dick Cheney to head a terrorism task force and created the Office of National Preparedness within the Federal Emergency Management

Agency."[88] Not noticed by the press was the fact (discussed in the last chapter) that Cheney, Rumsfeld, and FEMA had been working as a team throughout the 1980s and 1990s to develop plans and exercises for COG or "Continuity of Government.[89] These were extreme, controversial, and highly secretive plans "to establish a new American 'president' and his staff, outside and beyond the specifications of the U.S. constitution."[90]

In reporting this, James Mann noted correctly that the purpose of the plans was "to keep the federal government running during and after a nuclear war with the Soviet Union." He did not mention, however, that the planning eventually called for suspension of the Constitution, not just "after a nuclear war" but for any "national security emergency." This was defined in Executive Order 12656 of 1988 as "any occurrence, including natural disaster, military attack, technological emergency, or other emergency, that seriously degrades or seriously threatens the national security of the United States."[91] As noted in the last chapter, the COG plans were thought by many to have been downplayed or dropped in the 1990s under Clinton. But instead they were implemented by Cheney on September 11, 2001.[92]

It is of interest that the 1980s team of Cheney and FEMA was reconstituted and charged, five months before 9/11, with the assignment of *preparing* for how to deal with terrorist attacks. It is of further interest that the Bush administration appointed to head FEMA Joe Allbaugh, who in 2000 managed the Bush-Cheney campaign and later was involved in the so-called 19th Floor Riot that stopped the ballot recount in Miami-Dade County.[93] I consider the appointment of a dirty-tricks specialist to head the supposedly apolitical agency FEMA a symptom that Bush-Cheney had political designs for FEMA from the outset of their administration. It has been alleged that Cheney's terrorism task force accomplished little. But no one to my knowledge has challenged Ruppert's linking of Cheney's group to the issuance of the JCS memo "Aircraft Piracy (Hijacking) and Destruction of Derelict Airborne Objects."

After June 1, Cheney is said to have spent the entire month of August at his home in Teton Pines, Wyoming.[94] But this news item is less innocuous when we recall that Cheney, as part of his secret COG planning, had "regularly gone off to undisclosed locations in the 1980s."[95] On either August 4 or August 6, the president also left Washington "for his Crawford ranch for nearly a month-long vacation."[96] August 6 was of course the date of the now-famous memo warning "Bin Laden Determined to Strike in U.S." (after which the president reportedly "broke off work early and spent most of the day fishing").[97] Why at this point did the president and the vice president both stay out of town? Had Cheney resorted to his 1980s practice of planning in a parallel structure via outside channels?

Chapter 13 explores the possibility that Bush, Cheney, and Rumsfeld were communicating via outside channels on 9/11 itself as the best explanation for why there is no record of the single most important order given on that day. I argue that although much of the *9/11 Commission Report* is well researched, professional, and credible, on the matter of Cheney's orders, the report resorts to deceptive and contrived misrepresentations of the truth.

This raises the important question of what deeper truth is being concealed by these misrepresentations.

THIRTEEN

THE *9/11 COMMISSION REPORT*'S AND CHENEY'S DECEPTIONS ABOUT 9/11

> If we take these new regions, we shall be well entangled in that
> contest for territorial aggrandizement which distracts other
> nations and drives them far beyond their original design. So
> it will be inevitably with us. We shall want new conquests to
> protect that which we already possess. The greed of specula-
> tors working upon our government will push us from one
> point to another, and we shall have new conflicts upon our
> hands, almost without knowing how we got into them.
>
> **Carl Schurz, 1899**

WHY DID DICK CHENEY SPEND SO MUCH TIME IN THE PEOC TUNNEL?

Cheney's Two Evacuation Stories

As we saw in the last chapter, the 9:21 report of an approaching plane also corroborates Cheney's original account of his movements (that he arrived in the PEOC before Flight 77 hit the Pentagon at 9:37). It renders suspect the 9/11 report's estimate that an approaching plane at 9:34 or 9:35 "prompted the Secret Service to order the immediate evacuation of the Vice President [from his White House Office] 'just before 9:36.'"[1] It is time to compare his two divergent accounts more closely and to see that by both accounts his hurried departure from his office led to an unexplained pause in the tunnel. More important, Cheney made impor- tant phone calls to the president in the seclusion of the tunnel, rather than from the PEOC. I argue in this chapter that his reason for doing this is because in the phone calls important decisions were made about continuity of government, too highly classified to be made in front of witnesses.

According to Cheney's *Meet the Press* interview with Tim Russert on September 16, the Secret Service evacuated him from his office in response to "a report that an airplane was headed for the White House . . . which turned out to be Flight 77." As Cheney told Russert: "Once I got down into the shelter, the first thing I did—there's a secure phone there. First thing I did was pick up the telephone and call the president again, who was still down in Florida, at that point, and strongly urged him to delay his return. . . . Once I left that immediate shelter, after I talked to the president, urged him to stay away for now, well, I went down into what's call[ed] a PEOC. [Note the distinction here between the "shelter" and the PEOC bunker.] . . . But when I arrived there within a short order, we had word the Pentagon's been hit." In the same interview Cheney discussed continuity of government planning at some length, and he specified that the decision implementing it (made before 9:54, according to counterterrorism coordinator Richard Clarke) was made "later on that day."[2]

The different timeline in the report (evacuation at 9:36, arrival in the PEOC "shortly before 10 A.M.") relies on a later Cheney interview with *Newsweek* on November 19, 2001, the source of the following long account in *Newsweek* on December 31:

> At about 9:35 A.M., Vice President Cheney was standing by his desk, looking at the TV in the corner. A Secret Service agent said to him, in a tone that brooked no dissent, "Sir, we have to leave now." The agent grabbed the vice president by the back of his belt and aimed him at the door. . . . Down the hallway, past the empty Oval Office, the vice president was rushed into a tunnel outside a bombproof bunker known as the PEOC, the Presidential Emergency Operations Center. About 30 miles away, at Dulles airport, air-traffic controllers were watching agape as a plane raced toward Washington at 500 miles an hour. A controller looking at a radar screen had noticed the blip, heading straight for the White House, about 12 miles out. As ABC's *20/20* later reconstructed the scene, another controller called the Secret Service: "We have unidentified, very fast-moving aircraft inbound toward your vicinity, eight miles west." In the Dulles radar room, the horrified air-traffic controllers counted down the miles. Five, four, three—then the plane began to turn away. . . . Shortly before 10 A.M., the Cheneys [Dick and Lynne] were led into the PEOC conference room. . . . It was 9:58 A.M.[3]

Relying on the November *Newsweek* interview, the report (I believe correctly) talked of a fifteen-minute delay in the tunnel, part of which was consumed in establishing a phone call to the president, "advising that three planes were missing and one had hit the Pentagon." Offering no evidence, the report stated: "We believe that this is the same call in which the Vice President urged the President not to return to Washington."[4] But there is strong evidence (to which I will return) that this was the call Clarke says was made before 9:54, instituting a tripartite order for both COG and authority to shoot down planes. The report thus disregarded Cheney's own remarks to Russert on September 16 that his advice not to return and the order for COG were made at two different times. The simplest way to reconcile Cheney's two statements is to extract from them that there were two periods spent in the tunnel (one before the Pentagon was hit, and one after), and that one phone call to the president was made in each period of seclusion. I shall have more to say about the important second call.

The most obvious conclusion from this mess of conflicting evidence is that both of Cheney's conflicting accounts of his evacuation cannot be true; one must be at least partly false. This does not make Cheney a liar; he could simply on reflection have had a better memory of what happened. But the likelihood of a conscious and deliberate cover-up is enhanced by the *9/11 Commission Report*'s total suppression of Cheney's first story, its elaborate protection of Cheney's second story, and above all its blatant failure to mention important contradictory evidence against the second story from the three most important eyewitnesses in the White House: Mineta, Clarke, and (as I have just shown) Cheney himself.

I conclude that Cheney was in the tunnel twice. On first entering the tunnel, he called the president and, in response to the 9:21 alarm, told him not to return to Washington. Cheney later returned to the tunnel from the PEOC and made the phone call for which (as I show below) there is no PEOC record, instituting the tripartite order.

The National Ground Stop Order

In the same time period as the Mineta story of an incoming plane, the FAA's Herndon Command Center ordered a "national ground stop" at 9:25 A.M.[5] FAA administrator Jane Garvey later called it "a national ground stop . . . that prevented any aircraft from taking off."[6] An early report from *Time* claimed that this national ground stop was also a no-fly order:

> At 9:25, Garvey, in an historic and admirable step, and almost certainly after getting an okay from the White House, initiated a national ground

stop, which forbids takeoffs and requires planes in the air to get down as soon as reasonable. The order, which has never been implemented since flying was invented in 1903, applied to virtually every single kind of machine that can take off—civilian, military, or law enforcement. The Herndon command center coordinated the phone call to all major FAA sites, the airline reps in the room contacted all airlines, and so-called NOTAMS—notices to airmen—were also sent out. The FAA had stopped the world. . . . At 10:31, the FAA allowed all military and law enforcement flights to resume (and some flights that the FAA can't reveal that were already airborne).[7]

The last sentence of this uncorroborated but detailed account would coincide neatly with Major General Larry Arnold's order to NORAD at 10:31: "[The] Vice president has cleared us to intercept tracks of interest and shoot them down if they do not respond."[8]

The attribution of the ground stop order to Garvey should not surprise us. Mineta told the 9/11 Commission that on arrival in the PEOC, "I established contact on two lines, one with my chief of staff at the Department of Transportation, and the second with Monty Belger, the acting deputy administrator of the FAA, and Jane Garvey, both of whom were in the [Herndon] FAA operations center."[9] Nevertheless, FAA national operations manager Benedict Sliney, Belger, and Mineta all agree that the official order to land was issued at about 9:42 A.M., after the crash of Flight 77 into the Pentagon.[10] Thus at the time of Cheney's alleged orders in Mineta's story (concerning the incoming plane), the only order we know of was Garvey's national ground stop.

FAA Regulation 7210.3 establishes that a ground stop "is a process that requires aircraft that meet a specific criteria [sic] to remain on the ground."[11] As so defined, a ground stop does not affect planes in the air. However, there are other indications that Garvey did also order down planes in the air, as *Time* claimed. An earlier order had already done this regionally. At 9:03 the New York air control center issued an "ATC zero" order to clear the skies in the area: "And not just the skies over Manhattan. Controllers must clear the air from southern New England to Maryland, from Long Island to central Pennsylvania—every mile of the region they control."[12] Clarke in *Against All Enemies* wrote that he first asked Garvey, at some time before 9:28, to "order aircraft down" and "clear the airspace around Washington and New York." Soon afterward he asked her if she was "prepared to issue a national ground stop and no fly order."[13]

It is reasonable to ask whether Garvey's ground stop order at 9:25 A.M. was relevant to the orders Mineta claims to have heard Cheney refer to in the same time frame. As we saw in the last chapter, author David Ray Griffin raised the possibility that it was a *stand-down* order: "orders *not* to have the aircraft shot down."[14] Another possibility is that the *Time* story is correct, and that Cheney was reaffirming a "no-fly" order that prohibited the Langley fighters from entering the Washington area.

A no-fly order would have had the same effect of letting the plane approach Washington unhindered. This possibility, which Kean and Hamilton treat with ridicule, would have been worthy of investigation by the commission. After all, Garvey's order of 9:25, according to *Time*, required "planes in the air to get down as soon as reasonable" and "applied to virtually every single kind of machine that can take off— civilian, military, or law enforcement."[15]

Putting together all I have compiled so far, we see that after 9:21 there were two orders issued within minutes of each other: the Northeast Air Defense Sector (NEADS) order scrambling planes to defend Washington and Garvey's order from the FAA, which may have declared a no-fly zone in the same area. If what I have reconstructed is accurate, Cheney's order may have allowed Garvey's FAA order (if truly a no-fly order) to override the scramble ordered by NEADS.

Griffin assumed that there could be no innocent explanation for this interpretation of Cheney's orders. But we cannot exclude one possible one: that Cheney thought he knew the plane in question to be a phantom. Indeed, the report's chronology can be said to corroborate this otherwise fantastic notion. It attributes the activity just before 9:30 to the "phantom aircraft" identified at 9:21 A.M.[16] Kean and Hamilton also write that "the air force jets from Langley were thus pursuing a phantom aircraft—American 11, not United 93 or American 77."[17] According to what the public has been told about this flight, it was somewhere north of Baltimore when fighters from Langley were dispatched to meet it at 9:30 A.M.[18] The *9/11 Commission Report* never tells us what happened to the radar track then. Did it disappear because it was in truth a phantom, and Cheney (perhaps alone of those in the PEOC) knew it?

WERE CHENEY AND FEMA PLANNING THE MULTIPLE WAR GAMES ON 9/11?

We now know that on 9/11 air defense was made more difficult by simultaneous operations, war games, and exercises, including an exercise at the National Reconnaissance Office near Dulles Airport, testing responses "if a plane were to strike a building."[19] At least one of these war games did involve phantom flights.

Only one of these war games, Vigilant Guardian, is referred to by the *9/11 Commission Report*, in a footnote.[20] In addition, Donald Rumsfeld told *Washington Post* reporters Dan Balz and Bob Woodward of another exercise, Global Guardian.[21] Further war operations that day deployed U.S. Air Force fighters to Iraq, Iceland, and Northern Canada. In addition, the *Toronto Star* revealed that Operation Northern Vigilance, at least, also involved "simulated information, what's known as an 'inject' [that is, an input or false blip] on radar screens." There is also a reference on the NEADS tape at 9:05 A.M. to "a damn input," meaning (as *Vanity Fair* author Bronner explained), "a simulations input" as part of one of the exercises that day.[22]

The war games may help explain why on that day the civilian and possibly also the military operations managers for aircraft were performing that role for the first time in their lives. The two men were the FAA Command Center's national operations manager, Ben Sliney, and the National Military Command Center's deputy operations manager, recently promoted Admiral-Select Charles Leidig.[23] Leidig told the commission, "On 10 September 2001, Brigadier General Winfield, U.S. Army, asked that I stand a portion of his duty on the following day." Winfield thus was freed from his usual post to spend the next morning (9/11) in the Pentagon War Room.[24]

Unambiguously the response to the 9/11 hijackings was made more difficult by the confusion that arose from the hijack/exercise overlap. Lieutenant Colonel Dawne Deskins, regional airborne control and warning officer for the Vigilant Guardian exercise, said that everyone at NEADS initially thought the first call they received about the real 9/11 hijackings was part of the war games scenario.[25] Major General Larry Arnold, the NORAD commander, initially asked of the Boston hijacks, "Is this part of the exercise?"[26] So did other officers, including Colonel Robert Marr, the head of NEADS in Rome, New York.[27]

9/11 researcher Michael Kane, summarizing the work of fellow researcher Mike Ruppert, has charged that through the Office of National Preparedness set up on May 8, 2001, Cheney and FEMA were planning the coordinated war games of 9/11:

On May 8, 2001—four months prior to 9/11—the president placed Dick Cheney in charge of "[A]ll federal programs dealing with weapons of mass destruction consequence management within the Departments of Defense, Health and Human Services, Justice, and Energy, the Environmental

Protection Agency, and other federal agencies." This included all "*training and planning*" which needed to be "*seamlessly integrated*, harmonious and comprehensive" in order to "maximize effectiveness." This mandate created the Office of National Preparedness in FEMA, overseen by Dick Cheney.

Dick Cheney was placed directly in charge of managing the seamless integration of all training exercises throughout the entire federal government and all military agencies. On 9/11 Cheney oversaw multiple war games and terror drills, including several exercises of NORAD, the Air Force agency whose mandate is to "watch the sky."[28]

In my opinion such remarks about Cheney's and FEMA's responsibilities for the war games of 9/11 can only be posed as a question, not as an assertion. But there is some evidence to support Kane's thesis in the Pentagon's own descriptions of Amalgam Virgo 01 and 02, two war games planned before 9/11. They reveal that FEMA was indeed involved in the planning for both Amalgam Virgo 01 (which included response to an offshore guided missile), from May 31 to June 4, 2001,[29] and Amalgam Virgo 02 (the hijacking of a commercial airliner), planning for which was begun *before* 9/11.[30]

The report failed to consider the extent to which the strange inability of NORAD to engage the hijacked planes was because of an excessive number of phantoms introduced by "injects" (false radar blips) on that day. On September 11, FAA administrator Jane Garvey told Richard Clarke of "reports of eleven aircraft off course or out of communication, maybe hijacked."[31] The *9/11 Commission Report* concurred that "during the course of the morning, there were multiple erroneous reports of hijacked aircraft."[32] *Aviation Week* wrote that on September 11, "21 aircraft across the U.S. had been handled as 'tracks of interest.'"[33] Colonel Marr at NEADS has said: "I think at one time [on September 11] I was told that across the nation there were some 29 different reports of hijackings."[34]

At one point there was a record that could have established more conclusively how the government responded on September 11, and whether either war games or phantom airplanes helped account for the lack of response. Shortly after the attacks, air traffic controllers who handled two of the hijacked flights recorded their experiences on tape. But the tape cassette was deliberately destroyed by an unidentified FAA quality assurance manager, who "crushed the cassette in his hand, cut the tape into small pieces and threw them away in multiple trash cans."[35] Such an extreme and possibly illegal action adds to suspicions that the full story of responses to the 9/11 attacks is as yet untold.

CLARKE'S WHITE HOUSE TELECONFERENCE:
WHICH IS THE FALSE ACCOUNT?

Because of the president's strange odyssey that day, the National Command Authority effectively devolved in his absence to Vice President Cheney, acting in conjunction with Secretary of Defense Rumsfeld, and the acting chairman of the Joint Chiefs, Air Force general Richard Myers. Despite the prominence of these men, the movements of all three on that morning are surrounded by mystery and controversy—mystery and controversy that are greatly compounded rather than resolved by the account in the *9/11 Commission Report*. This is a matter of crucial importance. For the *9/11 Commission Report* attributes the breakdown of the NORAD defense system on September 11 to the claim that these men at the top of the National Command Authority were out of touch with each other, so that there was no meaningful coordination of military and FAA response to the hijackings.[36]

I offer a three-part alternative hypothesis that has circumstantial evidence, partly from the report itself and partly from other authoritative sources. First, Cheney directed his own decision-making network from in or near the presidential bunker below the White House (the Presidential Emergency Operations Center, or PEOC). Second, Bush, Cheney, and Rumsfeld were indeed in touch, and all three discussed at least the tripartite decision for a shoot-down order and COG—but at a key moment when Cheney and Rumsfeld were both in seclusion from their own staffs. Third, as I detail below, Cheney had access to a special secure communications system, possibly through the Secret Service, to maintain these contacts, outside regular channels. In short, National Command Authority was operating through Cheney at the PEOC, and key decisions from Cheney were transmitted from the PEOC to the three teleconferences: the White House (Clarke's), the National Military Command Center (NMCC), and the FAA.

The report focuses instead on these three lower-level multiagency teleconferences. It claims that none of these achieved meaningful coordination, because "none of these teleconferences—at least before 10:00—included the right officials from both the FAA and Defense Department." The report states: "At the White House, the video teleconference was conducted from the Situation Room by Richard Clarke, a special assistant to the president long involved in counterterrorism. Logs indicate that it began at 9:25 and included the CIA; the FBI; the departments of State, Justice, and Defense; the FAA; and the White House shelter. The

FAA and CIA joined at 9:40. The first topic addressed in the White House video teleconference—at about 9:40—was the physical security of the President, the White House, and federal agencies. Immediately thereafter it was reported that a plane had hit the Pentagon. . . . Indeed, it is not clear to us that the video teleconference was fully under way before 9:37, when the Pentagon was struck."[37]

As already mentioned, the commission should have obtained the actual videotape of the teleconference and not relied on the secondary evidence of the White House Situation Room Communications Log. The report's claim, furthermore, is at odds with Clarke's own detailed account in his book *Against All Enemies*. (This book, after being held up for three months by the White House, was published before the *9/11 Commission Report*, but it is cited only in three later chapters, not in connection with what happened on September 11.)[38] Clarke does not specify a time for the beginning of his teleconference, but he claims to have completed three conversations before 9:28 A.M. with "the right officials": specifically with Garvey, Mineta, and Myers. Before any of these conversations, Clarke claims to have already seen Rumsfeld and CIA director George Tenet in his conference video screen.[39]

THE SUPPRESSED SYNCHRONOUS PAUSE AT 9:45 A.M.

Rumsfeld, Myers, and Cheney: Where Were They?

Clarke's account cannot be reconciled with the *9/11 Commission Report*'s version of the whereabouts of Myers, Rumsfeld, and Cheney. The commission, citing an interview with Myers himself, claims that Myers was "on Capitol Hill when the Pentagon was struck" (at 9:37 A.M.) and "saw smoke as his car made its way back" to the Pentagon.[40] Clarke says that he had completed an important teleconference dialogue with Myers *at the Pentagon* by 9:28 A.M., nine minutes *before* the Pentagon was struck.[41]

The commission presents an elaborate account of Rumsfeld's movements. It claims that he was in his office when he heard of the second strike on the World Trade Center towers; then, after the Pentagon was struck at 9:37, he "went to the parking lot to assist with rescue efforts."[42] Later, "he went from the parking lot to his office (where he spoke to the President), then to the Executive Support Center, where he participated in the White House video teleconference. He moved to the NMCC shortly before 10:30."[43] Thus there was a period of almost an hour when Rumsfeld was not where one would have expected him to have been—in command at the NMCC. As a senior official told author Andrew Cockburn, "What was Rumsfeld doing on 9/11? He deserted his post. He disappeared. The country was under attack. Where was the guy who controls America's defense? Out of touch!"[44]

Once again, the discrepancy with Clarke's account is extreme. Clarke writes that when the Pentagon was struck (9:37 A.M.), he commented, "I can still see Rumsfeld on the screen."[45] If true, this would mean that Rumsfeld was *not* in his office when the Pentagon was hit, but in the Executive Support Center, more than twenty minutes before the *9/11 Commission Report* puts him there.

As we have seen, the greatest discrepancy is with respect to the whereabouts of Vice President Cheney, the most important man in Washington that day. Clarke's account, which has Cheney leaving for the White House bunker or the PEOC by about 9:10 A.M., is supported by an eyewitness, White House photographer David Bohrer ("just after 9 A.M.").[46] Norman Mineta described Cheney's activities in the PEOC starting from around 9:20 A.M. However, the *9/11 Commission Report* has Cheney entering the tunnel "at 9:37," arriving at the PEOC "shortly before 10:00, perhaps at 9:58."[47]

Why would it take twenty-one minutes to traverse the short tunnel? According to the report: "Once inside, Vice President Cheney and the agents paused in an area of the tunnel that had a secure phone, a bench, and television. The Vice President asked to speak to the President, but it took time for the call to be connected. He learned in the tunnel that the Pentagon had been hit, and he saw television coverage of smoke coming from the building."[48] This account of Cheney's pause parallels the similar synchronous pause or isolation at around 9:45 A.M. in the timelines that morning of Rumsfeld (when according to the report he was "in the parking lot" of the Pentagon, "to assist with rescue efforts")[49] and above all, inexplicably, of President Bush.

The first accounts of 9/11 suppressed all reference to this synchronous pause. Bob Woodward's *Bush at War* said of Cheney's trip through the tunnel that he "had been *whisked* from his West Wing office by the Secret Service to the Presidential Emergency Operations Center, or PEOC."[50] Of Rumsfeld's peregrinations in the fifty-three minutes the NMCC was looking for him, Woodward wrote: "'I'm going inside,' Rumsfeld said, and *hurried* to the National Military Command Center."[51] I have already explained my belief that Cheney *was* whisked rapidly to the PEOC (where Mineta claimed to have observed him around 9:20 A.M.) and *also* that he reentered the PEOC from the tunnel at 9:58

A.M., as noted in the PEOC Shelter Log (a source I have no reason to question).[52] For some period in between Cheney, like Rumsfeld, was by all accounts not at his command post.

At this time there is a similar discrepancy in accounts about Bush's activity in Florida, although you would never know this from statements by Woodward and White House officials. And Bush's ten-minute delay at Sarasota Bradenton Airport (from 9:45 to 9:54 A.M.) is particularly incongruous, because the Secret Service had reportedly learned of a terrorist threat to the president in Sarasota, "just minutes after Bush left Booker Elementary."[53] Chief of staff Andrew Card corroborated this: "As we were heading to Air Force One . . . [we] learned, what turned out to be a mistake, but we learned that the Air Force One package could in fact be a target."[54]

An ABC correspondent who was there described the "mad-dash motorcade out to the airport."[55] This urgency is reflected by Woodward in his account: "The President's motorcade raced to the Sarasota Bradenton International Airport. He dashed up the steps and into his private front cabin and office on Air Force One. 'Be sure to get the first lady and my daughters protected,' was his first order to the Secret Service agents. 'Mr. President,' one of the agents said nervously, 'we need you to get seated as soon as possible.' Bush strapped in, and the plane accelerated down the runway, almost standing on its tail as it climbed rapidly."[56]

Woodward's account is corroborated by White House sources like presidential adviser Karl Rove, who told ABC News: "Before we could, both of us, sit down [in the plane cabin] and put on our seat belts, they were rolling the plane. And they stood that 747 on its tail and got it about 45,000 feet as quick as I think you can get a big thing like that in the air."[57] But according to the *9/11 Commission Report*, Rove's eyewitness account is misleading if not incorrect. As there is so much corroboration from the principals for both the mad-dash motorcade and the near vertical takeoff, it is surprising to read in the 9/11 report that the plane paused on the runway for *ten minutes* while the president conferred with Cheney.

> The President's motorcade departed at 9:35, and arrived at the airport between 9:42 and 9:45. During the ride the President learned about the attack on the Pentagon. He boarded the aircraft, asked the Secret Service about the safety of his family, and called the Vice President. According to notes of the call, at about 9:45 the President told the Vice President: "Sounds like we have a minor war going on here, I heard about the Pentagon. We're at war . . . somebody's going to pay.". . .

Air Force One departed at approximately 9:54, without any fixed destination. The objective was to get up in the air—as fast and as high as possible—and then decide where to go.[58]

In fact, almost the entire ten-minute delay may have been consumed by the phone call: "According to contemporaneous notes [from Washington], at 9:55 the Vice-President was still on the phone with the President advising that three planes were missing [which would have included United 93] and one had hit the Pentagon."[59] Why, in the context of a threat, did the president not phone Cheney from the air? Was there a decision to be made that was too urgent to wait?

THE PAUSE AND THE TRIPARTITE ORDER: WAS IT FIRST MADE OUTSIDE CHANNELS?

Before we consider this question, we have to note that (according to Clarke) Cheney had little interest in Clarke's crisis management conference. Clarke described how Cheney kept hanging up on the open telephone line between them, while Cheney's wife Lynne kept turning down the volume on the teleconference, so as to hear CNN.[60]

Meanwhile, the report tells us that Cheney participated in the NMCC teleconference call "at various times, as did military personnel from the White House underground shelter."[61] Overall the record confirms that Cheney, possibly using the network of the Secret Service, had in effect his own adequate network of communication out of the PEOC, reaching not only the NMCC but Bush, Clarke, Rumsfeld, and the FAA. As already noted, Cheney himself told Tim Russert that "we had access, secured communications with Air Force One, with the secretary of Defense over in the Pentagon. We had also the secure videoconference that ties together the White House, CIA, State, Justice, Defense—a very useful and valuable facility. We have the counterterrorism task force up on that net. And so I was in a position to be able to see all the stuff coming in, receive reports and then make decisions in terms of acting with it."[62]

That Cheney's network was used for a shoot-down order before the downing of United 93 is the only conclusion compatible with the accounts of Donald Rumsfeld, James Bamford and Richard Clarke. Rumsfeld told the 9/11 Commission that "upon my return from the crash site and before going to the Executive Support Center (ESC), I had one or more calls in my office, one of which I believe was with the President."[63] He said further to *Washington Post* reporters Balz and Woodward that he discussed the shoot-down order and its rules of engagement "at some length" with both Bush *and Cheney.*

Q: One of the first conversations/decisions had to do with rules of engagement that you had with the president. Can you walk us through what went back and forth between you and the president on that and what those rules of engagement, the degree to which you talked about them with him.

Rumsfeld: We talked at some length about them. I talked about them with the president, I talked about them with Dick Cheney.

Q: Did you talk to the vice president first and then the president or vice versa, or do you remember?

Rumsfeld: I don't remember. I talked to General Myers about them. . . . So we ended up fashioning those and the president approved them and I gave the instructions to [General] Eberhart.[64]

There was so little time for this difficult decision making (between 9:45 and 10:14, according to the 9/11 report) that Rumsfeld probably spent more of his "missing" time on this matter, than in rescue efforts loading stretchers.

Bamford also wrote that, during their overlapping periods of seclusion, Cheney was in touch not only with the president but also with Rumsfeld (before Rumsfeld joined his own team at the NMCC): "As United 93 got closer and closer to the White House [that is, before 10:03 A.M.], covering a mile every seven seconds, Cheney conferred with Secretary of Defense Donald Rumsfeld and then asked Bush to order the United jetliner shot down."[65]

This is consistent with Clarke's report that *before Air Force One took off at 9:54 A.M.,* Bush had already given Cheney a shoot-down order, which was then transmitted by Clarke himself to Rumsfeld. In Clarke's own words: "At that moment Paul [Kurtz, from the White House counterterrorism team] handed me the white phone to the PEOC. It was [Clarke's representative at the PEOC, Major Michael] Fenzel. 'Air Force One is getting ready to take off. . . . Tell the Pentagon they have authority from the President to shoot down hostile aircraft, repeat, they have authority to shoot down hostile aircraft.'"[66] Clarke says that he then transmitted this information to Myers and Rumsfeld at the Pentagon, along with an order instituting continuity of government. Balz and Woodward later wrote that (as Cheney himself confirmed to Tim Russert) "from the bunker, Cheney officially implemented the emergency continuity of government orders."[67]

Cheney's call to Bush, according to Clarke, produced a decision before

Air Force One took off at 9:54 A.M.[68] Meanwhile the *9/11 Commission Report* suggests a time of 9:58 for Cheney's entry to the PEOC from the tunnel (citing the credible source of the PEOC Shelter Log).[69] That Cheney's calls to both Bush and Rumsfeld were made in the tunnel seems likely. ("Others nearby who were taking notes" in the PEOC have no record of a call to Bush, and the report has no record of Cheney's call with Rumsfeld either.)[70] To believe that the calls were made in the tunnel, one has to believe also that the vice president was indeed whisked to the PEOC, as Woodward claimed, and then *returned* from the PEOC to the tunnel at some later point to make calls *outside channels*. Thus the report's suggested time of 9:58 for Cheney's entry to the PEOC would be accurate, but only as a reentry time, not a time of arrival.[71]

The *9/11 Commission Report*, in addressing the much debated issue of the shoot-down order, makes no mention whatsoever of the call between Cheney and Rumsfeld—certainly an important call and possibly at least as important as the call obtaining approval from the marginalized president. This omission suggests to me only one of two things: Either on this issue the report is superficial and badly researched, or it is a misleading deception designed to cover up one of the more important events of that day. With the second possibility, the question arises again: Why?

TWO VERSIONS OF THE TRIPARTITE ORDER: WAS ONE FALSIFIED?

Clarke wrote that on receiving the order from Fenzel in the PEOC, he immediately transmitted it to Myers and Rumsfeld (who was not yet in the NMCC): " 'Three decisions: One, the President has ordered the use of force against aircraft deemed to be hostile. Two, the White House is also requesting fighter escort of Air Force One. Three, and this applies to all agencies, we are initiating COG. Please activate your alternate command centers and move to them immediately.' Rumsfeld said that smoke was getting into the Pentagon secure teleconferencing studio. . . . Gen. Myers asked. 'Okay, shoot down aircraft, but what are the ROE [Rules of Engagement]?'"[72]

This tripartite order is echoed in the *9/11 Commission Report* from a Defense Department transcript, in the same time period (that is, before Flight 93 crashed), but with a significant difference that rephrased, and in effect suppressed, the shoot-down order: "At 9:59, an Air Force lieutenant colonel working in the White House Military Office joined the [NMCC] conference and stated he had just talked to Deputy National

Security Advisor Stephen Hadley [who was with Cheney]. The White House requested (1) the implementation of continuity of government measures, (2) fighter escorts for Air Force One, and (3) *a fighter combat air patrol over Washington, D.C.*"[73]

The idea that the White House would authorize a combat air patrol for Washington at around 9:59 A.M. is hard to reconcile with the fact, not disputed, that fighters had already been ordered for this very purpose more than half an hour earlier.[74] (According to Clarke, he and Myers had agreed on the need for this CAP [Combat Air Patrol] on Clarke's same teleconference at 9:28 A.M.; and at 9:37 A.M. Clarke had ordered, "I want Combat Air Patrol over every major city in this country. Now."[75])

These significant divergences illustrate the need for historians to access all records, both those made available to the 9/11 Commission and those apparently never requested by them. Important in the second category would be all records about the implementation of COG that day, which presumably was recorded on the White House teleconference videotape. With respect to the tripartite order and its order for combat aircraft, it seems clear that someone, either Clarke or the DOD transcript cited by the *9/11 Commission Report*, has misrepresented it. I am not aware of any reason to mistrust the bona fides of Clarke, but the report has repeatedly been misleading with respect to decisions taken by Cheney. (What could be so sensitive about this issue is that, as David Ray Griffin has suggested, an order may have been given in time to shoot down Flight 93, possibly even after it was already known on the ground that the passengers of Flight 93 had overcome their hijackers.)[76]

WAS THERE A GAP IN THE PHONE LOGS?

Thus there is great significance to the divergence over the timing of the shoot-down order. The *9/11 Commission Report* claims that the relevant Cheney-Bush call, and the resulting shoot-down order, occurred after Cheney entered the PEOC (allegedly at about 10:00): "We believe this call would have taken place some time before 10:10 to 10:15. Among the sources that reflect other important events that morning there is no documentary evidence for this call, but the relevant sources are incomplete."[77] What were these relevant sources? The footnote tells us: "In reconstructing events that occurred in the PEOC on the morning of 9/11, we relied on (1) phone logs of the White House switchboard; (2) notes of Lewis Libby, Mrs. Cheney [in the PEOC], and Ari Fleischer [with the president]; . . . (4) Secret Service and White House Situation Room Logs, as well as four separate White House Military Office logs [including] the Communications Log."[78]

Commission chair Thomas Kean later complained that "the phone logs don't exist, because they evidently got so fouled up in communications that the phone logs have nothing. So that's the evidence we have." Vice chair Lee Hamilton added, "There's no documentary evidence here. . . . The only evidence you have is the statements of the president and vice president."[79] In their book *Without Precedent*, Kean and Hamilton write that "there was no documentary evidence of this call—either in log entries from the day or from the notes of the people sitting next to the vice-president."[80]

This paradox needs clarification. The commission did have phone log verification, from the Secure Switchboard Log, for Bush's call to Cheney at 9:15 and for an unimportant call made by the president about 9:20 to FBI director Robert Mueller.[81] The 9/11 report cites the Secure Switchboard Log again for what they call a second "confirmation call at 10:18 A.M."[82] Thus either there was a Watergate-like gap in the same log for the period of the Bush-Cheney phone call authorizing the tripartite order, around 10:00 A.M., or the call was made on some other channel.[83]

In the old-fashioned days of Watergate, the nonexistence of a particular White House phone log record would lead one to suspect that it had been suppressed or destroyed—"deep-sixed" in the language of that crisis—by the White House itself. In this case I believe there are four alternative hypotheses, of which I find the third and fourth the most likely:

1. Someone in the 9/11 Commission or its staff redacted the Secure Switchboard Log.

2. The record for the shoot-down phone call existed earlier on the Secure Switchboard Log but was eliminated before the log was seen by the 9/11 Commission or its staff.

3. There never was any Secure Switchboard Log record of this call because it was made on another channel: Cheney made it to the president from the area of the tunnel that had a secure phone. (This use of what is called a "back channel" would explain why "others nearby who were taking notes" in the PEOC have no record of such a call.[84])

4. The phone call was made outside channels but logged in a record with a higher security level than those of the records requested by and/or supplied to the commission.

I give most credit to the third and fourth possibilities, because the tripartite order specifically (according to both Clarke and the *9/11 Commission Report*) authorized COG.[85] COG was and remains an extremely sensitive matter. The 9/11 report has only one other reference to COG besides the tripartite order (on page 38) already noted: namely, that on 9/11 "contingency plans for the continuity of government and the evacuation of leaders had been implemented." A footnote adds: "The 9/11 crisis tested the U.S. government's plans and capabilities to ensure the continuity of constitutional government and the continuity of government operations. We did not investigate this topic, except as needed to understand the activities and communications of key officials on 9/11. The Chair, Vice Chair, and senior staff were briefed on the general nature and implementation of these continuity plans."[86] The other footnotes confirm that no information from COG files was used to document the 9/11 report. At a minimum these files might resolve the mystery of the missing phone call about the tripartite order. I suspect that they might tell us a great deal more.

The tripartite order instituting COG also transmitted a Secret Service request for planes to protect Air Force One, and the Secret Service appears to have had its own secure system and logs.[87] The question arises whether the "secure phone" in the White House tunnel belonged to the Secret Service or (as one might expect) was part of the secure network of the White House Communications Agency (WHCA). The WHCA is a military agency that functions closely with the Secret Service, whose agents of course were present with both Bush and Cheney that morning. The WHCA also had an open line to the FAA.[88] The *9/11 Commission Report* notes, for example, "at 10:02, the communicators in the [PEOC] shelter began receiving reports from the Secret Service of an inbound aircraft."[89]

Significantly, this important fact is footnoted to a Department of Defense transcript; the 9/11 Commission and report apparently had no access to Secret Service phone tapes. If the phone call was made outside channels, then we can say with some certainty that it was made before 9:58 A.M., when Cheney entered (or reentered) the PEOC. This would discredit the report's suggested time for the shoot-down phone discussion (between 9:58 and 10:15)[90] and corroborate Clarke's evidence that the shoot-down order was authorized in a phone call before the president's plane took off at 9:54 A.M. (Although the WHCA boasts on its Web site that the agency "was also a key player in documenting the assassination of President Kennedy," the WHCA logs and transcripts were in fact withheld from the purview of the Warren Commission and subsequent public investigations.[91] Were they withheld from Kean and Hamilton as well?)[92]

The *9/11 Commission Report* never cites the WHCA by name. However, the WHCA, according to its official Web site, is "under operational control of the White House Military Office."[93] One might conclude that the WHCA Communications Log would be one and the same as the White House Military Office Communications Log, which the report refers to. Yet the report, which cites phone logs to confirm the time of an uncontroversial presidential phone call to FBI director Mueller, does not so with the two most important of the four phone calls it reports between Cheney and Bush:

1. For a call at about 9:20 from Bush to Mueller, which has never been disputed, it cites a "White House record, Secure Switchboard Log, Sept. 11, 2001" (see footnote 204 on page 463).

2. For the two highly disputed calls, one from the tunnel (before the crash of Flight 93) and one soon after from the PEOC, it cites the "Vice President Cheney interview with *Newsweek*, Nov. 19, 2001, p. 5" (see footnote 211 on page 464).

3. Finally, for a two-minute "confirmation" call at 10:18, it cites a "White House record, Secure Switchboard Log, Sept. 11, 2001" (see footnote 221 on page 465).

Why did the 9/11 report authors not cite Log records for the two disputed calls about the shoot-down order? Were they denied them? Were they never entered in the Secure Switchboard Log? Or did these records never exist at all? One way or another, it would appear that either the evidence has again been cherry-picked on a key issue, or that Cheney may have taken unusual steps to sequester himself from the PEOC for a call or calls outside channels. The strange testimony of Karl Rove about the takeoff of Air Force One ("Before we could . . . put on our seat belts, they were rolling the plane") suggests that not just Cheney, but others in the White House as well, may have participated in a deceitful cover-up to suppress the details of the crucial ten-minute phone call with Bush at 9:45 A.M.

DID THE SHOOT-DOWN ORDER APPLY TO FLIGHT 93?

We know almost nothing about the unrecorded call, other than that (to judge from the subsequent tripartite order) it covered security for Air Force One, a disputed order about planes (either the shoot-down order or an order for a combat air patrol), and COG. It is possible that the most sensitive part of the call pertained to COG and covered matters still unknown to us, to which even the occupants of the PEOC were not cleared to listen.

The timing of the shoot-down order has been studied scrupulously by some critics of the 9/11 report, because of initial statements that United 93 was in fact shot down. Bamford is certain that the order was issued in time for NORAD and NEADS to go after United 93. In his book *Pretext for War*, he wrote: "A few minutes later, Cheney passed the order to . . . the Pentagon's War Room. . . . Sitting in the glassed-in Battle Cab of NORAD's Northeast Defense Sector Operations Center at Rome, New York, Air Force Colonel Robert Marr . . . sent out word to air traffic controllers to instruct fighter planes to destroy the United jetliner. . . . 'United Airlines Flight 93 will not be allowed to reach Washington, D.C.,' said Marr."[94]

According to the 9/11 report, NORAD learned about Flight 93 too late for Marr to have said this. The same was implied by the movie *United 93* in 2006. But the movie provoked General Larry Arnold to retort that NORAD had indeed been notified of United 93 "a short time before it crashed. . . . I advised Col. Marr to intercept UAL 93."[95] A number of stories confirmed that an F-16 went in pursuit of Flight 93, corroborating the statement by deputy secretary of defense Paul Wolfowitz that "we were already tracking that plane that crashed in Pennsylvania. I think it was the heroism of the passengers on board that brought it down but the Air Force was in a position to do so if we had to."[96]

There was also some circumstantial evidence of a shoot down. According to early reports, later disputed, one of the Flight 93 passengers reported by cell phone that "he heard some sort of explosion and saw white smoke coming from the plane," then contact with this passenger was lost.[97] A number of witnesses on the ground also heard a loud bang before the plane crashed.[98] Later, "according to sources, the last seconds of the cockpit voice recorder are the loud sounds of wind, hinting at a possible hole somewhere in the fuselage."[99] Debris from the plane was scattered over a wide area up to eight miles away, including a half-ton piece of one of the engines that was found two thousand yards from the crash site.[100] The FBI agent at the scene, Bob Craig, attributed the debris disposal to the prevailing wind.[101]

Ignoring these claims, the 9/11 report maintains that "by the time the military had learned about the flight [10:03, 10:06, or 10:07] . . . it had crashed. . . . NORAD did not even know the plane was hijacked until after it had crashed."[102] Citing NORAD's own sources, it claims that no shoot-down order was communicated to the military until 10:31. Ignoring Clarke's account that he heard the order from Cheney before Air Force One took off at 9:54, the report simply says "Clarke reported that they were asking the President for authority to shoot down aircraft. Confirmation of that authority came at 10:25."[103]

The issue of course was extremely sensitive. Flight 93 should not have been shot down, because by most accounts the passengers had, by about 9:56 A.M., wrested control of the aircraft away from the hijackers. Thus when General Myers testified to Congress on September 13, 2001, Senator Carl Levin asked him about "statements that the aircraft that crashed in Pennsylvania was shot down." Myers replied that "the armed forces did not shoot down any aircraft."[104]

Even if United 93 had been shot down, it could be seen as a tragic error or alternatively a grim but tragic necessity (if by any chance the heroic passengers were not successful as reported). In these cases the cover-up performance of the *9/11 Commission Report* would be at worst a cover-up of an embarrassment, not of a homicidal crime. When I bring up all these confusing and conflicting reports, it is not because I believe that Flight 93 was shot down (a question on which I am ignorant). It is once again to reinforce my general thesis that on key matters there has been a cover-up, and the public still does not know what happened on September 11, 2001.

WHAT IS THE REPORT COVERING UP ABOUT CHENEY?

My most important conclusions from the foregoing research have nothing to do with the fate of Flights 77 and 93. Rather, they are that on crucial matters Cheney misrepresented what really happened and that the *9/11 Commission Report*, by omitting some key evidence and by cherry-picking its sources, has created the false picture that Cheney's contested claims are substantiated by the available evidence. The story the report presented was embarrassing enough: of a multibillion-dollar defense system that broke down on September 11 and completely failed to perform its designated function. But the report's systematic and repeated distortions lead me to suspect that some even more embarrassing truth is being concealed and that this truth has to do with orders given on that day by the vice president.

Mineta's story of Cheney's orders at 9:25 A.M., as Flight 77 was approaching Washington, needs to be examined critically for the first time in an authorized investigation. The report's failure to deal with it seems inexcusable. So does its claim that "American 77 traveled undetected for 36 minutes" before its crash at 9:37 and that Cheney "arrived" (as opposed to reentered) the PEOC at about 9:58. If Mineta's story is true, then Cheney gave orders that have since been covered up and for which no presidential authorization is known.

Over the course of finalizing this manuscript, a number of mainstream articles and books have been published accusing Cheney of dishonesty and misleading statements about Iraq and weapons of mass destruction, about Iraq and the terrorist Mohamed Atta, about Iraq and aluminum tubes, about Iraq and uranium yellowcake.[105] This was brought to a head by Cheney's shameless lie to Senator John Edwards in the 2004 vice presidential debate: "The senator has got his facts wrong. I have not suggested there's a connection between Iraq and 9/11."[106]

Falsehoods are not necessarily lies. Condoleezza Rice, then national security adviser, tried to persuade the 9/11 Commission that her notorious statement of May 2002—"I don't think anybody could have predicted that . . . they would try to use . . . , a hijacked airplane as a missile"[107]— merely reflected her lack of knowledge about counterterrorism.[108] But, as former vice president Al Gore has observed, in accusing both Bush and Cheney of lying about Iraq and Osama bin Laden: "Bush's consistent and careful artifice is itself evidence that he knew full well that he was telling an artful and important lie."[109]

Lying about public policy, particularly foreign policy, is a familiar tradition in American politics, and one that spans both parties. What we are talking about here are misrepresentations, including possible lies, about a crime, the largest homicide in the history of the United States. So much remains unknown about that crime, from the identity of the hijackers to the circumstances that let them reach their targets, that the crime must be considered unsolved. In these circumstances the misrepresentations in the 9/11 Commission Report are not only evidence of a deception and cover-up, they justify grave suspicion as to what is being covered up. Although it is too early to reach a conclusion, it is at least possible that the misrepresentations also constitute obstruction of justice. I cannot refrain from observing that at least once before in U.S. history a major political crime was allowed to remain unsolved: the assassination of John F. Kennedy.[110] A number of studies have shown increasing mistrust, beginning in 1963, of American citizens in their government. To leave 9/11 in the same state of unresolved suspicion would be an even greater shock to the conditions of democratic government.

All this leaves us with important specific questions:

1. Who was responsible for the June 1, 2001, Joint Chiefs of Staff order making intercepts of off-course planes more difficult? What was the justification for it? The records of both the JCS and Cheney's National Preparedness Review should be consulted in this matter.

2. Was Mineta merely informed of the order to land by Sliney, or did the order come down to Sliney from Mineta when in the PEOC with Cheney?

3. What are the reasons for the commission's flagrant neglect of testimony about the events of September 11 from Mineta and Clarke?

4. Where is the videotape of the White House teleconference, which would resolve the question of when the shoot-down order was issued and whether Rumsfeld was participating in it before 10 A.M. (as Clarke claimed) or not (as the *9/11 Commission Report* implied)?

5. Did Cheney's series of responses to an incoming plane occur about 9:25 (as Mineta reported) or about 10:15 (as Lynne Cheney and Lewis Libby recalled)? If the earlier time, what orders was Cheney referring to?

6. What explains the apparent gap in the records concerning the day's most important phone call (in which Bush authorized both the implementation of COG and, allegedly, a shoot-down order)? Is there a record of that phone call from another source, such as the Secret Service?

7. Are there COG files extant somewhere that would expand on the limited story relayed by the 9/11 Commission?

At this stage the main accusation that can be based on all this evidence is that of cover-up—an ongoing cover-up among other matters of the most important orders given on September 11. The 9/11 Commission decided that its supporting evidence and records should be withheld from public view until January 2, 2009.[111] Kean and Hamilton, who wrote that "we decided to be open and transparent so the people could see how we reached our conclusions," offered no explanation in their book for this retreat from transparency.[112]

As it did belatedly in the case of the John F. Kennedy assassination, Congress should initiate a procedure for these records to be reviewed and released expeditiously. Records that should be released would include all of the phone logs from the White House on September 11, to determine, as a matter of priority, the precise time and circumstances of Cheney's orders respecting planes. They would also include materials (such as COG files and the videotape of the White House teleconference) that the commission apparently never requested. The public also needs to establish why other records requested by the commission did not initially reach them. The next step would be to depose important witnesses, such as Monte Belger and Richard Clarke, about the discrepancies in testimony that the 9/11 report failed to address.

Then it would be appropriate for a venue to be established in which the vice president would testify for the first time about 9/11 under oath. This inquiry would look critically at the vice president's responses to hijacked aircraft on September 11 and also ask an even more serious question: Did Cheney's activities with FEMA in the spring of 2001 contribute to the magnitude of the attacks? FEMA was an agency with which Cheney had been secretly involved since the 1980s. In that decade Cheney and Rumsfeld, who was not even in government, had been engaged with FEMA in highly secret preparations for what finally occurred on 9/11: the proclamation of rules for COG—continuity of government.[113]

Although we know almost nothing of COG since 2001, news stories in the 1980s indicated that COG planning, in conjunction with Oliver North, then included plans for warrantless detention and warrantless eavesdropping—plans that were swiftly implemented after 9/11.[114] We have to ask whether Cheney, both in May and on September 11, was not more focused on implementing his own earlier COG programs, than in stopping incoming planes.

When asked for my opinion of what happened on 9/11, I customarily answer that I am sure of one thing only: that there has been a significant cover-up of vital issues. But there is one other conclusion that can be drawn from the available evidence: At a moment when the nation was under attack, Cheney and Rumsfeld both simultaneously absented themselves for a period from their associates and their appointed posts, to hold a significant conversation about which (a) they have since been deceptive, (b) the report is silent or misleading, and (c) the facts are unknown. I find all this very suggestive. If Cheney and Rumsfeld were discussing issues too sensitive for even the audience in the PEOC to hear, the two of them were almost certainly not acting on their own. More probably they were the key figures in a highly classified operation that must have involved others.

Their behavior on 9/11 revives the question arising from their White House activity in the semiconspiratorial 1975 Halloween Massacre—an event that I argued in chapter 3 was critical in redefining America's posture in the world. The question in both events is whether Cheney and Rumsfeld could have contrived such a major change on their own within the White House, or whether they were acting in concert with other aspects of the deep state. That is a key question for 9/11. And it is a question made even more urgent by Cheney's and Rumsfeld's activities with respect to COG.

FOURTEEN

CHENEY, THE FEDERAL EMERGENCY MANAGEMENT AGENCY, AND CONTINUITY OF GOVERNMENT

> We annually spend on military security more than the net income of all United States corporations. This conjunction of an immense military establishment and a large arms indus- try is new in the American experience. The total influence— economic, political, even spiritual—is felt in every city, every State house, every office of the Federal government.
>
> **Dwight D. Eisenhower, Farewell Address, 1961**

THE SWIFT IMPLEMENTATION OF COG ON 9/11

In chapter 11 we saw that Cheney had a strong agenda for U.S. involve- ment in Iraq before 9/11, and that on 9/11 he argued for an immediate invasion. In this chapter I detail a similar pattern with respect to the 1980s plans for continuity of government (COG). These plans, secretly developed under President Reagan by Cheney and Rumsfeld, had as far as we know been given lower priority during the Clinton presidency, as FEMA became more focused on dealing with natural disasters. But COG was implemented at least partially on 9/11, before the last hijacked plane had hit the ground.

All sources agree that before 10 A.M. on that day, a central order from President Bush to Cheney contained three provisions, of which the first was, according to the *9/11 Commission Report*, "the implementation of continuity of government measures."[1] As James Mann has written: "On September 11, 2001, ... Cheney and Rumsfeld suddenly began to act out parts of a script they had rehearsed years before. Operating from the underground shelter beneath the White House, called the Presidential Emergency Operations Center, Cheney told Bush to delay a planned flight back from Florida to Washington. At the Pentagon, Rumsfeld instructed a reluctant Wolfowitz to get out of town to the safety of one of the underground bunkers, which had been built to survive nuclear attack. Cheney also ordered House Speaker Dennis Hastert, other congressional leaders, and several Cabinet members (including Agriculture Secretary Ann Veneman and Interior Secretary Gale Norton) evacuated to one of these secure facilities away from the capital."[2]

By 2:40 P.M. on September 11, deputy secretary of defense Paul Wolfowitz had left Washington by helicopter for a COG underground base. Both Cheney and Rumsfeld refused to leave on that day, however. This meant that for a time there were two parallel governments in place.[3]

Cheney himself frequently disappeared from public view after 9/11. At these times he too was working from a COG base—"Site R," the so-called Underground Pentagon at Raven Rock Mountain on the Maryland-Pennsylvania border.[4] As the *Washington Post* later reported, Cheney became in effect the leader of a U.S. "shadow government":

> President Bush has dispatched a shadow government of about 100 senior civilian managers to live and work secretly outside Washington, activating for the first time long-standing plans to ensure survival of federal rule after catastrophic attack on the nation's capital. . . . Known internally as the COG, for "continuity of government," the administration-in-waiting is an unannounced complement to the acknowledged absence of Vice President Cheney from Washington for much of the past five months. Cheney's survival ensures constitutional succession, one official said, but "he can't run the country by himself.". . . The White House is represented by a "senior-level presence," one official said, but well below such Cabinet-ranked advisers as Chief of Staff Andrew H. Card Jr. and national security adviser Condoleezza Rice.[5]

Meanwhile, Democratic Senate Majority Leader Thomas A. Daschle told the *Post* "he had not been informed about the role, location or even the existence of the shadow government that the administration began to deploy the morning of the Sept. 11 hijackings."[6]

It requires considerable prior planning to remove one hundred senior civilian managers. Displaced to form a parallel government outside Washington, these managers must have had some assignment; it is inconceivable that they were just sitting and waiting for developments. But about all we know of their activity is that it had been effectively removed from congressional review. It is disturbing that there has been no official report on the activities of this "shadow government," or even whether it is still activated.

CHENEY'S TERRORISM TASK FORCE, COG, AND MARTIAL LAW

Whether or not the shadow government is still active, many actions of the Bush presidency after 9/11 resembled not only what Nixon did in the 1970s, but what Cheney and Rumsfeld had planned to restore under COG in the 1980s in the case of an attack. As noted in chapters 11 and 13, news stories in the 1980s indicated that COG planning in the 1980s included plans for martial law and overriding the Posse Comitatus Act, plans for warrantless eavesdropping, including eavesdropping on domestic dissidents, warrantless detention, and the use of association as grounds for deportation.[7] We have to ask whether Cheney, in May and September 2001, was not crucial in implementing his own earlier COG programs.

Some of these ideas from the 1980s were incorporated almost immediately in the USA Patriot Act, which clearly had been drafted before 9/11.[8] The erosion of *posse comitatus*, which began right after 9/11, was consummated without debate, perhaps even without congressional awareness, in the October 2006 defense budget bill.[9] The suspension of the FISA Act, to eliminate judicial review of warrantless eavesdropping, was initiated with no legal justification at all.[10]

Cheney had long had it in mind to restore the untrammeled presidential style of Richard Nixon. As he told reporters on his return in December 2005 from Pakistan: "Watergate and a lot of things around Watergate and Vietnam, both during the '70s served, I think, to erode the authority . . . the legitimate authority of the presidency"—practices exercised by Nixon that were outlawed after Watergate.[11] As reporter Charlie Savage wrote in the *Boston Globe*:

> Cheney also offered a roadmap to his thinking about presidential power. He told reporters to read a 1987 report whose production he oversaw when he was a leading Republican in the House of Representatives. The report offered a dissenting view about the Iran-Contra scandal. . . . A congressional committee [had] issued a 427-page report concluding that a "cabal of zealots" in the administration who had "disdain for the law" had violated the statute.[12] But some of the Republicans on the committee, led by Cheney,

refused to endorse that finding. They issued their own 155-page report asserting the real problem was Congress passing laws that intruded into a president's authority to run foreign policy and national security. . . . Cheney's report includes a lengthy argument that the Constitution puts the president beyond the reach of Congress when it comes to national security.[13]

Cheney's minority report was drafted with the assistance of David Addington, a former CIA lawyer under CIA director William Casey. Under George W. Bush, Addington became the leading architect of the "signing statements" the president appended to more than 750 laws. After Lewis Libby was indicted and resigned over the Valerie Plame affair, Addington became Vice President Cheney's chief of staff.[14]

Cheney's comments in 2005 came in reply to questions about Bush's policy, just exposed by reporter James Risen in the *New York Times*, of warrantless eavesdropping. In the 1980s, back in the era of Iran-Contra, Cheney and Rumsfeld had discussed with FEMA just such emergency surveillance and detention powers. In May 2001, Cheney and FEMA were reunited: President George W. Bush appointed Cheney to head a terrorism task force and created a new office within FEMA to assist him. In effect, Bush was authorizing a resumption of the kind of planning that Cheney and FEMA had conducted under the heading of COG. We have to ask whether this second task force of Cheney was not crucial in designing policies of warrantless eavesdropping and detention, in addition to stymieing normal response to the hijackings of 9/11.[15]

Attorney General John Ashcroft took immediate steps after 9/11 to implement a central COG idea from the 1980s—arbitrary detention. Starting in September 2001, "hundreds of non-citizens were swept up on visa violations, . . . held for months in a much-criticized federal detention center in Brooklyn as 'persons of interest' to terror investigators, and then deported."[16] In some cases secretly detained and physically abused, none of the detainees in the New York area were ever linked to 9/11. Six of them returned in January 2006 to sue government officials, starting with Ashcroft. According to their attorney, warrantless eavesdropping may have figured in their detention.[17]

In May 2002 an American citizen, Jose Padilla, was first arrested and then, by a Bush executive order, removed from court jurisdiction to be held indefinitely in a U.S. Navy brig, without access to his lawyer. Three months later, in August, Ashcroft disclosed a plan that "would allow him to order the indefinite incarceration of U.S. citizens and summarily strip them of their constitutional rights and access to the courts by declaring them enemy combatants."[18] After widespread protests from legal scholars, the plan for military detention camps was not discussed publicly further. It seems clear, however, that the camps exist and that in the case of martial law the authority already exists for them to be used.

It is clear also that the number of camps will be expanded. In January 2006, KBR, the engineering and construction subsidiary of Halliburton, announced it had been awarded a contract from the Department of Homeland Security for $385 million, to provide "temporary detention and processing capabilities."[19] The contract (using Oliver North's justification of two decades earlier) envisaged preparing for "an emergency influx of immigrants, or to support the rapid development of new programs." However, the press release made clear that the facilities could be used for other emergencies, such as "a natural disaster."

On February 6, 2007, homeland security secretary Michael Chertoff announced that the fiscal year 2007 federal budget would allocate more than $400 million to add sixty-seven hundred additional detention beds (an increase of 32 percent over 2006). This $400 million allocation is more than a fourfold increase over the fiscal year 2006 budget, which provided only $90 million for the same purpose. Both the contract and the budget allocation were in partial fulfillment of an ambitious ten-year Homeland Security strategic plan, code-named Endgame, authorized in 2003. A forty-nine-page Homeland Security document on the plan explained, deadpan, that Endgame expanded "a mission first articulated in the Alien and Sedition Acts of 1798." Its goal was the capability to "remove all removable aliens," including "illegal economic migrants, aliens who have committed criminal acts, asylum-seekers (required to be retained by law) or potential terrorists."[20] (At the time there were approximately eleven million "illegal immigrants" in the United States.)

Is it possible that the managers sent outside Washington in the COG shadow government were responsible for initiating Endgame? One clue is that the group who prepared Endgame was, as the Homeland Security document put it, "chartered in September 2001." Endgame's goal of a capacious detention capability is remarkably similar to North's controversial Rex-84 "readiness exercise" for COG in 1984. This had reportedly envisaged a plan for FEMA to round up and detain four hundred thousand imaginary "refugees," in the context of "uncontrolled population movements" over the Mexican border into the United States.[21]

As I have detailed throughout this book, controversial plans for detention facilities or camps have a long history, going back to fears in the

1970s of a national uprising by black militants. Reportedly they were included in the executive order for continuity of government that had been drafted in 1982 by FEMA director Louis Giuffrida. This draft order advocated the use of martial law and detention camps. As Alfonso Chardy reported in the *Miami Herald* on July 5, 1987, the order called for "suspension of the Constitution, turning control of the government over to FEMA, emergency appointment of military commanders to run state and local governments and declaration of martial law during a national crisis."[22] The martial law portions of the plan were outlined in a memo by Giuffrida's deputy for national preparedness programs, John Brinkerhoff. According to Chardy, they resembled an earlier paper by Giuffrida, which prepared for the roundup and transfer to "assembly centers or relocation camps" of twenty-one million "American Negroes."[23]

After 9/11 it became clear that FEMA's COG martial law plans in the 1980s were being resurrected. In January 2002 the Pentagon submitted a proposal for deploying troops on American streets. One month later, Brinkerhoff, the author of the 1982 FEMA memo, published the second of two articles arguing for the legality of using U.S. troops for purposes of domestic security. Brinkerhoff, now with the quasi-governmental ANSER Institute for Homeland Security (a spin-off from RAND), claimed that the Posse Comitatus Act of 1878 did not apply to such deployments.[24]

Then in April 2002, Defense officials implemented a plan for domestic U.S. military operations by creating a new U.S. Northern Command (CINC-NORTHCOM) for the continental United States. Defense Secretary Rumsfeld called this "the most sweeping set of changes since the unified command system was set up in 1946."[25] It was announced that "the NORTHCOM commander is responsible for homeland defense and also serve[s] as head of the North American Aerospace Defense Command (NORAD). . . . He will command U.S. forces that operate within the United States in support of civil authorities. The command will provide civil support not only in response to attacks, but for natural disasters."[26] Brinkerhoff later commented on PBS that "the United States itself is now for the first time since the War of 1812 a theater of war. That means that we should apply, in my view, the same kind of command structure in the United States that we apply in other theaters of war."[27]

One declassified FEMA memo from 1982 stated that "a fully implemented civil defense program may not now be regarded as a substitute for martial law, nor could it be so marketed, but if successful in its execution it could have that effect."[28] By 2005 it was clear that the Bush administration was thinking seriously, not about civil defense but about martial law. In response to Hurricane Katrina, according to the *Washington Post*, White House senior adviser Karl Rove told the governor of Louisiana, Kathleen Babineaux Blanco, that she should explore legal options to impose martial law "or as close as we can get." The White House tried vigorously, but ultimately failed, to compel Governor Blanco to yield control of the state National Guard.[29]

In September 2006, as part of the 2007 Defense Authorization Bill, Congress made it easier for the president to declare martial law and to federalize the National Guard, even over the objections of the Nation's governors, as Section 1076 of the new law changed Section 333 of the "Insurrection Act," increasing the president's ability to deploy troops within the United States during a natural disaster, epidemic, serious public health emergency, terrorist attack, or "other condition." As Senator Patrick Leahy pointed out in February 2007, while moving to repeal the amendment, the change was merely slipped in at the administration's request as rider to a bill that was hundreds of pages long.[30]

In September 2005, meanwhile, NORTHCOM conducted a highly classified Granite Shadow exercise in Washington. As military affairs analyst William Arkin reported on his *Washington Post* blog: "Granite Shadow is yet another new Top Secret and compartmented operation related to the military's extra-legal powers regarding weapons of mass destruction. It allows for emergency military operations in the United States without civilian supervision or control." Arkin could learn little about the classified operation except that it involved activities "that are highly controversial and might border on the illegal."[31]

Many critics have alleged that FEMA's spectacular failure to respond to Katrina followed from a deliberate White House policy of paring back FEMA and instead strengthening the military for responses to disasters. Endgame's multimillion-dollar program for detention facilities will greatly increase NORTHCOM's ability to respond to any domestic disorders.

9/11 AS IMPLEMENTATION OF THE TOP-DOWN DEEP STATE

The administration seems quite aware that if opposition emerges to these programs, it will be organized principally through the Internet. Thus a recent U.S. war game, Cyber Storm, was waged, not just to protect the Internet but to safeguard the American people from "musings about current events":

The government concluded its "Cyber Storm" war game Friday [February 10, 2006], its biggest-ever exercise to test how it would respond to devastating attacks over the Internet from antiglobalization activists, underground hackers and bloggers.

Bloggers?

Participants confirmed parts of the worldwide simulation challenged government officials and industry executives to respond to deliberate misinformation campaigns and activist calls by Internet bloggers, whose Web logs include political rantings and musings about current events.[32]

A week later, in a speech to the Council on Foreign Relations on February 17, Defense Secretary Donald Rumsfeld also spoke of the danger to the country's security from misinformation, from what he called "news informers" who needed to be combated in "a test of wills."[33] Two days earlier, citing speeches critical of Bush by Al Gore, John Kerry, and Howard Dean, conservative columnist Ben Shapiro called for "legislation to prosecute such sedition."[34] No such provisions were submitted in the War Crimes Act subsequently passed by Congress. But, as I discuss in the next chapter, a proposal was submitted to revise the "network neutrality" in the Telecommunications Act of 1996. This threat to the traditional openness of the Internet apparently waned when the Democrats, in November 2006, resumed control of Congress.

The American Deep State in Historical Context

I do not consider it helpful in political discourse to use loaded terms like "fascism," whose original meanings have been overladen with propagandistic associations. But I do believe that U.S. citizens should study Germany in the 1930s, to see how a civilized nation, under stress, momentarily lost track of its inherent moral virtues and lapsed into a disastrous course of repression, xenophobia, and ultimately war. Most of us in America, including myself, have experienced the same powerlessness as the "good Germans" did under Hitler. They too were vaguely aware that members of another ethnic group were being rounded up and illegally detained, yet they too felt unable to do anything about it.

I recommend that Americans read Sebastian Haffner's self-critical account of his own inability to understand and stop Nazism in the 1930s. Although most of his memoir was written back in 1939, it has a chilling relevance to the situation "good Americans" find themselves in today: "It was just this automatic continuation of ordinary life that hindered any lively, forceful reaction against the horror. I have described how the treachery and cowardice of the leaders of the opposition prevented their organisations being used against the Nazis or offering any resistance. That still leaves the question why no individuals ever spontaneously opposed some particular injustice or iniquity they experienced, even if they did not act against the whole. . . . It was hindered by the mechanical continuation of normal daily life."[35]

Franz Neumann, who was arrested by the Nazis and then escaped to England, later wrote a famous analysis of the Nazi system as a behemoth: "a non-state, a chaos, a situation of lawlessness, disorder, and anarchy," in which the traditional order established by law broke down.[36] His friend and fellow refugee Ernst Fraenkel analyzed the Nazi system more charitably as a "dual state": a "normative state" (*Normenstaat*), a body endowed with "powers for safeguarding the legal order," together with a "prerogative state" (*Maßnahmenstaat*) "which exercises unlimited arbitrariness . . . unchecked by any legal guarantees."[37] In 1955 the notion of a dual state was transferred from totalitarian states to America, by the distinguished political scientist Hans Morgenthau, another refugee from Nazi Germany. Criticizing the paranoid purges of the State Department by bureaucratic allies of Senator Joseph McCarthy, Morgenthau deplored that the "authorities charged by law" with making decisions had effectively been subordinated to a hostile right-wing Bureau of Security within the department, which exerted "an effective veto over the decisions" of the former.[38]

Recently the European peace researcher Ola Tunander, recalling Morgenthau's analysis of the dual state, has applied it to America post 9/11: "After September 11, the U.S. 'democratic state' (characterized by openness, legal procedures and free elections) is forcefully . . . subsumed under a U.S. 'security state' (characterized by secrecy and military hierarchy). Much of public life is 'securitized' and the president and his close advisers are focused on the War on Terror, not on civilian matters. 'I am a war president. I make decisions . . . with war on my mind,' President Bush said."[39]

As I have showed throughout this book, this recent emergence of the security or deep state from the shadows is the fruition of processes in motion long before the George W. Bush administration came to power. The twentieth century everywhere saw both the spread of the democratic nation-state and also its subordination to the top-down deep state—not just in Germany and America, but also in Britain, France, Italy, Spain, many nations in Latin America and Africa, and of course the Soviet

Union and China.[40] In the same way that arms races create their own rationale (as I have argued), so the follies of deep-state paranoia create the conditions to justify them. If there is merit to this analysis, then we must say that the recommendations of the 9/11 Commission have taken us still further in the wrong direction. As I and many others have written, a change in U.S. policies in the Middle East would do far more to reduce terrorism than consolidating the security bureaucracies in Washington.

The phenomenon of subordination to paranoia is widespread, but we should not surrender to it passively as irreversible. On the contrary, there are two opposing tendencies in recent history: increasing powers for top-down domination of public opinion and also the rise of new technological resources, above all those embodied in the Internet, for popular resistance to ideological top-down domination. The twentieth century saw two dramatic reversals of the subordination process coupled with the creation or restoration, drawing in part on these new resources, of an autonomous public state. I am referring to the liberation movements of Poland and South Africa. In my final chapter I describe how these movements should serve as an inspiration to all Americans.

FIFTEEN

CONCLUSION

9/11 and the Future of America

If once the people become inattentive to public affairs, you
and I and Congress and Assemblies, Judges and Governors,
shall all become wolves. It seems to be the law of our general
nature in spite of individual exceptions.

Thomas Jefferson, *Notes on the State of Virginia*, 1800

With malice toward none; with charity for all; with firmness in
the right, as God gives us to see the right, let us strive on to fin-
ish the work we are in; to bind up the nation's wounds; to care
for him who shall have borne the battle, and for his widow,
and his orphan—to do all which may achieve and cherish a
just, and a lasting peace, among ourselves, and with all nations.

Abraham Lincoln, Second Inaugural Address, 1865

Truth being that which it is can never be destroyed.

Gandhi

AMERICA'S BEST DEFENSE:
STRENGTHENING OUR OPEN SOCIETY

9/11 represents a double challenge to the American way of life: the external threat of terrorist attacks and also the internal threat of subversion of
the Constitution by cabals and a deep state that are threatening to get out
of control. The United States faces a fundamental choice of what and in
whom to trust. Will we deal with the problem of terrorism primarily by

working to resolve issues that provoke conflict and projecting values that the rest of the world will wish to share? Or will we trust primarily in our own military power and become increasingly a garrison state and empire, conducting more and more of our global strategies in secret and projecting our military and covert strength into further and further corners of the earth?

The cult of secrecy in government, though necessary in some areas, has become counterproductive. On an operational level it makes it easy for special interests to falsify intelligence input and not be corrected. We saw this recently with Ahmed Chalabi's disastrous advice on Iraq, with the false stories linking Iraq to uranium from Niger, and with the hijacker Mohamed Atta.[1] This book has argued that secrecy has served America even worse on the policy level. We need to admit that the secret powers of our government helped to create and train this enemy, whose presence is now invoked to further augment the government's secret powers. Those secret powers themselves are becoming the major threat to the survival of the open republic. If we now want to strengthen democracy and reduce the threat of terrorism, we must look in a different direction.

What is urgently needed is not a reinforcement of Washington's inner citadels of secret decision making, but a totally different and more open approach. America's true strength is not its military and paramilitary resources, but what Harvard professor Joseph Nye has called its soft power—its ability to influence the rest of the world culturally and by example.[2] America's strongest resource is ultimately its people. The best antidote to Islamic terrorism will come when the chief contact of Muslims abroad is with American people, not GIs breaking down doors or bombing from the air with missiles.

This said, however, we are in 2006 a long way from such an alternative approach. The distinguished social scientist Chalmers Johnson, who once described himself as a former "spear carrier for the empire," has formulated succinctly the challenge that must be met if we are to preserve the American Republic:

> There is one development that could conceivably stop this process of over-reaching: the people could retake control of Congress, reform it along with the corrupted elections laws that have made it into a forum for special interests, turn it into a genuine assembly of democratic representatives, and cut off the supply of money to the Pentagon and the secret intelligence agencies. We have a strong civil society that could, in theory, overcome the entrenched interests of the armed forces and the military-industrial complex. At this late date, however, it is difficult to imagine how Congress, much like the Roman senate in the last days of the republic, could be brought back to life and

cleansed of its endemic corruption. Failing such a reform, Nemesis, the goddess of retribution and vengeance, the punisher of pride and hubris, waits impatiently for her meeting with us.[3]

Most readers have experienced, at a gut level, the fearful pessimism of Johnson's last two sentences. Many of us, like Johnson himself, are looking for ways not to succumb to it. In my view the correct starting point is, as he indicates, America's civil society, which I would characterize as indeed strong but not unified. Before we can dream of reforming Congress, an almost utopian goal, the first steps to be taken are to create greater cohesion in our civil society itself. And a necessary goal, however difficult, will be to lessen the growing disparity of income that has done so much to empower the deep state at the expense of the public one.

Let us look more closely at Johnson's claim that America has a strong civil society. It is true that U.S. traditions of decency and good neighborliness make for good local government and all manner of effective pro bono interest groups. But on the national political level American civil society is not and never has been strong. On the contrary, it is deeply and passionately divided, as can be seen for example in ongoing warfare over appointments to the U.S. Supreme Court. Despite (or because of) enormous recent improvements in human rights, consensus in favor of these rights has not been reached. The wounds of the Civil War are not yet fully healed.

The same divisions affect the public's ideas on foreign policy. The passions aroused by the Vietnam War have not abated either. This stasis, this absence of national consensus, has abetted (one might almost say forced) the growth of government by secrecy and cabal. Therefore the reform of Congress depends on healing the divisions in the civil society. This will involve strenuous efforts that I believe will be rewarding, whether in the end it is the existing American republic that is revived or some alternative future society.

CRISIS AS OPPORTUNITY
AND A GENERATOR OF NEW FORCES

Large numbers of Americans, on both the left and the right, agree that today's republic is threatened, from both without and within. Taking the long view, we recognize that America's history has in fact been a succession of such crises. We can think back to the threats faced by President John Adams, the hero of the revolutionary Congress, to which he responded with the Alien and Sedition Acts.[4] America's slow and bumpy progress toward democracy has been in response to alternating periods of quiescence and excess. In my own lifetime the excesses of McCarthyism resulted in the election of enough liberals to secure the passage of the long overdue Civil Rights Act in 1964.

But the whole of U.S. history has been dialectical. Periods of consensus, in which burning issues were ignored (like slavery in the early nineteenth century), have eventually generated concerted efforts to rectify and redefine the republic. In my youth these efforts came mostly from the left, beginning with the civil rights movement and ending with a brief phase of doomed, and in retrospect silly, revolutionary movements. From about 1980 to 2004 the momentum has been one of right-wing consensus, veering still further toward the right. American history has shown a rhythm, varying by stages from excessive quiescence to excessive innovation.[5]

These excesses have not been self-correcting. Instead they have been bypassed by the development of new compensatory forces. The excesses of wealth in the first Gilded Age after the Civil War were ultimately corrected by an agenda of progressive legislation, including antitrust laws, direct election of senators, and the income tax. But these reforms came only after unprecedented exposures by investigative journalists, or "muckrakers," such as Ida Tarbell and David Graham Phillips. Their contributions strengthened the powers of newspaper barons like William Randolph Hearst, until the media themselves came to constitute an important and ultimately dysfunctional part of the establishment. The Hearst who was seen as a reformer in the 1900s became an oppressive reactionary in the McCarthy era.[6] The corporate media today have become, collectively, less a vehicle of information than of mind control.

The civil rights legislation of the 1960s was the product of another new force: nonviolent grassroots organizing. But the very success of that movement has produced its dialectical opposite: the fundamentalist Christian right. Grassroots organizing on the conservative side ultimately snatched control of the Republican Party from elitist "liberals" such as Nelson Rockefeller. The current crisis has been caused by excessive government from the top down, the product of secrecy and off-the-books activity by irresponsible cabals. The correct response will be found in mobilization, once again, from the bottom up. But this must be mobilization to embody the prevailable public will of the whole nation—not to subvert or co-opt it in favor of a faction.

Thus I believe the old grassroots methods of both left and right are inappropriate. What is needed is a force uniting the American people against its unrepresentative government. To a distressing degree, the energies of the American populists of both left and right are focused on attacking each other. I suspect that most readers of this book admire the legacy of Abraham Lincoln, but how many can contemplate their fellow citizens as Lincoln exhorted us to do: "with malice toward none; with charity for all"?

To put it another way, the breakdown of democracy in America is not just a product of top-down deep state connivance on the political level; it is also a symptom of the incoherence of U.S. civil society on the national level. Many grassroots organizers, energized by their success in previous crises, are today aggravating that incoherence.[7] What is needed instead is a movement, like that of Solidarity in Poland, that unites the various elements in civil society instead of setting them against each other. I suspect that both left and right, by discarding preconceptions and learning more about those whom they presume to be adversaries, could discover that they may have more in common than they believe. For example, it is fashionable on the left to criticize the neocons of the Project for the New American Century for their intellectual adherence to the philosophy of Leo Strauss. Strauss in turn is characterized, even in mainstream texts, as an elitist and moral absolutist, who once criticized the historian and philosopher Isaiah Berlin as symptomatic of "the crisis of liberalism—of a crisis due to the fact that liberalism has abandoned its absolute basis and is trying to become entirely relativistic."[8]

But there is far more to Strauss than this cartoon of him, which ignores his defense of the moral and political imagination against the allegedly value-free (*Wertfrei*) social sciences that in his view abetted the nihilism of the modern age. As literary critic and scholar Robert Alter has commented, Strauss "strenuously resisted the notion that politics could have a redemptive effect by radically transforming human existence. Such thinking could scarcely be further from the vision of neoconservative policy intellectuals that the global projection of American power can effect radical democratic change."[9] I believe that capacious minds should be learning from Leo Strauss at the same time they are learning from the radical philosopher Herbert Marcuse. The more there are individuals who can think of themselves as both liberal and conservative, the easier it will be to heal the artificial divisions in our civil society.

Since I first began this book in 2002, there have been hopeful signs that the politics of America's left are moving toward rapprochement with the religion of America's right. The clearest example is in the emerging struggle over the future of the Internet, which has emerged as the most hopeful development for America's future (and the world's). As the ownership of U.S. media has become increasingly concentrated, the independence of mainstream journalism—the old media—has become radically reduced. The Internet has done much to fill the resulting vacuum, at every level.

In the important PBS special *The Net @ Risk*, aired in late 2006, veteran journalist Bill Moyers spelled out the opportunities created by the Internet for democracy and transparency: "The Internet is revolutionary because it is truly democratic, open to anyone with a computer and connection. We don't just watch; we participate, collaborate, and create." He also drew attention to the dangerous threat to open and equal Internet access from proposed legislation being lobbied for in 2006 by the powerful duopoly of the telephone and cable companies.[10]

Moyers focused further on the emerging coalition of grassroots liberal and conservative organizations, uniting MoveOn with the Christian Coalition, which has mobilized against this duopoly and also against the corporate takeover of local radio stations by huge top-down corporations like Clear Channel Communications.[11] As this book goes to press, it is impossible to predict the short-term successes of this coalition, whose chances clearly improved with the Democratic capture of Congress in November 2006. But the coalition's true importance will be established in the long run. It has the potential to repeat in this century what was achieved by the three great nonviolent revolutions of the twentieth century: the soft victories of the U.S. Civil Rights Movement, Solidarity in Poland, and anti-apartheid in South Africa. All three of these movements succeeded by commitment to abiding values and by the building of coalitions and consensus through persuasion.

THREE SOFT VICTORIES: THE U.S. CIVIL RIGHTS MOVEMENT, POLAND, AND SOUTH AFRICA

These three recent nonviolent victories for humanity, one domestic and two foreign, sustain my belief that the current world crisis, grounded as it is in false values and false hopes, can be dealt with by a concerted human response.[12] The first victory is that of the civil rights movement in the American South. That great step forward is still unfinished, and admittedly it has produced countercurrents that are a major part of America's civil problems today.[13] Nevertheless, the improvement in daily life in the South, for blacks and whites alike, has been both profound and irreversible. The second victory was that of Eastern Europe in the 1980s, particularly the victory of the Polish Solidarity alliance between labor, intellectuals, and the Roman Catholic Church. The third was the essentially nonviolent transition in South Africa from a repressive elitist white oligarchy to a more open multiracial democracy.

Contemplating these victories, I believe in the possibility of human progress. All three were victories by means of a soft politics of nonviolent persuasion.[14] The movements were contemporaneous with America's inevitable and predictable failures to impose nonprevailable regimes through violence in Vietnam and Iraq.[15] All three victories teach us a more concrete message: that tyrannical oppression from above, no matter how invincible it may outwardly appear, is vulnerable to organized nonviolent resistance when it is grounded in a sufficiently broad social base. Going one step further, I will say that oppression, in the context of modern communications, tends to threaten its own stability, by generating the resistance to itself. Although the parallels are far from exact, it is important to see that in the United States today, as in Poland and the American South in the past, government is increasingly a top-down deep state dominated by private interests. To this degree it is less responsive to the needs of civil society, just as are the nominally representative institutions that are supposed to rectify the situation.

In this book I present a coherent documented outline of how, over the past half century, the open politics and representative institutions of the American *res publica* (the public state) have been progressively subordinated to a *res privata* (a restrictively controlled locus of top-down decision making in the deep state). Within that restricted locus of top-down power, bureaucratic paranoia has tended to increase. By making the world secure for global capitalism and suppressing opposition at home and abroad, the resulting system has become dangerously inflexible in the short run, with the increasing long-run prospect of nightmare as needed reforms are endlessly postponed. It is neither subjective nor exaggerated to speak of nightmare. The current drift of the world is toward more and more intolerable inequality, an inequality of which most Americans are unaware. But the consequences of global inequality cannot be shielded from Americans forever, as this country learned with a shock on September 11, 2001.

The truth is that the apparent stability of global capitalism is deceptive. It has always bred its own opposition within it, beginning with individuals like the college-educated Unabomber or the American Taliban volunteer John Walker Lindh. On every continent rule by the wealthy has also bred organized resistance, first in the form of Marxist revolutionary movements and more recently in the form of reactionary fundamentalism.

The question is whether the American nation can develop resistance, sedated as it is by material comforts and insecurity. In my view the answer to this question is a moral and indeed spiritual one. In the three soft victories mentioned, success derived from what Solidarity theorist and organizer Adam Michnik prescribed for Poland: the solidarity between urban intellectuals and a spiritually united popular base—that is, religion.[16] The American Revolution itself was the fruit of such an alliance.[17] Will we see it in the United States again? As I commented in an essay on Czeslaw Milosz and the Solidarity movement, it will not be easy. Michnik's prescription was as difficult and startling as asking followers of libertarian socialist Noam Chomsky to have discourse with Southern Baptists.[18]

The role of religion in popular protest movements cannot be ignored in this book. Neither can it be adequately treated, however. Religion, like the weather or America itself, is endlessly polymorphous, a gigantic Rorschach blot evolving through time. In attempting to define religion's role in history, we succeed chiefly in defining ourselves. I am moved to write a brief belated digression in response to political commentator Kevin Phillips's book *American Theocracy*, a book that (like all of Phillips's recent work), I consider to be an excellent introduction to American politics. Writing explicitly in the spirit of Edward Gibbon's *Decline and Fall of the Roman Empire*, Phillips sees "renascent religion" as a potential liability, even a "danger" to the United States, just as "religious excess" has been one of the "prominent causes of the downfall of the previous leading world economic powers."[19]

The possibility that religion might be a "good danger" to empire is not raised by Phillips in his extended discussion. His use of evidence is formidable but also selective: he does not mention that religion helped end slavery in all the empires he discusses, nor that it contributed to the evolution of the British Empire into self-governing nations.[20] Phillips fears that "the interplay of imperialism and evangelicism . . . could propel the United States into war in the Middle East."[21] Despite his exhaustive documentation, he nowhere mentions the involvement of religious leaders in the antiwar movement, which helped America to extricate itself from the immoral folly of Vietnam.

My point is not that Phillips's observations are wrong, but (like my own throughout this book) they are one-sided. I see America's religiosity equally as a cause for concern and for hope.[22] For example, in April

2006 millions of Americans marched to protest the oppressive proposals to restrict and punish so-called illegal immigration. Religious leaders and others were prominent in organizing these protests, and possibly only a protest with religious support could have been mobilized so swiftly and effectively. If this is dangerous to the American empire, I say: Let us, for the sake of the republic, have more of such danger.

GLOBAL INEQUALITY AND THE NEED FOR VISIONARY REALISM

The late social critic Daniel Singer has written eloquently of global inequality. In the words of his 1999 book *Whose Millennium: Theirs or Ours?*:

> Looking at the global picture one gets a striking view of inequality. The fact that the combined wealth of the 225 richest people in the world nearly equals the annual income of the poorer half of the earth's population, that is to say more than 2.5 billion human beings, is more arresting than volumes of social criticism. Actually, inequality appears at the very center of the major issues of our time: international exploitation, racism, gender discrimination, and the hierarchical division of labor. And when polarization rhymes with stagnation, it is no longer possible to pretend that, because of the expanding pie, equality is irrelevant. Egalitarianism—not to be confused with leveling and uniformity—must be at the very heart of any progressive project.[23]

Singer concluded this essay optimistically, by calling for a "realistic utopia": "*Realistic*, since it must be rooted in current conflicts and in the potentialities of existing society. *Utopian*, because that is how any attempt to look beyond the confines of capitalism is branded."[24]

Singer formulated his goal of a realistic utopia as a nondoctrinaire Marxist, ignoring Marx's own strictures against utopian socialists. I am not a Marxist (or for that matter an anti-Marxist) but find that his twofold phrase neatly encapsulates what is needed. In case any critics deride the phrase as an oxymoron, we can talk of a *visionary realism*: the need to bring a fresh, visionary alternative from outside to bear on institutions that, although worthy of preservation and respect, are clearly not working as intended. The best way to make them work better is to first look beyond them, to see where we wish the world to go. With this in mind I distinguish between three different strategies for change in a world that is both socially deliquescent and politically immobilized. The three strategies will not always be distinguishable in practice, and I do not mean in the next paragraphs to praise one to the exclusion of the rest. We will need however to be mindful of the differences as we proceed.

First-Level Strategy

The first is the strategy of unmediated or direct political change: working for new programs to succeed with political institutions as they now exist. An example of this would be Chalmers Johnson's hope of reforming Congress. Another would be the recent book by Noreena Hertz, who has written compellingly of the need to break "the financial stranglehold corporations have on politics" and to address "the dominance of trade and corporate interests in the global sphere."[25] Pointing to the recent achievements of the global environmentalist movement, Hertz hopes that such countervailing energy can overcome President George W. Bush's efforts to roll back the "great progressive gains of the last three decades."[26]

I do not expect such an easy nonviolent evolution out of the present crisis. To begin with, such sanguine hopes underestimate the threats to democratic control presented by Bush and his colleagues. Bush's coming to power has been described, even by Chalmers Johnson himself, as a coup d'état.[27] The respected commentator Bill Moyers, a veteran of the Johnson White House, has called the Bush revolution the "most radical assault on the notion of one nation, indivisible, that has occurred in our lifetime."[28]

Even before Bush II, though, American electoral politics had become a caricature of its former vital self: a process in which money (mostly corporate) first bought both political parties and then graciously allowed the public to choose between them. Or, as distinguished American author Gore Vidal said memorably: there is now "only one political party, the Property Party, with two right wings, Republican and Democrat."[29] This was notably true in the 2004 election. Both presidential candidates promised to win with U.S. troops in Iraq. Both were competing with each other to show their support for Israeli Prime Minister Ariel Sharon, as he continued to build his wall in defiance of the UN and the International Court of Justice.

A great deal of well-intentioned and indeed inspired organization work, such as the creative MoveOn.org Web-based movement, must be described as first-level strategies: attempting to force change through the political filters of the status quo. Such strategies are not to be discouraged, just as I believe one should be ready to cooperate with the establishment itself if an opportunity arises to influence it.[30] Nevertheless, I suspect that it is unrealistic to expect MoveOn.org's current first-level strategies to change America by themselves.[31]

Third-Level Strategy

At the other extreme would be what I see as the third-level strategy of replacing or doing away with our existing institutions as the necessary precondition for meaningful social change. This is of course the alternative held out by revolutionaries past and present, whether red-flag Marxists or black-flag anarchists. I shall not waste much time rebutting this position. The history of the past century is, I think, adequate demonstration of the disasters that follow such a lobotomizing of society. The few successful examples of revolution—I would cite China and Vietnam—did not proceed in this fashion; they successfully developed alternative institutions and mobilized broad coalitions of support for a phased transition to a new social order. (Both China and Vietnam even found a temporary place for their respective emperors, Henry Pu-yi and Bao Dai, in their mustering of a broad social coalition.)

In retrospect it seems extraordinary that two generations ago, at the height of the Vietnam War, so many intellectuals were denouncing liberalism as the bar to third-level change. Books that were taken seriously then, such as Jacques Revel's elitist *Revolution Within the Revolution* or Carlos Marighella's *Manual of the Urban Guerrilla*, seem absurdly quaint and irrelevant today. Many of the organizers of America's peace movement are accused of still harboring such aspirations. Whether this is true I do not know, but the tolerance shown at demonstrations to black-flag anarchists is from my past experience a symptom of a fatal and self-defeating strategy. There may well be "third-level moments," extreme moments that invite immediate opposition without attention to the flag color of those you protest with. But in the United States such third-level tactics will never be elevated successfully into a third-level strategy. The answer lies in a middle path between absorption into the existing political process and futile rejection of it.

Visionary Realism and a Second-Level Strategy

Visionary realism, or realistic utopianism, favors a second-level strategy of restoring the political process by first strengthening civil society. This will require visionary cooperation with existing elements in society.

Drawing on the experience of the civil rights movement and Solidarity, the initial emphasis will be less on reforming or breaking down old top-down institutions than on developing and strengthening alternative ones from the ground up.[32]

Adam Michnik has described this process of creating alternative institutions as "the real value of Poland's peaceful transformation. How was it possible? It was preceded by an almost two-decade effort to build institutions of civil society. Political thought within the democratic opposition in Poland took as its main objective the creation of alternative structures in politics, labor, culture, media, and publishing. From this there emerged a complex network of communities independent from the state. Those communities developed alternative practices of thinking and acting, taught intellectual independence and a new kind of resourcefulness, along with self-reliant decision making, and a spirit of creativity."[33]

This emphasis on the creation of an alternative civil society reflects the views of John Adams, as expressed in his retirement to his correspondent Thomas Jefferson: "What do we mean by the revolution? The War? That was no part of the revolution; it was only an effect and consequence of it. The revolution was in the minds of the people, and this was effected from 1760 to 1775, in the course of fifteen years, before a drop of blood was shed at Lexington."[34]

In the background of both revolutions lies the emergence of Western civilization from one of the most successful of all alternative civil societies: the early Christian church. As noted by peace theorist Jonathan Schell, John Stuart Mill pointed to the success of the early Christians as proof of his principle that "opinion is itself one of the greatest active social forces": "They who can succeed in creating a general persuasion that a certain form of government, or social fact of any kind, deserves to be preferred, have made nearly the most important step which can possibly be taken towards ranging the powers of society on its side. . . . [St. Stephen was] stoned to death in Jerusalem while he who was to be Apostle to the Gentiles [St. Paul] stood by 'consenting unto his death.' . . . Would anyone have supposed that the party of that stoned man were then and there the strongest power in society? And has not the event proved that they were so? Because theirs was the most *powerful* of then existing beliefs."[35]

The quotations from Adams, Mill, and Michnik suggest a similar course of action for us today. There is widespread agreement that the political institutions of the West, saturated as they are with contributions from free-floating global wealth, are more efficient at resisting than generating a visionary alternative to the status quo. This does not mean we should turn our back on them. Ultimately, free elections were the defining moment when Poland was able to turn away from the declining Soviet empire. In other words, in recognizing that the political process is temporarily immobilized, energy is deflected into the task of developing alternative structures in civil society in preparation for eventual political change. America has the advantage (which for organizers is also a problem) of being an extremely articulated civil society, whose robustness protects it from the cultural sickness currently affecting the state. This civil society may be difficult to mobilize, but for organizers it offers a maximum degree of both opportunity and protection.

I wish in this brief conclusion to note some changes that have presented themselves as goals for organizing, both internationally and domestically, to limit and progressively cut back the unrepresentative deep state. None of these proposals is new, and each one already has groups campaigning for its implication. The novelty I propose is to see each as components of a larger movement for change, to focus on the deep state as the target, and to recognize that within the status quo none of the proposals can succeed by itself.

1. The first goal is to recognize income disparity as a threat to the public state and to address it on a number of fronts:

   a. Undo the recent regressive tax laws that have unduly favored the rich.

   b. Bring an end to the United States– and International Monetary Fund–imposed "Washington consensus," permitting capital flight out of smaller nations into the banks and economies of the United States and its closest allies.

   c. Work toward global regulations to reduce both the economic power of the supranational milieu and the tax advantages of moving offshore.

      What Mexican politician and author Jorge Castañeda wrote specifically of Latin America has application also to the world and to the United States: "Until the gaps between rich and poor are reduced, . . . democracy will simply not work."[36]

Journalist and author William Greider has said the same of the United States: "Since I am increasingly skeptical that regular politics will reform itself, I suspect that the best route to restoring our democracy might begin elsewhere, confronting the undemocratic qualities embedded in the economic system which are, in fact, a principal source of democracy's decline."[37] His latest book, *The Soul of Capitalism: Opening Paths to a Moral Economy*, has the potential to unite left and right in a number of local grassroots solutions.

2. A second organizing goal is to reform the electoral process in the light of the breakdowns in 2000 and 2004. This issue has the advantage of forcing individuals to think beyond the existing structures of the two main political parties.

3. A third goal is to restructure narcotics suppression strategies, to reduce the international drug traffic that has served, recurrently, as an underworld asset of the deep state. At present the police enforcement strategies of the "war on drugs" model maintain retail prices at such an elevated level that there will always be groups seeking to enter and dominate the market. What is needed is an alternate medical model for dealing with the problem, one that is explicitly designed to minimize rather than maximize the profits of drug trafficking. This issue, like the first, has the potential to unite church groups, legal reformers, and local grassroots activists in a campaign to ease prison crowding and purge so-called victimless crimes from the law books. As indicated earlier, reducing our bloated prison population will reduce the pool from which American terrorists are recruited.

4. A fourth organizing goal is to oppose U.S. involvement in Iraq and the doctrine of preemptive wars in general.[38]

The need to combat terror is currently being used as justification to increase the dominance of the deep state at home, and to justify ongoing oppressive U.S. occupation of such foreign territories as Afghanistan and Iraq. We need to develop the consciousness that such occupation in the long run is more a cause of terrorism than it is a remedy. Even Michael Scheuer, the ex-CIA officer, has agreed that the United States did not move toward solutions but took a big step backward by invading Iraq.[39]

The experience to date has amply corroborated this observation. Yet our leaders seem reluctant to acknowledge it. In 2004, for example, Senator John Kerry proposed an increase in U.S. troop levels as a solution for the chaos in Iraq. This is all too reminiscent of Lyndon Johnson's "solution" in 1965 for the chaos in Vietnam, followed by Richard

Nixon's goal of "peace with honor." The lesson to be learned from Vietnam, and even more from Thailand, is that those countries moved rapidly toward U.S.-friendly programs of economic development, but only *after* U.S. troops were withdrawn and covert operations were scaled back.[40]

AN OPEN POLITICAL APPROACH TO ISLAM

The perspective I present in this book is that the bottom-up institutions of American society are in better health than the bloated top-down institutions of the deep state. With respect to Islamist terrorism, those who know most about Islam and have no second agenda, such as support for Israel, have been sidelined. And counterterror policies have been evolved with minimal consultation by those who know next to nothing about Islam. I myself have no qualifications as an Arabist or a student of Islam, yet I have read enough books about al Qaeda to see biases and limits if not errors in just about all of them. Thus I will share my personal impression that the roots of Islamic jihadism are more situational than endemic to Islam itself.

The countries of Islam in the past century, particularly since the collapse of the caliphate, have seen themselves lose power to the West. More important, they have seen waves of political, economic, and cultural intervention in their home countries. Some of these interventions strike me as constructive, particularly with respect to education and health. Others, such as the record of economic exploitation by the oil companies, should offend Westerners as much as Muslims in Islam.

History tells us that such outside interventions are likely if not certain, in any culture, to produce reactions that are violent, xenophobic, and desirous of returning to a mythically pure past. This was predictably true of Christian Germany after the disastrous and punitive defeat of World War I. It was true in the 1990s of Peru's exploited Indians who responded briefly to the revolutionary appeal of the Shining Path. There are any number of examples where alien occupation has produced terrorism among typically nonviolent people, such as the Cambodians, the Basques, and the Irish.

If we go back in time, we see even more examples. The suppression of Christians by the Moors in Andalusia after the seventh century produced a reaction of militant Christianity that was apocalyptic, xenophobic, passionately vindictive, and murderous. Its desire to purge the Iberian peninsula of Moorish and Jewish traces became so extreme that the inquisition at one point punished those guilty of the Muslim tradition of habitually bathing. The experience of defeat in the American South after the Civil War helped nourish millenarian evangelist John Nelson Darby's similarly apocalyptic theology of Rapture, with its expectation of Armageddon, the backbone of Christian dispensationalist fundamentalism in the United States today.[41]

The suffering behind the apocalyptic rapturism of the South should be viewed with compassion, and this compassion should extend also to its mirror opposite in al Qaeda. Both Osama bin Laden and his detractors like to point to a jihadist tradition in Islam whose notable example is Imam Taki-d-Din bin Taymiyyah of the thirteenth century. We should not forget, however, that bin Taymiyyah's jihadism was also situational, in reaction to the Mongol destruction of Baghdad in 1258.[42]

In the wake of 9/11, Americans were encouraged not to think of al Qaeda with compassion, or even to consider the reasons why jihadists had attacked the United States. Many of those who did were attacked as "allies of terrorists."[43] Since then one professional counterterrorist, Michael Scheuer, has urged America to "proceed with relentless, brutal, and, yes, blood-soaked offensive military actions until we have annihilated the Islamists who threaten us."[44] Yet even Scheuer recognizes that bin Laden's popularity stems from American policies that are anathema to Muslims, notably uncritical U.S. support for Israel that is "radicalizing [Muslim] attitudes in such countries as Indonesia and Malaysia."[45]

I believe we have lost ground when so many Muslims have come to feel, not without justification, that the Muslim world has been targeted by insensitive U.S. military, diplomatic, and covert strategies. That impression has been strengthened by quasi-academic books with such titles as Samuel P. Huntington's *The Clash of Civilizations*.[46] In *The Road to 9/11*, I have tried to strengthen the opposite belief that it is the task of civilization to bring the world closer together, without annihilating cultural differences (as unrestricted top-down U.S. globalization threatens to do). From this perspective it is barbarisms that clash, not civilizations.

To be worthy of the term, "civilizations" (a product of urban culture) must learn from and communicate with each other. Medieval European culture became elevated to a new level of civilization in the twelfth and thirteenth centuries, as it began to learn from and incorporate the best of the advanced Muslim culture of Andalusia, from lyric poetry to the Arab-transmitted Aristotle, which so influenced St. Thomas Aquinas.

One faint cause for hope in our present embattled world is that even Osama bin Laden, the Wahhabi "fundamentalist" (as he is clumsily called in the press), recalls with nostalgia the lost greatness of al-Andalus. Al-Andalus was indeed a moment of peak civilization, not just for Islam but also for the Jews and ultimately Christian Europe.

Clashes arise from ignorance, deprivation, and resentment, which it is the task of civilization to overcome. It is a task for the public more than for governments, which are of necessity infected by the barbarisms of violence they have to deal with. It is my belief and hope that American society is civilized enough so that it can attain a tolerant and compassionate understanding of Islam. This would include responding to the legitimate complaints of Islam. This is a task for all Americans, not merely our governors. American society has the resources to rise to this challenge, and it must. Our current leaders, to put it politely, do not. Bin Laden in his hatred understands the West and its limitations far better than our leaders do the complexities of Asia.

We all have a lot to learn. For example, the Sudanese Muslim leader Hassan al-Turabi has recurrently been referred to in Western intelligence and right-wing circles as the "Pope of Terror" or "Pope of Terrorism."[47] He was also "accused by American intelligence officials of having an important political and financial relationship with Mr. bin Laden."[48] This fails to take into account the evolution in al-Turabi's relationship with bin Laden. In 1989 and 1990, as the "power behind the throne" in Sudan, he had invited bin Laden and other veterans of the Afghan war to set up bases in his country. He apparently hoped that bin Laden in particular would finance both Sudanese development and training camps for militants.[9] However, "by late 1995, al-Turabi and other senior figures in the Sudanese government were beginning to think that their bid to turn Sudan into a centre for Islamic radicalism was a miscalculation. . . . It was becoming increasingly clear that the benefits of bin Laden's presence in their country did not outweigh the international opprobrium it brought. The Sudanese were particularly angry when it emerged that men close to bin Laden had murdered a young boy suspected of collaborating with the Egyptian intelligence services."[50]

Almost unnoticed in America has been the fact that al-Turabi condemned the September 11 attacks.[51] About this time al-Turabi appears to have redefined his views on Islam in the world. In 2001 he was arrested in Sudan for his efforts to negotiate with warring Christian and animist rebels in the country's oil-rich south.[52] In March 2007, with respect to Darfur, al-Turabi said that the Sudanese government "should cooperate with the ICC [International Criminal Court], which Sudan has said has no jurisdiction over its nationals."[53]

On the Web we find al-Turabi talking of trying "to focus on the international human dialogue of religions generally, not only a dialogue, but further on, perhaps, an institution or machinery for cooperation as well."[54] In an interview in Arabic with the journalist Mohamed Elhachmi Hamdi, al-Turabi focused again on the need for dialogue: "I believe in dialogue as a religious duty, even if I do not like it or think it is useless, because God encourages it and recommends it. . . . We are all human beings and we must be in touch with one another. We are living in the global village, and contact between people has become a necessity for practical reasons. . . . Health has become global, the media have become global, security has become global, and the human experience has all but become one common experience. We must talk to one another."[55]

It is obvious that there is an information gap here that Western intelligence circles and Washington think tanks, many of them heavily oriented toward the perspectives of the deep state, oil companies, or Israel, have not managed to bridge. So I encourage people-to-people contacts with Muslim leaders who, like al-Turabi, talk of the need to talk. Contacts are needed also with the Muslim media, including stations like the Arabic news network al-Jazeera.

THE TRUTH MOVEMENT: 9/11 AS AN ORGANIZING ISSUE

I have left until last the question of how successfully a so-called truth movement can make an organizing issue of the 9/11 homicide itself. At first glance it would seem to lack the potential for becoming, like an antiwar movement, a mass movement with the potential to change society. But it is an issue that has certain big advantages nonetheless. Perhaps more clearly than any other, the truth movement uses verifiable issues of fact as a way to call into question the legitimacy of the present administration. It is clear that the largest homicide in American history has not yet been adequately investigated, and it is difficult for legislators in particular to back the Bush administration in its efforts to obstruct an honest investigation. This was shown by the recurring successes of the 9/11 families in securing a nongovernmental 9/11 Commission, followed by additional funds and time for its transactions.

No one should have ever expected the 9/11 Commission to challenge the legitimacy of the administration that appointed it. It was a first step. Similarly the Warren Commission was the first step in a process that led, more than thirty years later, to the release of the incriminating North-woods documents by the Assassination Records Review Board. Of course the Warren Commission, like the 9/11 Commission, was charged with ending inquiries rather than increasing them. But it was one of the strengths of American civil society that the *Warren Report* spawned a student-led movement, the Assassination Information Bureau (AIB) "that sought 'to politicize the question of John F. Kennedy's assassination.' The bureau's activism helped bring about a congressional committee that in 1979 concluded, on the basis of acoustic evidence, that a second gunman had in fact shot at Kennedy (although later findings cast doubt on that conclusion)."[56]

It is unlikely that the AIB would have had the clout it did, without the surrounding ambience of Watergate and a residual antiwar movement. But that is precisely a suggestive analogy with today's political crisis. Opposition to illegitimate power will be strengthened by a truth-based movement, however intellectual, that seeks to impeach the administration with historical facts.

The search for truth, both in itself and in its social implementation, is a powerful common denominator with the earlier issues mentioned. Journalist Amy Goodman has written how the so-called Battle of Seattle in 1999, the first mass challenge to top-down globalization policies of the World Trade Organization, spawned the creation of the first Independent Media Center, as an alternative to the top-down corporate media.[57] Before that millions had learned to use the Internet because of the late Gary Webb's series on CIA and crack cocaine, as promulgated in its Internet version on the *San Jose Mercury-News* Web site.[58] The U.S. invasion of Iraq, with the accompaniment of "embedded" journalists, has taught patriotic Americans that to learn the truth of what is happening there they must go to foreign sources.[59] With so many Americans now getting news from the Web, and from alternate and foreign media sources, it was possible in 2004 to mount a challenge to voting irregularities in the 2004 presidential election.[60]

In the long run, as Milton once wrote, the winning side tends to be the one whose weapon is the truth. Widespread use of the Internet and alternative media has done much to shorten the length of time it takes for political truths to be heard. As long as the alternate sources are there, the widespread recurrence of censorship and lies in the major media must be taken as a sign of the establishment's weakness, not its strength.

It will be important to monitor whether the Internet remains free, both economically and politically. I believe that if it does, the American republic will be secure, despite challenges from above. Thus Internet freedom is like a canary in the caverns of our modern mass society. It was indeed ominous when in December 2004 former CIA director George Tenet proclaimed: "Access to networks like the World Wide Web might need to be limited to those who can show they take security seriously."[61] That a former CIA director was proposing that the United States adopt the restrictive Web policies of China and Myanmar was barely mentioned in the mainstream U.S. press. But it was soon reported in fifteen hundred sources on Google, including sources in French, German, and Dutch.

This points to a second powerful commonalty between the truth-based movement surrounding 9/11 and other organizational movements. The Web has created the makings of a multinational civil society and public arena in which there is a shared global interest in matters of justice and injustice in and for all nations, perhaps especially the United States. Thus it is no accident that early books challenging the official account of 9/11 were published in other countries—in England, France, and Germany, most of them before comparable books were published in the United States.[62]

9/11 AND THE STRENGTHENING OF THE INTERNATIONAL COMMUNITY

The movement to expose 9/11 has helped strengthen an international community against the excesses of the Bush administration. It has also helped fortify researchers with the additional resources from blogs, Web sites, and international conferences. The movement to expose the truth has the potential to heal old divisions between the left and the right in the United States. Both the left and the right profess to love freedom, but on many issues the freedoms sought (for abortion and sexual preference on the left, for handguns and prayer on the right) are hard to reconcile.

However, the left and the right have shown they can speak as one against power grabs like the efforts to stifle the truth surrounding 9/11, the implementation of COG, and the push toward the passage of the Patriot Act. Throughout this book I have relied on the research and lawsuits of men like David Schippers of JudicialWatch and John Whitehead of the right-wing Rutherford Institute, men who are today resisting the power encroachments of Bush and Cheney with the same energy they once used to attack Clinton. On the issue of 9/11, Bush is threatened with a revolt from within the Republican Party. The revolt on other issues may be coming as well, particularly as the military worries more and more about the condition of U.S. defense forces and true conservatives worry about the subversion of the U.S. Constitution.

The opposition between the right and the left in America was exacerbated by the black and women's liberation movements of the 1960s as well as the antiwar movement during the Vietnam era. Before George W. Bush, it seemed unlikely that this confrontational opposition would ever diminish. But then Bush came to power with the promise that he would unite America; and it is still possible that he may do so, although in quite a different way than he intended. With a triumphalist Bush presidency it is possible that Americans of many differing opinions will be moved to unite in defense of the public realm of the republic, against the unpopular and indefensible overreaching of the deep state.

This book is dedicated to the strengthening of that possibility.

Glossary of Open Politics

archival history A chronological record of events, as reconstructed by archival historians from public records; as opposed to **deep history**, which is a chronology of events concerning which the public records are often either falsified or nonexistent.

cabal A network, often of **cliques**, operating within or across a broad social and bureaucratic base with an agenda not widely known or shared. According to many dictionary definitions, a cabal is a group of persons secretly united to bring about a change or overthrow of government. But in the deep state cabals can also operate within the status quo to sustain top-down rule, including interventions from the **overworld**.

clique A small group of like-minded people, operating independently within a larger social organization. Before the Iraq War the neocons in the Bush administration represented a **clique**; the faction preparing secretly for war (which included both neocons and veterans of the international petroleum industry, like Dick Cheney and Condoleezza Rice) represented a larger and more widespread **cabal**.

closed power, or top-down power Power derived from the **overworld**, as opposed to democratically responsive **open power**. See **power**.

continuity of government (COG) A term of art for secret arrangements for command and control in the event of an emergency.

deep history See **archival history**.

deep politics All those political practices and arrangements, deliberate or not, that are usually repressed in public discourse rather than acknowledged.

deep state A term from Turkey, where it is used to refer to a closed network said to be more powerful than the public state. The **deep state** engages in false-flag violence, is organized by the military and intelligence apparatus, and involves their links to organized crime.

See also **dual state** and **state**.

dual power See **power**.

dual state A **state** in which one can distinguish between a **public state** and a **top-down deep state**. Most developed states exhibit this duality, but to varying degrees. In America the duality of the state has become more and more acute since World War II.

globalization The trend toward a more unified world at two levels: (1) top-down globalization, a system imposed from above on peoples and cultures; and (2) bottom-up globalization, a geographic expansion of people-to-people contacts producing a more international civil society and community. Top-down globalization, if not balanced by bottom-up globalization, will result in increasing polarization.

Islamism A political Muslim movement with origins in the late nineteenth century, dedicated to jihad, or struggle for the political unification and purification of Islam, and restoration of its lost territories such as Spain. Often called **Islamic fundamentalism** but its relation to the fundamentals of Islam is problematic. Its main sources are Wahhabism in Saudi Arabia and Deobandism in the Indian subcontinent.

meta-group A private group collaborating with and capable of modifying governmental policy, particularly (but not exclusively) with respect to the international drug traffic. Over time meta-groups have tended to become more powerful, more highly organized, and more independent of their government connections.

milieu A location (not necessarily geographical) where private deals can be made. Relatively unimportant to proceedings and institutions of the **public state**, restricted milieus are of greater relevance to operations of the **deep state**.

open, public, cooperative, or **participatory power.** See **power, soft power**.

order There are two clusters of dictionary definitions of order, both relevant: (1) **top-down** or **coercive order**, meaning "a command or direction" (or their results); and (2) **public** or **participatory order**, meaning "a condition of arrangement among component parts, such that proper functioning or appearance is achieved."

overworld That realm of wealthy or privileged society that, although not formally authorized or institutionalized, is the scene of successful influence of government by private power. It includes both (1) those whose influence is through their wealth, administered personally or more typically through tax-free foundations and their sponsored projects, and (2) the first group's representatives. The term should be distinguished from Frederick Lundberg's "superrich," the sixty wealthiest families that he wrongly predicted in his 1967 book *Sixty Families* would continue to dominate America both as a class and as a "government of money." The recent *Forbes* annual lists of the four hundred richest Americans show that Lundberg's prediction was wrong on both counts: his richest inheritors of 1967 are mostly not the richest today, and today's richest are not necessarily those projecting their wealth into political power. The overworld is not a class but a category.

As a rule it is wrong to think of overworld influence institutionally, as exercised through the Bilderberg Society, the Trilateral Commission, or the Council on Foreign Relations. However, there are less known, usually secret, **cabals** (such as the Pinay Circle and the Safari Club) that flourish in these overworld **milieus**.

parallel government (or shadow government) A second government established in times of crisis to override or even replace the official government of the public state.

paranoia The irrational drive toward dominance that is motivated not by rational self-interest but by fear of being surpassed by a competitor. A paradox of civilization is that, as relative power increases (along with expansion and exposure), so does paranoia. The dominance over the **public state** by the **deep state** is based on (and also generates) paranoia. The paradox that power increases paranoia is seen *within* states as well as *between* them. It is not restricted to so-called totalitarian states.

paranoia, bureaucratic The dominance of bureaucratic policy planning by worst-case scenarios, calling for maximized bureaucratic responses and budgets. This leads to the paranoid style in bureaucratic politics.

parapolitics This term has two definitions: (1) "a system or practice of politics in which accountability is consciously diminished,"[1] and (2) the intellectual study of parapolitical interactions between public states and other forms of organized violence (or **parastates**): covert agencies, mafias, and so on.[2]

parastates Structurally organized violence (in the form of covert agencies, mafias, revolutionary movements, and so on) with some but not all of the recognizable features of a state.

power There are two definitions of power, both relevant: (1) **top-down, coercive, or closed power**, meaning "the ability or official capacity to exercise control; authority"; and (2) **public, cooperative, or open power**, meaning "the might of a nation, political organization, or similar group." This notion of **dual power** is reflected in Gandhi's distinction between **duragraha** (coercive force, "obtained by the fear of punishment") and **satyagraha** (obtained "by acts of love").[3] Jonathan Schell paraphrases this as the distinction between coercive and cooperative power: "Power is cooperative when it springs from action in concert of people who willingly agree with one another and is coercive when it springs from the threat or use of force. Both kinds of power are real. . . . Yet the two are antithetical."[4] This antithesis is embodied in the tension in the **dual state** between the **deep state** and the **public state**. The tension between **top-down** and **public power** exists to some degree in all developed states. It becomes more acute with increased income disparity: polarization of wealth or economic power is inevitably accompanied by polarization of political power.

prevailable will of the people That potential for solidarity that, instead of being checked by top-down repression, can actually be awakened and reinforced by it. It thus becomes the emerging sanction for a generally accepted social or political change. The more common term "will of the people," a refurbishing of Rousseau's "general will," is often invoked as the ultimate sanction of a generally accepted decision. However, even if not a total abstraction, the term has little or no meaning at the time of a major controversy; the "public will" must be established by events, not passively divined in advance of them. The "will of the majority" is an even more dangerous phrase; the opinions of majorities are often superficial and fickle, and destined not to prevail. (The Vietnam and Iraq wars are examples where the momentary will of the majority proved not to be the prevailable will.) The prevailable will can be said to be latent in a political crisis but not established or proven until its outcome. In the case of abolishing slavery in America, for example, the resolution took many decades, but it is hard to imagine any other prevailable outcome.

realism There are two prevailing and conflicting notions of political realism: (1) **realpolitik**, defined as "a usually expansionist national policy, having as its sole principle the advancement of the national interest"; and (2) what I call **visionary realism**, a vision of a public **order** conforming to the **prevailable will of the people**. I consider the latter more realistic than the former, because it can see more clearly the dialectical consequences of expansion and over-stretch.

second-level strategy A strategy of first strengthening civil society as a condition for social change.

security state See **state**.

soft power versus **open power** Soft power, as defined by Joseph Nye, works (in distinction to military and economic superiority) by persuasion; it is an "ability . . . that shapes the preferences of others" that "tends to be associated with intangible power resources such as an attractive culture, ideology, and institutions."[5] **Soft power** or **soft politics** puts more emphasis on a persuasive technique; **open power** or **open politics**, on a participatory process or result.

state There are two definitions, both relevant, both deriving ultimately from Machiavelli. What is being discussed here are dictionary definitions, which I culled and combined from a number of dictionaries: (1) a system of organized power controlling a society; and (2) a politically organized body of people under a single government. These correspond to two overlapping systems of statal institutions: the **deep state** (or **security state**) and the **public state**. The second interacts with and is responsive to civil society, especially in a democracy; the first is immune to shifts in public opinion.

Thus the deep state is expanded by covert operations; the public state is reduced by them. Following the same distinction as Hans Morgenthau in his discussion of the **dual state**, Ola Tunander talks of a "democratic state" and a "security state." His definitions focus more on the respective institutions of the **dual state**; mine, on their social grounding and relationship to the power of the **overworld**.

Deep state and **security state** are not quite identical. By the **deep state** I mean agencies like CIA, with little or no significant public constituency outside government. By the **security state** I mean above all the military, an organization large enough to have a limited constituency and even in certain regions to constitute an element of local civil society. The two respond to different segments of the **overworld** and thus sometimes compete with each other.

Notes

PREFACE. THE AMERICA WE KNEW AND LOVED: CAN IT BE SAVED?

1. However, it was alarming to read in the newspaper in 2003 that during a red alert in New Jersey, "You will be assumed by authorities to be the enemy if you so much as venture outside your home, the state's anti-terror czar says" (Tom Baldwin, "Red Alert? Stay Home Await Word," Gannett News Service, March 16, 2003).

2. John A. Hobson, *Imperialism* (London: Allen and Unwin, 1902; reprint, 1948). Cf. general discussion in Phillips, *Wealth and Democracy*, 397–98.

3. Marfa is not a typical Texas town, hosting many writers, artists, and summer residents escaping the heat of coastal Houston for the hills of West Texas. But many of my acquaintances during my stay were not from these categories. For example, I met a retired Republican who owned a private plane who was shocked that some of the private ranch airstrips nearby were being lengthened to accommodate jets.

4. Michael Lind, *Made in Texas: George W. Bush and the Southern Takeover of American Politics* (New York: Basic Books, 2003). Lind's analysis, too subtle in detail for me to do justice to it here, acknowledges its debt to the cultural theories of David Hackett Fischer, *Albion's Seed: Four British Folkways in America* (New York: Oxford University Press, 1989). In the eighteenth and early nineteenth centuries it was commonplace to analyze the difference in terms of "two competing economic systems: a nascent Northern industry . . . and the slave South with its plantation system" (see Michael Hudson, *Economics and Technology in 19th-Century American Thought* [New York: Garland, 1975], 55–73, 55).

5. Lind, *Made in Texas*, 143; citing Joseph A. Fry, *Dixie Looks Abroad: The*

South and U.S. Foreign Relations, 1789–1973 (Baton Rouge: Louisiana State University Press, 2002), 259: "The vast majority of southerners cast aside any pretense of internationalism. The South quickly became disillusioned with the United Nations after 1945 and persistently favored unilateral actions when U.S. interests were in question."

6. Lind, *Made in Texas*, 143. The last sentence of this quotation is too glib. The FBI and CIA are also separated by the Potomac, but historically the FBI and the military have tended to face off against the more internationalist CIA and State Department. See Herbert Franz Schurmann, *The Logic of World Power: An Inquiry into the Origins, Currents, and Contradictions of World Politics* (New York: Random House, 1974).

7. Lind, *Made in Texas*, 80.

8. Zinn, *People's History*, 147–56.

9. Garry Wills, *Henry Adams and the Making of America* (Boston: Houghton Mifflin, 2005), 396.

10. Walt Whitman, *Complete Poetry and Selected Prose* (New York: Library of America, 1982), 960. Quoted in Richard Rorty, *Achieving Our Country: Leftist Thought in Twentieth-Century America* (Cambridge: Harvard University Press, 1998), 19; and Peter Dale Scott, *Minding the Darkness: A Poem for the Year 2000* (New York: New Directions, 2000), 160.

11. I have visited all but three of the fifty United States and slept in all but six of them.

12. Phillips, *Wealth and Democracy*, 124. Even in Great Britain, the most extreme example after the United States, the richest group only earns 9.6 times more than the poorest group.

1. INTRODUCTION: WEALTH, EMPIRE, CABALS, AND THE PUBLIC STATE

Epigraphs: Phillips, *Wealth and Democracy*, 71, 309, and 312.

1. Project for the New American Century, *Rebuilding America's Defenses*, 51, 63, quoted in Griffin, *9/11 Commission Report: Omissions and Distortions*, 117–18.

2. Griffin, *9/11 Commission Report: Omissions and Distortions*, 116, quoting Bob Woodward, *Bush at War* (New York: Simon and Schuster, 2002), 32; "Secretary Rumsfeld Interview with the *New York Times*," October 12, 2001, http://www.defenselink.mil/Transcripts/Transcript.aspx?TranscriptID=2097 (Rumsfeld). Cf. Johnson, *Sorrows of Empire*, 229: "Within days, Condoleezza Rice called together members of the National Security Council and asked them 'to think about "How do you capitalize on these opportunities" to fundamentally change American doctrine, and the shape of the world, in the wake of September 11th.'"

3. Phillips, *Wealth and Democracy*, 408: "How the top 1 percent garnered over half of late-twentieth-century U.S. income gains went essentially unremarked upon."

4. Phillips, *Wealth and Democracy*, 422.

5. Paul Krugman, "Graduates Versus Oligarchs," *New York Times*, February 27, 2006. Krugman later used government figures to argue that about 40 percent of Bush's tax relief programs had gone to the richest 1 percent of the country (Paul Krugman, "Weapons of Math Destruction," *New York Times*, April 14, 2006).

6. Phillips, *American Theocracy*, 268. Phillips quotes from the British journalist Eamonn Fingleton, who deplores "financialism" as "the increasing tendency by the financial sector to invent gratuitous work for itself that does nothing to address society's real needs but simply creates jobs for financial professionals." Time-Warner president Richard Parsons is quoted in the *New Yorker* as saying: "We don't make things any more in this country. Look at the derivatives business. It's just people trading money and taking a piece for their effort" (Ken Auletta, "The Raid: How Carl Icahn Came Up Short," *New Yorker*, March 20, 2006, 134).

7. For example, Elizabeth Drew, *The Corruption of American Politics* (Woodstock, N.Y.: Overlook, 2000).

8. Brock, *Republican Noise Machine*, 39–45.

9. By "overworld" I mean the milieu of both (1) those who exert influence through their wealth, administered personally or more typically through tax-free foundations and their sponsored projects, and (2) the representatives of this group. The term should be distinguished from popular historian Frederick Lundberg's "superrich," the sixty wealthiest families that he wrongly predicted would continue to dominate America both as a class and as a "government of money" (Frederick Lundberg, *Sixty Families* [New York: Vanguard, 1937]). The recent *Forbes* annual list of the four hundred richest Americans shows that Lundberg's prediction was wrong on both counts: his richest inheritors of 1937 are mostly not the richest today, and today's richest are not necessarily projecting their wealth into political power. The overworld today is less a class than a category and a milieu. Especially since the Civil War, the northern U.S. establishment has continuously been opposed by an antiestablishment overworld, rooted in the South and associated not just with wealth but also with land ownership and the military.

10. The two terms overlap but are not quite identical. By the "deep state," I mean primarily agencies like CIA, with little or no significant constituency outside of government. By the "security state," I mean more specifically the deep state's resources in the military, an organization large enough to have a limited constituency, and even in certain regions to constitute an element of local civil society. The two milieus respond to different segments of the overworld and thus sometimes compete with each other.

11. There are two relevant definitions of the "state," both deriving from the Italian political philosopher Niccoló Machiavelli: (1) a system of organized power controlling a society; and (2) a politically organized body of people under a single government. These correspond to two overlapping systems of statal institutions. The first I call the "deep state"; the second, the "public state."

12. For more on the Endgame program, see chapter 14 in this book.

13. In this book I focus on the American responsibility for al Qaeda and related phenomena. Other governments and their intelligence agencies, notably Pakistan and Saudi Arabia, also played an important role. Undoubtedly a major

cause of Islamism in the world today is the rise of Wahhabism around the world as a result of direct Saudi subventions of overseas mosques (originally with the approval and support of CIA and U.S. oil companies). But the narrative in this book focuses on processes that Americans can most easily do something about.

14. Suskind, *One Percent Doctrine*, 62.

15. Frederick Lundberg, *The Rich and the Superrich* (New York: Lyle Stuart, 1968).

16. Phillips, *American Theocracy*, 80.

17. Peter Dale Scott, "The Vietnam War and the CIA-Financial Establishment," in *Remaking Asia: Essays on the American Uses of Power*, edited by Mark Selden (New York: Pantheon, 1974), 107–26; Sanders, *Peddlers of Crisis*, 137–45; Paul Ivan Joseph, "March 1968: A Study of Vietnam Decision-Making," Ph.D. dissertation, University of California at Berkeley, 1975; and Paul Joseph, *Cracks in the Empire: State Politics in the Vietnam War* (New York: Columbia University Press, 1987).

18. "From 1979 to 1990, Bruce Jackson served in the United States Army as a Military Intelligence Officer. From 1986 to 1990, he served in the Office of the Secretary of Defense in a variety of policy positions pertaining to nuclear forces and arms control. Upon leaving the Department of Defense in 1990, Mr. Jackson joined Lehman Brothers, an investment bank in New York, where he was a strategist in the firm's proprietary trading operations. Between 1993 and 2002, Mr. Jackson was Vice President for Strategy and Planning at Lockheed Martin Corporation" (Project for the New American Century, *Rebuilding America's Defenses: Strategy, Forces, and Resources for a New Century*, 2000, www.new americancentury.org/RebuildingAmericasDefenses.pdf).

19. For an evaluation of journalist Judith Miller's story with Michael R. Gordon in the *New York Times* ("Threats and Responses: The Iraqis," September 8, 2002) about Iraq and aluminum tubes for weapons of mass destruction (WMD), see John R. MacArthur, "The Lies We Bought: The Unchallenged 'Evidence' for War," *Columbia Journalism Review* (May–June 2003), http://www.cjr.org/issues/2003/3/lies-macarthur.asp.

20. I take the term "shadow government" from Richard Clarke's description of COG in Clarke, *Against All Enemies*, 10. See also Barton Gellman and Susan Schmidt, "Shadow Government Is at Work in Secret," *Washington Post*, March 1, 2002.

21. This is the story richly documented in Phillips, *Democracy and Wealth*, a book that should be read in every American college and university.

22. The paradox that power increases paranoia is seen *within* states as well as *among* them. It is not restricted to so-called totalitarian states. Even in the relatively open and peaceful country Thailand, for example, we saw Prime Minister Thaksin Shinawatra's increase in power produce both increased opposition and increased paranoid fear of opposition. This tension led in 2006 to a royally backed military coup.

23. The role of secrecy in Athens was not marked, apart from the treacherous machinations of Alcibiades with Sparta. For the role in the Roman empire of *agentes in rebus*, government agents whose duties ranged from postal inspection and tax collection to espionage and secret police work, see J. S. Reid, "Reorgani-

zation of the Empire," in *Cambridge Medieval History*, edited by H. M. Gwatkin and Rev. J. P. Whitney (New York: Macmillan Company, 1911), vol. 1, 36–38; also see Peter Dale Scott, "Deep Politics: Some Further Thoughts," http://roswell .fortunecity.com/angelic/96/pdscot~1.html.

24. In Porter, *Perils of Dominance*, 4: "In 1955, the index of U.S. military power was forty times greater than the index of Soviet power, and a decade later . . . still more than nine times greater. . . . This disparity . . . was far greater than any other disparity . . . since the modern state system came into existence in the seventeenth century."

25. Porter, *Perils of Dominance*, 71.

26. Scott, *Drugs, Oil, and War*, 129–37.

27. James K. Galbraith, "Did the U.S. Military Plan a Nuclear First Strike for 1963?" *American Prospect*, September 21, 1994.

28. Porter, *Perils of Dominance*, 15.

29. Galbraith, "Did the U.S. Military Plan," citing Nikita S. Khrushchev, *Khrushchev Remembers* (Boston: Little Brown, 1970), 497.

30. Porter, *Perils of Dominance*, 193.

31. "Iran-Contra Hearings; North's Testimony," *New York Times*, July 14, 1987; see also chapter 11 in this book.

32. Draper, *Very Thin Line*, 578, 579.

33. Peter Dale Scott, "Northwards without North: Bush, Counterterrorism, and the Continuation of Secret Power," *Social Justice* (San Francisco), 16, no. 2 (summer 1989): 1–30.

34. Kornbluh, "Crack, the Contras, and the CIA: The Storm over 'Dark Alliance,'" *Columbia Journalism Review* (January–February 1997), http://archives .cjr.org/year/97/1/d-alliance.asp (Webb).

35. See especially chapter 2 in this book for details relating to Pakistan, chapter 5 for Iran, and chapter 7 for Afghanistan.

36. Perhaps the most visible example, not analyzed in this book, is the Federal Reserve Board, whose governors represent both the public state and the private banking community. The Fed is in many ways a symbol for the convergence between private and public power in other aspects of the American polity.

37. CNN Special Assignment, "Investigative Report into the National Program Office (NPO) and the Continuity of Government (COG)," November 17, 1991.

38. Simpson, *Blowback*, 42–43. The other two men, Generals Walter Bedell Smith and Edwin Sibert, had risen through the ranks to become senior army officers.

39. Mark Riebling, *Wedge: The Secret War between the FBI and CIA* (New York: Knopf, 1994), 56–79.

40. See Shoup and Minter, *Imperial Brain Trust*, 61–62.

41. Hersh, *Old Boys*, 172. Journalist Joseph Trento transmits the rumor in Washington that at the time Dulles "was now running a private intelligence service out of an office at 44 Wall Street, using some of the biggest names in American business" (Trento, *Prelude to Terror*, 1). I have not found documentation for this claim, however. The closest might be Dulles's overseas work in 1949 as legal adviser to Overseas Consultants, Inc., whose "most promising venture was the

design of a long-range development program [for] Mohammed Reza Pahlavi, shah of Iran" (Grose, *Gentleman Spy*, 295).

42. Helms with Hood, *Look over My Shoulder*, 83. The following anecdote (in Saunders, *Who Paid the Piper*, 141) illustrates Dulles's easy relationships within the overworld: "On 21 January 1953, Allen Dulles, insecure about his future in the CIA under the newly elected Eisenhower, had met his friend David Rockefeller for lunch. Rockefeller hinted heavily that if Dulles decided to leave the Agency, he could reasonably expect to be invited to become president of the Ford Foundation. Dulles need not have feared for his future. Two days after this lunch, the *New York Times* broke the story that Allen Dulles was to become Director of Central Intelligence."

43. Helms with Hood, *Look over My Shoulder*, 82–83; cf. Hersh, *Old Boys*, 185. The six were Kingman Douglass, managing partner of Dillon Read; Robert Lovett of Brown Brothers Harriman; William H. Jackson and Frank Wisner of Carter, Ledyard and Milburn; Paul Nitze of Dillon Read; and former director of Central Intelligence Admiral Sidney Souers, who in 1946 retired to become a St. Louis investment banker.

44. Helms with Hood, *Look over My Shoulder*, 99; Hersh, *Old Boys*, 233. The other two lawyers were William H. Jackson and Mathias Correa.

45. Hersh, *Old Boys*, 233.

46. Scott, *Drugs, Oil, and War*, 187, 200–201. The seven deputy directors included William H. Jackson and Frank Wisner of Carter, Ledyard and Milburn, both of whom were listed in the New York Social Register.

47. Scott, *Deep Politics and the Death of JFK*, 54, 322.

48. David Wise, a veteran intelligence reporter, "Why the Spooks Shouldn't Run Wars," *Time*, February 3, 2003. The 1947 act, which created both the National Security Council and CIA to advise it, also empowered CIA to "perform such other functions and duties related to intelligence . . . as the National Security may from time to time direct" (Victor Marchetti and John D. Marks, *The CIA and the Cult of Intelligence* [New York: Knopf, 1974], 8).

49. NSC 10-2, which authorized OPC, provided it with a secret charter going far beyond the CIA's statutory responsibility for intelligence, including "subversion of hostile states . . . assistance to underground resistance and support of indigenous anti-Communist elements in threatened countries of the free world" (Helms with Hood, *Look over My Shoulder*, 113).

50. Ranelagh, *Agency*, 133; Hersh, *Old Boys*, 223–26.

51. David Wise and Thomas B. Ross, *The Espionage Establishment* (New York: Random House, 1967), 166; quoted in Scott, *Drugs, Oil, and War*, 187.

52. Grose, *Gentleman Spy*, 268–69, 292–93 (Kennan), 290–95 (Dulles). Kennan initially launched his doctrine of "containment" in a State Department cable from Moscow, then at a Council on Foreign Relations meeting, and still later, writing as "X," in the CFR journal *Foreign Affairs*.

53. Hersh, *Old Boys*, 215–16. In private practice Dulles was at Sullivan and Cromwell, Wisner at Carter, Ledyard, and Milburn. Both firms represented various Rockefeller and Standard Oil interests. According to Trento (*Secret History of the CIA*, 44–47): "Dulles arranged the job for Wisner, who quickly turned it into an intelligence power base. . . . By late 1947, Wisner, in an underhanded

way, wielded vast power in the State Department bureaucracy. He never asked permission to conduct his operations. Rather, he played a deceptive double game in which he informed either Secretary of State George Marshall or Secretary of Defense James Forrestal that the other secretary had approved his operation. Then he went ahead and carried it out. . . . The OPC's employees were largely handpicked by Wisner. . . . Under the guise of refugee administration, Wisner ran his covert operations. Dulles ran Wisner from his Sullivan and Cromwell law offices." A secret Dulles-Wisner connection at this time through "frequent meetings and phone calls" is acknowledged by Grose (*Gentleman Spy*, 301).

54. The OPC officer overseeing this project in Italy was Carmel Offie (Rowse, "Gladio," 21).

55. Ganser, *NATO's Secret Armies*.

56. Calvi and Laurent, *Piazza Fontana*, 109.

57. Griffin, *New Pearl Harbor*, 101.

58. Bamford, *Body of Secrets*, 82.

59. Hersh, *Old Boys*, 243, 252.

60. McCoy, *Politics of Heroin*, 166–74; Scott, *Drugs, Oil, and War*, 59–64, 191–93.

61. See Scott, *Drugs, Oil, and War*.

62. Scott, *Drugs, Oil, and War*, 7, 60–61, 198, 207; citing Penny Lernoux, *In Banks We Trust* (Garden City, N.Y.: Anchor / Doubleday, 1984), 84.

63. Scott, *Drugs, Oil, and War*.

64. Jack Blum, testimony before the Senate Intelligence Committee, October 23, 1996, quoted in Daniel Brandt and Steve Badrich, "Pipe Dreams: The CIA, Drugs, and the Media," *Lobster* 30 (summer 1997): 30, http://www.namebase .org/news16.html.

65. Fineman, *Special Relationship*, 179; Brown, *Last Hero*, 821–25.

66. Peter Dale Scott, Paul Hoch, and Russell Stetler, editors, *The Assassinations: Dallas and Beyond* (New York: Vintage, 1976), 395; Scott and Marshall, *Cocaine Politics*, 25. I should make it clear that the vast majority of Bay of Pigs recruits had no underworld involvement.

67. McCoy, *Politics of Heroin*, 122; Scott, *Drugs, Oil, and War*, 40.

68. McCoy, *Politics of Heroin*, 16; Emdad-ul Haq, *Drugs in South Asia*, 187.

69. *New York Times*, March 2, 2007.

70. Scott, *Drugs, Oil, and War*, 45–46; Griffin, *Reaping the Whirlwind*, 150–51.

71. In addition, America's own "war on drugs" has had a disastrous impact on the domestic security of ordinary U.S. citizens, devastating both inner cities and affluent suburbs with family tragedies and increased crime rates.

72. McCoy, *Politics of Heroin*, 178.

73. Lord Acton, "Prospectus for Cambridge Modern History," in *Selected Writings of Lord Acton*, edited by J. Rufus Fears, vol. 3 (Indianapolis, Ind.: Liberty Classics, 1988), 678.

74. Jürgen Habermas, *The Structural Transformation of the Public Sphere: An Inquiry into a Category of Bourgeois Society* (Cambridge, Mass.: MIT Press, 1991).

75. See Blum, *Killing Hope*, 64–72; Yergin, *Prize*, 450–78.

76. Shoup and Minter, *Imperial Brain Trust*, 196. CFR member Adolf Berle recorded in his diary how the 1954 overthrow in Guatemala was endorsed back in October 1952 at a CFR meeting. He added: "I am arranging to see Nelson Rockefeller, who knows the situation and can work a little with General Eisenhower on it."

77. In contrast, the governments elected with CIA help in France and Italy were able to survive because they were conformable to a prevailable will in those countries. I explore further what I mean by "prevailable will" in chapter 2.

78. This can be compared to the Soviet overreaches in Hungary in 1956 and again in Czechoslovakia in 1968. These attempts to preserve regimes that lacked the support of a prevailable will among their people doomed the chances, which until then had seemed quite possible, of a democratic Communist victory in Western Europe.

79. Burnham, in a book publicized widely by Luce, wrote of "rolling back" Communism and of supporting Chiang Kai-shek to, at some future point, "throw the Communists back out of China." See James Burnham, *The Coming Defeat of Communism* (New York: John Day, 1951), 256–66.

80. *NSC-68: United States Objectives and Programs for National Security*, April 14, 1950, http://www.fas.org/irp/offdocs/nsc-hst/nsc-68.htm; Carroll, *House of War*, 185; cf. 176: "Forrestal had hired [Nitze] at the investment firm of Dillon, Read in 1929 and then brought him to Washington in 1940."

81. Carroll, *House of War*, 152 (repeated paranoia); Fred Kaplan, "Paul Nitze: The Man Who Brought Us the Cold War," *Slate*, October 12, 2004, http://www.slate.com/id/2108510/ (missile gap). The Gaither Report was leaked in 1957, possibly by Nitze himself; leaks would be used again in the 1970s by CPD supporters, including Defense Secretary Donald Rumsfeld.

82. Paul Kennedy, *The Rise and Fall of the Great Powers* (New York: Vintage, 1989), 384.

83. For example, the largest shareholder in General Dynamics was Henry Crown, said to have invested profits from figures allied with the Chicago mob (Scott, *Deep Politics and the Death of JFK*, 155). Likewise, no one has ever satisfactorily explained the involvement in the affairs of military-industrial magnate Howard Hughes with both CIA and its sometime asset Robert Maheu, longtime friend of mafia figure John Rosselli (Donald L. Barlett and James B. Steele, *Empire: The Life, Legend, and Madness of Howard Hughes* [New York: W. W. Norton, 1979], 281–87).

84. In language not declassified until 1976, this committee concluded: "It is now clear that we are facing an implacable enemy whose avowed objective is world domination by whatever means and at whatever cost. There are no rules in such a game. If the United States is to survive, long-standing American concepts of 'fair play' must be reconsidered. We must develop effective espionage and counterespionage services and must learn to subvert, sabotage, and destroy our enemies by more clever, more sophisticated and more effective methods than those used against us. It may become necessary that the American people be made acquainted with, understand, and support this fundamentally repugnant philosophy" (Church Committee Report, Book 4, 54). As a Canadian Foreign Service officer in the late 1950s, I was able to observe the new ruthlessness in a

breed of foreign policy officials, skilled in affecting and exploiting bureaucratic paranoia, who were less interested in knowing about the world outside the United States than in knowing how to manipulate power both abroad and at home.

85. Scott, *Drugs, Oil, and War*, 4, 11, 40.

86. Church Committee Report, Book 1, 192.

87. Remark of CIA operative to Philip Graham, editor of the *Washington Post* (cited in Deborah Davis, *Katharine the Great* [New York: Sheridan Square Press, 1991], 131).

88. Church Committee Report, Book 1, 198.

89. Church Committee Report, Book 1, 189–90.

90. More precisely, a powerful antiglobal force of domestic oil independents— such as the Hunts, Murchisons, and Basses in Texas—also became caught up in the increasing search for fossil fuels overseas.

91. Ovid Demaris, *Dirty Business: The Corporate-Political-Money-Power-Game* (New York: Avon, 1975), 191. For the emergence of AIPAC in opposition to the oil lobby, see Umut Uzer, "The Impact of the Jewish Lobby on American Foreign Policy in the Middle East," *Perceptions: Journal of International Affairs* 6, no. 4 (December 2001–February 2002), http://www.sam.gov.tr/perceptions/Volume6/December2001-February2002/uuzer.PDF; partially quoted in Scott, *Drugs, Oil, and War*, 20–21.

92. "Resisting the Global Domination Project: An Interview with Prof. Richard Falk," *Frontline* 20, no. 8 (April 12–25, 2003); Richard Falk, "Global Ambitions and Geopolitical Wars," in *9/11 and American Empire*, edited by Griffin and Scott, 117–27; and Bacevich, *American Empire*, 72.

93. "Full-spectrum dominance" is the key term in *Joint Vision 2020*, the May 2000 U.S. Department of Defense blueprint for the future: "The ultimate goal of our military force is to accomplish the objectives directed by the National Command Authorities. For the joint force of the future, this goal will be achieved through full-spectrum dominance—the ability of U.S. forces, operating unilaterally or in combination with multinational and interagency partners, to defeat any adversary and control any situation across the full range of military operations" (http://www.dtic.mil/jointvision/jv2020.doc).

94. USSPACECOM, *Vision for 2020*, 1998, http://www.fas.org/spp/military/docops/usspac/lrp/ch02.htm.

95. Lester W. Grau, "Hydrocarbons and a New Strategic Region: The Caspian Sea and Central Asia," *Military Review* (May–June 2001).

96. Sheila Heslin, testimony before the Senate Hearings into Illegal Fund-Raising Activities, September 17, 1997, reported in Rashid, *Taliban*, 174.

97. Robert Baer, *See No Evil: The True Story of a Ground Soldier in the CIA's War on Terrorism* (New York: Crown, 2002), 243–44.

98. See the useful discussion by Godfrey Hodgson, "The Establishment," *Foreign Policy* No. 10 (spring 1983): 3–40.

99. Sanders, *Peddlers of Crisis*, 141–45, 174, and passim. The useful distinction between "traders" and "Prussians" was introduced by Michael Klare, *Beyond the "Vietnam Syndrome"* (Washington, D.C.: Institute for Policy Studies, 1981). Among the Prussians in the late 1960s and 1970s were Albert Wohlstetter, Richard Perle, and Paul Wolfowitz.

100. Kristol as quoted in Lewis H. Lapham, "Tentacles of Rage: The Republican Propaganda Mill, a Brief History," *Harper's Magazine*, September 2004, 36.

101. Lapham, "Tentacles of Rage," 33.

102. Lewis Powell, "Confidential Memorandum: Attack on the American Free Enterprise System," quoted in Lapham, "Tentacles of Rage," 34. Cf. Brock, *Republican Noise Machine*, 39–41.

103. Lapham, "Tentacles of Rage," 34.

104. ABC News, May 2, 2002, quoted in Phillips, *American Theocracy*, 244–45. Tim LaHaye, founder and first president of the Council for National Policy, was also a member of the executive board of Moral Majority.

105. Phillips, *Wealth and Democracy*, 92.

106. Brock, *Republican Noise Machine*, 171.

107. Parry, *Lost History*, 5–22.

108. Alfonso Chardy, "Reagan Aides and the 'Secret' Government," *Miami Herald*, July 5, 1987, http://www.theforbiddenknowledge.com/hardtruth/secret_white_house_plans.htm. In October 1984, investigative journalist Jack Anderson is said to have reported that FEMA's plans would "suspend the Constitution and the Bill of Rights, effectively eliminate private property, abolish free enterprise, and generally clamp Americans in a totalitarian vise."

109. Gelbspan, *Break-ins, Death Threats, and the FBI*, 184; cf. *New York Times*, November 18, 1991.

110. Bamford, *Pretext for War*, 74; cf. Mann, *Rise of the Vulcans*, 138–45.

111. "IRAN-CONTRA HEARINGS; North's Testimony," *New York Times*, July 14, 1987; Gelbspan, *Break-ins, Death Threats, and the FBI*, 184. Congressman Jack Brooks, who had asked North the question, was referring to the article by Alfonso Chardy in the *Miami Herald* on July 5, 1987. It "revealed Oliver North's involvement in plans for the Federal Emergency Management Agency to take over federal, state and local functions during an ill-defined national emergency."

112. Ben Bradlee Jr., *Guts and Glory: The Rise and Fall of Oliver North* (New York: Donald I. Fine, 1988), 132.

113. Bamford, *Pretext for War*, 74; cf. Clarke, *Against All Enemies*, 8–9.

114. Bamford, *Pretext for War*, 72; Mann, *Rise of the Vulcans*, 138.

115. Mann, *Rise of the Vulcans*, 209–13. The 1992 *Defense Planning Guidance* was redrafted after the document was leaked and raised considerable controversy, particularly for its ambition of discouraging all challenges through unmatchable military strength.

116. Project for the New American Century, *Rebuilding America's Defenses*, 51 (63). That the PNAC report said this does not of course implicate the authors in the planning of 9/11. But it is important as a symptom of a widely accepted truism, that it would take something like a Pearl Harbor to get America to accept an aggressive war. See, for example, Brzezinski, *Grand Chessboard*, 24–25.

117. "Report of the Commission to Assess United States National Security Space Management and Organization," January 7, 2001, http://www.defenselink.mil/pubs/spaceintro.pdf, quoted in Griffin, *9/11 Commission Report: Omissions and Distortions*, 121. In June 2001, Wolfowitz delivered a commencement address that focused on the lessons of Pearl Harbor, as analyzed by Roberta

Wohlstetter, the wife of Wolfowitz's thesis adviser and mentor, Albert Wohlstetter. In keeping with her observation that "interestingly, that 'surprise attack' was preceded by an astonishing number of unheeded warnings and missed signals," Wolfowitz commented, "Surprise happens so often that it's surprising that we're still surprised by it. . . . [America needs to] replace a poverty of expectations with an anticipation of the unfamiliar and the unlikely" (Mann, *Rise of the Vulcans*, 291).

118. "Full-spectrum dominance" is a term of art made popular by the U.S. Space Command in its *Vision for 2020*: "The emerging synergy of [U.S.] space superiority with land, sea, and air superiority, will lead to Full Spectrum Dominance" (quoted in Griffin, *9/11 Commission Report: Omissions and Distortions*, 119).

119. The estimate of a trillion dollars is in Griffin, *9/11 Commission Report: Omissions and Distortions*, 120, citing the *Global Network Space Newsletter* no. 14 (fall 2003), http:// space4peace.org/newsletter/gnnews14.htm. The March 28, 2005, edition of the *New York Times* (Tim Weiner, "Drive to Build High-Tech Army Hits Cost Snags") reported on the Pentagon's plans to build more than seventy major weapons systems at a cost of more than $1.3 trillion.

120. Cumings, *Origins of the Korean War*, 2:431–32. On the deceits of the Tonkin Gulf, see Ellsberg, *Secrets*, 7–20.

121. Ola Tunander, "The Use of Terrorism to Construct World Order," paper presented at the Fifth Pan-European International Relations Conference, The Hague, September 9–11, 2004, http://www.sgir.org/conference2004/papers/ Tunander%20-%20Securitization,%20dual%20state%20and%20US-European %20geopolitical%20divide.pdf.

122. Alexis de Tocqueville, *Democracy in America*, translated by Harvey C. Mansfield and Delba Winthrop (Chicago: University of Chicago Press, 2000), 3.

2. NIXON, KISSINGER, AND THE DECLINE
OF THE PUBLIC STATE

Epigraphs: "House of Lords Journal Volume 5: 24 May 1642," *Journal of the House of Lords*, vol. 5, 1642–1643 (1802): 80–3, http://www.british-history .ac.uk/report.asp?compid=34806. Richard Chambers, a leading merchant, was in 1629 fined two thousand pounds and imprisoned for speaking out against the illegal taxes levied by Charles I. The Huston Memorandum is quoted in Emery, *Watergate*, 25. The Huston Plan, incorporating this provision for surreptitious entries, was temporarily blocked by FBI director J. Edgar Hoover, but President Nixon continued to support and promote the idea, which led to the break-in at the office of Daniel Ellsberg's psychiatrist and eventually to the Watergate incident.

1. Nixon in turn ran the most paranoid administration, with bugging and spying in all directions. From a 2002 *Slate* article: "That Kissinger was bugging Nixon at the same time that Nixon was bugging (and, on occasion, tormenting) Kissinger provides further evidence, if any were needed, that the twin themes of the Nixon White House were paranoia and betrayal" (Tom Blanton, "Kissinger's

Revenge: While Nixon Was Bugging Kissinger, Guess Who Was Bugging Nixon," *Slate*, February 18, 2002, http://www.slate.com/?id=2062229).

2. The 1964 Republican presidential candidate Barry Goldwater caught the prevailing mood of many beyond the right in his memorable oversimplification: "Extremism in the defense of liberty is no vice; moderation in the pursuit of justice is no virtue." See Goldwater's acceptance speech at the 28th Republican National Convention, http://www.washingtonpost.com/wp-srv/politics/daily/may98/goldwaterspeech.htm.

3. Juan Williams, *Eyes on the Prize: America's Civil Rights Years, 1954–1965* (New York: Penguin, 1988); Diane McWhorter, *A Dream of Freedom: The Civil Rights Movement from 1954 to 1968* (New York: Scholastic, 2004).

4. From Schell, *Unconquerable World*, 227: "I suggest that power that is based on support might be called cooperative power. . . . Power is cooperative when it springs from action in concert of people who willingly agree with one another and is coercive when it springs from the threat or use of force." Cf. 231: "The power that flows upward from the consent, support, and nonviolent activity of the people is not the same as the power that flows downward from the state."

5. Nye, *Paradox of American Power*, 9.

6. The prevailable will of the people is the emerging sanction of a generally accepted social or political change. The more common term "will of the people," a refurbishing of Rousseau's "general will," is often invoked as the ultimate sanction of a generally accepted decision. However, even if not a total abstraction, the term has no meaning at the time of a major controversy; the "public will" will be established by events, not passively divined. The "will of the majority" is an even more dangerous phrase; the opinions of majorities are often superficial and fickle, and destined not to prevail. (The Vietnam and Iraq wars are examples where the momentary will of the majority proved not to be the prevailable will.) The prevailable will can be said to be latent in a political crisis but will not be established or proven until its outcome. In the case of abolishing slavery in America, for example, the resolution took decades, but it is hard to imagine any other prevailable outcome.

7. U.S. Army Field Manual, *FM 100–19*, chapter 3, "Legal Considerations and Constraints," http://www.fas.org/irp/doddir/army/fm100-19/fm100-19_3.html. See also Keith Earle Bonn and Anthony E. Baker, *Guide to Military Operations Other Than War: Tactics, Techniques, and Procedures for Stability* (Mechanicsburg, Pa.: Stackpole Books, 200), 51.

8. Ridenhour with Lubow, "Bringing the War Home," 20, http://www.namebase.org/ppost14.html; cf. Ron Ridenhour, "Garden Plot and the New Action Army," *CounterSpy* (1975). Ridenhour attributed the policies to the recommendations of Cyrus Vance to the Kerner Commission. Vance testified twice to the Kerner Commission, but I have not seen his testimony. The only Vance recommendations I have run across are in a more moderate vein, in a report submitted to the president recommending a more professional training in riot control for the National Guard. I can find no acknowledgment that Vance recommended a surveillance role for army intelligence either to the Pentagon or to the Kerner Commission. See Lyndon Baines Johnson Library, "Oral Histories—Cyrus R.

Vance," http://www.lbjlib.utexas.edu/Johnson/archives.hom/oralhistory.hom/Vance-C/Vance1.pdf.

9. Ridenhour with Lubow, "Bringing the War Home," 18.

10. From Halperin et al., *Lawless State*, 2: "Investigations have shown that every intelligence agency had one or more surveillance programs that spied on law-abiding American citizens, in violation of the laws, the Constitution, and the traditions of the country. Their ominous scope is best portrayed by the code names used by the agencies: the CIA ran CHAOS, SETTER, HT-LINGUAL, MERRIMAC, and RESISTANCE, the FBI added COMINFIL, VIDEM, STUDEN; the military had CABLE SPLICER and GARDEN PLOT; the NSA managed MINARET and SHAMROCK; the IRS had LEPRECHAUN and the SSS (Special Service Staff). All the techniques associated with secret police bureaus throughout history were used to gather information: black-bag break-ins, wiretaps and bugs, mail openings, cable and telegram interceptions, garbage covers, and informers." Cf. Scott, Hoch, and Stetler, *Assassinations*, 443–46 (Secret Service). In this source I document the role of two other political assassinations besides that of Martin Luther King Jr., those of the two Kennedy brothers, in supplying the pretext and authorization for these programs.

11. Churchill and Wall, *Agents of Repression*, 48, 219.

12. Michael P. Wright, "Stephen Jones, the FBI, & the Tinker 12," http://members.aol.com/mpwright9/index1.html.

13. Fred Cook, "The Real Conspiracy Exposed," *Nation*, October 1, 1973; Frank Donner, "The Confession of an FBI Informer," *Harper's* (December 1972): 54–62. While in Thailand, I received a friendly e-mail from Pablo Fernandez, saying that his views had changed. I promised him a book when I returned, but I have since lost his address. If he gets to read this, the offer still stands.

14. Scott, *Deep Politics and the Death of JFK*, 278–79.

15. William F. Pepper, *Orders to Kill: The Truth behind the Murder of Martin Luther King* (New York: Carroll and Graf, 1995), 414–15. Most of what Pepper writes about army surveillance of King is documented and corroborated (cf. Steve Tompkins, "Army Feared King, Secretly Watched Him. Spying on Blacks Started 75 Years Ago," *Memphis Commercial Appeal*, March 21, 1993). Unfortunately, Pepper also transmitted the claim made to him that the 20th Special Forces Group had a sniper team in Memphis on April 4, 1968, to ensure that King was murdered. I believe from my own research that the sniper team story was disinformation from high sources designed to discredit Pepper. In particular, an alleged authorizing cable, citing Operation Garden Plot, is to a trained reader a self-revealing forgery (photo #33, see 424). Cf. *Memphis Flyer*, July 17, 1997.

16. J. Anthony Lukas, *Nightmare: The Underside of the Nixon Years* (New York: Viking, 1976), 32–37; Helms with Hood, *Look over My Shoulder*, 279–84.

17. Lukas, *Nightmare*, 195–96; Ellsberg, *Secrets*, 451.

18. Lapham, "Tentacles of Rage," 33.

19. Powell, "Confidential Memorandum," quoted in Lapham, "Tentacles of Rage," 34. Cf. Brock, *Republican Noise Machine*, 39–41. *American Prospect* columnist Mark Schmitt has argued that Powell's memo, even if influential, should not be seen as launching a right-wing trend by itself; there were "a lot of

people writing their own memos" (see Schmitt, "The Legend of the Powell Memo," *American Prospect Online*, April 27, 2005, http://www.prospect.org/web/page.ww?section=root&name=ViewWeb&articleId=9606).

20. H. R. Haldeman, *The Haldeman Diaries: Inside the Nixon White House* (New York: G. P. Putnam's, 1994), 193.

21. Parry, *Secrecy & Privilege*, 72; cf. Blumenthal, *Rise of the Counter-Establishment*, 45.

22. "Assault on Free Enterprise" pamphlet quoted in Sampson, *Seven Sisters*, 271: "Scores of senators and congressmen rushed to propose new legislation to control the oil companies; according to one count, there were almost 800 bills concerned with the energy crisis." The only serious challenge to the industry came from Senator Church's Subcommittee investigating multinational corporations. It reported: "In a democracy, important questions of policy with respect to a vital commodity like oil, the life blood of an industrial society, cannot be left to private companies acting in accord with private interests and a closed circle of government officials." Senator Church was defeated by huge sums of outside money when he came up for reelection in 1980.

23. Brewery magnate Joseph Coors was reportedly "stirred up" by Lewis Powell's memorandum (Micklethwait and Wooldridge, *Right Nation*, 77–78).

24. Nelson Rockefeller blamed his brother John for having "allowed the family's influence to be diminished and then extinguished at the Rockefeller Foundation" (Rockefeller, *Memoirs*, 342). In 1983, Henry Ford II resigned in disgust from the board of the Ford Foundation.

25. Anthony Summers and Robbyn Swan, *Sinatra: The Life* (New York: Alfred A. Knopf, 2005), 350–53.

26. Sanders, *Peddlers of Crisis*, 174. I have written elsewhere how by 1968 the war's costs threatened the convertibility of the dollar under the Bretton Woods Agreement of 1944 and thus occasioned a split between the "military-industrial complex" and the "CIA-financial establishment" (see Scott, "Vietnam War and the CIA-Financial Establishment," 107–26). Cf. Robert Buzzanco, "What Happened to the New Left? Toward a Radical Reading of American Foreign Relations," *Diplomatic History* 23 (fall 1999): 593–95. Buzzanco agrees that by 1968 many of America's financial elite had concluded that the Vietnam War was "damaging the economy" and causing "economic instability on an international scale." Under the guise of calling for reduced expenditure on the war, the bankers effectively endorsed U.S. military withdrawal from Vietnam. See also Kirkpatrick Sale, *Power Shift: The Rise of the Southern Rim and Its Challenge to the Eastern Establishment* (New York: Random House, 1975), 266–67.

27. Sanders, *Peddlers of Crisis*, 141–45 and passim.

28. Kissinger, *White House Years*, 11, quoted in Hersh, *Price of Power*, 27–28.

29. Hersh, *Price of Power*, 27, supplies important details, often overlooked, about Nixon's probable contacts with Kissinger in the 1950s.

30. Phillips, *Wealth and Democracy*, 313–14.

31. Hersh, *Price of Power*, 67–73.

32. Bill, *Eagle and the Lion*, 328. Besides being a paid consultant to the Rockefellers, Kissinger also received sizable cash gifts.

33. Phillips, *Wealth and Democracy*, 86.

34. Yergin, *Prize*, 590–91. In 1972 the United States imported 28 percent of its oil, and by 1977, 47 percent ("The Decline of U.S. Power: The New Debate over Guns and Butter," *Business Week*, March 12, 1979).

35. As Nixon told the American people on April 30, 1970, he had ordered troops into Cambodia because America would otherwise become "a pitiful, help-less giant." In the next years he had to deal with a socialist revolution in Portu-gal, destabilizing its former colonies, and with the election of Salvador Allende in Chile.

36. Woodward, *State of Denial*, 407.

37. Woodward, *State of Denial*, 406–8, citing Kissinger's August 12, 2005, column in *Washington Post*. Kissinger himself long peddled the image that he was the sane man preventing Nixon from "going off to extremes" (Rothkopf, *Running the World*, 128). But in 2005, Kissinger revealed to Bush's speechwriter Mike Gerson that at one point "he had proposed to President Nixon a major ultimatum to the North Vietnamese with dire consequences if they did not nego-tiate peace. But it didn't happen, [Kissinger] said wistfully. 'I didn't have enough power'" (Woodward, *State of Denial*, 409–10).

38. Haldeman, *Haldeman Diaries*, 316–17; Hersh, *Price of Power*, 372–73.

39. James A. Bill, "U.S.-Iran Relations: Forty Years of Observations," lecture, February 20, 2004, the Middle East Institute, http://www.mideasti.org/articles/doc183.html. Cf. Bill, *Eagle and the Lion*, 201. Little, *American Orientalism*, 143–45, 222.

40. Sampson, *Arms Bazaar*, 252.

41. Little, *American Orientalism*, 5; cf. 140, 143–45, 222. The twin pillars referred to Iran and Saudi Arabia, but underlying them were two more funda-mental pillars of U.S. policy: arms and oil. The groundwork for this policy was actually laid by Presidents Kennedy and Johnson, but it only became fully embodied with the Nixon Doctrine.

42. See Nitzan and Bichler, *Global Political Economy of Israel*.

43. Stanley Hoffman, "Washington, Ripe for Disaster," *New York Times*, June 16, 1985. The shah, when interviewed about his role in increasing oil prices in the first OPEC oil crisis, repeatedly maintained that he had been encouraged to do so by the Americans.

44. James K. Galbraith, "The Unbearable Costs of Empire," *The American Pros-pect*, November 18, 2002, http://www.prospect.org/print/V13/21/galbraith-j.html.

45. Walter Russell Mead, review of *American Dynasty* by Kevin Phillips, *For-eign Affairs* 83, no. 2 (March–April 2004): 155: "Phillips' central idea is inter-esting and important. The twentieth century, he argues, saw a fusion of three major interests: the energy industry, Wall Street, and the defense industry. Four generations of Bushes have participated in and furthered the emergence of this finance-security-hydrocarbon complex."

46. J. P. Smith, "International Oil Market Faces an Uncertain Future!" *Wash-ington Post*, July 1, 1979.

47. Dreyfuss, *Devil's Game*, 131.

48. Brisard and Dasquié, *Forbidden Truth*, 79; Labévière, *Dollars for Terror*, 42.

49. David Holden and Richard Johns, *The House of Saud* (New York: Holt, Rinehart and Winston, 1981), 262.

50. Cordovez and Harrison, *Out of Afghanistan*, 16. Selig S. Harrison heard about the program in 1975 from the shah's ambassador to the United Nations, "who pointed to it proudly as an example of Iranian-American cooperation."

51. Summers with Swan, *Arrogance of Power*, 283 (Salinger); Baer, *Sleeping with the Devil*, 43 (briefcase). In 1972, Khashoggi is said to have held deposits of $200 million in the bank of Nixon's crony Bebe Rebozo (in Renata Adler, "Searching for the Real Nixon Scandal," *Atlantic* [December 1976], 76–84). Khashoggi admitted publicly to a gift of $43,000 in 1972.

52. Marshall, Scott, and Hunter, *Iran-Contra Connection*, 19–24.

53. Summers with Swan, *Arrogance of Power*, 164; cf. Sampson, *Arms Bazaar*, 252.

54. Sampson, *Arms Bazaar*, 204.

55. Kessler, *Richest Man in the World*, 29 (Yassin), 175–78, 275–78 (Khashoggi). A friend of Khashoggi's, Larry Kolb, reports that Khashoggi himself essentially corroborated the story that Khashoggi and John Kennedy had a friendship in the 1950s that "evolved primarily out of whoring together" (Larry J. Kolb, *Overworld: The Life and Times of a Reluctant Spy* [New York: Riverhead/Penguin, 2004], 236). The woman who destroyed the presidential aspirations of Senator Gary Hart in 1987 was one of Khashoggi's many girls.

56. *Kerry-Brown BCCI Report*, 299.

57. Kolb, *Overworld*, 238, 242–43.

58. Investigative reporter Jim Hougan reports the incredulity of congressional investigators that Lockheed was the only large corporation not to have made a contribution to Nixon's 1972 election campaign (Hougan, *Spooks: The Haunting of America—The Private Use of Secret Agents* [New York: William Morrow, 1978], 457–58).

59. Standard Shaefer, "Duck, Duck, Goose: Financing the War, Financing the World," *Counterpunch*, April 23, 2003, summarizing Michael Hudson, *Super Imperialism* (London: Pluto Press, 2003). Shaefer's interview of Hudson here is of great interest.

60. In *Drugs, Oil, and War* (15), I gave the example of the use of defoliant herbicides like Agent Orange in Vietnam: a program that continued at full blast, to the enrichment of U.S. corporations with Department of Defense contracts, long after expert evaluations had determined that the program was arousing much hostility "and might well be counterproductive."

61. In 1980, Iranian specialist Barnett Rubin would call the 1972 arms deal with Iran "short-sighted and almost criminally careless" (Rubin, *Paved with Good Intentions*, 261).

62. David J. Louscher and Michael D. Solomon, "Set and Drift," *Naval War College Review*, November–December 1980, 82. A U.N. conference in 2001 attempted to limit the global trade in small arms, of which there are now over five hundred million, more than half of them illicit. At the conference "the U.S. under secretary of state for arms control, John Bolton, said the Bush administration rejected any move to restrict the right of citizens to bear arms. He also warned that America would oppose plans to restrict arms trading to rebel

groups. . . . America made clear yesterday that Washington would oppose measures to constrain legal trade and manufacture. 'The vast majority of arms transfers in the world are routine and not problematic,' Mr Bolton stressed" (Anne
Penketh, "U.S. Hinders Global Effort to Cut Small Arms Trade," *Independent*,
July 10, 2001, http://www.globalpolicy.org/security/smallarms/articles/2001/
0710us.htm).

63. From Johnson, *Sorrows of Empire*, 280: "Pentagon planners hoped that
the sales of armaments and munitions to new NATO members might amount to
$35 billion over ten years."

64. Johnson, *Sorrows of Empire*, 280–81.

65. Scott, *Drugs, Oil, and War*, 41, 53–54.

66. David E. Spiro, *The Hidden Hand of American Hegemony: Petrodollar
Recycling and International Markets* (Ithaca, N.Y.: Cornell, 1999), x, quoted in
Scott, *Drugs, Oil, and War*, 53.

67. "Colombia was the largest supplier of illegal drugs in Latin America in the
1980s, although estimates of the value of these drugs varied tremendously. From
1981 to 1986, annual receipts from the drug trade ranged from US$1 billion to
US$4 billion. The actual amount of money that was laundered back into the
economy each year, however, was much lower; estimates varied from
US$200,000 to more than US$1 billion. Regardless of the precise dollar figure,
most analysts agreed that drug money had a significant effect on foreign
exchange reserves. Many believed that narcotics accounted for as much as the
equivalent of 50 percent of officially recorded exports" (in "Relations with the
United States," *Country Studies: Colombia*, U.S. Library of Congress, Federal
Research Division, http://countrystudies.us/colombia/77.htm).

68. In Little, *American Orientalism*, 222: "While the shah flexed his new-
found military muscle, his multi-billion spending spree spawned inflation at
home that eroded the earnings of tenant farmers, oil workers, and shopkeepers."

69. Sick, *All Fall Down*, 21.

70. Rockefeller, *Memoirs*, 237, 242; cf. Kissinger/David Rockefeller telcon
of March 17, 1972, http://www.gwu.edu/~nsarchiv/NSAEBB/NSAEBB123/
telcon-19720313.pdf (China).

71. Rockefeller, *Memoirs*, 274, 276, 281, 298, and passim.

72. Hougan, *Spooks*, 435. Later, just as Kermit Roosevelt parlayed his 1953
CIA coup in Iran into longtime service with Gulf Oil, so Kissinger followed his
White House stint with consultations for oil companies like Unocal in Afghan-
istan (Joe Conason, "Regarding Henry: Will He Explain His Job for Unocal
When the Oil Giant Was Cozying Up to the Taliban?" *Salon*, December 3, 2002,
http://dir.salon.com/story/politics/conason/2002/12/03/bush/index.html.

73. Rockefeller, *Memoirs*, 331. This discussion occurs in his disarmingly frank
chapter on "Family Turmoil" because of the alienation his children experienced
over Vietnam.

74. Oval Office transcript, May 2, 1972, National Security Archive, http://
www.gwu.edu/~nsarchiv/NSAEBB, 717-20; Ellsberg, *Secrets*, 418.

75. Isaacson, *Kissinger*, 248. National Security Council staffer Tony Lake
sensed that Kissinger was in favor of a military blow in 1969 and "was disap-
pointed Nixon was not as tough as [Nelson] Rockefeller would have been. 'He

kept muttering afterwards, "Nelson would have cracked them"'" (Isaacson, *Kissinger*, 247).

76. Suhail Islam and Syed Hassan, "The Wretched of the Nations: The West's Role in Human Rights Violations in the Bangladesh War of Independence," in *Genocide, War Crimes, and the West*, edited by Jones, 206–9, summarizing Hitchens, *Trial of Henry Kissinger*, 37. Cf. Scott, *Drugs, Oil, and War*, 169; Hersh, *Price of Power*, 121–22. Haldeman noted in his diary on December 22, 1970, that "Henry . . . has to use the P[resident] to force Laird and the military to go ahead with the P[resident]'s plans, which they won't carry out without direct orders" (Haldeman, *Haldeman Diaries*, 224). Although critics from Hersh to Hitchens have blamed Kissinger for this bombing, he was actually "downgrading" angry orders from Nixon to tell the Air Force to "really go in [with] everything that can fly and crack the hell out of them" (Hanhimäki, *Flawed Architect*, 111, citing "Telcons: Nixon-Kissinger, Kissinger-Haig," December 9, 1970, National Security Archive Web site, http://www.gwu.edu/~nsarchiv/NSAEBB/NSAEBB123/index.htm).

77. Asad Ismi, "An Unpunished War Criminal: Not All Terrorists Are Muslim Fundamentalists," *Canadian Centre for Policy Alternatives (CCPA) Monitor* (December 2001–January 2002), http://141.117.225.2/~asadismi/kissinger.html. The Joint Chiefs of Staff bombing expert whose recommendations were overruled "recalls one constant Kissinger directive: that the secret missions avoid civilian casualties and thus, it was hoped, a public protest from the Sihanouk government" (Hersh, *Price of Power*, 122). But Cambodia is not Antarctica, and the bombed areas were not "unpopulated."

78. Scott, *Drugs, Oil, and War*, 167–70. There I describe the role in 1963 of Mobil, a Rockefeller company, in lobbying for a "final [U.S.] commitment" to Southeast Asia, meaning "that we must be prepared to fight . . . at a minimum" (100). After the final expulsion of the United States from Vietnam in 1975, Mobil switched swiftly from lobbying for war with Vietnam to lobbying for a resumption of United States–Vietnam relations. It was perhaps the first U.S. oil company to win rights to continue exploring for oil and gas off Vietnam. With the resumption of United States–Vietnam relations in 1994, Mobil has been producing from Vietnam's Big Bear field, estimated to contain six hundred million barrels (John Pomfret, "Contested Islands Chains a Security Concern for the 1990s," Associated Press, July 15, 1992; *USA Today*, January 19, 1994; *Chicago Tribune*, May 3, 1996).

79. Scott, *Drugs, Oil, and War*, 178, quoting *San Francisco Examiner*, May 21, 1970. At the same time, when a number of aides resigned in protest against the Cambodia invasion, Kissinger roared at one of them: "Your views represent the cowardice of the Eastern Establishment" (in John Prados, *Keeper of the Keys: A History of the National Security Council from Truman to Bush* [New York: Morrow, 1991], 297–98).

80. Hersh, *Price of Power*, 270.

81. See Hersh, *Price of Power*, 264, 275–77; also 269–70: "In future planning in the Chilean crisis, Kissinger wrote, Nixon 'sought as much as possible to circumvent the bureaucracy.' Kissinger neglected to note that he too was . . . as eager as Nixon to circumvent the bureaucracy." In Kissinger's *Years of Renewal*

(315) he reiterated that the origin of the controversial "Track II" option in Chile "was Nixon's reluctance to do combat with an obstreperous bureaucracy."

82. Hersh, *Price of Power*, 296, 268n: After their testimony to Congress about Chile in 1973, Helms was ultimately indicted and convicted for misleading Congress. At the same time "Geneen, Parkinson, and Kendall were each under investigation on felony charges" in connection with their testimony.

83. Rockefeller, *Memoirs*, 431.

84. Rockefeller, *Memoirs*, 432; Hersh, *Price of Power*, 262.

85. Hanhimäki, *Flawed Architect*, 101. On another occasion Kissinger is said to have told a Chilean visitor: "Latin America is not important. Nothing important can come from the South. History has never been produced in the South" (Hanhimäki, *Flawed Architect*, 101). In 1969, Nixon disliked both the Chilean regime of Christian Democrat Eduardo Frei (whom he saw as a Kennedy man) and also "the Georgetown set in the CIA," who, with Kennedy encouragement and support, had helped subsidize Frei's election in 1964 (Hersh, *Price of Power*, 261). His response was to slash the U.S. support to Chile that had been supplied with the goal of keeping Frei in power.

86. Hanhimäki, *Flawed Architect*, 102.

87. Kissinger, *Years of Renewal*, 314; cf. Hanhimäki, *Flawed Architect*, 101.

88. Rockefeller, *Memoirs*, 432. In August 1971, David Rockefeller also asked Kissinger to discuss the Chilean election with his former colleague John Place, who had recently become president of Anaconda Copper (Letter from Rockefeller to Kissinger of August 17, 1971, http://www.gwu.edu/~nsarchiv/NSAEBB/NSAEBB193/hak-8-17-71.pdf). Anaconda, which Allende had pledged to nationalize, "owed a quarter of a billion dollars to a group of banks led by Chase Manhattan" (in Howard Zinn, "The CIA, Rockefeller, and the Boys in the Club," http://www.thirdworldtraveler.com/Zinn/Rockefeller_BoysClub.html).

89. Helms with Hood, *Look over My Shoulder*, 399–400.

90. Trento, *Prelude to Terror*, 367. The secret history of the CLA was prepared by Enno Hobbing, a CIA officer on assignment to the Council.

91. Hersh, *Price of Power*, 260, cf. 266. See also Trento, *Secret History of the CIA*, 206: "The Group's job was to provide a cover organization to which corporations could contribute money to pay for bribes and other political activities in Latin America."

92. Hersh, *Price of Power*, 266.

93. Hersh, *Price of Power*, 268n.

94. Rockefeller, *Memoirs*, 432.

95. Hersh, *Price of Power*, 273.

96. Isaacson, *Kissinger*, 289.

97. Trento, *Prelude to Terror*, 62. The sensitivity of David Rockefeller's CIA collaboration helps explain why President Ford assigned an investigation of the CIA's operations to David's brother Nelson Rockefeller.

98. Rockefeller, *Memoirs*, 433.

99. Hanhimäki, *Flawed Architect*, 154–84; Faqir Syed Aijazuddin, *The White House and Pakistan: Secret Declassified Documents, 1969–74* (New York: Oxford University Press, 2003).

100. Hersh, *Price of Power*, 447–48. Kissinger's words at a top-level White

House meeting ("The President . . . wants us to tilt in favor of Pakistan") were soon reproduced in journalist Jack Anderson's syndicated column, "U.S. Tilts to Pakistan," (December 14, 1971). A resulting investigation by the White House Plumbers unit failed to find the source but revealed that the Joint Chiefs were spying on the White House (Lukas, *Nightmare*, 104–6).

101. Hitchens, *Trial of Henry Kissinger*, 47; Islam and Hassan, "Wretched of the Nations," 206–9.

102. Hitchens, *Trial of Henry Kissinger*, 45; Islam and Hassan, "Wretched of the Nations," 208–9.

103. Later, after East Pakistan was invaded by India and became "a sovereign Bangladesh . . . [Kissinger] compared Sheikh Mujibur Rahman, the [Awami League leader and] first President of Bangladesh, to Allende and prepared a similar fate for him. In an account which adds significant new information, Hitchens details a U.S.-sponsored military coup against Mujib in August 1975 which led to his murder and that of forty of his family members" (in Ismi, "Unpunished War Criminal").

104. Sean P. Winchell, "Pakistan's ISI: The Invisible Government," *International Journal of Intelligence and Counterintelligence* 16, no. 3 (2003): 374–88; Jaideep Saikia, "The ISI Reaches East: Anatomy of a Conspiracy," *Studies in Conflict and Terrorism* (May–June 2002): 185–97.

105. The CIA's and Kissinger's exploitation of Muslim paranoia for massacre in 1970 had a precedent: the 1965 massacre of Communist Party supporters in Indonesia, also encouraged and facilitated by CIA but carried out by the Indonesian army together with Islamic madrassas. See Peter Dale Scott, "The U.S. and the Overthrow of Sukarno, 1965–67," *Pacific Affairs* (summer 1978): 239–264, http://www.namebase.org/scott.html.

106. Hitchens, *Trial of Henry Kissinger*, 50–51.

107. Hitchens, *Trial of Henry Kissinger*, 52–53, citing an unpublished review of the U.S.-Pakistan tilt by the Carnegie Endowment for International Peace, 1973.

108. B. Raman, "Pakistan's Inter-Services Intelligence (ISI)," South Asia Analysis Group (SAAG), Paper No. 287, August 1, 2001, http://www.saag.org/papers3/paper287.html.

109. Dreyfuss, *Devil's Game*, 73–79. Ramadan's Muslim Brotherhood associates in Palestine and Jordan were the organizers of first Hizb-ut-Tahrir, now powerful in Central Asia, and later Hamas (Dreyfuss, *Devil's Game*, 75, 191–92). Some Russians suspect Hizb-ut-Tahrir of serving a U.S. intelligence plan to foment Muslim secession in Russia. See Peter Dale Scott, "The Global Drug Meta-Group: Drugs, Managed Violence, and the Russian 9/11," *Lobster* (October 2005), http://lobster-magazine.co.uk/articles/global-drug.htm.

110. Dreyfuss, *Devil's Game*, 75, 79, quoting Sylvain Besson, "When the Swiss Protected Radical Islam in the Name of Interests of State," *Le Temps* (Geneva), October 26, 2004.

111. Cooley, *Unholy Wars*, 43.

112. Dreyfuss, *Devil's Game*, 151; emphasis added, citing Holden and Johns, *House of Saud*, 289; Kissinger, *White House Years*, 1293.

113. Cf. Coll, *Ghost Wars*, 63: By 1981 the "ISI and the CIA had collaborated

secretly for decades." The ISI had been originally established in the 1940s by the British, but many Pakistanis believe it would never have become as massive as it did without CIA support for it and Gen. Mohammed Zia-ul-Haq in the 1970s.

114. M. B. Naqvi, "The Crisis Prone U.S.-Pakistan Ties," *Defence Journal* (January 2003), http://www.defencejournal.com/2003/jan/crisis.htm.

115. Dreyfuss, *Devil's Game*, 109–11: "Ayatollah Seyyed Abolqassem Kashani, the chief representative of the Muslim Brotherhood in Iran and Ayatollah Ruhollah Khomeini's mentor . . . was a central figure in the campaign." For the role of British intelligence in securing cooperation with the mullahs as part of this joint MI6-CIA project, see Mark Curtis, *The Ambiguities of Power: British Foreign Policy since 1945* (London: Zed Press, 1995), chapter 4.

116. Aburish, *Brutal Friendship*, 60–61. Cf. Miles Copeland, *The Game Player: Confessions of the CIA's Original Political Operative* (London: Aurum Press, 1989), 149–54.

117. International Crisis Group, "Pakistan: Madrasas, Extremism, and the Military," Asia Paper No. 36, July 29, 2002, http://www.crisisweb.org/home/index.cfm?id=1627&l=1.

118. Hersh, *Price of Power*, 451.

119. "Comity" is defined in most dictionaries as civility or courtesy. In politics the term carries the unique sense of a shared recognition of the respect and trust due to political institutions and personages. Richard Helms later told Stanley Kutler that "Nixon never trusted anyone in the Executive Branch" (Summers with Swan, *Arrogance of Power*, 330).

120. Kutler, *Wars of Watergate*, 478. John Doar, the special counsel to the House Judiciary Committee, duly investigated the Cambodia bombing, but House liberals failed in their efforts to have Cambodia included among the articles of impeachment (Kutler, *Wars of Watergate*, 481, 530).

121. Emery, *Watergate*, 9–12; Kutler, *Wars of Watergate*, 119–20.

122. The most celebrated leak of this period was of course Daniel Ellsberg's leak of the Pentagon Papers concerning Vietnam, and the Plumbers' response to it became a major factor in Nixon's downfall. But the leak did not concern Nixon-Kissinger excesses, and Ellsberg's motives in leaking the documents were to end the Vietnam War, not to curb or bring down the president.

123. Emery, *Watergate*, 83–84; Kutler, *Wars of Watergate*, 116–19; and Lukas, *Nightmare*, 104–6.

124. Kutler, *Wars of Watergate*, 117, cf. 457–58. Lukas (*Nightmare*, 105) calls the JCS espionage "a natural response to the increasing concentration of national security-making in Kissinger's NSC." But the objection to Kissinger had to do with policy as well as with procedures. Suspicion that Kissinger was some kind of Soviet agent for détente was widespread at this time in right-wing circles, including the military. See Phyllis Schlafly and Chester Ward, *Kissinger on the Couch* (New Rochelle, N.Y.: Arlington House, 1975).

125. This is the easiest explanation for the unnecessary "dead giveaway" retaping of the latch on the B-2 level door to the Watergate, which McCord falsely assured the burglars he had removed. See Hougan, *Secret Agenda*, 200; Emery, *Watergate*, 132. Although there were for a long time mutual recriminations as to who was responsible for the retaping, McCord admitted on TV in

1993 that it was he (Emery, *Watergate*, 505). Not only did McCord needlessly tape or retape a number of doors inside the building (which opened without a key from the inside), he apparently affixed the tape horizontally in a way that made it easily visible when the door was shut (Lukas, *Nightmare*, 204). Hard also to explain is the prompt arrival at the scene of Carl Shoffler, a junior police officer whose regular shift that night (for desk work) had already ended and who "had assisted the CIA in the past" (Hougan, *Secret Agenda*, 320–23). Finally, how can one explain the burglars' possession of easily traceable, sequentially numbered $100 bills, which led investigators within days to burglar Bernard Barker's bank account in Miami? The bills had been issued there in exchange for four Mexican checks traceable to the Finance Committee for the Re-election of the President (Lukas, *Nightmare*, 190, 229; Emery, *Watergate*, 111–12, 148, 162, 188). Like an oak tree in an acorn, the whole subsequent drama of Watergate was implanted in the unnecessary giveaway evidence of that day.

126. Hougan, *Secret Agenda*, 24. Cf. James McCord, *A Piece of Tape* (Rockville, Md.: Washington Media Services, 1974).

127. Hougan, *Secret Agenda*, 16.

128. One of Angleton's preferred Soviet defectors, the controversial Michal Goleniewski, "insisted that Kissinger had been recruited by the Soviets in the aftermath of World War II" (Hougan, *Secret Agenda*, 63); cf. Kutler, *Wars of Watergate*, 457. Paranoia was widespread during this time in Washington. Kissinger himself used to call Defense Secretary Laird "a crook"; Nixon adviser Alexander Haig reportedly called Laird "a traitor to the country" (Hersh, *Price of Power*, 90).

129. Powers, *Man Who Kept the Secrets*, 242.

130. It is alleged that CIA was eavesdropping on Nixon in the Oval Office, as Charles Colson and others in the White House believed, and that Nixon's knowledge of this explains why he complied, disastrously, with orders to hand over his tapes. See Hougan, *Secret Agenda*, 59–61 (CIA bug), 133, and passim; Scott, *Deep Politics and the Death of JFK*, 234–37.

131. At the time of the Watergate break-in, Hunt was in a "current relationship" with the CIA's Central Cover staff (CIA memo of June 19, 1972, NARA #104-10103-10057, p. 3).

132. A particularly important example of these crimes was the 1971 break-in at the office of Daniel Ellsberg's psychiatrist, Dr. Lewis Fielding, the event that led to the indictment and conviction of John Ehrlichman, Assistant to the President for Domestic Affairs, as well as of the White House Plumbers. Hunt deposited at CIA "photos of the doctor's office from all angles, with Liddy in the foreground. . . . They included the parking space marked DR. FIELDING as well as the doctor's car license plate" (Emery, *Watergate*, 64). What function, other than to prove a crime, was served by these photos?

133. From Emery, *Watergate*, 441: Colson "revealed to a journalist that in January 1974 Nixon had wanted to dismiss CIA Director William Colby because of suspicions the agency was deeply involved in Watergate. . . . Colson also testified similarly to the House Judiciary Committee. He said that Nixon had told him in January that he had received a lot of information about the CIA's involvement that was very peculiar."

134. See Hougan, *Secret Agenda*, 59–61 (CIA bug), 133, 271–74 (Colson), 277 (Baker); and Scott, *Deep Politics and the Death of JFK*, 234–37.

135. Hougan, *Secret Agenda*, 294. "Reportedly, it was at the urging of Welander—who had yet to be implicated in 'the Moorer-Radford affair'—that Woodward extended his tour of duty in 1969, going to the Pentagon to serve as Communications Duty Officer to then-CNO [Chief of Naval Operations] Tom Moorer. In that capacity, Woodward presided over the CNO's code-room, reading every communication that went in and out, while acting, also, as a briefer and a courier. This, he tells us, is how he met Deep Throat, while cooling his heels outside the Situation Room in the White House. It was 1970 and, according to Woodward, Mark Felt was sitting in the next chair" (Jim Hougan, "Deep Throat, Bob Woodward, and the CIA: Strange Bedfellows," *Counterpunch*, June 8, 2005, http://www.counterpunch.org/hougan06082005.html).

136. Hougan, *Secret Agenda*, 296–97.

137. Scott, *Deep Politics and the Death of JFK*, 304.

138. Thomas M. Troy Jr., review of *A Look over My Shoulder*, by Richard Helms with William Hood, https://www.cia.gov/csi/kent_csi/docs/v48i1a08p .htm. Cf. Powers, *Man Who Kept the Secrets*, 271–308.

139. John Prados, *Lost Crusader: The Secret Wars of CIA Director William Colby* (New York: Oxford, 2003), 297–330.

3. THE PIVOTAL PRESIDENCY:
FORD, RUMSFELD, AND CHENEY

Epigraph: The Franklin Delano Roosevelt quotation is from his 1936 Madison Square Garden Speech, http://history.sandiego.edu/gen/text/us/fdr1936.html.

1. Emery, *Watergate*, 469–70. Haig in 1979 raised a much more dramatic possibility. Asked by an interviewer "what he felt was his 'main accomplishment' while in the Nixon White House, Haig replied: 'With respect to Watergate and its consequences, clearly one of the most dangerous periods in American history, change occurred within the provisions of our Constitution and established rule of law. *This was not a foregone conclusion during those difficult days.*' [emphasis added]" (Hougan, *Secret Agenda*, quoting *Newsweek*, July 16, 1979, 54). But Haig's objectivity demands to be questioned, especially if (as Hougan speculates in *Secret Agenda*, 286–89), Haig may himself have been an active co-conspirator in a Watergate plot to unseat the president.

2. Kissinger, *Years of Renewal*, 826.

3. Ferguson and Rogers, *Right Turn*, 68–69.

4. Rockefeller, *Memoirs*, 392–96.

5. The term "intellectual counterrevolution" was prominent neoconservative Irving Kristol's (quoted in Lapham, "Tentacles of Rage," 36).

6. Ferguson and Rogers, *Right Turn*, 103.

7. Ferguson and Rogers, *Right Turn*, 103–4; Sanders, *Peddlers of Crisis*, 221–25. Disclaimer: I was a reader of the dissertation that became Sanders's excellent book.

8. Sanders, *Peddlers of Crisis*, 193–94.

9. A. James Reichley, *Conservatives in an Age of Change* (Washington, D.C.: Brookings Institution, 1981), 295, quoting Rumsfeld interview of November 25, 1978.

10. Reichley, *Conservatives in an Age of Change*, 303.

11. David Rockefeller (*Memoirs*, 337) wrote later that "Ford's decision devastated Nelson. The stark reality was that his hopes of becoming president were now permanently dashed." It was also a strong signal of the waning Rockefeller influence in the Republican Party.

12. T. D. Allman, "The Curse of Dick Cheney," *Rolling Stone*, August 25, 2004, http://www.rollingstone.com/politics/story/6450422/the_curse_of_dick_cheney/: "Having turned Ford into their instrument, Rumsfeld and Cheney staged a palace coup. They pushed Ford to fire Defense Secretary James Schlesinger, tell Vice President Nelson Rockefeller to look for another job and remove Henry Kissinger from his post as national security adviser." Cf. Sidney Blumenthal, "The Long March of Dick Cheney," *Salon*, November 24, 2005, http://www.salon.com/opinion/blumenthal/2005/11/24/cheney/print.html: "Rumsfeld and Cheney quickly gained control of the White House staff, edging out Ford's old aides. From this base, they waged bureaucratic war on Vice President Nelson Rockefeller and Henry Kissinger, a colossus of foreign policy, who occupied the posts of both secretary of state and national security advisor. Rumsfeld and Cheney were the right wing of the Ford administration, opposed to the policy of détente with the Soviet Union, and they operated by stealthy internal maneuver. . . . In 1975, Rumsfeld and Cheney stage-managed a Cabinet purge called the 'Halloween massacre' that made Rumsfeld secretary of defense and Cheney White House chief of staff."

13. Rockefeller, *Memoirs*, 337; John Osborne, *White House Watch: The Ford Years* (Washington, D.C.: New Republic Books, 1977), xxiv–xxv. But the ever power-hungry Kissinger (*Years of Renewal*, 176–77), quoting Osborne, added that "with the passage of time, I grew more mellow about Rumsfeld's brilliant single-mindedness."

14. Reichley, *Conservatives in an Age of Change*, 350. Author and journalist Walter Isaacson (*Kissinger*, 669) agrees that the decision arose from a Ford meeting with his kitchen cabinet, where Harlow argued that unity was needed even if "you have to fire them all." Historian Jussi Hanhimäki (*Flawed Architect*, 427) has written that the downgrading of Kissinger was suggested to Ford by "Howard Calloway and some other members of the President Ford Committee." Ford's press secretary Ron Nessen endorsed Ford's claim that he "made his decisions . . . alone in the family room of his living quarters" (Ron Nessen, *It Sure Looks Different from the Inside* [New York: Playboy Press, 1978], 155).

15. However, the Rumsfeld-Cheney preference for presidential privilege over congressional legislation clearly dates from the Nixon era. Terry Lenzner, head of the legal aid program in Nixon's Office of Economic Opportunity, later recalled that an order came down for him to fire certain lawyers who were challenging the administration. Lenzner protested that to do so would violate the law. "Still, in November 1970, Rumsfeld summoned Lenzner to his office, and, with Cheney at his side, fired Lenzner because he was unwilling to follow orders" (Charlie Savage, "Hail to the chief," *Boston Globe*, May 28, 2006).

16. Rockefeller, *Memoirs*, 337.

17. Persico, *Casey*, 96–97, 169, 187, and passim.

18. Originally Ford intended to announce that he would not be a candidate for election in 1976. Kissinger dissuaded him from this step, however, which would have made Ford in effect a weak lame-duck president.

19. Adam Smith, *The Wealth of Nations* (New York: Modern Library, 1937), 423.

20. Memo, Robert Teeter to Richard Cheney, November 12, 1975, Box 62, Robert Teeter Papers, Gerald R. Ford Library, http://www.ford.utexas.edu//library/exhibits/campaign/themes.htm.

21. Blumenthal, "Long March of Dick Cheney."

22. Hanhimäki, *Flawed Architect*, 447.

23. David Plotz, "Kissinger's Comeback Tour," a review of *Years of Renewal* by Henry Kissinger, *Slate*, June 11, 1999, http://slate.msn.com/id/30301/. Kissinger's responsibility for the Basket III on human rights has been disputed, but see Hanhimäki, *Flawed Architect*, 433–34.

24. Henry Kissinger, "The Pitfalls of Universal Jurisdiction: Risking Judicial Tyranny," *Foreign Affairs* (July–August 2001), http://www.globalpolicy.org/intljustice/general/2001/07kiss.htm.

25. Anatoly Dobrynin, *In Confidence: Moscow's Ambassador to America's Six Cold War Presidents (1962–1986)* (New York: Times Books/Random House, 1995), 346.

26. Gates, *From the Shadows*, 89, quoted in Powers, *Intelligence Wars*, 333.

27. Kissinger, *Years of Renewal*, 662–63, citing "Summit in Helsinki," *Newsweek*, August 11, 1975; *Department of State Bulletin*, September 15, 1975, 392. Kissinger's speech rebuts neoconservative Robert Kagan's claim that neither Kissinger nor anyone else could have strategized or even predicted Helsinki's effects (Robert Kagan, "The Revisionist," *New Republic*, June 21, 1999).

28. A Polish uprising in 1976 was easily quashed. But three years later the irreversible movement of Solidarnosc began when the Pope came to Poland with the message "Don't be afraid" (Richard Bernstein, "Did John Paul Help Win the Cold War? Just Ask the Poles," *New York Times*, April 6, 2005).

29. Timothy Garton Ash, *The Polish Revolution: Solidarity* (New Haven, Conn.: Yale University Press, 2002), 19.

30. Hanhimäki, *Flawed Architect*, 434.

31. For this Cheney-Rumsfeld memo, see Mann, *Rise of the Vulcans*, 65.

32. Robert G. Kaiser, "A Power over Arms Policy; Senate Staffer Richard Perle," *Washington Post*, June 26, 1977.

33. Nessen, *It Sure Looks Different from the Inside*, 150.

34. Years later Kissinger recalled: "In 1973, when I served as Secretary of State, David Rockefeller showed up in my office one day to tell me that he thought I needed a little help. I must confess, the thought was not self-evident to me at the moment. He proposed to form a group of Americans, Europeans, and Japanese to look ahead into the future. . . . When I thought about it, there actually was a need" (Trilateral Commission, "Tributes to David Rockefeller," December 1, 1998, http://www.trilateral.org/nagp/regmtgs/98/1201tribs.htm.

35. Sanders, *Peddlers of Crisis*, 176, citing "An Outline for Remaking World Trade and Finance," *Christian Science Monitor*, February 15, 1977.

36. Sanders, *Peddlers of Crisis*, 150.

37. Carroll, *House of War*, 152. The pattern began with James Forrestal, who "consistently exaggerated the dangers posed by the Soviet Union. . . . This pattern would be repeated in 1950, with the secret review of Soviet purposes called *NSC-68*; in 1957, with the Gaither Report, which demanded an urgent U.S. buildup; in 1960, with the 'missile gap' crisis; in 1969, with warnings of a Soviet 'first strike'; in the 1970s . . . and in the 1980s, with the Committee on the Present Danger" (Carroll, *House of War*, 152).

38. Sanders, *Peddlers of Crisis*, 45, 61–65.

39. Tom Barry, "The 'Present Danger' War Parties," International Relations Center, June 16, 2006, http://www.irc-online.org/content/3297, citing Boies, *Buying for Armageddon*, 126: "In sum, the 141 founding directors of the CPD formed an insidious web with links to 110 major corporations. Leading CPD members included three former treasury secretaries—Henry Fowler, C. Douglas Dillon, and John Connally—two former high officials of the Export-Import Bank, numerous private bankers, partners in leading New York investment firms, the former president of Time, Inc., the chairman of Prudential Insurance, the director of the Atlantic Council, Citibank's chief international business adviser, and many other corporate figures whose interests reached beyond military budget increases."

40. Mann, *Rise of the Vulcans*, 31–32.

41. Hersh, *Price of Power*, 150.

42. Carroll, *House of War*, 321–27.

43. Ranelagh, *Agency*, 280, 622–23. General Graham in an interview told Jerry Sanders that he concluded from his years of work with CIA that they were "antimilitary": "There are more liberals per square foot in the CIA than [in] any other part of government" (Sanders, *Peddlers of Crisis*, 198).

44. Anne Hessing Cahn, "Team B: The Trillion-Dollar Experiment," *Bulletin of the Atomic Scientists* (April 1993).

45. Cahn, "Team B," citing William E. Colby to President Ford, November 21, 1975: "The PFIAB [President's Foreign Intelligence Advisory Board] first raised the issue of competitive threat assessments in 1975, but Director of Central Intelligence William Colby was able to ward them off, partly on procedural grounds (an NIE [National Intelligence Estimate] was in progress). But Colby, a career CIA officer, also said, 'It is hard for me to envisage how an ad hoc "independent" group of government and non-government analysts could prepare a more thorough, comprehensive assessment of Soviet strategic capabilities—even in two specific areas—than the intelligence community can prepare.'"

46. Kennedy had declined to reappoint Anderson as chief of naval operations during the Cuban Missile Crisis. He was succeeded as head of the President's Foreign Intelligence Advisory Board in 1976 by Leo Cherne, who in 1981 would join the interventionist Committee for a Free World, along with neocons Midge Decter, Michael Ledeen, and Norman Podhoretz.

47. Ironically, Evans and Novak were initially cool to Bush's nomination, reporting the opinion that "any identified politician, no matter how resolved to be politically pure, would aggravate the CIA's credibility gap" (Webster G. Tarpley and Anton Chaitkin, *George Bush: The Unauthorized Biography*, chapter 15, http://www.tarpley.net/bush15.htm).

48. Cahn, "Team B"; and Hicks, *Big Wedding*, 122; both quoting Bush's sign-off on a memo from George Carver, May 26, 1976. Bush later told an aide: "It wasn't my doing" (Mark Perry, *Eclipse: The Last Days of the CIA* [New York: William Morrow, 1992], 140).

49. Thirty years later the Team B assessment is still being either defended or reviled. Veteran journalist and author Tom Wicker has written that "Team B and the CPD were egregiously wrong, as forthcoming events in Eastern Europe and the Soviet Union were to demonstrate" (Tom Wicker, *George Herbert Walker Bush* [New York: Lipper/Viking, 2004], 47). Neocons have been just as adamant in their defense. Robert Gates, who at the time was a CIA Soviet analyst seconded to the White House, tactfully declines even to mention this important disagreement. My uninformed opinion is that the USSR was indeed expanding its nuclear strength, to avoid ever again being forced to back down as in 1962. But that this was for defensive purposes I think should have been obvious then, and became more so with time.

50. Cahn, *Killing Détente*, 148, 150, quoting Sidney Blumenthal, "Richard Perle's Nuclear Legacy," *Washington Post*, November 24, 1987.

51. Sanders, *Peddlers of Crisis*, 197–202. Another quiet supporter of Team B was Defense Secretary Rumsfeld, the leading opponent of détente in the Ford administration. In this he was backed by his protégé Cheney, who was by 1976 the White House chief of staff (Mann, *Rise of the Vulcans*, 241, 57–62).

52. Cahn, "Team B": "The first press leak occurred two days after the first meeting of the CIA and Team B members who were examining Soviet strategic policy and objectives. . . . After the Democrats won the election and President-elect Jimmy Carter had ignored Bush's hint that up to now, CIA directors had not changed with an incoming administration, George Bush, the foe of leaks, agreed to meet with David Binder of the *New York Times*. The same director who wrote to President Ford in August 1976, 'I want to get the CIA off the front pages and at some point out of the papers altogether,' now made sure that Team B would become front-page news." Cf. Jason Vest, "Darth Rumsfeld," *The American Prospect*, February 26, 2001, http://www.prospect.org/print/V12/4/vest-j.html: "Two days before Jimmy Carter's inauguration, Rumsfeld fired parting shots at Kissinger and other disarmament advocates, saying that 'no doubt exists about the capabilities of the Soviet armed forces' and that those capabilities 'indicate a tendency toward war fighting . . . rather than the more modish Western models of deterrence through mutual vulnerability'" (citing Sanders, *Peddlers of Crisis*, 203, who in turn quotes from "Rumsfeld Says Russia Could Become Dominant Power," *San Francisco Chronicle*, January 19, 1977).

53. Cahn, in her appearance on "The Power of Nightmares," a BBC three-part television series, 2005.

54. From Mann, *Rise of the Vulcans*, 73: "While Rumsfeld and Cheney were eviscerating Kissinger's Soviet policies at the top levels of the Ford administration and the Republican party, Paul Wolfowitz was engaged in a parallel effort [Team B] inside the U.S. intelligence community."

55. Mann, *Rise of the Vulcans*, 33. In the summer of 1969, while still graduate students, Perle and Wolfowitz were brought by Professor Albert Wohlstetter to Washington, as unpaid workers for hardliners Dean Acheson and Nitze in

their successful campaign to win congressional support for the antiballistic missile. Perle never returned to graduate school; Wolfowitz did. In 1974, Perle became noted in Washington when he drafted the 1974 Jackson-Vanik Amendment linking trade issues to freedom of emigration. For this he is said to have received numerous awards from Israel.

56. By contrast, the CPD provided thirty-three officials of the Reagan administration, including William Casey, Richard Allen, Jeane Kirkpatrick, John Lehman, George Shultz, and Richard Perle. Reagan himself was a CPD member in 1979.

56. Cf. Jim Lobe, "Neocons Revive Cold War Group," Antiwar.com, July 21, 2004, http://www.antiwar.com/lobe/?articleid=3075: "A bipartisan group of 41 mainly neoconservative foreign-policy hawks has launched the third Committee on the Present Danger (CPD) . . . whose new enemy will be "global terrorism." . . . Prominently represented are fellows from the American Enterprise Institute (AEI), such as former United Nations Ambassador Jeane Kirkpatrick, Joshua Muravchik, Laurie Mylroie, Danielle Pletka, Michael Rubin and Ben Wattenberg. Members from Pentagon chief Donald Rumsfeld's Defense Policy Board (DPB) include Kenneth Adelman, Newt Gingrich, and [former CIA director James] Woolsey himself. Committee members from the Center for Security Policy (CSP), include CSP President Frank Gaffney, Charles Kupperman, William Van Cleave, and Dov Zakheim, who just stepped down as an undersecretary of defense under Rumsfeld."

58. From 1973 to 1976, Helms testified to Congress on more than thirty separate occasions, for a total of one hundred hours or more (Powers, *Man Who Kept the Secrets*, 295).

59. Under Nixon, CIA was already offloading assets to former CIA officer Edwin Wilson's Task Force 157, which Kissinger allegedly used to protect his secret China communications from Admiral Moorer (Trento, *Prelude to Terror*, 51-53). In turn, Wilson developed connections to both the Nugan Hand Bank in Australia and Tongsun Park, who was distributing money to members of Congress on behalf of the Korean CIA (Trento, *Power House*, 100-104).

60. Kevin Phillips, "The Barrelling Bushes," *Los Angeles Times*, January 11, 2004. Phillips continues: "After leaving the CIA in January 1977, Bush became chairman of the executive committee of First International Bancshares and its British subsidiary, where, according to journalists Peter Truell and Larry Gurwin in their 1992 book 'False Profits' [p. 345], Bush 'traveled on the bank's behalf and sometimes marketed to international banks in London, including several Middle Eastern institutions.'" Trento claims that through the London branch of this bank, which Bush chaired, "Adham's petrodollars and BCCI money flowed for a variety of intelligence operations" (Trento, *Prelude to Terror*, 139).

61. Truell and Gurwin, *False Profits*, 120-21.

62. Cooley, *Unholy Wars*, 24-28. The Safari Club took its name from the famous lodge on Mount Kenya, where the leaders first met. The lodge was developed by gambler and oilman Ray Ryan and later owned by Adnan Khashoggi.

63. Cooley, *Unholy Wars*, 26.

64. Prince Turki bin Faisal is quoted in Trento, *Prelude to Terror*, 102. Citing the same speech, Coll adds Britain to the list (Coll, *Ghost Wars*, 81).

65. Kessler, *Richest Man in the World*, 239-41.

66. Trento, *Prelude to Terror*, 104. Bush may have used CIA connections to

lend a helping hand. In 1976 a law firm in the Cayman Islands, Bruce Campbell & Company, which was already the registered agent for the CIA bank Nugan Hand, "set up BCCI's most secretive unit: International Credit & Investment Company (ICIC)" (Truell and Gurwin, *False Profits*, 125). French customs officials, when they raided the Paris branch of the BCCI in 1991, claim to have discovered an account in Bush's name (Trento, *Prelude to Terror*, 104).

67. Trento, *Prelude to Terror*, 101. Trento quotes a Wilson associate, Mike Pilgrim, as saying: "It got to the point that we were used to support GID operations when the CIA could not." Richard Secord, discussed in chapter 10, became part of this group.

68. Truell and Gurwin, *False Profits*, 130. The courts eventually conceded that Wilson had been working for Shackley in CIA: "In 1984 Wilson was found not guilty of trying to hire Raphael Quintero and other Cubans to kill a Libyan dissident. However, he was found guilty of exporting guns and conspiracy to murder and was sentenced to 52 years in prison. Wilson claimed he had been framed and claimed that he was working on behalf of the CIA. He employed David Adler, a former CIA agent, as his lawyer. Adler eventually found evidence that Wilson was indeed working for the CIA after he retired from the agency. In October 2003 a Houston federal judge, Lynn Hughes, threw out Wilson's conviction in the C-4 explosives case, ruling that the prosecutors had 'deliberately deceived the court' about Wilson's continuing CIA contacts, thus 'double-crossing a part-time informal government agent'" (*Spartacus Educational: The Biography of Edwin P. Wilson*, http://www.spartacus.schoolnet.co.uk/JFKwilson E2.htm).

69. Marshall, Scott, and Hunter, *Iran-Contra Connection*, 24, 48–49, 76–82; Trento, *Prelude to Terror*, 78–82. It is noteworthy that just as de Marenches was the man who formalized the Safari Club agreement, so his close friend Vernon Walters, Bush's deputy director of central intelligence, became the chief U.S. contact of the CAL/Condor coalition. Operation Condor was responsible for the 1976 murder in Washington of former Chilean ambassador Orlando Letelier and young researcher Ronni Moffit. The assassins were two former CIA terrorists, whose arrest was delayed for two years, in part because Bush as CIA director did not turn over their files to the FBI.

70. Trento, *Prelude to Terror*, 138–44 and passim. Cf. Trento, *Secret History of the CIA*, 410, 467, and passim. Cf. also Loftus and Aarons, *Secret War against the Jews*, 397: "After Jimmy Carter became president in 1977, a number of people suddenly resigned from the CIA, went through the 'revolving door,' and acquired connections to the BCCI." Trento once wrote of the off-loaded agents "working for the Israelis" (Trento, *Secret History*, 410). Loftus and Aarons saw Bush shifting away from Israel and moving "closer to the Arabs" (*Secret War against the Jews*, 396). We shall see that both accounts are partially true. It was through these double contacts that "the Club was able to bring about President Sadat's historic peacemaking visit of November 1977 to Jerusalem, leading eventually to the U.S.-Egyptian-Israeli peace treaty of 1979" (Cooley, *Unholy Wars*, 27).

71. Trento, *Prelude to Terror*, 249 (Clines); Truell and Gurwin, *False Profits*, 123 (Shorafa).

72. Parry, *Secrecy & Privilege*, especially 136 (Clines-Shackley-Bush).

4. BRZEZINSKI, OIL, AND AFGHANISTAN

Epigraph: U.S. Congress, Senate Committee on Foreign Relations, Subcommittee on Multinational Corporations, *Multinational Corporations and U.S. Foreign Policy*, Report, 1975, 17–18, quoted in Little, *American Orientalism*, 72.

1. Hanhimäki, *Flawed Architect*, 450. These attacks were made "in numerous speeches authored partly by Zbigniew Brzezinski."

2. Sanders, *Peddlers of Crisis*, 235.

3. Sanders, *Peddlers of Crisis*, 263.

4. By contrast, the CPD provided thirty-three officials of the Reagan administration, including William Casey, Richard Allen, Jeane Kirkpatrick, John Lehman, George Shultz, and Richard Perle. Reagan himself was a member in 1979.

5. Ferguson and Rogers, *Right Turn*, 103.

6. Sanders, *Peddlers of Crisis*, 193–94.

7. Sanders, *Peddlers of Crisis*, 244–45.

8. From Robert G. Kaiser, "Memo Sets Stage in Assessing U.S., Soviet Strength; Memo Sets Stage for Debate on U.S., Soviet Capabilities," *Washington Post*, July 6, 1977: "Several of the people whom Huntington asked to help with the project said privately during its early stages that they hoped to create a document that would scare the Carter Administration into greater respect for the Soviet menace."

9. Sanders, *Peddlers of Crisis*, 247, quoting Hedrick Smith, "Carter Study Takes More Hopeful View of Strategy of U.S.," *New York Times*, July 8, 1977.

10. For example, see Murray Marder, "'Cooperation, Competition' Seen in U.S.-Soviet Ties," *Washington Post*, October 19, 1977; Brzezinski, *Power and Principle*, 519–20.

11. Rothkopf, *Running the World*, 168.

12. Strobe Talbott, "Zbig-Think," *Time*, May 2, 1983.

13. Brzezinski, *Power and Principle*, 177. Brzezinski argued against those who wished "to consider reducing our forces" by pointing to "the vulnerability of the oil-rich region around the Persian Gulf."

14. From Sanders, *Peddlers of Crisis*, 236: "On December 12, 1979 . . . the President, in a speech before the Business Council, committed the nation to an average real increase in defense spending of 5 percent for the next 5 years. In 1976, candidate Carter promised to cut defense spending by $5 to $7 billion."

15. Bernard Gwertzman, *New York Times*, December 21, 1978, 3; Jim Hoagland, "Shah to Name Regency Council," *Washington Post*, January 12, 1979.

16. Dreyfuss, *Devil's Game*, 240.

17. For example, see Memo to President Carter from Zbigniew Brzezinski, December 26, 1979, http://www.eurolegal.org/neoconwars/interafghan.htm: "With Iran destabilized, there will be no firm bulwark in Southwest Asia against the Soviet drive to the Indian Ocean."

18. Mann, *Rise of the Vulcans*, 74–75.

19. Brzezinski, *Power and Principle*, 66. Brzezinski's memoir lists thirty-five index entries for the Persian Gulf, starting in 1977. By contrast, Kissinger's memoir lists none.

20. Cordovez and Harrison, *Out of Afghanistan*, 33, emphasis added, citing Brzezinski, *Power and Principle*, 73.

21. Cordovez and Harrison, *Out of Afghanistan*, 54.

22. Cordovez and Harrison, *Out of Afghanistan*, 6.

23. Cordovez and Harrison, *Out of Afghanistan*, 6.

24. My personal suspicion is that the trilateralist ideology, with its rhetoric about North-South issues and diminishing poverty in the third world, was at least in part designed to take control of the Democratic Party away from the McGovernites, at the time that Nelson Rockefeller was losing control of the Republican Party to Ronald Reagan. Once Carter was in power, the trilateralist ideology became less and less relevant.

25. Prestowitz, *Rogue Nation*, 98–99; Yergin, *Prize*, 663–64.

26. Jimmy Carter, State of the Union Address 1980, January 23, 1980, http://www.jimmycarterlibrary.org/documents/speeches/su8ojec.phtml.

27. Yergin, *Prize*, 702.

28. Brzezinski, *Power and Principle*, 456.

29. For Saudi agreement with the United States to secure denomination in U.S. dollars for OPEC oil sales, see Scott, *Drugs, Oil, and War*, 41–42; Spiro, *Hidden Hand of American Hegemony*, x, 103–12. The agreement proved a long-term solution to the crisis of a dollar weakening so rapidly that there was a threat to the global trading system. From "The Decline of U.S. Power: The New Debate over Guns and Butter," *Business Week*, March 12, 1979: "The dollar's decline proved so rapid in late 1978 that an impending crash of the world's financial system pushed the Federal Reserve on Nov. 1 into raising interest rates to defend the currency. This was perhaps one of the most important events in the recent history of the country: The international position of the dollar suddenly became a burden adversely affecting domestic policy rather than an advantage helping it."

30. Back in 1957, writing on military-civilian relations, Huntington concluded that Americans "may eventually find redemption and security in making [the military standard] their own" (Samuel P. Huntington, *The Soldier and the State* [Belknap Press / Harvard University Press, 1957], 466).

31. Michel Crozier, Samuel Huntington, and Joji Watanuki, *The Crisis of Democracy* (New York: New York University Press, 1975), 105, 115.

32. Brzezinski, *Grand Chessboard*, 24–25.

33. Brzezinski, *Grand Chessboard*, 211.

34. The creation of FEMA was authorized by President Carter's Executive Order 12148, dated July 20, 1979, and retroactively made effective July 15. According to critics, Executive Order 12148 became law simply by its publication in the Federal Registry. In other words Congress was bypassed for FEMA's authorization as well as its funding.

35. Brzezinski, *Power and Principle*, 470–73.

36. Tim London, "Emergency Management in the Twenty-first Century," http://www.homestead.com/emergencymanagement/files/21STCEN2.HTM: "FEMA's name may have changed in 1979, but the organization was still focused primarily on civil defense, with a secondary mission of natural and man-made disasters starting to emerge. In December, 1980, FEMA published a pamphlet, *War Survival Focus*, drawn from a speech given by John W. Macy, Jr., the director of FEMA, to the American Civil Defense Association on October 23, 1980. In his speech, Macy said, 'Clearly, the Congress, the administration, and the American public have shown a new consensus in 1980 favoring greater protective measures for the United States' (3). Macy went on to say, 'An important turning

point, again reflecting new congressional support for civil defense, is almost completed action on the hill toward the appropriation of $120 million for civil defense purposes in the current fiscal year 1981' (5). 'The leadership of the Federal Emergency Management Agency will be moving quickly to deploy an enhanced Civil Defense program providing protection against both peacetime and wartime crises, but focusing especially on counterforce areas' (5). In an 18 page speech, Macy devotes only one paragraph to FEMA's natural disaster capabilities, preferring to center his speech around the country's nuclear, biological, and terrorist threats instead."

37. Gene Sosin, *Sparks of Liberty: An Insider's Memoir of Radio Liberty* (University Park: University of Pennsylvania Press, 1999), 115, quoted in Dreyfuss, *Devil's Game*, 251.

38. See especially Alexandre Bennigsen and Marie Broxup [his daughter], *The Islamic Threat to the Soviet State* (New York: St. Martin's Press, 1983); discussion in Dreyfuss, *Devil's Game*, 252.

39. Dreyfuss, *Devil's Game*, 256.

40. Dreyfuss, *Devil's Game*, 254.

41. Coll, *Ghost Wars*, 46.

42. See "Les Révélations d'un ancien conseiller de Carter," interview with Zbigniew Brzezinski, *Le Nouvel Observateur*, January 15–21, 1998, http://www.globalresearch.ca/articles/BRZ110A.html (French version: http://www.confidentiel.net/breve.php3?id_breve=1862), quoted at length in Scott, *Drugs, Oil, and War*, 35.

43. National Security Archive, "Interview with Dr. Zbigniew Brzezinski," June 13, 1997, http://www2.gwu.edu/~nsarchiv/coldwar/interviews/episode-17/brzezinski2.html.

44. Rahul Bedi, "Why? An Attempt to Explain the Unexplainable," *Janes.com*, September 14, 2001, http://www.janes.com/regional_news/americas/news/jdw/jdw010914_1_n.shtml.

45. Lloyd Cutler, Exit Interview, March 2, 1981, Jimmy Carter Library, http://www.jimmycarterlibrary.org/library/exitInt/exitcutl.pdf; Scott, *Drugs, Oil, and War*, 30, 35.

46. "Washington's 'Realistic' View of Soviet Aims," *Christian Science Monitor*, January 7, 1980, quoted in Sanders, *Peddlers of Crisis*, 240.

47. National Security Archive, Interview with Dr. Zbigniew Brzezinski, June 13, 1997; cf. Gates, *From the Shadows*, 90–96. Although Brzezinksi's primary focus appears to have been Eastern Europe, Gates clarifies that in response to Brzezinski's initiative CIA had forwarded to the White House special coordinating committee "a covert program targeting Soviet Muslims" (Gates, *From the Shadows*, 92).

48. Gates, *From the Shadows*, 91–92. Brzezinski later pointed to the Ukraine as "a geopolitical pivot because its very existence as an independent country helps to transform Russia. Without Ukraine, Russia ceases to be a Eurasian empire" (Brzezinski, *Grand Chessboard*, 46). Brzezinski, however, fails to mention the Ukraine in his White House memoir, *Power and Principle*.

49. It is indisputable that the IIRO was distributing Korans in such former Soviet republics as Tajikistan (Baer, *Sleeping with the Devil*, 144, 141, 140).

According to London's *The Tablet* (July 3, 2004), "Osama bin Laden first saw action in Afghanistan fighting under Abd al-Rab al-Rasul Sayyaf," whom earlier the Saudis picked to administer the Central Asian Koran project. In the 1990s the IIRO's Philippines regional director was Mohammed Jamal Khalifa, said to be Osama bin Laden's brother-in-law. Indisputably, Khalifa used IIRO funds to support the terrorist Abu Sayyaf organization, regarded as an affiliate of al Qaeda (Lance, *1000 Years for Revenge*, 235).

50. Yousaf and Adkin, *Bear Trap*, 193; Rashid, *Jihad*, 223. Arabic Korans came from Saudi Arabia. In addition, "the CIA commissioned an Uzbek exile living in Germany to produce translations of the Koran in the Uzbek language. . . . About five thousand books [crossed] the Soviet border by early 1985" (Coll, *Ghost Wars*, 104).

51. "The Crescent of Crisis," *Time*, January 15, 1979. In this book I focus on U.S. complicity in Saudi-financed campaigns to promote Wahhabi fundamentalism throughout the Muslim world. We must however recognize that the primary source for this state-promoted Wahhabism is in Saudi Arabia itself.

52. Texas oilmen, in conjunction with the U.S. Army Intelligence Reserve, had been researching this possibility since the 1960s. Chevron bought into the rich Tengiz oilfield of Kazakstan in the late 1980s, before the break-up of the Soviet Union (Seymour M. Hersh, "The Price of Oil: What Was Mobil up to in Kazakhstan and Russia?" *New Yorker*, July 9, 2001, 48–65, http://www.whatreally happened.com/mobil.html).

53. Chalmers Johnson, "Abolish the CIA!" *London Review of Books*, October 21, 2004; "Les Révélations d'un ancien conseiller de Carter," *Le Nouvel Observateur*, January 15–21, 1998. In his extremely intelligent book *Ghost Wars*, Coll writes that in the light of Brzezinski's contemporary memos, "very worried that the Soviets would prevail," "any claim that Brzezinski lured the Soviets into Afghanistan warrants deep skepticism" (Coll, *Ghost Wars*, 581n). I would respond that in his determined drive to reduce Soviet influence in the world, Brzezinski in his memos consistently exaggerated the Soviet menace beyond what saner heads at the time were estimating. We should not assume that he believed what he wrote.

54. Anonymous [Mike Scheuer], *Imperial Hubris: Why the West Is Losing the War on Terror* (Washington, D.C.: Brassey's, 2004), 25. The Pakistan-Afghanistan Golden Crescent, which was not part of the American drug picture until 1979, was supplying 60 percent of U.S. heroin by 1980 (in McCoy, *Politics of Heroin*, 472).

55. Banafsheh Zand-Bonazzi and Elio Bonazzi, "The Sorcerer's Apprentice," Institute for the Secularisation of Islamic Society, http://www.secularislam.org/articles/bonazzi.htm (accessed February 2005).

56. Carter and Brzezinski initiated the movement to the mujahideen of captured Soviet arms from Egypt, which was renegotiated after Sadat's death by Casey (Persico, *Casey*, 225).

57. Haq identified himself as a Brzezinski contact when in a 1989 interview he had pressured Brzezinski to back the ISI's clients in Afghanistan: "I told Brzezinski you screwed up in Vietnam and Korea; you better get it right this time" (Scott, *Drugs, Oil, and War*, 48, citing Lamb, *Waiting for Allah*, 222).

58. Scott, *Drugs, Oil, and War*, 48, citing Beaty and Gwynne, *Outlaw Bank*, 52 (CIA).

59. Scott, *Drugs, Oil, and War*, 48, citing Lawrence Lifschultz, "Pakistan: The Empire of Heroin," in *War on Drugs: Studies in the Failure of U.S. Narcotics Policy*, edited by Alfred W. McCoy and Alan A. Block (Boulder, Colo.: Westview, 1992), 342 (Interpol). Bengali political scientist M. Emdad ul-Haq speculates further that Haq was the "foreign-trained adviser" who, according to the *Hindustani Times*, had suggested to General Zia that he use drug money to meet the Soviet challenge (Scott, *Drugs, Oil, and War*, 48; Emdad ul-Haq, *Drugs in South Asia*, 187; N. C. Menon, *Hindustan Times*, October 1, 1994, 14).

60. Scott, *Drugs, Oil, and War*, 48, quoting Beaty and Gwynne, *Outlaw Bank*, 48. Compare Phillips, *American Dynasty*, 316.

61. Scott, *Drugs, Oil, and War*, 57, quoting Gates, *From the Shadows*, 144, 146.

62. McCoy, *Politics of Heroin*, 461–62.

63. Scott, *Drugs, Oil, and War*, 46, 49; McCoy, *Politics of Heroin*, 475–78.

64. Brzezinski, for example, writes that "I pushed a decision through the SCC to be more sympathetic to those Afghans who were determined to preserve their country's independence" (Brzezinski, *Power and Principle*, 427). On the same page he writes that "I also consulted with the Saudis and the Egyptians regarding the fighting in Afghanistan." He is silent about the early, decisive, and ill-fated contact with Pakistan.

65. Tim Weiner, "Blowback from the Afghan Battlefield," *New York Times*, March 13, 1994.

66. Kaplan, *Soldiers of God*, 68–69.

67. McCoy, *Politics of Heroin*, 475–77.

68. *9/11 Commission Report*, 145–50.

69. Weiner, "Blowback from the Afghan Battlefield." Sheikh Omar Abdel Rahman, a ringleader, first obtained a U.S. visa in 1990 "to fly to New York and assist U.S. agencies in recruiting Islamist guerrillas" (John Cooley, "Islamic Terrorists: Creature of the U.S. Taxpayer?" *International Herald Tribune*, March 13, 1996). In Afghanistan, Abdel Rahman befriended Hekmatyar, who offered the sheikh asylum in Afghanistan after his indictment (Griffin, *Reaping the Whirlwind*, 132). The technical mastermind of the first World Trade Center bombing in 1993 was Ramzi Yousef, Khalid Shaikh Mohammed's nephew.

70. McCoy, *Politics of Heroin*, 475–77.

71. Letter to *New York Times*, May 22, 1980, discussed in McCoy, *Politics of Heroin*, 461–62. Musto and a colleague, unable to get a White House response to their warnings about Afghan opium, went public with a *New York Times* op-ed piece on May 22, 1980: "We worry about the growing of opium in Afghanistan or Pakistan by rebel tribesmen. . . . Are we erring in befriending these tribes as we did in Laos when Air America . . . helped transport opium from certain tribal areas?" This public appeal also met with no establishment response (Alexander Cockburn and Jeffrey St. Clair, *Whiteout: The CIA, Drugs, and the Press* [London: Verso, 1998], 259–60).

72. Scott, *Drugs, Oil, and War*, 48, citing Beaty and Gwynne, *Outlaw Bank*, 48. Cf. Truell and Gurwin, *False Profits*, 160.

73. Scott, *Drugs, Oil, and War*, 48, citing Beaty and Gwynne, *Outlaw Bank*, 52.

74. B. Raman, "Heroin, Taliban and Pakistan," *Financial Times* (Asian edition), August 10, 2001, http://www.wanttoknow.info/010810ft.isiheroin. Raman's crude calculations estimated that "Pakistan's heroin economy was 30 per cent larger than its legitimate State economy."

75. Barbara Leitch LePoer, "Pakistan-U.S. Relations," Order Code IB94041, http://fpc.state.gov/documents/organization/7859.pdf.

76. Eric Alterman, "Blowback: The Prequel," *Nation*, October 25, 2001, http://www.thenation.com/doc.mhtml%3Fi=20011112&s=alterman, emphasis mine. The comments from Horelick are not in Gates's account (Gates, *From the Shadows*, 144–45).

77. Alterman, "Blowback," emphasis mine.

78. Cordovez and Harrison, *Out of Afghanistan*, 32.

79. The complexities of the PDPA Taraki coup are misrepresented in mono-chromatic accounts from the United States, both left and right. Throughout the twentieth century, Afghan politics had alternated between progressive (chiefly Tajik and urban middle-class) and reactionary (chiefly Pashtun, peasant, and rural) tendencies. After World War I this tension had become difficult to recon-cile, due to Soviet support for the former and British support for the latter. The Taraki reform program ("measures to create a ceiling on landholdings, reduce rural indebtedness, limit the brideprice and [begin] a mass literacy campaign") was reasonable enough. What doomed it from the outset was the speed and insensitivity with which the PDPA attempted to implement it. See Peter Marsden, *The Taliban: War, Religion, and the New Order in Afghanistan* (London: Zed Books, 1998), 19–25; Cordovez and Harrison, *Out of Afghanistan*, 25–32.

80. Hammond, *Red Flag over Afghanistan*, 49–55. See the assessment by for-mer CIA deputy director for intelligence Douglas MacEachin, "Predicting the Soviet Invasion of Afghanistan: The Intelligence Community's Record," http://www.fas.org/irp/cia/product/afghanistan/#link5: "From Washington's perspective, the Soviets' obvious motivation to . . . re-establish a more compliant client regime led naturally to suspicions that Moscow had engineered the government takeover. The fact that the USSR was the first state to formally recognize the new govern-ment reinforced this view. U.S. embassy officers also had reported seeing Soviet advisors mingling with some of the Afghan military units carrying out the opera-tions. U.S. intelligence assessments, however, said there was no evidence the Sovi-ets had been involved in launching the coup, although Moscow had moved quickly to exploit the situation once it began. The assessments said that the more fervent Soviet ideologues and military officials probably saw the developments as offering an opportunity to create another allied Communist regime on the borders of the USSR." Cf. Sam Vaknin, "Afghan Myths: An Interview with Anssi Kullberg [of Finnish Intelligence]," http://www.usamemorial.org/sept11078.htm. General Vladimir Kruichkov, then deputy head of the KGB, later told CNN: "Brezhnev and the Politburo tried to talk sense into Kabul. We couldn't understand how they could build socialism in just five years. We said, 'You can't do that. We've been building socialism for sixty years and we're still not finished.' But they thought it was us that had got it wrong. Naivete was coming out of their every orifice. It was

in their every word" ("Encore Presentation: Soldiers of God," *CNN.com*, September 29, 2001, http://cnnstudentnews.cnn.com/TRANSCRIPTS/0109/29/cp.00 .html). Even the small Maoist party in Afghanistan attacked the 1978 coup, with some justification, as bourgeois.

81. Vance, *Hard Choices*, 384.

82. Little, *American Orientalism*, 223; Cordovez and Harrison, *Out of Afghanistan*, 17, 23–28.

83. Cordovez and Harrison, *Out of Afghanistan*, 16.

84. Fred Weston, review of *Reaping the Whirlwind: The Taliban Movement in Afghanistan* by Michael Griffin, http://www.marxist.com/Asia/taliban_review .html.

85. Marsden, *Taliban*, 24.

86. Brzezinski, *Power and Principle*, 520; Cooley, *Unholy Wars*, 17.

87. Marsden, *Taliban*, 26.

88. Gaddis, *Cold War*, 208; cf. Cordovez and Harrison, *Out of Afghanistan*, 35–36.

89. The Soviet Union also attempted to make contact with the former Afghan king, Mohammad Zahir Shah, exiled in Rome, to find a political solution (Michael T. Kaufman, *New York Times*, August 14, 1979).

90. Little, *American Orientalism*, 150.

91. Marsden, *Taliban*, 26.

92. Brzezinski, *Power and Principle*, 420; Cooley, *Unholy Wars*, 29 (Brzezinski).

93. William Casey, speech of October 27, 1986; in William Casey, edited by Herbert E. Meyer, *Scouting the Future: The Public Speeches of William J. Casey* (Washington, D.C.: Regnery Gateway, 1989), 35, quoted in Coll, *Ghost Wars*, 97.

94. Yergin, *Prize*, 702; Scott, *Drugs, Oil, and War*, 30.

95. From Asian studies scholar Lawrence E. Grinter: "Concurrent with Mr. Carter's pronouncement came an intensified search by Defense and State Department officials for new military arrangements with Kenya, Somalia, Oman, Egypt, and Pakistan. Diego Garcia, the British territory in the Indian Ocean, also received new attention. On 1 March 1980, the United States Rapid Deployment Joint Task Force (RDJTF) was formally established by Secretary of Defense Harold Brown at MacDill Air Force Base, Florida. Its primary mission was subsequently focused exclusively on deployment to the Middle East and Southwest Asia. By early 1981, when Ronald Reagan took office as President, the RDJTF was estimated to have grown to more than 200,000 CONUS-based forces, including 100,000 Army troops, 50,000 Marines, and additional Air Force and Navy personnel" (Lawrence E. Grinter, "Avoiding the Burden: The Carter Doctrine in Perspective," *Air University Review* [January–February 1983], http://www.airpower.maxwell.af.mil/airchronicles/aureview/1983/jan-feb/grinter.html).

96. National Security Archive, Interview with Dr. Zbigniew Brzezinski, June 13, 1997. The proposal for an RDF was first put forward in Presidential Directive 18 (PD-18) of August 24, 1977 (Brzezinski, *Power and Principle*, 177–78).

97. Cordovez and Harrison, *Out of Afghanistan*, 55.

98. From Australian political journalist Doug Lorimer: "According to his official Pentagon biography, Paul Wolfowitz, the present U.S. deputy defence secretary, who was a deputy assistant secretary in the Carter administration,

'helped create the force that later became the United States Central Command and initiated the Maritime Pre-positioning Ships, the backbone of the initial U.S. deployment twelve years later' in preparation for the 1991 Gulf War" (in Doug Lorimer, "Iraq: Oil and the Bush Plan for Global Domination," *Green Left Weekly*, http://www.greenleft.org.au/back/2003/535/535p14.htm). Cf. Mann, *Rise of the Vulcans*, 79–83.

5. CARTER'S SURRENDER TO
THE ROCKEFELLERS ON IRAN

Epigraphs: Fouad Ajami, "The Roots of Rage," *Washington Post*, November 28, 2004; and Carter as quoted in Jordan, *Crisis*, 31.

1. Alan Tonelson, "The Peacock Throne," *New Republic*, August 1, 1988.

2. William J. Daugherty, "Jimmy Carter and the 1979 Decision to Admit the Shah into the United States," *AmericanDiplomacy.org*, 3, March 16, 2003, http://www.unc.edu/depts/diplomat/archives_roll/2003_01-03/dauherty_shah/dauherty_p3.html. Daugherty was himself a hostage taken from the Tehran Embassy in 1979. In Daugherty's informed and balanced insider account, there is not a word about the role of CIA. No doubt this is because, as he has revealed, he was a CIA operations officer in the Tehran Embassy. He has just published *Executive Secrets*.

3. Nelson Rockefeller died on January 26, 1979, in the midst of the crisis. Brzezinski records receiving from him in November 1978 "a worried call . . . urging a clear-cut U.S. stand in support of the Shah" (Brzezinski, *Power and Principle*, 363). Earlier, Brzezinski (*Power and Principle*, 96) recommended to Carter that he solicit Nelson Rockefeller's assistance on Middle East policy "since that would have the added benefit of keeping Kissinger in line."

4. American charge d'affaires Bruce Laingen had warned from Tehran that the shah should not be admitted until the embassy had been provided with a protective force, as "the danger of hostages being taken in Iran will persist" (Rubin, *Paved with Good Intentions*, 296–97).

5. Bernard Gwertzman, *New York Times*, November 18, 1979; Salinger, *America Held Hostage*, 25. Hamilton Jordan, who was one of those present and advising for the shah's admission, later gave a more hypothetical version: "What are you guys going to advise me to do if they overrun our embassy and take our people hostages" (Jordan, *Crisis*, 32). Earlier, on July 27, Carter had commented that "he did not wish the Shah to be here playing tennis while Americans in Tehran were being kidnapped or even killed" (Brzezinski, *Power and Principle*, 474).

6. It also augmented, and possibly prolonged unnecessarily, the so-called Second Oil Shock of 1979 and 1980, which led to a permanent increase in crude oil prices and contributed significantly to Carter's electoral defeat in 1980.

7. Ledeen and Lewis, *Debacle*, 143. In 1980 an important article by Michael Ledeen and William Lewis, summarized in *Newsweek*, revealed how Carter and Vance had been opposed by Brzezinski: "At this critical juncture, a fundamental split developed in Washington. According to the authors, national-security

adviser Zbigniew Brzezinski 'believed that the nature of the Shah's regime was a distinctly secondary question, and that Iran was of such pre-eminent importance to American Middle East policy that the Shah should be encouraged to do whatever was necessary to preserve control of the country.' This view was opposed by human-rights enthusiasts in the State Department, including Iran desk chief Henry Precht who, the authors say, 'had disliked the Shah's regime for years.' Ledeen and Lewis say that secretary of state Cyrus Vance gave his 'full backing' to Precht and others who argued that the U.S. could not support 'repression in Iran.' "(Russell Watson, "Who Lost Iran," *Newsweek*, April 28, 1980, summarizing Michael Ledeen and William Lewis, "Carter and the Fall of the Shah: The Inside Story," *Washington Quarterly: A Review of Strategic and International Issues* [spring 1980]: 3–40). Cf. Ledeen and Lewis, *Debacle*, 143–48, and passim.

8. From their roles as the shah's bankers at the Chase Manhattan Bank, David Rockefeller and McCloy had known the shah and had had business interests and contacts in Iran for almost two decades. Kissinger in 1979 "was, among other enterprises, in the employ of David Rockefeller's Chase Manhattan Bank as chairman of its International Advisory Committee" (Daugherty, "Jimmy Carter and the 1979 Decision to Admit the Shah"). Nelson Rockefeller had also pressured the administration on behalf of the shah until his death in January 1979. Behind the scenes was a sixth Rockefeller man, Archibald Roosevelt, a CIA Iranian operative and "old boy" who had moved on to become an adviser to David Rockefeller at Chase Manhattan Bank (Robert Parry, "David Rockefeller and October Surprise Case," *Consortiumnews.com*, April 15, 2005, http://www.consortiumnews.com/2005/041505.html).

9. Bill, *Eagle and the Lion*, 331. Brzezinski later tried to downplay his role in the Iran debacle (Brzezinski, *Power and Principle*, 473–74). U.S. ambassador William Sullivan accused him of playing the principal role, going outside channels to do so ("Brzezinski . . . established his own 'embassy' in Iran . . . in the person of Ardeshir Zahedi, the Shah's ambassador to Washington"; William H. Sullivan, "Dateline Iran: The Road Not Taken," *Foreign Policy* no. 40 [fall 1980]: 178; cf. Allan Mayer, "Zbig on the Griddle," *Newsweek,* September 22, 1980). Sullivan's claims are corroborated in the very hostile account by Henry Precht of the State Department's Iran desk, of which I will quote only a fraction: "Brzezinski throughout the revolution was communicating with [Ambassador] Zahedi or the Shah himself, to give his own personal opinions of how Iran should conduct itself during the revolution without coordinating with Vance. . . . During a meeting with Brzezinski, the latter told Sullivan that the Shah was our man, and we had to stand behind him at whatever cost. There would be no compromise, and we would do whatever was necessary to support him. Brzezinski's position was much tougher than Sullivan's. . . . [In February 1979] As fighting between military units was still going on, I spoke to Sullivan on the phone. He said he had just come off the line with Brzezinski, who had told him to tell General Gast, who was our MAAG Chief and chief military officer, to tell the Iranian leadership now was the time for a coup. They must overthrow Bakhtiar and take control of the country and do whatever is necessary to restore order. Sullivan said, 'I can't understand you. You must be speaking Polish. General Gast is in the basement of

the Supreme Commander's headquarters pinned down by gunfire and he can't save himself, much less the country.' That was the last gasp, for the Iranian regime collapsed at that point" (Charles Stuart Kennedy, "The Iranian Revolution: An Oral History with Henry Precht, Then State Department Desk Officer," Middle East Institute, http://www.mideasti.org/pdfs/mejprecht5801.pdf).

10. From *Newsweek*, September 22, 1980: "Former U.S. Ambassador to Teheran William H. Sullivan has accused [Brzezinski] of contributing to the Iran crisis by first refusing to accept that the Shah's regime was doomed—and then blocking efforts to open talks with the Ayatollah Khomeini."

11. Rubin, *Paved with Good Intentions*, 214. Cf. Bill, *Eagle and the Lion*, 248: "Brzezinski's distorted views . . . came from his friend, Iranian Ambassador Ardeshir Zahedi, with whom he maintained close contact throughout the crisis. Brzezinski and Zahedi spent the last half of 1978 reinforcing one another's opinions on the situation in Iran." In 1978, Zahedi returned from his Washington post to Tehran, where he told U.S. ambassador William Sullivan that first Brzezinski and then Carter had encouraged his return to "stiffen the shah's spine" (Sullivan, *Mission to Iran*, 171–72).

12. From Bill, *Eagle and the Lion*, 251: "The shah was also incredulous when he heard that Brzezinski had vetoed [U.S. Ambassador William] Sullivan's proposal that the United States make direct contact with Khomeini in Paris. . . . Later, in February 1979, Brzezinski was as disgusted with the Iranian military as he had been earlier with the shah, since 'the Iranian military evidently did not have the will to act.' Ultimately, in Brzezinski's eyes everyone was vacillating: Ambassador Sullivan, the shah, and the Iranian military itself." In his memoir, much more subdued than his *Foreign Policy* article, Sullivan wrote that in response to his "short, sharp" message of protest at the cancellation of plans to deal with Khomeini, he was notified that the decision was the president's, backed by "the vice-president [Mondale], the secretary of state [Vance], the secretary of defense [Brown], the secretary of the treasury [Miller], the head of CIA [Turner], and the national-security advisor [Brzezinski]" (Sullivan, *Mission to Iran*, 224–25).

13. Rubin, *Paved with Good Intentions*, 215, 223, 229–32, 235–38.

14. Daugherty, "Jimmy Carter and the 1979 Decision to Admit the Shah," 2. This is only the short list, which also included neocons. "The rogues' gallery includes not only Michael Ledeen and Richard Secord, but Kissinger, David Rockefeller, and John McCloy, whose frantic lobbying to admit the cancerstricken Shah into the United States undoubtedly reflected a peculiar combination of considerations that fogged their strategic vision—the financial interests of Chase Manhattan and a sentimental attachment to the former monarch. Indeed, one of [Bill's] book's most valuable features is its description of America's 'Pahlavites,' those political and media luminaries, including Jacob Javits and his wife, Marian, Abraham Ribicoff, Barry Goldwater, Barbara Walters, Joseph Kraft, and Arnaud de Borchgrave, who promoted the Shah's image as tirelessly as if they were hired guns. (Mrs. Javits, of course, was just that.)" (Tonelson, "Peacock Throne").

15. Rockefeller, *Memoirs*, 374–75 (quotation marks in original).

16. Bird, *Chairman*, 644. The academic engaged was Professor George Lenczowski but apparently no such book was ever published.

17. Brzezinski, *Power and Principle*, 474.

18. Bird, *Chairman*, 646–48.

19. The Rockefeller-McCloy Project Alpha invites comparison with the private intelligence operations allegedly launched by Allen Dulles and William Donovan out of their law offices in the 1940s. See chapter 1 in this book.

20. Mark Hulbert, *Interlock: The Untold Story of American Banks, Oil Interests, the Shah's Money, Debts, and the Astounding Connections between Them* (New York: E. P. Dutton, 1982), 117–18.

21. Terence Smith, "Why Carter Admitted the Shah," *New York Times*, May 17, 1981.

22. Jordan, *Crisis*, 31.

23. It was recently observed that "the Democrats . . . were ill-served by Jimmy Carter's being in office for the Iran hostage crisis and the Soviet invasion of Afghanistan" (Drake Bennett, "Losing It," *Boston Globe*, October 31, 2004). But the author of this comment fails to note that some Democrats, and specifically Brzezinski, calculatedly encouraged both events.

24. Bird, *Chairman*, 644. Cf. Rockefeller, *Memoirs*, 367. Without directly naming Reed, political historian David Harris has called him "the principal unofficial contact" between the shah and the U.S. government (Harris, *Crisis*, 190, cf. 167). Also advising the shah was McCloy's law partner William E. Jackson (Walter Pincus and John M. Goshko, "U.S. Officials Had 'Understanding' with the Shah," *Washington Post*, March 26, 1980).

25. "Robert Armao's Recollection of the Shah of Iran," http://www.iranian voice.org/article1302.html. Nelson Rockefeller died in the middle of the Iran crisis, on January 26, 1979. Cf. Alan Richman, "The Shah Gets a Public Relations Man and City Hall Loses an Official Greeter; Armao Sees No Conflict," *New York Times*, August 14, 1979, B6.

26. "The Shah's Flight into Egypt," *Newsweek*, April 7, 1980.

27. Daugherty, "Jimmy Carter and the 1979 Decision to Admit the Shah."

28. "Kean, whose examination of Pahlavi in Mexico two months ago at the behest of banker David Rockefeller led to the shah's admission to the United States on medical grounds" (Don Oberdorfer, "Shah Flown to Sanctuary in Panama," *Washington Post*, December 16, 1979). See also Bird, *Chairman*, 644: "Rockefeller dispatched a close personal friend, Dr. Benjamin Kean."

29. From Terence Smith, "Why Carter Admitted the Shah," *New York Times*, May 17, 1981: "In late September, Joseph Reed, David Rockefeller's assistant, asked Dr. Benjamin H. Kean, a tropical-disease specialist, to examine the Shah in Cuernavaca. Dr. Kean learned from Armao about the Shah's history of cancer. Arriving in Mexico, Dr. Kean also found that the Shah was suffering from advanced jaundice and fever. Unsure what else might be wrong, Dr. Kean recommended that the Shah undergo extensive tests to complete the diagnosis and proposed that it be done at New York Hospital–Cornell Medical Center or one of several other hospitals in the United States."

30. From Lawrence K. Altman, "The Shah's Health: A Political Gamble," *New York Times*, May 17, 1981: "Robert Armao, a protégé of Nelson Rockefeller, and Joseph V. Reed, an aide to David Rockefeller, had both been sent to assist the Shah. Both were patients of Dr. Benjamin H. Kean, an internist at New

York Hospital who specializes in malaria and tropical medicine. When the Shah's condition did not improve, they summoned him to Mexico to consult on the Shah's case."

31. Daugherty, "Jimmy Carter and the 1979 Decision to Admit the Shah," 2.

32. Richard D. Lyons, "Physician Sues Magazine over Article on Care of Ex-Shah," *New York Times*, January 27, 1981: "Dr. Kean charged in the suit, in which he is asking $4 million, that the article accused him of 'making superficial diagnoses, rendering flawed and incomplete medical advice and either deliberately or negligently misjudging the capacity of Mexican doctors and medical facilities to treat the Shah's illness.' The suit, filed Jan. 2 [1981] in Federal District Court, also contended that the article implied that Dr. Kean's 'diagnoses were dictated or otherwise improperly influenced by David Rockefeller,' the chairman of the Chase Manhattan Bank and a friend of the late Shah, thus portraying Dr. Kean 'as a "pawn" of Mr. Rockefeller.' "

33. Smith, "Why Carter Admitted the Shah," *New York Times*, May 17, 1981

34. Yergin, *Prize*, 700.

35. Brzezinski, *Power and Principle*, 476. The event inspired Sunni extremists as well. "Only two weeks after radical students seized the American Embassy in Tehran on November 5, 1979, a similar group of Islamic radicals burned to the ground the American Embassy in Islamabad as Zia's troops stood idly by" (Chalmers Johnson, "Are We to Blame for Afghanistan?" *History News Network*, November 22, 2004, http://hnn.us/articles/8438.html).

36. "Abolhassan Bani-Sadr, newly-appointed foreign minister of Iran and a member of the governing Revolutionary Council, defended his government's plan to withdraw its assets from the U.S. on the ground that American banking interests were responsible for the admission of the shah to the U.S. He singled out David Rockefeller, head of Chase Manhattan Bank, as well as former Secretary of State Henry Kissinger. Rockefeller had acknowledged that he interceded with the Carter Administration to admit the shah to the U.S. for medical treatment" (Facts on File World News Digest, November 16, 1979; cf. John M. Goshko, "U.S. Firmly Refuses to Extradite the Shah," *Washington Post*, November 6, 1979).

37. John M. Goskho and Victor Cohn, "Shah Quits Panama Despite U.S. Effort," *Washington Post*, March 24, 1980.

38. This explains the appalling lack of U.S. knowledge of the shah's deteriorating position. An August 1978 preliminary CIA study had said "Iran is not in a revolutionary or even a 'prerevolutionary' situation"; a month later, the Defense Intelligence Agency predicted that the shah would "remain actively in power over the next ten years" (Michael A. Ledeen and William H. Lewis, "Carter and the Fall of the Shah: The Inside Story," *Washington Quarterly* [April 1980]: 10). Earlier Carter had proclaimed Iran "an island of stability" when he celebrated New Year's Eve of 1978 with the shah.

39. James A. Bill, "U.S.-Iran Relations: Forty Years of Observations," lecture of February 20, 2004, Middle East Institute, Washington, D.C., http://www.mideasti.org/articles/doc183.html.

40. As reported in Terence Smith, "Putting the Hostages' Life First," *New York Times*, May 17, 1981: "On Nov. 5 [1979], the day after the embassy was

seized, David Rockefeller, a leader of the network, had taken up his telephone, called the White House and asked Susan Clough, Carter's secretary, to put him through to the President. There were at least two unusual aspects to the call: David Rockefeller does not customarily do his own dialing, and those accustomed to dealing with the White House know that Presidents are not likely to be immediately available, even to a Rockefeller. Nonplussed, Carter's secretary put Rockefeller off and then called him back to make sure the call was genuine."

41. Hulbert, *Interlock*, 85, quoted, with minor qualification, in Bill, *Eagle and the Lion*, 330, cf. 496.

42. Mark D. Lew, "Letters: Chase Manhattan Follow-Up," *Benzene* 4, http://radio.weblogs.com/0134204/2004/02/21.html, summarizing Hulbert, *Interlock*. Hulbert is an insider. According to a recent Web biography (which has since vanished): "Mr. Hulbert is a regular columnist for *Forbes* magazine, and is on the editorial board for the *Journal of the American Association of Individual Investors*. He is often quoted in the *Wall Street Journal, Barron's, USA Today* and many other newspapers and magazines. He has appeared several times on public television's *Wall Street Week with Louis Rukeyser*, and is a frequent guest on CNBC and Cable News Network." Yet his book has all but vanished from our collective electronic memory. I can find no references to it *at all* in Lexis Nexis, and only passing references to it on Web sites in Google. There is only one cited reference to the book in the *Social Sciences Citation Index* (in a 1994 article by the equally important and marginalized author R. T. Naylor). Compare this, for example, to forty-two citations for Noam Chomsky's *American Power and the New Mandarins* (New York: Pantheon, 1969).

43. Roy Assersohn, *The Biggest Deal* (London: Methuen, 1982), 272. Chase's total loan exposure was $1,930 billion; the next largest exposure, that of Chemical of New York, was $260 billion (Hulbert, *Interlock*, 96, citing *Euromoney* [November 1980]: 14, 16).

44. Terry Robards, *New York Times*, February 1, 1976, section 3, p. 1; Rockefeller, *Memoirs*, 305–10.

45. Bill, *Eagle and the Lion*, 341–44, quoting Hulbert, *Interlock*, 156. The freeze of Iranian assets was controversial and dangerous. From the *New York Times*, May 17, 1981: "Ten days after the embassy takeover, the United States froze the estimated $6 billion in Iranian assets on deposit in American banks. The decision had been put off for several days out of fear that other countries—Saudi Arabia, for example—would view the move as a precedent that endangered international banking understandings. If these nations had reacted by withdrawing their huge deposits in American banks, it could have caused a run on the dollar and a collapse of the banking system. In a recent interview, Lloyd N. Cutler, the urbane, silver-haired Washington lawyer who had become White House counsel, remembered: 'It seemed a very real fear at the time. We had some terrific arguments in the Administration about whether we were about to cause the "Crash of '79."'"

46. See chapter 4 in this book.

47. Dreyfuss with LeMarc, *Hostage to Khomeini*, 62.

48. Bill, *Eagle and the Lion*, 343, quoting Hulbert, *Interlock*, 196.

49. From Assersohn, *Biggest Deal*, 82: "European and Japanese bankers were outraged and gave their tacit approval, at least, to the litigation started by the Iranians when they challenged the legality of the President's extra territorial actions which seemed to threaten the stability of the world's sophisticated financial machinery."

50. Robert Carswell, "Economic Sanctions and the Iran Experience," *Foreign Affairs* (winter 1981–82): 257, quoted in Hulbert, *Interlock*, 195.

51. Hulbert, *Interlock*, 195. Economic analyst Roy Assersohn has commented that "throughout the whole transaction the hardest nosed and most aggressive of all the banks was probably the Chase Manhattan, which . . . was . . . quite prepared to push aside all other considerations and other banks to secure what it deemed to be its own targets" (Assersohn, *Biggest Deal*, 273).

52. Hulbert, *Interlock*, 196.

53. Bill, *Eagle and the Lion*, 346–47; Hulbert, *Interlock*, 108–9.

54. Hulbert, *Interlock*, 34; cf. 31–37. The twenty-five-year contract negotiated in 1953 between the Iranian government and BP, representing the Western oil majors, expired in 1978. The shah and his National Iranian Oil Consortium refused the new contract BP offered, creating the opportunity for Iran to market its oil to France, Brazil, and other countries on a state-to-state basis. A highly tendentious book published by the Lyndon Larouche organization in 1981 argued that these signs of growing independence by the shah led to a decision by Washington and London to drop him. See Dreyfuss and LeMarc, *Hostage to Khomeini*, 19–20, 34–35, and passim.

55. Hulbert, *Interlock*, 35, 105–7.

56. Yergin, *Prize*, 702.

57. Benjamin J. Cohen, *In Whose Interest? International Banking and American Foreign Policy* (New Haven, Conn.: Yale University Press, 1986), 153, citing Karin Lissakers, "Money and Manipulation," *Foreign Policy* 44 (fall 1981): 112.

58. Hobart Rowen, "Rockefeller Sees U.S. Losing Influence Abroad," *Washington Post*, August 20, 1978.

59. Cohen, *In Whose Interest?* 154. Without mentioning Hulbert, Cohen attacks the "somewhat sensationalist" thesis that David Rockefeller "played a key role" in the decision to forestall an Iranian withdrawal (Cohen, *In Whose Interest?* 155). But as Bill points out (Bill, *Eagle and the Lion*, 498), Cohen and other skeptics have failed to address the important issue of the legality of the loans to the shah.

60. As reported in the *Washington Post*, "U.S. Freeze of Iran's Assets Gets Test in French Court," on December 12, 1979: "At the monthly meeting of major central banks in Basel, Switzerland, yesterday, Federal Reserve Chairman Paul Volcker reportedly was subjected to almost universal criticism of the American action as endangering the international banking system." A French court on January 16, 1980, before ruling on the U.S. freeze of Iranian assets, temporarily ordered a retaliatory freeze on $ 51.7 million in Citibank funds deposited in the French Central Bank and a small private bank ("France Seizes Citibank Funds," *Facts on File*, January 25, 1980).

61. Parry, *Secrecy & Privilege*, 87.

62. Rockefeller, *Memoirs*, 374; Parry, *Secrecy & Privilege*, 102–3.

63. "U.S. Aides Describe '79 Coup Plan," *New York Times*, April 20, 1980. The *Times* reported senior U.S. officials as saying that the Carter administration in January 1979 attempted to lay the groundwork for a possible military coup in Iran. The rapid disintegration of Iran's military forces made the plans unworkable before they could be carried out.

64. Smith, "Putting the Hostages' Lives First," *New York Times*, May 17, 1981.

65. Only recently have we learned of a second military coup plot in July 1980, coordinated with Iranian exile and outspoken Khomeini critic Ali Akbar Tabatabai in Washington: "The most serious of the real [conspiracies] was led by military officers at the Nojeh air base in western Iran. It had the support of the main opposition leader, former prime minister Shahpour Bakhtiar, who was exiled in Paris—and whose main spokesman in America was Ali Akbar Tabatabai. On July 10, the Khomeini government moved to preempt the 'Nojeh coup' by arresting 300 suspects, most of them military officers" (David B. Ottaway, "The Lone Assassin," *Washington Post*, August 25, 1996). Cf. also Jack Anderson, *Peace, War, and Politics: An Eyewitness Account* (New York: Forge, 1999), 333.

66. Smith, "Putting the Hostages' Lives First," *New York Times*, May 17, 1981.

67. Parry, *Trick or Treason*, 142–43.

68. Larry Everest, "Fueling the Iran-Iraq Slaughter," *ZNet*, September 5, 2002, http://www.zmag.org/content/showarticle.cfm?SectionID=40&ItemID=2292, citing Abol Hassan Bani-Sadr, *My Turn to Speak: Iran, the Revolution, and Secret Deals with the U.S.* (Washington, D.C.: Brassey's, 1991), 13, 70, 94: "This plan to reestablish a royalist regime also mentioned a meeting in Jordan between Zbigniew Brzezinski, President Carter's national security adviser, and Saddam Hussein, two months before the Iraqi attack. . . . We knew that Zbigniew Brzezinski, Carter's national security adviser, and Saddam Hussein had met in the first week of July 1978. . . . I also happened to know that Brzezinski had assured Saddam Hussein that the United States would not oppose the separation of Khuzestan from Iran, despite the fact that Carter had promised to prevent our defeat." In noting these facts, Larry Everest also cites journalist Robert Parry for a report ["October Surprise X-Files (Part 5): Saddam's 'Green Light,'" http://www.consortiumnews.com/archive/xfile5.html] that in a secret 1981 memo summing up a trip to the Middle East, then Secretary of State Al Haig noted, "It was also interesting to confirm that President Carter gave the Iraqis a green light to launch the war against Iran through [then Prince, later King] Fahd." Parry repeats this information in *Secrecy & Privilege* (180–81), without either confirming it or discounting it.

69. Lacey, *Kingdom*, 450–54; Loftus and Aarons, *Secret War against the Jews*, 342–48. "[Menachem] Begin loathed Carter for the peace agreement forced upon him at Camp David" (Ben-Menashe, *Profits of War*, 48).

70. Parry, *Secrecy & Privilege*, 103–7.

71. Brzezinski, *Power and Principle*, 296–301.

72. Will Banyan, "Rockefeller Internationalism," *Nexus Magazine* 11, no. 1 (December–January 2004), citing David Rockefeller, "In Pursuit of a Consistent Foreign Policy: The Trilateral Commission," *Vital Speeches of the Day*, June 15, 1980, 518.

73. Banyan, "Rockefeller Internationalism," *Nexus Magazine*, (December–

January 2004), citing David Rockefeller, "America's Future: A Question of Strength and Will," *The Atlantic Community Quarterly* (spring 1979): 15–18.

74. Parry, *Secrecy & Privilege*, 117. A fourth member of the party was Owen Frisbie, Rockefeller's chief lobbyist in Washington. The campaign log entry can be seen online at http://www.consortiumnews.com/2005/Rockefeller-Casey.pdf.

75. Parry, *Secrecy & Privilege*, 115–16.

76. Jimmy Carter, *Keeping Faith: Memoirs of a President* (New York: Bantam Books, 1982), 559.

77. The Republicans' concern was brought up by vice presidential candidate George H. W. Bush with a group of reporters on October 2: "One thing that's at the back of everybody's mind is, 'What can Carter do that is so sensational and so flamboyant, if you will, on his side to pull off an October Surprise?'" (Parry, *Secrecy & Privilege*, 125).

78. Parry, *Secrecy & Privilege*, 86, 123–24, 136–37.

79. Parry, *Secrecy & Privilege*, 137; cf. 171.

80. Bani-Sadr escaped the Revolutionary Guards who had come to kill him and found refuge in France. Qotbzadeh was imprisoned and eventually executed by a firing squad.

81. The possibility of treason was raised tentatively by the title and final chapter of Robert Parry's groundbreaking book *Trick or Treason*.

6. CASEY, THE REPUBLICAN COUNTERSURPRISE, AND THE BANK OF CREDIT AND COMMERCE INTERNATIONAL, 1980

Epigraph: Response of January 11, 1993, from Sergey Vadimovich Stepashin, chairman of the Supreme Soviet's Committee on Defense and Security Issues, to a query dated October 21, 1992, from Representative Lee Hamilton (D-Ind.), chair of the House task force investigating the October Surprise, "October Surprise X-Files (Part 1): Russia's Report," *ConsortiumNews.com*, http://www.consortium news.com/archive/xfile1.html.

1. Loch K. Johnson, "Spymasters and the Cold War," *Foreign Policy* no. 105 (winter 1996–1997): 179.

2. Brown, *Last Hero*, 22–29.

3. Persico, *Casey*, 132–33. After David Rockefeller became CFR chairman in 1970, he invited Casey to join; Casey accepted, but with ambivalence (Persico, *Casey*, 157).

4. Bird, *Chairman*, 457.

5. Phillips, *Wealth and Democracy*, 87.

6. Block and Weaver, *All Is Clouded by Desire*, 28.

7. Peter Dale Scott, "The United States and the Overthrow of Sukarno, 1965–1967," *Pacific Affairs* (summer 1985), http://www.namebase.org/scott.html, citing "I Like Everybody to Do What They Are Told," *Fortune*, July 1973, 154; cf. *Wall Street Journal*, April 18, 1967.

8. Truell and Gurwin, *False Profits*, 384. This claim is fleshed out in Block and Weaver, *All Is Clouded by Desire*.

9. Block and Weaver, *All Is Clouded by Desire*, 27.

10. Block and Weaver, *All Is Clouded by Desire*, 6–8 and passim.

11. Martin J. Rivers, "A Wolf in Sheikhs Clothing: Bush Business Deals with 9 Partners of bin Laden's Banker," *GlobalResearch*, March 27, 2004, http://global research.ca/articles/MAR403A.html; Block and Weaver, *All Is Clouded by Desire*, 111–12; cf. Unger, *House of Bush, House of Saud*, 120–21 (Harken and BCCI).

12. Beaty and Gwynne, *Outlaw Bank*, 309.

13. Parry, *Secrecy & Privilege*, 97.

14. Demaris, *Dirty Business*, 92; Persico, *Casey*, 166.

15. Jude Wanniski, "Memo to Richard Lugar, Chairman, Senate Foreign Relations," May 8, 2005, http://wanniski.com/showarticle.asp?articleid=4345. Wanniski is a former associate editor of the *Wall Street Journal*. From Phillips, *Wealth and Democracy*, 87: "After 1968 . . . every passing year gave the principal Sun Belt states of California, Texas, and Florida a steadily higher ratio of the major U.S. fortunes, especially in oil, aerospace, real estate, construction, technology, and 'conglomerate' money."

16. Phillips, *Wealth and Democracy*, 92.

17. In his now unobtainable book *The Master Speaks* (1967), Moon allegedly wrote: "My dream is to organize a Christian political party including the Protestant denominations, Catholics and all the religious sects." The Christian dispensationalist Tim LaHaye, founder of the Council for National Policy and later the author of the best-selling *Left Behind* rapture novels, once wrote to thank Moon's assistant, Colonel Bo Hi Pak of the *Washington Times*, for a contribution of more than $500,000 to LaHaye's American Coalition for Traditional Values (Carolyn Weaver, "Unholy Alliance," *Mother Jones* [January 1986]).

18. Moon's organization was also associated with the Korean CIA in more disreputable forms of influence, remembered as Koreagate (Parry, *Secrecy & Privilege*, 75–85). Cf. David Ignatius, "Tension of the Times," *Washington Post*, June 18, 2004 ($1 billion). At the time of the Korean CIA's Koreagate crisis in the 1970s, Viguerie was paid nearly a million dollars for a direct-mail campaign on behalf of the Koreans. Trento has reported that Shackley and Tom Clines's company EATSCO then became tenants of Viguerie at 7777 Leesburg Pike in Falls Church, Virginia. A former associate of Ed Wilson's is quoted as saying: "The reality is that 7777 Leesburg Pike became the headquarters for the private CIA" (Trento, *Prelude to Terror*, 171–72).

19. Carl Oglesby, *The Yankee-Cowboy War: Conspiracies from Dallas to Watergate* (Mission, Kans.: Sheed Andrews and McMeel, 1976); cf. Sale, *Power Shift*.

20. David Brock, *Blinded by the Right* (New York: Crown, 2002), 71. As Olin Foundation president, Simon once wrote that "business leaders can direct corporate giving along constructive lines by playing an active role on the boards of the foundations their enterprise has made possible. . . . [C]orporate leaders have abdicated far too much day-to-day operational control of their giving to a philanthropic managerial class which sets their giving priorities for them. . . . While businesses may understandably wish to give to traditional charities of interest to local employees and customers, it is also their responsibility to nurture

the efforts of individuals and institutions which strive to strengthen the very freedoms that allow business to thrive in the first place. . . . Companies should give as though their futures depended on it, for in a very real sense, they do" (William E. Simon, preface to Marvin Olasky, Daniel T. Oliver, and Stuart Nolan, *Patterns of Corporate Philanthropy: The Progressive Deception* [Washington, D.C.: Capital Research Center, 1992], quotation from Simon is included in "Funder of Lott 1996 CCW Study Has Links to the Gun Industry," http://www.vpc .org/fact_sht/lottlink.htm).

21. Sanders, *Peddlers of Crisis*, 196–97. The NISC interlocked with the American Security Council through such men as former admiral Thomas H. Moorer.

22. See Martin Morse Wooster, review of *Antony Fisher: Champion of Liberty* by Gerald Frost, *Philanthropy* (July–August 2003). Cf. "Chuck Brunie's Hamilton Award Acceptance Speech," 2003, http://www.manhattan-institute .org/html/ah_2003.htm. According to Brunie, Hayek told Fisher, "'If you want to do something more for your country, DON'T go into politics, since politicians always lag behind public opinion. And public opinion always lags behind the tide of intellectual thought. So try to change elite intellectual opinion.' Which, he added, is a 20–30 year process."

23. Lapham, "Tentacles of Rage," 34. Brewery magnate Coors was reportedly "stirred up" by Lewis Powell's memorandum (Micklethwait and Wooldridge, *Right Nation*, 77–78).

24. Ferguson and Rogers, *Right Turn*, 88.

25. Earlier Crozier had been director of Forum World Features, "a classic CIA [and British Secret Intelligence Service] undercover operation," which by the 1960s "was the most widely circulated of the CIA-owned news services" (Frances Stonor Saunders, *The Cultural Cold War: The CIA and the World of Arts and Letters* [New York: The New Press, 1999], 311–12). In his review of Brian Crozier's *Free Agent: The Unseen War, 1941–1991* (London: HarperCollins, 1993), British intelligence researcher Robin Ramsay summarizes, with quotations from Crozier, the evolution whereby "Forum World Features in which, 'with the full agreement of SIS [he] would deal directly with CIA personnel' (p. 71), was succeeded by the Institute for the Study of Conflict. After Sir Dennis Greenhill, Permanent Under-Secretary at the Foreign Office, vetoed British state money for ISC and the CIA felt obliged to follow suit, 'the Agency came up with' Richard Mellon Scaife, who provided $100,000 a year' (p. 90)." (Robin Ramsay, "Crozier Country," *Lobster* 26 [December 1993], http://www.lobster-magazine.co.uk/online/issue26/lob26-11 .htm).

26. Stephen Dorril and Robin Ramsay, *Smear! Wilson and the Secret State* (London: Grafton/HarperCollins, 1992), 212–13.

27. For de Marenches's seminal meeting with Reagan on December 16, 1980, see the firsthand account, "Reagan's recipe for downing Evil Empire," by de Marenches's relative, Arnaud de Borchgrave, who was also present, in *Washington Times*, June 9, 2004.

28. Dorril and Ramsay, *Smear!*, 212; Robin Ramsay "Brian Crozier, the Pinay Circle and James Goldsmith," *Lobster* 17 (November 1988), 14.

29. Karen Armstrong, *The Battle for God: A History of Fundamentalism* (New York: Ballentine Books, 2001), 309: "The original inspiration for the

group . . . came not from the fundamentalists themselves but from three professional right-wing organizers, Richard Viguerie, Howard Phillips, and Paul
Weyrich."

30. Diamond, *Spiritual Warfare*, 30: "Weyrich proposed that if the Republican Party could be persuaded to take a firm stance against abortion, that would
split the strong catholic voting block within the Democratic Party. The New
Right leaders wanted [Jerry] Falwell to spearhead a visibly Christian organization
that would apply pressure to the GOP. Weyrich proposed that the name have
something to do with the moral majority."

31. Penny Lernoux, *People of God: The Struggle for World Catholicism* (New
York: Viking, 1989), 200.

32. Persico, *Casey*, 174.

33. Persico, *Casey*, 180.

34. Unger, *House of Bush, House of Saud*, 10–11. I believe that we should
distinguish the arrangements made to extricate the bin Ladens from those at the
same time for extricating members of the Saudi royal family. Removing members
of the Saudi royal family from America can be understood as affairs of state: it
was essential to secure Saudi cooperation for the campaign against al Qaeda, and
this was an understandable quid pro quo. But at least two of the bin Ladens permitted to leave, Osama's nephews Abdullah and Omar bin Laden, had been targets of an FBI antiterrorist investigation in 1996 that was reopened after their
departure in September 2001 (Unger, *House of Bush, House of Saud*, 178–79).

35. Draft section of 1993 *House October Surprise Task Force Report*, as
quoted in Parry, *Secrecy & Privilege*, 110–11.

36. Maureen Dowd, "I Spy a Screw-Up," *New York Times*, March 30, 2005;
Michael Ledeen, "Intelligence Failures: Virtues and Sins of Commission,"
National Review Online, April 7, 2005, http://www.nationalreview.com/ledeen/
ledeen200504070808.asp.

37. Bush's words were: "One thing that's at the back of everybody's mind is,
'What can Carter do that is so sensational and so flamboyant, if you will, on his
side to pull off an October Surprise?'" (Parry, *Secrecy & Privilege*, 125).

38. Nixon famously declined to contest the 1960 election result, telling the
press that "no one steals the presidency of the United States." Yet he worked
hard to get even in 1968.

39. Exhaustive proof of this is supplied by Summers with Swan, *Arrogance of
Power*, 299–308. There is a summary account in Scott, *Drugs, Oil, and War*,
121–23. Richard Allen, who described himself to Robert Parry as a "highly
reluctant" participant in 1980 Republican meetings over the hostages, said "he
was leery about such a meeting because he had been burnt by the controversy
over the [*sic*] Nixon's Vietnam peace-talk interference in 1968" (Parry, *Secrecy &
Privilege*, 119).

40. Nixon in turn privately believed, with reason, that his defeat in 1960 had
been secured in part by illegal ballot-stuffing by Democrats in Illinois and Texas.

41. Sick, *October Surprise*, 12; Parry, *Trick or Treason*; and Phillips, *American Dynasty*, 289.

42. Walter Pincus, "House Panel Finds 'No Credible Evidence' of an 'October
Surprise,'" *Washington Post*, January 14, 1993.

43. Parry, *Secrecy & Privilege*, 169.

44. *Kerry-Brown BCCI Report*, Appendixes.

45. Parry, *Secrecy & Privilege*, 139.

46. Parry, *Secrecy & Privilege*, 108–9, 123–25.

47. Parry, *Secrecy & Privilege*, 98–99. Arrangements were made to receive the funds in a new offshore bank in the small Caribbean nation of Antigua, where the chief banking eminence was Casey's close friend Bruce Rappaport.

48. Parry, *Secrecy & Privilege*, 99–100. In July 1980, amid fears of a military coup, Admiral Madani was forced into retirement, and several other people were executed (Rubin, *Paved with Good Intentions*, 334).

49. Parry, *Secrecy & Privilege*, 106–7. Gregg had been a deputy of Carter's enemy Ted Shackley in Vietnam. In the spring of 1980, when he joined Carter's NSC staff, he was close to Bush the elder. Gregg's fellow staffer David Aaron later told the *Village Voice*: "I think most people were unaware of [these connections]. . . . Zbig hired him . . . if Zbig was aware of it, he's never told anybody that" (*Village Voice*, May 21, 1991).

50. In October 1980 the FBI initiated surveillance of Cyrus Hashemi's offices because he was suspected of illegal arms sales, but in February 1981 the taping was terminated ahead of schedule by the incoming Reagan administration. The full transcripts of these tapes have never been released, despite many Freedom of Information Act (FOIA) requests and the death of Hashemi (Warren Cohen, review of *October Surprise: America's Hostages in Iran and the Election of Ronald Reagan*, by Gary Sick in *Fletcher Forum of World Affairs* [summer 1992], http://wjcohen.home.mindspring.com/otherclips/sick.htm). Cf. Parry, *Secrecy & Privilege*, 136–38.

51. Steven Emerson, "No October Surprise," *American Journalism Review* (March 1993), http://eightiesclub.tripod.com/id53.htm.

52. The "Bohemian Grove alibi" was actually a second effort to discredit the story of Casey's presence at the July meeting. Before this the same Steven Emerson had claimed that Casey spent the morning of July 27 at a conference in London (Steven Emerson and Jesse Thurman, "What October Surprise?" *New Republic*, November 18, 1991). Eventually a number of witnesses, including the historian Robert Dallek, corroborated written evidence that he "came at 4 P.M. that afternoon" (Parry, *Secrecy & Privilege*, 147–51).

53. Parry, *Secrecy & Privilege*, 159–63. Cf. Robert Parry, "The Bushes & the Death of Reason," *ConsortiumNews.com*, http://consortiumnews.com/2005/050905.html, May 9, 2005: "The task force adopted this Bohemian Grove alibi even though the documentary evidence showed that Casey actually had attended the Grove on the first weekend of August and could not have gone on the last weekend in July. The evidence established the following: In the summer of 1980, Casey's host, Darrell Trent, recalled traveling with Casey from Los Angeles to San Francisco and then to the Grove, but Trent wasn't sure which weekend. Grove financial records, however, showed that Trent was at the Grove on Friday, July 25, while Casey was still engaged in campaign business back in the Washington, D.C., area. There was also no evidence that Casey flew to the West Coast that weekend. Indeed, the House task force found a receipt showing that Casey had flown on the Washington-to-New York shuttle that Friday. Casey's calendar

also showed a meeting on Saturday morning, July 26, with a right-to-life activist, who said she met with Casey at his home in Roslyn Harbor, N.Y. Other records made clear that Casey did go to the Bohemian Grove the following weekend. According to Republican campaign records, Casey traveled to Los Angeles on Aug. 1, 1980, and met Darrell Trent at a campaign strategy meeting. By that evening, Grove financial records documented Casey and Trent making purchases at the Grove. In addition, there was a diary entry from Matthew McGowan, one of the Grove members at the Parsonage cottage. He wrote on Aug. 3, 1980, that 'we had Bill Casey, Gov. Reagan's campaign mgr., as our guest this last weekend.' "

54. Parry, Secrecy & Privilege, 112–13.

55. Parry, Trick or Treason, 142–43; Carter, Keeping Faith, 559.

56. Parry, Secrecy & Privilege, 118–19.

57. Parry, Secrecy & Privilege, 123.

58. Parry, "The Ladies' Room Secrets," ConsortiumNews.com, http://www .consortiumnews.com/archive/xfile2.html. Cf. Parry, Secrecy & Privilege, 137: "The curious BCCI money flight on the Concorde has never been explained."

59. Parry, Secrecy & Privilege, 124.

60. Truell and Gurwin, False Profits, 137.

61. Block and Weaver, All Is Clouded by Desire, 86. The first BCCI attempt to take over an American bank was made in 1975 by Abbas Gokal (Truell and Gurwin, False Profits, 35).

62. Block and Weaver, All Is Clouded by Desire, 86–87, emphasis in original; cf. Truell and Gurwin, False Profits, 138.

63. Parry, Secrecy & Privilege, 136. Hassan Yassin was the son of Yussuf Yassin, mentioned in chapter 2 as procurer to Saudi king Abdul Aziz.

64. Parry, Secrecy & Privilege, 137; Truell and Gurwin, False Profits, 129.

65. Parry, Secrecy & Privilege, 137.

66. Parry, Secrecy & Privilege, 117.

67. Parry, Secrecy & Privilege, 137–38; Parry, "Ladies' Room Secrets."

68. [Deputy Treasury Secretary] Robert Carswell, "Economic Sanctions against Iran," Foreign Affairs 60 (winter 1981–82): 257, quoted in Hulbert, Interlock, 195.

69. Hulbert, Interlock, 195.

70. Parry, Secrecy & Privilege, 118, citing an unpublished section of the House Task Force Report.

71. Parry, Secrecy & Privilege, 119–21; Trento, Prelude to Terror, 208. Cf. Curtiss, "Reprise of the October Surprise," http://www.washington-report.org/ backissues/0591/9105011.htm: "Bob Woodward and Walter Pincus of The Washington Post were the first to report that one such meeting took place in Washington, D.C. It was held Oct. 2 at the L'Enfant Plaza Hotel. Reagan campaign participants were Richard Allen, subsequently the Reagan administration's first national security adviser; Marine Lt. Col. Robert (Bud) McFarlane, then an aide to Senator John Tower but subsequently also a Reagan administration national security adviser; and Allen aide Lawrence Silberman, who apparently set up the meeting and who presently is a judge on the Federal Court of Appeals in

the national capital. A shadowy Iranian Jewish arms dealer, Hushang Lavie, says he was the Iranian principal. Allen says he was not, but that he has forgotten the name of the Iranian they met."

72. Former Mossad operative Ari Ben Menashe testified under oath to Congress that at Casey's October meeting in Paris there were also three active CIA officers present along with former CIA director George Bush. These were Bush's associate Donald Gregg, Robert Gates, and the CIA's Iran expert George Cave. (In 1980 both Gates and Gregg had been assigned to the Carter/Brzezinski National Security Council, and Gregg was still there.) But Bush, Gregg, Gates, and Cave have all denied participating in the meeting.

73. Cf. Curtiss, "Reprise of the October Surprise": "For doubters who still find it hard to believe that Americans of any political persuasion would, to be elected, enter into a cynical bargain to leave American hostages at risk through the harsh Tehran winter in an unheated embassy while Iranian mobs howled for their blood in the streets outside, there is a chilling, clinching argument in the report of John Anderson, the independent candidate for president in 1980. Officials of his campaign were approached by Iranians who offered them a deal to trade hostages for arms. The Anderson officials said no, and complied with the law by reporting the Iranian overture to the FBI. The FBI received no report of any kind from McFarlane, Allen, Silberman, Casey, or Admiral Garrick, who had been designated the sole Reagan campaign spokesman on all hostage matters. The idea that Iranians would approach dark-horse Anderson officials, and not approach Reagan campaign officials, is absurd."

74. See Robin Ramsey, "Brian Crozier, the Pinay Circle, and James Goldsmith," *Lobster* 17 (November 1988); David Teacher, "The Pinay Circle and Destabilization in Europe," *Lobster* 18 (October 1989).

75. Cooley, *Unholy Wars*, 24–28. Cf. Beaty and Gwynne, *Outlaw Bank*, 167.

76. Parry, "Ladies' Room Secrets." Cf. Parry, *Secrecy & Privilege*, 171. Some accounts, based on allegations from Ari ben Menashe, Richard Brenneke, Heinrich Rupp, and Oswald LeWinter, have placed George Bush at the Paris meetings. Most of these sources are extremely controversial, and the effect of their contributions has been to poison a story that had much stronger corroboration with respect to Casey's participation in the meeting. After having personally interviewed Brenneke for two days on another matter (drug trafficking through Central America), I am strongly inclined not to trust him on any subject. LeWinter later told Robert Parry that he had been "hired by elements in U.S. intelligence" to add bogus information to his story (Parry, *Secrecy & Privilege*, 145–46).

77. Robert Parry, "Lost History (Part 4): Pierre Salinger & a 1980 Taboo," *ConsortiumNews.com*, http://www.consortiumnews.com/archive/lost4.html. Parry comments: "Ironically, Salinger's account of his October Surprise reporting would suffer a similar fate, excised from his memoirs and 'disappeared' from official American history—like so much of the other October Surprise evidence." Cf. Phillips, *American Dynasty*, 287.

78. Parry, *Secrecy & Privilege*, 109–10.

79. Parry, "Ladies' Room Secrets."

80. Robert Parry, "October Surprise: Finally, Time for the Truth," *Consor-tiumNews.com*, http://www.consortiumnews.com/archive/xfile9.html.

81. John Walcott and Jane Mayer, "Israel Said to Have Sold Arms to Iran since 1981," *Wall Street Journal*, November 28, 1986. Cf. Fred Kaplan, "A 10-Year-Old Quandary: Should We Deal with Terrorists?" *Boston Globe*, November 5, 1989: "The hostages were released on Jan. 20, 1981, just minutes after Reagan took the oath of office. It is now well known that Israel started delivering weapons to Iran shortly after. Sick says a list of these weapons was reported to the U.S. government, with no apparent objection."

82. Daniel Schorr, " 'No Deal' on Hostages This Time," *St. Petersburg Times*, July 30, 1988.

83. Harry V. Martin, "Israelis Hold the Key to October Surprise," *Napa Sentinel*, May 1991, http://www.american-buddha.com/israelis.hold.key.htm#ISRAELIS%20HOLD%20THE%20KEY%20TO%20OCTOBER%20SURPRISE. Cf. Noam Chomsky, *What Uncle Sam Really Wants* (Berkeley, Calif.: Odonian Press, 1992), quoting David Nyham, "Israel Plan Was Aimed at Toppling Khomeini," *Boston Globe*, October 21, 1982.

84. Parry, *Secrecy & Privilege*, 107.

85. Parry, *Secrecy & Privilege*, 131.

86. Curtiss, "Reprise of the October Surprise."

87. Other Americas Radio, "The October Surprise," transcript http://www.informationclearinghouse.info/article3862.htm: "On July 18th, 1981, an Argentine cargo plane crashed on the Soviet-Turkish border. It was loaded with weapons in transit from Israel to Iran. High-level Israeli officials have said that the Reagan administration knew and approved of the arms dealings the crash exposed. The cargo of spare parts and ammunition were all American-made. From reports in the *New York Times* and *Wall Street Journal*, we know of two separate groups of shipments to Iran in 1981. The first, as we have already heard, was shipped through Israel with authorization from the Reagan administration officials. The second group of arms was shipped by an Iranian-born arms merchant, Cyrus Hashemi. Hashemi had worked for the CIA beginning in 1975. He died suddenly of a rare form of acute leukemia in 1986."

88. Robert Parry, "October Surprise X-Files (Part 3): Bill Casey's Iranian," *ConsortiumNews.com*, http://www.consortiumnews.com/archive/xfile3.html.

89. Parry, *Trick or Treason*, 282; Draper, *Very Thin Line*, 132–54. Also involved were three other figures alleged by some to have attended Casey's October 1980 meetings in Paris: Manucher Ghorbanifar, Adnan Khashoggi, and George Cave. Khashoggi intimate Larry Kolb has described attending the meeting in Hamburg with Ghorbanifar, along with Al Schwimmer, David Kimche, Hassan Karoubi, and two others not usually mentioned elsewhere: his friends Adnan Khashoggi and ex-CIA officer Miles Copeland, said by Parry to have been on the periphery of the countersurprise (Kolb, *Overworld*, 244–45; Parry, *Secrecy & Privilege*, 113–14; Draper, *Very Thin Line*, 126–31). Draper says (*Very Thin Line*, 131) that the Khashoggi-Schwimmer-Kimche connection grew out of an earlier Khashoggi-Israeli plan for offshore covert operations and arms deals hatched "at a safari resort in Kenya owned by Khashoggi"—i.e., the Safari Club.

90. Block and Weaver, *All Is Clouded by Desire*, 89–90.

91. Pelletiere, *Iraq and the International Oil System*, 197.

92. Persico, *Casey*, 311; Crile, *Charlie Wilson's War*, 131, 141–42.

93. Beaty and Gwynne, *Outlaw Bank*, 80; cf. 53.

94. *Kerry-Brown BCCI Report*, "BCCI, the CIA, and Foreign Intelligence," 320, http://www.fas.org/irp/congress/1992_rpt/bcci/11intel.htm: "BCCI may have been moving money through the National Bank of Oman to fund the war in Afghanistan. British journalists have written: 'BCCI's role in assisting the U.S. to fund the Mujaheddin guerrillas fighting the Soviet occupation is drawing increasing attention. The bank's role began to surface in the mid-1980's when stories appeared in the *New York Times* showing how American security operatives used Oman as a staging post for Arab funds. This was confirmed in the *Wall Street Journal* of 23 October 1991 which quotes a member of the late General Zia's cabinet as saying "It was Arab money that was pouring through BCCI." The Bank which carried the money on from Oman to Pakistan and into Afghanistan was National Bank of Oman, where BCCI owned 29%.' The National Bank of Oman and its CEO, Case Zawawi, also did business with Bruce Rappaport. Jerry Townsend, the President of Colonial Shipping in Atlanta, told the Subcommittee that his former employer, Bruce Rappaport, had business relations in Oman with Case Zawawi at the National Bank of Oman. Townsend, who claims to have worked as a soviet analyst with the CIA, was employed by Rappaport between 1981 and 1990. Townsend recalled that Rappaport flew Zubin Mehta and the London Philharmonic to Oman on one occasion to entertain the Sultan and other members of the royal family. More importantly, according to Townsend, Rappaport and Zawawi had numerous 'contracts with the Saudis.' The consolidated loan report for BCCI of March 3, 1991 shows a loan authorization of almost $11 million to the Zawawi group with an outstanding balance of nearly $8 million."

95. Block and Weaver, *All Is Clouded by Desire*, 85, emphasis in original. The authors cite two Townsend associates, one of them Bert Lance, who "had no doubt that Townsend was CIA during his tenure with Rappaport." According to the online version of the *Kerry-Brown BCCI Report*, posted by the Federation of American Scientists (at http://www.fas.org/irp/congress/1992_rpt/bcci/11intel .htm): "Jerry Townsend, the President of Colonial Shipping in Atlanta, told the Subcommittee that his former employer, Bruce Rappaport, had business relations in Oman with Case Zawawi at the National Bank of Oman." In the final published version, this text reads: "A former CIA agent, now based in Atlanta, Georgia and in private business, told the Subcommittee that his former employer, Bruce Rappaport, had business relations in Oman with Qais-Al Zawawi at the National Bank of Oman. . . . The former CIA officer, who worked for the operations directorate, was employed by Rappaport between 1981 and 1990" (*Kerry-Brown BCCI Report*, 320).

96. Truell and Gurwin, *False Profits*, 123.

97. Truell and Gurwin, *False Profits*, 120–21.

98. Adams and Frantz, *Full Service Bank*, 48–54. Carter took a personal interest in his friend's problems and asked Washington's prominent attorney, Clark Clifford, to represent Lance.

99. Truell and Gurwin, *False Profits*, 122.

100. Truell and Gurwin, *False Profits*, 125; Parry, *Secrecy & Privilege*, 111.

101. Beaty and Gwynne, *Outlaw Bank*, 357.

102. By 1989, at the time of the bank's exposure, some of the key countersurprise figures had died: Shaheen in 1985, Cyrus Hashemi in 1986, Casey in 1987, and Abedi in 1988. Parry has written that he does not believe Hashemi was murdered (Parry, *Secrecy & Privilege*, 147).

103. Eleanor Clift, on the NBC television talk show *The McLaughlin Group*, May 12, 1991.

104. In 1984, Hamilton received all but $500 of the $14,500 in pro-Israel PAC money that went to Indiana House contests (Paul Findlay, *They Dare to Speak Out: People and Institutions Confront Israel's Lobby* [Chicago: Lawrence Hill Books, 1989], 46, cf. 69).

105. Scott and Marshall, *Cocaine Politics*, 179–81.

106. Parry, *Trick or Treason*, 281–85.

107. Brisard and Dasquié, *Forbidden Truth*, 117, cf. 135–39; Truell and Gurwin, *False Profits*, 397–402. A libel proceeding has since been instituted against Jean Charles Brisard by Khalid bin Mahfouz, one of the Arabs he named (Thompson, *Terror Timeline*, 260). The Banque de Commerce et de Placements, chaired by BCCI director Alfred Hartmann, the vice president of Rappaport's Inter Maritime Bank, was affiliated with the Lebanese branch of the huge National Commercial Bank of Saudi Arabia, in which bin Mahfouz was a major stockholder (Brisard and Dasquié, *Forbidden Truth*, 193).

108. Stansfield Turner quoted in "An Election Held Hostage," *Playboy*, October 1988, http://history.eserver.org/the-october-surprise.txt.

109. Parry, *Secrecy & Privilege*, 95, quoting senior CIA analyst George Carver.

110. Trento, *Secret History of the CIA*, 344 (private); Trento, *Prelude to Terror*, 61, cf. 101, 104–5, 140–41 (Adham, Safari Club).

111. Parry, *Secrecy & Privilege*, 49, 114.

112. Parry, *Secrecy & Privilege*, 132–33.

113. Parry, *Secrecy & Privilege*, 98.

114. *Kerry-Brown BCCI Report*, 320, http://www.fas.org/irp/congress/1992_rpt/bcci/; Truell and Gurwin, *False Profits*, 384; Beaty and Gwynne, *Outlaw Bank*, 311–12.

115. We learn this from the lament of former FBI assistant director W. Raymond Wannall (in "Undermining Counterintelligence Capability," *International Journal of Intelligence and Counterintelligence* 15, no. 3 [fall 2002], http://cicentre.com/Documents/DOC_Wannall_Undermining_Intel.htm): "On 18 February 1976, President Gerald R. Ford Jr. issued an order directing the Attorney General to prepare guidelines under which the FBI would carry out its investigatory and security functions. A decade later, in referring to this order during testimony on 20 May 1986 before the National Committee to Restore Internal Security, former Subversive Activities Control Board director Francis J. McNamara stated: 'Now, these guidelines, promulgated in March 1976 by Attorney General Edward H. Levi, said that in conducting domestic security investigations, the Bureau was strictly limited to investigating groups and individuals "which involve or will

involve the use of force or violence and which involve or will involve the viola-tion of Federal law." So intelligence as such was out.' Explaining the impact of the guidelines on the FBI, McNamara pointed out that, in mid-1973, more than 21,400 domestic security matters were pending. After the guidelines were issued, the number had been reduced to 4,868. This number was continuously reduced under the new rules, so that by 1982, only 43 cases were being handled, 23 on organizations and 20 on individuals. Commented McNamara, 'And this is in a nation of over 200 million people that is the main target of Soviet subversion and espionage efforts.' This drastic reduction in the caseload led to the abolition of the internal security branch of the FBI's intelligence division in 1976.

"A comparable de-emphasis on Communist matters took place in the CIA. In 1977 President Jimmy Carter appointed Admiral Stansfield Turner as the new Director of Central Intelligence (DCI). He soon dismissed several hundred of the Agency's experts on Communism. Turner, in his memoirs, justified the reduction in staff by pointing to a previous study, conducted in mid-1976 under DCI, later President, George H. W. Bush, which recommended the abolition of 1,350 posi-tions in the Agency's espionage branch. Turner claimed that, of the final total of 820 positions vacated largely by attrition, only 17 people were actually dis-missed, while 147 took an early forced retirement. But the CIA has never fully recovered from the Turner-era reductions in this critical area."

116. For example, Richard Viguerie, one of the cofounders of Moral Major-ity, "was paid nearly a million dollars for a direct-mail campaign on behalf of the Koreans" (Trento, *Prelude to Terror*, 171).

117. Scott and Marshall, *Cocaine Politics*, 148–49; Scott, *Drugs, Oil, and War*, xviii.

118. See chapter 7 in this book.

119. For example, Allen Dulles and CIA actively misrepresented to Eisen-hower the situation in Laos that CIA gradually teased into a full-blown war. See Scott, *Drugs, Oil, and War*, 128–32, 146n.

120. Lawrence E. Walsh, Independent Counsel, *Final Report of the Indepen-dent Counsel for Iran/Contra Matters*, volume 1: *Investigations and Prosecutions*, August 4, 1993, Part 4, "The Flow of Funds: The Prosecution of the Private Oper-atives," http://www.fas.org/irp/offdocs/walsh/part_v.htm; emphasis added.

7. AFGHANISTAN AND THE ORIGINS OF AL QAEDA

Epigraphs: Clark Clifford [a drafter of the 1947 National Security Act], Church Committee Hearings, December 5, 1975, 51, quoted in *Church Committee Report*, Book 1, 153. The Afghan exile is quoted in Coll, *Ghost Wars*, 182.

1. Crile, *Charlie Wilson's War: The Extraordinary Story of the Largest Covert Operation in History*.

2. Springman quoted in "Has Someone Been Sitting on the FBI?" BBC, November 6, 2001, http://news.bbc.co.uk/1/hi/events/newsnight/1645527.stm.

3. Consider, for example, the fate of state department officer Edmund McWilliams, who warned in a twenty-eight-paragraph cable against the U.S. and ISI policy of favoring the Islamist Gulbuddin Hekmatyar. The result was to

provoke the wrath of the embassy's three most powerful figures, who arranged for McWilliams to be relieved from his post and transferred abruptly back to Washington (Coll, *Ghost Wars*, 180–84, 198–99). In 1998, McWilliams belatedly received the American Foreign Service Association's Christian Herter Award for creative dissent by a senior foreign service officer.

4. Cordovez and Harrison, *Out of Afghanistan*; Crile, *Charlie Wilson's War*; and Coll, *Ghost Wars*.

5. Persico, *Casey*; Peter and Rochelle Schweizer, *The Bushes: Portrait of a Dynasty* (New York: Doubleday, 2004). However, the BCCI now gets some attention in two other Bush biographies: Phillips, *American Dynasty*, and Unger, *House of Bush, House of Saud*.

6. Truell and Gurwin, *False Profits*, 132; cf. Unger, *House of Bush, House of Saud*, 109.

7. Beaty and Gwynne, *Outlaw Bank*, 301. The two authors wrote in *Time* ("Cover Story: The Dirtiest Bank of All," July 29, 1991) "of a clandestine division of the bank called the 'black network,' which functions as a global intelligence operation and a Mafia-like enforcement squad. Operating primarily out of the bank's offices in Karachi, Pakistan, the 1,500-employee black network has used sophisticated spy equipment and techniques, along with bribery, extortion, kidnapping and even, by some accounts, murder. The black network—so named by its own members—stops at almost nothing to further the bank's aims the world over. . . . The black network, which is still functioning, operates a lucrative arms-trade business and transports drugs and gold."

8. Truell and Gurwin, *False Profits*, 133–34. Cf. *Kerry-Brown BCCI Report*, 306–8, http://www.fas.org/irp/congress/1992_rpt/bcci.

9. Scott and Marshall, *Cocaine Politics*, 161–64, 179–81; Peter Dale Scott, *Drugs, Contras, and the CIA: Government Policies and the Cocaine Economy. An Analysis of Media and Government Response to the Gary Webb Stories in the San Jose Mercury News (1996–2000)* (Los Angeles: From the Wilderness Publications, 2000), chapter 4.

10. In a preface Brown congratulated Kerry for having had the courage to produce the report, when so many of his own party had enjoyed BCCI patronage. That patronage extended even to the Democratic Senate Campaign Committee, which was cochaired by Kerry and by David L. Paul of the notorious S&L CenTrust Savings Bank of Miami. CenTrust's major stockholder and close associate of Paul was Ghaith Pharaon of BCCI (Truell and Gurwin, *False Profits*, 71–72).

11. McCoy, *Politics of Heroin*; Scott, *Drugs, Oil, and War*, 33, 43–46.

12. Mohamad Bazzi, "Black Hawk Likely Shot Down by Rocket-Propelled Grenade," *Seattle Times*, November 8, 2003.

13. The responsibility of al Qaeda for the shoot-down of the Black Hawks was affirmed in June 2004 by the 9/11 Commission, Staff Statement #15, "Overview of the Enemy," 4. This conclusion has been considerably debated but was reaffirmed by the FBI agent who investigated the matter, Mary Deborah Doran. See Wright, *Looming Tower*, 188–89, 411.

14. Mark Bowden, *Black Hawk Down* (New York: Atlantic Monthly Press, 1999), 110.

15. Bergen, *Holy War, Inc.*, 82.

16. Crile, *Charlie Wilson's War*, 335.

17. Lance, *Triple Cross*, 141–43. Saif al-Masry, a member of al Qaeda's *shura*, or ruling council, also fought in Somalia. Mohamed's confession rebuts Burke, *Al-Qaeda*, 148–49: "Given the number of 'Arab Afghan' veterans in east Africa at the time, there seems to me to be no particular reason why it would have to be bin Laden's fighters, or even Islamic Jihad's, who transferred their skills to the Somalis."

18. Lance Williams and Erin McCormick, "Al Qaeda Terrorist Worked with FBI," *San Francisco Chronicle*, November 4, 2001: "The CIA . . . warned other U.S. government agencies about Mohamed and urged them to detain him if possible, the official said. The next year, in 1985, Mohamed managed to get a visa to enter the United States. One year later, he enlisted as a regular soldier in the U.S. Army at the age of 34, unusually old for a recruit. He was assigned to the U.S. Special Operations Command in Fort Bragg, the home of the Green Berets and the Delta Force, the elite counterterrorism squad. . . . In 1993, he trained Somali clansmen in the months leading up to a furious gun battle that took the lives of 18 U.S. soldiers."

19. Lance, *1000 Years for Revenge*, 29–31; Andrew Marshall, "Terror 'Blowback' Burns CIA," *Independent*, November 1, 1998.

20. See note 2, this chapter. Michael Springman, the former head of the American visa bureau in Jeddah, told the BBC that since 1987 CIA had been illicitly issuing visas to unqualified applicants from the Middle East and bringing them to the United States for training in terrorism for the Afghan war in collaboration with bin Laden.

21. Rashid, *Taliban*, 19–29.

22. Burke, *Al-Qaeda*, 72–86. "Throughout the 1980s, the 'Arab Afghans' or 'Afghan Arabs' called themselves 'Anssar,' or 'supporters' in Arabic. *Anssar* was first used to describe a group of Muslims that supported the Prophet Muhammad against his enemies more than 1,400 years ago. Bin Laden's organization used the name until early 1990, when it was changed to al Qaeda, which means 'the base'" (Jalal Ghazi, "'Arab Afghan' Primer—Who Are the Ones Who Got Away?" *Pacific News Service*, March 29, 2002, http://news.ncmonline.com/news/view_article.html?article_id=582).

23. Rashid, *Taliban*, 84–85. Like many authors Crile has explained that CIA backed Hekmatyar because he "was the darling of Zia and the Pakistan intelligence service" (Crile, *Charlie Wilson's War*, 222). But according to Coll, CIA officers "concluded independently that [Hekmatyar] was the most efficient at killing Soviets." Coll also makes it clear that ISI support for Hekmatyar was firmly endorsed by Milt Bearden, the Pakistan CIA station chief, and that Edmund McWilliams, a vigorous State Department opponent of Hekmatyar, was for his objections hustled out of the Islamabad embassy by Bearden and U.S. ambassador Robert Oakley (Coll, *Ghost Wars*, 120, 195–202).

24. Cordovez and Harrison, *Out of Afghanistan*, 61, emphasis added.

25. Kepel, *Jihad*, 142.

26. Cordovez and Harrison, *Out of Afghanistan*, 161.

27. Cordovez and Harrison, *Out of Afghanistan*, 62.

28. Rashid, *Taliban*, 84–85; Griffin, *Reaping the Whirlwind*, 57.

29. Hassan N. Gardezi, "Jihadi Islam: The Last Straw on the Camel of Pakistan's National Unity," paper presented at the World Sindhi Institute conference, Washington, D.C., May 20, 2000. Gardezi claims CIA as well as ISI backing for the Jamaat-e-Islami. In the 1980s the direct Zia-ISI-CIA dealings were exclusively with the Jamaat-e-Islami and its Afghan clients; however, Zia's policy of funding madrassas of all persuasions was an enormous boost to the militant Deobandis of the Jamiat-e-Ulema-Islam (Rashid, *Taliban*, 86, 89–90).

30. Cordovez and Harrison, *Out of Afghanistan*, 163.

31. Cordovez and Harrison, *Out of Afghanistan*, 162, quoting Congressman Wilson. Hekmatyar talked to British journalist and author Dilip Hiro of "rolling back communism by freeing the Muslim lands of Bukhara, Tashkent, and Dyushanbe" (Hiro, *Holy Wars*, 259, quoted in Dreyfuss, *Devil's Game*, 268).

32. This claim, widely repeated overseas but not in the United States, was challenged in June 2004 by the *9/11 Commission Report* (171) and its Staff Report #15, "Overview of the Enemy," 10: "No persuasive evidence exists that al Qaeda relied on the drug trade as an important source of revenue, or funded itself by trafficking in diamonds from African states engaged in civil wars." But Pakistani journalist and author Ahmed Rashid heard from officials in Washington that the Islamic Movement of Uzbekistan (IMU), which had earlier gravitated to the radicalism of Hekmatyar, had by 2000 become a "virtual partner in Al Qaeda's global jihad," providing "drug smuggling, military training, and support for Al Qaeda to extend its cells into Central Asia" (Rashid, *Jihad*, 173; cf. 45, 165). Ralf Mutschke, assistant director of the Criminal Intelligence Directorate of the International Criminal Police Organization (Interpol), testified to the U.S. Congress in 2000 that "according to some estimations IMU may be responsible for 70% of the total amount of heroin and opium transiting through the area" (Mutschke, "The Threat Posed by the Convergence of Organized Crime, Drugs Trafficking, and Terrorism," written testimony before a hearing of the Committee on the Judiciary, Subcommittee on Crime, December 13, 2000, http://judiciary.house.gov/Legacy/muts1213.htm).

33. B. Raman, "Musharraf, Viewed through Moscow's Eyes," *Asia Times Online*, December 10, 2002: "Moscow has reasons to be concerned about the reappearance of Gulbuddin Hekmatyar and his Hizb-e-Islami in Afghanistan and over the possibility of its teaming up with remnants of the Taliban and al Qaeda against allied troops in Afghanistan and the Hamid Karzai regime. There are strong grounds for believing that Pakistan's ISI, or at least sections of it, have been helping Hekmatyar, their blue-eyed mujahid of the 1980s."

34. Rahul Bedi, "Washington's Pakistani Allies: Killers and Drug Dealers," *Sydney Morning Herald*, September 27, 2001: "Opium cultivation and heroin production in Pakistan's northern tribal belt and adjoining Afghanistan were a vital offshoot of the ISI-CIA co-operation. It succeeded in turning some of the Soviet troops into addicts. Heroin sales in Europe and the U.S., carried out through an elaborate web of deception, transport networks, couriers and payoffs, offset the cost of the decade-long war in Afghanistan."

35. Scott, *Drugs, Oil, and War*.

36. Rashid, *Taliban*, 129. Cf. Coll, *Ghost Wars*, 90.

37. Rashid, *Taliban*, 131.

38. Roberto Montoya, "Tiempos de Guerra: El Imperio Global," *El Mundo* (Madrid), February 16, 2003, http://www.el-mundo.es/cronica/2003/383/1045 404347.html. For more on de Marenches, the Safari Club, and Afghanistan, see Doug Vaughan, "French Bull: Spies for Profit and Glory," *Covert Action Quarterly* (fall 1993): 44–49; and Cooley, *Unholy Wars*, 25–28.

39. Burke, *Al-Qaeda*, 59.

40. *9/11 Commission Report*, 56.

41. "What Good Friends Left Behind," *Guardian*, September 20, 2003, http://www.guardian.co.uk/afghanistan/story/o,1284,1044925,oo.html.

42. Lance, *1000 Years for Revenge*, 41–42.

43. Coll, *Ghost Wars*, 157 (host); Crile, *Charlie Wilson's War*, 521 (bags of money).

44. Burke, *Al-Qaeda*, 59.

45. Bergen, *Holy War, Inc.*, 66–67.

46. Cooley, *Unholy Wars*, 41.

47. Coll, *Ghost Wars*, 103; cf. 161–62.

48. Robert I. Friedman, *Village Voice*, April 15, 1993, summarizing and quoting from McCoy, *Politics of Heroin*, 479.

49. Cooley, *Unholy Wars*, 128–29; Beaty and Gwynne, *Outlaw Bank*, 305–6.

50. Beaty and Gwynne, *Outlaw Bank*, 306, cf. 82; also Stéphane Allix, *La petite cuillère de Scheherazade* (Paris: Jean-Claude Roux, 2001), 35, 95.

51. Maureen Orth, "Afghanistan's Deadly Habit," *Vanity Fair* (March 2002): 170–71. A Tajik sociologist added that she knew "drugs were massively distributed at that time" and that she often heard how Russian soldiers were "invited to taste."

52. B. Raman, "Assassination of Haji Abdul Qadeer in Kabul," South Asia Analysis Group (SAAG), Paper No. 489, http://www.saag.org/papers5/paper489 .html.

53. Raman, "Assassination of Haji Abdul Qadeer in Kabul."

54. Smucker's journalistic credibility on other matters has been challenged. On August 6, 1998, Smucker reported in the *Washington Times* concerning a mass grave of Serbians in Orahovac, Kosovo; many journalists reported the story, which was soon retracted. In June 2003 the *Monitor* had to apologize for a story by Smucker (April 25, 2003) that claimed the antiwar British MP George Galloway had been funded for eleven years by Saddam Hussein. The documents obtained by Smucker from an Iraqi general were soon shown to be forgeries (Cliff Kincaid, "Christian Science Monitor Apologizes," *Media Monitor, Accuracy in Media.org*, July 9, 2003, http://www.aim.org/media_monitor/A312_0 _2_0_C/). Despite this, I consider Smucker's book to be one of the best on America's Afghan campaign of 2001.

55. Smucker, *Al Qaeda's Great Escape*, 9. This decision by British and American officials (the latter almost certainly CIA) may have contributed to bin Laden's escape from Tora Bora in December 2001. Cf. CNN, "Afghan Official Believes bin Laden in Pakistan," December 29, 2001: "Abdullah Tawheedi, a deputy head of intelligence in Afghanistan, says he has received 'reliable infor-

mation' that the terrorist leader paid a 'large amount' of money to buy his way out of Afghanistan. Tawheedi named Haji Zaman—a well-known independent military commander—as the man responsible for taking bin Laden across the border to Pakistan. Ironically, Haji Zaman had recently been fighting against bin Laden and his al Qaeda organization. But Tawheedi says he believes Haji Zaman was apparently persuaded—by money—to help the terrorist leader."

56. Syed Saleem Shahzad, "U.S. Turns to Drug Baron to Rally Support," *Asia Times Online*, December 4, 2001; Peter Dale Scott, "Pre-1990 Drug Networks Being Restored Under New Coalition?" http://socrates.berkeley.edu/~pdscott/qf5.html.

57. Steve Coll, "Anatomy of a Victory: CIA's Covert Afghan War," *Washington Post*, July 19, 1992. Some CIA officials were less opposed. Charles Cogan, who oversaw the Afghan operation from Washington, later told Australian television: "Our main mission was to do as much damage as possible to the Soviets. We didn't really have the resources or the time to devote to an investigation of the drug trade. I don't think that we need to apologize for this" (quoted in McCoy, *Politics of Heroin*, 486).

58. Coll, *Ghost Wars*, 104, quoting from unpublished manuscript by Robert Gates.

59. Cordovez and Harrison, *Out of Afghanistan*, 159. The original plan "was to utilize Afghans belonging to the same ethnic groups that were dominant in adjacent parts of Central Asia, especially Uzbeks and Tajiks." But at some point Arab Afghans also became involved.

60. Schweizer, *Victory*, 29.

61. Rashid, *Jihad*, 43–44; cf. Reeve, *New Jackals*, 167.

62. Yousaf and Adkin, *Bear Trap*, 189.

63. Rashid, *Taliban*, 129.

64. Emdad-ul Haq, *Drugs in South Asia*, 189.

65. It is indisputable that the IIRO with Sayyaf's assistance were distributing Korans in former Soviet republics like Tajikistan. Baer, *Sleeping with the Devil*, 144, 141, 140. For more on the United States and bin Laden family connections to the IIRO, see Brisard and Dasquié, *Forbidden Truth*, 83–86.

66. Yousaf and Adkin, *Bear Trap*, 193; Rashid, *Jihad*, 223; and Coll, *Ghost Wars*, 90, 104.

67. Coll, *Ghost Wars*, 119.

68. Allix, *La petite cuillère*, 100.

69. Burke, *Al-Qaeda*, 168.

70. Griffin, *Reaping the Whirlwind*, 20.

71. The general consensus is that Hekmatyar was the principal drug trafficker among mujahideen leaders. However, John Cooley transmits the Soviet assessment that the "real 'king of heroin'" was Pir Sayad Ahmed Gailani (Cooley, *Unholy Wars*, 132). Gailani was used by the ISI to counter the influence of the Northern Alliance in the first postwar Hamid Karzai government of 2001 (Benjamin Soskis, "Circle Game," *New Republic*, November 12, 2001).

72. Cordovez and Harrison, *Out of Afghanistan*, 191–93. The principal of these "bleeders" at the time was Richard Perle (Cordovez and Harrison, *Out of Afghanistan*, 191–99, 207).

73. Cordovez and Harrison, *Out of Afghanistan*, 194–95.

74. Cordovez and Harrison, *Out of Afghanistan*, 6; cf. 268.

75. Cordovez and Harrison, *Out of Afghanistan*, 197.

76. Bamford, *Pretext for War*, 178.

77. Ahmed Rashid, "Afghanistan Heroin Set to Flood West," *Independent* (London), March 25, 1990. In early 1988 the State Department negotiators had been preparing to accept an end to CIA assistance. They then reversed themselves and held out for a matching of Soviet and CIA support to the two factions. Apparently the policy shift was motivated by an unscripted remark by Reagan to a television interviewer (Coll, *Ghost Wars*, 176–77).

78. Coll, *Ghost Wars*, 225–26; 226.

79. Coll, *Ghost Wars*, 225.

80. Coll, *Ghost Wars*, 181.

81. Coll, *Ghost Wars*, 211–12, 226–27, 231. The CIA station chief in Islamabad "met face-to-face with Hekmatyar" and helped organize supplies to his forces. As late as 1989, Azzam and bin Laden are said to have received a consignment of U.S. sniper rifles.

82. Alan J. Kuperman, "The Stinger Missile and U.S. Intervention in Afghanistan," *Political Science Quarterly* (summer 1999): 219–63, quoted with further discussion in Peter Dale Scott, "The CIA's Secret Powers: Afghanistan, 9/11, and America's Most Dangerous Enemy," *Critical Asian Studies* 35, no. 2 (2003): 242.

83. In addition, Milton Bearden, CIA station chief in Islamabad, had contempt for the Westernized Afghan rebel leaders and encouraged ISI chief Hamid Gul in his policy of giving the Stingers and other support chiefly "to Hekmatyar and other Islamists" (Coll, *Ghost Wars*, 175).

84. Walter Pincus, "Panels to Probe Afghan Arms Fund," *Washington Post*, January 13, 1987.

85. Cordovez and Harrison, *Out of Afghanistan*, 198.

86. Christina Lamb, "My Door Was Forced Open and I Was Grabbed," (London) *Daily Telegraph*, November 11, 2001.

87. During testimony in court regarding the 1998 attacks on the U.S. embassies in Kenya and Tanzania, al Qaeda defector Essam al-Ridi said bin Laden took $230,000 and transferred it to Arizona to acquire a plane that was supposed to fly Stinger missiles from Pakistan to Sudan. It is hard to imagine how a plane-load of Stingers could leave Pakistan without ISI knowledge.

88. Rashid, *Taliban*, 176–77; Johnson, *Sorrows of Empire*, 176–80; and Brisard and Dasquié, *Forbidden Truth*, 17–46. See also Labévière, *Dollars for Terror*, passim.

89. Hugh Pope, "Afghan Mutiny Boosts Islamist Fighters, Chances for Western-Built Oil Pipelines," *Wall Street Journal*, May 20, 1997.

90. Brisard and Dasquié, *Forbidden Truth*, 97–102, 155–59. A leader in the plot was Anas al-Liby, who was later given political asylum in Great Britain despite suspicions that he was a high-level al Qaeda operative. He was trained in terrorism by the triple agent Ali Mohamed, while Mohamed was still on the payroll of the U.S. Army (Lance, *Triple Cross*, 104; see also chapter 9 in this book).

91. Scott, *Drugs, Oil, and War*, 7; Thomas Goltz, *Azerbaijan Diary* (Armonk,

N.Y.: M. E. Sharpe, 1999), 274–75; and Mark Irkali, Tengiz Kodrarian, and Cali Ruchala, "God Save the Shah: American Guns, Spies, and Oil in Azerbaijan," *Sobaka*, May 22, 2003. See chapter 10 in this book.

92. Mutschke, "Threat Posed by the Convergence of Organized Crime, Drugs Trafficking, and Terrorism"; Scott, *Drugs, Oil, and War*, 29, 34.

93. *Halifax Herald*, October 29, 2001. Cf. Bodansky, *Bin Laden*, 298: "In late 1998, despite the growing pressure from U.S. intelligence and its local allies . . . a new network made up of bin Laden's supporters was being established in Albania under the cover of various Muslim charity organizations. . . . Bin Laden's Arab 'Afghans' also have assumed a dominant role in training the Kosovo Liberation Army." Bodansky adds that by mid-March 1999 the Kosovo Liberation Army (UCK) included "many elements controlled and/or sponsored by the U.S., German, British, and Croatian intelligence services. . . . In early April [1999] the UCK began actively cooperating with the NATO bombing—selecting and designating targets for NATO aircraft as well as escorting U.S. and British special forces detachments into Yugoslavia" (397–98). Cf. also Scott Taylor, "Bin Laden's Balkan Connections," *Ottawa Citizen*, December 15, 2001, http://www.unitedmacedonians.org/newspaper/ndo1/ottawa.htm.

94. Nick Wood, "U.S. 'Covered up' for Kosovo Ally," *Observer*, September 10, 2000, http://observer.guardian.co.uk/print/0,,4061661-102275,00.html (asset); "Prosecutor Berates Ex-Leader of Kosovo at Trial," AP, *New York Times*, March 6, 2007 (indicted).

95. Tom Walker and Aidan Laverty, "CIA Aided Kosovo Guerrilla Army All Along," *Sunday Times*, March 12, 2000, http://www.globalpolicy.org/security/issues/kosovo1/ksv17.htm.

96. Bergen, *Holy War, Inc.*, 136–37. Mir Aimal Kasi, the Pakistani who killed two CIA employees at CIA headquarters in January 1993, had also been with the mujahideen in Afghanistan and returned there after the killings (Jeff Stein, "Convicted Assassin: 'I Wanted to Shoot the CIA Director'" *Salon*, January 22, 1998, http://www.salon.com/news/1998/01/22news_kasi.html).

97. CIA deputy director for operations John McMahon in particular was concerned that escalation in Afghanistan might induce the Soviet Union to retaliate against Pakistan. Cf. Crile, *Charlie Wilson's War*, 251, 417, and passim.

98. Cordovez and Harrison, *Out of Afghanistan*, 158; Coll, *Ghost Wars*, 150.

99. Crile, *Charlie Wilson's War*, 517–19: As the sum was matched by an equal contribution from Saudi Arabia, "that meant another $400 million for the mujahideen."

100. Griffin, *9/11 Commission Report: Omissions and Distortions*, 104–7; Ahmed, *War on Truth*, 137–44; and Peter Dale Scott, "The CIA's Secret Powers: Afghanistan, 9/11, and America's Most Dangerous Enemy," *Critical Asian Studies* 35, no. 2 (2003): 233–58.

101. Julian Borger and John Hooper, "Trail Links Bin Laden Aide to Hijackers," *Guardian*, October 1, 2001, http://www.guardian.co.uk/wtccrash/story/0,,561001,00.html. Cf. Griffin, *9/11 Commission Report: Omissions and Distortions*, 109–10. The investigators were later identified as the FBI (*Wall Street Journal*, October 10, 2001; CNN, October 28, 2001; and *Times* [London], November 16, 2001).

102. For example, Daniel Klaidman, "Federal Grand Jury Set to Indict Sheikh," *Newsweek*, March 13, 2002: U.S. officials suspect "that Sheikh has been a 'protected asset,' of Pakistan's shadowy spy service, the Inter-Services Intelligence, or ISI." The story was enhanced by Indian intelligence sources with a more sensational claim: that Saeed Sheikh had wired the money to hijacker Mohamed Atta at the direction of Lieutenant-General Mahmoud Ahmad, the director of the ISI at the time (*Wall Street Journal*, October 10, 2001). Indian sources later downplayed this anti-Pakistani allegation by suggesting that the money came instead from a ransom paid to another terrorist, Aftab Ansari in Dubai, when a Kolkata businessman, Partha Roy Burman, was kidnapped in July 2001 (B. Muralidhar Reddy, "Omar Sheikh Arrested, Says Pearl Is Alive," *The Hindu*, February 13, 2002).

103. "Did Pearl Die Because Pakistan Deceived CIA?" *Pittsburgh Tribune-Review*, March 3, 2002, http://www.pittsburghlive.com/x/pittsburghtrib/s_20141 .html: "There are many in Musharraf's government who believe that Saeed Sheikh's power comes not from the ISI, but from his connections with our own CIA. The theory is that with such intense pressure to locate bin Laden, Saeed Sheikh was bought and paid for."

104. Ahmed, *War on Truth*, 142; cf. John Newman, "Omissions and Errors in the Commission's Final Report: Rep. McKinney 9/11 Congressional Briefing," August 18, 2005, http://911readingroom.org/bib/whole_document.php?article _id=422; Musharraf, *In the Line of Fire*, 225: "It is believed in some quarters that while Omar Sheikh was at the LSE [London School of Economics] he was recruited by the British intelligence agency MI6. It is said that MI6 persuaded him to take an active part in demonstrations against Serbian aggression in Bosnia and even sent him to Kosovo to join the jihad. At some point he probably became a rogue or double agent."

105. Maria A. Ressa, "India Wants Terror Spotlight on Kashmir," CNN, October 8, 2001, http://archives.cnn.com/2001/WORLD/asiapcf/south/10/08/ india.ressa/.

106. "Sources: Suspected Terrorist Leader Was Wired Funds through Pakistan," CNN, October 1, 2001, http://archives.cnn.com/2001/US/10/01/inv .pakistan.funds/: "As much as $100,000 was wired in the past year from Pak- istan to Mohamed Atta." Subsequent developments lent weight to the Pakistani connection, such as the arrest of Atta's alleged controls, Ramzi Binalshibh and Khalid Shaikh Mohammed, in Pakistan.

107. United States District Court for the Eastern District of Virginia, Alexan- dria Division. *United States of America v. Zacarias Moussaoui*, #108.

108. "India Helped FBI Trace ISI-Terrorist Links," *Times of India*, October 9, 2001; *Wall Street Journal*, October 10, 2001.

109. The appendixes note, in a list of names, a "Sheikh Saeed al Masri" as an "Egyptian; head of al Qaeda finance committee." Instead, following a previous reversal in the U.S. media, the financial role attributed earlier to Sheikh Saeed is now given to "Mustafa al Hawsawi," the name (or pseudonym) used for the financial transactions (*9/11 Commission Report*, 436). The only reference to any Sheikh Saeed in the text says that the Egyptian (or Kenyan) Sheikh Saeed "argued that al Qaeda should defer to the Taliban's wishes" and *not* attack the United

States directly (*9/11 Commission Report,* 251). The report treats Sheikh Saeed and al-Hawsawi as two people, whereas earlier they had been identified in U.S. media reports as the same person.

110. *9/11 Commission Report,* 172.

111. "Pakistan Weekly Spills 9/11 Beans," *Telegraph* (Calcutta), March 13, 2006, http://www.telegraphindia.com/1060313/asp/nation/story_5962372.asp. The *Telegraph* story cited the *Friday Times,* a Pakistani weekly, which claimed the story was based on "disclosures made by foreign service officials to the Public Accounts Committee at a secret meeting in Islamabad."

112. Kamran Khan and Molly Moore, "Leader Purges Top Ranks of Military, Spy Services," *Washington Post,* October 8, 2001; Thompson, *Terror Timeline,* 260–61. It was widely reported that Mahmoud was let go for being too sympathetic to the Taliban (for example, Alan Sipress and Vernon Loeb, "CIA's Stealth War Centers on Eroding Taliban Loyalty and Aiding Opposition," *Washington Post,* October 10, 2001).

113. Newman, "Omissions and Errors in the Commission's Final Report."

114. For example, Ahmed, *War on Truth,* 137–46; Griffin, *9/11 Commission Report: Omissions and Distortions,* 103–9.

115. Crile, *Charlie Wilson's War,* 521. However, the United States did not attack Haqqani until after CIA had failed in a major attempt to persuade him to change sides (Syed Saleem Shahzad, "U.S. Explores Its Afghanistan Exit Options," *Asia Times Online,* October 15, 2003, http://www.atimes.com/atimes/Central_Asia/EJ15Ago1.html).

116. One who escaped was Tahir Yuldashev, the number two Islamic Movement of Uzbekistan (IMU) leader at this time, who is now said to lead a new and larger clandestine Islamic Movement of Turkestan (or Central Asia). According to the U.S. private research firm Stratfor, the movement is headquartered in Badakhshan, northeastern Afghanistan, close to the mountainous Pakistani border. The number one IMU leader, Namangani, was reportedly injured at Kunduz and is supposed by most to have died later at Mazar-i-Sharif.

117. Seymour M. Hersh, "The Getaway," *New Yorker,* January 21, 2002.

118. Arnaud de Borchgrave, "Pakistan Replaces Afghanistan as Al-Qaeda's Haven," *Washington Times,* June 18, 2002.

119. Bodansky, *Bin Laden,* 319; cf. 320–21.

120. Napoleoni, *Terror Incorporated,* 90–93.

121. John Ward Anderson and Peter Baker, "Killers Likely Never Intended to Free Pearl," *Washington Post,* February 23, 2002.

122. Sheikh Saeed, who assisted Pearl in setting up interviews in Pakistan, was later convicted of masterminding his kidnap (Steve LeVine, "Killing of Pearl Fit into Pakistani Web of Radical Islam," *Wall Street Journal,* January 23, 2003; Thompson, *Terror Timeline,* 264).

123. Robert Sam Anson, "The Journalist and the Terrorist," *Vanity Fair,* August 2002. Khawaja was eventually detained in connection with Pearl's murder.

124. "Pearl Tracked al Qaida," UPI, September 30, 2002. Baer's claim was

disputed by a spokesman for the *Wall Street Journal*, but CNN confirmed on January 31, 2003 that Pearl was hunting for an al Qaeda cell in Pakistan that included Reid and was headed by Khalid Shaikh Mohammed. Mohammed, whose role as a mastermind is not disputed, is apparently a Kuwaiti-born Pakistani (Richard Leiby, "Looking Back and Seeing the Future of Terror," *Washington Post*, September 10, 2003). In March 2007, "Khalid Sheikh Mohammed, the suspected planner of the Sept. 11 attacks, admitted during a military tribunal . . . that he personally killed *Wall Street Journal* reporter Daniel Pearl, according to a revised transcript of the hearing that confirmed long-held suspicions about his role in the slaying" (Peter Spiegel, "Al-Qaida Operative Says He Beheaded Pearl," *Baltimore Sun*, March 16, 2007).

125. "Pakistan Juggles with U.S. and al-Qaida" [leader], *Guardian*, October 8, 2002.

126. Arnaud de Borchgrave, "Pakistan Replaces Afghanistan as Al-Qaeda's Haven," *Washington Times*, June 17, 2002.

8. THE AL-KIFAH CENTER, AL QAEDA, AND THE U.S. GOVERNMENT, 1988–98

Epigraph: "The Road to Sept. 11," *Newsweek*, October 1, 2001.

1. Presidential Proclamation of March 21, 1983: "The resistance of the Afghan freedom fighters is an example to all the world of the invincibility of the ideals we in this country hold most dear, the ideals of freedom and independence." In addition to funding the "Arab Afghans" in Afghanistan, CIA after 1986 "funneled millions of dollars in money and equipment to anti-Kadafi rebels" in Libya (Ken Silverstein, "How Kadafi Went from Foe to Ally," *Los Angeles Times*, September 4, 2005).

2. Crile, *Charlie Wilson's War*, 521. By 2006, Haqqani was known as "deputy chief of the Taliban movement" (Syed Saleem Shahzad, "Taliban Lay Plans for Islamic Intifada," *Asia Times*, October 6, 2006).

3. Coll, *Ghost Wars*, 225.

4. Berger, *Ali Mohamed*, 6, 205.

5. Marshall, "Terror 'Blowback' Burns CIA."

6. Berger, *Ali Mohamed*, 3.

7. Emerson, *American Jihad*, 130, 131. Azzam traveled in America without difficulty, even though, according to *Jane's Intelligence Review*, he was an "influential figure in the Muslim Brotherhood [and] regarded as the historical leader of Hamas" (Phil Hirschkorn, Rohan Gunaratna, Ed Blanche, and Stefan Leader, "Osama Bin Laden and the Al Qaeda Group," *Jane's Intelligence Review*, August 1, 2001, http://www.webspawner.com/users/islamicjihad15/).

8. Lance, *1000 Years for Revenge*, 40. Cf. Emerson, *American Jihad*, 128–30. Also recruiting for the Afghan jihad was an international organization headquartered in Pakistan, the Tablighi Jamaat. The 1988 Tablighi Jamaat convention in Chicago "managed to attract over 6,000 Muslims from around the world" (Cooley, *Unholy Wars*, 83).

9. There is disagreement as to when both the MAK and its branch in Brooklyn were founded. Some argue that Azzam established the MAK in Peshawar as early as 1979 (Williams, *Al Qaeda*, 76). *Jane's* suggests 1982–1984 (Hirschkorn et al., "Osama Bin Laden and the Al Qaeda Group"). The usual suggested date is 1984 (Burke, *Al-Qaeda*, 73; Bergen, *Holy War, Inc.*, 51).

10. "The CIA, concerned about the factionalism of Afghanistan made famous by Rudyard Kipling, found that Arab zealots who flocked to aid the Afghans were easier to 'read' than the rivalry-ridden natives. While the Arab volunteers might well prove troublesome later, the agency reasoned, they at least were one-dimensionally anti-Soviet for now. So bin Laden, along with a small group of Islamic militants from Egypt, Pakistan, Lebanon, Syria and Palestinian refugee camps all over the Middle East, became the 'reliable' partners of the CIA in its war against Moscow" (Michael Moran, "Bin Laden Comes Home to Roost," MSNBC, August 24, 1998, http://www.msnbc.msn.com/id/3340101/). Cf. Barnett Rubin, "Sheikh Azzam Was 'Enlisted' by the CIA to Unite Fractious Rebel Groups Operating in Peshawar" (quoted in Robert Friedman, "The CIA's Jihad," *New Yorker*, March 17, 1995).

11. Hirschkorn et al., "Osama Bin Laden and the Al Qaeda Group," *Jane's Intelligence Review*, August 1, 2001. One way Egypt cooperated was by releasing jailed terrorists and their backers to take part in the war. A key example was Dr. Ayman al-Zawahiri, bin Laden's future adviser and possibly mentor (Burke, *Al-Qaeda*, 153).

12. *9/11 Commission Report*, 56.

13. I accept the important founding date of 1988 for the al-Kifah Center in Brooklyn based on a story by Amanda Garrett about the interesting Muslim leader Fawaz Damra in the *Cleveland Plain-Dealer*, "Prelude to Terror: How Damra Misled FBI," September 16, 2004: "Damra's radical history dates to the Cold War, when the United States spent billions of dollars training and arming the Muslim mujahedin fighting the Soviets in Afghanistan. In 1988, when he was imam of Al Farooq mosque in Brooklyn, he wrote to the New York Commissioner of Deeds announcing plans for a humanitarian nonprofit organization called MAK that would help the Muslim fighters. It was later incorporated under the name Afghan Services Bureau and ultimately changed its name to Alkifah Refugee Center." Cf. the vague reference to the "mid-1980s" in the *9/11 Commission Report*, 58.

14. Rahman was issued two visas, one of them "by a CIA officer working undercover in the consular section of the American embassy in Sudan" (Bergen, *Holy War, Inc.*, 67; cf. 218 [Khalifa]). FBI consultant Paul Williams writes that Ali Mohamed "settled in America on a visa program controlled by the CIA" (Williams, *Al Qaeda*, 117). Others allegedly admitted to the country, despite being on the State Department "watch list," were Mohamed Atta and possibly Ayman al-Zawahiri (Ahmed, *War on Truth*, 205, 46).

15. Former State Department officer Michael Springmann, BBC 2, November 6, 2001; Ahmed, *War on Truth*, 10.

16. Cooley, *Unholy Wars*, 83, 195, 203–4. Cooley claims further (85) that "perhaps occasionally, if among the thousands of Algerians, Egyptians, Sudanese,

Saudis and others, an individual would stand out for his special skills, he would be singled out for attention by American or allied European visitors and travel to the West for special cadre training, though this was rare."

17. Lance, *Cover Up*, 25.

18. Lance, *1000 Years for Revenge*, 42. Cf. Bergen, *Holy War, Inc.*, 66–67. Cf. James C. McKinley Jr., "Islamic Leader on U.S. Terrorist List Is in Brooklyn," *New York Times*, December 16, 1990.

19. Robert I. Friedman, "The CIA and the Sheikh," *Village Voice*, March 30, 1993, http://www.textfiles.com/conspiracy/wtcbomb1.txt.

20. Wright, *Looming Tower*, 177.

21. Clarke, *Against All Enemies*, 52.

22. *New York Times*, June 6, 2002; cf. Lance, *1000 Years for Revenge*, 211.

23. South Asia Terrorism Portal (SATP), "Rabita Trust," http://www.satp .org/satporgtp/countries/pakistan/terroristoutfits/rabita_trust.htm. Jalaidan, who once was a student at the University of Arizona, left Tucson around 1986 (*Arizona Daily Star*, November 5, 2001) to fight the Russians. Evan Kohlmann has described Jalaidan as one of the first volunteers at Azzam's earlier training camp for Arab Afghans in 1985 (Kohlmann, *Al-Qaida's Jihad in Europe*, 7). Cf. Farah, *Blood from Stones*, 143: "Julaidan attended the 1988 meeting where al Qaeda was founded and was on al Qaeda's first finance committee."

24. *9/11 Commission Report*, 55–56. On September 6, 2002, Jalaidan's personal assets were finally frozen by the U.S. Treasury Department (Office of Public Affairs, United States Treasury Department, "Treasury Department Statement on the Designation of Wa'el Hamza Julidan," September 6, 2002. Document #PO-3397); Thompson, *Terror Timeline*, 297. The United States and Saudi Arabia jointly announced Jalaidan's designation as a terrorist, but "within twenty-four hours two senior Saudi officials publicly disowned the designation" (Farah, *Blood from Stones*, 143).

25. "Arabian Gulf Financial Sponsorship of Al-Qaida via U.S.-Based Banks, Corporations and Charities," testimony of Matthew Epstein with Evan Kohlmann before the House Committee on Financial Services Subcommittee on Oversight and Investigations, *Progress Since 9/11: The Effectiveness of U.S. Anti-Terrorist Financing Efforts*, March 11, 2003, http://financialservices.house.gov/ media/pdf/031103me.pdf. Cf. Kohlmann, *Al-Qaida's Jihad in Europe*, 7.

26. SATP, "Rabita Trust."

27. Coll, *Ghost Wars*, 203–4.

28. Hirschkorn et al., *Jane's Intelligence Review*, August 1, 2001. Author Lawrence Wright has since claimed that bin Laden remained personally close to Azzam, even after Azzam broke with Hekmatyar and endorsed Massoud. Instead of breaking with Azzam, though, bin Laden returned to Saudi Arabia to consult with Saudi intelligence about whether to back Massoud or Hekmatyar. "Price Turki's chief of staff, Ahmed Badeeb, told him, 'It's better to leave'" (Wright, *Looming Tower*, 142–43).

29. Griffin, *Reaping the Whirlwind*, 133.

30. "In October 2001, a U.S.-led NATO contingent, with the cooperation of local authorities, raided the Sarajevo office of the Saudi High Commissioner for

Aid to Bosnia, which had spent $600 million of the kingdom's money on Bosnia over the previous 10 years. . . . Domestic opposition to the policy shift diminished markedly when the NATO contingent discovered computer files containing marked photographs and maps of government buildings in Washington" (Damjan de Krnjevic-Miskovic, "Assessing Militant Islamist Threats in the Balkans," Woodrow Wilson International Center for Scholars, Southeast Europe Project, Commentaries, http://www.wilsoncenter.org/index.cfm?topic_id=109941&fuse action=topics.documents&doc_id=119921&group_id=115869). Cf. Kohlmann, *Al-Qaida's Jihad in Europe*, 43.

31. SATP, "Rabita Trust."

32. Mira L. Boland, "Sheikh Gilani's American Disciples," *Weekly Standard*, March 18, 2002.

33. Lance, *1000 Years for Revenge*, 211–12, 374–76. Wadih el-Hage administered the MAK center in Tucson before being dispatched in 1991 to help direct the Al-Kifah Center in Brooklyn (Oriana Zill, "A Portrait of Wadih el-Hage, Accused Terrorist," *Frontline*, http://www.pbs.org/wgbh/pages/frontline/shows/binladen/upclose/elhage.html).

34. Kohlmann, *Al-Qaida's Jihad in Europe*, 72–74. There is understandably little press interest in Jamaat-al-Fuqra compared with al Qaeda. But Mira L. Boland ("Sheikh Gilani's American Disciples," *Weekly Standard*, March 18, 2002) has written that "Fuqra members are suspects in at least 10 unsolved assassinations and 17 firebombings between 1979 and 1990. Nor is Fuqra's criminal activity all in the past. In the last year [2001] alone, a resident of the California compound was charged with first degree murder in the shooting of a sheriff's deputy; another was charged with gun smuggling; the state of California launched an investigation into the fate of more than a million dollars in public funds given to a charter school run by Fuqra leaders; and two residents of the Red House community were convicted of firearms violations, while a third awaits trial." See also Jessica Stern, "The Protean Enemy," *Foreign Affairs* (July–August 2003): "Another organization now active in U.S. prisons is Jamaat ul-Fuqra, a terrorist group committed to purifying Islam through violence. (Daniel Pearl was abducted and murdered in Pakistan while attempting to interview the group's leader, Sheikh Gilani, to investigate the claim that Richard Reid—who attempted to blow up an international flight with explosives hidden in his shoes—was acting under Gilani's orders.)"

35. B. Raman, "Dagestan: Focus on Pakistan's Tablighi Jamaat," South Asia Analysis Group (SAAG), Paper No. 80, http://www.saag.org/papers/paper80.html; cf. Dreyfuss, *Devil's Game*, 277 (jihadi recruiting campaign). For the historical origins of Tablighi Jamaat in India, see Mumtaz Ahmad, "Islamic Fundamentalism in South Asia: The Jamaat-i-Islami and the Tablighi Jamaat of South Asia," in *Fundamentalisms Observed*, edited by Martin E. Marty and R. Scott Appleby (Chicago: University of Chicago Press, 1991), 529ff.

36. The multigovernmental involvement to some extent explains and perhaps even extenuates the current cover-up concerning 9/11. In the wake of 9/11 it was urgent for the United States to secure the cooperation of the Saudi and Pakistani governments. It is thus not surprising that the names of Jalaidan and

Gilani are not found in mainstream U.S. analyses of what happened that day. This illustrates the easy way in which secrecy leads to collusion, and eventually dishonesty.

37. Ahmad, "Islamic Fundamentalism in South Asia," 518. According to former CIA official Graham Fuller, Tablighi Jamaat is a "peaceful and apolitical preaching-to-the-people movement" ("The Future of Political Islam," *Foreign Affairs* [March–April 2002]: 49). For historian Barbara Metcalf, Tablighi Jamaat is "an apolitical, quietist movement of internal grassroots missionary renewal" (Metcalf, "Traditionalist Islamic Activism: Deoband, Tablighis, and Talibs," *Social Service Research Council*, January 1, 2004, http://www.ssrc.org/sept11/essays/metcalf.htm). Political consultant Olivier Roy has described Tablighi Jamaat as "completely apolitical and law abiding" (*Le Monde Diplomatique*, May 15, 2002). Discussion by Alex Alexiev, "Tablighi Jamaat: Jihad's Stealthy Legions," *Middle East Quarterly* (January 2005), http://www.meforum.org/article/686.

38. *Le Monde*, January 25, 2002.

39. Susan Sachs, "A Muslim Missionary Group Draws New Scrutiny in U.S.," *New York Times*, July 14, 2003. The FBI mentioned Tablighi Jamaat in the 2002 indictment of Mukhtar al-Bakri and five other Tablighi Jamaat Yemeni members from Lackawanna, New York, alleged to have used the group as a pretext for a voyage to Peshawar to join al Qaeda.

40. Burke, *Al-Qaeda*, 155.

41. Cooley, *Unholy Wars*, 83; cf. 6, 84–85. The 1988 Tablighi Jamaat convention in Chicago "managed to attract over 6,000 Muslims from around the world" (Cooley, *Unholy Wars*, 83).

42. Raman, "Dagestan."

43. *Washington Post*, October 16, 1995; Alexiev, "Tablighi Jamaat."

44. Alexiev, "Tablighi Jamaat." Alexiev is a member of PNAC neocon Frank Gaffney's hawkish Center for Security Policy.

45. Coll writes of Arab Afghan terrorist "Muslim Brotherhood–inspired networks" (Coll, *Ghost Wars*, 145). Cf. Baer, *Sleeping with the Devil*, 98–100, 180, and passim (Muslim Brotherhood). An Arab source, however, writes of Ayman al-Zawahiri's criticism of the Muslim Brotherhood in his book *The Bitter Harvest* (al-Zayyat, *Road to Al-Qaeda*, 100). On August 5, 2005, U.K. prime minister Tony Blair "said Britain would ban two radical groups from operating in the country. One of them was the British branch of Hizb ut-Tahrir" (Reuters, August 9, 2005).

46. There are authorities who agree that imprisoned African-American males commonly convert to Islam and that this creates a pool for recruitment by extremist Islamist groups: "Jamaat al-Fuqra is an extremist Islamic organization largely composed of African-Americans recruited from United States prisons" (Zachary Crowley, "Jamaat al-Fuqra Dossier," Center for Policing Terrorism, March 16, 2005, http://www.cpt-mi.org/pdf_secure.php?pdffilename=JAMAAT AL-FUQRA2); "The tendency to convert to Islam is common among African American male [prison] inmates" (Felecia Dix-Richardson, "Resistance to Conversion to Islam among African American Women Inmates [Abstract]," *Journal of Offender Rehabilitation* 35, no. 4 [December 4, 2002], 109).

47. Salem "had ties to Egyptian intelligence" (Laurie Mylroie, "Iraqi Complicity in the World Trade Center Bombing and Beyond," *Middle East Intelligence Bulletin* [June 2001], http://www.meib.org/articles/0106_ir1.htm); cf. Lance, *1000 Years for Revenge*, 51–59; Lance, *Triple Cross*, 79; and Russ Baker, "The Past as Prologue," *Salon*, October 29, 2001, http://www.russbaker.com/Salon%20-%20The%20Past%20As%20Prologue.htm. In April 1993 Egyptian president Hosni Mubarak told reporters in Washington his intelligence services had tipped off the United States that the World Trade Center attack was coming. "It could have been prevented if you listened to our advice," he said. Asked if he had specific information about individuals involved, he responded: "That's right. And this information has been exchanged with American intelligence" (Elaine Sciolino, "Egypt Warned U.S. of Terror, Mubarak Says," *New York Times*, April 5, 1993).

48. *United States of America v. Usama Osama bin Laden et al., Defendants*, Transcript, February 6, 2001, 165–70, 234–38, http://cns.miis.edu/pubs/reports/pdfs/binladen/060201.pdf.

49. Lance, *1000 Years for Revenge*, 51–59 (Salem), cf. 374 (Mohamed). Lance has argued strenuously that "rumors that Salem was an Egyptian intelligence agent" were "a fabrication that Salem himself spun" (54). But he concedes that Salem had "a few acquaintances in Egyptian intelligence" and apparently does not dispute that Salem was as he claimed a member of the elite corps of bodyguards defending Anwar Sadat (some of whom also killed him). As I explore further, CIA had trained Sadat's bodyguards (Woodward, *Veil*, 169).

50. Lance, *1000 Years for Revenge*, 207. In a wiretapped conversation between al-Kifah militant Siddiq Ali and FBI informant Emil Salem, Siddiq said, "Our goal is that these people get extensive and very, very, very good training, so that we can get started at any place where Jihad is needed" (Kohlmann, *Al-Qaida's Jihad in Europe*, 73).

51. Journalist Jason Burke has written that after 1989 the United States was "uninterested" in Afghanistan, adding that "the State Department . . . was simply not that concerned by events in Afghanistan" (Burke, *Al-Qaeda*, 128–29). But Steve Coll gives details of the CIA's efforts in the winter of 1990 "to coordinate broad attacks against Afghanistan's major cities and roads" (Coll, *Ghost Wars*, 210–11, cf. 225).

52. Coll, *Ghost Wars*, 232.

53. Coll, *Ghost Wars*, 233. A comparison can be made with the year 1971, when Nixon and the U.S. government, struggling to disengage from the U.S. drug proxies in Laos and Vietnam, belatedly publicized the heroin problems there and declared war on the heroin traffic. See McCoy, *Politics of Heroin*, 380–81. (I do not agree with McCoy's claim there, however, of U.S. "ignorance about the logistics of the Laotian heroin trade.")

54. Edward A. Gargan, "The New Struggle for Afghanistan," *New York Times*, May 10, 1992.

55. Coll, *Ghost Wars*, 235–36; cf. Burke, *Al-Qaeda*, 142. The *9/11 Commission Report*, following Peter Bergen (*Holy War, Inc.*), writes (57): "With help from a dissident member of the royal family, [bin Laden] managed to get out of the country [Saudi Arabia] under the pretext of attending an Islamic gathering in

Pakistan in April 1991. . . . Bin Laden moved to Sudan in 1991." But bin Laden's presence in Peshawar was no pretext and was consonant with mainstream Saudi policy objectives at the time. The Saudi-Pakistani mediation took place in April and/or May 1992, not 1991 (Andrew Roche, "Kabul Guerrillas Agree Peace Deal," *Independent*, May 26, 1992; "Afghan Rebels Announce Peace Accord," *Houston Chronicle*, May 26, 1992). Thus I agree with Burke (*Al-Qaeda*, 142) that bin Laden "after around three months in Peshawar" arrived in Sudan in 1992, not 1991. If so, the widespread claim that bin Laden "went rogue" in 1990 (Griffin, *Reaping the Whirlwind*, 133) must be revised.

56. Kathy Evans, "Pakistan Clamps Down on Afghan Mojahedin," *Guardian*, January 7, 1993; Kohlmann, *Al-Qaida's Jihad in Europe*, 16.

57. Evans, "Pakistan Clamps Down," *Guardian*, January 7, 1993; cf. Kohlmann, *Al-Qaida's Jihad in Europe*, 16.

58. Kohlmann, *Al-Qaida's Jihad in Europe*, 16. The FBI was secretly recording "a senior Egyptian *jihad* leader" (possibly Ali Mohamed).

59. Bodansky, *Bin Laden*, 333, 385; cf. 22–23 (Pakistan-Iran-Hekmatyar). The statement is particularly absurd with respect to the Taliban, a nationalist force bitterly opposed to Iran.

60. Coll, *Ghost Wars*, 252; cf. Kohlmann, *Al-Qaida's Jihad in Europe*, 161, 199. I agree on this question with Michael Griffin: "The literature dealing with state-sponsored terrorism at an international level, or *Hizballah* International as it is known, is as suspect as it is sensational, being based on information leaked by one or another intelligence service in the countries most affected by Islamist subversion. It needs to be treated with extreme caution, rather like CIA estimates of the Soviet military capability in the 1980s, particularly at a time when Tehran had largely replaced Moscow as Washington's foremost cause of insecurity" (Griffin, *Reaping the Whirlwind*, 129–30). The example Griffin then cites is by Yossef Bodansky. The intelligence service usually given as a source for Bodansky is Israel's Mossad.

61. Kenneth R. Timmerman, "Iran Cosponsors Al-Qaeda Terrorism," *Insight*, November 9, 2001, http://www.kentimmerman.com/news/insight_iran-obl_011112.htm. A competing right-wing view, long argued by Laurie Mylroie, with support from her friend Mrs. [Clare] Paul Wolfowitz, was that the cosponsoring state is not Iran but Iraq. See Mylroie, *War Against America*. In the book, published by the American Enterprise Institute, Mylroie acknowledges the help of both Clare and Paul Wolfowitz.

62. *9/11 Commission Report*, 241.

63. Wright, *Looming Tower*, 262.

64. Kux, *United States and Pakistan*, 322.

65. Napoleoni, *Terror Incorporated*, 89. Napoleoni charged also that the ISI and bin Laden jointly backed the insurgency in Chechnya (*Terror Incorporated*, 94–95).

66. Kohlmann, *Al-Qaida's Jihad in Europe*, 16.

67. Kohlmann, *Al-Qaida's Jihad in Europe*, 45.

68. Martin S. Indyk, "Back to the Bazaar," *Foreign Affairs* (January–February 2002), quoted in Ahmed, *War on Truth*, 128.

69. Kohlmann, *Al-Qaida's Jihad in Europe*, 18–19.

70. Marshall, "Terror 'Blowback' Burns CIA," *Independent*, November 1, 1998. In September 2001, when President Bush finally denounced the MAK as a terrorist group, it was reported that the MAK in America generally, and Boston specifically, had raised money for Muslims in Bosnia (Michael Kranish and Stephen Kurkjian, "Charity Tied to Bin Laden," *Boston Globe*, September 26, 2001).

71. Kohlmann, *Al-Qaida's Jihad in Europe*, 41, citing Steve Coll and Steve LeVine, "Global Network Provides Money, Haven," *Washington Post*, August 3, 1993. After the 1993 World Trade Center bombing, several documents from Zagreb were found in the New York al-Kifah office, and Ramzi Yousef, the lead bomber, was determined to have placed many calls to Yugoslavia.

72. Kohlmann, *Al-Qaida's Jihad in Europe*, 39, 40.

73. *United States v. Omar Ahmad Ali Abdel Rahman et al.*, Federal Court, SDNY, 15629-30, 15634-35, 15654, 15667-68, 15671, 15673; Kohlmann, *Al-Qaida's Jihad in Europe*, 72–74; and J. M. Berger, "Al Qaeda Recruited U.S. Servicemen: Testimony Links Plot to Saudi Gov't," *Intelwire.com*, http://intelwire.egoplex.com/hamptonel010604.html.

74. Clement Rodney Hampton-El, testimony, *United States v. Omar Ahmad Ali Abdel Rahman et al.*, Federal Court, SDNY, August 3, 1995. Fort Belvoir was the site of the army's Land Information Warfare Activity (LIWA), whose Information Dominance Center was "full of army intelligence 'geeks'" targeting Islamic jihadists (Lance, *Triple Cross*, 331).

75. "The Islam Scholar Who Defies Iranian Clerics," *South China Morning Post*, August 12, 1994; Harvey Shepherd, "Muslim Scholar Calls for Unity," (Montreal) *Gazette*, January 17, 1998. Bilal Philips has also rejected allegations during the Day of Terror trial that he recruited U.S. soldiers as mujahideen, claiming that "the talk that I was the one who persuaded them to do that . . . is not true" ("Tablighi Jamaat Convert and Saudi Agent of Influence Claims to Have Converted Thousands of U.S. Troops," Global News Wire, August 3, 2003). Testifying to Congress about the recruitment of U.S. military personnel into foreign terrorist networks, J. Michael Waller testified that Philips himself had been "recruited in the U.S. by Tablighi Jamaat." But his supporting appendix made it clear that, in his own words, Philips (an alleged "Saudi agent of influence") "did not benefit much" from his three months with Tablighi Jamaat; he preferred to study with the more shari'a-oriented schools of Saudi Arabia. See Statement of J. Michael Waller, *Terrorist Recruitment and Infiltration in the United States: Prisons and Military as an Operational Base*, testimony before the Subcommittee on Terrorism, Technology, and Homeland Security, Senate Committee on the Judiciary, October 14, 2003, http://www.globalsecurity.org/security/library/congress/2003_h/031014-waller.htm.

76. J. M. Berger, "Al Qaeda Recruited U.S. Servicemen": "In May 1993, Bilal Philips sent for Hampton-El, who was flown first to Saudi Arabia for a week, then to the Philippines for a week. In Manila, Hampton-El testified, he met with Philips at an Islamic conference that Hampton-El said was sponsored by wealthy Saudis and the Islamic Da'wah Council of the Philippines. The Da'wah Council was one of Khalifa's charities, according to an intelligence report compiled on Khalifa by the Philippines government."

77. Kohlmann, *Al-Qaida's Jihad in Europe*, 30.
78. Clarke, *Against All Enemies*, 88.

9. THE PRE-9/11 COVER-UP
OF ALI MOHAMED AND AL QAEDA

Epigraphs: Both are from *United States v. Omar Ahmad Ali Abdel Rahman et al.*, S5 93 Cr. 181 (MBM), Exhibit Nosair JJJ-1, videotape of Ali Mohamed.

1. Terrorism researcher J. M. Berger lists sixteen variant names and aliases for Ali Abdelsaoud Mohamed (Berger, *Ali Mohamed*, 35). His list does not include Ali Abu-al-Saud Mustafa (Bodansky, *Bin Laden*, 105) or Ali Abdel Suud Mohammed Mustafa (Sageman, *Understanding Terror Networks*, 35).

2. The report describes Ali Mohamed as "a former Egyptian army officer who had moved to the United States in the mid-1980s, enlisted in the U.S. Army, and become an instructor at Fort Bragg" (*9/11 Commission Report*, 68; cf. 62, al-Fadl).

3. Lance writes that "Ali Mohamed was regular army, not a member of the Special Forces" (Lance, *Triple Cross*, 34). Yet on the same page he quotes Mohamed's commanding officer as saying that Mohamed was "assigned to a Special Forces unit at Fort Bragg." There he trained officers destined for the Middle East in Islamic studies.

4. Berger, *Ali Mohamed*, 1, 205; Lance, *Triple Cross*, 47–49; and Marshall, "Terror 'Blowback' Burns CIA," *Independent*, November 1, 1998; cf. Bergen, *Holy War, Inc.*, 127–36.

5. Cf. Johnson, *Sorrows of Empire*, 124.

6. Berger, *Mohamed Ali*, 14; cf. Wright, *Looming Tower*, 181.

7. *San Francisco Chronicle*, September 21, 2001; *Toronto Globe and Mail*, November 22, 2001.

8. Lance, *Triple Cross*, 11–12 (allegiance); Wright, "Man behind Bin Laden"; Lance Williams and Erin McCormick, "Bin Laden's Man in Silicon Valley," *San Francisco Chronicle*, September 21, 2001 (money). Ali Mohamed was also known to his al-Kifah trainees as "Abu Omar" (Lance, *Triple Cross*, xxvii, 48). This, along with his admitted connection to al-Zawahiri, has led some to identify Mohamed (Abu Mohamed al-Amriki) with the Abu-Umar al-Amriki alleged by Yossef Bodansky to have acted as go-between between al-Zawahiri and CIA: "In the first half of November 1997 Ayman al-Zawahiri met a man called Abu-Umar al-Amriki (*al-Amriki* means 'the American') at a camp near Peshawar, on the Pakistan-Afghanistan border. High-level Islamist leaders insist that in this meeting Abu-Umar al-Amriki made al-Zawahiri an offer: The United States would not interfere with or intervene to prevent the Islamists' rise to power in Egypt if the Islamist mujahideen currently in Bosnia-Herzegovina would refrain from attacking the U.S. forces there. Moreover, Abu-Umar al-Amriki promised a donation of $50 million (from unidentified sources) to Islamist charities in Egypt and elsewhere. This was not the first meeting between Abu-Umar al-Amriki and Zawahiri. Back in the 1980s Abu-Umar al-Amriki openly acted as an emissary for the CIA with various Arab Islamist militant and terrorist movements . . . then operating under the wings of the Afghan jihad. . . . In the late 1980s, in one of his

meetings with Zawahiri, Abu-Umar al-Amriki suggested that Zawahiri would need '$50 million to rule Egypt.' At the time, Zawahiri interpreted this assertion as a hint that Washington would tolerate his rise to power if he could raise this money. The mention of the magic figure, $50 million, by Abu-Umar al-Amriki in the November 1997 meeting was interpreted by Zawahiri and the entire Islamist leadership, including Osama bin Laden, as a reaffirmation of the discussions with the CIA in the late 1980s about Washington's willingness to tolerate an Islamic Egypt. In 1997 the Islamist leaders were convinced that Abu-Umar al-Amriki was speaking for the CIA—that is, the uppermost echelons of the Clinton administration" (Bodansky, *Bin Laden*, 212–13).

9. *9/11 Commission Report*, 68.

10. Patrick Fitzgerald, testimony before the 9/11 Commission, *Twelfth Public Hearing of the National Commission on Terrorist Attacks upon the United States*, June 16, 2004, http://www.9-11commission.gov/hearings/hearing12.htm, emphasis added. Actually Mohamed was in Santa Clara, California, by 1993 (Lawrence Wright, "The Man behind Bin Laden," *New Yorker*, September 16, 2002). Fitzgerald was flagrantly dissembling. Even the mainstream account by writers Daniel Benjamin and Steven Simon (*The Age of Sacred Terror* [New York: Random House, 2002], 236) records that "when Mohamed was summoned back from Africa in 1993 [*sic*, Mohamed in his confession says 1994] to be interviewed by the FBI in connection with the case against Sheikh Rahman and his coconspirators, he convinced the agents that he could be useful to them as an informant."

11. Lance, *Triple Cross*, 95. Cf. Wright, *Looming Tower*, 181–82; Benjamin and Simon, *Age of Sacred Terror*, 236; Lawrence Wright, "The Man Behind Bin Laden," *New Yorker*, September 16, 2002: "In 1989 . . . Mohamed talked to an F.B.I. agent in California and provided American intelligence with its first inside look at Al Qaeda."

12. Joseph Neff and John Sullivan, "Al-Qaeda Terrorist Duped FBI, Army," *Raleigh News & Observer*, October 24, 2001, http://www.knoxstudio.com/shns/story.cfm?pk=ALIMOHAMED-10-24-01&cat=AN.

13. Johnson quoted in Williams and McCormick, *San Francisco Chronicle*, November 4, 2001: "Al Qaeda Terrorist Worked with FBI." What is clear to Johnson cannot be clear to the American public, however. We have no way of knowing whether or not Mohamed forewarned his American handlers about the embassy bombings, or even (since his current whereabouts are a mystery) about 9/11.

14. "Ali Mohammed . . . went to work as a CIA 'contract' agent, before being dismissed because of his ties to the radical terrorist group Hizbollah" (Lance, *1000 Years for Revenge*, 30); Mohamed "worked briefly as a CIA informant in the early 1980s" (Bergen, *Holy War, Inc.*, 67).

15. Lance, *1000 Years for Revenge*, 30 (watch list); Williams, *Al Qaeda*, 117; Paul Quinn-Judge and Charles M. Sennot, "Figure Cited in Terrorism Case Said to Enter U.S. with CIA Help," *Boston Globe*, February 3, 1995 (visa program); and Bergen, *Holy War, Inc.*, 128 (security officer). James Risen in the *New York Times* ("C.I.A. Said to Reject Bomb Suspect's Bid to Be a Spy," October 31,

1998) wrote that there was no evidence that CIA arranged for Mohamed's visa: "Officials could not, however, rule out the possibility that some other Federal agency helped Mr. Mohamed."

16. From 1987 to 1989, Mohamed "walked the halls of the U.S. military's top warfare planning center at Fort Bragg for more than two years as an Army sergeant" (John Sullivan and Joseph Neff, "An al Qaeda Operative at Fort Bragg," *Raleigh News & Observer*, November 13, 2001, http://www.s-t.com/daily/11-01/11-14-01/a01wn017.htm). "He was assigned to the U.S. Special Operations Command in Fort Bragg, the home of the Green Berets and the Delta Force, the elite counterterrorism squad" (John Sullivan and Joseph Neff, "Al Qaeda Terrorist Duped FBI, Army," *Raleigh News & Observer*, October 21, 2001).

17. Richard H. Shultz Jr. and Ruth Margolies Beitler, "Tactical Deception and Strategic Surprise in al-Qai'da's Operations," *Middle East Review of International Affairs* (June 2004), http://meria.idc.ac.il/journal/2004/issue2/jv8n2a6.html; cf. Lance, *Triple Cross*, 43.

18. A notorious example is the Marine Gerry Patrick Hemming, who served with Fidel Castro. Hemming is often accused of having worked with or for CIA. See, for example, http://www.spartacus.schoolnet.co.uk/JFKhemming.htm.

19. Wright, *Looming Tower*, 181.

20. Estanislao Oziewicz and Tu Thanh Ha, "Canada Freed Top al-Qaeda Operative," *Toronto Globe and Mail*, November 22, 2001, http://www.mail-archive.com/hydro@topica.com/msg00224.html; Lance, *Triple Cross*, 123–25; Peter Dale Scott, "How to Fight Terrorism," *California Monthly* (September 2004), http://www.alumni.berkeley.edu/Alumni/Cal_Monthly/September_2004/How_to_fight_terrorism.asp. Mohamed's companion, Essam Marzouk, is now serving fifteen years of hard labor in Egypt, after having been arrested in Azerbaijan. Mohamed's detention and release was months after the first World Trade Center bombing in February 1993, and after the FBI had already rounded up two of the plotters whom they knew had been trained by Ali Mohamed.

21. Judy Aita, "Ali Mohamed: The Defendant Who Did Not Go to Trial," U.S. State Department, International Information Programs, May 15, 2001, http://usinfo.state.gov/is/Archive_Index/Ali_Mohamed.html. In his confession Mohamed also testified that he arranged security for a meeting in Sudan between Hezbollah's security chief, Imad Mughniyeh, and bin Laden (*U.S. v. Ali Mohamed*, United States District Court S[7], 98 Cr. 1023 LBS, October 20, 2000; in J. M. Berger, *Ali Mohamed*, 305).

22. National Geographic Presents *Triple-Cross: Bin Laden's Spy in America*, National Geographic Society, 2006, http://channel.nationalgeographic.com/channel/triplecross/.

23. Dave Shiflett, "How Bin Laden's Spy Suckered the CIA, FBI, and Army: TV Review," Bloomberg News, August 28, 2006, http://www.bloomberg.com/apps/news?pid=20601088&sid=aNWwkZYujCIs&refer=home.

24. Glenn Garvin, "Author: Terror Spy Show a TV Whitewash," *Miami Herald*, http://www.miami.com/mld/miamiherald/entertainment/columnists/glenn_garvin/15310462.htm.

25. Wright, *Looming Tower*, 181. The *9/11 Commission Report* (56) claims

that "Bin Ladin and his comrades had their own sources of support and training, and they received little or no assistance from the United States."

26. J. M. Berger, "Unlocking 9/11: Paving the Road to 9/11," *Intelwire.com*, http://intelwire.egoplex.com/unlocking911-1-ali-mohamed-911.html; Berger, *Ali Mohamed*, 14. Cf. Lance, *Triple Cross*, 382.

27. Aita, "Ali Mohamed."

28. Lance, *Triple Cross*, 23. According to publicity for the National Geographic special *Triple-Cross: Bin Laden's Spy in America*, Mohamed is "currently in U.S. custody," but "his whereabouts and legal status are closely guarded secrets" (*Rocky Mountain News*, August 28, 2006, 2D). Lance wrote that Mohamed was put into the witness protection program. "David Runke [Ruhnke], a defense attorney in the African embassies bombing case, says, 'I think the most likely thing that will happen is he'll be released, he'll be given a new name and a new identity, and he will pick up a life someplace.'" (Shiflett, "How Bin Laden's Spy Suckered the CIA, FBI, and Army").

29. "Ali Mohamed had stayed in [El-Hage's] Kenyan home in the mid 90's as they plotted the bombings. Another agent in Fitzie's squad, Dan Coleman, had searched El-Hage's home a year before the bombings and found direct links to Ali Mohamed and yet Fitzgerald failed to connect the dots" (Lance, "Triple Cross," *Huffington Post*, August 29, 2006). Cf. Lance, *Triple Cross*, 274–79, 298–301, 355, and passim.

30. Lance, *1000 Years for Revenge*, 29–37.

31. Dreyfuss, *Devil's Game*, 278; Cooley, *Unholy Wars*, 87–88; Lance, *1000 Years for Revenge*, 29–31; and Marshall, "Terror 'Blowback' Burns CIA."

32. Rahman was issued two visas, one of them "by a CIA officer working undercover in the consular section of the American embassy in Sudan" (Bergen, *Holy War, Inc.*, 67). FBI consultant Paul Williams has written that Ali Mohamed "settled in America on a visa program controlled by the CIA" (Williams, *Al Qaeda*, 117). Others allegedly admitted in the country, despite being on the State Department watch list, were Osama bin Laden's brother-in-law Mohamed Jamal Khalifa, Mohamed Atta, and possibly Ayman al-Zawahiri (Ahmed, *War on Truth*, 205, 46).

33. Wright, *Looming Tower*, 177.

34. Lance, *1000 Years for Revenge*, 34.

35. Lance, *1000 Years for Revenge*, 31; Lance, *Cover Up*, 25.

36. Karen Freifeld and David Kocieniewski, "The Fateful Hours," *Newsday*, November 8, 1990, quoted in Lance, *1000 Years for Revenge*, 35.

37. John Kifner, "Police Think Kahane Slaying Suspect Acted Alone," *New York Times*, November 8, 1990; Friedman, "The CIA and the Sheikh."

38. James C. McKinley Jr., "Islamic Leader on U.S. Terrorist List Is in Brooklyn," *New York Times*, December 16, 1990.

39. Joint Inquiry into Intelligence Community Activities before and after the Terrorist Attacks of September 11, 2001, Statement, October 8, 2002, 3; quoted in Lance, *Triple Cross*, 58.

40. Lance, *Triple Cross*, 59.

41. Lance, *Triple Cross*, 171.

42. *United States v. Omar Ahmad Ali Abdel Rahman et al.*, S5 93 Cr. 181 (MBM), 19122; in Berger, *Ali Mohamed*, 205.

43. *United States v. Omar Ahmad Ali Abdel Rahman et al.*, 19133; in Berger, *Ali Mohamed*, 217.

44. *United States v. Omar Ahmad Ali Abdel Rahman et al.*, 14128, 14282, 14291, and passim; in Berger, *Ali Mohamed*, 93, 138, 147, and passim.

45. Lance, *Triple Cross*, 177, cf. 174.

46. *United States v. Omar Ahmad Ali Abdel Rahman et al.*, Government Exhibit 153; in Berger, *Ali Mohamed*, 235–36.

47. Lance, *Triple Cross*, 177. Nosair's cousin and fellow accused, Ibrahim El-Gabrowny, later alleged that Mohamed told him precisely this (Lance, *Triple Cross*, 175–76).

48. Usually the CIA's interference is not even made public. One dramatic exception was the 1982 San Diego indictment for car theft of a top CIA asset in Mexico, Miguel Nazar Haro. After an associate U.S. attorney general (acting on instructions from CIA and the FBI) refused to permit the indictment, the U.S. attorney in San Diego publicly protested the CIA's role in obstructing justice. He was summarily fired. See Scott and Marshall, *Cocaine Politics*, 36. For the CIA's long-term arrangements not to report to the Justice Department on drug traffickers, see Scott, *Drugs, Contras, and the CIA*, 39–40.

49. Lance, *Triple Cross*, 301.

50. Lance, *Triple Cross*, 317–18.

51. Berger, "Unlocking 9/11: Paving the Road to 9/11." FBI Agent Cloonan said on the National Geographic special *Triple-Cross: Bin Laden's Spy in America*, that "if you look at the six- or seventeen sentences that are in there, from what I've seen, all that information came from Ali" (Berger, *Ali Mohamed*, 20). But Cloonan's statement exaggerates; one section of the presidential daily brief is clearly from Millennium plotter Ahmed Ressam.

52. *9/11 Commission Report*, 261–62.

53. Lance, *Triple Cross*, 374–75.

54. The company was Globe Aviation Services, a subsidiary of the Burns International Security Agency, where Mohamed started to work in 1995 and where he applied just one month after his mysterious interview with McCarthy and Bell. Globe provided security at both Logan (Boston) and Reagan (Washington, D.C.) airports. From Berger, *Ali Mohamed*, 18–20, 32: "Shortly after September 11, the FBI arrested a Burns employee from the Washington, D.C. area named Mohammed Abdi. . . . When the FBI found the car left behind [by] the five 9/11 hijackers who departed from Dulles airport near Washington, they discovered a map of the D.C. area with Abdi's name and phone number written with a yellow highlighter. . . . Investigators discovered Abdi had removed five Burns security jackets from his workplace before September 11. He attempted to give them to the Salvation Army three days after the attack. . . . [Yet] Abdi was never convicted of any crime related to terrorism."

55. J. M. Berger, "Paving the Road to 9/11," *IntelWire.com*, http://intelwire.egoplex.com/unlocking911-1-ali-mohamed-911.html.

56. *9/11 Commission Report*, 72. This praise for the superb prosecutorial

effort of Patrick Fitzgerald was presumably drafted by his former colleague Dietrich Snell.

57. Fitzgerald is of course the U.S. attorney who for years has been investigating the leak of the name of CIA covert operative Valerie Plame.

58. Kean and Hamilton, *Without Precedent*, 273 (chapters); Lance, *Cover Up*, 212–20 (reports). Snell was assisted by Douglas MacEachin, the former CIA deputy director for intelligence.

59. *9/11 Commission Report*, 72.

60. Lance, *1000 Years for Revenge*, 31–35.

10. AL QAEDA AND THE U.S. ESTABLISHMENT

Epigraph: *Iran-Contra Affair*, 20.

1. Western governments and media apply the term "al Qaeda" to the entire "network of co-opted groups" that have at some point accepted leadership, training, and financing from Osama bin Laden (Burke, *Al-Qaeda*, 7–8). From a Muslim perceptive the term "al Qaeda" is clumsy and has led to the targeting of a number of Islamist groups opposed to bin Laden's tactics. See al-Zayyat, *Road to Al-Qaeda*, 100 and passim. I am reminded of certain right-wing hypostatizations of the Vietnam antiwar "movement" in which I took part, which saw foreign-funded conspiracy where I could only see chaos. For this reason, where possible, I will try to use instead the clumsy but widely accepted term (and misnomer) "Arab Afghans."

2. Kathy Evans, "Pakistan Clamps Down on Afghan Mojahedin," *Guardian*, January 7, 1993; Kohlmann, *Al-Qaida's Jihad in Europe*, 16. Despite this public stance, ISI elements "privately" continued to support Arab Afghans who were willing to join Pakistan's new covert operations in Kashmir.

3. Al-Zayyat, *Road to Al-Qaeda*, 55.

4. Barnett Rubin, "Afghanistan, Armed and Abandoned, Could Be the Next Bosnia," *New York Times*, December 28, 1992.

5. Baer, *Sleeping with the Devil*, 143–44. Former CIA officer Robert Baer, who in 1993 was posted to Tajikistan, describes a raid at that time in which "a Tajik Islamic rebel group . . . from Afghanistan . . . managed to overrun a Russian border post and cut off all the guards' heads." According to Baer, the local Russian intelligence chief was convinced that "the rebels were under the command of Rasool Sayyaf's Ittehad-e-Islami, bin Laden's Afghani protector," who in turn was backed by Saudi Arabia and the IIRO. More commonly, it is claimed that Hekmatyar's terrorist drug network was supporting the Tajik resistance (Hugh Pope, "Russia Takes Sides in Tajikistan War," *Independent*, February 17, 1993). For Casey's encouragement of these ISI-backed raids in 1985, see Coll, *Ghost Wars*, 104.

6. Griffin, *Reaping the Whirlwind*, 150 (Tajik rebels); Coll, *Ghost Wars*, 225 (U.S. aid).

7. Rashid, *Jihad*, 140–44.

8. Griffin, *Reaping the Whirlwind*, 115. Exploration in the 1990s has considerably downgraded these estimates.

9. Rashid, *Taliban*, 145. In 1992, Chevron struck a deal to spend $10 billion over four decades in Kazakhstan (Steven Greenhouse, "Chevron to Spend $10 Billion to Seek Oil in Kazakhstan," *New York Times*, May 19, 1992).

10. Scott, *Drugs, Oil, and War*, 30–31.

11. Martha Brill Olcott, "The Caspian's False Promise," *Foreign Policy*, no. 111 (summer 1998): 96, quoted in Klare, *Blood and Oil*, 129. Cf. Scott, *Drugs, Oil, and War*, 8, 64–66.

12. Robert Burns, "Rumsfeld Assured U.S. Won't Lose Kyrgyz Base," Associated Press, April 14, 2005.

13. Martha Brill Olcott, "In Uzbekistan, the Revolution Won't Be Pretty," *Washington Post*, May 22, 2005. In July 2005, Uzbekistan, moving back into the Russian orbit, ordered U.S. troops to leave the country.

14. Goltz, *Azerbaijan Diary*, 272–75. Cf. Irkali, Kodrarian, and Ruchala, "God Save the Shah," *Sobaka*, May 22, 2003. A fourth operative in MEGA Oil, Gary Best, was also a veteran of North's Contra support effort. For more on General Secord's and Major Aderholt's role as part of Ted Shackley's team of offloaded CIA assets and capabilities, see Marshall, Scott, and Hunter, *Iran-Contra Connection*, 26–30, 36–42, 197–98.

15. It was also a time when Congress, under pressure from Armenian voters, had banned all military aid to Azerbaijan (under Section 907 of the Freedom Support Act). This ban, reminiscent of the congressional ban on aid to the Contras in the 1980s, ended after 9/11. "In the interest of national security, and to help in 'enhancing global energy security' during this War on Terror, Congress granted President Bush the right to waive Section 907 in the aftermath of September 11th. It was necessary, Secretary of State Colin Powell told Congress, to 'enable Azerbaijan to counter terrorist organizations'" (Irkali, Kodrarian, and Ruchala, "God Save the Shah").

16. Secord with Wurts, *Honored and Betrayed*, 53–57.

17. Secord with Wurts, *Honored and Betrayed*, 211–16.

18. Secord with Wurts, *Honored and Betrayed*, 233–35.

19. Goltz, *Azerbaijan Diary*, 272–75; Scott, *Drugs, Oil, and War*, 7. As part of the airline operation, Azeri pilots were trained in Texas. Dearborn had previously helped Secord advise and train the fledgling Contra air force (Marshall, Scott, and Hunter, *Iran-Contra Connection*, 197). These important developments were barely noticed in the U.S. press, but a *Washington Post* article did belatedly note that a group of American men who wore "big cowboy hats and big cowboy boots" had arrived in Azerbaijan as military trainers for its army, followed in 1993 by "more than 1,000 guerrilla fighters from Afghanistan's radical prime minister, Gulbuddin Hekmatyar" (Steve LeVine, "Azerbaijan Throws Raw Recruits into Battle," *Washington Post*, April 21, 1994). Richard Secord was allegedly attempting also to sell Israeli arms, with the assistance of Israeli agent David Kimche, another Iran-Contra associate of Oliver North. See Scott, *Drugs, Oil, and War*, 7, 8, 20. Whether or not the Americans were aware of it, the al Qaeda presence in Baku soon expanded to include assistance for moving jihadis onward into Dagestan and Chechnya.

20. Cooley, *Unholy Wars*, 180; Scott, *Drugs, Oil, and War*, 7.

21. Napoleoni, *Terror Incorporated*, 89–97; Griffin, *Reaping the Whirlwind*, 150; Cooley, *Unholy Wars*, 176.

22. As the *9/11 Commission Report* (58) notes, the bin Laden organization established an NGO in Baku, which became a base for terrorism elsewhere. It also became a transshipment point for Afghan heroin to the Chechen mafia, whose branches "extended not only to the London arms market, but also throughout continental Europe and North America" (Cooley, *Unholy Wars*, 176).

23. Irkali, Kodrarian, and Ruchala, "God Save the Shah." As we have just seen, they were not the first.

24. *9/11 Commission Report*, 58. Ibrahim Eidarous, later arrested in Europe by the FBI for his role in the 1998 embassy bombings, headed the Baku base of al Qaeda between 1995 and 1997 (United States Information Service, "U.S. Indicts Suspects in East Africa Embassy Bombings," May 9, 2000, http://www.fas.org/irp/news/2000/05/000509-terror-usia1.htm). An Islamist in Baku claimed that they did not attack the U.S. Embassy there so as "not to spoil their good relations in Azerbaijan" (*Bill of Indictment in U.S.A. vs. Bin Laden et. al.*, April 2001; Vernon Loeb, "U.S. Prosecutor Details Day of Bombings," *Washington Post* May 3, 2001).

25. Cooley, *Unholy Wars*, 176.

26. From Frank Viviano, "Drug Trade Feeds World's Rebellions," *San Francisco Chronicle*, December 18, 1992: "According to police sources in the Russian capital, 184 heroin processing labs were discovered in Moscow alone last year. 'Every one of them was run by Azeris, who use the proceeds to buy arms for Azerbaijan's war against Armenia in Nagorno-Karabakh,' [Russian economist Alexandre] Datskevitch said." The estimate of 184 labs has been dismissed as wildly exaggerated. But the DEA has acknowledged the recent involvement of Azeris in Russia's burgeoning heroin traffic (DEA, "Heroin Trafficking in Russia's Troubled East," Drug Intelligence Brief, October 2003, http://www.shaps.hawaii.edu/drugs/dea03053/dea03053.html).

27. *9/11 Commission Report*, 58.

28. Jamal Ahmed al-Fadl, transcript of testimony, "United States of America v. Usama bin Laden et al., Defendants" February 6, 2001, 300–303, http://cns.miis.edu/pubs/reports/pdfs/binladen/060201.pdf.

29. Levon Sevunts, "Who's Calling the Shots?" (Montreal) *Gazette*, October 26, 1999; cf. Michel Chossudovsky, "Who Is Osama bin Laden?" Centre for Research on Globalisation, September 12, 2001, http://www.globalresearch.ca/articles/CHO109C.html. Those trained by the ISI included the main rebel leaders Shamil Basayev and Emir al Khattab. Cf. Sharma, *Pak Proxy War*, 84, 86, 89, 91.

30. Griffin, *Reaping the Whirlwind*, 115, 149–51.

31. "BP Oiled Coup with Cash, Turks Claim" (London) *Sunday Times*, March 26, 2000. The U.S. private research firm Stratfor agrees that "Western energy companies splashed cash about in an attempt to squeeze the country for its oil and natural gas" (Stratfor, "Azerbaijan Elections: All in the Family," October 16, 2003, http://www.stratfor.com/products/premium/read_article.php?id=223646).

32. European sources have also alleged that CIA meetings with the Algerian fundamentalist leader Anwar Haddam in the period 1993–95 were responsible

for the surprising lack of Islamist attacks on U.S. oil and agribusiness installations in Algeria. See Labévière, *Dollars for Terror*, 182–89. For partial corroboration, cf. Cooley, *Unholy Wars*, 207.

33. From Dan Morgan and David B. Ottaway, "Fortune Hunters Lured U.S. into Volatile Region," *Washington Post*, October 4, 1998: "Before the meeting ended, Amoco—the largest U.S. investor in Azerbaijan's oil boom—had what it wanted: a promise from Clinton to invite the Azerbaijani president to Washington. Six months later the company, which traditionally donated heavily to the Republicans, contributed $50,000 to the Democratic Party. In August 1997, Clinton received President Heydar Aliyev with full honors, witnessed the signing of a new Amoco oil exploration deal and promised to lobby Congress to lift U.S. economic sanctions on Azerbaijan."

34. White House Press Statement, August 1, 1997, quoted in Klare, *Resource Wars*, 4; Scott, *Drugs, Oil, and War*, 30.

35. Johnson, *Sorrows of Empire*, 174; Mann, *Rise of the Vulcans*, 224–25 (Aliyev visit).

36. Olivier Roy, quoted in Labévière, *Dollars for Terror*, 280.

37. Senator Hank Brown was a supporter of the Unocal project and welcomed the fall of Kabul as a chance for stable government (Rashid, *Taliban*, 166).

38. Griffin, *Reaping the Whirlwind*, 124; cf. "Timeline of Competition between Unocal and Bridas for the Afghanistan Pipeline," http://www.worldpress .org/specials/pp/pipeline_timeline.htm.

39. Scott, *Deep Politics and the Death of JFK*, 203.

40. "Uzbekistan Has Difficulties Finding Venues for Its Gas," *Alexander's Gas & Oil Connections*, October 12, 1998, http://www.gasandoil.com/goc/news/ ntc85031.htm.

41. Enron's losses on its Dabhol project approached $900 million and were a major factor in Enron's bankruptcy. "Cheney, Secretary of State Colin Powell and a series of other top Bush administration officials and diplomats reportedly lobbied Indian leaders to save Dabhol. OPIC documents released in January 2002 revealed that the National Security Council had intervened on behalf of Enron on the Dabhol issue" (M. Asif Ismail, "A Most Favored Corporation," Center for Public Integrity, July 29, 2005, http://www.publici.org/report.aspx?aid=104 &sid=200). Earlier, according to Chalmers Johnson (*Sorrows of Empire*, 166), CIA, using its advanced signals intercept program, Echelon, had tracked British offers on the Dabhol contract in order to give a competitive advantage to Enron.

42. Brisard and Dasquié, *Forbidden Truth*, 41–44.

43. Johnson, *Sorrows of Empire*, 176.

44. Phillips, *American Theocracy*, 83. Cf. Pepe Escobar, "The War for Pipelineistan," *Asian Times*, January 26, 2002.

45. Scott, *Drugs, Oil, and War*, 55n.

46. According to *Nation* correspondent David Corn, George W. Bush "claimed he had not gotten to know disgraced Enron chief Ken Lay until after the 1994 Texas gubernatorial election. But Lay had been one of Bush's larger contributors during that election and had—according to Lay himself—been friends with Bush for years before it" (Corn, "The Other Lies of George Bush,"

Nation Online, September 25, 2003, http://www.thenation.com/doc/20031013/corn).

47. Judah, *Kosovo*, 120.

48. Michel Chossudovsky, "Macedonia: Washington's Military-Intelligence Ploy," Transnational Foundation for Peace and Future Research, http://www.transnational.org/SAJT/forum/meet/2001/Chossudov_WashingtPloy.html.

49. Kohlmann, *Al-Qaida's Jihad in Europe*, 79. Al-Qahtani, who was killed by U.S. ordinance in Afghanistan in 2001, had previously fought in Afghanistan, Bosnia, Chechnya, Israel, and Kosovo.

50. In 2001 the U.S. press paid brief attention to the case of David Hicks, an Australian al Qaeda fighter and convert to Islam. Captured when fighting with the Taliban, Hicks had previously been with Lashkar-e-Taiba, a Pakistan force targeting Kashmir. Before training at an al Qaeda camp, Hicks had joined the KLA in mid-1999. See Grant Holloway, "Australia Mulls Fate of al Qaeda Fighter," December 13, 2001, *CNN.com*, http://archives.cnn.com/2001/WORLD/asiapcf/auspac/12/12/ret.australia.capture.latest/.

51. Isabel Vincent, "U.S. Supported al-Qaeda Cells during Balkan Wars," *National Post*, March 15, 2002. Contrast, for example, Michael Ignatieff, *Virtual War: Kosovo and Beyond* (New York: Metropolitan/Henry Holt, 2000), 13: "the KLA, at first a small band of poorly trained and amateurish gunmen." For the al Qaeda background to the KLA and its involvement in heroin trafficking, see also Marcia Christoff Kurop, "Al Qaeda's Balkan Links," *Wall Street Journal Europe*, November 1, 2001; "The KLA and the Heroin Craze of the 90s," (Montreal) *Gazette*, December 15, 1999.

52. Steiner is quoted in Vincent, "U.S. Supported al-Qaeda Cells during Balkan Wars," *National Post*, March 15, 2002.

53. Scott, *Drugs, Oil, and War*, 29. "According to Michel Koutouzis, the DEA's Web site once contained a section detailing Kosovar trafficking, but a week before the U.S.-led bombings began, the section disappeared" (Peter Klebnikov, "Heroin Heroes," *Mother Jones* (January–February 2000), http://www.motherjones.com/news/feature/2000/01/heroin.html). Speaking in Kosovo in February 1998, Robert Gelbard, the U.S. special envoy to the region, said publicly that the KLA "is, without any questions, a terrorist group" (Judah, *Kosovo*, 138).

54. Jerry Seper, "KLA Finances War with Heroin Sales," *Washington Times*, May 3, 1999. Cf. Frank Viviano, "KLA Linked to Enormous Heroin Trade," *San Francisco Chronicle*, May 5, 1999: "Officers of the Kosovo Liberation Army and their backers, according to law enforcement authorities in Western Europe and the United States, are a major force in international organized crime, moving staggering amounts of narcotics through an underworld network that reaches into the heart of Europe."

55. From McCoy, *Politics of Heroin*, 517: "The most militant of these local commanders, Muhamed Xhemajli, had reportedly been a major drug trafficker in Switzerland before joining the KLA in 1998."

56. Wood, "U.S. 'Covered Up' for Kosovo Ally"; and Chossudovsky, "Macedonia."

57. "In a Place of Extremes, West Seeks Middle Ground Too Late," *Irish Times*, June 24, 1998.

58. George Monbiot, "A Discreet Deal in the Pipeline," *Guardian*, February 15, 2001.

59. BBC News, December 28, 2004. Those who charged that such a pipeline was projected were initially mocked but gradually vindicated (Monbiot, "Discreet Deal in the Pipeline"; Scott, *Drugs, Oil, and War*, 34). See also Marjorie Cohn, "NATO Bombing of Kosovo: Humanitarian Intervention or Crime against Humanity?" *International Journal for the Semiotics of Law* (March 2002): 79–106.

60. Phillips, *American Theocracy*, 82.

61. Colin Brown, "Attack on Afghanistan: Bin Laden Linked to Albanian Drug Gangs," *Independent*, October 21, 2001. Cf. Bodansky, *Bin Laden*, 298: "In late 1998, despite the growing pressure from U.S. intelligence and its local allies . . . a new network made up of bin Laden's supporters was being established in Albania under the cover of various Muslim charity organizations. . . . Bin Laden's Arab 'Afghans' also have assumed a dominant role in training the Kosovo Liberation Army." Bodansky adds that "in early April [1999] the UCK began actively cooperating with the NATO bombing—selecting and designating targets for NATO aircraft as well as escorting U.S. and British special forces detachments into Yugoslavia" (Bodansky, *Bin Laden*, 397–98). Cf. also Bill Wallace, "Opium Trade Keeps Taliban in Business, Experts Charge," *San Francisco Chronicle*, October 4, 2001.

62. Cliff Kincaid, "Remember Kosovo?" Media Monitor, *AccuracyinMedia.org*, December 28, 2004, http://www.aim.org/media_monitor/2393_0_2_0_C/.l. Bodansky, *Bin Laden*, 298.

63. Kurop, "Al Qaeda's Balkan Links," *Wall Street Journal Europe*, November 1, 2001.

64. Bodansky, *Bin Laden*, 397–98.

65. Wood, "U.S. 'Covered Up' for Kosovo Ally" ("asset"); Jenny Booth, "Profile: Ramush Haradinaj," (London) *Times Online*, March 8, 2005, http://www.timesonline.co.uk/article/0,,3-1516562,00.html (charged).

66. Klebnikov, "Heroin Heroes."

67. Baer, *See No Evil*, 243–44. Cf. Scott, *Drugs, Oil, and War*, 31.

68. Rashid, *Jihad*, 83.

69. Scott, *Drugs, Oil, and War*, 65; Johnson, *Sorrows of Empire*, 172–73.

70. Rashid, *Taliban*, 173–75, 182.

71. Johnson, *Sorrows of Empire*, 137. Cf. 169: "During the 1990s and especially after Bush's declaration of a 'war on terrorism,' the oil companies again needed some muscle and the Pentagon was happy to oblige."

72. Klare, *Blood and Oil*, 6–7.

73. Scott, *Drugs, Oil, and War*, 1–105, 185–207.

74. Lacey, *Kingdom*, 374 (Faisal); Brisard and Dasquié, *Forbidden Truth*, 79 (Aramco); and Labévière, *Dollars for Terror*, 42 (Aramco). Labévière (*Dollars for Terror*, 77–78) attaches significance to the fact that Prince Turki, the Saudi intelligence chief and MAK funder, is the son of Crown Prince Faisal, the founder of the MWL.

75. Aburish, *Rise, Corruption, and Coming Fall of the House of Saud*, 130–31; cf. 162–63. Aburish notes that Faisal initially acted without the support of Kennedy, who "instinctively liked Nasser." But "the Johnson years were the

golden years of the Saudi pan-Islamic policy. The Secretary General of the Muslim World League, Muhammad Sabbah, was elevated to the post of minister"; and Walt Rostow, Special Assistant for National Security Affairs to Lyndon Baines Johnson, tried in 1968 to put together "a pro-American Muslim alliance between Saudi Arabia, Turkey, Iran and Pakistan" (Aburish, *Rise, Corruption, and Coming Fall of the House of Saud*, 162–63).

76. Bergen, *Holy War, Inc.*, 55. Cf. Hirschkorn et al., *Jane's Intelligence Review*, August 1, 2001: "Both the fighting and relief efforts [for MAK] were assisted by two banks—Dar al Mal al Islami, founded by Turki's brother Prince Mohammad Faisal in 1981 and Dalla al Baraka founded by King Fahd's brother-in-law in 1982. The banks channeled funds to 20 non-governmental organizations (NGOs), the most famous of which was the International Islamic Relief Organization (IIRO). With IIRO and the Islamic Relief Agency functioned under the umbrella of the World Islamic League led by Mufti Abdul Aziz bin Baz."

77. Sharma, *Pak Proxy War*, 144; Rashid, *Taliban*, 92. In 1997 the United States declared the HuA a terrorist organization, and Fazlur Rehman Khalil became leader of the new Harkat-ul-Mujahideen (HuM).

78. Sharma, *Pak Proxy War*, 145–46.

79. Paul Watson and Mubashir Zaidi, "Militant Flourishes in Plain Sight in Pakistan," *Los Angeles Times*, January 25, 2004.

80. John Loftus, "What Congress Does Not Know about Enron and 9/11," May 31, 2002, http://www.john-loftus.com/enron3.asp.

81. Greg Palast and David Pallister, "Intelligence: FBI Claims Bin Laden Inquiry Was Frustrated," *Guardian*, November 7, 2001; Thompson, *Terror Timeline*, 279.

82. Steven Emerson, testimony before the *Hearings of the 9/11 Commission, Third Public Hearing: Terrorism, al Qaeda, and the Muslim World*, July 9, 2003, 66; Thompson, *Terror Timeline*, 279.

83. Kevin Cullen and Andrea Estes, "Family Weighed Staying in U.S.," *Boston Globe*, September 21, 2001; Thompson, *Terror Timeline*, 288.

84. Stephen Schwartz, "Wahhabis in the Old Dominion," *Weekly Standard*, April 8, 2002 (chaplains).

85. Jonathan Wells, Jack Meyers, Maggie Mulvihill and Kevin Wisniewski, "Under Suspicion: Hub Mosque Leader Tied to Radical Groups," *Boston Herald*, October 29, 2003.

86. Jonathan Wells, "Local Islamic Leader Has Ties to Raided Quincy Co. Founder," *Boston Herald*, January 16, 2004. In response to this article, the Islamic Society of Boston brought a defamations suit against Wells and the *Boston Herald*. The suit was still unresolved two years later.

87. Greg Palast, "See No Evil," *TomPaine.com*, March 1, 2003, http://greg palast.com/detail.cfm?artid=195&row=0.

88. Ahmed, *War on Truth*, 99–100; cf. Thompson, *Terror Timeline*, 281.

89. CNN, October 15, 2001, http://www.cnn.com/2001/WORLD/meast/10/15/inv.saudi.frozen.assets/.

90. William A. Mayer, *PipelineNews.org*, March 10, 2004, http://www.pipelinenews.org/index.cfm?page=rabinowitz2.htm, citing Jodi Wilgoren and Judith Miller, "Trail of Man Sought in 2 Plots Leads to Chicago and Arrest,"

New York Times, September 21, 2003. Mayer calls Salah the "head" of the QLI. The *LA Weekly* (Jim Crogan, "Another FBI Agent Blows the Whistle," July 31, 2002), in an article generally sympathetic to Wright and hostile to the QLI, describes Salah only as a computer analyst for the group.

91. "Three Muslim Charities Ordered to Pay $156 Million to Parents of Teenager Killed in Jerusalem Bombing," *American Muslim Perspective*, December 8, 2004, http://www.archives2005.ghazali.net/html/three_muslim_charities .html: "The institute's attorney, John Beal, refused to take any active part in the trial. He said the judge didn't provide enough time to prepare a defense. Beal repeatedly insisted there was an innocent explanation for each of the allegations."

92. Ralph Ranalli, "FBI Reportedly Didn't Act on Ptech Tips," *Boston Globe*, December 7, 2002; WBZ4, December 9, 2002; Janet Parker, "The Ptech Story," *The New Criminologist*, June 17, 2005, http://www.newcriminologist.co.uk/ article.asp?aid=-526089048.

93. From a White House Press Briefing by Ari Fleischer: "The products that were supplied by this company [Ptech] to the government all fell in the nonclassified area. None of it involved any classified products used by the government. The material has been reviewed by the appropriate government agencies, and they have detected absolutely nothing in their reports to the White House that would lead to any concern about any of the products purchased from this company [Ptech]." Briefing, December 6, 2002, http://www.whitehouse.gov/news/ releases/2002/12/20021206-4.html, quoted in Michael Kane, "Ptech, 9/11, and USA-Saudi Terror, Part 2," *FromTheWilderness.com*, http://www.fromthe wilderness.com/free/ww3/012705_ptech_pt2.shtml.

94. Indira Singh, testimony before the *9/11 Citizens' Commission—September 9, 2004, Symphony Space, New York, NY*, 128, http://www.justicefor911 .org/September-Hearings.doc.

95. From "Whose War on Terror?" *Newsweek*, April 9, 2003: "The FBI-Justice move, pushed by DOJ Criminal Division chief Michael Chertoff and Deputy Attorney General Larry Thompson, has enraged Homeland Security officials, however. They accuse the bureau of sabotaging Greenquest investigations— by failing to turn over critical information to their agents—and trying to obscure a decade-long record of lethargy in which FBI offices failed to aggressively pursue terror-finance cases." Note that in 2005 Chertoff was named to succeed Tom Ridge as head of the Department of Homeland Security.

96. Farah, *Blood from Stones*, 184.

97. Steve Inskeep, "FBI's Continuing Investigation of Boston-Area Software Company Ptech and Its Possible Ties to Terrorism," NPR Weekend, *All Things Considered*, December 8, 2002, http://www.globalsecurity.org/org/news/2002/ 021208-secure01.htm.

98. Indira Singh, testimony before the *9/11 Citizen's Commission*, 130.

99. Indira Singh, testimony before the *9/11 Citizen's Commission*, 124.

100. James Ridgeway, "This Made Ashcroft Gag," *Village Voice*, May 25, 2004.

101. Daniel Hopsicker, "FBI's Role in 9/11 Investigation Needs Investigation," *Mad Cow Morning News*, http://www.madcowprod.com/mc4522004.html.

102. Griffin, *9/11 Commission Report: Omissions and Distortions*, 90–91 (Wright); Thompson, *Terror Timeline*, 284 (O'Neill).

103. Griffin, *9/11 Commission Report: Omissions and Distortions*, 90–91; Thompson, *Terror Timeline*, 282; "Wall Street Whistleblower Singh on Kean's Saudi/Ptech Connections," Total 911 Info, March 6, 2005, http://www.total911 .info/2005/03/wall-street-whistleblower-singh-on.html: "'When Agent Wright said he was investigating a company with 26 subsidiaries, it was BMI, and Ptech was their crown jewel.' Though Ptech wasn't a direct subsidiary of the New Jersey Islamic banking firm BMI, Dr. Hussein Ibrahim, Ptech's chief scientist who inexplicably asked Indira [Singh] to develop JP Morgan's software on his laptop, was vice president of BMI from 1989 to 1995. BMI had also leased computer equipment to Ptech, and as mentioned earlier, it was BMI that introduced Ptech to Yasin Al Qadi."

104. Ranalli, "FBI Reportedly Didn't Act on Ptech Tips," *Boston Globe*, December 7, 2002; Thompson, *Terror Timeline*, 282 (Ibrahim).

105. Farah, *Blood from Stones*, 160.

106. Adam Gorlick, "Muslim Charity Officer Pleads Not Guilty," Associated Press, May 16, 2005. Care International was housed in the Boston office of al-Kifah.

107. Thomas Walkom, "Did bin Laden Have Help from U.S. Friends?" *Toronto Star*, November 27, 2001.

108. Beaty and Gwynne, *Outlaw Bank*, 229.

109. Phillips, *American Dynasty*, 269. Cf. Truell and Gurwin, *False Profits*, 369–70.

110. Unger, *House of Bush, House of Saud*, 120. In 1977 the Saudi investors in the BCCI also bought the Main Bank of Houston in conjunction with former Texas governor John Connally, at a time when he too seemed like a serious possible candidate for the presidency in 1980 (Unger, *House of Bush, House of Saud*, 34–35).

111. Ben. C. Toledano, "A League of Bushes," *Chronicles* (June 2004), http://www.chroniclesmagazine.org/Chronicles/June2004/0604Toledano.html; cf. Phillips, *American Dynasty*, 272–73, 276–77, 291–92, 315–16.

112. Phillips, *American Dynasty*, 292, 315.

113. Securacom has attracted attention because of the frequently encountered speculation that the collapse of three World Trade Center buildings on 9/11 was from a controlled demolition, rather than an external attack. This would have required hours if not days of preparation. See Griffin, *New Pearl Harbor*, 21–22, 180; Griffin, *9/11 Commission Report: Omissions and Distortions*, 26–27.

114. Unger, *House of Bush, House of Saud*, 53.

115. Beaty and Gwynne, *Outlaw Bank*, 355. The other principal purchaser was Rafik Hariri, the Saudi-born billionaire who later became prime minister of Lebanon. In 2005, Hariri was assassinated by a car bomb in Beirut.

116. Beaty and Gwynne, *Outlaw Bank*, 357.

117. Toledano, "League of Bushes."

118. Truell and Gurwin, *False Profits*, 71–72.

119. Phillips, *American Dynasty*, 347–48.

120. Toledano, "League of Bushes."

121. "Has Someone Been Sitting on the FBI?" BBC, November 6, 2001, http://news.bbc.co.uk/1/hi/events/newsnight/1645527.stm.

122. For example, Kevin Phillips, "Bush Saudi Connection: Part I," *Houston Chronicle*, January 23, 2004. In 2001, I too was one of the pack writing about Khalid bin Mahfouz as a possible al Qaeda supporter. I have since retracted claims I made at the time, for three reasons. One is that allegations which I then treated as fact have since been retracted or radically restated by my original sources. Another reason, just as important, is that I now perceive there has been a sustained and dubious ideological campaign, not based simply on hard evidence, to link the Saudi overworld to al Qaeda. See, for example, Posner, *Why America Slept*. A third reason is that some of my original sources, notably James Woolsey, themselves had a discernible bias that I failed to note at the time.

123. Rivers, "Wolf in Sheikh's Clothing"; Block and Weaver, *All Is Clouded by Desire*, 111–12; Unger, *House of Bush, House of Saud*, 120–21.

124. Prince Alwaleed Bin Talal Bin AbdulAziz Alsaud is chairman of Saudi-based Kingdom Holding Co., whose primary investments include major stakes in Citigroup, News Corp., as well as a host of resorts and hotels across the United States. The Olayan Group of Suliman Olayan acquired more stock in Chase Manhattan than any other holder except David Rockefeller. The group also has major holdings in Mellon and Bankers Trust.

125. Block and Weaver, *All Is Clouded by Desire*, 3, quoting editorial, "The Russian Money Trail," *New York Times*, August 31, 1999.

126. Until recently, news stories about the international backers for Neil Bush's firm Ignite have focused on Taiwanese businessmen and Middle East billionaires, such as the defense minister and crown prince of Dubai, Sheikh Mohammed bin Rashid al Maktoum. But in September 2005, "exiled Russian tycoon Boris Berezovsky was in Riga along with Neil Bush, the brother of the U.S. president, to discuss an educational project with Latvian businessmen" ("Berezovsky, Neil Bush, Latvian Businessmen Meet," *Baltic Times*, September 23, 2005). In an interview with Interfax, Berezovsky pointed out that he is one of the shareholders of Ignite! Inc. ("Berezovsky Comes to Latvia over 'Education Projects," Interfax, September 21, 2005).

127. Scott, "Global Drug Meta-Group," *Lobster* (October 2005), http://lobster-magazine.co.uk/articles/global-drug.thm, citing John B. Dunlop, " 'Storm in Moscow': A Plan of the Yeltsin 'Family' to Destabilize Russia," Hoover Institution, October 8, 2004, http://www.sais-jhu.edu/programs/res/papers/Dunlop%20paper.pdf (note: this paper has been withdrawn).

128. Scott, "Global Drug Meta-Group."

11. PARALLEL STRUCTURES AND PLANS FOR CONTINUITY OF GOVERNMENT

Epigraphs: Secretary of Defense Dick Cheney (1990), quoted in Ted Koppel, "Will Fight for Oil," *New York Times*, February 24, 2006. Judge Robert H. Jackson, Nuremberg War Crimes Tribunal, October 1, 1946, judgment. Bush is quoted in Clarke, *Against All Enemies*, 24.

1. Ganser, *NATO's Secret Armies*, 63–83; Willan, *Puppetmasters*, 122–31, 160–67.

2. Thomas Sheehan, "Italy: Terror on the Right," *New York Review of Books*, January 22, 1981, http://www.nybooks.com/articles/7178.

3. Willan, *Puppetmasters*, 26.

4. William Scobie, *Observer*, August 11, 1990. For a detailed analysis, see Calvi and Laurent, *Piazza Fontana*.

5. "Italian General Alleges CIA Link to Bombings," Reuters, August 4, 2000: " 'We cannot say that the CIA had an active and direct role in the bombings, but it is true that they knew the targets and culprits,' General Gianadelio Maletti told *la Repubblica* newspaper in an interview from Johannesburg, where the former spy is in self-imposed exile."

6. One of the alleged documents, "U.S. Field Manual 30-31B," turned up in a number of countries and was claimed by CIA to be a KGB forgery. See House Permanent Select Committee on Intelligence Hearing, "Soviet Covert Action (The Forgery Offensive)," February 1980, 12, 13, and appendix: "CIA Study: Soviet Covert Action and Propaganda," 66, 67; cf. Ganser, *NATO's Secret Armies*, 234–35. Ganser has again argued for the authenticity of Annex 30-31B in "The CIA in Western Europe and the Abuse of Human Rights," *Intelligence & National Security* (fall 2006), 760–81; I remain unconvinced.

7. "The CIA in Western Europe," http://www.wakeupmag.co.uk/articles/cia6.htm, viewed October 2005; cf. *Wikipedia*, s.v., "Greek military junta of 1967–1974," http://en.wikipedia.org/wiki/Greek_military_junta_of_1967-1974; Ganser, *NATO's Secret Armies*, 215–23; Blum, *Killing Hope*, 215–21.

8. Blum, *Killing Hope*, 217.

9. "Rising Criticism of the Leaks," *Time*, February 9, 1976, http://www.time.com/time/magazine/article/0,9171,917960,00.html. Arthur E. Rowse claims the money came from Kissinger; see Rowse, "Gladio," http://www.mega.nu:8080/ampp/gladio.html, citing Pike Report (unavailable at my library). "The [CIA] advised [Martin] against giving money to SID director Vito Miceli and warned of Miceli's links to Pino Rauti, the Ordine Nuovo founder" (Willan, *Puppetmasters*, 116).

10. Ganser, *NATO's Secret Armies*, 76–78.

11. Ganser, *NATO's Secret Armies*, 81.

12. A similar attack is the campaign of violence and murder sanctioned by General Douglas MacArthur against the left in Japan, using forces allied with the Japanese organized criminal societies known as *yakuza*.

13. Rowse, "Gladio"; Willan, *Puppetmasters*, 38, quoting Roberto Faenza and Marco Fini, *Gli Americani in Italia* (Milan: Feltrinelli, 1976), 276.

14. Calvi and Laurent, *Piazza Fontana*, 109; Laurent, *L'orchestre noir*, 193; cf. Jeffrey M. Bale, "The 'Black' Terrorist International: Neo-Fascist Paramilitary Networks and the 'Strategy of Tension' in Italy, 1968–1974," (Ph.D. dissertation, University of California, Berkeley), 177. There is confusion both about the lecturer and more important the date. Bale identifies as the lecturer Giannettini's coconspirator the Ordine Nuovo founder Pino Rauti, and 1962 as the date. It is possible that there were two different lectures given.

15. David Ruppe, "U.S. Military Wanted to Provoke War With Cuba," ABC News, January 5, 2001; cf. Bamford, *Body of Secrets*, 82. The documents are in

the National Archive as document RIF #202-10002-10104, pp. 128–41, accessible from the Mary Ferrell Foundation website, http://www.maryferrell.org. They are reprinted in Ruppert, *Crossing the Rubicon*, 595–608. There are other unpublished Northwoods documents in the same file, from February 7 to July 25, 1962.

16. John Prados, foreword to Ganser, *NATO's Secret Armies*, xiii.

17. Willan, *Puppetmasters*, 26–27, 100–101. General Vito Miceli, who later headed Italy's secret service (SID), said he set up the separate structure "at the request of the Americans and NATO" (Rowse, "Gladio").

18. "News from Post-Constitutional America" *Progressive Review*, http://prorev.com/coup12.htm.

19. Bamford, *Pretext for War*, 70–72. According to Bamford (*Pretext for War*, 72), "the Eisenhower White House failed to pass on details of their secret government to the incoming Kennedy administration, which discovered it by accident." On October 30, 1969 President Nixon issued Executive Order 11490, consolidating twenty-one executive orders and two defense mobilization orders, assigning emergency preparedness functions to federal departments and agencies. In 1976, with Executive Order 11921, President Ford further consolidated these functions in the Federal Emergency Preparedness Agency (FEPA).

20. Gelbspan, *Break-ins, Death Threats, and the FBI*, 184.

21. Gelbspan, *Break-ins, Death Threats, and the FBI*, 184; Jonathan Vankin and John Whalen, *The 80 Greatest Conspiracies of All Time* (New York: Citadel Press, 2004), 32.

22. For text of the exchange, see transcript of hearing in *New York Times*, July 14, 1987. Although the *Times* reproduced the transcript of Congressman Brooks's exchange with Senator Inouye, the accompanying eleven-hundred-word story by R. W. Apple did not mention it. Neither did the *Washington Post* on the same day (or, according to Lexis-Nexis, any other newspaper). *Congressional Quarterly*'s 480-page volume, *The Iran-Contra Puzzle*, reprints only Brooks's subsequent angry exchange with Sullivan. Brooks was referring to an article by Alfonso Chardy in the *Miami Herald* on July 5, 1987. It "revealed Oliver North's involvement in plans for the Federal Emergency Management Agency to take over federal, state and local functions during an ill-defined national emergency" ("The Ronald Reagan Myth," *Progressive Review*, http://prorev.com/reagan.htm).

23. Gelbspan, *Break-ins, Death Threats, and the FBI*, 184.

24. Vankin and Whalen, *80 Greatest Conspiracies of All Time*, 32. Cf. Peter Dale Scott, "Northwards without North: Bush, Counterterrorism, and the Continuation of Secret Power," *Social Justice* (San Francisco) 16, no. 2 (summer 1989): 1–30; Bradlee, *Guts and Glory*, 132.

25. Barton Gellman and Susan Schmidt, "Shadow Government Is at Work in Secret," *Washington Post*, March 1, 2002, reporting in part on National Security Decision Directive 188, "Government Coordination for National Security Emergency Preparedness." For the text of NSDD-188, go to http://www.fas.org/irp/offdocs/nsdd/nsdd-188.htm. The planning took the place of an earlier Emergency Mobilization Preparedness Board established by President Reagan in a December 1981 announcement ("Announcement of Establishment of the Emergency Mobilization Preparedness Board," December 29, 1981, http://www.reagan.utexas.edu/archives/speeches/1981/122981a.htm).

26. James Mann, "The Armageddon Plan," *Atlantic Monthly* (March 2004), http://www.theatlantic.com/doc/prem/200403/mann; Mann, *Rise of the Vulcans*, 138–45. Mann in his book also names as team leaders in COG planning James Woolsey, later head of CIA, and Kenneth Duberstein, Reagan's final chief of staff.

27. Bamford, *Pretext for War*, 72. According to CNN, the list eventually grew to seventeen names and also included Howard Baker, Richard Helms, Jeanne Kirkpatrick, James Schlesinger, Richard Thornberg, Edwin Meese, and Tip O'Neill ("Undernews: The Amazing, Scary History of FEMA," *Progressive Review*, September 11, 2005, http://prorev.com/2005/09/amazing-scary-history-of-fema.htm). Schlesinger was also president of Mitre Corporation, a defense industry that some have suspected of a role in 9/11 because of its collaboration with Ptech on the command and control systems of the Department of Defense, NORAD, the Air Force, and the FAA. Those who, like myself, have known Schlesinger personally find the notion of his possible involvement highly unlikely.

28. Gellman and Schmidt, "Shadow Government Is at Work in Secret," *Washington Post*, March 1, 2002.

29. "Some Secret Activities," *Miami Herald*, July 5, 1987, http://www.theforbiddenknowledge.com/hardtruth/secret_white_house_plans.htm. In October 1984 columnist Jack Anderson is said to have reported that FEMA's plans would "suspend the Constitution and the Bill of Rights, effectively eliminate private property, abolish free enterprise, and generally clamp Americans in a totalitarian vise."

30. *Singapore Straits-Times*, July 17, 2002; Rodger Herbst, "Poised for a COUP: Bush Regime Struggles to Retain Power in an Increasingly Alienated America," *Washington Free Press*, no. 70 (July–August 2004): " 'The Mysterious Mountain,' an article appearing in the March 1976 issue of *The Progressive*, was based on the Senate Subcommittee on Constitutional Rights hearings in 1975, and several off-the-record interviews. The article noted that Mount Weather [the home of one of the COG alternative government sites] at that time contained a parallel 'government-in-waiting' ready to take control of the United States upon word from the President or his successor. The subcommittee learned that Congress has almost no knowledge and no oversight—budgetary or otherwise—on Mount Weather, and that the 'facility held dossiers on at least 100,000 Americans'" Cf. Richard Pollack, "The Mysterious Mountain," *The Progressive*, March 1976, 12–16.

31. Mann, "Armageddon Plan"; cf. Mann, *Rise of the Vulcans*, 145; Bamford, *Pretext for War*, 74: "The existence of the secret government was so closely held that Congress was completely bypassed. Rather than through legislation, it was created by Top Secret presidential fiat. In fact, Congress would have no role in the new wartime administration. 'One of the awkward questions we faced,' said one of the participants, 'was whether to reconstitute Congress after a nuclear attack. It was decided that no, it would be easier to operate without them.'"

32. The provisions of Executive Order 12656 of November 18, 1988, appear at 53 FR 47491, 3 CFR, 1988 Comp., p. 585, "Executive Order 12656—Assignment of Emergency Preparedness Responsibilities," http://www.archives.gov/federal-register/codification/executive-order/12656.html. The *Washington Post* (Gellman and Schmidt, "Shadow Government Is at Work in Secret," March 1,

2002) later claimed, incorrectly, that Executive Order 12656 dealt only with "a nuclear attack."

33.Clarke, *Against All Enemies*, 165–75.

34. Tim Weiner, "Pentagon Book for Doomsday Is to Be Closed," *New York Times*, April 17, 1994.

35. Mann, *Rise of the Vulcans*, 144. Cf. Bamford, *Pretext for War*, 74: "The existence of the secret government was so closely held that Congress was completely bypassed . . . but with the Cold War over, President Bill Clinton decided to end it."

36. Andrew Cockburn, *Rumsfeld: His Rise, Fall, and Catastrophic Legacy* (New York: Scribner, 2007), 88.

37. Clarke, *Against All Enemies*, 8, 165–75.

38. Steve Perry, "The CIA Leak Investigation: Bigger Fish, Deeper Water," *Minneapolis/St. Paul City Pages*, November 2, 2005, http://silverback.gnn.tv/headlines/5879/The_CIA_Leak_Investigation_Bigger_Fish_Deeper_Water.

39. Lawrence B. Wilkerson, "Cheney Cabal Runs Foreign Policy, Ex-aide to Powell Reiterates," *Los Angeles Times*, October 25, 2005, http://www.unknownnews.org/051028-Wilkerson.html.

40. Jane Mayer, "Contract Sport: What Did the Vice-President Do for Halliburton?" *New Yorker*, February 16–23, 2004, http://www.newyorker.com/fact/content/articles/040216fa_fact.

41. Linda McCuaig, "Crude Dudes," *Toronto Star*, September 20, 2004; cf. McQuaig, *It's the Crude, Dude*, 84–85, quoting Mayer, "Contract Sport."

42. McQuaig, "Crude Dudes"; cf. McQuaig, *It's the Crude, Dude*, 79–80. The documents can be seen on-line at "Maps and Charts of Iraqi Oil Fields," http://www.judicialwatch.org/printer_iraqi-oil-maps.shtml.

43. One of the Baker task force members was Kenneth Lay, the former chief executive of Enron, which went bankrupt after carrying out massive accountancy fraud. The report begins with references to "recent energy price spikes" and "electricity outages in California," which are now known to have been engineered by Enron market manipulations for which two Enron energy traders later pleaded guilty to conspiracy charges (*Forbes*, February 5, 2003).

44. "Strategic Energy Policy: Challenges for the Twenty-first Century," 40; http://www.rice.edu/energy/publications/docs/TaskForceReport_Final.pdf. In an earlier draft of a Web site essay I quoted extensively (as have many other writers) from an October 6, 2002, news story by Neil Mackay in the *Scotland Sunday Herald*. This story claimed that Vice President Cheney himself commissioned the second task force report, and that former secretary of state James Baker delivered the report to Cheney. I have since been assured that neither claim is true.

45. Greg Palast, "Secret U.S. Plans for Iraq's Oil," BBC News, March 17, 2005, http://news.bbc.co.uk/1/hi/programmes/newsnight/4354269.stm.

46. AEI chairman Christopher Demuth, quoted in Woodward, *State of Denial*, 84.

47. "Rumsfeld: It Would Be a Short War," CBS News, November 15, 2002. For other examples, see Peter Dale Scott, "Bush's Deep Reasons for War on Iraq: Oil, Petrodollars, and the OPEC Euro Question," http://ist-socrates.berkeley.edu/~pdscott/iraq.html; Phillips, *American Theocracy*, 69.

48. Pepe Escobar, "China, Russia, and the Iraqi Oil Game," *Asia Times*, November 1, 2002. Woolsey voiced similar sentiments to the *Washington Post* (cited in Tom Cholmondeley, "Comment & Analysis: Over a Barrel," *Guardian*, November 22, 2002).

49. Scott, "Bush's Deep Reasons for War on Iraq."

50. Scott, *Drugs, Oil, and War*, 41–42, 53–54; Spiro, *Hidden Hand of American Hegemony*, x, 103–12, 121.

51. Scott, "Bush's Deep Reasons for War on Iraq." The U.S. failure in Iraq has seen the threat to the dollar increase: "Between 2001 and 2004 OPEC nations dropped the share of their reserves held in dollars from 75 percent to 61.5 percent. Major OPEC producers such as Iran and Venezuela held fewer dollars because their hostility to the United States had become overt, but even moderates in OPEC ranks saw the growing wisdom of putting reserves into a wider array of currencies" (Phillips, *American Theocracy*, 358).

52. "Executive Order Protecting the Development Fund for Iraq and Certain Other Property in Which Iraq Has an Interest," Executive Order 13303 of May 22, 2003, *Federal Register*, 31931, http://www.whitehouse.gov/news/releases/2003/05/20030522-15.html. The order was issued ten days after Paul Bremer arrived in Iraq to head the Coalition Provisional Authority that would enforce it. But the *Irish Times* had correctly predicted the outcome on April 17, noting Washington was making dollars the short-term currency within Iraq and putting the Iraqi oil industry under U.S. direction: "This makes it certain that the future sale of Iraqi oil will be in dollars, the international currency for oil transactions, once the UN lifts anti-Saddam sanctions that provide that only the UN can approve Iraqi oil sales" (Conor O'Clery, "Dollar to Replace Dinar, for Now," *Irish Times*, April 17, 2003).

53. Carola Hoyos and Kevin Morrison, "Iraq Returns to International Oil Market," *Financial Times*, June 5, 2003: "Iraq stepped back into the international oil market yesterday for the first time since the war, offering 10m barrels of oil from its storage tanks for sale to the highest bidder. . . . The tender, for which bids are due by June 10, switches the transaction back to dollars—the international currency of oil sales—despite the greenback's recent fall in value." Cf. Krassimir Petrov, "The Proposed Iranian Oil Bourse," *Gold Eagle*, January 20, 2006, http://www.countercurrents.org/us-petrov200106.htm: "Two months after the United States invaded Iraq, the Oil for Food Program was terminated, the Iraqi Euro accounts were switched back to dollars, and oil was sold once again only for U.S. dollars."

54. Charles Clover and Arkady Ostrovsky, "Economic Reform Plan Will Push Iraq towards Sell-offs," *Financial Times*, May 27, 2003; Ed Vulliamy and Faisal Islam, "And Now for the Really Big Guns," *Observer*, June 29, 2003; Tim Shorrock, "Selling (Off) Iraq," *Nation*, June 23, 2003.

55. Charles Krauthammer, "Our Instant Experts," *Washington Post*, October 3, 2003.

56. From Alan Beattie and Charles Clover, "Iraq Minister Announces Plan to End Almost All Curbs on Foreign Investment," *Financial Times*, September 22, 2003: "The new laws, which will make Iraq one of the most open economies in the developing world and go beyond even legislation in many rich countries, were

immediately attacked by Iraqi business representatives. Wadi Surab, a member of the Iraqi Businessman's Union in Baghdad, told the BBC Arabic service yesterday that the proposed reforms would 'destroy the role of the Iraqi industrialist,' as Iraqi business groups would be unable to compete in privatisation tenders with richer foreign companies. 'I suggest you take a poll of whether Iraqis support this, and I guarantee 100 per cent will say no,' he said."

57. Ricks, *Fiasco*, 158. The most obvious example was de-Baathification, the purging from leadership of those in Saddam Hussein's Baath Party. The NSC had decided to purge "senior Baath leadership and intelligence officials" (Woodward, *Plan of Attack*, 339, 343). But Bremer extended the notion of "senior Baathist" to include any Baath member holding a position in the top three management layers of any ministry, state corporation, university, or hospital (Ricks, *Fiasco*, 159). This decision was immediately opposed by Bremer's predecessor, Lieutenant General Jay Garner, and the local CIA chief as an order that would encourage not only chaos but insurgency.

58. Rothkopf, *Running the World*, 414.

59. Tim Shorrock, "Selling (Off) Iraq," *Nation*, June 23, 2003.

60. The 1996 document, "A Clean Break: A New Strategy for Securing the Realm," was drafted by among others PNAC author Richard Perle and his neocon ally Douglas Feith (both later connected to the second Bush administration). It advised an attack on Syria. "Syria challenges Israel on Lebanese soil," they wrote, calling for "striking Syrian military targets in Lebanon, and should that prove insufficient, *striking at select targets in Syria proper.*" Perle approved of the Israeli strike in 2003. "It will help the peace process," he told the *Washington Post*, adding later that the United States itself might have to attack Syria. See editorial, "Is Syria Next?" *Nation*, November 3, 2003.

61. Palast, "Secret U.S. Plans for Iraq's Oil"; Greg Palast, "OPEC on the March," *Harper's* (April 2005): 74–76. As financial journalist John Dizard predicted in May 2004: "Military sources say Feith will resign his Defense Department post by mid-May. His removal was reportedly a precondition imposed by Ambassador to the UN John Negroponte when he agreed to take over from Paul Bremer as the top U.S. official in Iraq. . . . Feith's boss, Undersecretary of Defense Paul Wolfowitz, may follow" (John Dizard, "How Ahmed Chalabi Conned the Neocons," *Salon*, May 4, 2004, http://www.salon.com/news/feature/2004/05/04/chalabi/). Feith's departure was in fact delayed until January 2005.

62. Palast, "OPEC on the March," 76; Palast, *Armed Madhouse*, 83–106.

63. Bamford, *Pretext for War*, 72. Cf. chapter 11 in this book.

64. "The Plan: Were Neo-Conservatives' 1998 Memos a Blueprint for Iraq War?" ABC News, March 10, 2003.

65. Project for the New American Century, *Rebuilding America's Defenses*.

66. There were a number of other PNAC appointments. Dov Zakheim became Pentagon comptroller. Abram Shulsky became head of the Pentagon's Office of Special Plans.

67. David E. Sanger, "Threats and Responses," *New York Times*, September 20, 2002. In an important article Noam Chomsky traces the origins of this strategic doctrine back to the plans "to achieve military and economic supremacy" outlined by the War and Peace Studies Project of the Council on Foreign Rela-

tions, in the early days of World War II (Noam Chomsky, "Dominance and Its Dilemmas: The Bush Administration's Imperial Grand Strategy," *Boston Review* 28, no. 5 [October–November 2003], http://bostonreview.net/BR28.5/chomsky .html; cf. Shoup and Minter, *Imperial Brain Trust*, 117–87). The "significant difference" Chomsky sees is the determination of the current administration to *declare* "full-spectrum dominance" over all others, including those once considered allies. For someone of my generation another difference is also important: the planners of 1940 wished to assert supremacy over a totalitarian enemy by which they felt *threatened*. Rightly or wrongly, this perception of being threatened continued to affect American thinking in at least the early years of the Cold War, at least until the facts of the missile gap became known about 1960. There is no such threat to the United States today.

68. William W. Keller and Gordon R. Mitchell, *Hitting First: Preventive Force in U.S. Security Strategy* (Pittsburgh, Pa.: University of Pittsburgh Press, 2006), chapter 1, n15.

69. Hersh, *Chain of Command*, 207–8. In a firsthand and sophisticated rebuttal to Hersh's claims, Michael Rubin, of the Office of Special Plans and the American Enterprise Institute, replied in the *National Review* (May 18, 2004): "We had never called ourselves that, although we were aware that Defense Intelligence Agency official W. Patrick Lang (whom Hersh cites openly), Defense Intelligence Agency official Bruce Hardcastle, and some Central Intelligence Agency officials used the term to describe Jewish colleagues."

70. Hersh, *Chain of Command*, 177, 207–9: "Special Plans was created in order to find evidence of what Wolfowitz and his boss, Defense Secretary Donald Rumsfeld, believed to be true—that Saddam had close ties to Al Qaeda, and that Iraq had an enormous arsenal of chemical, biological, and possibly even nuclear weapons" (209). Also serving in the Office of Special Plans were neocons Douglas Feith and Michael Rubin of the AEI and the Jewish Institute for National Security Affairs.

71. Robert Dreyfuss, "More Missing Intelligence," *Nation*, July 7, 2003; Peter Dale Scott, "Bush's Misguided Post-War Military Policy in Iraq Based on Falsification of Evidence," http://ist-socrates.berkeley.edu/~pdscott/iraqje.html.

72. Project for the New American Century, *Rebuilding America's Defenses*, 51 (63).

73. The same opinion had been voiced by the Democrat Zbigniew Brzezinski in his blueprint for projecting U.S. power into Central Asia: "The pursuit of power is not a goal that commands popular passion, except in conditions of a sudden threat or challenge to the public's sense of domestic well-being. . . . Democracy is inimical to imperial mobilization. . . . The public supported America's engagement in World War II largely because of the shock effect of the Japanese attack on Pearl Harbor." See Brzezinski, *Grand Chessboard*, 24–25. However Brzezinski presciently warned against a unilateral American invasion of Iraq; and he later judged that "the war in Iraq has been a geopolitical disaster," eroding America's influence or soft power (Michiko Kakutani, "When a Leader Missteps, a World Can Go Astray," *New York Times*, March 6, 2007; reviewing Zbigniew Brzezinski, *Second Chance: Three Presidents and the Crisis of American Superpower* [New York: Basic Books, 2007]).

12. THE *9/11 COMMISSION REPORT*
AND VICE PRESIDENT CHENEY

Acknowledgment: I wish to express my gratitude to David Ray Griffin, Matt Everett, and Paul Thompson for their help in drafting and revising chapters 12 and 13. *Epigraph*: Niccolò Machiavelli, *The Prince*, in Peter Bondanella and Mark Musa, eds., *The Portable Machiavelli* (New York: Penguin Books, 1979), 148.

1. "Bush Asks Daschle to Limit Sept. 11 Probes," *CNN.com*, January 29, 2002, http://archives.cnn.com/2002/ALLPOLITICS/01/29/inv.terror.probe/.

2. Commission cochairs Thomas Kean and Lee Hamilton later acknowledged the crucial role of the 9/11 families in securing congressional support for a commission (Kean and Hamilton, *Without Precedent*, 15-19, 25-29). The Jersey Girls who thus impacted history were Kristen Breitweiser, Patty Casazza, Mindy Kleinberg, and Lori Van Auken ("9/11 Widows Speak," PBS, September 12, 2003, http://www.pbs.org/now/politics/911widows.html; cf. "9/11: Press for Truth," DVD, http://www.911PressForTruth.com).

3. Sheryl Gay Stolberg, "9/11 Widows Skillfully Applied the Power of a Question: Why?" *New York Times*, April 1, 2004.

4. Kean and Hamilton, *Without Precedent*, 15. The commission eventually obtained a budget of $14 million.

5. *9/11 Commission Report*, 34.

6. Bronner, "9/11 Live," 271, referring to the testimony of Major General Larry Arnold and William Scott, May 23, 2003. Arnold and Scott are omitted from the list of witnesses supplied by the *9/11 Commission Report* in Appendix C, 441.

7. John Farmer, "'United 93': The Real Picture," *Washington Post*, April 30, 2006. Cf. Kean and Hamilton, *Without Precedent*, 87: "The staff front office suggested that the NORAD situation bordered on willful concealment."

8. *9/11 Commission Report*, xvii.

9. Kean and Hamilton, *Without Precedent*, 268.

10. Jersey Girl Lori Van Auken later said of the *9/11 Commission Report*: "We don't know the whole story, not at all" ("9/11: Press For Truth," DVD).

11. Richard Clarke heard that the FBI had the list at 9:59 A.M., the time of the collapse of World Trade Center Tower 2. See Clarke, *Against All Enemies*, 13-14. This investigative tour de force is even more amazing when we consider that in the FBI, according to the *9/11 Commission Report* (77), "prior to 9/11 relatively few strategic analytic reports about counterterrorism had been completed. Indeed, the FBI had never completed an assessment of the overall terrorist threat to the U.S. homeland." Number 4 of the Jersey Girls' top 20 questions was "Are all 19 people identified by the government as participants in the Sept. 11 attacks really the hijackers?" (William Bunch, "Why Don't We Have Answers to These 9/11 Questions?" *Philadelphia Daily News*, September 11, 2003, www.truthout .org/docs_03/091203A.shtml).

12. The mainstream U.S. press, such as the *New York Times*, later attributed the confusion about the hijackers' identity to the number of different Arabs sharing the same names. But at least five men shared histories as well as names with the alleged hijackers. Waleed al-Shehri told the BBC "that he attended flight

training school at Daytona Beach in the United States, and is indeed the same Waleed Al Shehri to whom the FBI has been referring. But, he says, he left the United States in September last year, became a pilot with Saudi Arabian airlines and is currently on a further training course in Morocco" (BBC, September 23, 2001). Saeed al-Ghamdi, alive and flying planes in Tunisia, also studied at Florida flight schools, as late as 2001. According to the London *Telegraph* (David Harrison, "Revealed: The Men with Stolen Identities," September 23, 2001), CNN used his photograph in describing the hijacker with his name. Abdulaziz al-Omari acknowledged the same date of birth as the accused hijacker al-Omari but claimed his passport was stolen when he was living in Denver, Colorado (London *Telegraph*, September 23, 2001; Thompson, *Terror Timeline*, 497).

13. "Hijack 'Suspects' Alive and Well," BBC, September 23, 2001. The editor of BBC News Online has since partially retracted the original BBC article (Steve Herrman, "9/11 Conspiracy Theory," October 27, 2006, http://www.bbc.co.uk/blogs/theeditors/2006/10/911_conspiracy_theory_1.html).

14. *9/11 Commission Report*, 1–14, 215–42. Discussion in Griffin, *9/11 Commission Report: Omissions and Distortions*, 19–23.

15. "12. Why did 7 World Trade Center collapse?" in Bunch, "Why Don't We Have Answers to These 9/11 Questions?" *Philadelphia Daily News*, September 11, 2003.

16. James Glanz, "Wounded Buildings Offer Survival Lessons," *New York Times*, December 4, 2001. Experts assembled by FEMA prepared an extensive report on the World Trade Center disaster. With respect to WTC-7, this said: "The specifics of the fires in WTC-7 and how they caused the building to collapse remain unknown at this time. Although the total diesel fuel on the premises contained massive potential energy, *the best hypothesis has only a low probability of occurrence.* Further research, investigation, and analyses are needed to resolve this issue" (FEMA, World Trade Center Building Performance Study, Chap. 5, Sect. 5.7 "Observations and Findings," http://911research.wtc7.net/mirrors/guardian2/wtc/WTC_ch5.htm, emphasis added). The mystery is still unresolved.

17. Steven E. Jones, "Why Indeed Did the WTC Buildings Collapse?" in *9/11 and American Empire*, edited by Griffin and Scott, 33–62; cf. Steven E. Jones, "Why Indeed Did the WTC Buildings Completely Collapse?" *Journal of 9/11 Studies*, http://www.journalof911studies.com/volume/200609/Why_Indeed_Did _the_WTC_Buildings_Completely_Collapse_Jones_Thermite_World_Trade _Center.pdf.

18. *9/11 Commission Report*, 36–38: "None of these teleconferences . . . succeeded in meaningfully coordinating the military and FAA response to the hijackings" (*9/11 Commission Report*, 36).

19. Co-chairs quoted from their appearance on *Jim Lehrer News*, PBS, July 22, 2004.

20. "Vice President Appears on *Meet the Press* with Tim Russert," September 16, 2001.

21. Clarke, *Against All Enemies*, 8.

22. Scott, *Deep Politics and the Death of JFK*, 60.

23. *9/11 Commission Report*, 29; Clarke, *Against All Enemies*, 5 (first day).

24. 9/11 Commission, Hearing of June 17, 2004, "National Commission on Terrorist Attacks upon the United States: Twelfth Public Hearing," http://www.9-11commission.gov/archive/hearing12/9-11Commission_Hearing_2004-06-17.htm.

25. Alan Levin, Marilyn Adams, and Blake Morrison, "Part I: Terror Attacks Brought Drastic Decision: Clear the Skies," *USA Today*, August 12, 2002, http://www.usatoday.com/news/sept11/2002-08-12-clearskies_x.htm.

26. U.S. Congress, Senate, Committee on Commerce, Statement by Norman Y. Mineta, Hearing on Federal Aviation Security Standards, September 20, 2001, http://lobby.la.psu.edu/_107th/136_Aviation%20Security/Congressional_Hearings/Testimony/S_CST_Mineta_09202001.htm.

27. Dan Balz and Bob Woodward, "America's Chaotic Road to War," *Washington Post*, January 27, 2002, http://www.washingtonpost.com/ac2/wp-dyn/A42754-2002Jan26. There is no trace of this important command in Woodward's subsequent book, *Bush at War*.

28. "Mineta Exclusive: In Conversation with the Secretary," *Aviation Security International Magazine*, October 2002, http://www.asi-mag.com/editorials/norman_mineta.htm.

29. Norman Mineta, testimony before the *National Commission on Terrorist Attacks upon the United States, Second Public Hearing: Congress and Civil Aviation Security*, May 23, 2003, http://www.globalsecurity.org/security/library/congress/9-11_commission/030523-transcript.htm.

30. He had previously been interviewed on April 20, 2004 (*9/11 Commission Report*, 463).

31. Griffin, *9/11 Commission Report: Omissions and Distortions*, 221.

32. *9/11 Commission Report*, 40. In fact, as we shall soon see, these were exactly the two times mentioned by the Cheneys themselves in November 2001 interviews with *Newsweek*.

33. David Griffin, "9/11, the American Empire, and Common Moral Norms," *9/11 & American Empire: Intellectuals Speak Out*, edited by David Ray Griffin and Peter Dale Scott (Northampton, Mass.: Olive Branch Press, 2006), 8.

34. Clarke, *Against All Enemies*, 2, 5.

35. "The Vice President Appears on *Meet the Press* with Tim Russert," September 16, 2001, http://www.whitehouse.gov/vicepresident/news-speeches/speeches/vp20010916.html: "I went down into what's call[ed] a PEOC, the Presidential Emergency Operations Center, . . . But when I arrived there within a short order, we had word the Pentagon's been hit." To minimize the issues in this chapter, I have accepted the report's revised time for the hit (9:37 A.M.). The time for Flight 77's crash was originally announced as 9:45 A.M. (Elaine Sciolino and John H. Cushman Jr., "After the Attacks: American Flight 77; A Route out of Washington, Horribly Changed," *New York Times*, September 13, 2001, A21).

36. "'Sir, we have to leave now,' a Secret Service agent told Vice President Dick Cheney. He grabbed Cheney by the back of his belt and forcibly propelled him to the underground bunker known as the Presidential Emergency Operations

Center. Minutes later the hijacked jet smashed into the Pentagon" ("Inside Cheney's Bunker," *Newsweek*, December 31, 2001).

37. Evan Thomas, "The Story of September 11," *Newsweek*, December 31, 2001.

38. Statement of Secretary of Transportation Norman Y. Mineta before the National Commission on Terrorist Attacks upon the United States, May 23, 2003, quoted in Griffin, *9/11 Commission Report: Omissions and Distortions*, 220.

39. Thompson, *Terror Timeline*, 409.

40. *9/11 Commission Report*, 25; cf. Thompson, *Terror Timeline*, 409. The report's authority for overruling the accounts by Mineta and ABC News is a single interview with air traffic controller John Hendershot (460n146).

41. "'Countdown with Keith Olbermann' for August 3," MSNBC, August 3, 2006, http://www.msnbc.msn.com/id/14184586/; Bronner, "9/11 Live," 270. Bronner adds: "20 months later, when the military presents to the 9/11 commission what is supposed to be a full accounting of the day, omitted from the official time line is any mention of this reported hijacking and the fevered chase it engenders." This verbatim transcript is not in the *9/11 Commission Report* either, which quotes instead a less urgent account from a different NEADS channel (*9/11 Commission Report*, 26).

42. *9/11 Commission Report*, 27.

43. *9/11 Commission Report*, 39; citing 464n209.

44. Clarke, *Against All Enemies*, 7.

45. *Newsweek*, December 31, 2001; *Meet the Press*, NBC, September 16, 2001:

> **Vice. Pres. Cheney:** [They] grabbed me and... you know, your feet touch the floor periodically. But they're bigger than I am, and they hoisted me up and moved me very rapidly down the hallway, down some stairs, through some doors and down some more stairs into an underground facility under the White House, and, as a matter of fact, it's a corridor, locked at both ends, and they did that because they had received a report that an airplane was headed for the White House.
> **Mr. Russert:** This is Flight 77, which had left Dulles.
> **Vice. Pres. Cheney:** Which turned out to be Flight 77.

46. *9/11 Commission Report*, 39, 464n209, 464n213. For the time of evacuation, the report cites instead the White House transcript of Cheney's interview with *Newsweek* on November 19, 2001, an interview with Secret Service agent Rocco Delmonico, and notes from Cheney's aide Mary Matalin of the White House.

47. Larry Arnold, testimony before the *National Commission on Terrorist Attacks upon the United States, Second Public Hearing: Congress and Civil Aviation Security*, May 23, 2003, http://www.globalsecurity.org/security/library/congress/9-11_commission/030523-transcript.htm.

48. *9/11 Commission Report*, 34, 26.

49. *9/11 Commission Report*, 31.

50. *Aviation Security International Magazine* (October 2002), http://www.asi-mag.com/editorials/norman_mineta.htm, viewed October 15, 2006. The *9/11 Commission Report* cited instead a minor FAA person's impression that the

plane was "somewhere over, uh, New Jersey or somewhere further south" (*9/11 Commission Report*, 26).

51. Kean and Hamilton intensified this picture, in carefully drafted language that without being false created the misleading impression that there was no awareness of Flight 77's approach to Washington, D.C., before 9:36 A.M. (Kean and Hamilton, *Without Precedent*, 258).

52. Bronner, "9/11 Live," 275; MSNBC, "'Countdown with Keith Olbermann' for August 3 [2006]"; cf. *9/11 Commission Report*, 26.

53. *9/11 Commission Report*, 27.

54. *9/11 Commission Report*, 34.

55. Kean and Hamilton, *Without Precedent*, 258, 259.

56. Compare Richard Nixon's taped description of the Warren Report as "the greatest hoax that has ever been perpetuated" (Kevin Anderson, "Revelations and Gaps on Nixon Tapes," BBC News, March 1, 2002, http://news.bbc.co.uk/2/hi/americas/1848157.stm).

57. "Cheney Recalls Taking Charge from Bunker," *CNN.com*, September 11, 2002, http://archives.cnn.com/2002/ALLPOLITICS/09/11/ar911.king.cheney/index.html.

58. *9/11 Commission Report*, 30–31, 40–41.

59. *9/11 Commission Report*, 41, 464–65.

60. However, Richard Clarke did write of hearing via the Secret Service, sometime after 9:45 A.M., reports of "a hostile aircraft ten minutes out," followed by "hostile aircraft eight minutes out" (*Against All Enemies*, 9, 10).

61. The same would be true of any available records still extant of CNN's interviews with Cheney and Bolten.

62. Griffin, *9/11 Commission Report: Omissions and Distortions*, 220. Many critics have seen Mineta's testimony as evidence of a stand-down order. But the order Mineta talks about is with respect to one plane only. Furthermore, because of the existence of phantom flights on that day, we cannot assume Cheney's order applies specifically to Flight 77.

63. *9/11 Commission Report*, 40.

64. *9/11 Commission Report*, 31.

65. Clarke, *Against All Enemies*, 8. Clarke's book was released on March 22, 2004, the date of his testimony before the 9/11 Commission. The commission wanted to review the book before Clarke's testimony, but the publisher did not provide copies until an agreement had been made, limiting access to three designated staff members. "The agreement specified that our executive director (Philip Zelikow) could not review the book—Clarke and Zelikow had apparently not gotten along when Zelikow worked on the NSC's transition from the Clinton administration to the Bush administration" (Kean and Hamilton, *Without Precedent*, 154–55). However, the *9/11 Commission Report*, written primarily by Zelikow, was not released until July 22, 2004. Apart from four footnote references, it did not deal with Clarke's testimony in his book.

66. *9/11 Commission Report*, 36, citing 463n190: "Patrick Gardner interview (May 12, 2004). . . . On the absence of Defense officials, see John Brunderman interview (May 17, 2004). The White House video teleconference was not connected into the area of the NMCC [National Military Command Center, or War

Room] where the crisis was being managed. . . . Moreover when the Secretary [Rumsfeld] and Vice Chairman [Myers] later [N.B.] participated in the White House video teleconference they were necessarily absent from the NMCC and unable to provide guidance to the operations team."

67. Brunderman is cited on the Air Force Web site as "Air Force mobility division chief for global reach programs" (C. Todd Lopez, "C-5 Galaxy Aircraft Engine Test Successful," http://www.af.mil/news/story.asp?storyID=123016154).

68. A later footnote in the report would seem to indicate that (as one would expect) Brunderman was instead part of the military NMCC teleconference (*9/11 Commission Report*, 463n196).

69. *9/11 Commission Report*, 37.

70. Leslie Miller, "Military Now Notified Immediately of Unusual Air Traffic Events," Associated Press Online, June 13, 2002.

71. Linda Slobodian, "Norad on Heightened Alert," *Calgary Herald*, October 13, 2001.

72. The following is taken from the U.S. National Transportation Safety Board's account of the flight: "At 0933:38 EDT (6 minutes and 20 seconds after N47BA acknowledged the previous clearance), the controller instructed N47BA to change radio frequencies and contact another Jacksonville ARTCC controller. The controller received no response from N47BA. The controller called the flight five more times over the next 4½ minutes but received no response. About 0952 CDT, a USAF F-16 test pilot from the 40th Flight Test Squadron at Eglin Air Force Base (AFB), Florida, was vectored to within 8 nm [nautical miles] of N47BA. About 0954 CDT, at a range of 2,000 feet from the accident airplane and an altitude of about 46,400 feet, the test pilot made two radio calls to N47BA but did not receive a response."

73. In fact, on that day there was one successful interception: that of a Korean airliner over Alaska that had accidentally transmitted a hijack signal (Shawn McCarthy, "PM Says U.S. Attitude Helped Fuel Sept. 11," (Toronto) *Globe and Mail*, September 12, 2002, http://www.ctv.ca/special/sept11/hubs/canadian/mccarthy01.html).

74. Colonel Robert Bowman, USAF (Ret.), "9/11 Was Treason," address delivered at the July 22–23, 2005, Emergency Truth Conference.

75. Personal communication of December 2, 2005.

76. *9/11 Commission Report*, 17, citing a JCS instruction of June 1, 2001, entitled "Aircraft Piracy (Hijacking) and Destruction of Derelict Airborne Objects"; cf. 458n101.

77. *9/11 Commission Report*, 17–18.

78. *9/11 Commission Report*, 17, citing a JCS instruction of June 1, 2001, entitled "Aircraft Piracy (Hijacking) and Destruction of Derelict Airborne Objects"; cf. 458n101.

79. Major Snyder of NORAD quoted in Glen Johnson, "Facing Terror Attack's Aftermath: Otis Fighter Jets Scrambled Too Late to Halt the Attacks," *Boston Globe* (September 15, 2001), emphasis added. Snyder's remarks can be used to rebut the claim in *Popular Mechanics* (Benjamin Chertoff, "9/11: Debunking Myths," March 2005) that the only interception in the decade before 9/11 was that of Payne Stewart's plane.

80. Miller, "Military Now Notified Immediately."

81. *9/11 Commission Report*, 42; 465n229, citing the DOD chat log.

82. *9/11 Commission Report*, 42–43; 465n230.

83. "Vice President Appears on *Meet the Press* with Tim Russert," September 16, 2001:

> **Mr. Russert:** What's the most important decision you think he made during the course of the day?
>
> **Vice. Pres. Cheney:** Well, the — I suppose the toughest decision was this question of whether or not we would intercept incoming commercial aircraft.
>
> **Mr. Russert:** And you decided?
>
> **Vice. Pres. Cheney:** We decided to do it. We'd, in effect, put a flying combat air patrol up over the city; F-16s with an AWACS, which is an airborne radar system, and tanker support so they could stay up a long time.

84. Kean and Hamilton, *Without Precedent*, 109, 161, 265–66.

85. Interview with former air controller Robin Hordon, February 25, 2007.

86. "Statement by the President: Domestic Preparedness against Weapons of Mass Destruction," White House Press Release, May 8, 2001, http://www.whitehouse.gov/news/releases/2001/05/20010508.html; Ruppert, *Crossing the Rubicon*, 333.

87. Cheney appointed retired Admiral Steve Abbot to be the executive director of his National Preparedness Review. But the *Washington Post* (Susan B. Glasser and Michael Grunwald, "Department's Mission Was Undermined From Start," December 22, 2005) reported that Abbot "did not start work until a few days before Sept. 11." Subsequently, in October, 2001, Abbot became deputy director of the Office of Homeland Security.

88. Bennett Roth, "Bush Adds Terrorism to FEMA's Task List," *Houston Chronicle*, May 9, 2001.

89. Mann, *Rise of the Vulcans*, 138–45 (Cheney); Bamford, *Pretext for War*, 70–81 (Cheney); and Bradlee, *Guts and Glory*, 132–34 (FEMA).

90. Mann, *Rise of the Vulcans*, 138.

91. The provisions of Executive Order 12656 of November 18, 1988, appear at 53 FR 47491, 3 CFR, 1988 Comp., p. 585, "Executive Order 12656—Assignment of Emergency Preparedness Responsibilities," http://www.archives.gov/federal-register/codification/executive-order/12656.html. The *Washington Post* (Gellman and Schmidt, "Shadow Government Is at Work in Secret") later claimed, wrongly, that Executive Order 12656 dealt only with "a nuclear attack." Earlier there was a similar misrepresentation of COG in the *New York Times* (Eric Schmitt, "President's Plan to Name Successors Skirted Law," November 18, 1991).

92. Clarke, *Against All Enemies*, 8–9; Mann, *Rise of the Vulcans*, 139.

93. "Floridagate, or 'Hey, What's 2.5 Million Votes between Friends?'" http://www.geocities.com/goretothecore/floridagate/. For the importance of the Miami-Dade results to the election outcome, see Peter Dale Scott, "Miami-Dade Reversal—A Cuban Terrorist Payback to Bush Family?" Pacific News Service, December 7, 2000, http://pacificnews.org/jinn/stories/6.24/001207-miami-dade.html.

94. Thompson, *Terror Timeline*, 100, citing Angus M. Thuermer Jr., "A

Working Vacation: Vice President Cheney Plans to Fish, Travel during Month-Long Valley Sojourn," *Jackson Hole News and Guide*, August 15, 2001. The response of both the president and the vice president was to leave town.

95. Mann, *Rise of the Vulcans*, 139.

96. Woodward, *Plan of Attack*, 153.

97. Frank Rich, "Thanks for the Heads-Up," *New York Times*, May 25, 2002.

13. THE *9/11 COMMISSION REPORT*'S AND CHENEY'S DECEPTIONS ABOUT 9/11

Epigraph: Schurz, *Pictorial History of America's New Possessions*, 1899.

1. *9/11 Commission Report*, 39, citing page 464n209, one of the most important pages of the report.

2. "Vice President Appears on *Meet the Press* with Tim Russert," September 16, 2001:

> Vice. Pres. Cheney: I said, "Delay your return. We don't know what's going on here, but it looks like, you know, we've been targeted." . . . And one of the things that we did later on that day were [*sic*] tied directly to guaranteeing presidential succession, and that our enemies, whoever they might be, could not decapitate the federal government and leave us leaderless in a moment of crisis.

3. "The Day That Changed America," *Newsweek*, December 31, 2001. Ironically, the same issue of *Newsweek*, as mentioned earlier, ran a much shorter story reporting that Cheney reached the PEOC before the Pentagon was hit at 9:37.

4. *9/11 Commission Report*, 40, 464n210.

5. *9/11 Commission Report*, 25.

6. U.S. Congress, House, Committee on Transportation, "Aviation Security Following the Terrorist Attacks on September 11th," Hearing, 107th Cong., 1st Sess., Statement of Jane Garvey, Administrator, Federal Aviation Administration.

7. Donnelly, "Day the FAA Stopped the World," *Time*, September 14, 2001.

8. *9/11 Commission Report*, 42–43; 465n229, citing the DOD chat log.

9. Norman Mineta, testimony before the *National Commission on Terrorist Attacks upon the United States, Second Public Hearing: Congress and Civil Aviation Security*, May 23, 2003, http://www.globalsecurity.org/security/library/congress/9-11_commission/030523-transcript.htm.

10. *9/11 Commission Report*, 29, citing an FAA memo of October 2003.

11. FAA Regulation 7210.3, http://www.faa.gov/ATpubs/FAC/Ch17/s1709.html.

12. Alan Levin, Marilyn Adams, and Blake Morrison, "Part I: Terror Attacks Brought Drastic Decision: Clear the Skies," *USA Today*, August 12, 2002, http://www.usatoday.com/news/sept11/2002-08-12-clearskies_x.htm.

13. Clarke, *Against All Enemies*, 4, 5.

14. Griffin, *9/11 Commission Report: Omissions and Distortions*, 220.

15. Donnelly, "Day the FAA Stopped the World," *Time,* September 14, 2001.

16. *9/11 Commission Report*, 34.

17. Kean and Hamilton, *Without Precedent*, 259.

18. *9/11 Commission Report*, 27, citing NEADS audio tape, and interview with Ken Nasypany. Cf. Michael Bronner, "9/11 Live: The NORAD Tapes," *Vanity Fair*, September 2006, 276. But Clarke reports hearing from General Myers about this time that "we have three F-16s from Langley over the Pentagon" (Clarke, *Against All Enemies*, 12).

19. Other war operations and exercises that day were Northern Watch, Northern Guardian, Northern Vigilance, Vigilant Guardian, and Global Guardian. Details are available at "Complete 911 Timeline: Military Exercises Up to 9/11," http:// www.cooperativeresearch.org/timeline.jsp?timeline=complete_911_timeline&before_9/11=militaryExercises: "Vigilant Guardian is described as being held annually, and is one of NORAD's four major annual exercises [GlobalSecurity.org 'Vigilant Guardian' page, 4/14/02 . . .]. However, another report says it takes place semi-annually [*Aviation Week and Space Technology*, 6/3/02]. Accounts by participants vary on whether 9/11 was the second, third, or fourth day of the exercise [Newhouse News Service, 1/25/02; *Ottawa Citizen*, 9/11/02; *Code One Magazine*, 1/02]. Vigilant Guardian is a command post exercise (CPX) and in at least some previous years was conducted in conjunction with Stratcom's Global Guardian exercise and a U.S. Space Command exercise called Apollo Guardian [Committee on Armed Services, *Exercise Program FY 1999*; GlobalSecurity.org 'Vigilant Guardian' page, 4/14/02; *Code Names*, by William M. Arkin, 2005, pp 545]. All of NORAD is participating in Vigilant Guardian on 9/11 [*Aviation Week & Space Technology*, 6/3/02]. At NEADS, most of the dozen or so staff on the operations floor have no idea what the exercise is going to entail and are ready for anything [*Utica Observer-Dispatch*, 8/5/04]. NORAD is also running a real-world operation named Operation Northern Vigilance." In addition, Clarke speaks in *Against All Enemies* (5) of a seventh war game—Vigilant Warrior. This is possibly a reference to Amalgam Warrior.

20. *9/11 Commission Report*, 458n116.

21. Rumsfeld Interview with Balz and Woodward, "America's Chaotic Road to War."

22. Scott Simmie, "The Scene at NORAD on Sept. 11: Playing Russian War Games," *Toronto Star*, December 9, 2001, quoted in Ruppert, *Crossing the Rubicon*, 339; Bronner, "9/11 Live," 268; cf. 264.

23. "Ben Sliney arrived for his first day of work as national operations manager" (Bamford, *Pretext for War*, 42); cf. Clarke, *Against All Enemies*, 5.

24. Bamford, *Pretext for War*, 65.

25. Michael Kane, "9/11 War Games—No Coincidence," http://911review .org/brad.com/batcave/WarGames.html, citing John O'Brien, "Reporting from the Rooftop, Shovel in Hand," Newhouse News, January 25, 2002, http://www .newhousenews.com/archive/story1a012802.html.

26. General Arnold on ABC News, September 11, 2002; cf. further quotations in Thompson, *Terror Timeline*, 367. The *9/11 Commission Report* claims in a footnote that the response to the hijackings "was, if anything, expedited . . . because of the scheduled exercise" (458n116).

27. William B. Scott, "Exercise Jump-Starts Response to Attacks," *Aviation Week & Space Technology*, June 3, 2002. Cf. *9/11 Commission Report*, 20: "NEADS: Is This Real-World or Exercise?"

28. Michael Kane, "Crossing the Rubicon: Simplifying the Case against Dick Cheney," http://www.911truth.org/article.php?story=20050119084227272, citing Ruppert, *Crossing the Rubicon*, 333. For the exact text of the president's order of May 8, see "Statement by the President: Domestic Preparedness against Weapons of Mass Destruction," http://www.whitehouse.gov/news/releases/2001/05/20010508.html.

29. "The Amalgam Virgo exercise of June 2001," http://www.911exposed.org/Almalgam.htm.

30. Gerry J. Gilmore, "NORAD-Sponsored Exercise Prepares for Worst-Case Scenarios," American Forces Press Service, http://www.defenselink.mil/news/Jun2002/n06042002_200206043.html.

31. Clarke, *Against All Enemies*, 4. At 9:40 A.M. the FAA Command Center was tracing ten possible hijackings (MSNBC, September 11, 2002; Thompson, *Terror Timeline*, 428).

32. *9/11 Commission Report*, 28.

33. *Aviation Week & Space Technology*, June 3, 2002, quoted in Ruppert, *Crossing the Rubicon*, 348. Cf. the New York FAA Center at 9:01–02 A.M.: "We have several situations going on here. It's escalating big, big time" (*9/11 Commission Report*, 22). According to the official timeline, at this point there were only two planes that had caused concern.

34. O'Brien, "Reporting from the Rooftop." Cf. Bronner, "9/11 Live," 285.

35. Matthew L. Wald, "F.A.A. Official Scrapped Tape of 9/11 Controllers' Statements," *New York Times*, May 6, 2004.

36. *9/11 Commission Report*, 36 and passim. By official definition the National Command Authority consists of "the U.S. President and the Secretary of Defense or their duly deputized alternates or successors" (see *MilitaryPeriscope.com* at http://www.periscope.ucg.com/terms/t0000206.html); cf. *9/11 Commission Report*, 37.

37. *9/11 Commission Report*, 36, 462n189, citing White House record, Situation Room Communications Log.

38. The report refers to Clarke's claim in his book that Bush on September 12 asked Clarke to "see if Saddam did this," along with Bush's denial of the details in Clarke's account (*9/11 Commission Report*, 334, 559n60). Other footnoted citations refer to events in 1998 and 2000 (*9/11 Commission Report*, 482n56, 484n103, 508n149). Thus the failure to cite Clarke on the crucial events of September 11 itself is all the more glaring.

39. Clarke, *Against All Enemies*, 4–17. Cf. Griffin, *9/11 Commission Report: Omissions and Distortions*, 207. Clarke's account, as well as the *9/11 Commission Report*'s, has problems. Tenet is said by Woodward to have reached his office "by 9:50," a revision of an earlier estimate, "after 9:30." See Woodward, *Bush at War*, 7; Dan Balz and Bob Woodward, "America's Chaotic Road to War," *Washington Post*, January 27, 2002. Clarke writes of seeing Tenet in his office significantly before 9:30. Rumsfeld by all other accounts was

either in a Pentagon dining room or in his office at this time, not in a teleconference room. See Donald H. Rumsfeld, testimony before the *National Commission on Terrorist Attacks upon the United States*, Eighth Public Hearing, Counterterrorism Policy, March 23, 2004, http://www.defendamerica.mil/articles/mar2004/a032304f1.html.

40. *9/11 Commission Report*, 463n199; Griffin, *9/11 Commission Report: Omissions and Distortions*, 213.

41. Clarke, *Against All Enemies*, 5.

42. *9/11 Commission Report*, 37. Although Rumsfeld was interviewed by the commission at least three times, including once under oath, the report cites instead for this claim a memo of an earlier Department of Defense interview, plus a commission interview of Undersecretary of Defense Stephen Cambone on July 8, 2004, two weeks before the release of the report. I conclude that the commission did not want to press Rumsfeld on his account of "helping put people on stretchers [for] about half an hour," a length of time that many have been doubted (Griffin, *9/11 Commission Report: Omissions and Distortions*, 217, citing Department of Defense releases of October 12 and September 15, 2001).

43. *9/11 Commission Report*, 43; Griffin, *9/11 Commission Report: Omissions and Distortions*, 218. The report sentence is not footnoted, but the context suggests that the source is a Rumsfeld interview on January 30, 2004. The *9/11 Commission Report* (43) places Rumsfeld's call with the president "shortly after 10:00" and quotes from a phone call with Cheney "at 10:39."

44. Andrew Cockburn, *Rumsfeld: His Rise, Fall, and Catastrophic Legacy* (New York: Simon & Schuster, 2007), 3–4.

45. Clarke, *Against All Enemies*, 7.

46. "Sept. 11 Scramble," ABC News, September 14, 2002 (Bohrer); Thompson, *Terror Timeline*, 399. I am prepared to believe that these times are too early and that Cheney did indeed leave his office at 9:21, at the time of the first report of a plane approaching Washington. At 9:15, Bush and Cheney discussed the statement that Bush would make at 9:30, and the consensus of all the evidence is that Cheney was still in his office when this call was made (*9/11 Commission Report*, 39, 463n204, citing the President's Daily Diary).

47. *9/11 Commission Report*, 40.

48. *9/11 Commission Report*, 40, citing White House transcript of Vice President Cheney interview with *Newsweek*, November 19, 2001; President Bush and Vice President Cheney meeting with the 9/11 Commission, April 29, 2004. This timing issue is crucial to shoot-down and other orders issued that day. Yet the *9/11 Commission Report* makes no reference to the conflict with Clarke's account, even though it heard testimony from Secretary of Transportation Mineta, that when he arrived in the PEOC "at about 9:20 A.M.," Cheney was already there and in charge. As David Griffin has pointed out in *9/11 Commission Report: Omissions and Distortions*, a videotape of Clarke's White House teleconference ought to exist, establishing who has been telling the truth about events on 9/11. The *9/11 Commission Report* does not refer to such a videotape. To justify a 9:25 starting time for the conference, it cites instead a "White House

record, Situation Room Communications Log." As Richard Nixon learned to his sorrow, it is far easier to edit a log than a tape.

49. *9/11 Commission Report*, 37. Cf. Kean and Hamilton, *Without Precedent*, 464: "Rumsfeld . . . did not get on the Air Threat Conference until 10:39 because he had been assisting Pentagon rescue efforts."

50. Woodward, *Bush at War*, 17. Cf. Balz and Woodward, "America's Chaotic Road to War": "9:32 A.M. . . . Before Cheney could respond, the agents grabbed the vice president under his arms—nearly lifting him off the ground—and propelled him down the steps into the White House basement and through a long tunnel that led to the underground bunker."

51. Woodward, *Bush at War*, 25, emphasis added.

52. *9/11 Commission Report*, 464n213.

53. Chris Davis, "Bush Visit Makes Sarasota Footnote in Disaster Story," *Sarasota Herald-Tribune*, September 16, 2001; cf. Thompson, *Terror Timeline*, 418–19.

54. "White House Chief of Staff Andy Card Discusses Bush Administration's Actions on 9/11," MSNBC, September 9, 2002; Thompson, *Terror Timeline*, 419. The mistaken information was received by Cheney from the Secret Service, before his advice to the president to stay out of Washington ("Vice President Appears on *Meet the Press* with Tim Russert," September 16, 2001).

55. BBC News, September 1, 2002; Thompson, *Terror Timeline*, 419.

56. Woodward, *Bush at War*, 16.

57. Rove quoted in ABC News, September 11, 2002; quoted in Bamford, *Pretext for War*, 63.

58. *9/11 Commission Report*, 39.

59. *9/11 Commission Report*, 40.

60. Clarke, *Against All Enemies*, 6, 17, 18: "I picked up the open line to the PEOC. I got a dial tone. . . . [After 11:45 A.M.] I picked up the open line to the Presidential Emergency Operations Center, only to find that once again it had a dial tone. When I punched the PEOC button [on another phone], the person answering the line grunted and passed the phone to [Clarke's representative] Major Fenzel. 'Who's the asshole answering the phone for you, Mike?' I asked. 'That would be the Vice-President, Dick. And he'd like you to come over.' [Later, after Clarke's arrival in the PEOC] I grabbed Mike Fenzel. 'How's it going over here?' I asked. 'It's fine,' Major Fenzel whispered, 'but I can't hear the crisis conference because Mrs. Cheney keeps turning down the volume on you so she can hear CNN . . . and the Vice President keeps hanging up the open line to you.'"

61. *9/11 Commission Report*, 37.

62. "Vice President Appears on *Meet the Press* with Tim Russert," September 16, 2001.

63. Rumsfeld, testimony before the 9/11 Commission, March 23, 2004.

64. Balz and Woodward, "America's Chaotic Road to War," interview with Rumsfeld.

65. Bamford, *Pretext for War*, 64–65.

66. Clarke, *Against All Enemies*, 8.

67. Balz and Woodward, "America's Chaotic Road to War."

68. Clarke, *Against All Enemies*, 8

69. *9/11 Commission Report*, 40, 464n213.

70. *9/11 Commission Report*, 41.

71. *9/11 Commission Report*, 40, 464n213.

72. Clarke, *Against All Enemies*, 8–9.

73. *9/11 Commission Report*, 38, citing "DOD transcript, Air Threat Conference Call, Sept. 11, 2001," emphasis added.

74. "After consulting with NEADS command, the crew commander [Marr] issued the order at 9:23: 'Okay . . . scramble Langley. Head them toward the Washington area.' . . . Radar data show the Langley fighters airborne at 9:30" (*9/11 Commission Report*, 27).

75. Clarke, *Against All Enemies*, 5, 7–8.

76. Griffin, *9/11 Commission Report: Omissions and Distortions*, 232, 252–54.

77. *9/11 Commission Report*, 40–41. The report's first post-attack phone call between Cheney and Rumsfeld is at 10:39 A.M., by which time Rumsfeld was in the NMCC (*9/11 Commission Report*, 44).

78. *9/11 Commission Report*, 464n216.

79. 9/11 Commission, Hearing of June 17, 2004, http://www.9-11commission .gov/archive/hearing12/9-11Commission_Hearing_2004-06-17.pdf.

80. Kean and Hamilton, *Without Precedent*, 260; cf. 264.

81. *9/11 Commission Report*, 463n204: "White House record, Secure Switchboard Log, Sept. 11, 2001 call [about 9:20 A.M. from Bush to FBI Director] Mueller."

82. For the two-minute "confirmation" call at 10:18, the report cites a "White House record, Secure Switchboard Log, Sept. 11, 2001" (*9/11 Commission Report*, 41 and 465n221).

83. The report's footnotes also cite a "9:15 call to Vice President" from the President's Daily Diary (*9/11 Commission Report*, 463n204). Does the President's Daily Diary contain a similar gap at the time of the shoot-down order?

84. *9/11 Commission Report*, 41.

85. Clarke, *Against All Enemies*, 8; *9/11 Commission Report*, 38.

86. *9/11 Commission Report*, 326; 555n9.

87. The *9/11 Commission Report*'s documentation includes Secret Service shift logs, plus other Secret Service logs and timelines. There are no citations of Secret Service phone logs or tapes, in marked contrast to the heavy citation of FAA and NEADS audio tapes.

88. A further possibility, that Bush and Cheney were already using an independent COG channel, seems unlikely: Clarke speaks of ordering the activation of the National Communications System more than an hour and a half later, after 12:30 P.M. (Clarke, *Against All Enemies*, 91). For the Secret Service line to the FAA, see *9/11 Commission Report*, 464n208 and 464n217; Thompson, *Terror Timeline*, 375; Clarke, *Against All Enemies*, 7: "Secret Service had a system that allowed them to see what FAA's radar was seeing." This could have been a responsibility for Ptech, which had interoperability contracts with both the FAA and Secret Service.

89. *9/11 Commission Report*, 41. Paul Thompson, citing *USA Today* (August 13, 2002), says that Chris Stephenson, head controller at Washington's Reagan

National Airport, says that about 9:30 A.M. he was notified by the Secret Service of an incoming flight just outside Washington. Others claimed that the FAA warned the Secret Service (Thompson, *Terror Timeline*, 414).

90. *9/11 Commission Report*, 40.

91. In the 1990s the Assassination Records Review Board attempted to obtain from the WHCA the unedited original tapes of conversations from Air Force One on the return trip from Dallas, November 22, 1963. (Edited and condensed versions of these tapes had been available since the 1970s from the Lyndon Baines Johnson Library in Austin, Texas.) The attempt was unsuccessful: "The Review Board's repeated written and oral inquiries of the White House Communications Agency did not bear fruit. The WHCA could not produce any records that illuminated the provenance of the edited tapes." See *Assassinations Records Review Board: Final Report*, chapter 6, Part 1, 116, http://www.archives.gov/research/jfk/review-board/report/chapter-06-part1.pdf.

92. The WHCA public affairs office, contacted several times about these issues, provided no information and suggested instead that the problems be resolved by filing an FOIA request.

93. Department of Defense, Defense Information Systems Agency, White House Communications Agency, http://www.disa.mil/main/whca.html.

94. Bamford, *Pretext for War*, 64–66; Bamford is quoting Marr's own words on ABC News, September 11, 2002. Cf. discussion in an op-ed by commission senior counsel John Farmer ("'United 93': The Real Picture," *Washington Post*, April 30, 2006). Farmer claimed that what Marr on the ABC show recalled saying was "almost completely untrue," but he offered no explanation as to why Marr would have spoken a falsehood. Farmer did not reply to my query to him about this.

95. Larry Arnold, "MG Larry Arnold on UAL Flight 93," *NavySEALs.com*, June 8, 2006, http://www.navyseals.com/community/articles/article.cfm?id=9723.

96. Wolfowitz quoted in Matthew L. Wald, "Pentagon Tracked Deadly Jet but Found No Way to Stop It," *New York Times*, September 15, 2001; Thompson, *Terror Timeline*, 494.

97. ABC News, September 11, 2001; Associated Press, September 12, 2001. The story was later denied by a *New York Times* reporter, Jere Longman, in *Among the Heroes* (New York: HarperCollins, 2002), 264. The person who took what was probably the phone call in question was not allowed to speak to the public ([London] *Mirror*, September 13, 2002; Thompson, *Terror Timeline*, 439).

98. Thompson, *Terror Timeline*, 447–49.

99. (London) *Mirror*, September 13, 2002; cf. CNN, April 19, 2002.

100. *Philadelphia Daily News*, December 28, 2001; Thompson, *Terror Timeline*, 492–93.

101. Longman, *Among the Heroes*, 264.

102. *9/11 Commission Report*, 34, 44.

103. *9/11 Commission Report*, 37. The citation is not to Clarke's book but to National Security Council Notes, the notes of Paul Kurtz. As we have seen, Clarke's account has him promulgating the shoot-down order thirty minutes earlier.

104. Senate Armed Services Committee, Hearing on Nomination of General Richard Myers to be Chairman of the Joint Chiefs of Staff, September 13, 2001.

105. See, for example, Joan Didion, "Cheney: The Fatal Touch," *New York*

Review of Books, October 5, 2006, 54: "What the Vice President was doing . . . was not cherry-picking the evidence but rejecting it, replacing it with whatever self-interested rumor better advanced his narrative line." Lewis Lapham concludes from his list of Bush-Cheney-Rumsfeld lies, falsehoods, and deceptions that "conspiracy to commit fraud would seem reason enough to warrant the President's impeachment" (Lapham, *Pretensions to Empire*, 270), citing "the legal precedent for finding a conspiracy to commit fraud [in] the Supreme Court ruling *Hammerschmidt v. United States.*"

106. Cheney quoted in Glenn Kessler and Jim VandeHei, "Misleading Assertions Cover Iraq War and Voting Records," *Washington Post*, October 6, 2004, A15.

107. Rice quoted in "Report Warned of Suicide Hijackings," CBS News, May 17, 2002.

108. Condoleezza Rice, testimony before the 9/11 Commission, April 8, 2004.

109. Al Gore, "Democracy Itself Is in Grave Danger," *CommonDreams.org*, June 24, 2004, www.commondreams.org/views04/0624-15.htm.

110. This can hardly be doubted in 2006, now that we know that Lyndon Johnson was convinced Kennedy was killed by a conspiracy, and Richard Nixon was taped saying of the Warren Report, "it was the greatest hoax that has ever been perpetuated" (Anderson, "Revelations and Gaps in Nixon Tapes," BBC, March 1, 2002) cf.

111. 9/11 Commission, Media Advisory, August 20, 2004; Kean and Hamilton, *Without Precedent*, 312: "All of our records were transferred to the National Archives, with an agreement that they would be made public at the beginning of 2009."

112. Kean and Hamilton, *Without Precedent*, 253; cf. 319. The Warren Commission, often criticized for its lack of transparency, at least made most of its supporting evidence available immediately and published a great deal of it.

113. *9/11 Commission Report*, 38; cf. Clarke, *Against All Enemies*, 8. Bamford specifies that only part of the plan was initiated on September 11 (Bamford, *Pretext for War*, 74).

114. Chardy, "Reagan Aides and the 'Secret' Government." See chapter 11 in this book.

14. CHENEY, FEDERAL EMERGENCY MANAGEMENT AGENCY, AND CONTINUITY OF GOVERNMENT

Epigraph: Eisenhower's farewell address is on the Internet at http://www.eisenhower.archives.gov/farewell.htm.

1. *9/11 Commission Report*, 38.

2. Mann, "Armageddon Plan." Hastert, next in line after Cheney to succeed the president, had previously been unaware of the program (Bamford, *Pretext for War*, 74).

3. Clarke, *Against All Enemies*, 9; cf. Mann, "Armageddon Plan"; and Mann, *Rise of the Vulcans*, 296.

4. Bamford, *Pretext for War*, 77; Steve Goldstein, 'Undisclosed Location'

Disclosed," *Boston Globe*, July 20, 2004. Congressional leaders and representatives from intelligence agencies were also briefly installed in another COG location, Mount Weather in Virginia (Bamford, *Pretext for War*, 81).

5. Barton Gellman and Susan Schmidt, "Shadow Government Is at Work in Secret," *Washington Post*, March 1, 2002.

6. Amy Goldstein and Juliet Eilperin, "Congress Not Advised of Shadow Government," *Washington Post*, March 2, 2002; cf. Thompson, *Terror Timeline*, 541. Daschle was third in line of succession to the presidency, after House Speaker Hastert.

7. Alfonso Chardy, "Reagan Aides and the 'Secret' Government," *Miami Herald*, July 5, 1987, http://www.theforbiddenknowledge.com/hardtruth/secret_white_house_plans.htm. See chapter 11 in this book.

8. David Cole and James X. Dempsey, *Terrorism & the Constitution: Sacrificing Civil Liberties in the Name of National Security* (New York: New Press, 2006); Jennifer Van Bergen, "The USA PATRIOT Act Was Planned before 9/11," May 20, 2002, http://www.truthout.org/docs_02/05.21B.jvb.usapa.911.htm.

9. Editorial, "Making Martial Law Easier," *New York Times*, February 19, 2007.

10. James Risen and Eric Lichtblau, "Bush Secretly Lifted Some Limits on Spying in U.S. after 9/11, Officials Say," *New York Times*, December 15, 2005.

11. Richard W. Stevenson and Adam Liptak, "Cheney Defends Eavesdropping Without Warrants," *New York Times*, December 21, 2005.

12. *Iran-Contra Affair*. The volume includes Cheney's lengthy minority report, which no Republican senators signed.

13. Charlie Savage, "Cheney Aide Is Screening Legislation," *Boston Globe*, May 28, 2006.

14. Chitra Ragavan, "Cheney's Guy," *U.S. News and World Report*, May 29, 2006, http://www.usnews.com/usnews/news/articles/060529/29addington.htm.

15. On June 4, 2006, William Arkin reported in the *Washington Post* that "on Monday, June 19, about 4,000 government workers representing more than 50 federal agencies from the State Department to the Commodity Futures Trading Commission will . . . set off for dozens of classified emergency facilities . . . in an 'evacuation' that my sources describe as the largest 'continuity of government' exercise ever conducted."

16. Nina Bernstein, "Held in 9/11 Net, Muslims Return to Accuse U.S.," *New York Times*, January 23, 2006.

17. Bernstein, "Held in 9/11 Net," *New York Times*, January 23, 2006.

18. Jonathan Turley, "Camps for Citizens: Ashcroft's Hellish Vision," *Los Angeles Times*, August 14, 2002, http://www.commondreams.org/views02/0814-05.htm. Cf. Anita Ramasastry, "Do Hamdi and Padilla Need Company? Why Attorney General Ashcroft's Plan to Create Internment Camps for Supposed Citizen Combatants Is Shocking and Wrong," *FindLaw.com*, August 21, 2002, http://writ.news.findlaw.com/ramasastry/20020821.html.

19. Peter Dale Scott, "Homeland Security Contracts for Vast New Detention Camps," Pacific News Service, January 31, 2006, http://news.pacificnews.org/news/view_article.html?article_id=eed74d9d44c30493706fe03f4c9b3a77.

20. Peter Dale Scott, "Ten-Year U.S. Strategic Plan for Detention Camps

Revives Proposals from Oliver North," Pacific News Service, February 21, 2006; cf. U.S. Immigration and Customs Enforcement (ICE), "ENDGAME: Office of Detention and Removal Strategic Plan, 2003–2012—Detention and Removal Strategy for a Secure Homeland," http://www.ice.gov/graphics/dro/endgame.pdf. (Note: As of this writing, the Endgame strategic plan is no longer posted on a government Web site, but it can still be read online at http://gothinkblog.com/gblog/wp-content/uploads/2006/03/endgame.pdf.)

21. Vankin and Whalen, *80 Greatest Conspiracies of All Time*, 30. Before North's ambitious exercise there was also James McCord's plan for the preventive detention of civilian "security risks," who would be placed in military "camps" (Hougan, *Secret Agenda*, 16).

22. Chardy, "Reagan Aides," *Miami Herald*, July 5, 1987.

23. Chardy, "Reagan Aides," *Miami Herald*, July 5, 1987.

24. John R. Brinkerhoff, "Restore the Militia for Homeland Security," ANSER Institute for Homeland Security, November 12, 2001; Brinkerhoff, "The Posse Comitatus Act and Homeland Security," *Journal of Homeland Security* (February 2002), http://www.homelandsecurity.org/journal/Articles/brinkerhoff possecomitatus.htm. Cf. Ritt Goldstein, "Foundations Are in Place for Martial Law in the U.S.," *Sydney Morning Herald*, July 27, 2002, http://www.smh.com.au/articles/2002/07/27/1027497418339.html.

25. Rumsfeld, quoted in Jim Garamone, "U.S. Northern Command to Debut in October," American Forces Press Service, April 17, 2002, http://www.defense link.mil/news/Apr2002/n04172002_200204175.html.

26. U.S. Department of Defense, "U.S. Northern Command," http://www.globalsecurity.org/military/agency/dod/northcom.htm.

27. Brinkerhoff, PBS, Online Newshour, September 27, 2002.

28. FEMA memo cited in Sam Smith, "Mind Wars: 'X-Files' Gets It Right," *Progressive Review*, June 1998.

29. From Spencer S. Hsu, Joby Warrick, and Rob Stein, "Documents Highlight Bush-Blanco Standoff," *Washington Post*, December 5, 2005: "Thus began what one aide called a 'full-court press' to compel the first-term governor to yield control of her state National Guard—a legal, political and personal campaign by White House staff that failed three days later when Blanco rejected the administration's terms, 10 minutes before Bush was to announce them in a Rose Garden news conference, the governor's aides said."

30. Statement of Senator Patrick Leahy on Legislation to Repeal Changes to the Insurrection Act (S. 513), February 7, 2007, http://leahy.senate.gov/press/200702/020707.html.

31. William M. Arkin, "Today in D.C.: Commandos in the Streets?" *Early Warning* (*Washington Post* blog), http://blog.washingtonpost.com/earlywarning/2005/09/today_in_dc_commandos_in_the_s.html. Compare Arkin's revelations about Power Geyser, "a small group of super-secret commandos . . . ready with state-of-the-art weaponry to swing into action to protect the presidency" (Eric Schmitt, "Commandos Get Duty on U.S. Soil," *New York Times*, January 23, 2005).

32. Ted Bridis, "U.S. Concludes 'Cyber Storm' Mock Attacks," Associated Press, February 10, 2006.

33. Nat Parry, "Bush's Mysterious 'New Programs,'" *ConsortiumNews.com*, http://www.consortiumnews.com/2006/022106a.html.

34. Ben Shapiro, "Should We Prosecute Sedition?" *Townhall.com*, http:// www.townhall.com/columnists/BenShapiro/2006/02/15/should_we_prosecute _sedition.

35. Sebastian Haffner, *Defying Hitler: A Memoir*, translated by Oliver Pretzel (London: Weidenfeld and Nicolson, 2002), 114.

36. Franz Neumann, *Behemoth: The Structure and Practice of National Socialism, 1933–1944* (Oxford: Oxford University Press, 1944), 459.

37. Ernst Fraenkel, *The Dual State: A Contribution to the Theory of Dictatorship*, translated by E. A. Shils et al. (New York: Oxford University Press, 1941), xiii.

38. Hans J. Morgenthau, *Politics in the Twentieth Century*, volume 1, *The Decline of Democratic Politics* (Chicago: University of Chicago Press, 1962), 400. (This article, "The Corruption of Patriotism," was first published in 1955 in the *New Republic* and in the *Bulletin of the Atomic Scientists*.) Morgenthau rightly did not attribute the Security Bureau's power to the overworld, but to the demagogy of the "Senator and his friends in Congress." But today we can see more clearly how McCarthyism as a phenomenon first began inside the Office of Strategic Services and was originally encouraged by Wall Street Republicans, who were determined to cleanse America's bureaucracies of the last remnants of Roosevelt's New Deal.

39. Ola Tunander, "The Use of Terrorism to Construct World Order," paper to be presented at the Fifth Pan-European International Relations Conference, Netherlands Congress Centre, The Hague, 9-11 September 2004, http://www.sgir .org/conference2004/papers/Tunander%20-%20Securitization,%20dual% 20state%20and%20US-European%20geopolitical%20divide.pdf; quoting Bush, BBC News, 2/8/04; and citing Jules Lobel, "Emergency Power and Decline of Liberalism," *Yale Law Journal* 8 (1981): 1385-1433. See also Ola Tunander, "Democratic State versus Deep State: Approaching the Dual State of the West," in *Government of the Shadows: Parapolitics and Criminal Sovereignty*, edited by Eric Wilson and Tim Lindsey (London: Pluto Press, 2008).

40. Other large organizations besides the dual state (including the European Union) exhibit the same tension between top-down and bottom-up power. In the American Roman Catholic Church, for example, the episcopal hierarchy, representing local community interests, has at times found itself opposed by top-down organizations, like the Knights of Malta and Opus Dei, that like the deep state operate in secrecy and represent overworld interests. See Lernoux, *People of God*, 200–4, 283–346. It is possible that a similar tension could be traced in the postwar American and Italian Communist Parties.

15. CONCLUSION: 9/11
AND THE FUTURE OF AMERICA

Epigraphs: The Jefferson quotation is from Richard Hofstader's *The American Political Tradition and the Men Who Made It* (New York: Vintage, 1967), 33. The

Lincoln quotation is from the White House Web site, http://www.whitehouse
.gov/history/presidents/al16.html. The Gandhi quotation is from Mahatma Gandhi, *Selected Works*, edited by Shriman Narayan (Ahmedabad: Navajivan, 1968),
vol. 2, 389, quoted in Schell, *Unconquerable World*, 206.

1. *9/11 Commission Report*, 228–29.

2. Joseph S. Nye Jr., *The Paradox of American Power: Why the World's Only
Superpower Can't Go It Alone* (Oxford: Oxford University Press, 2002), 9.

3. Johnson, *Sorrows of Empire*, 312. In his sequel *Nemesis* (p. 9), while still
hopeful for change, Johnson wrote darkly that "our political system may no
longer be capable of saving the United States as we know it, since it is hard to
imagine any president or Congress standing up to the powerful vested interests of
the Pentagon, the secret intelligence agencies, and the military-industrial complex
[i.e., the vested interests of the deep state]. Given that 40 percent of the defense
budget is now secret as is every intelligence agency budget, it is impossible for
Congress to provide effective oversight even if its members wanted to."

4. John Adams is usually thought of as a canny revolutionary but a bad president because of his stubborn refusal to indulge in the rabble-rousing party politics that brought Thomas Jefferson to power. My prayer for this country is that
someday party politics will become less central to American politics, and Adams's
distaste for them will be judged more favorably.

5. These periodical searches for American renewal have thus far mostly been
accompanied by waves of renewed interest in the Founding Fathers as sources of
inspiration. As American historian Garry Wills has observed, "Such piety has, of
course, prompted revisionist attempts to bring the idols back down to our level,
but they float magically back up again" (Wills, *Henry Adams and the Making of
America*, 396).

6. Hearst's choice for Hearst Corporation president Richard Berlin was in fact
a manipulator behind the McCarthy phenomenon (Carey McWilliams, "Double
Exposure: Woltman on McCarthy," *Nation*, July 31, 1954).

7. By 2006 the Iraq War had become roughly as unpopular as the Vietnam
war was in the late 1960s, but American protesters were not marching in equal
numbers. Perhaps those who didn't march were thinking back to what followed
the violent antiwar protests at the Democratic Convention in 1968: five Republican presidencies, plus two more Democratic presidencies in which the defense
budget also continued to rise. What is needed is an antiwar strategy that will persuade America, not alienate it.

8. See Mann, *Rise of the Vulcans*, 26, quoting from Leo Strauss, *What Is
Political Philosophy?* (Westport, Conn.: Greenwood Press, 1959, 1973), 41.

9. Robert Alter, review of *Reading Leo Strauss: Politics, Philosophy, Judaism*,
by Steven B. Smith, *New York Times Book Review*, June 25, 2006.

10. Bill Moyers, Moyers on America, *The Net @ Risk*, PBS, aired in October
2006, http://www.pbs.org/moyers/moyersonamerica/print/netatrisk_transcript
_print.html.

11. See also Eric Klinenberg, *Fighting for Air: The Battle to Control America's
Media* (New York: Metropolitan Books, 2007).

12. There are other recent examples of tyranny that was ended by sustained
popular resistance. I was marginally involved in the liberation of East Timor

from Indonesia in 2001. I have chosen not to foreground this example because (like the overthrow of the Marcos regime in the Philippines) popular resistance received significant help from other quarters. Nonetheless, this event can be adduced as evidence that nonviolence can result in revolutionary transfers of power. (Although the resistance movement Fretilin in East Timor was not nonviolent in principle, the worldwide movement in support of it was.) I still think of the self-described "political realist" who assured me, only three years before the Indonesian withdrawal from East Timor, that "you guys will never get what you're hoping for." Violence, however, has fewer and fewer successful examples of social change to show for itself.

13. These countercurrents include the sophisticated Jim Crow tactics of segregation and disenfranchisement to deny African Americans the vote, which many believe cost the Democrats the 2000 and 2004 elections. See Palast, *Armed Madhouse*.

14. Solidarity in particular was a powerful answer to the realpolitik of Stalin's famous question "How many divisions has the Pope got?"

15. I make the case for this inevitability in Peter Dale Scott, "Why the U.S. Must Withdraw from Iraq," *Salon*, October 28, 2004, http://dir.salon.com/story/opinion/feature/2004/10/28/overstretch/index.html.

16. Michnik, *The Church and the Left*. For the American South, see David L. Chappell, *A Stone of Hope: Prophetic Religion and the Death of Jim Crow* (Chapel Hill: University of North Carolina Press, 2005); Charles Marsh, *The Beloved Community: How Faith Shapes Social Justice, from the Civil Rights Movements to Today* (New York: Basic Books, 2005).

17. Cedric B. Cowing, *The Great Awakening and the American Revolution: Colonial Thought in the 18th Century* (New York: Rand McNally, 1971).

18. Peter Dale Scott, "Milosz and Solidarity," *Brick* 78 (fall 2006): 67–74.

19. Phillips, *American Theocracy*, ix, 99, 221–22, 375. Phillips supports his case with a telling remark from the historian Michael Grant, but Grant attributed the collapse of Rome not to religion, or even religious excess, but to persecution of religion, which from a religious perspective is something quite different (Phillips, *American Theocracy*, 221, citing Grant, *The Fall of the Roman Empire* [New York: Collier Books, 1990], 171). Similarly his two citations from Charles Freeman's *Closing of the Western Mind* appear to make Freeman see "faith" as an enemy to logic, whereas Freeman's compelling argument was that the problem was not faith, but imperial meddling with and persecution of it (Phillips, *American Theocracy*, 226, 228; cf. Freeman, *The Closing of the Western Mind* [New York: Vintage Books, 2002], 178–201).

20. See, for example, Adam Hochschild, *Bury the Chains: Prophets, and Rebels in the Fight to Free an Empire's Slaves* (Boston : Houghton Mifflin, 2005); Geoff A. Oddie, *Social Protest in India: British Protestant Missionaries and Social Reforms, 1850–1900* (New Delhi: Manohar Publications, 1978).

21. Phillips, *American Theocracy*, 375.

22. Phillips's passing references to what he calls the "American Disenlightenment," or dialectic of enlightenment (*American Theocracy*, 217), raise profound issues that go beyond both his book and my own. I have tried to grapple with them in my poem *Minding the Darkness*.

23. Daniel Singer, *Whose Millennium: Theirs or Ours?* (New York: Monthly Review Press, 1999), introduction, http://www.monthlyreview.org/millen.htm. His statistics about wealth are taken from the 1998 *Human Development Report* (New York: Oxford University Press), which put the wealth of the 225 richest people in 1997 at more than $1 trillion, nearly equaling the annual income of 47 percent of the world's poorest people.

24. Singer, *Whose Millennium*, Introduction, emphasis in original.

25. Noreena Hertz, *The Silent Takeover: Global Capitalism and the Death of Democracy* (New York: Free Press, 2001), 209, 210.

26. Hertz, *Takeover*, 208.

27. Chalmers Johnson, in interview, "Militarism and Imperialism in the United States," *Critical Asian Studies* 35, no. 2 (2003): 303.

28. Bill Moyers, "This Is Your Story—The Progressive Story of America. Pass It On," *CommonDreams.org*, http://www.commondreams.org/views03/0610-11 .htm.

29. Gore Vidal, "State of the Union, 2004," *Nation*, September 13, 2004, http://www.thenation.com/doc/20040913/vidal.

30. It was in this spirit that in 1987 I spent six months at a think tank in Washington, researching and writing in support of the so-called Kerry Committee's investigation of allegations linking the Contras and their supporters to drug trafficking. See Scott and Marshall, *Cocaine Politics*.

31. Howard Dean, thanks largely to MoveOn.org, briefly emerged as the leading Democratic candidate in 2003. At one point even he characterized his foreign policy differences from Bush as being "all about nuance" (David E. Sanger and Jody Wilgoren, "Dean Strives for a Nuanced Approach to Foreign Policy," *New York Times*, December 14, 2003).

32. Polish Solidarity is greatly admired today in America but much less understood. The historian John Lewis Gaddis attributes Solidarity to the leadership of Pope John Paul and Lech Walesa, without mentioning intellectuals like Adam Michnik (Gaddis, *Cold War*, 218–22). The intellectual Jonathan Schell offers an inspiring and appreciative discussion of Solidarity, in which there are fifteen page references to the Polish writer Adam Michnik, but none to either Lech Walesa or Pope John Paul (Schell, *Unconquerable World*, 191–95, 201–5, and passim). Schell's intellectual bias underlies his statement—extraordinary, if he has Solidarity in mind—that "the Eastern Europeans demonstrated that revolution without violence did not have to depend on religious faith" (201). Clearly this was true of many individuals. But one can hardly reach this conclusion about Solidarity if one has read what many consider to be Michnik's most important book and proposition, *Church-Left Dialogue* (translated as *The Church and the Left*). I had hoped in this book to say more about Michnik's case that the left must learn to work with a difficult and sometimes reactionary Church. The subject is too important; it must await treatment elsewhere.

33. Adam Michnik, "The Montesinos Virus," *Social Research* (winter 2001), http://findarticles.com/p/articles/mi_m2267/is_4_68/ai_83144752. If this was possible in Poland, which at the time was becoming more and more a police state, surely it should be possible in America.

34. John Adams, *The Works of John Adams* (Boston: Little, Brown, 1956),

volume 10, 85, quoted in Schell, *Unconquerable World*, 160. Schell also quotes on the same page from page 180 of the Adams volume: "The revolution was in the mind of the people, and in the union of the colonies, both of which were accomplished before the hostilities commenced."

35. John Stuart Mill, "Considerations on Representative Government" in *Utilitarianism* (London: J. M. Dent, 1972), 196–97, quoted in Schell, *Unconquerable World*, 229–30, emphasis in original. Cf. Acts 7:59, 8:1.

36. Jorge Castañeda, *The Mexican Shock: Its Meaning for the United States* (New York: New Press, 1995), 221.

37. Greider, *Soul of Capitalism*.

38. Cf. Jeffrey D. Sachs in "A Better Use for Our $87b," *Boston Globe*, September 12, 2003: "The world is out of kilter when President Bush asks for $87 billion for Iraq and only $200 million for the Global Fund to Fight AIDS, tuberculosis, and malaria. The administration displays profound confusion regarding national security as well as moral purpose. It is ready to pump tens of billions of dollars into a middle-income oil-rich country of 24 million people, while utterly neglecting 500 million impoverished Africans, 10 million of whom will actually die this year of extreme poverty, too poor to buy the drugs, bed nets, fertilizers, tube wells, and other basic contrivances that could keep them alive."

39. "Experts Fears 'Endless' Terror War," MSNBC, July 9, 2005, http://www.msnbc.msn.com/id/8524679. Peter Bergen agrees: "Many jihadists are so happy that the Bush administration invaded Iraq. Without the Iraq war, their movement—under assault from without and riven from within—would have imploded a year or so after Sept. 11" (Bergen, "The Jihadists Export Their Rage to Book Pages and Web Pages," *Washington Post*, September 11, 2005). So does Richard Clarke (*Against All Enemies*, 246): "Nothing America could have done would have provided al Qaeda and its new generation of cloned groups a better recruitment device than our unprovoked invasion of an oil-rich Arab country."

40. Scott, "Why the U.S. Must Withdraw from Iraq."

41. Armstrong, *Battle for God*, 137–39; Phillips, *American Theocracy*, 252–54.

42. Burke, *Al-Qaeda*, 29. Cf. Ladan Boroumand and Roya Boroumand, "Terror, Islam, and Democracy," *Journal of Democracy* 13, no. 2 (2002): 5–20, n29: "Bin Laden's declaration of jihad mentions Ibn Taymiyya's authority and yet clearly contradicts the latter's ideas on jihad. Ibn Taymiyya explicitly forbids the murder of civilians and submits jihad to strict rules and regulations. See Henri Laoust, *Le traité de droit public d'Ibn Taimiya* (annotated translation of *Siyasa shar'iya*)" (Beirut: Institut Français de Damas, 1948), 122–35.

43. I myself was denounced as such an ally: "Berkeley Professor Peter Dale Scott telephonically imparted to [a class of] students, 'what goes around comes around' and defended the terrorists by proclaiming, 'they aren't cowards, if nothing else, it surely isn't cowardly to ride the plane in for something you believe'" (Dan Flynn, "Terrorists Find Allies on Campus," *Academia.org*, October 5, 2001, http://www.academia.org/news/terrorists.html). Although the thrust of my remarks was wildly misrepresented, the cherry-picked text was for the most part

accurate. At the time I suspected that someone had attended the class with a tape recorder; we had not yet learned about Bush's authorization of warrantless wiretaps. To wiretap ordinary nonviolent people and then leak selected results to right-wing hate media was an old trick of FBI director J. Edgar Hoover in the Cointelpro era of the 1960s.

44. [Michael Scheuer], *Imperial Hubris: Why the West Is Losing the War on Terror* (Washington, D.C.: Brassey's, 2004), 85. Some of the best left-wing books critical of America's dalliance with jihadis betray a similar secularist repugnance for Islam in general.

45. [Michael Scheuer], *Imperial Hubris*, 228, quoting Clyde Prestowitz, "Why Don't We Listen Anymore?" *Washington Post*, July 7, 2002.

46. Samuel P. Huntington, *The Clash of Civilizations and the Remaking of World Order* (New York: Simon and Schuster, 1996). From 1989 to 1999, Huntington and his John M. Olin Institute for Strategic Studies at Harvard received a total of $4,719,832 from the John M. Olin Foundation, a right-wing think tank established by a chemicals and munitions business (Center for Media & Democracy, "John M. Olin Institute for Strategic Studies," http://www.sourcewatch .org/index.php?title=John_M._Olin_Institute_for_Strategic_Studies). However, the inventor of the phrase "clash of civilizations" is said to be Islamic historian Bernard Lewis (Dreyfuss, *Devil's Game*, 332).

47. *Daily Telegraph* (London), March 7, 2001; Thomas Joscelyn, "The Pope of Terrorism," *Weekly Standard*, July 25, 2005; Dan Darling, "Why the West Should Never Kowtow to al Qaeda's Demands on Darfur," *Weekly Standard*, April 25, 2006.

48. Jane Perlez, "In the Sudan: For This Islamic Tactician, Battle with U.S. Has Begun," *New York Times*, August 24, 1998.

49. Burke, *Al-Qaeda*, 145.

50. Burke, *Al-Qaeda*, 155–56.

51. Fawaz A. Gerges, "Is Political Islam on the March?" *Christian Science Monitor*, June 6, 2006.

52. AFP (Agence France-Presse), "Sudan Arrests More Partisans of Top Islamist," *New York Times*, February 23, 2001.

53. Sean Maguire and Andrew Marshall, "Pressure Sudan and It Will Bow on Darfur–Turabi," *San Diego Union Tribune* [Reuters], March 5, 2007.

54. Muriel Mirak-Weissbach, "Sudanese Leaders Deal with the Issues," *Executive Intelligence Review* (1994), http://www.aboutsudan.com/interviews/hassan _al_turabi.htm. Al-Turabi's remarks were made at a 1994 Inter-Religious Dialogue conference organized by the Schiller Institute. See also Mohamed Elhachmi Hamdi, *The Making of an Islamic Political Leader: Conversations with Hasan al-Turabi* (Boulder, Colo.: Westview, 1998).

55. Hamdi, *Making of an Islamic Political Leader*, 74. On March 31, 2004, the Sudanese government arrested al-Turabi again and accused him of supporting the rebels in the Darfur area to the west of Sudan ("Inter-Sudanese Peace Negotiations in Kenya Extended; Turabi Detained, Accused of Supporting Darfour's Rebels," *ArabicNews.com*, April 1, 2004, http://www.arabicnews.com/ansub/ Daily/Day/040401/2004040110.html).

56. David Greenberg, "Dallas through the Looking Glass," *Slate*, November

20, 2003, http://www.slate.com/id/2091462/. The AIB's leader, former Students for a Democratic Society president Carl Oglesby, was no longer a student, but most of his younger followers were.

57. Goodman with Goodman, *Exception to the Rulers*, 295–99: "During the 'Battle of Seattle,' there were more hits on the brand-new Web site indymedia.org than on cnn.com. . . . IMCs [independent media centers] are cropping up all the time, all over the world. Today there are more than a hundred IMCs across the globe. . . . This media and democracy movement is a budding revolution. It is a bold new grassroots media for a new millennium of resistance" (298–99).

58. Bill Weinberg, "Farewell, Gary Webb," *WorldWar 4 Report*, November 17, 2001, http://www.WW4Report.com; Robert Parry, "America's Debt to Journalist Gary Webb," *ConsortiumNews.com*, http://www.consortiumnews.com/2004/121304.html.

59. Goodman with Goodman, *Exception to the Rulers*, 152–57, has an excellent chapter on spin and censorship in the corporate media with respect to Iraq. Cf. Michael Massing, "Now They Tell Us: The American Press and Iraq," *New York Review of Books*, February 26, 2004.

60. One can contrast this movement with the frustrations in 2000 of reporter Greg Palast, an American who could only tell his important stories about Florida voting improprieties in the British press. See Palast, *Best Democracy Money Can Buy*.

61. Shaun Waterman, "Tenet Calls for Internet Security," *Washington Times*, December 2, 2004.

62. Nafeez Mosaddeq Ahmed (England), *The War on Freedom* (Joshua Tree, Calif.: Media Messenger Books, 2002); Thierry Meyssan (France), *L'Effroyable Imposture* (Chatou, France: Éditions Carnot, 2002, translated into twenty-eight languages); Andreas von Bülow (Germany), *Die CIA und der 11.September: Internationaler Terror und die Rolle der Geheimsdientse* (Munich: Piper Verlag, 2003); Pilar Urbano (Spain), *Jefe Atta* (Madrid: Plaza y Janes, 2003) and others.

GLOSSARY OF OPEN POLITICS

1. Scott, *War Conspiracy*, 171; cf. Scott, *Deep Politics and the Death of JFK*, 6–8; and Scott, *Drugs, Oil, and War*, xx.

2. See Robert Cribb and Peter Dale Scott, "Introduction," in *Government of the Shadows: Parapolitics and Criminal Sovereignty*, edited by Eric Wilson and Tim Lindsey (London: Pluto Press, 2007).

3. Gandhi is quoted in Schell, *Unconquerable World*, 226.

4. Schell, *Unconquerable World*, 227.

5. Joseph S. Nye Jr., *The Paradox of American Power: Why the World's Only Superpower Can't Go It Alone* (New York: Oxford University Press, 2002), 9.

Bibliography

ARTICLES

Balz, Dan, and Bob Woodward. "America's Chaotic Road to War." *Washington Post*, January 27, 2002, http://www.washingtonpost.com/ac2/wp-dyn/A42754-2002Jan26.

Bronner, Michael. "9/11 Live: The NORAD Tapes: Politics & Power." *Vanity Fair*, August 2006.

Chardy, Alfonso. "Reagan Aides and the 'Secret' Government." *Miami Herald*, July 5, 1987, http://www.theforbiddenknowledge.com/hardtruth/secret_white_house_plans.htm.

Curtiss, Richard H. "Reprise of the October Surprise: Is the Worst Surprise Still to Come?" *Washington Report on Middle East Affairs* (May–June 1991).

Daugherty, William J. "Behind the Intelligence Failure in Iran." *International Journal of Intelligence and Counterintelligence* 14, no. 4 (winter 2001–2002): 449–84.

Gellman, Barton, and Susan Schmidt. "Shadow Government Is at Work in Secret." *Washington Post*, March 1, 2002.

Looney, Robert. "From Petrodollars to Petroeuros: Are the Dollar's Days as an International Reserve Currency Drawing to an End?" *Center for Contemporary Conflict* 3 (November 2003).

Marshall, Andrew. "Terror 'Blowback' Burns CIA." *Independent*, November 1, 1998.

Moss, Robert. "Who's Meddling in Iran?" *New Republic*, December 2, 1978.

Ridenhour, Ron, with Arthur Lubow. "Bringing the War Home." *New Times*, November 28, 1975.

Rowse, Arthur E. "Gladio: The Secret U.S. War to Subvert Italian Democracy." *Covert Action Quarterly* 49 (summer 1994).

Teacher, David. "The Pinay Circle and Destabilisation in Europe." *Lobster* 18 (October 1989).

Tunander, Ola. "The Use of Terrorism to Construct World Order." Paper to be presented at the Fifth Pan-European International Relations Conference, Netherlands Congress Centre, The Hague, September 9–11, 2004, http:// www.sgir.org/conference2004/papers/Tunander%20-%20Securitization,% 20dual%20state%20and%20US-European%20geopolitical%20divide.pdf.

Williams, Lance, and Erin McCormick. "Al Qaeda Terrorist Worked with FBI." *San Francisco Chronicle*, November 4, 2001.

Wright, Lawrence. "The Man behind Bin Laden." *New Yorker*, September 16, 2002.

BOOKS

Aburish, Saïd K. *A Brutal Friendship: The West and the Arab Elite*. London: Indigo, 1998.

———. *The Rise, Corruption, and Coming Fall of the House of Saud*. New York: St. Martin's Press, 1995.

Abuza, Zachary. *Militant Islam in Southeast Asia: Crucible of Terror*. Boulder, Colo.: Lynne Rienner Publishers, 2003.

Adams, James Ring, and Douglas Frantz. *A Full Service Bank: How BCCI Stole Billions around the World*. New York: Pocket Books, 1992.

Ahmad, Muntaz. "Islamic Fundamentalism in South Asia: The Jamaat-i-Islami and the Tablighi Jamaat of South Asia." In *Fundamentalisms Observed*, edited by Martin E. Marty and R. Scott Appleby. Chicago: University of Chicago Press, 1991.

Ahmed, Nafeez Mosaddeq. *The London Bombings: An Independent Inquiry*. London: Gerald Duckworth, 2006.

———. *The War on Truth: 9/11, Disinformation, and the Anatomy of Terrorism*. Northampton, Mass.: Olive Branch Press, 2005.

Bacevich, Andrew J. *American Empire: The Realities and Consequences of U.S. Diplomacy*. Cambridge: Harvard University Press, 2003.

———. *The New American Militarism: How Americans Are Seduced by War*. New York: Oxford University Press, 2005.

Baer, Robert. *Sleeping with the Devil: How Washington Sold Our Soul for Saudi Crude*. New York: Crown, 2003.

Bamford, James. *Body of Secrets*. New York: Doubleday, 2001.

———. *A Pretext for War: 9/11, Iraq, and the Abuse of America's Intelligence Agencies*. New York: Doubleday, 2004.

Barnet, Richard J. *The Roots of War*. New York: Viking Press, 1973.

Barrett, Laurence I. *Gambling with History: Ronald Reagan in the White House*. Garden City, N.Y.: Doubleday, 1983.

Beaty, Jonathan, and S. C. Gwynne. *The Outlaw Bank: A Wild Ride into the Secret Heart of BCCI*. New York: Random House, 1993.

Beckwith, Charles A., and Donald Knox. *Delta Force: The Army's Elite Counterterrorist Unit*. New York: Avon, 2000.

Ben-Menashe, Ari. *Profits of War*. New York: Sheridan Square Press, 1992.

Bergen, Peter L. *Holy War, Inc.: Inside the Secret World of Osama bin Laden*. New York: Free Press, 2001.

Berger, J. M., ed. *Ali Mohamed: An Intelwire Sourcebook*. Intelwire Press, 2006.

Bill, James A. *The Eagle and the Lion: The Tragedy of American-Iranian Relations*. New Haven, Conn.: Yale University Press, 1988.

Bird, Kai. *The Chairman: John J. McCloy, the Making of the American Establishment*. New York: Simon and Schuster, 1992.

Block, Alan A., and Constance A. Weaver. *All Is Clouded by Desire: Global Banking, Money Laundering, and International Organized Crime*. Westport, Conn.: Praeger, 2004.

Blum, William. *Killing Hope: U.S. Military and CIA Interventions since World War II*. Monroe, Maine: Common Courage Press, 1995.

Blumenthal, Sidney. *The Rise of the Counter-Establishment*. New York: Times Books, 1986.

Bodansky, Yossef. *Bin Laden: The Man Who Declared War on America*. Roseville, Calif.: Prima, 2001.

Boies, John L. *Buying for Armageddon: Business, Society, and Military Spending since the Cuban Missile Crisis*. New Brunswick, N.J.: Rutgers University Press, 1994.

Boland, B. J. *The Struggle of Islam in Modern Indonesia*. The Hague: Nijhoff, 1982.

Brenner, Robert. *The Boom and the Bubble: The U.S. in the World Economy*. New York: Verso, 2002.

Brisard, Jean-Charles, and Guillaume Dasquié. *Forbidden Truth: U.S.-Taliban Secret Diplomacy and the Failed Hunt for Bin Laden*. New York: Thunder's Mouth Press/Nation Books, 2002.

Brock, David. *The Republican Noise Machine: Right-Wing Media and How It Corrupts Democracy*. New York: Crown, 2004.

Brown, Anthony Cave. *The Last Hero: Wild Bill Donovan*. New York: Times Books, 1982.

Brzezinski, Zbigniew. *The Choice: Global Domination or Global Leadership*. New York: Basic Books, 2004.

———. *The Grand Chessboard: American Primacy and Its Geostrategic Imperatives*. New York: Basic Books, 1997.

———. *Power and Principle: Memoirs of the National Security Advisor, 1977–1981*. New York: Farrar, Straus, and Giroux, 1983.

Burke, Jason. *Al-Qaeda: The True Story of Radical Islam*. London: I. B. Tauris, 2004.

Buruma, Ian, and Avishai Margalit. *Occidentalism: The West in the Eyes of Its Enemies*. New York: Penguin, 2004.

Byman, Daniel. *Deadly Connections: States That Sponsor Terrorism*. New York: Cambridge University Press, 2005.

Cahn, Anne H. *Killing Détente: The Right Attacks the CIA*. University Park: Pennsylvania State University Press, 1998.

Calvi, Fabrizio, and Frédéric Laurent. *France États-Unis: Cinquante ans de coups tordus*. Paris: Albin Michel, 2004.

————. *Piazza Fontana: La Verità su una Strage.* Milan: Mondadori, 1997.

Carroll, James. *House of War: The Pentagon and the Disastrous Rise of American Power.* Boston: Houghton Mifflin, 2006.

Cashill, Jack, and James Sanders. *First Strike: TWA Flight 800 and the Attack on America.* Nashville, Tenn.: Thomas Nelson, Inc., 2003.

Chatterjee, Pratap. *Iraq, Inc.: A Profitable Occupation.* New York: Seven Stories, 2004.

Chomsky, Noam. *American Power and the New Mandarins.* New York: Vintage Books, 1969.

Chua, Amy. *World on Fire: How Exporting Free Market Democracy Breeds Ethnic Hatred and Global Instability.* New York: Doubleday, 2003.

Churchill, Ward, and Jim Vander Wall. *Agents of Repression: The FBI's Wars against the Black Panther Party and the American Indian Movement.* Boston: South End Press, 1990.

Clark, William R. *Petrodollar Warfare: Oil, Iraq, and the Future of the Dollar.* Gabriola Island, B.C.: New Society, 2005.

Clarke, Jonathan, and Stefan Harper. *America Alone: The Neo-conservatives and Global Order.* Cambridge: Cambridge University Press, 2004.

Clarke, Richard A. *Against All Enemies: Inside America's War on Terrorism.* New York: Simon and Schuster, 2004.

Cockburn, Andrew. *Rumsfeld: His Rise, Fall, and Catastrophic Legacy.* New York: Scribner, 2007.

Cohen, Elliot D. *News Incorporated—Corporate Media Ownership and Its Threat to Democracy.* Amherst, Mass.: Prometheus Books, 2005.

Coll, Steve. *Ghost Wars: The Secret History of the CIA, Afghanistan, and Bin Laden, from the Soviet Invasion to September 10, 2001.* New York: Penguin Press, 2004.

Cooley, John K. *Unholy Wars: Afghanistan, America, and International Terrorism.* London: Pluto Press, 1999.

Cordovez, Diego, and Selig S. Harrison. *Out of Afghanistan: The Inside Story of the Soviet Withdrawal.* New York: Oxford University Press, 1995.

Crile, George. *Charlie Wilson's War: The Extraordinary Story of the Largest Covert Operation in History.* New York: Atlantic Monthly Press, 2003.

Cumings, Bruce. *The Origins of the Korean War.* Vol 2. Princeton, N.J.: Princeton University Press, 1990.

Daalder, Ivo H., and Michael E. O'Hanlon. *Winning Ugly: NATO's War to Save Kosovo.* Washington, D.C.: Brookings Institution Press, 2000.

Daugherty, William J. *Executive Secrets: Covert Action and the Presidency.* Lexington: University of Kentucky Press, 2004.

————. *In the Shadow of the Ayatollah: A CIA Hostage in Iran.* Annapolis, Md.: Naval Institute Press, 2001.

Davis, Jayna. *The Third Terrorist: The Middle East Connection to the Oklahoma City Bombing.* Nashville, Tenn.: WND Books/Thomas Nelson, 2004.

Diamond, Sara. *Roads to Dominion: Right-Wing Movements and Political Power in the United States.* New York: Guilford Press, 1995.

————. *Spiritual Warfare: The Politics of the Christian Right.* Boston: South End Press, 1989.

Draper, Theodore. *A Very Thin Line: The Iran-Contra Affairs.* New York: Hill and Wang, 1991.

Dreyfuss, Robert. *Devil's Game: How the United States Helped Unleash Fundamentalist Islam.* New York: Metropolitan Books/Henry Holt, 2005.

Dreyfuss, Robert, with Thierry LeMarc. *Hostage to Khomeini.* New York: New Benjamin Franklin House, 1981.

Durandin, Catherine. *La CIA en guerre: Allende, Gorbatchev, Ben Laden, Saddam Hussein.* Paris: Grancher, 2003.

Ehrenfeld, Rachel. *Funding Evil: How Terrorism Is Financed—And How to Stop It.* Chicago: Bonus Books, 2003.

Ellsberg, Daniel. *Secrets: A Memoir of Vietnam and the Pentagon Papers.* New York: Viking, 2002.

Emdad ul-Haq, M. *Drugs in South Asia: From the Opium Trade to the Present Day.* New York: St. Martin's Press, 2000.

Emerson, Steven. *The American Jihad: The Terrorists Living among Us.* New York: Free Press, 2002.

Emery, Fred. *Watergate: The Corruption of American Politics and the Fall of Richard Nixon.* New York: Random House/Times Books, 1994.

Engdahl, William. *A Century of War: Anglo-American Oil Politics and the New World Order.* London: Pluto Press, 2004.

Farah, Douglas. *Blood from Stones: The Secret Financial Network of Terror.* New York: Broadway Books, 2004.

Feffer, John, ed. *Power Trip: U.S. Unilateralism and Global Strategy after September 11.* New York: Seven Stories Press, 2003.

Ferguson, Thomas, and Joel Rogers. *Right Turn: The Decline of the Democrats and the Future of American Politics.* New York: Hill and Wang, 1986.

Findlay, Mark. *The Globalisation of Crime.* Cambridge: Cambridge University Press, 1999.

Fineman, Daniel. *A Special Relationship: The United States and Military Government in Thailand, 1947–1958.* Honolulu: University of Hawaii Press, 1997.

Fisk, Robert. *The Great War for Civilisation: The Conquest of the Middle East.* New York: Knopf, 2005.

Gaddis, John Lewis. *The Cold War: A New History.* New York: Penguin Press, 2005.

Ganser, Daniele. *NATO's Secret Armies: Operation Gladio and Terrorism in Western Europe.* London: Frank Cass Publishers, 2005.

Gates, Robert. *From the Shadows: The Ultimate Insider's Story of Five Presidents and How They Won the Cold War.* New York: Simon and Schuster, 1996.

Gavin, Francis J. *Gold, Dollars, and Power: The Politics of International Monetary Relations, 1958–1971.* Chapel Hill: University of North Carolina Press, 2004.

Gelbspan, Ross. *Break-ins, Death Threats, and the FBI: The Covert War against the Central America Movement.* Boston: South End Press, 1991.

Gerges, Fawaz. *America and Political Islam: Clash of Cultures or Clash of Interests?* Cambridge: Cambridge University Press, 1999.

Goff, Stan. *Full Spectrum Disorder: The Military in the New American Century*. Brooklyn, N.Y.: Soft Skull Press, 2004.

Goodman, Amy, with David Goodman. *The Exception to the Rulers: Exposing Oily Politicians, War Profiteers, and the Media That Love Them*. London: Arrow, 2004.

Greider, William. *The Soul of Capitalism: Opening Paths to a Moral Economy*. New York: Simon and Schuster, 2003.

Griffin, David Ray. *The New Pearl Harbor: Disturbing Questions about the Bush Administration and 9/11*. Northampton, Mass.: Olive Branch Press, 2004.

———. *The 9/11 Commission Report: Omissions and Distortions*. Northampton, Mass.: Olive Branch Press/Interlink, 2004.

Griffin, David Ray, and Peter Dale Scott, eds. *9/11 and American Empire: Intellectuals Speak Out*. Northampton, Mass.: Olive Branch Press, 2006.

Griffin, Michael. *Reaping the Whirlwind: The Taliban Movement in Afghanistan*. London: Pluto Press, 2001.

Grose, Peter. *Gentleman Spy: The Life of Allen Dulles*. Boston: Richard Todd/Houghton Mifflin, 1994.

Gunaratna, Rohan. *Inside Al Qaeda: Global Network of Terror*. New York: Columbia University Press, 2002.

Halperin, Morton, Jerry Berman, Robert Borosage, and Christine Marwick. *The Lawless State: The Crimes of the U.S. Intelligence Agencies*. New York: Penguin Books, 1976.

Hammond, Thomas. *Red Flag over Afghanistan: The Communist Coup, the Soviet Invasion, and the Consequences*. Boulder, Colo.: Westview, 1984.

Hanhimäki, Jussi. *The Flawed Architect: Henry Kissinger and American Foreign Policy*. New York: Oxford University Press, 2004.

Haqqani, Husain. *Pakistan: Between Mosque and Military*. Washington, D.C.: Brookings Institution Press, 2005.

Harris, David. *The Crisis: The President, the Prophet, and the Shah: 1979 and the Coming of Militant Islam*. New York: Little Brown, 2004.

Hartnett, Stephen John, and Laura Ann Stengrim. *Globalization and Empire: The U.S. Invasion of Iraq, Free Markets, and the Twilight of Democracy*. Tuscaloosa: University of Alabama Press, 2006.

Helms, Harry. *Inside the Shadow Government: National Security and the Cult of Secrecy*. Los Angeles: Feral House, 2003.

Helms, Richard, with William Hood. *A Look over My Shoulder: A Life in the Central Intelligence Agency*. New York: Random House, 2003.

Hersh, Burton. *The Old Boys: The American Elite and the Origins of the CIA*. New York: Scribner's, 1992.

Hersh, Seymour. *Chain of Command: The Road from 9/11 to Abu Ghraib*. New York: HarperCollins, 2004.

———. *The Price of Power: Kissinger in the White House*. New York: Summit, 1983.

Hicks, Sander. *The Big Wedding: 9/11, the Whistle-Blowers, and the Cover-Up*. Brooklyn, N.Y.: Vox Pop, 2005.

Hiro, Dilip. *Holy Wars: The Rise of Islamic Fundamentalism*. New York: Routledge, 1989.

Hitchens, Christopher. *The Trial of Henry Kissinger*. London: Verso, 2001.

Hougan, Jim. *Secret Agenda: Watergate, Deep Throat, and the CIA*. New York: Random House, 1984.

Isaacson, Walter. *Kissinger: A Biography*. New York: Simon and Schuster, 1992.

Jacquard, Roland. *In the Name of Osama bin Laden: Global Terrorism and the bin Laden Brotherhood*. Durham, N.C.: Duke University Press, 2002.

Johnson, Chalmers. *Nemesis: The Last Days of the American Republic*. New York: Metropolitan Books/Henry Holt, 2006.

———. *The Sorrows of Empire: Militarism, Secrecy, and the End of the Republic*. New York: Metropolitan Books/Henry Holt, 2004.

Jones, Adam, ed. *Genocide, War Crimes, and the West: History and Complicity*. London: Zed Books, 2004.

Jordan, David C. *Drug Politics: Dirty Money and Democracies*. Norman: University of Oklahoma Press, 1999.

Jordan, Hamilton. *Crisis: The Last Year of the Carter Presidency*. New York: Putnam, 1982.

Judah, Tim. *Kosovo: War and Revenge*. New Haven, Conn.: Yale University Press, 2002.

Judis, John. *The Folly of Empire: What George W. Bush Could Learn from Theodore Roosevelt and Woodrow Wilson*. New York: Scribner's, 2004.

Kaplan, Robert D. *Soldiers of God: With Islamic Warriors in Afghanistan and Pakistan*. New York: Random House, 1990.

Kean, Thomas H., and Lee H. Hamilton, with Benjamin Rhodes. *Without Precedent: The Inside Story of the 9/11 Commission*. New York: Knopf, 2006.

Kennedy, Paul. *The Rise and Fall of the Great Powers*. New York: Random House, 1988.

Kepel, Gilles. *Jihad: The Trail of Political Islam*. Cambridge, Mass.: Belknap Press, 2002.

Kessler, Ronald. *The Richest Man in the World*. New York: Warner Books, 1986.

Khalidi, Rashid. *Resurrecting Empire: Western Footprints and America's Perilous Path in the Middle East*. Boston: Beacon, 2004.

Kissinger, Henry. *White House Years*. Boston: Little, Brown, 1979.

———. *Years of Renewal*. New York: Simon and Schuster, 1999.

Klare, Michael T. *Blood and Oil: The Dangers and Consequences of America's Growing Dependency on Imported Petroleum (The American Empire Project)*. New York: Metropolitan Books, 2004.

———. *Resource Wars: The New Landscape of Global Conflict*. New York: Metropolitan Books/Henry Holt, 2001.

Kochan, Nick. *The Washing Machine: How Money Laundering and Terrorist Financing Soils Us*. Mason, Ohio: Thomson, 2005.

Kohlmann, Evan F. *Al-Qaida's Jihad in Europe: The Afghan-Bosnian Network*. Oxford: Berg Publishers, 2004.

Kutler, Stanley I. *The Wars of Watergate: The Last Crisis of Richard Nixon*. New York: W. W. Norton, 1990.

Kux, Dennis. *The United States and Pakistan, 1947–2000: Disenchanted Allies.* Washington, D.C.: Woodrow Wilson Center Press, 2000.

Labévière, Richard. *Dollars for Terror: The United States and Islam.* New York: Algora Publishing, 2000.

Lacey, Robert. *The Kingdom: Arabia and the House of Sa'ud.* New York: Avon, 1981.

Lamb, Christina. *Waiting for Allah: Pakistan's Struggle for Democracy.* London: H. Hamilton, 1991.

Lance, Peter. *Cover Up: What the Government Is Still Hiding about the War on Terror.* New York: Regan Books, 2004.

———. *1000 Years for Revenge: International Terrorism and the FBI— the Untold Story.* New York: Regan Books, 2003.

———. *Triple Cross: How Bin Laden's Chief Security Adviser Penetrated the CIA, the FBI, and the Green Berets.* New York: Regan, 2006.

Lapham, Lewis H. *Pretensions to Empire: Notes on the Criminal Folly of the Bush Administration.* New York: New Press, 2006.

Laurent, Frédéric. *L'orchestre noir.* Paris: Stock, 1978.

Ledeen, Michael, and William Lewis. *Debacle: The American Failure in Iran.* New York: Knopf, 1981.

Leeb, Stephen. *The Oil Factor: Protect Yourself—and Profit—from the Coming Energy Crisis.* New York: Warner Business Books, 2004.

Lerner, Michael. *The Left Hand of God: Taking Back Our Country from the Religious Right.* San Francisco: HarperSanFrancisco, 2006.

Little, Douglas. *American Orientalism: The United States and the Middle East since 1945.* Chapel Hill: University of North Carolina Press, 2002.

Loftus, John, and Mark Aarons. *The Secret War against the Jews.* New York: St. Martin's Press, 1994.

Mann, James. *The Rise of the Vulcans: The History of Bush's War Cabinet.* New York: Viking, 2004.

Marshall, Jonathan, Peter Dale Scott, and Jane Hunter. *The Iran-Contra Connection: Secret Teams and Covert Operations in the Reagan Era.* Boston: South End Press, 1987.

McCoy, Alfred W. *The Politics of Heroin: CIA Complicity in the Global Drug Trade.* Chicago: Lawrence Hill Books/Chicago Review Press, 2003.

McQuaig, Linda. *It's the Crude, Dude: War, Big Oil, and the Fight for the Planet.* Toronto: Doubleday Canada, 2004.

Merry, Robert M. *Sands of Empire: Missionary Zeal, American Foreign Policy, and the Hazards of Global Ambition.* New York: Simon and Schuster, 2005.

Michnik, Adam. *The Church and the Left.* Translated by David Ost. Chicago: University of Chicago Press, 1993.

Micklethwait, John, and Adrian Wooldridge. *The Right Nation: Conservative Power in America.* New York: Penguin Press, 2004.

Morgan, Rowland, and Ian Henshall. *9/11 Revealed: The Unanswered Questions.* New York: Carroll and Graf, 2005.

Murphy, Paul. *The Wolves of Islam: Russia and the Faces of Chechen Terror.* Washington, D.C.: Brassey's Inc., 2004.

Musharraf, Pervez. *In the Line of Fire: A Memoir.* New York: Free Press, 2006.

Mylroie, Laurie. *Bush vs. the Beltway: How the CIA and the State Department Tried to Stop the War on Terror.* New York: Regan Books, 2003.

———. *The War against America.* Washington, D.C.: AEI Press, 2000.

Napoleoni, Loretta. *Terror Incorporated: Tracing the Dollars behind the Terror Networks.* New York: Seven Stories Press, 2005.

Nitzan, Jonathan, and Shimshon Bichler. *The Global Political Economy of Israel.* London: Pluto Press, 2002.

Nye, Joseph S., Jr., *The Paradox of American Power: Why the World's Only Superpower Can't Go It Alone.* Oxford: Oxford University Press, 2002.

Odell, John S. *U.S. International Monetary Policy.* Princeton, N.J.: Princeton University Press, 1982.

Palast, Greg. *Armed Madhouse.* New York: Dutton, 2006.

———. *The Best Democracy Money Can Buy: An Investigative Reporter Exposes the Truth about Globalization, Corporate Cons, and High-Finance Fraudsters.* New York: Plume, 2004.

Parmar, Inderjeet. *Think Tanks and Power in Foreign Policy: A Comparative Study of the Role and Influence of the Council on Foreign Relations and the Royal Institute of International Affairs, 1939–1945.* New York: Palgrave Macmillan, 2004.

Parry, Robert. *Lost History: Contras, Cocaine, and Other Crimes.* Arlington, Va.: Media Consortium, 1997.

———. *Secrecy & Privilege: Rise of the Bush Dynasty from Watergate to Iraq.* Arlington, Va.: Media Consortium, 2004.

———. *Trick or Treason: The October Surprise Mystery.* New York: Sheridan Square Press, 1993.

Pelletiere, Stephen C. *Iraq and the International Oil System: Why America Went to War in the Gulf.* Washington, D.C.: Maisonneuve Press, 2004.

Perkins, John. *Confessions of an Economic Hit Man.* San Francisco: Berrett-Koehler Publishers, 2004.

Persico, Joseph E. *Casey: From the OSS to the CIA.* New York: Viking/Penguin, 1991.

———. *The Imperial Rockefeller: A Biography of Nelson A. Rockefeller.* New York: Simon and Schuster, 1982.

Phillips, Kevin. *American Dynasty: Aristocracy, Fortune, and the Politics of Deceit in the House of Bush.* New York: Viking, 2004.

———. *American Theocracy: The Peril and Politics of Radical Religion, Oil, and Borrowed Money in the 21st Century.* New York: Viking, 2006.

———. *Wealth and Democracy: A Political History of the American Rich.* New York: Broadway Books, 2002.

Pisani, Sallie. *The CIA and the Marshall Plan.* Lawrence: University Press of Kansas, 1996.

Porter, Gareth. *Perils of Dominance: Imbalance of Power and the Road to War in Vietnam.* Berkeley: University of California Press, 2005.

Posner, Gerard. *Why America Slept: The Failure to Prevent 9/11.* New York: Random House, 2003.

Potts, Mark, Nick Kochan, and Robert Whittington. *Dirty Money: BCCI, the*

Inside Story of the World's Sleaziest Bank. Washington, D.C.: National Press Books, 1992.

Powers, Thomas. *Intelligence Wars: American Secret History from Hitler to al-Qaeda.* New York: New York Review of Books, 2004.

——. *The Man Who Kept the Secrets: Richard Helms and the CIA.* New York: Knopf, 1979.

Prestowitz, Clyde. *Rogue Nation: American Unilateralism and the Failure of Good Intentions.* New York: Basic Books, 2003.

Quigley, Carroll. *The Anglo-American Establishment: From Rhodes to Cliveden.* New York: Books in Focus, 1981.

——. *Tragedy and Hope: A History of the World in Our Time.* New York: Macmillan, 1966.

Ranelagh, John. *The Agency: The Rise and Decline of the CIA.* New York: Simon and Schuster, 1986.

Rashid, Ahmed. *Jihad: The Rise of Militant Islam in Central Asia.* New Haven, Conn.: Yale University Press, 2002.

——. *Taliban: Militant Islam, Oil, and Fundamentalism in Central Asia.* New Haven, Conn.: Yale University Press, 2001.

Reeve, Simon. *The New Jackals: Ramzi Yousef, Osama bin Laden, and the Future of Terrorism.* Boston: Northeastern University: 1999.

Ressa, Maria A. *Seeds of Terror: An Eyewitness Account of al-Qaeda's Newest Center of Operations in Southeast Asia.* New York: Free Press, 2003.

Ricks, Thomas. *Fiasco: The American Military Adventure in Iraq.* New York: Penguin Press, 2006.

Ridgeway, James. *The March to War.* New York: Four Walls Eight Windows, 1991.

Ritter, Scott. *Iraq Confidential: The Untold Story of the Intelligence Conspiracy to Undermine the UN and Overthrow Saddam Hussein.* New York: Nation Books, 2005.

Rockefeller, David. *Memoirs.* New York: Random House, 2002.

Rothkopf, David J. *Running the World: The Inside Story of the National Security Council and the Architects of American Power.* New York: Public Affairs/Perseus, 2005.

Rubin, Barnett. *Paved with Good Intentions: The American Experience in Iran.* New York: Oxford University Press, 1980.

——. *The Search for Peace in Afghanistan: From Buffer State to Failed State.* New Haven, Conn.: Yale University Press, 1995.

Ruppert, Michael C. *Crossing the Rubicon: The Decline of the American Empire at the End of the Age of Oil.* Gabriola Island, B.C.: New Society Publishers, 2004.

Sageman, Marc. *Understanding Terror Networks.* Philadelphia: University of Pennsylvania Press, 2004.

Saighal, Vinod. *Dealing with Global Terrorism: The Way Forward.* New Delhi: Sterling, 2003.

Salinger, Pierre. *America Held Hostage: The Secret Negotiations.* Garden City, N.Y.: Doubleday, 1981.

Sampson, Anthony. *The Arms Bazaar: From Lebanon to Lockheed.* New York: Viking, 1977.

———. *The Seven Sisters: The Great Oil Companies and the World They Shaped*. New York: Viking, 1975.

Sanders, Jerry. *Peddlers of Crisis: The Committee on the Present Danger and the Politics of Containment*. Boston: South End Press, 1983.

Saul, John Ralston. *The Collapse of Globalism and the Reinvention of the World*. London: Atlantic, 2005.

Saunders, Frances Stonor. *Who Paid the Piper? The CIA and the Cultural Cold War*. London: Granta, 1999.

Schell, Jonathan. *The Unconquerable World: Power, Nonviolence, and the Will of the People*. New York: Metropolitan Books/Henry Holt, 2003.

Schroen, Gary. *First In: An Insider's Account of How the CIA Spearheaded the War on Terrorism in Afghanistan*. New York: Presidio/Ballantine, 2005.

Schwartz, Stephen. *The Two Faces of Islam: The House of Sa'ud from Tradition to Terror*. New York: Doubleday, 2002.

Schweizer, Peter. *Victory—The Reagan Administration's Secret Strategy That Hastened the Collapse of the Soviet Union*. New York: Atlantic Monthly Press, 1994.

Scott, Peter Dale. *Deep Politics and the Death of JFK*. Berkeley: University of California Press, 1998.

———. *Drugs, Oil, and War: The United States in Afghanistan, Colombia, and Indochina*. Lanham, Md.: Rowman and Littlefield, 2003.

———. *The War Conspiracy*. New York: Bobbs Merrill, 1972.

Scott, Peter Dale, and Jonathan Marshall. *Cocaine Politics: Drugs, Armies, and the CIA in Central America*. Berkeley: University of California Press, 1998.

Secord, Richard, with Jay Wurts. *Honored and Betrayed: Irangate, Covert Affairs, and the Secret War in Laos*. New York: John Wiley, 1992.

Sharma, Rajeev. *Pak Proxy War: A Story of ISI, bin Laden, and Kargil*. New Delhi: Kaveri Books, 2002.

Shawcross, William. *The Shah's Last Ride: The Fate of an Ally*. New York: Simon and Schuster, 1988.

Shevtsova, Lilia. *Putin's Russia*. Translated by Antonina Bouis. Washington, D.C.: Carnegie Endowment for International Peace, 2003.

Shoup, Laurence H., and William Minter. *The Imperial Brain Trust: The Council on Foreign Relations and United States Foreign Policy*. New York: Monthly Review Press, 1977.

Sick, Gary. *All Fall Down: America's Tragic Encounter with Iran*. New York: Random House, 1985.

———. *October Surprise: America's Hostages in Iran and the Election of Ronald Reagan*. New York: Times Books, 1991.

Simpson, Christopher. *Blowback: America's Recruitment of Nazis and Its Effect on the Cold War*. New York: Collier Books/Macmillan, 1988.

Sklar, Holly, ed. *Trilateralism: The Trilateral Commission and Elite Planning for World Management*. Boston: South End Press, 1980.

Smith, Steven B. *Reading Leo Strauss: Politics, Philosophy, Judaism*. Chicago: University of Chicago Press, 2006.

Smucker, Philip. *Al Qaeda's Great Escape: The Military and the Media on Terror's Trail*. Washington, D.C.: Brassey's, 2004.

Solomon, Robert. *The International Monetary System, 1945–1981*. New York: Harper and Row, 1982.

Sullivan, William H. *Mission to Iran*. New York: W. W. Norton, 1981.

Summers, Anthony, with Robbyn Swan. *The Arrogance of Power: The Secret World of Richard Nixon*. New York: Viking, 2000.

Summers, Anthony, and Robbyn Swan. *Sinatra: The Life*. New York: Alfred A. Knopf, 2005.

Suskind, Ron. *The One Percent Doctrine: Deep Inside America's Pursuit of Its Enemies since 9/11*. New York: Simon and Schuster, 2006.

Thompson, Paul. *The Terror Timeline: Year by Year, Day by Day, Minute by Minute*. New York: HarperCollins/Regan Books, 2004.

Thorn, Victor. *9-11 on Trial: The World Trade Center Collapse*. State College, Pa.: Sisyphus Press, 2005.

Trento, Josephy J. *Prelude to Terror: The Rogue CIA and the Legacy of America's Private Intelligence Network*. New York: Carroll and Graf, 2005.

———. *The Secret History of the CIA*. New York: Forum/Prima/Random House, 2001.

Trento, Susan B. *The Power House: Robert Keith Gray and the Selling of Access and Influence in Washington*. New York: St. Martin's Press, 1992.

Truell, Peter, and Larry Gurwin. *False Profits: The Inside Story of BCCI, the World's Most Corrupt Financial Empire*. Boston: Houghton Mifflin, 1992.

Unger, Craig. *House of Bush, House of Saud: The Secret Relationship between the World's Two Most Powerful Dynasties*. New York: Scribner, 2004.

Vance, Cyrus. *Hard Choices: Critical Years in American Foreign Policy*. New York: Simon and Schuster, 1983.

Van der Pijl, Kees. *The Making of an Atlantic Ruling Class*. London: Verso, 1984.

Willan, Philip. *Puppetmasters: The Political Use of Terrorism in Italy*. London: Constable and Company, 1991.

Williams, Paul L. *Al Qaeda: Brotherhood of Terror*. Upper Saddle River, N.J.: Alpha/Pearson Education, 2002.

Winks, Robin. *Cloak and Gown: Scholars in the Secret War, 1939–1961*. New York: William Morrow, 1987.

Woodword, Bob. *Plan of Attack*. New York: Simon and Schuster, 2004.

———. *Shadow: Five Presidents and the Legacy of Watergate*. New York: Simon and Schuster, 1999.

———. *State of Denial: Bush at War, Part III*. New York: Simon and Schuster, 2006.

———. *Veil: The Secret Wars of the CIA, 1981–1987*. New York: Simon and Schuster, 1987.

Wright, Lawrence. *The Looming Tower: Al-Qaeda and the Road to 9/11*. New York: Knopf, 2006.

Yergin, Daniel. *The Prize: The Epic Quest for Oil, Money, and Power*. New York: Simon and Schuster, 1991.

Yousaf, Muhhamed, and Mark Adkin. *The Bear Trap: Afghanistan's Untold Story*. London: Leo Cooper, 1992.

Al-Zayyat, Montasser. *The Road to Al-Qaeda: The Story of Bin Laden's Right-Hand Man.* London: Pluto Press, 2004.

Zepezauer, Mark. *Boomerang! How Our Covert Wars Have Created Enemies across the Middle East and Brought Terror to America.* Monroe, Maine: Common Courage Press, 2003.

Zinn, Howard. *A People's History of the United States: 1492–Present.* New York: HarperPerennial, 1984.

REPORTS

Church Committee Report: U.S. Congress, Senate, Select Committee to Study Governmental Operations with Respect to Intelligence Activities. *Final Report,* April 26, 1976. 94th Cong., 2nd Sess., Senate Report No. 94-755.

Iran-Contra Affair: U.S. House Select Committee to Investigate Covert Arms Transactions with Iran, U.S. Senate Select Committee on Secret Military Assistance to Iran and the Nicaraguan Opposition. *Iran-Contra Affair: Report of the Congressional Committees Investigating the Iran-Contra Affair: With Supplemental, Minority, and Additional Views.* 100th Cong., 1st Sess., House Report No. 100-433, Senate Report No. 100-216.

Kerry-Brown BCCI Report: U.S. Congress, Senate. *The BCCI Affair: A Report to the Senate Committee on Foreign Relations from Senator John Kerry, Chairman, and from Senator Hank Brown, Ranking Member, Subcommittee on Terrorism, Narcotics, and International Operations. . . .* December 1992, 102nd Cong., 2nd Sess., Senate Report No. 102-140.

9/11 Commission Report: The 9/11 Commission Report: Final Report of the National Commission on Terrorist Attacks on the United States. Authorized Edition. New York: W. W. Norton, 2004.

Pike Report: A report submitted to Congress in 1974 by the House Special Select Committee on Intelligence. The House of Representatives voted 246 to 124 to direct that the Pike report not be released if not certified by the President not to contain classified information. However *The Village Voice* published it in full on February 16, 1976. It was also published in England as *CIA: Pike Report* (Nottingham: Spokesman Books, 1977). This book is not currently available in the United States from either Amazon or Abebooks.com.

Index

Text: 10/13 Sabon
Display: Akzidenz Grotesk
Compositor: BookMatters, Berkeley
Printer and Binder: Maple-Vail Manufacturing Group